International Relations and World Politics

Fifth Edition

PAUL R. VIOTTI
University of Denver

MARK V. KAUPPI
Georgetown University

Boston   Columbus   Indianapolis   New York   San Francisco   Upper Saddle River
Amsterdam   Cape Town   Dubai   London   Madrid   Milan   Munich   Paris   Montreal   Toronto
Delhi   Mexico City   São Paulo   Sydney   Hong Kong   Seoul   Singapore   Taipei   Tokyo

Senior Acquisitions Editor: Vikram Mukhija
Editorial Assistants: Isabel Schwab, Beverly Fong
Associate Development Editor: Corey Kahn
Executive Marketing Manager: Wendy Gordon
Senior Digital Media Producer: Paul DeLuca
Production Manager: S. S. Kulig

Project Coordination, Text Design, and Electronic Page Makeup: S4Carlisle Publishing Services
Cover Design: Suzanne Behnke
Cover Art: iStockphoto
Senior Manufacturing Buyer: Dennis J. Para
Printer/Binder: R.R. Donnelley
Cover Printer: Lehigh Phoenix Color Corp.

Credits and acknowledgments borrowed from other sources and reproduced, with permission, in this textbook appear on the appropriate page within text or on page 530.

Library of Congress Cataloging-in-Publication Data

Viotti, Paul R.
  International relations and world politics / Paul R. Viotti and Mark V. Kauppi. — 5th ed.
    p. cm.
  ISBN-13: 978-0-205-85464-6—ISBN-10: 0-205-85464-8   1. World politics—1989–
2. International relations.   3. Security, International.   4. International trade.
5. Nationalism.   I. Kauppi, Mark V.   II. Title.
  D860.V56 2013
  327.101—dc23

                                              2011049061

10 9 8 7 6 5 4 3 2 1—DOC—15 14 13 12

www.pearsonhighered.com

ISBN 10:   0-205-85464-8
ISBN 13: 978-0-205-85464-6

DEDICATION

*To three scholars, the late James N. Rosenau,
Kenneth N. Waltz, and the late Ernst B. Haas, whose
diverse perspectives on international relations and world
politics developed in the last half of the 20th century
have so profoundly influenced the writing of this volume
on 21st-century opportunities and challenges posed by
globalization.*

BRIEF CONTENTS

DETAILED CONTENTS

PREFACE

E. H. Carr, the renowned English scholar, observed how academics and policymaker practitioners typically live in different worlds—the former stepping back from day-to-day events to ask (and try to answer) the big questions, the latter consumed by the immediacy and press of current events that pose challenges also requiring answers. The authors have had (and continue to have) experiences in both worlds in university and government positions they have held both at home and abroad.

In our government careers, one of us served in the diplomatic world as a political adviser, and the other has sought to make the world a safer place by working on ways to counter terrorist threats. We are also educators both in government and on university campuses, committed as we are to helping the current and future generations of policy practitioners enhance their understandings and develop their practical skills in making and implementing policy.

What motivates us to write this book is to bring a real-world policy perspective to the study of international relations and world politics. We build bridges in this volume in our effort to connect the academic and policy worlds, filling the gap between theory and practice and demonstrating how we can apply IR theory to the making and implementation of policy. Readers planning careers as practitioners will find that there is nothing more practical than good theory.

We live in an age of globalization made possible by technological advances, particularly in transportation and telecommunications, that bring us not only the benefits but also the downsides of coming closer together. Aspects of globalization have transformed the way individuals relate to one another and how firms and other organizations conduct their business from the local and the national to the regional and the global. There are many challenges, and you may be a player in many of these efforts, large or small. To play that role well requires an understanding of how we got to the current state of international relations and world politics and what that might mean for the future. *International Relations and World Politics* is a book that will help you—the new generation of leaders, practitioners, and participants in governments, international and nongovernmental organizations, multinational corporations, and more—prepare for that role.

NEW TO THIS EDITION

The fifth edition was significantly updated, rewritten, and reorganized to support all of the goals described above. Our broader commitment in undertaking this major redesign was to ensure that *International Relations and World Politics* retained a high level of intellectual content appropriate for an introduction to the field but was also more reader friendly and policy relevant. As such, key revisions include:

- A toolbox of theory, history, geography, and globalization chapters provides essential background on world affairs. Equipped with these tools, one can use them to develop a fuller understanding of the security, economy, and identity issues that are subsequently covered.

- Chapter 4, "Geography," is entirely new to this fifth edition; we introduce both physical and human geography as a central influence on international relations and world politics.

- Chapter 5, "Globalization," is another new chapter that brings diverse political, economic, and social threads together in one place and offers a holistic examination of the present-day complexity of global issues.

- More detailed coverage of the intersecting worlds of national and international security is now provided in separate chapters on power (Chapter 6), diplomacy and foreign policy (Chapter 7), international law and organization (Chapter 8), interstate conflict (Chapter 9), and asymmetric conflict (Chapter 10).

- Separate chapters are also provided on trade and finance (Chapter 11), development (Chapter 12), human rights (Chapter 13), and the environment (Chapter 14), bringing the number of chapters down from 17 to 14 but without a sacrifice in comprehensive coverage. We hope this makes the fifth edition easier to use in the course of a semester.

- Each chapter focuses on two primary opportunities for hands-on critical thinking. First, "Case & Point" boxes demonstrate how key concepts from theory, history, and geography are used to interpret international relations. Then, "Argument-Counterargument" boxes offers a chance to practice analysis by encouraging the application of international relations theory to current world problems.

- Each chapter integrates learning architecture to ensure comprehension. Learning objectives are listed in the beginning, tracked throughout the narrative, and a chapter review at the end organizes key terms and suggested readings by learning objective. In addition, a short multiple-choice test provides an opportunity for self-testing.

- Visuals play a more central role in the fifth edition. A chapter-opening anecdote and photo tells a story of an international relations practitioner at work. Later, a slideshow of four images are assembled into a visual narrative that illustrates an important conceptual or empirical issue from the chapter. Figures and tables now include detailed captions to help one interpret the data that are displayed. And last, world and regional maps are included as a reference for readers.

- Related to both theory and practice is coverage not just of historic, but also present-day events related to three sets of issues on the global agenda—security, economy, and identity—that reflect the dynamism of 21st-century international relations and world politics. Among the *security* challenges we take up are the proliferation of weapons of mass destruction, terrorism, intercommunal strife, and global crime, including human and drug trafficking across national borders. A focus on *economy* brings us to global trade and investment imbalances, development challenges faced by capital-poor countries, an uneven distribution of "sovereign" debt obligations owed by states, and the ongoing effort to maintain international liquidity and thus sustain currency exchange essential to global commerce. Finally, we address national and ethnic *identity* crises that result in genocide and other human rights violations as well as popular uprisings by people in the Arab world and elsewhere against authoritarian regimes.

FEATURES

This textbook includes coverage that surveys the entire field of international relations. As noted above, the first five chapters constitute the reader's toolbox. Chapter 1, "Engaging International Relations and World Politics," begins with an overview of the field and the book's goals, which provides context for the entire volume. Chapter 2, "Theory," presents the alternative images offered by realism, liberalism, economic structuralism, and the English School as well as interpretive understandings drawn from constructivist, feminist, postmodern, and critical theory. Chapter 3, "History," assesses the past's relevance to understanding present-day globalization. Chapter 4, "Geography," identifies the physical, human, and cultural factors that influence how different actors relate in this globalized era. Chapter 5, "Globalization," addresses political, economic, and social dimensions of globalization.

The balance of the chapters encourages students to apply their toolkit to analyze—and propose solutions to—current and future world issues. Chapter 6, "Power," focuses on national interests and objectives as well as the use of national capabilities or power to secure opportunities and counter threats. Chapter 7, "Diplomacy and Foreign Policy," represents the state as principal actor in efforts to maintain security and achieve other objectives—the relations governmental authorities as agents of states establish with their counterparts in other states and the ways and means they employ for national purposes in an increasingly complex, globalized policy space.

Chapter 8, "International Law and International Organization," examines the global institutions and the complex processes by which states as members and nongovernmental organizations as "outside" participants engage not just in collective-security and collective-defense (alliance) matters, but also in a wide range of political, social, and economic issues related to human security.

Chapter 9, "Interstate Conflict," proceeds not just with a strategic discussion on the use of force by states in warfighting, deterrence, and coercive diplomacy, but also consideration of both moral limits in just-war doctrine and the pursuit of arms control as a means to reduce the likelihood of war, reduce damage should war occur, and seek economic gains or achieve other goals. Chapter 10, "Asymmetric Conflict," covers two key concerns—terrorism and crime—that are some of the various forms of political and criminal violence and other actions that challenge political authorities and populations worldwide. The term *asymmetry* captures the uneven dimensions of seemingly very powerful states confronting socially grounded insurgencies, movements, and criminal groups usually lacking the same material might possessed by states.

Chapter 11, "Trade and Money," discusses the exchange of goods and services (imports and exports) that depends on finance—the entire chapter an application of the capitalist economy "tool" found in Chapter 5, "Globalization." Chapter 12, "Development," focuses on the marshaling of land, labor, and capital to increase economic production and level of living.

Chapter 13, "Human Rights," takes up an issue linked to our identity as human beings—our right to life, human dignity, and justice as fairness. We also examine the current state of international and regional efforts with regard to human rights and refugees. Finally, Chapter 14, "The Environment," addresses various environmental challenges and trends that are related to international security issues such as the potential for resource wars. We also look at the roles of international and nongovernmental organizations in addressing this complex transnational issue.

MYPOLISCILAB FOR *INTERNATIONAL RELATIONS AND WORLD POLITICS*

The Moment You Know

Educators know it. Students know it. It's that inspired moment when something that was difficult to understand suddenly makes perfect sense. Our MyLab products have been designed and refined with a single purpose in mind—to help educators create that moment of understanding with their students.

MyPoliSciLab delivers *proven results* in helping individual students succeed. It provides *engaging experiences* that personalize, stimulate, and measure learning for each student. And it comes from a *trusted partner* with educational expertise and a deep commitment to helping students, instructors, and departments achieve their goals.

MyPoliSciLab can be used by itself or linked to any learning management system. To learn more about how MyPoliSciLab combines proven learning applications with powerful assessment, visit **www.mypoliscilab.com**.

MyPoliSciLab Delivers *Proven Results* in Helping Individual Students Succeed

- Pearson MyLabs are currently in use by millions of students each year across a variety of disciplines.
- MyPoliSciLab works, but don't take our word for it. Visit **www.pearsonhighered .com/elearning** to read white papers, case studies, and testimonials from instructors and students that consistently demonstrate the success of our MyLabs.

MyPoliSciLab Provides *Engaging Experiences* That Personalize, Stimulate, and Measure Learning for Each Student

- *Assessment.* Track progress and get instant feedback on every chapter, video, and multimedia activity. With results feeding into a powerful gradebook, the assessment program identifies learning challenges early and suggests the best resources to help.

- *Personalized Study Plan.* Follow a flexible learning path created by the assessment program and tailored to each student's unique needs. Organized by learning objectives, the study plan offers follow-up reading, video, and multimedia activities for further learning and practice.
- *Pearson eText.* Just like the printed text; highlight and add notes to the eText online or download it to a tablet.
- *Flashcards.* Learn key terms by word or definition.
- *Video.* Analyze current events by watching streaming video from major news providers.
- *Mapping Exercises.* Explore interactive maps that test basic geography, examine key events in world history, and analyze the state of the world.
- *Simulations.* Engage world politics by experiencing how political actors make decisions.
- *PoliSci News Review.* Join the political conversation by following headlines in *Financial Times* newsfeeds, reading analysis in the blog, taking weekly current events quizzes and polls, and more.
- *ClassPrep.* Engage students with class presentation resources collected in one convenient online destination.

MyPoliSciLab Comes from a *Trusted Partner* with Educational Expertise and an Eye on the Future

- Pearson support instructors with workshops, training, and assistance from Pearson Faculty Advisors so you get the help you need to make MyPoliSciLab work for your course.
- Pearson gathers feedback from instructors and students during the development of content and the feature enhancement of each release to ensure that our products meet your needs.

To order MyPoliSciLab with the print text, use ISBN 0-205-85896-1.

Supplements

Pearson is pleased to offer several resources to qualified adopters of *International Relations and World Politics* and their students that will make teaching and learning from this book even more effective and enjoyable. Several of the supplements for this book are available at the Instructor Resource Center (IRC), an online hub that allows instructors to quickly download book-specific supplements. Please visit the IRC welcome page at **www.pearsonhighered.com/irc** to register for access.

PASSPORT   Choose the resources you want from MyPoliSciLab and put links to them into your course management system. If there is assessment associated with those resources, it also can be uploaded, allowing the results to feed directly into your course management system's gradebook. With MyPoliSciLab assets like videos, mapping exercises, *Financial Times* newsfeeds, current events quizzes, politics blog, and much more, Passport is available for any Pearson political science book. To order Passport with the print text, use ISBN 0-205-20865-7.

INSTRUCTOR'S MANUAL/TEST BANK   This resource includes learning objectives, lecture outlines, multiple-choice questions, true/false questions, and essay questions for each chapter. Available exclusively on the IRC.

PEARSON MYTEST   This powerful assessment generation program includes all of the items in the instructor's manual/test bank. Questions and tests can be easily created, customized, saved online, and then printed, allowing flexibility to manage assessments anytime and anywhere. Available exclusively on the IRC.

POWERPOINT PRESENTATION   Organized around a lecture outline, these multimedia presentations also include photos, figures, and tables from each chapter. Available exclusively on the IRC.

SAMPLE SYLLABUS   This resource provides suggestions for assigning content from this book and MyPoliSciLab. Available exclusively on the IRC.

LONGMAN ATLAS OF WORLD ISSUES (0-205-78020-2)   From population and political systems to energy use and women's rights, the *Longman Atlas of World Issues* features full-color thematic maps that examine the forces shaping the world. Featuring maps from the latest edition of *The Penguin State of the World Atlas*, this excerpt includes critical thinking exercises to promote a deeper understanding of how geography affects many global issues.

GOODE'S WORLD ATLAS (0-321-65200-2)   First published by Rand McNally in 1923, *Goode's World Atlas* has set the standard for college reference atlases. It features hundreds of physical, political, and thematic maps as well as graphs, tables, and a pronouncing index.

RESEARCH AND WRITING IN INTERNATIONAL RELATIONS (0-205-06065-X)   With current and detailed coverage on how to start research in the discipline's major subfields, this brief and affordable guide offers the step-by-step guidance and the essential resources needed to compose political science papers that go beyond description and into systematic and sophisticated inquiry. This text focuses on areas where students often need help—finding a topic, developing a question, reviewing the literature, designing research, and last, writing the paper.

ACKNOWLEDGMENTS

We, the authors, are educators who have had the privilege to teach thousands of students—graduate and undergraduate—over many years. We thank them for the insights that they, our colleagues, and our editors kindly have shared with us—inputs duly reflected in the pages of this volume. We also thank the reviewers for their invaluable feedback: Roberto Dominguez, Suffolk University; Amy Eckert, Metropolitan State College of Denver; Jeannie Grussendorf, Georgia State University; Lionel Ingram, University of New Hampshire; Rolin G. Mainuddin, North Carolina Central University; Richard Stoll, Rice University; Michael Struett, North Carolina State University; and Thomas C. Walker, State University of New York at Albany. Finally, our spouses and family members not only have given us precious time, but also shared their substantive comments for which we are, as always, most grateful.

PAUL R. VIOTTI
MARK V. KAUPPI

MAPS

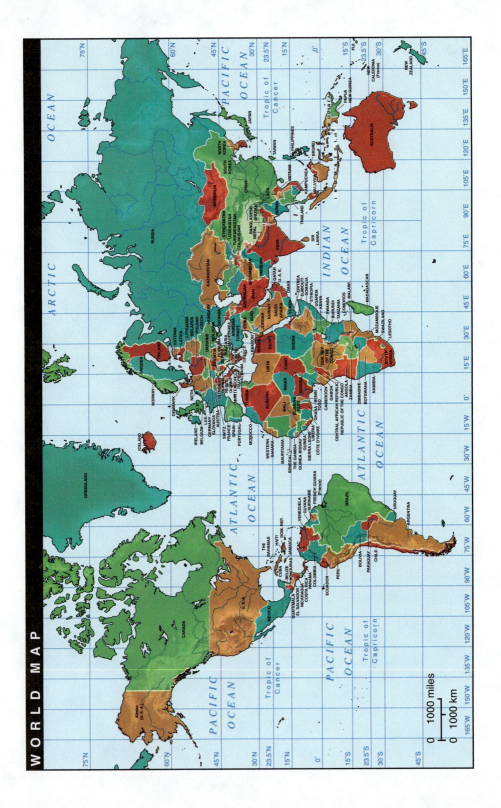

WORLD MAP

xviii

NORTH AMERICA

ARCTIC OCEAN

GREENLAND

Nuuk (Godthab)

CANADA

Brooks Range

Mt Mckinley

Mt Logan

Gulf of Alaska

Mackenzie Mountains

Great Bear Lake

Great Slave Lake

Lake Athabasca

Hudson Bay

Baffin Bay

Hudson Strait

Ungava Bay

Labrador Sea

Davis Strait

Denmark Strait

Norwegian Sea

Greenland Sea

Rocky Mountains

Vancouver

Calgary

Lake Winnipeg

Gulf of St. Lawrence

Montreal

Ottawa

Olympic Mts.

Seattle

Portland

Vancouver

Spokane

Lake Sakakawea

Great Salt Lake

Minneapolis

Lake Oahe

L. Superior

L. Michigan

L. Huron

Ontario

Rochester

Buffalo

Milwaukee

L. Erie

Detroit

Cleveland

New York

Philadelphia

Baltimore

Washington D. C.

U.S.A.

San Francisco

Oakland

Death Valley

Mojave Desert

Los Angeles

San Diego

Boulder

Great Plains

Omaha

Chicago

Kansas City

St. Louis

Louisville

Ohio R.

Appalachian Mts.

Norfolk

Charlotte

ATLANTIC OCEAN

Memphis

Dallas

Birmingham

Jacksonville

San Antonio

Houston

New Orleans

Gulf of Mexico

Orlando

Tampa

West Palm Beach

Miami

THE BAHAMAS

Nassau

Tropic of Cancer

Baja California

Gulf of California

Sierra Madre Occidental

MEXICO

Sierra Madre Oriental

Sierra Madre Del Sur

Mexico City

Havana

CUBA

HAITI

Port-au-Prince

Kingston

JAMAICA

Santo Domingo

San Juan

DOM. REP.

Yucatan Peninsula

Belize City

BELIZE

Belmopan

Gulf of Tehuantepec

Guatemala

GUATEMALA

HONDURAS

Tegucigalpa

San Salvador

EL SALVADOR

L. Nicaragua

NICARAGUA

Managua

San Jose

COSTA RICA

PANAMA

Panama

Willemstad

Caribbean Sea

PACIFIC OCEAN

0   500 miles

0   500 km

SOUTH AMERICA

Caribbean Sea

Barranquilla

Maracaibo • Valencia
Barquisimeto

VENEZUELA

GUYANA

Medellin •

Georgetown

SURINAME

Paramaribo

Río Orinoco

Cayenne

Bogotá •

Cali •

**FRENCH
GUIANA
(France)**

COLOMBIA

ECUADOR

Río Negro

Quito

**Amazon
Basin**

Río Amazonas

Manaus •

Amazon R.

Marajo
Island

Belém

Gulf of
Guayaquil

Guayaquil

Río Juruá

Río Madeira

Teresina •

Fortaleza

Río Purus

PERU

Río Japurá

Río Xingu

Río Tocantins

BRAZIL

Recife

San Martín de Porres

Lima

Río Tapajós

Río Araguaia

Río São Francisco

**Mato Grosso
Plateau**

Lake
Titicaca

BOLIVIA

La Paz •

Goiania •

★ *Brasília*

Salvador

Sucre

Belo Horizonte •

Atacama Desert

PARAGUAY

Río Paraguay

Campinas •

Río
de
Janeiro

CHILE

Tropic of
Capricorn

Asunción

São Paulo •

Cabo Frio

23.5°S

Río Pilcomayo

Curitiba •

Andes Mountains

**PACIFIC

OCEAN**

Porto
Alegre •

Rosario •

ARGENTINA

Río Paraná

Río Uruguay

URUGUAY

*Cerro
Aconcagua*

Santiago

Pampas

Buenos Aires

Montevideo

Patagonia

**ATLANTIC

OCEAN**

Isla Grande
de Chiloe

Gulf of
San Matias

**Valdes
Penninsula**

Gulf of
San Jorge

Taitao
Penninsula

**FALKLAND
ISLANDS**

Strait of
Magellan

*Port
Stanley*

**SOUTH
GEORGIA
ISLAND**

Tierra Del Fuego

0   500 miles

0   500 km

**ATLANTIC

OCEAN**

Caribbean Sea

80°W 70°W 60°W 50°W 40°W 30°W

10°N

0°

10°S

20°S

23.5°S Tropic of
Capricorn

30°S

40°S

50°S

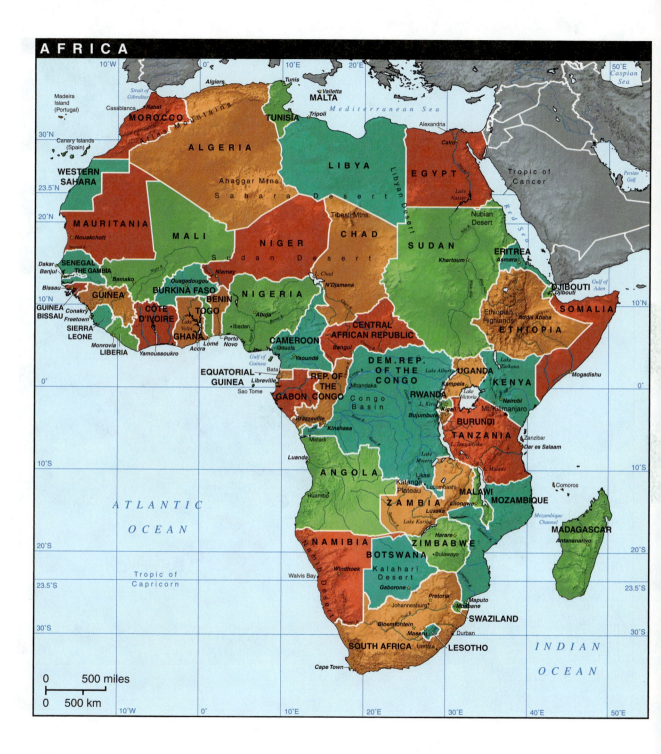

AFRICA

10°W · 0° · 10°E · 20°E · 50°E Caspian Sea

Madeira Island (Portugal)

Algiers · Tunis · Valletta · MALTA · Mediterranean Sea

Strait of Gibraltar

Casablanca · Rabat · Tripoli · Alexandria

MOROCCO · TUNISIA · Cairo

Canary Islands (Spain) · Atlas Mountains · ALGERIA · LIBYA · EGYPT · Tropic of Cancer · Persian Gulf

WESTERN SAHARA · Ahaggar Mtns. · Lake Nasser · Red Sea

Sahara Desert · Nubian Desert

MAURITANIA · Tibesti Mtns.

Nouakchott · Senegal R. · MALI · NIGER · CHAD · SUDAN · ERITREA · Asmara

Dakar · SENEGAL · Niger R. · Niamey · Sudan Desert · Khartoum · DJIBOUTI · Gulf of Aden

Banjul · THE GAMBIA · Bamako · Ouagadougou · Chad · N'Djamena · Nile R. · Djibouti

Bissau · GUINEA · BURKINA FASO · NIGERIA · White Nile · Addis Ababa · SOMALIA

GUINEA-BISSAU · Conakry · Freetown · CÔTE D'IVOIRE · TOGO · BENIN · Abuja · Benue R. · Ethiopian Highlands · ETHIOPIA

SIERRA LEONE · GHANA · Lake Volta · Ibadan · CENTRAL AFRICAN REPUBLIC

Monrovia · LIBERIA · Yamoussoukro · Accra · Lomé · Porto Novo · CAMEROON · Douala · Bangui

EQUATORIAL GUINEA · Bata · Yaoundé · Mogadishu

Gulf of Guinea · Libreville · DEM. REP. OF THE CONGO · Lake Albert · UGANDA · Lake Turkana

Sao Tome · GABON · REP. OF THE CONGO · Mbandaka · Kampala · KENYA

Congo Basin · RWANDA · Lake Victoria · Nairobi

Brazzaville · Kinshasa · Kasai R. · Bujumbura · Kigali · Mt. Kilimanjaro

Matadi · Lake Kivu · BURUNDI

Luanda · L. Tanganyika · TANZANIA · Zanzibar · Dar es Salaam

ANGOLA · Lake Mweru · Lake Malawi

Huambo · Likasi · Katanga Plateau · Lubumbashi · MALAWI · MOZAMBIQUE · Comoros

ZAMBIA · Lilongwe · Mozambique Channel · MADAGASCAR

Lusaka · Lake Kariba · Zambezi R. · Antananarivo

NAMIBIA · ZIMBABWE · Harare

Namib Desert · BOTSWANA · Bulawayo

Windhoek · Kalahari Desert

Walvis Bay · Tropic of Capricorn · Gaborone · Pretoria · Maputo · Mbabane · SWAZILAND

Johannesburg · Vaal R. · Bloemfontein · Maseru · Durban · LESOTHO

SOUTH AFRICA · Umtata

Cape Town

ATLANTIC OCEAN

INDIAN OCEAN

0 500 miles
0 500 km

xxi

EUROPE

ICELAND
Reykjavik
Faroe Islands (Denmark)
Torshavn
Shetland Islands
Orkney Islands
Hebrides
U.K.
Glasgow
Edinburgh
Belfast
IRELAND
Dublin
Limerick
Cork
Sunderland
Leeds
Liverpool · Manchester
Birmingham
London
DENMARK
Copenhagen
NETH.
Amsterdam
The Hague
Rotterdam
BELGIUM
Brussels
Luxembourg
LUX.
Bonn
Frankfurt
Nurnberg
GERMANY
Berlin
Leipzig
Hamburg
NORWAY
Oslo
SWEDEN
Stockholm
Goteborg
FINLAND
Helsinki
Tallinn
ESTONIA
St. Petersburg
Riga
LATVIA
Vilnius
LITHUANIA
Kaliningrad
Gdansk
POLAND
Poznan
Warsaw
Lodz
Krakow
Minsk
BELARUS
Kiev
UKRAINE
L'viv
Moscow
RUSSIA
Rostov
Jaroslavl
Gorkiy
Kazan
Perm
Izevsk
Saratov
Volgograd
Tol Yatti
Voronez
Kharkov
Krivoy Rog
Donetsk
Sea of Azov
Krasnodar
Caucasus Mts.
PRAGUE
CZECH
Brno
SLOVAKIA
Bratislava
LIECHTENSTEIN
Vaduz
Zurich
Bern
SWITZERLAND
Geneva
Lyon
Mont Blanc
AUSTRIA
Vienna
Budapest
HUNGARY
SLOVENIA
Ljubljana
Zagreb
CROATIA
Cluj-Napoca
Timisoara
ROMANIA
Bucharest
MOLDOVA
Chisinau
Frunze
Odessa
Black Sea
ATLANTIC OCEAN
FRANCE
Nantes
Strasbourg
Paris
Bordeaux
Bay of Biscay
Bayonne
Porto
Valladolid
PORTUGAL
Lisbon
Madrid
SPAIN
Cordoba
Gibraltar
Barcelona
Valencia
ANDORRA
Marseille
Corsica
Sardinia
Majorca
ITALY
Monaco
Milano
Genova
Firenze
Rome
Naples
Vesuvius
Appennines
Adriatic Sea
BOSNIA HERZE-GOVINA
Sarajevo
SERBIA
Belgrade
KOSOVO
Pristina
MONTENEGRO
Podgorica
MACEDONIA
Skopje
Tirana
ALBANIA
BULGARIA
Sofia
Varna
Burgas
GREECE
Thessaloniki
Agrinion
Athens
Peloponnesus
Lesbos
Aegean Sea
Rhodes
Crete
Palermo
Monte Etna
Sicily
Tyrrhenian Sea
Ionian Sea
Mediterranean Sea
Red Sea

Greenland Sea
Jan Mayen
Denmark Strait
Norwegian Sea
Barents Sea
Kolgujev
White Sea
L. Ladoga
Gulf of Bothnia
Gulf of Finland
Baltic Sea
North Sea
English Channel
Carpathian Mountains
Ural Mountains

500 miles
500 km

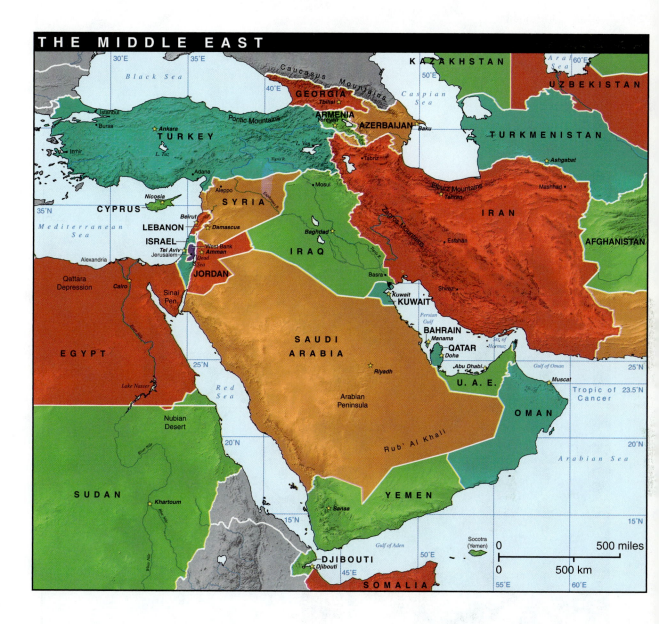

THE MIDDLE EAST

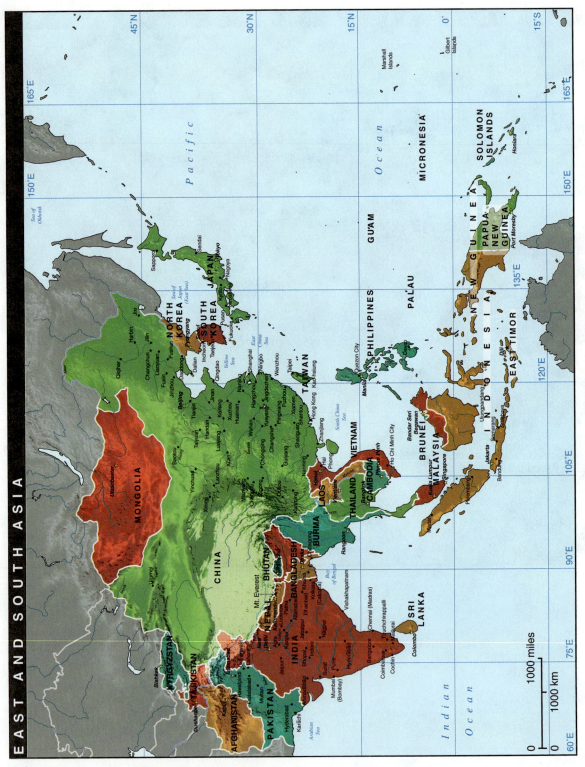

Pacific

Ocean

Sea of
Okhotsk

MONGOLIA

Ulaanbaatar

Qiqihar

Harbin

Jilin

NORTH
KOREA

SOUTH
KOREA

JAPAN

Sapporo

Sendai

Tokyo

Nagoya

Kyoto

Fukuoka

Pusan

Taegu

Seoul

Inchon

Pyongyang

Changchun

Liaoyuan

Fushun

Dalian

Qingdao

Jinan

Yellow
Sea

Sea of
Japan
(East Sea)

Shanghai

Ningbo

Wenzhou

Fuzhou

Xiamen

Shantou

Hong Kong

TAIWAN

Taipei

Kao-hsiung

East
China
Sea

Beijing

Tianjin

Shijiazhuang

Taiyuan

Handan

Zhengzhou

Luoyang

Kaifeng

Xuzhou

Wuhan

Hefei

Nanjing

Hangzhou

Changsha

Nanchang

CHINA

Baotou

Yinchuan

Lanzhou

Xining

Xian

Chengdu

Chongqing

Guiyang

Kunming

Nanning

Guangzhou

Liuzhou

Zhanjiang

South China
Sea

VIETNAM

Hanoi

Hai
Phong

Ho Chi Minh City

LAOS

Vientiane

THAILAND

Bangkok

CAMBODIA

Phnom
Penh

BURMA

Rangoon

Mandalay

BHUTAN

NEPAL

BANGLADESH

Dhaka

Chittagong

Kolkata
(Calcutta)

Mt. Everest

Kathmandu

Patna

Kanpur

Lucknow

Delhi

New Delhi

INDIA

Jaipur

Ahmadabad

Indore

Bhopal

Nagpur

Surat

Mumbai
(Bombay)

Pune

Hyderabad

Bangalore

Chennai (Madras)

Coimbatore

Tiruchirappalli

Madurai

Cochin

SRI
LANKA

Colombo

Vishakhapatnam

Bay
of Bengal

PAKISTAN

Karachi

Hyderabad

Multan

Lahore

Faisalabad

Islamabad

Peshawar

AFGHANISTAN

Kabul

Arabian
Sea

TAJIKISTAN

Dushanbe

KYRGYZSTAN

Bishkek

Ürümqi

PHILIPPINES

Quezon City

Manila

Davao

GUAM

PALAU

MICRONESIA

Marshall
Islands

Gilbert
Islands

SOLOMON
ISLANDS

Honiara

PAPUA
NEW
GUINEA

Port Moresby

NEW GUINEA

INDONESIA

EAST TIMOR

Ujungpandang

Surabaya

Jakarta

Bandung

Semarang

Palembang

Medan

MALAYSIA

Kuala Lumpur

Singapore

BRUNEI

Bandar Seri
Begawan

Indian
Ocean

45°N

30°N

15°N

0°

15°S

165°E

150°E

135°E

120°E

105°E

90°E

75°E

60°E

1000 miles

1000 km

0

0

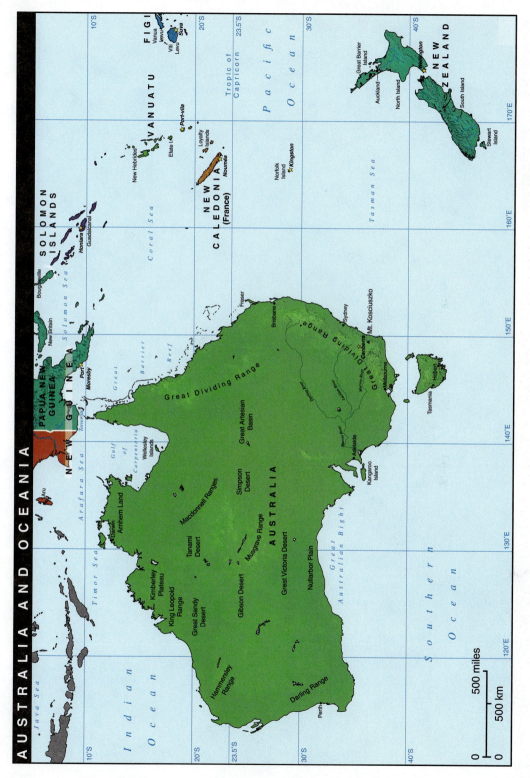

AUSTRALIA AND OCEANIA

Engaging International Relations and World Politics

"*The emerging international system is likely to be quite different from those that have preceded it.... At the politico-military level, we remain in a single-superpower world. But in every other dimension—industrial, financial, educational, social, cultural—the distribution of power is shifting, moving away from American dominance. That does not mean we are entering an anti-American world. But we are moving into a post-American world, one defined and directed from many places and by many people.*"—Fareed Zakaria, Editor-at-Large of Time Magazine

LEARNING OBJECTIVES

1.1 Illustrate specific aspects of globalization in the economic, social, and cultural realm and the role of technology.

1.2 Define and provide examples of the key actors in international relations and world politics—states, international organizations,

nongovernmental organizations, and individual practitioners.

1.3 Explain the difference between the terms international relations and world politics and define security, economy, and identity.

Read and Listen to **Chapter 1** at **mypoliscilab.com**

Study and Review the **Pre-Test & Flashcards** at **mypoliscilab.com**

The town of Sidi Bouzid is approximately one hundred fifty miles from Tunis, capital of the North African country of Tunisia. On December 17, 2010, a fruit seller by the name of Mohamed Bouazizi set a fire in an act of self-immolation outside the local government building. His extreme action was a protest against police abuse and a bureaucratic decision to deny him the right to sell his fruit as he did not have a proper license. As a relatively tight-knit rural community, demonstrators gathered that afternoon outside the mayor's office to protest. When Bouazizi died two weeks later on January 4, Tunisians across the country were politically galvanized as his private suffering turned into shared outrage.

Government militias shot and clubbed protestors in a number of towns. These actions drew young bloggers and amateur cell phone videographers from Tunis, which was well wired for the internet age compared to the rural areas of the country. Some of these individuals had participated for several years in online dissent through the website Nawaat.org. When the authoritarian government of Ben Ali cracked down on video-sharing websites, activists turned to Facebook, which boomed in popularity. Fearful of alienating moderates, the government only tried to shut down the Facebook Web pages of well-known activists. By early January, labor unions joined with political activists to stage massive protests in Tunis and other cities. Social media continued to encourage civil and political protest and became a way to tell the world what was going on in Tunisia. As pressure mounted on the regime, the Tunisian army made the decision not to fire on the protestors calling for the end of the Ben Ali regime. Twenty-eight days after Bouazizi's self-immolation, President Ben Ali and his family fled the country.

We live in an era of increasing globalization, and people have ambivalent feelings about it. Globalization advocates point to the great gains for human welfare, interaction among ourselves, and liberties many of us enjoy. Others, however, point out some of the downsides of globalization: environmental degradation, labor exploitation, rapid spread of viruses and other diseases across national borders, and the transnational reach of criminal and terrorist groups. On an even broader scale there is perhaps the ultimate question: Is the world becoming characterized more by peace or by war, and how has globalization affected the possible outcome?

The purpose of this textbook is to help our readers gain a better understanding of the shape of the current and emerging world order. It is specifically geared toward students who aspire to be practitioners of international relations (IR) and world politics. We define "practitioners" broadly. They include those interested in working in their country's foreign ministry and diplomatic corps like the U.S. State Department and its foreign service as well as any number of governmental organizations that deal with such matters abroad as defense, homeland security, foreign aid, agricultural assistance, trade and investment, intelligence and security services as well as various congressional or parliamentary committees and state and local organizations, which may also engage in international affairs. International organizations (IOs) such as the United Nations and its affiliated agencies would also count as well as nongovernmental organizations (NGOs) such as Doctors Without Borders, Amnesty International, Oxfam, and the Canadian Council for International Cooperation.

Some of you may find your way to positions in multinational corporations, banks, and other commercial enterprises that do business abroad, playing substantial roles in an increasingly globalized world. Like the co-authors of this book, some of you may become college or university professors who conduct research and teach classes in international relations and world politics, economics, geography, history, and related fields. Others may become educators in elementary or high schools, teaching your successor generations the history or social studies classes that convey important understandings about the world outside the country's national borders. Still others may pursue careers in journalism—a dynamic field that no doubt will take forms quite different from the traditional newspaper, radio, television, and internet that are the principal carriers of the spoken and written word today.

Do any of these positions or career paths interest you? There also may be other opportunities not mentioned here that come to mind. Whatever course you choose to pursue, the authors will lay out as clearly as we can what we think useful for you to know were you to pursue any of these opportunities. Even those who wind up in positions dealing primarily with domestic matters at national, state, or local levels will find value in grasping how the world "out there" matters, whether in business, government, or as a private citizen in an increasingly globalized world.

Toward that end, we devote the first chapters to what we think any practitioner of international relations and world politics should be familiar with: basic actors, theories and concepts that help make the world intelligible, a brief historical overview to reveal recurrent patterns, and a primer on international economy.

Taken together, these chapters can be seen as a toolbox designed to aid your understanding of global politics and economics.

In this chapter we begin our discussion of globalization and then turn to an overview of key actors who will reappear throughout the text. We conclude with a discussion of the title of the book: *International Relations and World Politics: Security, Economy, and Identity.*

GLOBALIZATION

1.1 Illustrate specific aspects of globalization in the economic, social, and cultural realm and the role of technology.

Watch the **Video "Global Migration and Employment"** at **mypoliscilab.com**

globalization ■ the continual increase in worldwide economic, social, and cultural interactions that transcend the boundaries of states and the resultant political implications

The key trend we wish to emphasize is increasing globalization. For many social scientists the concept of globalization suffers from a myriad of definitions, is fraught with emotional if not ideological connotations, and is so general and all-encompassing that it lacks utility as an analytical concept. From our perspective, however, it is important as useful shorthand for a number of interrelated and important developments in the modern world. Therefore, in this book the term **globalization** refers to the continual increase in worldwide economic, social, and cultural interactions that transcend the boundaries of states and which have significant political implications. These interactions are aided by advances in technologies. This definition does not presume globalization has a uniform impact on any one particular society, group, or class. Nor does it assume its political impact is necessarily a force for peace or conflict.

Globalization is exemplified in the economic realm by the formation and accelerated growth of a global capitalist economy that increasingly disregards state boundaries and makes economic self-sufficiency virtually impossible. International trade moves across the globe at historically unprecedented volumes. Containerized shipping has resulted in the rapid movement of goods from ships to trucks and on to inland cities and towns. Every convenience shop in North America undoubtedly has items for sale that were manufactured in Asia.

Global finance continues to accelerate with the formation and integration of financial markets around the world. New York may still be number one, but nightly business programs report closings in London, Frankfurt, Paris, and Hong Kong as well. Due to communication breakthroughs and the commonplace use of computers, billions of dollars in trades occur each day. Teleconferencing is standard operating procedures for banks, investment houses, and companies whether they are making cars or MP3 players.

Due to acquisitions and mergers, it is difficult to identify what is an American, British, or Canadian company. Longman, the publisher of this book, is based in New York City yet is a subsidiary of the British publishing firm Pearson. In the car industry even well-known national firms such as General Motors (GM) and Ford are as much foreign focused as they are domestically. For example, 70 percent of GM's sales are made overseas with China the number one market. Due to the fact that so many companies are partially owned by foreign firms, it is a challenge for individuals who would prefer to only "buy American" or "Canadian" or "British."

Globalization is also evident in the social realm. Satellites facilitate virtually instantaneous Cable News Network (CNN), British Broadcasting Company

(BBC), Al-Jazeera, and other worldwide network coverage of day-to-day news from around the globe. Such events may include famines, civil wars, and terrorist bombings from heretofore seemingly remote spots on the globe, altering our perception of time and space. Whether easy access to news coverage of such events has an impact on one's conception of self and place in the world is subject to speculation. On the more personal level, Facebook, Skype, and smartphone applications like FaceTime allow long-distance friendships to be sustained on a daily basis. It is no longer necessary to rely on snail mail letters sent by air or costly overseas phone calls.

The cultural impact of communication technologies associated with globalization is also subject to political debate. Satellites, cable programs, and internet feeds from different countries and cultures are broadcast into student union buildings and homes. This exposure allows for the possibility that people of different backgrounds can see what they have in common as much as what differentiates them. Such global access, however, can often distress parents, ethnic and religious leaders, and governments worried about "cultural pollution" and the allegedly pernicious effects of foreign values—concerns usually directed against Western popular culture. Minority cultures in particular may view such foreign programming as a threat to group identity and traditional values.

There is a pervasive sense that the world is rapidly growing more integrated, resulting in ongoing assessments of the impact of economic, social, and cultural interactions and, in turn, the political implications for international relations and world politics. It must be emphasized, however, that all states and peoples do not experience equally the impact of globalization. Globalization is neither a uniform nor a homogeneous process. There is no doubt that advanced industrial states in Europe, North America, and Japan are much more economically and politically interdependent with one another than they are with the countries of sub-Saharan Africa. Although commercials for computer firms would have us believe that the communications revolution is already well entrenched in Tibetan monasteries and Brazilian rain forests, this is simply not the case. Similarly, the poorer countries and their peoples in the euphemistically termed "developing world" are not equal players in the global economy. In fact, they are dependent on and sometimes see themselves as exploited by better-off countries and hence are victims of globalization.

Finally we want to note that the critical element of globalization—interactions across political boundaries—is not limited in its applicability to the contemporary era. Interdependence, as we will see in Chapter 3, characterizes a number of historical international systems over the past two thousand years. What is different today, however, is the extent and depth of globalization. Two hundred years ago, letters took weeks if not months to make their way from one end of Europe to another, just as cultural and political influences and trends took time to affect distant societies. The French Revolution, for example, had a profound historical impact, but not immediately on the Asian, African, and Latin American continents. But today the collapse of the nuclear-armed Pakistani government and the accession to power of Islamist extremists would have an immediate and profound ripple effect well beyond the South Asian subcontinent.

ACTORS

1.2 Define and provide examples of the key actors in international relations and world politics—states, international organizations, nongovernmental organizations, and individual practitioners.

Collective efforts are the primary means by which people achieve security, economic welfare, or a common identity. Indeed, throughout history humanity has recognized that a pooling of resources and energy is generally the most efficient way for individuals or groups to fulfill their wants and needs. In other words, the weak *I* becomes the strong *WE*. The expression of this collective effort—whether at the local, tribal, state, or international level—will vary depending on the importance of the issue and the time available for its resolution. In this book, therefore, we emphasize the following actors in terms of international relations and world politics (see Figure 1.1):

1. States
2. International organizations
3. Nongovernmental organizations
4. Individuals

◉—Watch the Video "IMF Conditionality and the Irish Bailout" at mypoliscilab.com

✴—Explore the "Why Study International Relations" at mypoliscilab.com

States

As is evident throughout this book, much of our discussion revolves around states. A geographical entity governed by a central authority, the state is traditionally viewed as the most important of the three basic organizations in the previous list. A state takes the lead in attempting to defend the physical security of the population, ensures the economic welfare of its citizens, provides a focus for loyalty and identity, and claims sovereignty. This means its leaders claim to represent and exercise authority over all persons within the state's territory and claim a right to autonomy internationally.

sovereignty ■ a claim to political authority to make policy or take actions domestically or abroad; based on territory and autonomy, historically associated with the modern state

When it comes to international relations, states dominate conventional discourse. Nongovernmental movements such as insurgencies and terrorist groups may attack particular states, but very often their goal is either to take over the reins of power in an existing state or to create a new state. Even if broad-based political-cultural-religious movements transcend state borders, a political-military

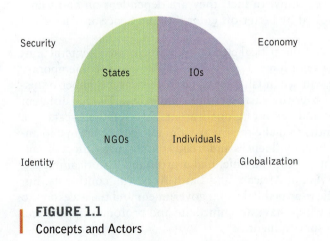

FIGURE 1.1
Concepts and Actors

entity is needed to carry out the agenda. Finally, in those areas of the world burdened by overpopulation, environmental degradation, and mass migration, states are expected to take the lead in developing and implementing policies to deal with these problems.

States, however, can be viewed as obstacles to the achievement of security, economy, and identity when they persecute their own citizens, pursue counterproductive economic policies, and demand complete and undivided loyalty to the point where no dissent is allowed. In addition, in their pursuit of security, states clash with one another, leading to international tension and perhaps war. A key domestic role of states—to adjudicate domestic disagreements—is difficult to perform in the international arena. There is no world government, international courts are weak, and states often resort to the use of force.

International Organizations

Second, states are not the only prism through which to view international relations, particularly in the current era of globalization in which it is apparent that no single state can hope to be the sole agent of collective action to solve global problems. International organizations (IOs)—also known as *intergovernmental organizations* (or *IGOs*)—play a role. IOs can be bilateral (between two states, as in the U.S.–Canada North American Aerospace Defense Command), but most are multilateral because three or more states are members. Examples include organizations with limited membership, such as the North Atlantic Treaty Organization (NATO), the European Union (EU), the Organization of American States (OAS), the Association of Southeast Asian Nations (ASEAN), and the African Union (AU). The best-known universal IO is the United Nations (UN). Membership in the UN is open to all states. Nongovernmental organizations (NGOs) and even individuals try to influence the United Nations and other international organizations and governments by lobbying or persuading international and national decision makers and their staffs, holding conferences of their own, and publicizing their views in the mass media, including internet websites, blogs, and social networking sites.

A dramatic expansion of IOs and NGOs occurred in the 20th century, ranging from military alliances in the security realm to UN-related organizations concerned not just with security, but also with economic and social issues. Organizations such as the Food and Agricultural Organization (FAO), the International Monetary Fund (IMF), the World Health Organization (WHO), the World Bank (known more formally as the IBRD, the International Bank for Reconstruction and Development), and the United Nations International Children's Emergency Fund (UNICEF) barely begin to cover the veritable "alphabet soup" of UN-related agencies and other international organizations pursuing specific objectives on the global agenda. The growth in numbers and activities of IOs has also been accompanied by a proliferation of NGOs actively pursuing their own objectives or agendas.

Though IOs were created by and for states, it is interesting to consider the extent to which they have come to be significant actors in their own right. Do IOs simply reflect states' interests and at best provide a forum for debate? Do they become a source of financial aid or other assistance when economic or other problems arise? Do they offer an international diplomat when states come into conflict

international organization (IO) ■ an institution composed of states as members (for example, the United Nations [UN], European Union [EU], and the North Atlantic Treaty Organization [NATO]) with one another? Or have IOs over time come to the point at which they now actually influence states' interests, preferences, and objectives? Whatever influence IOs may have in particular functional areas such as financial loans or mediation efforts, their key role may come to be purveyors of global **norms**—basic values that over time states come to take seriously.

norms ■ values that states or people take seriously and that influence behavior, such as human rights

For example, while many states around the world continue to violate human rights, over the years norms have evolved that allow outsiders to make this issue a matter of international and foreign policy discussion and even punishment or sanction. Despite vigorous protest from the Chinese government, many states and human rights groups continue to condemn Beijing for its harsh treatment of political dissidents. Another example involves NATO military action against Yugoslavia in 1999, a sovereign state that did not invade another country but whose officials committed or allowed ethnic cleansing and other human rights violations against its own citizens. Such action was a key reason that NATO launched the air war against authorities in the former Yugoslavia—a campaign motivated to serve human rights and related humanitarian goals rather than for such traditional purposes as seizing territory or repulsing an invader.

Pursuit of those responsible for these atrocities continues to the present day with arrest and trial of the alleged perpetrators—the likes of the late Serb President Slobodan Milošević, Bosnian Serb President Radovan Karadzic, and his military commander, General Ratko Mladić. More than bringing them to justice, these arrests and trials underscore the growing strength of increasing global commitment to norms against genocide and other human rights violations.

CASE & POINT | Global Governance and the Ratko Mladić Case

CASE　Born in 1943, Serbian General Ratko Mladić rose as a commander to lead the Serb Army in Bosnia as its chief of staff in the early 1990s. Under his command his troops conducted a four-year campaign against Sarajevo, blockading and bombarding the city, producing terror from seemingly random attacks that struck civilian targets, killing or wounding citizens there. Under fire from NATO air strikes in 1995, Mladić's forces overran UN safe areas at Žepa and Srebrenica—some 8,300 were murdered, allegedly on his orders, for which he was indicted shortly afterward at the International Criminal Tribunal for the Former Yugoslavia (ICTFY)—genocide, war crimes, and crimes against humanity were the charges levied against him. An international arrest warrant was issued by the ICTFY in 1996. Long in hiding—some sixteen years—Mladić finally was arrested in 2011 and brought to

trial before the ICTFY in The Hague, located in the capital of the Netherlands. The Hague is also the location for the International Criminal Court (ICC) and the International Court of Justice (ICJ).

The Hague is a center for international jurisprudence, current institutions building on a legacy established initially by the Permanent Court of Arbitration (PCA) established by The Hague Conventions in 1899, reaffirmed in 1907, and still in existence as a mechanism for the peaceful settlement of international disputes. The World Court, which was part of the post-World War I League of Nations system, operated in the interwar period until it was finally succeeded in 1945 by the ICJ. Like the World Court before its time, the ICJ—a principal organ of the United Nations—has jurisdiction over cases brought before it by other states. The ICC, ICTFY,

(continued)

and other special tribunals hear cases against individuals like Mladić and the late Serb President Slobodan Milošević.

Specific charges against Mladić—all violations of international law—include (1) genocide against Bosniaks (Muslims) and Bosnian Croats—killing men and boys found at Srebrenica, forcing women, children, and older people to leave the area; (2) crimes against humanity—persecutions directed against Bosniaks and Bosnian Croats including murder, torture, beatings, and rape; (3) mass murders (extermination) of Bosniaks and Bosnian Croats living in the cities his forces attacked, namely Srebrenica and Sarajevo; (4) forcible deportation of Bosniaks, Bosnian Croats, and other non-Serbs from cities, namely Srebrenica and Sarajevo; (5) terror and unlawful attacks against civilians, sniping and shelling against people living in Sarajevo; and (6) hostage-taking of United Nations military observers and peacekeepers.

The United States is not yet a member of the ICC, although Washington initially was instrumental in its establishment as a standing court with jurisdiction in cases against individuals accused of aggression: starting unjust or illegal wars, war crimes, genocide, and other crimes against humanity. Arguments made by those Americans opposed to joining the ICC rested mainly on two grounds: first, allowing such a court involves too great a transfer of authority from the sovereign jurisdiction of U.S. courts; second, at some future time the ICC could issue arrest warrants and prosecute American military members or civilian officials for alleged criminal violations.

Advocates of American ICC membership argue that protections are already present to prevent any such abuse. The very limited jurisdiction set out in the Rome Statute (the treaty under which the ICC operates that went into force in 2002) also makes the ICC a court of last resort, taking up cases when domestic courts have not, or cannot, do so. A state having jurisdiction in a particular case need not refer the case to the ICC.

Nevertheless, to date the American preference remains one in which tribunals like the ICTFY are created for specified purposes and are customized to particular wars or other contingencies that call for international legal action against perpetrators of such crimes.

Upon the arrest of Mladić, U.S. President Barack Obama underscored his support of the forthcoming prosecution:

> I applaud President Tadić and the government of Serbia on their determined efforts to ensure that Mladić was found and that he faces justice. We look forward to his expeditious transfer to The Hague. . . . Today is an important day for the families of Mladić's many victims, for Serbia, for Bosnia, for the United States, and for international justice. While we will never be able to bring back those who were murdered, Mladić will now have to answer to his victims, and the world, in a court of law.

Former Secretary of State Madeline Albright, who held office when these crimes were committed, added her comments.

> Ratko Mladić deserves to be tried and convicted. He was the military commander who ordered the murder of thousands and attempted to destroy Bosnian society. His trial should teach again the grim reality of ethnic cleansing and, I hope, bring some comfort to those who survived. . . . Mladić tried to become a conquering hero. Instead, he lived as a fugitive in obscurity and now faces years in custody. Justice works.

POINT Although there are still differences in views on how (or before which courts or tribunals) to hold individuals legally accountable for crimes against peace, war crimes, and crimes against humanity, widespread agreement has grown in the decades since World War II that this should be done. We are witnessing the slow growth of global governance on matters of criminal accountability. However limited such developments are, some say they are indicative of the ongoing emergence of a global civil society—the rule of law even beyond the jurisdiction of particular states. ◢

Nongovernmental Organizations

nongovernmental organizations (NGOs) ■
transnational organizations that have a standing independent of governments, often with a diverse membership that works to fulfill specific political, social, or economic objectives

Third, as noted earlier, in recent years there has been a veritable explosion in the number of **nongovernmental organizations (NGOs)**. As the term suggests, NGOs are composed of private, nonstate international actors that cut across national boundaries. In this regard, we identify four categories of NGOs of interest and importance to us in the study of international relations and world politics.

Private-Sector Economic Organizations   Although some writers reserve the term *NGO* for nonprofit organizations, we apply it to all nongovernmental organizations, including multinational corporations (MNCs), most of which are private-sector and thus nongovernmental organizations. Multinational business corporations and banks are understandably primarily motivated by enhancing the economic well-being of their stock- and other stakeholders, not necessarily the economic well-being of any one particular state. Interest in MNCs is not new. Indeed, with the U.S. Central Intelligence Agency (CIA) at the helm, the United Fruit Company played a role in the overthrow of the Arbenz regime in Guatemala in 1954, just as British Petroleum and the CIA were implicated in the overthrow of the Mossadegh government in Iran in 1953. Of particular interest to many observers of world politics, however, is the influence major corporations and banking institutions routinely have on the economies of states, particularly those in the developing world dependent on foreign investment. Does working in the corporate, banking, or import and export sectors appeal to you?

Transnational NGOs   Or would you rather work in nonprofit transnational NGOs with explicit political, economic, or social agendas, such as Amnesty International, Greenpeace, and religious organizations whose diverse memberships and global perspectives make it difficult to associate them with any one particular state? Transnational NGOs claim to have a broader constituency than MNCs or international banks. In their attempt to help define the international agenda, they often act as pressure groups to influence international organizations' or states' behavior. More generally, NGOs increase global awareness of such diverse topics as ozone-layer depletion, deforestation, epidemics, malnutrition and famine, religious persecution, genocide, and human rights in general. They also advance agendas for dealing with such problems.

Though such organizations do attempt to influence world politics by lobbying states and influencing state-sponsored meetings (such as those held during the early to mid-1990s in places like Rio de Janeiro, Cairo, and Beijing on economic development and environment, population, and the role and rights of women), their influence is actually much more pervasive and their goals much more sweeping. Activists aim at nothing less than shaping public affairs and how people perceive national and global problems. As a result, **global civil society** and the rule of law (domestic and international) associated with this term are increasingly prevalent in discussions of international relations, as are efforts to spread democratic forms of governance.

global civil society ■
the gradual worldwide emergence of the rule of law and networks or relationships among people in a world composed of both state and nonstate actors

Global civil society consists of states as well as individuals and organizations that aggregate individual interests within or outside particular states but operate typically beyond the border of any single state. That is, certain organizations may originate in a particular country, but their global agenda makes them, in effect, stateless. Their memberships also tend to be multinational. Along with states, international and nongovernmental organizations play important roles in global governance—coordinating, cooperating, and even collaborating on social, economic, and political matters that cannot so easily be resolved or managed by any one state or other actor alone. Indeed, multilateralism among diverse state and nonstate actors is characteristic of 21st-century globalization efforts.

Humanitarian Nongovernmental Organizations   Humanitarian nongovernmental organizations attempt to avoid overtly political roles. The best examples are humanitarian relief organizations such as Doctors Without Borders and a myriad of transnational programs in Africa and Asia that seek to improve the quality of life of the poor. If such an NGO engaged in politics and took sides in civil and international conflicts, it would most likely be denied access to combat zones. This and the previous category are what many people think of when the term *NGO* is used. In recent years there has been a phenomenal explosion in the number of such NGOs, from approximately 6,000 in 1990 to more than 40,000 today. NGOs have existed for centuries—the British and Foreign Anti-Slavery Society, for example, was around in the early 1800s. But the process of globalization—spurred further by the end of the Cold War and subsequent efforts to spread democratic and market-oriented values and structures, technological change, and economic integration—has also encouraged the growth of NGOs.

Nonstate Armed Groups   Terrorists often claim to represent a broader constituency, whereas transnational criminal organizations (TCOs) prefer to focus on their narrow economic agendas, becoming involved in politics only when the pursuit of their ill-gotten gains is threatened. In the past, terrorist activity tended to be more localized, often contained by the borders of a particular state. More recent is the globalization of terrorism by such networks as al-Qaeda, whose affiliates are said to operate in more than a dozen countries. TCOs like the Sicilian and American Mafias, the Russian "mafia," Japanese *Yakusa*, and Chinese "Triads" have also established regional and global networks essential to sustaining their "business" activities in drugs, gambling, human trafficking, prostitution, and the like.

In sum, these groups of actors—states, international organizations/IGOs, and nongovernmental organizations (NGOs)—can be viewed as a means by which people strive to attain their individual and collective goals of security, economic well-being, and identity. As already noted, states are not the only means by which security can be attained. In fact, where authoritarian governments are in power, it may be the state that poses the greatest threat to one's physical security. In such cases, IOs and NGOs might be called upon to help protect human rights, or individuals may turn to organizations or revolutionary movements dedicated to the overthrow of the existing regime.

Similarly, even if one accepts the argument that the state should work to enhance the economic well-being of its citizenry, the globalization of the economy has made this a much more difficult task. Indeed, the governments of some countries lacking financial reserves have turned to such international organizations as the International Monetary Fund for financial relief and in the process

States, often viewed in terms of their political leaders, are seen by most observers as the key actors in international relations. Here President Barack Obama meets with Canadian prime minister Stephen Harper during the president's visit to Ottawa in February 2009.

Although consisting of state actors, international organizations can also play key roles in international relations and world politics. Secretary-General Ban Ki-moon of the United Nations addresses a Security Council meeting in New York City.

Osama bin Laden, former head of the al-Qaeda terrorist organization, exemplifies the power of a nonstate actor. The instigator of the 9/11 attacks, he eluded efforts to kill or capture him for over twenty years. He was finally killed in May 2011 by U.S. Special Forces in Pakistan.

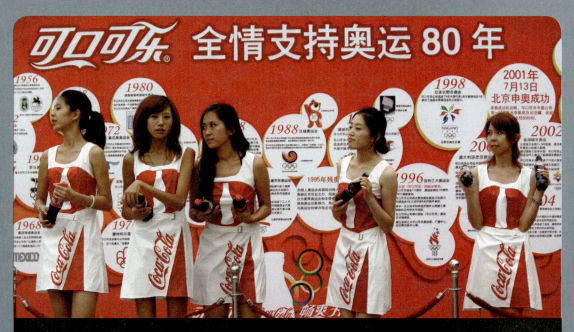

Multinational corporations increasingly became key nongovernmental actors during the twentieth century. The American firm Coca-Cola has been viewed not only as a financial giant, but also as the purveyor of American and Western values in China and throughout the world.

have had to swallow the subsequent bitter economic "medicine" imposed by the IMF as a condition for loans: cuts in government spending, increased taxes, higher interest rates, and restrictive fiscal and monetary policies intended to curb inflation, effectively slowing short-term business growth and thus reducing employment opportunities.

Finally, just as states have traditionally been the focal point of citizen identity and loyalty, at least in the Western world, other entities such as the United Nations and the European Union (EU) hold the potential to be foci of loyalty beyond the state. On the other hand, and much more prevalent today, in some parts of the world where state political authority is tenuous, religious or ethnic identification seems to be becoming a more important bond among people than any sense of loyalty or identification with a particular state.

Individuals

Our focus has been on the three broad categories of organizations in international relations, but what about the average human being? Individuals certainly make a difference, whether a Mahatma Gandhi in India or a Nelson Mandela in South Africa. But even those illustrious leaders found that a cause must be associated with an organization if the former is to be achieved. The same is true of Osama bin Laden, killed in 2011, who relied on the al-Qaeda organizational network and affiliated groups. We wish to emphasize, however, that while states, international organizations, and nongovernmental organizations are viewed as key actors in world politics, such entities are made up of flesh-and-blood human beings.

States do not make the decision to go to war; people in their governments or societies do. For example, would the United States have invaded Iraq in March 2003 if Al Gore had won the 2000 presidential election instead of George Bush? Would the United States and its allies and coalition partners have decided to draw down their forces in Iraq and Afghanistan as much or as rapidly as they have had John McCain defeated Barack Obama in the 2008 presidential campaign? Similarly, states do not decide to engage in genocide or provide famine relief to parts of Africa; people in their governments or societies do. So it is with the people who make up IOs and NGOs.

But the fact of the matter is that while individuals as practitioners can have a tremendous impact on the short-term course of world events—witness Mikhail Gorbachev, the former president of the former Soviet Union, whose actions contributed to the end of the Cold War—it is extremely difficult to identify such individuals until after their impact has been felt. For example, in 1985 experts initially saw Gorbachev as merely the latest in a long line of Soviet officials or Communist Party *apparatchiks,* not the agent of radical change in the global order he would become. Nor, for that matter, did Gorbachev initially see himself as precipitating these events merely by calling for greater openness (in Russian, *glasnost*) or restructuring state and society (in Russian, *perestroika*) within his own country. As things turned out, pursuit of this essentially domestic agenda had the unintended consequence of the breakup of the Soviet Union and its Warsaw Pact alliance in Central and Eastern Europe.

Most people who want to influence world politics must do so in an indirect manner through collective actors such as states, IOs, or NGOs. Gorbachev had at his disposal the Communist Party and the bureaucratic machinery of the Soviet state. Even Nelson Mandela of South Africa, longtime leader and symbol of the anti-apartheid movement, found it useful to be supported by the African National Congress in the presidential election campaign following his release from prison. Former U.S. president Jimmy Carter's leadership on election monitoring, conflict resolution, and other humanitarian causes is facilitated through his NGO, the Carter Center, in association with states and IOs. In short, while individuals can and do act on their own, they usually are more effective when they operate from an organizational base—states, international organizations, or nongovernmental organizations.

Whether acting on their own or as agents of states or nonstates, actors can make a difference. Put simply, human agency matters.

apartheid ■ a state policy of discrimination and strict racial segregation in a society

SECURITY, ECONOMY, IDENTITY

We now offer a few comments concerning the title of this book. To be precise, the concept international relations should refer to relations among nations—people with a common identity such as the French or Japanese nation. However, over the years, conventional discourse has come to equate the term *international* with *interstate* relations. When we use the term *international relations*, we are principally referring to relations among states, as we believe it is necessary to emphasize that states continue to be the primary actors on the world stage and central players in global governance—managing, if not resolving, issues on the security, economy, and identity agendas worldwide: problems, challenges, and opportunities. Even international organizations such as the United Nations, International Monetary Fund, and the World Bank are composed of member states. Similarly, much of international law deals with regulating relations among states. Realists who put emphasis on states, power, and balance of power among states tend to feel most comfortable with this use of the term *international relations*.

1.3 Explain the difference between the terms international relations and world politics and define security, economy, and identity.

international relations ■ conventionally refers to relations among states

We believe the term world politics is a more inclusive term as it captures much of today's reality to include not only states and international organizations, but also a wide range of transnational actors, the phenomenon of globalization, vast social and economic global inequalities, and emergent global norms. One must be wary, however, as to the assumed connotations of "world" politics. First, the term does not necessarily equate to "peaceful." Second, although a case can be made that the trends we discuss in this book are indeed found throughout the world or at least have global ramifications, not every one we address is equally salient or important to all peoples or regions of the globe.

world politics ■ refers to relations among states but also international organizations and nongovernmental organizations

Sweeping generalizations about the condition of the entire world should be viewed with suspicion. Environmental degradation, for example, may be a global concern, but its manifestations are certainly much worse in some areas of the world than in others. The same is true of population and refugee issues. Similarly, economic conditions vary widely across the globe. One could, in fact, simply divide the world into spheres. In North America, Europe, Australia, New Zealand, and Japan, high or increasing standards of living prevail.

Added to these are rising powers like Brazil, Russia, India, and China—the so-called "BRIC" countries that constitute a middle category between the relatively

ARGUMENT The state is the key actor in international relations.

Observers of international relations known as *realists* (who will be discussed at some length in Chapter 2) argue that the state is the key actor in international relations. Whether we're talking about Greek city states of the 5th century B.C.E. or the rise of the territorially expansive modern state in the 16th century, states are the starting point for analysis. This is particularly true for realists interested in developing theories of international relations.

COUNTERARGUMENT Nonstate actors are key in international relations. Students of international relations and world politics obviously cannot ignore states and their interactions. To say the least, states have not yet withered away, however desirable they may or may not be. Most observers thus concede that states remain central players.

Important academic research in the early 1970s, however, made the case for taking nonstate actors seriously. This work has come to be associated with the *liberal* school of thought, also discussed in Chapter 2. Robert O. Keohane and Joseph S. Nye, Jr.* are two prominent academics associated with this literature. They have emphasized the actual and potential roles of international organizations as well as nongovernmental organizations. Both authors have continued over the years to investigate the complexity of world politics, recognizing the centrality of the state yet sensitive to the impact of transnational interdependence and nonstate actors on world politics. Thousands of international NGOs lobby states and international organizations, some to promote international cooperation, others to keep states from interfering with the activities of private citizens. There are also thousands of multinational corporations (MNCs) with subsidiaries that have gross sales larger than the gross domestic product (GDP) of even some major countries. More recently, the term transnational corporation (TNC) has been coined to account for global firms that do not associate themselves with a home country.

The biggest problem with most works on transnational actors is that they tend to be highly descriptive but with low theoretical content. The key question to ask about transnational actors is, "How and when can transnational actors change state policy?"

APPLICATION The International Criminal Court (ICC) in The Hague, Netherlands was established in 2002. It is an independent IO and not part of the United Nations, yet it receives funding from states, other IOs, individuals, and corporations. The court's statutes permit it to prosecute people for suspected genocide, crimes against humanity, and war crimes committed in any signatory state when that state is unwilling or unable to do so. But it can also investigate atrocities in nonmember states if the United Nations Security Council decides such actions are a threat to regional or international peace or security. Such actions are often encouraged by nongovernmental organizations such as relief agencies on the ground in places like Darfur and also by human rights organizations such as Amnesty International. The current (and expanding) role of the ICC is an excellent example of the interaction of states, international organizations, and transnational nongovernmental organizations that pressure state authorities who might otherwise be reluctant to pursue justice against certain indivuduals (often state officials) accused of committing or authorizing atrocities. For more on the role of the ICC and its relations with states and IOs, go to http://icc-cpi.int ◤

*Robert O. Keohane and Joseph S. Nye, Jr., eds., *Transnational Relations and World Politics* (Cambridge, MA: Harvard University Press, 1971) and their subsequent *Power and Interdependence*, 3rd ed. (New York: Longman, 1977, 2000).

few capital-rich and the many capital-poor countries. The small upper-, but growing middle classes in the BRIC countries are doing relatively well (perhaps as much as 30 percent of the population), but they still have large numbers at lower socio-economic levels to include those living in abject poverty.

Take China, for example. With rapidly growing economies that have substantial wealth and opportunity concentrated in the upper rungs of society, the larger mass of the population is not so advantaged. Some 55 percent of the Chinese people still live in the countryside as peasants even as a growing percentage concentrated in the urban areas enjoy a level of living comparable to those in North America, Europe, and Japan. Also in this middle category are South Korea, Taiwan, Singapore, and other new industrialized or industrializing countries (NICs) in which gains from economic development have been distributed more widely.

Some analysts have added South Africa, Chile, Argentina, and, most recently, Indonesia to the list. Malaysia, Vietnam, and the Philippines clearly want to make and stay on this diverse, middle-category list. Apart from relatively privileged elites, much of the rest of the world, home to the mass of humanity, suffers from varying degrees of poverty, low levels of economic development, and high rates of population growth, disease, and environmental pollution. Moreover, a number of these countries are also plagued by collapsing social and political orders.

As is clear in earlier discussion, we use three key concepts in international relations or world politics to organize much of the material we present—*security, economy,* and *identity*. Security is often viewed in terms of the basic survival, welfare, and protection of the state existing in an international "system" of states characterized by self-help—each securing its own position in the global order as best it can. But states may place varying degrees of faith in the role of international organizations, alliances, and negotiated agreements—ranging from trade and commerce to controlling armaments—as a means to enhance security. Others argue that since states are often the cause of insecurity through the use of force or conduct of war, we ought to focus on *human* security, defined in group and individual terms and associated with socioeconomic well-being and human rights. However defined, state policymakers or practitioners working for an international organization or nongovernmental organization may all play a role in building (or restoring) and maintaining international peace and security.

Discussions of the international economy generally revolve around trade, monetary issues (the relative value and reserves of currencies held or available to treasury and central bank officials), finance for trade and investment, foreign aid, health, and the environment. Economic issues are particularly important as they influence a state's overall power. For many observers, the international economy is a critical aspect of world politics and raises issues of global disparities and inequalities. Economic matters may be viewed as individual security concerns such as feeding one's family, which may dominate every waking moment for many people in the world's most impoverished countries. For them, global economic trends, growth rates, balance-of-payments problems, and exchange rates are irrelevant abstractions. Indeed, achieving minimum economic subsistence is the goal of the vast majority of humanity. How can practitioners of international relations and world politics help attain this goal?

Identity involves the answer to the question, "Who am I, and with whom do I identify?" In terms of international relations and world politics, identity is most

security ■ the basic survival and protection of a state, but can also refer to individuals

economy ■ The production, distribution, and consumption of goods and services. While conventionally focusing on the state, it can also be applied to the economic well-being of individuals.

identity ■ Consists of the answer to the question "Who am I?" May be associated with a state, religion, ethnicity, and have political implications.

often associated with the state and nation and the values, culture, and people who fall within that state's borders, although some ethnic, tribal, or other identities may extend beyond the borders of any one state. Thus, transnational movements may also be purveyors of emergent identities that parallel or transcend those associated with the state. Some people, for example, may identify strongly with an international movement concerned with such goals as protection of the global environment. These people may see themselves more as citizens of the world rather than as citizens of any single country. For others, identification with a particular religion such as Islam is more important than association with any one state. Identity may also be based on economic class and hence may also transcend any state boundary.

More than factory or farm workers, owners or managers of capital may have strong, common identities even as they compete for business globally. This is not surprising, we suppose, in a capitalist world economy that is so much a part of globalization or, as some would say, a globalization *project* that allows capital interests, acting in their own interests worldwide, to find gains from labor and natural-resource savings. As profits grow, share values in stock markets increase. Does money make the world go round? What do you think?

Whatever the basis for identity, it will play some role in how a practitioner engages in international relations and world politics. What identities do you have or are you likely to acquire? How about fellow students? Faculty and administrators at your college or university? Do you think these identities are fixed or do they change (or, perhaps, expand to other areas) over time and depending on where one is in one or another career path?

A useful metaphor that captures our approach to the study of international relations and world politics is a chessboard. Just as chess consists of different actors—kings, queens, rooks, bishops, pawns—so too does international relations and world politics. In fact, the realm of international relations and world politics is a three-level game of chess, with at least three games in progress at once—security, economy, and identity. Within and between each game various levels of interdependencies exist. But to make the game even more of an analytical challenge, the actual size and boundaries of the chessboards are unclear. The constituent elements and complex, multidimensional nature of contemporary world politics are continually evolving.

Most observers agree that the state continues to be the preeminent actor in world politics, but because of globalization and crises of authority in world politics, this may or may not be the case at the end of the 21st century. For now, at least, the challenges of security, economy, and identity remain with us, providing the principal themes of this book. The struggle over these three issues and their interrelations—particularly the security dimensions of economy and identity—define much of what is important and interesting today about international relations and world politics. As noted, all three concepts relate not just to the desires of individuals, but also to the collective aspiration of peoples in states and societies throughout the world. A substantial challenge is how to satisfy and attempt to reconcile common aspirations for security, economic welfare, and identity. Accordingly, human behavior in international relations and world politics involves goal-seeking behavior and the processes of deciding who gets what, when, and how.[1]

---

[1]Harold D. Lasswell, *Politics: Who Gets What, When, How* (Cleveland, OH: World Publishing, 1958).

In sum, these three themes represent three universal concerns. In this book we examine the means by which states, organizations, and the individual practitioners who comprise these entities have attempted to achieve security, economic welfare, and identity—however defined—and overcome the obstacles to this achievement. In a world of scarcity, the means for some to achieve these goals can be an obstacle to their achievement by others. Similarly, while some states at a minimum may seek to be left alone, other states have a more expansive definition of security or the pursuit of other opportunities abroad, the fulfillment of which might come at the expense of their neighbors. One must therefore be wary of thinking that such common concerns are necessarily a force for universal harmony. In fact, the manner in which these concerns for security, economic welfare, and identity are specifically defined and pursued can vary widely. Indeed, they can just as easily divide people as unite them and be a source of domestic, regional, or global conflict. Still, there may be grounds for hope if professionals or practitioners like you, the readers of this book, will see and lead the way to improving the human condition. There is much to be done.

CONCLUSION

The Tunisian people's revolution had a galvanizing effect on populations across North Africa and other countries of the Middle East. The next domino to fall was Egypt. In this case the role of social media and international telecommunications played an even larger role than in Tunisia. Facebook, YouTube, Al Jazeera (a satellite news organization based in Doha, Qatar), and the ability of protestors to send cell phone photos and videos around the globe encouraged the world to pay attention. For supporters of democratic freedoms in authoritarian states it was an exhilarating and heartening moment. For leaders of these states, it was a cause of real concern as anti-regime movements subsequently emerged in Libya, Bahrain, Yemen, and Syria. This "Arab Spring" was fraught with crises of authority that many observers saw as long overdue in a region dominated by anti-democratic, authoritarian elites often backed by and relying on military and police forces to keep them in power.

Communication technology was obviously critical in the development of popular democratic movements. This is not always the case. Iran successfully repressed demonstrators and access to the internet in 2009. In the late 1980s and early 1990s democratic social and political movements appeared in central and Eastern Europe. Despite not having access to the extensive social media of today, these movements were eventually successful. But nothing can match the speed and pervasiveness of today's communication and transportation capabilities. As a critical aspect of globalization, such technology will undoubtedly continue to play a major role for practitioners in the organization of social and political protest movements throughout the world. At the same time governmental policymakers will have to ponder how to deal with such technology and its social, economic, cultural, and political impact.

This book applies international relations and world politics theory and conceptual understandings to real-world issues by capturing much of today's reality to include not only states and international organizations, but also a wide range of transnational actors, the phenomenon of globalization, divergent approaches to security, and varying social and economic global conditions. Our focus is on real-world ideas and real-world implications. The first five chapters provide important foundational material for aspiring practitioners to improve their understanding of international relations and world politics. Key concepts involving theory, history, geography, and globalization are introduced and developed as tools for dealing with the subject matter that follows—not just in this volume, but also in the world in which readers of this book likely will be deeply engaged. After assembling these tools, we turn to discussions on power, foreign policy, international organizations, and international law. Subsequent chapters analyze interstate and asymmetric war, followed by an in-depth examination of international trade, finance, and development issues. We conclude with discussions in chapters on human rights and the global environment.

Our increasingly globalized world is in a state of flux, exhibiting a number of disturbing trends. Some of these trends certainly existed during the Cold War, but the forty-five-year-long East-West confrontation between the democratic capitalist and communist worlds overshadowed them. Observers of international relations through the centuries have made similar observations about their unique and troubling times.

Study and **Review** the **Post-Test & Chapter Exam** at **mypoliscilab.com**

Our task as authors is to provide a toolbox for international studies and present as objective and balanced a presentation of key global issues as we can. We try to be even-handed, not taking sides—providing you, the reader, with an opportunity to weigh different arguments as you try (as we do) to make the world around us more intelligible. After all, we're in this together! We all live in a globalized world. We invite readers to examine critically what we present. For most readers of this volume, it is *your* generation more than ours that will have to deal with the problems that face us throughout much of the 21st century.

LEARNING OBJECTIVES REVIEW

1.1 Illustrate specific aspects of globalization in the economic, social, and cultural realm and the role of technology.

Globalization refers to the continual increase in world-wide economic, social, and cultural interactions that transcend the boundaries of states and the resultant political implications. These interactions are aided by technologies that enhance financial and trade transactions and encourage the rapid dissemination of political as well as cultural ideals and values. The resultant impact could have either negative or positive consequences in terms of peace, stability, and conflict.

KEY TERM
Globalization 4

ADDITIONAL READINGS
John Micklethwait and Adrian Woolridge, *A Future Perfect: The Challenge and Promise of Globalization* (New York: Random House, 2003). This book examines the social, economic, cultural, and political impact of globalization using real-world examples.
Thomas L. Friedman, *The World Is Flat: A Brief History of the Twenty-first Century* (New York: Farrar, Straus and Giroux, 2005). Discusses globalization and provides fascinating case studies.

1.2 Define and provide examples of the key actors in international relations and world politics—states, international organizations, nongovernmental organizations, and individual practitioners.

The key organizational actors in international relations and world politics are *states* (the dominant actors), *international organizations* (such as the United Nations and its associated organizations), and *nongovernmental organizations* (multinational business corporations; organizations with explicit political, economic, or social agendas, such as Amnesty International; nonpolitical organizations such as Doctors Without Borders; and nonstate armed groups such as terrorist and criminal organizations and networks). Yet flesh-and-blood individuals are the actual policymakers and practitioners who make decisions in the name of these organizations.

KEY TERMS
Sovereignty 6
International organizations (IOs) 7
Norms 8
Nongovernmental organizations (NGOs) 10
Global civil society 10
Apartheid 15

ADDITIONAL READING
Robert O. Keohane and Joseph S. Nye, Jr., eds., *Transnational Relations and World Politics* (Cambridge, MA: Harvard University Press, 1972). This is the first systematic examination of nongovernmental organizations written by two prominent theorists and observers of international relations and world politics.

1.3 Explain the difference between the terms international relations and world politics and define security, economy, and identity.

International relations is a term that generally refers to relations among states. World politics is a more encompassing term that also includes nonstate actors. Security, economy (well-being), and identity can be viewed as three basic goals or concerns that organizations and individuals seek to achieve. The struggle over these three goals helps to explain much of the conflict and cooperation evident today in international relations and world politics.

KEY TERMS
International relations 15
World politics 15
Security 17
Economy 17
Identity 17

ADDITIONAL READING
Dan Smith, *The Penguin State of the World Atlas,* 8th ed. (New York: Penguin Books, 2008). A unique visual survey of political, economic, and social trends that is superior to the usual charts and tables.

CHAPTER REVIEW

1. Globalization has
   a. increased substantially over the decades.
   b. decreased slightly in recent decades.
   c. remained about the same over the decades.
   d. decreased substantially over the last century.

2. Globalization is evident in the
   a. economic realm.
   b. social realm.
   c. cultural realm.
   d. all of the above.

3. The impact of globalization on international relations and world politics
   a. is minimal.
   b. is entirely negative, especially in the economic realm.

   c. is entirely positive, especially in the social
       realm.
   d. may be positive or negative in terms of
       peace and conflict.

4. The major actor in world politics is
   a. the state.
   b. the international organization.
   c. the multinational corporation.
   d. global civil society.

5. A multilateral institution created by states in
   order to pursue common objectives is called a(n)
   a. nongovernmental organization (NGO).
   b. system of global governance.
   c. world government.
   d. international (or intergovernmental)
       organization.

6. The World Bank is an example of a(n)
   a. unilateral organization.
   b. world government.
   c. international (or intergovernmental)
       organization.
   d. nongovernmental organization.

7. Amnesty International is an example of a(n)
   a. unilateral organization.
   b. world government.
   c. nongovernmental organization.
   d. international (or intergovernmental)
       organization.

8. "Global civil society" refers to
   a. increasing levels of democratization in
       countries around the world.
   b. decreasing levels of crime and an increase in
       civil discourse among citizens of a state.
   c. the gradual worldwide emergence of the
       rule of law and networks or relationships
       among people.
   d. countries that are more "civil" to one
       another and therefore less warlike.

9. As concepts, international relations and world
   politics
   a. have the same meaning as they emphasize
       the same international actors.
   b. are complementary as world politics
       encompasses the state.
   c. are both primarily defined in terms of the
       globalization process.
   d. both exclude the role of the individual
       policymaker or practitioner.

10. The theoretical framework provided by the
    authors of this text includes
    a. security, economy, and identity.
    b. power, interdependence, and decision
        making.
    c. democracy, totalitarianism, and dictatorship.
    d. politics, economics, and international
        relations.

Theory

"Not everything that can be counted counts, and not everything that counts can be counted." —Thomas Edison, Inventor

"The philosophers have only interpreted the world, in various ways; the point is to change it." —Karl Marx, Philosopher

LEARNING OBJECTIVES

2.1 Define the concept of theory and formulate and test hypotheses (using both qualitative and quantitative methods) on various aspects of international relations such as how arms races between states may increase the chances of war.

2.2 Apply the levels of analysis framework to current international events, like U.S. troop levels in Afghanistan, to generate hypotheses that help you determine the factors affecting decisions about world politics.

2.3 Compare and contrast the essential elements of four images of international relations and world politics—realism, liberalism, economic structuralism, and the English School.

2.4 Describe the different interpretive understandings and the critique of the four images offered by constructivists, feminists, critical theorists, and postmodernists.

2.5 Evaluate the relevancy of normative or value theory to policymakers.

▣▣ Read and Listen to **Chapter 2** at **mypoliscilab.com**

✔● Study and Review the **Pre-Test & Flashcards** at **mypoliscilab.com**

Gene Sharp is a political scientist and philosopher who for decades has argued that nonviolent political action is the best means for overthrowing corrupt and repressive regimes. His *From Dictatorship to Democracy: A Conceptual Framework for Liberation* has been translated into twenty-four languages including Arabic and can be downloaded from the Albert Einstein Institution website. His basic hypothesis, which he tests against extensive historical cases studies, is that violence, even if serving a just cause, often creates more problems than it solves, often leading to greater injustice and more suffering. Nonviolent resistance requires dedication and courage, and does not guarantee success.

In his book he develops a theory of political power, defines key terms, relates means to ends, hypothesizes four ways in which nonviolent action produces change, and analyzes specific weaknesses of regimes that render dictatorships highly vulnerable to skillfully implemented nonviolent strategies. He also analyzes what history tells us in terms of what strategies should be pursued once a dictatorship collapses. Perhaps the best evidence of his success is that he has been personally condemned by the authoritarian president of Venezuela, Hugo Chavez, as well as Iranian officials who fear popular unrest.

The overthrowing of the authoritarian regimes in Tunisia and then Egypt in early 2011 have been dubbed Twitter revolutions based upon the role of social media. Yet the most salient characteristics of these movements is the fact that they were relatively peaceful. These outcomes would seem to vindicate Gene Sharp's theory of nonviolent resistance. As he would be the first to acknowledge, however, the circumstances were conducive to the application of a nonviolent strategy in both Tunisia and Egypt. Other situations, Syria for example, are more problematic. The point, however, is that theories can help not only to explain international outcomes, but also provide insight as to the circumstances under which such outcomes are more or less likely to be achieved. The ability to develop hypotheses, testing them against real-world data, and being aware of the implicit images and assumptions one brings to the study of international relations are critical skills for any aspiring practitioner of world politics.

Let's be frank. Studying theory is tougher for those of us who are more comfortable with the here and now than others who like to deal with abstractions. Nothing, however, is more practical than a good theory that tells us how the world works, explains causally why things happen, and gives us an ability to anticipate or predict what is likely to happen in different circumstances. Still, some of us are just not as theoretically oriented as others.

Those who like to think theoretically[1] tend always to ask questions about the world around them, and they try to figure out what is going on. They are prone to generalize about what they see by asking, "What is this an instance of?" Or maybe they think something to be true, but look at the world to see if what is going on conforms to their expectations. Such theoretically oriented persons tend to deal well with uncertainty. Things do not have to be nailed down. They tend to have a high tolerance for ambiguity and their theories help them cut through this uncertainty. Wouldn't these theorizing virtues be of benefit to anyone attempting to navigate the complex world of international relations and world politics?

The ability to think theoretically is an important element in your conceptual toolbox and informs your approach to our world. Focusing on the key aspects of theory, we'll cover the subject with as little jargon as possible:

- *Theory-building*—what it takes to make the world more intelligible by explaining and anticipating or predicting the phenomena we observe.
- *Levels of analysis*—a useful checklist for considering possible explanations of international events.
- *World images*—various lenses through which the world as a whole is seen, as we seek approaches to understanding what is important and what is not in international relations or world politics.
- *Interpretive understandings*—challenges to long-established "scientific" or "positivist" premises in the four images that present the world as if it were a "reality" quite apart from the subjective way we perceive and make sense of what we see.
- *Normative theory*—the values or norms that inform judgments about what *ought to be* so in international relations and world politics, quite apart from the way things *are*.

---

[1]We owe this perspective on the propensity to think theoretically by drawing inferences from what we observe to both James Rosenau and Ernst Haas.

WHAT IS A THEORY?

2.1 Define the concept of theory and formulate and test hypotheses (using both qualitative and quantitative methods) on various aspects of international relations such as how arms races between states may increase the chances of war.

Many people make the assumption that theory is divorced from reality, is merely an intellectual exercise, and is most likely a complete waste of time. In common parlance, something may be true in theory but not in fact. Another meaning, consistent with usage in this book, has a much more positive view of theory—that it is simply a way of making the world or some part of it more intelligible or better understood. Theories dealing with international relations and world politics aspire to achieve this goal. Making things more intelligible, of course, may amount to nothing more than better or more precise descriptions of the things we observe. Although accurate description is essential, theory is something more. Theory makes the world more intelligible by offering interrelated statements or hypotheses which, taken together, purport to explain what we observe. Explanation involves accounting for, or understanding causes of, such phenomena as war, arms races, and global poverty. For some, theories also aim to make generalized predictions of future patterns or trends, given the presence (or absence) of certain factors. To think theoretically, however, is not to engage in point predictions like *"A will attack B the first week of the year,"* however much we may want the answers to such questions. Natural scientists face the same problem. They cannot predict the precise time a particular leaf may fall and can only predict, for example, that leaves will fall in the autumn depending on variations in daylight, temperature, weather conditions, and other factors. Likewise international relations theorists may have to be content with specifying, for example, conditions or factors that increase or decrease the probability of war between State A and State B.

👁 **Watch** the **Video** *"Obama Controversial Anti-Terrorism Policies"* at **mypoliscilab.com**

theory ■ an intellectual construct that helps us explain or predict what we observe—interpreting facts and identifying regularities and recurrences or repetitions of observed phenomena

dependent variable ■ the thing that is to be explained or accounted for

independent variable ■ a factor used to explain some outcome or effect

intervening variable ■ a factor that comes between the cause (independent variable) and the outcome or effect (dependent variable)

Formulating and Testing Hypotheses

What one is trying to explain—such as the existence of interstate war—is known as the dependent variable. Factors we suspect as being causally related to what we are trying to explain typically are termed independent variables. Sometimes other factors—dubbed intervening variables—may facilitate or, conversely, block the effects of the independent variables on each other or on the dependent variable.

According to mainstream social science, the theoretical task is to engage in causal explanation or prediction based on certain prior occurrences, patterns, or conditions. Thus, whenever X is present, then Y can be expected to follow. "If X, then Y" is a hypothesis or educated guess that should be subject to empirical testing—that is, the rigorous, systematic testing of the hypothesis with evidence or data gathered from the real world.

The example outlined in Figure 2.1 should clarify what we mean by the causal relations in our hypothesis among independent, dependent, and intervening variables. Let's state the hypothesis in general form: "If states engage in arms races (X), then the likelihood of war (Y) increases." If we test this proposition in the Pakistan-India case, it becomes: If Pakistan (X1) and India (X2) both increase their military spending, then the likelihood of war (Y) increases. Put another way, we are suggesting there may be a direct causal relation between X and Y (as one increases so does the other). The likelihood of war is the *dependent variable* affected by whether or not Pakistan and India engage in arms races—the *independent*

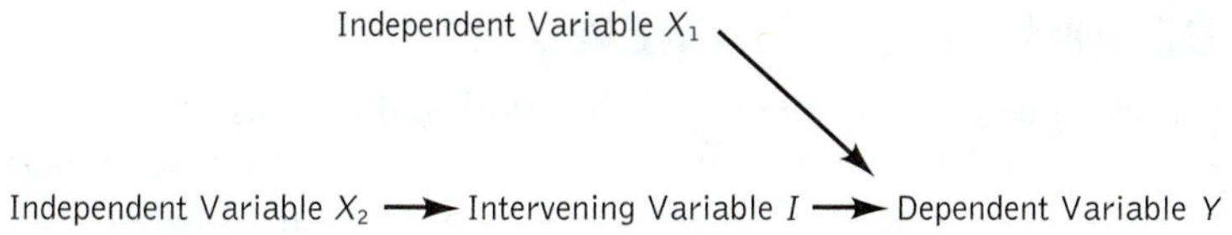

Independent Variable X_1

Independent Variable X_2 ⟶ Intervening Variable I ⟶ Dependent Variable Y

hypothesis ■
an explanatory
proposition subject to
empirical test for its
veracity

FIGURE 2.1
Causal Analysis

Another example of a hypothesis might be: "If states in a region become democratic (X), then the likelihood of war among them (Y) decreases"—an inverse causal relation between X and Y (as one increases, the other decreases). Question: What might be a possible intervening variable in this hypothesis that would affect the outcome (Y)?

variable. Let's assume this causal relation holds except for circumstances in which an important *intervening variable* is present—in this case the United States engaging in vigorous diplomacy to reduce the escalating tensions between India and Pakistan.

Indeed, formal statement and tests of hypotheses through the use of statistical or **quantitative methods** are seen by many scholars as central to the theory-building process. Others prefer to rely on nonquantitative case and comparative case studies, historical methods, and reasoned arguments—the so-called traditional or **qualitative methods** of theory building. Quite apart from the methods used, it is the testing with data of propositions or hypotheses grounded in theory that gives meaning to the "facts" about the world and the sense we make of them. It is a fact, for example, that the Soviet Union and its empire or sphere of influence collapsed in the early 1990s; good theory would help us understand why this occurred—an explanation for what happened. Scholars of international relations would agree that theory is necessary and unavoidable when it comes to explaining and attempting to foresee the future of international relations or world politics. Theory is unavoidable in that all people approach their subject matter from prior assumptions, perspectives, or images. An analyst needs to be theoretically self-conscious—aware of the perspective or even bias he or she might bring to a problem.

Theory also tells us what to focus on and what to ignore in making sense of the world around us. Without theory we would be overwhelmed and immobilized by an avalanche of mere facts. The sense we make of what we observe is informed by the perspectives, concepts, and theories we hold. *A theory thus is an intellectual construct that helps us explain or predict what we observe—interpreting facts and identifying regularities and recurrences or repetitions of observed phenomena.* Fitting pieces into a larger whole makes theory building analogous to puzzle solving.

The bottom line is that thinking theoretically is important, necessary, and very satisfying when one achieves better understanding of international relations or world politics. Thinking theoretically—seeking explanations or predictions for what we observe in the world around us—can be done by any of us.

Consider how often you contemplate if–then hypotheses in your own life when you analyze an experience or outcome. How might applying causal analysis impact your future actions?

quantitative methods
■ the use of statistical
data and measures to
explain outcomes

qualitative methods
■ comparative case
studies, historical
methods, and
reasoned arguments to
develop explanations
of outcomes

THE LEVELS OF ANALYSIS FRAMEWORK

2.2 Apply the levels of analysis framework to current international events, like U.S. troop levels in Afghanistan, to generate hypotheses that help you determine the factors affecting decisions about world politics.

Let's turn now to a more specific analytical tool that will make it easier to think theoretically. The **levels of analysis framework** is useful precisely because it provides a checklist that allows us to make educated guesses as to what factors might account for the international behavior we are trying to explain or predict. How, for example, do we explain major national security and foreign policy decisions? Table 2.1 illustrates a number of possible factors or levels of analysis worthy of consideration—individual and group, state and society, and international or global. Applying it to the U.S. troop presence in Afghanistan, we'll see how this tool works.

> Why did the United States decide in 2009 to increase the number of U.S. troops in Afghanistan?

✦─[**Explore** the **"The Prisoner's Dilemma: You Are a Presidential Advisor"** at **mypoliscilab.com**

levels of analysis framework ■ A way to organize thinking about world politics and generate hypotheses. Individuals, groups, states and their societies, or the overall international system are points of focus.

This question is our dependent variable—perhaps part of an even broader, more theoretical question on what explains policy changes. Possible answers to this question are our independent variables. One explanation (X_1) is that the critical explanatory factor in this case was the *individual* role, personality, and understandings of President Obama, the key and ultimate decision maker. Another possible explanation involves the impact of the president's closest advisers (X_2)—for example, the secretary of state, defense secretary, national security adviser, and chairman of the Joint Chiefs of Staff. This would be the group level of analysis. In this regard, we may try to identify the relation between X_2 and X_1—the influence advisers had on the president or whether he acted independently of those giving him advice. A third possibility might be the influence of other individuals or groups in the larger national security and foreign policy bureaucracy, the Congress, or other policy-oriented elites in government or in the private sector (X_3).

At the *state and national* level (X_4), we might ask if public opinion mattered—on balance, would most Americans likely support or oppose increasing the troop commitment and, if so, for how long? Moving up one more level, we might look at the broader *international* environment and the threats and challenges posed by instability in Afghanistan and neighboring Pakistan (X_5). From this perspective, the United States naturally took the lead as the world's sole superpower because it was in its national interest to increase troop levels in Afghanistan—the state is a rational, self-serving actor that we expect will seek to achieve national (or international) objectives through available means to include, if it deems necessary, the use of force. Moreover, the superpower saw no other states (or alliances) with the capabilities to stop this action were they prone to do so—the presence or absence of obstacles or external constraints was a sixth variable (X_6). This focus on rational choice and cost-benefit analysis related to the decision to "up the ante" in Afghanistan will be treated in greater detail in Chapter 6 when we discuss the role of power in international relations and world politics.

In sum, the levels of analysis—individual, group, state and society, and international or global—are useful to students of international relations or world politics because they constitute a comprehensive framework that focuses our attention on a diverse set of factors or independent variables that may be causally

TABLE 2.1

Levels of Analysis: A More Detailed Look

Individual Level (domain of psychology)

Human nature and psychology
Leaders and beliefs systems
Personality of leaders
Cognition and perception or misperception

Group Level (domain of social psychology)

Government bureaucracies
Policy making groups
Interest groups
Other nongovernmental organizations

State and Societal (or National) Level

Governmental
    Structure and nature of political system
    Policymaking process
Societal (domain of sociology)
    Structure of economic system
    Public opinion
    Nationalism and ethnicity
    Political culture
    Ideology

International—World (or Global) Level

Anarchic quality of international or world politics
Number of major powers or poles
Distribution of power/capabilities among states
Level and diffusion of technology
Patterns of military alliances
Patterns of international trade and finance
International organizations and regimes
Transnational organizations and networks
Global norms and international law

related to what we are trying to explain, the dependent variable. This could be a state's foreign policy behavior (the decisions and actions it takes) or, more generally, such international outcomes as the outbreak of war between or among states. Put another way, using levels of analysis helps us along the road to the major goal of theory—explanation and, perhaps, even prediction. If we have at least a general understanding of what conditions tend to cause certain phenomena to occur, we may also be in a better position to anticipate or predict likely outcomes when we observe the presence or absence of certain factors our theory has helped us

ARGUMENT-COUNTERARGUMENT | Generating Hypotheses

ARGUMENT   The levels of analysis framework provides a useful checklist for generating hypotheses about international decisions and behavior.

The levels move on a continuum from the individual to smaller, then larger groups, and conclude with analysis at the global level. Throughout this process it is important to evaluate both the psychological and sociological factors impacting the decision and behavior being evaluated.

Attempts to explain why wars occur have led theorists to look for factors that are present (or absent) prior to the outbreak of war. In a now classic explanation offered by Kenneth Waltz in his book *Man, the State and War*, he considers psychological and social-psychological factors involving individuals and groups (Are human beings naturally aggressive?),

societal differences (Do dictatorships have a higher propensity to go to war than democracies?), and the international condition of anarchy (States can go to war as there is nothing such as a world government to prevent them.).

COUNTERARGUMENT   While a useful checklist and source of hypotheses, the levels of analysis framework does not tell us what is the relative importance of these various levels.

APPLICATION   Choose a current international issue involving a state making headlines such as a decision to crack down on domestic demonstrators or threaten a neighboring state. Generate two hypotheses utilizing the levels of analysis framework that might conceivably explain that behavior.

identify. Using levels of analysis broadens our focus, provides a way of organizing the factors that may influence outcomes, and helps us avoid overlooking or ignoring factors that should be part of our explanation.

WORLD IMAGES

2.3 Compare and contrast the essential elements of four images of international relations and world politics—realism, liberalism, economic structuralism, and the English School.

The critical importance of the image or perspective we have stems from the fact that everyone, even implicitly or unconsciously, has or holds one—sometimes more than one depending on the issues or circumstances at hand. Such sets of assumptions about international relations or world politics influence the approaches we take to studying and understanding the world around us—the types of questions asked and how we answer them. As such, images help to orient our reading and research by highlighting certain actors or concepts and discounting or ignoring others, as well as influencing the interpretation of particular international trends.

Images can be compared to what we see when we wear a pair of glasses to look at the world around us. We may prefer a particular pair of glasses because it gives what we think is the clearest vision—a correct understanding of what is going on. Sometimes, however, we may decide to change glasses, looking through an alternative set of lenses that may lead us to see, or interpret what we see, differently. Doing so leads us to ask which image or set of lenses gives us the clearest vision—the most accurate view of how the world works.

👁—**Watch** the **Video**
"Churchill's Iron Curtain Speech" at
mypoliscilab.com

The images we are about to discuss are not the only ones that can be used to view the world, but they have many adherents among students of international relations and world politics. First, we will discuss three long-established, basic perspectives: (1) *realism* that focuses on power and a balance of power among states in international relations; (2) *liberalism*—a pluralist perspective that includes states, but looks beyond them to observe the roles individuals play as well as the activities of both international and nongovernmental organizations in world politics; and (3) *economic structuralism* that emphasizes the importance of such material factors or structures as capital-owning classes or capital-rich countries that explain much of what we observe in international relations or world politics. A fourth perspective is that of *English School "rationalists"*—those who portray international or global society in which one finds operative not only realist ideas of power and balance of power emphasized in the writings of Machiavelli or Hobbes, but also the rules, ideas, and institutions one finds in the writings of Grotius, the "father" of international law.

For readers interested primarily in the practical side of politics, pay particular attention to realism and liberalism as these images are most often held by practitioners—foreign and national security policymakers. For their part, theorists in the English School combine the two images, drawing from both realist and liberal understandings. In short, power and the balance of power (important to realists) also matter to those in the English School, but so do the rules states follow, the norms with which they comply, and the institutions they create to facilitate the conduct of international relations (important to liberals). Economic structuralists, by contrast, paint a different vision of the world, one in which the economically powerful dominate those lacking these resources.

In our quest to think theoretically, we will look at the world image through various lenses to see which ones give us a more accurate view depending on what we are trying to explain or, conversely, which ones we consider misleading or distorting our understanding of international relations and world politics. To complete the metaphor, feel free to try on all four pairs of glasses before deciding which one to wear. Is there even a fifth or sixth pair you can imagine—yet other images or perspectives not identified by the authors or of which they may not be aware? Whichever lens you now think best captures the essence of international relations or world politics, you may want to reevaluate your initial choice during the course of your studies and afterward.

Also affecting these images are several alternative approaches to interpretive understanding of international relations or world politics that challenge many of the assumptions, orientations, and findings of the four basic images we have identified: (1) *constructivism* that underscores the importance of ideas and *ideational structures* in establishing or constituting the world we understand around us; (2) *feminism* that focuses on gender as key to our understandings not only of politics within state and society, but also of international relations or world politics; (3) *postmodernism* that emphasizes the subjective dimension of what we think we see in the world around us—a view that leads us to deconstruct or unpack the text of spoken or written communications to find underlying meanings; and (4) *critical theory* that probes beneath the cover stories we are given to reveal underlying calculations of interest or exploitation. In this section we also take up the degree

image ■ a general perspective of international relations and world politics

to which the four basic images and the four challenges in interpretive understanding we identify are open to (or critical of) modernist or "positivist" social science methods as they are sometimes called—quantitative, nonquantitative, or "qualitative" approaches to formulating and testing hypotheses. We ask whether science provides the means to understanding the world around us, explaining and predicting the phenomena we see as well as the degree to which we need to interpret the phenomena we observe. Put another way, subjectivity matters—"facts" cannot be identified with complete objectivity, but are always dependent upon understandings we gain from interpreting them.

Realists

realism ■ An image of international relations or world politics that can be traced back more than two thousand years. Realists tend to hold a rather pessimistic view, emphasizing the struggle for power and influence among political units acting in a rational, unitary manner in pursuit of objectives grounded in their separate, often divergent interests.

The tradition of political thought known as **realism** has dominated thinking about international politics over the millennia. As the term suggests, writers and political theorists associated with realism claim to view the world as it *is*, not as it *ought to be*. In terms of domestic politics, a primary concern for any ruler is stability—the ways and means of gaining and staying in power. Without some degree of order or internal stability, it is difficult to pursue other political, economic, or social objectives. Hence the challenge of establishing authority has drawn the attention of many realist writers. In terms of international relations, realists emphasize the struggle for power and influence among states, empires, and principalities. At a minimum, all such political entities seek security. Some, however, may have a more extensive agenda of opportunities to pursue and may even aspire to regional or world conquest.

All realists agree, however, that the mere existence of independent states, empires, or principalities—all of which reject the notion of being subject to the authority of any other political unit—creates a dynamic that encourages competition and violence. In other words, international relations are conducted in a condition of international **anarchy** or, as the seventeenth-century writer Thomas Hobbes also termed it, a world in which there is "no common power." No central, global power exists to enforce peace among the various political units, whether they are city-states, empires, principalities, or modern states. As a result, a political leader's primary concern is to protect the national security of the country. At a minimum this means defending the physical and territorial integrity of the state.

anarchy ■ The absence of political authority. International politics or the international system is said to be anarchic as there is no world government—no central or superordinate authority over states, which retain their sovereign rights.

For many realists, the competitive and often warlike condition of international relations is essentially the result of some combination of factors—human nature or the psychology of individuals and dynamics of small groups; the nature of certain types of states or societies; and the structure or distribution of power among states. Structural realists, sometimes called neorealists, look to this distribution of power among states or "structure" as affecting the behavior of states within an international system of states: a unipolar structure in which one dominant state has capabilities or power well above all of the others, such as the United States in the present period; a bipolar structure such as the United States and the former Soviet Union during the Cold War (1945–1991); and a multipolar structure, the most common form historically, such as Europe in the nineteenth century, the period between World War I and World War II (1919–1939), and what appears to be reemerging in the 21st century.

Power is important to achieving the objectives or satisfying the interests of states. International organizations, alliances, and other coalitions are merely mechanisms used by states to exercise their power in the conduct of their international relations. For some realists, the pursuit of power by states is not so much a means to achieving these ends; indeed, it becomes an end in itself. The state's concern both for its security in an anarchic world and its capacity to achieve its other purposes make it focus on its relative power position in relation to other states; it wishes to strengthen rather than weaken its power position in relation to other states. To realists, whether power is sought as a means or an end in itself, it is the acquisition and use of power by states that tends to produce or result in an equilibrium or balance of power. Some realists see states, particularly the most powerful (or great powers as they are sometimes called), as actively constructing power balances to assure the best position they can in such balances. Other realists see balance of power as something that simply occurs, whether or not states will seek such an outcome.

Liberals

An alternative image of world politics is most commonly referred to as liberalism. The liberal image is of a very complex world in which multiple kinds of actors are active players engaged in international relations or world politics in an increasingly global society—an understanding compatible with a very rich tradition of liberal thought that can be traced back to the ancient Greek and Roman Stoics. We're careful to note that classical liberal thought should not be confused with present-day debates in the United States or elsewhere between social liberals or conservatives on the domestic role of the state in assuring welfare to the citizenry in a particular society.

liberalism ■ an image of world politics that emphasizes the multiplicity of international actors—states, international organizations, and transnational organizations—and the conditions under which international cooperation can be achieved

Liberals adopt an inclusive view of world politics that takes a multiplicity of actors into account. States are usually recognized as key actors in world politics, but they are not the only important ones. Hence while realists tend to prefer the term *international relations* because they see it as putting emphasis on states as the key actors, liberals often prefer to use the term *world politics* that take place in an increasingly globalized context—a world or global society composed of both state and nonstate actors. Even when they use the term *international relations*, they do not confine themselves primarily to states as realists are prone to do. Instead, liberals tend to see international relations as going beyond just the state to include individuals as well as both international and nongovernmental organizations that engage in activities that do indeed move internationally both between and transnationally across national borders.

To liberals, institutions matter. International organizations such as the United Nations and the European Union (EU) are not simply arenas within which states compete for influence, but often independent actors in their own right that increasingly set the international or global issue agenda. This trend has accelerated in the almost seven decades since the end of World War II. The economic and political clout of cities both within their states and across their borders also makes such urban conglomerates as Los Angeles, New York, and Tokyo significant players. In the capital-poor countries in the developing world, underemployed urban populations suffering in sordid living conditions provide the breeding ground for unrest and demands for political change.

A growing number of liberal scholars therefore debate the privileged position in which realists place the state. Increasing globalization is an important factor. They note that the emergence of the modern state is, historically speaking, a relatively recent phenomenon, going back to perhaps the 15th century. Other forms of political and social relations develop and are carried on across state borders in the form of transnational organizations. Indeed, far from seeing the state as a unitary, rational, power-oriented actor, liberals also see the state as a battleground for conflicting bureaucratic interests, subject to the pressures of both domestic and transnational interest groups.

The term *global civil society* not only refers to growth in international law, but also describes the multitude of institutions, voluntary organizations, and networks ranging from women's groups and human rights organizations to environmental activists and chambers of commerce that have multiplied rapidly since the beginning of the 20th century. Whereas most originated and confined their interests to the capital-rich, industrial countries, this is no longer the case. Today such organizations are found not only in capital-poor, developing countries, but also in the Russian Federation, the former Soviet republics, and the former communist countries of Eastern Europe. Liberals note that such organizations are more than special interest groups attempting to influence state policies. These groups play an important role in forming an international consciousness among peoples around the globe on such diverse issues as the environment, human rights, and weapons proliferation. Indeed, it allows one to speak, at least in terms that originated in the Western world, of a growing liberal-capitalist civic identity.

The realist and liberal views of the possibilities of peaceful international change are also at odds. Realists tend to be more pessimistic about future prospects, viewing international relations as "more of the same old thing"—conflict and competition in a world constantly threatened with instability and threats to peace. Liberals, by contrast, tend to be much more optimistic, especially in terms of their underlying view of human nature—one that allows for cooperation and accommodation on a person-to-person level, fostering the spread of democratic ideals that over time will tend to have a pacifying effect on peoples and states.

As a practical matter, liberals are interested in the ways issues on the global agenda will be addressed. These issues reach well beyond the capability of individual states to resolve; they often call for regional or global approaches. Hence liberals are interested in the modalities of global governance and the role of global institutions in these processes. In this regard, global governance does not mean world government, but refers to the ways and means by which state and nonstate actors deal authoritatively with issue on global and regional agendas.

According to the 18th-century German writer Immanuel Kant in his essay "Perpetual Peace," a world of good, morally responsible states would be less likely to engage in wars. Thus, many liberals argue that the realist emphasis on international anarchy and the consequent insecurity is excessive. International cooperation and peaceful engagement among states and other actors are possible; there are no insuperable obstacles to block us, although achieving such progress takes decisive actions by both state and nonstate actors—international and nongovernmental organizations as well as individuals and groups of one kind or another. Indeed, liberals tend optimistically to rely on the ability of political leaders and nations to learn from mistakes—the past is not necessarily prologue. State interests can be redefined and new identities—not restricted to loyalty to the state—can be created. Policymakers and others who adopt this more optimistic perspective, seeking to universalize gains through peaceful engagement and international cooperative and collaborative efforts of all kinds, are sometimes referred to as *liberal internationalists*.

Economic Structuralists

A third image is economic structuralism—the operation of material factors or structures in a truly global context. Not to be confused with the term *globalization*, this image of world politics is also fundamentally different from the realist and liberal images. First, those we identify as economic structuralists, both Marxists and non-Marxists, argue that one must comprehend the global context within which states and other entities interact. Economic or material structures matter— whether these take the form of capital-owning classes of people or capital-rich blocks of countries arrayed respectively against other classes or blocks of countries. References such as rich vs. poor, capitalists vs. peasants and workers, the capital-rich North vs. the capital-poor South, and exploitation by the privileged of those without such advantages are reflective of economic-structuralist understandings.

economic structuralism ■ an image of world politics that argues one must comprehend the global context within which states and other entities interact—a context defined by class or other materially defined structures and exploitative relations

Seeing the overall economic or class structure of the international system means one must examine more than just the distribution of power among states (realists) or chart the movements of transnational actors and the internal political processes of states (liberals). Though important, such actors, processes, and relations are part of a world shaped by global social and economic structures or forces whose impact is not always readily apparent in the day-to-day world of domestic and international political competition. These forces condition and predispose actors (state as well as nonstate) to act in certain ways; they also account for the generation of these actors in the first place. In other words, while realists tend to view state actors and their interests as givens, economic structuralists are interested in explaining how they came into existence in the first place.

By structure, Marxists typically mean global class formations as in the *bourgeoisie* or capitalists in various countries that occupy a position of dominance over the "downtrodden"—the worker (proletarian) and peasant classes. Another Marxist, or modified, "neo"-Marxist, understanding sees global capitalist structures of dominance by the core of advanced capitalist countries over the periphery of capital-poor countries with some countries caught in between—the semiperiphery. Both Marxist and non-Marxist economic structuralists also paint a picture of exploitative relations in which the capital-poor countries of the South are kept in a position of dependency or bondage by the capital-rich countries of the North through various discriminatory practices adverse to these countries caught on the downside of the global economic structure of world capitalism.

So what is the difference between Marxists and non-Marxists on economic structuralism? A short answer is that Marxists tend to focus on class structure;

non-Marxists look to other forms of structure. Put another way, Marxists refer readily to the bourgeoisie or capitalist class that establishes a structure of global dominance over the working class or peasantry; non-Marxists, less concerned with relations among classes or class conflict, generally prefer to describe economic structures of dependency as between the capital-rich countries of the North and the capital-poor countries of the South or, more simply, North versus South, rich versus poor, haves versus have-nots.

Following from this discussion, economic structuralists argue that it is absolutely necessary to view international relations in historical perspective. Realists and liberals would agree. But while realists tend to emphasize the timeless and repetitive nature of world politics dating back to ancient times, economic structuralists tend to use as a benchmark the historical emergence of capitalism. They argue that the emergence of capitalism in 16th-century Europe was a fundamental breaking point in the structure and dynamics of world politics. Indeed, some date the origins of the concept we now call globalization to this era, although others see even earlier historical roots for this phenomenon. Be that as it may, capitalism has continued to spread today to the point some economic structuralists describe as a capitalist world system.

Similarly, while liberals tend to emphasize the growing transnational nature of world politics and foresee the possibility of a fundamental change in the nature of international politics and modes of global governance occurring, economic structuralists instead emphasize how the continual, incremental evolution of capitalism goes a long way toward accounting for recent changes in world politics. While individual countries over the years may claim to base their domestic economic systems on something other than capitalism—such as socialism—many economic structuralists argue they nevertheless must operate internationally as part of a global or capitalist world system that conditions and constrains the behavior of all states and societies.

While recognizing the importance of states as actors (as do realists) and non-state actors such as international organizations, multinational corporations, and banks (as do liberals), economic structuralists frequently view these entities in light of how they act as mechanisms of dominance in a capitalist world order. Specifically, economic structuralists examine how some capitalist states, elites, or transnational classes—given their privileged economic-structural position—manage to extract profits and other benefits from the capitalist world system at the expense of others.

LDC ■ less-developed country, a euphemism for an economically poor country

The exploited occupy the euphemistically termed "developing" or capital-poor, economically less-developed countries (LDCs), which are characterized by large, poverty-stricken sections of their populations. Using the term *Third World* to describe these countries seems offensive in particular to many liberals who politely refrain from using it nowadays. On the other hand, economic structuralists are more prone to see it as capturing an unpleasant, but certain reality suffered by the downtrodden that is lost when we substitute the more optimistic term *developing world* preferred by liberals. Indeed, some economic structuralists argue that these countries and populations are kept in a dependent status by capital-rich countries, not because they have failed to develop capitalist economic systems or because they are poorly integrated into the capitalist world system. In fact, it is quite the opposite: These less-developed countries play an important role in the capitalist world system, acting as a source of cheap labor and raw materials. Far from being outside the capitalist world system, they are an integral part of it—their exploitation helping to account for the continual economic dominance of the northern capitalist states in North America, Europe, and parts of Asia.

LDCs are unable to choose their own path toward economic development, ensnared in the structure of the capitalist world system net and often poorly served by their own elites or *comprador* class (capitalists constituting the local bourgeoisie in an LDC, seen as subordinated to the bourgeoisie in advanced capitalist countries), who derive selfish benefits due to these dependency relations. It is apparent, therefore, that even more so than the realists and liberals, these economic structuralists emphasize the critical importance of economic or material factors. For economic structuralists, economic considerations in the form of global structures of dominance are the key starting point for understanding international relations or world politics and the creation and development of the capitalist world system or global society within which these structures operate.

English School "Rationalists"

Scholars in what is called the English School draw on elements of the other images, particularly realism and liberalism. Their image is of an international society composed of both state and nonstate actors. Indeed, the world can be understood as an anarchical society—one composed of independent sovereign states and other actors but lacking in central authority or the degree of governance one typically finds in the domestic society within a state. Order in this anarchical society may come from the exercise of power one finds in the writings of the Italian Niccoló Machiavelli (1469–1527), or power and the balance of power described by the Englishman Thomas Hobbes (1588–1679).

English School
■ an image that combines aspects of realism and liberalism in the context of international society

---

CASE & POINT | Agriculture and the Developing World

CASE The farmers of Mekeni in central Sierra Leone signed a contract with a Swiss company granting the firm a 50-year lease on 154 square miles of land to grow biofuels for Europe. In exchange the Mekeni were promised 2,000 jobs. Three years later fifty jobs had been created. Other similar deals had been brokered throughout other poor areas of the world. The promise was to provide not only jobs, but also technology, capital, and better infrastructure. Recent studies, including one on some hundred such land deals, resulted in a damning indictment of the foreign companies. Virtually none of the promised benefits have occurred. It was estimated that some 310,000 square miles (more than half in Africa) had been subject to some sort of negotiation with a foreign investor. This amount of land is more than the farmland of Britain, France, Germany, and Italy combined.

POINT Economic structuralists would argue that such a dismal outcome was to be expected, given the exploitive nature of international capitalism.

Source: *The Economist*, May 7, 2011, pp. 65–66.

TABLE 2.2

Comparing Perspectives: Realism, Liberalism, & Economic Structuralism

The three dominant images of international relations and world politics vary in their underlying assumptions on a number of dimensions. Each image will therefore influence how you interpret events. Which image do you find most insightful in terms of grasping the essentials of globalization?

Realism	Liberalism	Economic Structuralism
View of International System		
A system or society of states engaged in struggle for power	States plus global civil society	Patterns of economic domination
Globalization		
Impact overstated	Impact dramatic; historically unprecedented	Dates back to 16th century
Actors		
STATES: Key actors	States plus nonstate actors	States, nonstate actors must be viewed in context of global economic structures
IOs: Reflect state interests	Increasingly independent role	Reflect class interests
NGOs: Secondary importance	Increasingly important	Corporations reflect class interests
Possibility of System Transformation		
Pessimistic	Cautiously optimistic	Pessimistic due to power of capitalist world system

But order also can derive from the rules or norms accepted by states and other actors as being in their enlightened self-interest, many of which attain the standing of international law as in the writings of the Hollander Hugo Grotius (1583–1645)—widely recognized as the "father" of international law. There is, then, in its rules or norms a rational or rule-oriented basis for order in this anarchic international society that lacks central governance.

To this rationalism we can add—as in the writings of the East Prussian Immanuel Kant (1724–1804)—the moral or ethical principles that come to be accepted internationally and thus contribute to some degree to a more orderly form of international anarchy—the absence of central authority over states that remain sovereign entities. Should order internationally one day become grounded primarily in moral principles or ethical norms—the Kantian ideal—some English School theorists refer to this in essence as the emergence of world society (in effect replacing the state-centric international society that describes present-day circumstances). Other English School scholars disagree, however, referring to such thinking as idealistic or utopian.

Understanding international relations as occurring within international society also puts emphasis on the human dimension rather than on what some see as mechanistic relations among abstract units—a system of states in structural-realist understandings or a capitalist world system of classes and states one finds in economic-structuralist formulations. That international society can become a global civil society under the rule of law is also compatible with such English School thinking.

This idea that international relations or world politics occur in an international society is not limited to the English School. It is also compatible with classical realism's focus on the pursuit of interest using state power or capabilities as well as with acknowledgment of roles played by multiple state and nonstate actors in liberal understandings. For that matter, many Marxist and neo-Marxist scholars are quite comfortable with portraying classes and class struggles as occurring not only in domestic society, but also more broadly in international or global contexts.

INTERPRETIVE UNDERSTANDINGS

Though realism, liberalism, economic structuralism, and English School rationalism have become fairly well-established, mainstream images and approaches to international relations or world politics, they are by no means the only ways to look at the world. We owe to the late-19th- and early-20th-century German scholar Max Weber the insight that we need to take account of the deeper understandings tied to the terms we create or use to describe the world around us. Indeed, Weber used the German word *verstehen* to capture the empathetic bases of deep understandings that human beings can attach to the descriptions they advance and the words they use. Interpretive understandings, therefore, question what the four images take for granted concerning our ability to use mainstream social scientific methods to comprehend world politics. From the policy perspective, you're unlikely to find many practitioners even acknowledging awareness of their existence. Indeed, interpretive understandings challenge the objectivity on which most policymakers pride themselves—as if being so completely "objective" were possible among essentially subjective human beings. However committed to objectivity policymakers (or we) may be, they (and we) need at least a basic comprehension of these interpretive understandings that emphasize the subjective component of how we see the world and, as a result, the decisions we make. At the very least, they sensitize the practitioner to the diverse meanings different observers may draw from what we observe in international relations or world politics.

2.4 Describe the different interpretive understandings and the critique of the four images offered by constructivists, feminists, critical theorists, and postmodernists.

Constructivists

In recent years constructivism (or, more precisely, social constructivism) has provided a provocative and intriguing challenge to realist and liberal conceptions in particular. The starting point for constructivists is the claim that what realists and

constructivism
■ Ideas and concepts about international relations are not essential attributes but are rather of human origin and humanly constructed. The world is the image that states and others choose to make it.

liberals take for granted—interests and the identities of actors—are actually quite malleable, constructed and subject to change by the actors themselves. Constructivists take on the typical realist claim that actors have a more or less fixed nature—that they are and seemingly always will be self-interested and security-conscious. Whether due to what they see as an unbending or essentially unchanging human nature or the eternal existence of an anarchic international environment, realists tend to see states continuing to compete for power, influence, and prestige.

Constructivists, by contrast, argue that states don't simply react to their environment but dynamically engage it. Just as the environment influences the behavior of the actors, so too do the actors or agents who over time affect the environment that surrounds them. As essentially subjective persons, human beings develop ideas among themselves, thus constructing their knowledge of (giving meaning to) the external world around them. States—the agents or persons acting for them—can and do redefine their interests, objectives, and individual courses of action. Collectively it is they who effectively construct the norms that influence international relations or world politics.

These ideas can become so deeply set or widely accepted over time that they in effect become structures that either facilitate or serve as obstacles to courses of action states choose to follow. To constructivists, ideas are important particularly when they take such structural form—in effect becoming ideational structures that can impact the behavior of both state and nonstate actors at least as much as the materially based power or class structures one finds respectively in realist and economic-structuralist thought.

Several examples may help to clarify what constructivists mean. As people we are the ones who formulate the ideas and construct the norms that define the context within which states and nonstate actors operate. Consider how slavery was once an accepted aspect of international relations. From the standpoint of the United States and many European countries, slavery was considered an economic imperative—an institution of critical importance to the economic interests of the slave-trading states as late as the 18th and well into the 19th centuries. Fortunately, this is no longer the case. Sadly, however, various forms of human bondage persist to the present day, but global and national norms make such practices not only morally illegitimate, but also illegal.

Or consider that, in the first half of the 20th century, European states were engaged in two major world wars, supposedly in defense of their respective national interests. But now Europe has created what amounts to a zone of peace, and it is hard nowadays to imagine that for centuries Germany and France had been bitter, war-prone rivals. How could a realist explain these developments? From a constructivist perspective, actors or "agents" constitute or shape over time their own social context, and this context in turn shapes the behaviors, interests, and identities we observe. Concepts such as "interests," "sovereignty," and "anarchy" are exactly that—concepts given meaning by actors, not eternal, unchanging aspects of reality beyond the control of these agents.

feminism ■ provides an alternative lens—gender—through which to view world politics and offers insights on the often-overlooked political, social, and economic roles that women play in IR

Feminists

Feminist scholars focus on gender as a category of analysis or factor in order to highlight an overlooked perspective on social political, and economic issues. Much of contemporary **feminism** is committed to progressive goals, particularly achieving equality for women through the elimination of discrimination and unequal gender relations. Gender, which embodies relationships of power inequality, is understandably the starting point. Feminists who define gender as a set of socially and culturally constructed characteristics share an affinity with the social constructivists.

Masculinity is stereotypically associated with power, a rationality often cold to human concerns, self-empowered autonomy, and assumption of leadership in public roles. Conversely, socially constructed feminine characteristics include less assertive or less aggressive behavior, willful dependence on or interdependence in nurturing relationships with others, sensitivity to emotional aspects of issues, and a focus on the private realm.

The two gender categories are dependent upon one another for their meaning. Indeed, society reinforces the idea that to be a "real man" means not to display "feminine" characteristics. Hence the emphasis on gender is not just about women, but men and masculinity as well. From the feminist perspective, gender is particularly important as a primary way to signify relationships of power, not only in the home, but also in the world of foreign policy and international relations. By privileging masculinity, women can be socially and also legally cast into a subordinate status.

Feminist theorists claim that as gender permeates social life, it has profound and largely unnoticed effects on the actions of states, international organizations, and transnational actors. These scholars seek to develop a research agenda and associated concepts to trace and explain these effects. In recent years feminism has cast its net much more widely, examining the interplay of gender with race and class. What connects all three is a concern for the nature of power relationships and points of both convergence and divergence in relation to the study of international relations and world politics.

Since feminism as an approach to international relations first began to appear in the international relations literature in the 1980s, scholars with a feminist perspective have been critical of "masculinist" approaches to conflict that tend to emphasize coercive diplomacy, unilateralism, and the use of force. From this perspective, conduct in international relations seems similar to schoolyard conflicts, particularly among boys, in which the strong do what they will and the weak do what they must. By contrast, feminist approaches to conflict tend to look for common ground—a search for positive gains for all parties. However we react to this mode of thinking, feminist writers have made us more aware of how gender—both feminine and masculine constructions—affect not only the way we understand and conduct relationships in daily life, but also in international relations and world politics.

Critical Theorists and Postmodernists

The dominant approach to knowledge has been referred to as modernism. A comparable term is positivism, which has been under assault by critical and postmodern theorists for its attempts in international relations and other social sciences to (1) separate facts from values, (2) define and operationalize concepts into precisely and accurately measurable variables, and (3) test truth claims in the form of hypotheses drawn from theories. Whether using quantitative or statistical methods, or such nonquantitative (or qualitative) methods as case and comparative-case studies, those who have tried to be scientific have been criticized for ignoring or taking insufficient account of the personal or human dimension of scholarship.

Critical theorists and postmodernists make the assumption that facts, concepts, and theories may not be separated from values, as all three stem from their observation and construction by human agency. To postmodernists, what we see, what we choose to see or measure, and the mechanisms or methods we employ are all of human construction and essentially rely on perception and cognitive processes influenced as well by prior understandings and meanings. Even the language we use constitutes an embedded set of values that are an integral part of any culture. What we observe in either the natural or social sciences is heavily influenced by the interpretive understanding we have of the concepts we employ. The same holds for the causal relations we infer when we specify the relations among variables, theories, hypotheses, and the observed behavior of states and nonstate actors in the political and social milieu in which they are immersed. If the central question of **epistemology** is how we know what we think we know, critical and postmodernist theorists set aside as problematic the abstract, universalist, scientific claims of positivists.

Some critical theorists argue that beliefs held by theorists necessarily bias their truth claims and may well be part of global ideological schemes to legitimize particular world orders. In supporting an alleged agenda of dominance (whether based on class, power, ethnicity, gender, or values), it may be convenient to advance ideologies often masquerading as scientifically based theories. Critical theorists do not reject science or the scientific method as such, but they do subject theoretical and other truth claims to greater scrutiny.

One of the tasks of critical theorists is to unmask deceptions, probe for deeper understandings or meanings, and expose the class or other interests these ideologies or alleged theories are designed to serve. Power is a core concept for critical theorists, particularly in relation to those who wield it. Given the focus on human perception and understandings that give diverse meanings to the concepts and theories we formulate and the behaviors we observe, it should not be surprising that some authors associated with economic structuralism, constructivism, and feminism are sympathetic to the assumptions of critical theory.

Critical theory may be viewed separately from **postmodernism** because most critical theorists retain scientific, strict methodological criteria to guide their work. Nevertheless, some critical theory does overlap with, or can be understood more broadly as, part of a postmodernist understanding. In this regard, postmodernist ontology (or assumptions about being—the way things are—that inform an individual's worldview) is prone to find the subtexts and to deconstruct—unpack and take apart—the meanings embedded in what we say or write and even in the ways we act.

Human beings are essentially subjective creatures. To postmodernists, claims made to empirically based, objective truth are necessarily hollow. Our understandings and meanings are, after all, humanly constructed. In the extreme, no knowledge or truth is possible apart from the motivations and purposes people put into their construction. From this extreme postmodernist perspective, truth is entirely relative.

epistemology ■
a theory of knowledge about how we come to know what we think we know about the world and what we observe in it; a pursuit that leads us to adopt various methods and methodologies for testing and expanding our knowledge

critical theory ■
Argues that theory must be connected to practice. This also entails a critique of positivist–empiricist approaches to knowledge, with critical theorists claiming all knowledge is historical and political in nature.

postmodernism ■
What we see and how we analyze international phenomena rely on our perception, which is particularly influenced by prior understandings and meanings. Even the language we use reflects values.

Assessing the Challenges to Mainstream Science and Positivism

These are, to say the least, significant challenges to "modernist" or "positivist" science more generally and to international relations theory in particular. It is difficult, however, simply to deny or dismiss scientific methodologies that have produced so much accumulated knowledge in so many diverse fields of human inquiry. Defenders quite simply see postmodernist thinkers as misrepresenting science; the scientific method is, after all, a skeptical enterprise that subjects all truth claims to both logical and empirical tests.

What constructivist, feminist, critical, and postmodernist perspectives do contribute to theorizing about international relations and world politics, however, is an ever-increased epistemological sensitivity to, and caution concerning, the fragility of what we think to be true. For example, is war among states an inevitable aspect of international relations? Or is it a phenomenon that can be essentially eliminated? The values we hold influence the interpretive understanding that leads us to formulate the concepts we adopt. Interpretive understanding thus has its place in international-relations theorizing by aiding in the ongoing search for new syntheses in human understandings of our political world. Even for the policymakers with little interest in theorizing, such understandings are a useful caution that we take our human subjectivity explicitly into account—that we look skeptically at claims that the world necessarily conforms to some reality set forth by a theorist or, for that matter, a policymaker claiming objectively to have a firm grip on what she or he sees as reality.

NORMATIVE THEORY

Mainstream social science attempts to explain *what is*. **Normative theory** is driven by a concern for what *ought to be* or should be. Because normative theory deals explicitly with norms and values, it has particular relevance to policymakers who must make the hard choices, particularly those involving moral or ethical questions. Indeed, normative theory strives to provide moral or ethical guidelines not only for policymakers, but also for any individual who is engaged or interested in international relations and world politics. Normative theorists, however, fully realize that choice is constrained by circumstance. Applying normative theory to practice crosses a wide diversity of global issues now confronting humankind. Consider the following questions that normative theory uses to attempt to provide guidance for policymakers:

2.5 Evaluate the relevancy of normative or value theory to policymakers.

Watch the **Video "Conflict Diamonds and the Kimberley Process"** at mypoliscilab.com

normative theory
■ Value-oriented or philosophical theory that focuses on what *ought to be* as opposed to *what is*. As such, it is usually different from empirical theories, which try to explain the way things *are* or predict what they will be.

- Can a war be "just"? And if so, under what conditions?
- When, if ever, some would say, is it legitimate to use force?
- Do the wealthy countries of the world have a responsibility to alleviate poverty in the developing world?
- Despite sovereignty's injunction that states should not interfere in the domestic affairs of other states, under what circumstances should the international community intervene to protect the human rights of people abused by their own governments?

President Theodore Roosevelt (1901–1909) was known for his progressive domestic policies. In terms of foreign affairs, however, he is best characterized as a realist and is known for his observation "Speak softly and carry a big stick." A former secretary of the Navy, as president he sent the U.S. Navy on a world tour to demonstrate U.S. military power.

President Woodrow Wilson (1913–1921) was also a progressive on domestic issues. Although the term wasn't even used at the time, in retrospect he shares an affinity with the perspective of the English School. He led the United States into World War I in 1917, yet after the war he was instrumental in creating the multilateral League of Nations.

Swedish diplomat Dag Hammarskjold (1905–1961) epitomized the values and perspective of the IR liberalism tradition. As an activist UN Secretary-General, he was a mediator during the 1956 Suez crisis and also following the capture of a U.S. reconnaissance plane by the Soviet Union in 1960. He also established the first UN peacekeeping force.

Hugo Chavez is the populist president of Venezuela. Under his rule he has aggressively implemented the nationalization of key industries. A self-professed anti-imperialist and critic of capitalism and U.S. foreign policy in particular, he would undoubtedly find merit in the basic assumptions of the Economic Structuralist image of world politics.

And for individuals:

- Do we owe our primary allegiance to our family, community, ethnic group or tribe, state or nation, or to a broader humanity of more than six billion persons? What obligations and duties do we as individuals have beyond the territorial boundaries of states in which we live?
- How should we live in an era of increasing globalization?
- Is there a natural limit to politically relevant ethics? Is it possible to balance politics and ethics?

Why are such questions important? One reason is that many students of international relations and world politics have felt a growing sense of intellectual inadequacy resulting from the collective failure to foresee the rapid end of the Cold War over a several-year period. If unable to anticipate such a major event, how confident can we be that we have an intellectual handle on where the world might be heading in the early 21st century as globalization continues apace, the environment deteriorates in many areas of the globe, diseases become more threatening, malnutrition remains prevalent, religious extremism seems on the rise, and the technology of mass destruction appears to be making its way into the hands of groups and individuals? Depending on the issue, normative concerns may well play a role in helping all of us think through the appropriate responses.

Fortunately, there is a vast and still-growing literature (with roots in the ancient world as well) to help guide practitioners properly concerned with doing the right thing. Normative theory also underlies international law, which draws moral insights that inform the general principles, customary practice, treaties or conventions, and writings of jurists.

CONCLUSION

Thinking critically and theoretically does not mean a flight from reality, but is actually a way to engage reality systematically in an attempt to understand some aspect of it. That is why this chapter is termed a "toolbox chapter." Certainly Gene Sharp and other practically oriented theorists approach the issue of overthrowing dictatorships and other questions from an empirical, historical, and conceptual standpoint. No one need accuse him or others like him of being excessively abstract and engaged in work divorced from reality and the major concerns of the day. At the same time, of course, all theory need not be so policy-relevant. It may be enough for many of us merely to understand better how the world works, based on insights from both explanatory and predictive theories.

Thinking theoretically helps to get you to ask key questions about international politics, sensitize you to patterns of behavior, and identify anomalies. In some ways, it is an endeavor similar to puzzle-solving. Theory, therefore, may actually help the policymaker navigate through the troubled waters of international relations. At a minimum, knowledge of basic images, interpretive understandings, and normative principles makes one more aware of potential biases and blind spots. As noted, however, critical theorists and postmodernists challenge the positivist assumptions that underlie most of the theoretical work in international relations, but they do bring us to understand better the essentially subjective nature of

✓• Study and Review
the Post-Test & Chapter
Exam at mypoliscilab.com

human beings whether in policymaking positions or not. Finally, normative theory is important to policymakers as it asks value questions, emphasizing the what "ought to be" as a way to challenge what "is" or may be the case.

LEARNING OBJECTIVES REVIEW

2.1 Define the concept of theory and formulate and test hypotheses (using both qualitative and quantitative methods) on various aspects of international relations such as how arms races between states may increase the chances of war.

Theory makes the world more intelligible by offering interrelated statements or hypotheses which taken together purport to explain what we observe. Explanation involves accounting for, or understanding causes of, such phenomena as war, arms races, and global poverty. Causal explanation or prediction is based on certain prior occurrences, patterns, or conditions. What one is trying to explain—such as the existence of interstate war—is known as the dependent variable. Factors we suspect as being causally related to what we are trying to explain typically are termed independent variables.

KEY TERMS

Theory 26
Dependent variable 26
Independent variable 26

Intervening variable 26
Hypothesis 26
Quantitative methods 27
Qualitative methods 27

ADDITIONAL READINGS

See Richard Ned Lebow and Mark Irving Lichbach, eds., *Theory and Evidence in Comparative Politics* (New York: Palgrave Macmillan, 2007) for information on methodological challenges and theory building.

Hartmut Behr, *A History of International Politics Theory: Ontologies of the International* (New York: Palgrave Macmillan, 2010); Stephen Hobden and John M. Hobson, *Historical Sociology of International Relations* (Cambridge, UK: Cambridge University Press, 2002); and Barry Buzan and Richard Little, *International Systems in World History* (Oxford, UK: Oxford University Press, 2000) provide historical overviews.

2.2 Apply the levels of analysis framework to current international events, like U.S. troop levels in Afghanistan, to generate hypotheses that help you determine the factors affecting decisions about world politics.

The levels of analysis framework is useful because it provides us a checklist that allows us to make educated guesses as to what factors might account for the international behavior we are trying to explain or predict. It focuses our attention on a diverse set of factors (independent variables) that may be causally related to what we are trying to explain (the dependent variable). Levels

include the individual and group, state and society, and international or global.

KEY TERM

Levels of analysis framework 28

ADDITIONAL READING

Kenneth N. Waltz, *Man, the State and War* (New York: Columbia University Press, 1954, 1959) and J. David Singer, "The Level-of-Analysis Problem in International Relations," *World Politics*, Vol. 14, No. 1 (Oct. 1961): 77–92, provide classic statements on the analytical value of levels of analysis in developing theory.

2.3 Compare and contrast the essential elements of four images of international relations and world politics—realism, liberalism, economic structuralism, and the English School.

Images are sets of assumptions about international relations or world politics that influence the approaches we take to studying and understanding the world around us—the types of questions asked and how we answer them. As such, images help to orient our reading and research by highlighting certain actors or concepts and discounting or ignoring others, as well as influencing the interpretation of particular international trends. Four major images are realism, liberalism, economic structuralism, and the English School.

KEY TERMS

Image 30
Realism 32
Anarchy 32
Liberalism 33
Economic structuralism 35
LDC 36
English school 37

ADDITIONAL READINGS

Paul R. Viotti and Mark V. Kauppi, *International Relations Theory*, 5th ed. (New York: Longman, 2011). Our own work, this volume goes into much greater depth on images, interpretive understandings, and normative theory than space allows here.

Scott Burchill et al., *Theories of International Relations*, 4th ed. (New York: Palgrave Macmillan, 2009) is another useful anthology of articles on various theoretical approaches to IR.

REALISM: Kenneth N. Waltz, *Theory of International Politics* (New York: Random House, 1979), is now a classic work on structural realism.

Jack Donnelly's *Realism and International Politics* (New York: Routledge, 2008) is a useful anthology that contains selected articles in this genre.

LIBERALISM: Robert O. Keohane, *Power and Governance in a Partially Globalized World* (New York: Routledge, 2002). A major work on global governance.

ECONOMIC STRUCTURALISM: Immanuel Wallerstein, *World-Systems Analysis: An Introduction* (Raleigh, NC: Duke University Press, 2004). A major theorist on world system theory.

ENGLISH SCHOOL: Andrew Linklater and Hidemi Suganami, *The English School of International Relations* (Cambridge, UK: Cambridge University Press, 2006). A solid overview.

Barry Buzan, *From International to World Society?: English School Theory and the Social Structure of Globalisation* (Cambridge, UK: Cambridge University Press, 2004). A creative attempt to reformulate major concepts within the English School.

2.4 Describe the different interpretive understandings and the critique of the four images offered by constructivists, feminists, critical theorists, and postmodernists.

Interpretive understandings question what the four images take for granted concerning our ability to use mainstream social scientific methods to comprehend world politics. Constructivists, for example, claim that what realists and liberals take for granted—interests and the identities of actors—are actually quite malleable, constructed and subject to change by the actors themselves. Critical theorists are skeptical about the truth claims made by mainstream scholars as well as the statements made by political leaders. Postmodernists have severe doubts as to our ability even to comprehend the supposed self-evident reality of international relations. By utilizing the concept of gender, feminists have provided an insightful and unconventional way to analyze and interpret world politics.

KEY TERMS

Constructivism 39
Feminism 40
Epistemology 42
Critical theory 42
Postmodernism 42

ADDITIONAL READINGS

CONSTRUCTIVISM: Maja Zehfuss, *Constructivism in International Relations* (Cambridge, UK: Cambridge University Press, 2002). One of the most accessible overviews on constructivism.

Alexander Wendt, *Social Theory of International Politics* (Cambridge, UK: Cambridge University Press, 1999). A pioneering theoretical work.

POSTMODERNISM: Francis A. Beer and Christ'l de Landtsheer (eds.), *Metaphorical World Politics* (East Lansing, MI: Michigan State University Press, 2004). A compendium on the various elements of postmodern thought.

David Campbell, *Writing Security*: *United States Foreign Policy and the Politics of Identity*, rev. ed. (Minneapolis, MN: Univ of Minnesota Press, 1998). An interesting analysis of the language of international security.

CRITICAL THEORY: James Der Derian, *Critical Practices in International Theory: Selected Essays* (New York:

Routledge, 2009). A collection of articles by a prominent postmodern and critical theorist.

Ken Booth, *Theory of World Security* (Cambridge, UK: Cambridge University Press, 2007). A spirited critique of realism.

FEMINISM: J. Ann Tickner and Laura Sjoberg (eds.), *Feminism and International Relations*: *Conversations About the Past, Present and Future* (New York: Routledge, 2011). An overview of the development and trials and tribulations of feminist IR theory.

Christine Sylvester (ed.), *War, Feminism & International Relations* (New York: Routledge, 2011). An excellent thematic collection.

2.5 Evaluate the relevancy of normative or value theory to policymakers.

Normative theory is concerned with what *ought to be* or should be. Because normative theory deals explicitly with norms and values, it has particular relevance to policymakers who must make the hard choices, particularly those involving moral or ethical questions. Major topics include just war, humanitarian intervention, conditions for the use of force, and responsibilities to a broader humanity.

KEY TERM
Normative theory 43

ADDITIONAL READINGS
Chris Brown, *Practical Judgement in International Politics Theory: Selected Essays* (New York: Routledge, 2010). A diverse collection of articles by a thoughtful observer of the role of normative theory in international relations and world politics.

Simon Caney, *Justice Beyond Borders* (New York: Oxford University Press, 2006). A cosmopolitan approach to global political theory that critiques realism, nationalism, and the society-of-states tradition.

CHAPTER REVIEW

1. Theory attempts to
   a. tell us how the world works.
   b. explain why things happen.
   c. anticipate what might happen in different circumstances.
   d. all of the above.

2. This chapter covers
   a. theory-building.
   b. levels of analysis.
   c. world images.
   d. interpretive understandings.
   e. all of the above.

3. What a theorist is trying to explain is the
   a. independent variable.
   b. intervening variable.
   c. dependent variable.
   d. constant variable.

4. A possible factor to explain a phenomenon is
   a. independent variable.
   b. non-constant variable.
   c. dependent variable.
   d. constant variable.

5. An hypothesis is
   a. a proven empirical fact.
   b. a dependent variable.
   c. an educated guess.
   d. none of the above.

6. Individuals and small groups, state and society, and the international system are
   a. levels of analysis
   b. economic structuralist categories.
   c. liberal references of multiple actors.
   d. social constructivist categories.

7. Political scientists who claim to view the world as it is, not as it ought to be, are often called
   a. liberals.
   b. utopians.
   c. realists.
   d. idealists.

8. Political scientists who claim to view the world in terms of a multiplicity of different kinds of actors engaged in transactions in multiple paths or channels of interaction are called
   a. optimists.
   b. economic structuralists.
   c. pluralists or liberals.
   d. realists.

9. Thomas Hobbes was concerned with the security implications of
   a. anarchy.
   b. political equality.
   c. assuring due process of law.
   d. global civil society.

10. Realists tend to see world politics as a result of the combination of
    a. power, democracy and human nature.
    b. human nature, conflict and power, and the structure of the state.
    c. human nature, ethics, and the characteristics of political organization.
    d. human nature, the characteristics of states, and the distribution of power or structure of the international system.

11. Liberals tend to
    a. dispute the claim that to understand international relations or world politics one need only focus on the state.
    b. see the state as a unitary, rational actor.

    c. downplay the importance of international organizations.
    d. see international organizations only as arenas in which states compete with each other.

12. Conventional discourse, particularly among realists, has come to equate the term international relations with
    a. global politics.
    b. global government.
    c. interstate government.
    d. interstate relations.

13. A focus on mechanisms of domination in a capitalist world order is most closely associated with
    a. realism.
    b. pluralism or liberalism.
    c. economic structuralism.
    d. social constructivism.

14. Which of the following is associated with economic structuralism?
    a. Marx
    b. Hobbes
    c. Kant
    d. Greek Stoics

15. Those in the English School tend to see international politics in terms of
    a. class struggle conducted on a global scale.
    b. interactions within a worldwide or international society.
    c. global ideals that ultimately will displace realist balance-of-power understandings.
    d. an almost mechanical system of states.

16. Which of the following is not true of the English School?
    a. Realist thought is associated with the writings of Thomas Hobbes.
    b. Writings by Grotius on international law are associated with rules that influence the behavior of states.
    c. The social contract in the writings of Locke and Rousseau is key to understanding anarchy in international society.
    d. Moral or ethical principles that come to be accepted internationally as in the writings of the East Prussian Immanuel Kant.

17. That states don't simply react to their environment, but dynamically engage it—that anarchy in international politics is what states make of it—is a view most closely associated with
    a. economic structuralism.
    b. feminism.
    c. both realism and pluralism or liberalism.
    d. social constructivism.

18. Feminism involves
    a. using gender as a category of analysis, focusing on differences between feminine and masculine understandings and actions.
    b. an understanding of women making decisions in a highly rational way, often cold to human concerns.

    c. a view of women as typically exhibiting assertive, often aggressive behavior.
    d. a perspective that sees women as customarily assuming leadership positions in society.

19. Postmodernists are most closely associated with
    a. critical theorists.
    b. realists.
    c. social constructivists.
    d. liberals.

20. Normative theory is associated with
    a. just war.
    b. a concern with what should be.
    c. use of force.
    d. all of the above.

History

"One age cannot be completely understood if all the others
are not understood. The song of history can only be sung as a whole."

LEARNING OBJECTIVES

3.1 Compare and contrast the four types of international systems we identify — independent, hegemonic, imperial, feudal — and explain the benefits of applying this conceptual understanding to the history of international relations.

3.2 Apply, the four categories or types of international systems to the cases of ancient Persia, Greece, India, Rome, and feudal Europe.

3.3 Explain the key developments that led to the rise of the European independent state system and how it eventually became globalized as a form of international politics.

3.4 Evaluate and explain the relative success and failure of attempts by states to develop collective security arrangements.

3.5 Evaluate the impact of the rising economic strength of the European Union and the four rising BRIC powers on future international developments.

At the end of major regional or world wars, there is often a reshuffling of the relative power capabilities of the participants whether one is referring to the end of the Napoleonic wars in Europe (1815), World War I (1918), or World War II (1945). In the latter case, Germany, Japan, and Italy were defeated. Great Britain, France, and Russia were exhausted from their efforts. The single strongest power remaining was the United States. American statesmen were faced with the basic question, how should the country proceed from this point forward? One suggestion was pushing for continual preeminence, assisted by a monopoly on atomic weapons. Another idea was to multilateralize security by creating a United Nations. Or, alternatively, the United States could encourage economic, political, and military alliances in conjunction with a weakened western Europe in the hope of assisting their recovery and providing an added bulwark against a potentially ambitious Soviet Union.

Deciding which way to go was argued and debated and reflected upon by such individuals as President Truman and some of the leading statesmen of the day. Termed "The Wise Men," they were six friends—two lawyers, two bankers, and two diplomats[1]—who were instrumental in not only devising the containment policy against the Soviet Union, but such institutions as the World Bank and International Monetary Fund, the North Atlantic Treaty

Read and Listen to **Chapter 3** at **mypoliscilab.com**

Study and Review the **Pre-Test & Flashcards** at **mypoliscilab.com**

---

[1]The six were Dean Acheson (lawyer), Averell Harriman (banker), George Kennan (diplomat), John McCloy Jr. (lawyer, also banker), Charles ("Chip") Bohlen (diplomat), and Robert Lovett (banker). See Walter Isaacson and Evan Thomas, *The Wise Men: Six Friends and the World They Made* (New York: Simon & Schuster, 1997).

Organization, and the Marshall Plan, which aimed to revitalize Europe economically. Their approach to engaging a new international environment with its new distribution of international power was pragmatic and nonpartisan and devoid of ideological fervor. Despite being criticized by some contemporaries as an East Coast elite, they nevertheless succeeded in devising a series of policies aimed at protecting American interests, which included the broad goal of international stability.

A legitimate question is: Why should one care about history? Assuming you have some interest in pursuing a career as a practitioner engaged in international politics, the rationale for the importance of this historical overview as part of our toolkit is as follows. First, history contributes to our contemporary understanding of international politics. How can policymakers understand what is unique or different about the current ways in which international relations and world politics take place unless they know what it has in common with (or how it differs from) earlier practice? Second, a study of history should make us careful in applying historical analogies or comparisons to current events. Rarely are circumstances exactly the same and hence it is dangerous to assume that the lessons of history are always clear-cut. Third, a discussion of historical forms of relations among states, city-states, or other units allows us to mention some of the political theorists who have influenced contemporary thinking about world politics. Finally, our discussion will expose the would-be practitioner to a conceptual and theoretical understanding of international relations and world politics beyond historical facts and figures. In other words, to think historically and conceptually is to be better prepared to anticipate future international developments such as closer integration or disintegration among European Union (EU) members, a resurgent Russia, and the rise to major-power status of China, India, and Brazil.

INTERNATIONAL SYSTEMS: DEFINITION AND SCOPE

3.1 Compare and contrast the four types of international systems we identify—independent, hegemonic, imperial, feudal—and explain the benefits of applying this conceptual understanding to the history of international relations.

How does one think about international relations in a conceptual and historical perspective? The contemporary era is the only one that is truly global. Historically most peoples' lives—economic, social, and political—revolved around an isolated village, clan, or tribe. Identity derived from these small communities, not some larger entity. Similarly, the local economy was usually insulated, particularly in subsistence economies, with little trade among communities. Hence political and economic—indeed, any—interactions outside of one's own community were minimal or nonexistent.

The same is true of relations among different civilizations. When the Spanish and Portuguese explorers set forth in the 15th and 16th centuries, they had little idea what other cultures and civilizations they would encounter. Similarly, it was not until adventurers and traders trekked to China along what came to be known as the Silk Road that economic exchanges occurred between West and East. Therefore it makes little sense to begin speaking of global politics until after the rise of the modern state that encouraged and sponsored the outward expansion of capitalism through both trade and an exploitative colonialism. The concept of what we now call globalization, however, did not take hold until the worldwide expansion of markets, transportation, and communications penetrated national borders globally, especially during the last half of the 20th century.

Given the fact the world has not always been organized the way it is today, it makes more sense to speak historically of different types of international systems— systems that were limited in geographic scope and hence cannot accurately be described as global or world systems. The concept of system used here is defined as an aggregation of diverse entities linked by regular interaction that sets them apart from other systems.[2] The idea of diverse entities is useful in that it allows not only for different types of state actors, such as city-states, empires, and modern states, but also international organizations and such nonstate actors as corporations and humanitarian relief organizations. The definition of regular interaction varies depending on the nature and intensity of the interactions. For example, the nature of the interaction could be war, with such conflict being of greater or lesser intensity. Or the interaction could be trade, ranging from minimal to a large volume. Finally the nature of the system's units and their relative capabilities or positions in relation to each other give the system structure and set the system apart from other systems. This also allows us to speak of a system having boundaries. For example, we can speak of relations in the contemporary European Union (EU) as a political-economic system or view commercial interactions in the North American Free Trade Agreement (NAFTA) among firms and consumers in Canada, Mexico, and the United States as a separate North American economic system.

In this regard it can be said that today a world or global system also exists, as the distinct boundaries between separate international systems of earlier historical periods are lacking. Furthermore the current global system—although dominated by states—is also characterized by extensive economic and technological interdependence and interconnectedness among a diverse set of international and transnational actors. From this perspective the EU and NAFTA examples could be termed regional subsystems of the larger global system. It should be remembered, however, that a system is simply an analytic device to allow an observer to deal with an aspect of international relations that is of interest. It is not meant to be a precise description of reality.

To summarize, while we characterize the world today as a global system, we can also focus on various subsystems. Such subsystems may be geographically oriented—for example, relations among members of the EU, NAFTA, or ASEAN (the Association of Southeast Asian Nations). Or the subsystems may be defined in functional terms—a telecommunications subsystem, a trading subsystem, a transportation subsystem, a financial transaction subsystem. These latter types of subsystems could be depicted visually, with lines crisscrossing the globe, illustrating the density of transactions. Instead of the globe being divided into geographic entities—the image with which we began this chapter—it would look more like a cobweb or latticework.

⊙—❙Watch the **Video** **"The Berlin Blockade"** at mypoliscilab.com

international system ■ an aggregation of similar or diverse entities linked by regular interaction that sets them apart from other systems, for example, the interstate or international system of states, or world politics understood as a system composed of both state and nonstate actors

structure ■ In realist usage, structure usually refers to the distribution of power among states. Thus, a world subject to the influence of one great power is unipolar, to two principal powers is bipolar, and to three or more is multipolar.

global system ■ encompasses the entire globe and is characterized by economic and technological interdependence and diverse actors

---

[2]This definition is modified from that provided by Robert A. Mundell and Alexander K. Swoboda (eds.), *Monetary Problems of the International Economy* (Chicago: University of Chicago Press, 1969), 343.

When did the global system come about? It is difficult to determine a precise date, as the globalization process occurred incrementally over many centuries. We would suggest, however, that the globalization of the European state system (i.e., the state as the key political unit) began in earnest in the 19th century at the same time that global economic interdependence began to accelerate. It has been only since 1945, or the end of World War II, that the technological and communications revolutions in transportation, communications, information transfer, and other technologies have gathered speed and had a global impact. The internet, dubbed appropriately the World Wide Web, now connects people, their governments, corporations, and both international and nongovernmental organizations in ways that were inconceivable to most just a few decades ago.

Up until the 19th century it makes more sense to speak of various regional or international systems, meaning they were not global in scope. In historical references we prefer, however, the term *international* to *regional*. In ancient times people had no idea that other civilizations existed in other parts of the world. As far as they knew, they were the world if not the center of the universe. This was as true in Europe as it was in the Americas, Africa, China, or elsewhere in Asia and the Pacific.

In this chapter we examine four different types of historical international systems.[3]

Independent State System

independent state system ■ political entities that each claim to be sovereign with the right to make both foreign policy and domestic decisions

First, an independent state system consists of political entities that each claim to be sovereign—the right to make both foreign policy and domestic decisions. No superior power is acknowledged and other states recognize these claims. Simply by interacting with other units (the system), some interdependence exists, resulting in a certain degree of constraint on any one state's actions. States are equal in terms of their claims to sovereignty, though they obviously differ in their capabilities and power. An ambitious and rising power may be viewed as a threat to the independence of other states, resulting in the formation of a counterweight or countervailing coalition or alliance. The rising power is constrained by the actions of the others, just as the members of the alliance will witness some degree of limitation on their freedom to maneuver by agreeing to work together to deter or defeat the ambitious state and maintain a balance of power.

Hegemonic State System

Second, there is the hegemonic state system (see Figure 3.1). By hegemony we mean one or more states dominate the system, set the "rules of the game," and thus have some degree of direct influence on the external affairs of member states.

[3]The first three systems we discuss follow the categorization of Adam Watson, *The Evolution of International Society* (London: Routledge, 1992).

FIGURE 3.1

Hegemonic State System: Historical Examples

Many writers refer in structural terms to what we call hegemony as having three variants:

1. *Unipolarity:* "One pole," or a single dominant state such as the United States in the aftermath of the collapse of the Soviet Union in the early 1990s
2. *Bipolarity* or *dual hegemony:* Two dominant states, such as Athens and Sparta in the second half of the 5th century B.C.E. or the United States and the Soviet Union during the Cold War (1945–1991)
3. *Multipolarity* or *collective hegemony:* Three or more states dominate international relations, such as the five great European powers after 1815 (Great Britain, France, Russia, Austria, and Prussia)

In any of these hegemonic systems, the less powerful members may interact with one another, but they take their cues from the hegemonic authorities. They may even derive important benefits such as security by aligning with the more powerful states. The domestic affairs of states, however, are generally left untouched by the hegemonic powers. While political leaders are not installed by the hegemonic powers, they have little room for maneuvering in their state's foreign policy.

hegemonic state system ■ One or more states dominate the system. Variants include unipolar, bipolar or dual hegemony, multipolar or collective hegemony.

Imperial System

The third type of international system is evident in recent centuries as well as in ancient times—imperial systems such as those of Assyria, Persia, Macedonia, and Rome. An empire consists of separate societal units associated by regular interaction, but one among them asserts political supremacy and the others formally or tacitly accept this claim. The difference between this and the hegemonic system, however, is that in an empire the dominant state is more likely to manage subject colonies' or territorial units' affairs, appointing local political officials, collecting taxes, drafting recruits into the imperial military, and creating and maintaining a system of roads and other transportation networks to enhance economic, military, and political interdependence.

These three systems can be depicted as a set of alternative types as shown in Figure 3.2. Historically there has been a tendency for one or more states to attempt to move from an independent system to a hegemonic state system or to an empire, with other states attempting to prevent this from happening or forming

imperial system ■ consists of separate societal units associated by regular interaction, but one among them asserts political supremacy and tends to manage the affairs of a subject state or colony

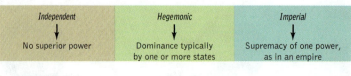

Independent	Hegemonic	Imperial
↓	↓	↓
No superior power	Dominance typically by one or more states	Supremacy of one power, as in an empire

FIGURE 3.2
Three Types of Historical Systems

empires of their own. Military conquest historically has been the principal means by which empires have been established. But authority crises within a particular political system can make it weak and vulnerable to foreign pressure. Within any particular geographic area, any of these three types of systems can ebb and flow, rise and decline, evolve from one into another and back again.

Feudal System

feudal system ■
power is claimed by a diverse group of governmental units including kings, barons, trading houses, and popes in a very decentralized system

The fourth type of international system is the feudal system from about the 9th to the 14th centuries. What makes the feudal system so unusual is the diversity of the entities that comprised it and the manner in which the relations among these units were structured. Power was decentralized and claimed by a diverse group of governmental units, only some of which evolved into modern states. Other actors included trading associations, the great houses of merchant bankers, and local feudal barons. The one institution to claim universal or global jurisdiction was the pre-Reformation Christian Church in Rome, now the Roman Catholic Church. As scholars point out, the feudal system reminds us that the key actors of international politics have not always been, and in the future may not necessarily be, states.

All four categories of international systems—independent, hegemonic, imperial, and feudal—are ideal or pure types, meaning actual historical examples placed within any single category will not line up exactly, but will have their variations in relation to what a pure type would be. As such, the ideal or pure type is a yardstick or standard against which we measure real-world examples. Moreover, it is possible for such systems to coexist and overlap, as was the case during the period of Spartan–Athenian hegemony and their relations with the Persian Empire to the east. Such systems remained important even as the globalization process was beginning to emerge in the 18th and 19th centuries. Roughly the first half of the 20th century, for example, most closely resembled collective hegemony (or a multipolar system), but the Cold War had many of the hallmarks of a dual hegemonic (or bipolar) state system because of the dominance then of both the United States and the Soviet Union as superpowers.

How do such international systems develop, evolve, and decay over time? Why do such systems come to be viewed as legitimate, meaning their particular distribution of power and authority is accepted (decentralized in an independent state system, centralized in an empire)? We should keep these questions in mind as we consider the problematic integration of European countries in the European Union (EU) and the current rise of China, India, Brazil, and a resurgent Russia—a Eurasian power.

Just as we must be wary of assuming that the past was somehow predetermined, we must also realize that the future is not inevitably a mere continuation of present trends. It is extremely difficult to judge how various political, economic, social, and technological forces may come together to influence the evolution of the world or world politics. History is full of surprising twists and turns that few could have foreseen: the collapse of the Soviet Union and end of the Cold War in 1991 is one example. The popular uprisings against authoritarian regimes in North Africa and the Middle East is a more recent case. This should give pause to anyone who assumes the dominance or hegemony of the United States is now a fixed characteristic of the international system or, for that matter, that the continuing rise of China is somehow inevitable.

A related point we wish to make is that some of the most critical concepts and ideas that have shaped contemporary thinking about the nature of international relations have deep historical roots. One should not underestimate the power of ideas in influencing the course of history. Human beings do not just passively react to their environment, whether ecological, economic, social, or political; they also shape it.

Ideas about international relations are sometimes used to justify the status quo in any era. But ideas can also help to overturn that status quo by providing inspiration and guidance to those who seek an alternative world future. Consider, for example, how the concept of democracy has gripped the imaginations of many people all over the world to include portions of the Middle East and North Africa in 2011 and afterward. It has motivated them to take up a struggle against authoritarianism even though in many countries the quest would appear to be nearly hopeless. Ideas about democracy, political economy, social justice, and other concerns do matter, sometimes succeeding against enormous odds. At the same time, of course, those holding conservative or reactionary views—in the extreme calling for a return to some idealized golden age of the past—challenge those committed to a more forward-looking, progressive future in which liberal, democratic regimes displace authoritarian ones that for so long have dominated the region.

HISTORICAL INTERNATIONAL SYSTEMS

We now turn to a discussion of historical international systems. Our purpose is to illustrate the diversity of systems, actors, and processes of world politics. The application of the concept of system also allows us to compare and contrast how political authority was organized in different times and geographic regions. This also encourages aspiring practitioners of international relations to judge how past periods of history may enlighten us as to the current and future direction of international relations and world politics.

3.2 Apply the four categories or types of international systems to the cases of ancient Persia, Greece, India, Rome, and feudal Europe.

The Persian Empire

Persia is one of the best examples of imperial organization in the ancient world. Centered in present-day Iran, Persia was founded on the ruins of the Assyrian empire (about 1100–600 B.C.E.), but was much larger, extending from the eastern

Mediterranean south to Egypt and all the way to the western borders of India. The Persians were particularly adept at assimilating those local customs that eased the expansion and efficient control of their empire. The Assyrian network of roads, for example, was extended, and Egyptian advances in administration and science were also adopted. In order to communicate more effectively with locals, they used Aramaic as the common language—Emperor (*Shahenshah*) Darius the Great having ordered this the official language about 500 B.C.E.[4]

The best way to visualize the political aspect of the Persian Empire is as a series of concentric circles. The inner core was directly administered, but as one moved farther away from the capital of Persepolis (in present-day Iran), control was more decentralized. In outlying areas the client territorial units were quasi-autonomous. The threat of imperial military forces was always there; garrisons were established at key locations, and local troops were trained and armed. But the Persian overlords preferred to rely on persuasion to maintain control. Indeed, historians note the relative moderation of Persian rule over other peoples. Local governors, termed satraps, were either Persians brought in from outside or members of the local royalty. Aided by advisory councils, political rulers had jurisdiction separate from that of the local garrison commander and the representative of the imperial intelligence service. To accommodate regional and cultural differences across the far-flung empire, local administrative customs were generally adopted without substantial change. Administrators below the imperial level ranged from priests and kings to land-owning aristocrats or merchant families, depending on the custom of the area.

satraps ■ local Persian governors

The Persian rulers were successful in avoiding conflict among the diverse members of their empire. After failing to conquer the Greeks directly, the Persians astutely supplied money and ships to whatever Greek coalition was formed to counter the strongest Greek city-state. During the reigns of Cyrus and Darius, the Persians extended their authority over the Greek and Phoenician cities located along the Mediterranean shore. These trading cities brought the Persians considerable economic benefits, so the Greeks and Phoenicians were allowed to retain almost complete control over their internal affairs. Special rules also were devised for the government of Egypt, which by some estimates accounted for one-fifth of the population of the Persian Empire.

In sum, the Persian approach to empire—providing internal autonomy to constituent territorial units as a means to lower military, administrative, and financial costs—established a practical precedent followed subsequently by leaders of the Macedonian and Roman empires.

Classical Greece

The Greek world of the 6th to the 1st century B.C.E. was composed of a variety of political entities that today we call city-states. Their small populations, limited control of territory beyond city walls, and proximity to each other were similar

---

[4]This section relies on insights and is adapted from commentary in Watson, *Evolution of International Society*, 40–46.

to the Italian Renaissance city-state system, not to modern states, most of which consist of comparatively large populations and often vast territorial expanses. The political forms of Greek city-states, as discussed by Plato and Aristotle, included monarchies that often degenerated into despotism (both of which involved dominance by a powerful individual) and other forms of rule. These ranged from leadership by enlightened aristocracies to exploitative oligarchies (rule by the few) and in some cases democracy, although participation was limited to those deemed worthy of the title "citizen."

However they were organized, all of the city-states worked assiduously to maintain their independence. Some city-states were naturally more powerful than others, dominating weaker city-states and sometimes extracting tribute in return for military protection. Diplomatic practices were rudimentary, generally consisting of delegations that traveled to other city-states in order to present demands, resolve disputes, or negotiate trade agreements. Aside from its cultural and artistic impact, the classical Greek period also served as a model of interstate relations for European and American diplomats in the 18th and 19th centuries.

Although all city-states desired to be independent, during the 5th century B.C.E. the rise of two city-states—Sparta and Athens—turned the Greek independent state system into a dual hegemony. The Spartans played a minor role in repelling the Persian invasion of northern Greece in 490 B.C.E., which ended with the spectacular Greek victory at the battle of Marathon. Ten years later, however, the Spartans reluctantly agreed to accept the command of combined Greek forces to repel the second Persian invasion led by King Xerxes in 480 B.C.E. Spartan forces were unable to hold back the Persians at Thermopylae. The city-state of Athens, known for its navy as well as its democratic form of government, argued for a naval confrontation and, at the battle of Salamis, the Persian fleet was defeated. The following year the Spartan army routed the Persians at the battle of Plataea, and Xerxes' forces retreated.

With the repulse of the Persians, Sparta returned to its traditional concerns and more limited sphere of influence on the Peloponnese (the peninsula or mainland of present-day Greece). At this point Athens came to the fore and, hoping to prevent the Persians from launching another invasion of Greece, proposed the creation of the Delian League. This alliance was composed principally of the city-states most vulnerable to Persian pressure, including those along the west coast of Asia Minor (present-day Turkey) and islands in the Aegean. In order to protect these city-states and sweep the Persians out of northern Greece, Athens continued to expand the size of its navy and other military forces. In the process it became a major military power.

Delian League ■
alliance of city-states headed by Athens

After a series of victories against Persian forces, the Delian League of city-states totaled some two hundred members. But, as so often happens in alliances, once the foreign threat had been neutralized, problems among the member city-states soon began to appear. This was in part due to resentment and fear of Athenian domination. These states, although formally autonomous political units, or polities, were forced to pay tribute to Athens, which determined not only their foreign policies, but also important domestic policies.

Following a peace treaty between the Greeks and Persians in 449 B.C.E., the Athenians and Spartans in effect recognized spheres of influence and what amounted to a balance of power between the two city-states and their respective allies. The ensuing peace allowed the two hegemonic rivals to consolidate control in their respective spheres. It was at this point, in 435 B.C.E., that the historian Thucydides (c. 460–406 B.C.E.) took up the story in detail and discussed the specific events that led to the outbreak of the second Peloponnesian War. The Greek international system was essentially an Athenian–Spartan dual hegemony, but other states such as Corcyra, Thebes, Argos, and Corinth also had significant capabilities that distinguished them from the vast majority of city-states.

The final defeat of Athens in 404 B.C.E. at first seemed to usher in a return to the independent state system. But Sparta soon began to assert hegemony over the rest of Greece, interfering in the internal affairs of other city-states and losing the support of its former allies.

The Persian Empire, alarmed by Sparta's attempts to extend its rule to city-states in Asia Minor, joined in this new alliance. Unable to control Greece directly, they realized that the next best thing was to support whatever anti-hegemonic coalition was formed as a way to be sure no single Greek city-state could threaten Persia itself. But their primary concern was stability on the western border of their empire. Hence they pushed for a negotiated peace with Sparta and later a general peace conference among all the belligerents. The resultant international system was composed of independent states with a balance of power among them.

The peace, however, was fragile. The Spartans, Athenians, and Thebans maintained their respective hegemonic ambitions. This international system, therefore, can be characterized as one with several states vying for hegemonic control, but thwarted in their effort by shifting state coalitions or balances of power. A common Greek identity did not prevent war among them. It is no wonder that later European political leaders found many parallels between their condition and the classical Greek international system.

With the rise to power of Philip of Macedon to the north and his son, Alexander the Great (356–323 B.C.E.), both the Persian Empire and the Greek system ultimately came under Macedonian imperial rule.

India

Prior to the sixth century B.C.E., ancient India drew much of its common identity from geographic isolation and the impact of Hinduism. More than a religion, Hindu ideas represent a broad-based set of values that became deeply embedded in Indian culture. As such, Hinduism influenced social and economic life in one of the world's great civilizations. Despite a common civilization, however, the Indian subcontinent was divided into a number of independent political units. Some were more powerful than others, and warfare and expansionism were common. But, aided by Hinduism, there was a degree of common cultural identity and interdependence that encouraged the development of common rules and customs to guide relations among the various states. Although some were ruled by elected leaders and a few were republics, most were governed by kings belonging to the second-highest *kshatriya* caste, who believed their primary role in life was to govern and to fight.[5]

---

[5]Watson, *Evolution of International Society*, 77–84.

As is so often the case, however, it was Hindu contact with the outside world that led to fundamental changes in the Indian international system of independent states. As the Persian Empire expanded eastward, it eventually conquered what is present-day Pakistan. It was at this point that the concept of empire began to circulate among Indian rulers and the educated castes. The Persians showed how a vast territory could be governed from an imperial center and how an extensive road network could facilitate interdependence through commerce and the movement of people. Some two centuries of Persian influence (520–327 B.C.E.) were followed by the invasion of Alexander's armies. With them they brought new Greek ideas (Alexander, after all, was one of Aristotle's students). This influx of foreign ideas followed hard on the heels of the spread of Buddhism (the Buddha—Gautama Siddhartha—having lived about 563–483 B.C.E.), which also had a major impact on Hindu life.

Out of this intellectual, social, and economic turmoil arose Chandragupta Maurya, who managed to transform an independent Indian state system into an empire. Although it was similar in scope to Persia, day-to-day rule of the Indian Empire was heavily infused with indigenous values and customs. This man of action was accompanied in his rise to power by a man of intellect who worked to provide Maurya an extensive treatise on the ways and means of governing. That man was Kautilya.

With the death of Alexander, Chandragupta and Kautilya seized the opportunity to put their plans and ideas into motion and eventually established the Mauryan Empire. Although not all of India was brought under Chandragupta's control, most of it was. An attempt to reclaim what had been the Persian part of India was turned back in 305 B.C.E. Domestic security and the neutralization of foreign threats encouraged the expansion of trade. But, against Kautilya's advice, Chandragupta's rule became heavy-handed, and not surprisingly he made enemies. He became isolated and withdrawn, surrounding himself with a large personal bodyguard of armed women for protection.

Empire building continued under his son and grandson. The grandson, Asoka (272–231 B.C.E.), initially expanded the empire by brutal methods, but once he became a devout Buddhist, he was known for his concern over the welfare of his subjects. Upon his death, however, the bonds of the empire began to loosen. The desire for independence was reasserted by elements throughout the empire, a crisis of authority ensued, and the empire eventually collapsed. India reverted to a series of independent warring states, the very condition Chandragupta had surmounted more than a hundred years before.

The Roman Empire

At least to those educated in the West, Rome represents the ultimate historical expression of the imperial international system. Rome started out, however, as a city-state, indistinguishable from its neighbors on the Italian peninsula. Over several centuries it gradually expanded its control to all points of the compass: north and west to present-day Germany, Britain, Spain, and France; south to North Africa and Egypt; and east to Iran. The importance of the Roman Empire, however, lies not in its size, but in the fact that it came to be viewed as the legitimate authority by the vast majority of its diverse communities. For two centuries, beginning with Augustus (63 B.C.E.–14 B.C.E), the Roman Empire provided internal stability, two common languages (Latin and Greek), and a conduit for the dissemination of Greek and Eastern culture that helped to establish the foundations of European civilization. In terms of world politics, Rome shaped current thought and practice about the state, international law, and international society.

In its early years, Rome was ruled by kings, but with the development of aristocratic rule came the rise of the Senate with executive authority residing in two consuls. The lower class, or plebeians, also elected tribunes to keep watch over their interests. Internal strife assuredly occurred, but as Roman rule expanded outward, so did Rome's wealth. Increased wealth combined with able rulers strengthened the power of the Senate.[6]

To conquer territory is a difficult feat, but to retain it is perhaps even harder. The senators were shrewd enough to realize that their long-term interests would suffer if they abused the newly subjected communities. Instead they bestowed upon these populations the advantages of Roman order and law, co-opting certain individuals via the extension of Roman citizenship. As with such earlier empires as Persia, the degree of direct rule lessened with increased distance from the imperial capital, allowing more distant communities substantial self-rule.

Rome's interest in Sicily brought it into contact with the Phoenician trading city of Carthage, now the capital city of Tunis located on the Mediterranean coast of present-day Tunisia. From approximately 250 to 200 B.C.E., Rome and Carthage vied for supremacy in the western Mediterranean. With ultimate victory in the Punic wars, Rome absorbed the Carthaginian Empire. As this struggle concluded, Rome looked to the east toward Greece and the Macedonian kingdoms. With the Greeks and Macedons unable to form an anti-hegemonic coalition, Rome soon gained control of the region. At this point the Roman imperial lands were divided into provinces, ruled and taxed by Roman governors. As long as they pledged loyalty, these kingdoms were granted local autonomy, and indigenous customs were generally respected. In fact it was due to Roman occupation that the values and culture of these Eastern civilizations made their way back to Rome.

The rapid expansion of the empire, however, made it difficult to control territories effectively, particularly as the central government was constrained by a weak executive authority and a small bureaucracy. Attempts to fill this executive vacuum were made by various military leaders who promised stability but generally brought unrest and near civil war to Rome.

Ruthless in battle, as a ruler Caesar (Emperor) Augustus was a moderate who brilliantly reorganized the empire and provided it with a respite from internal strife. Although he retained ultimate power, Augustus helped to legitimate his authority by allowing for the restoration of the Senate and some of its privileges and responsibilities. His successors helped to consolidate his basic achievement, which was to improve dramatically the governance of the empire. Periods of instability spurred the further growth of a centralized bureaucracy that encouraged the development of Roman law and, in turn, helped to streamline and rationalize the legal and administrative systems throughout the empire.

---

[6]The rest of this section is based on Watson, 94–106.

Problems began to arise in the 3rd century, however. Armies of the Persian Sassanid Empire invaded Roman territory; when Roman troops in Germany were called back, the northern frontier of the empire became open to attack. Not surprisingly a series of Roman generals came to power, vowing to restore order. Imperial authority became even more concentrated in the hands of the emperor at the expense of the Senate. To those parts of the empire under threat from foreign armies, such a development was welcome. But gradually, following the death of the emperor Constantine in C.E. 337, the western half of the empire began to crumble. The stronger eastern half of the empire, based in Constantinople (present-day Istanbul, Turkey) remained politically, economically, and culturally vibrant for several more centuries. But in the West, the Roman Empire came to a formal end in C.E. 476 as Germanic invaders swept south. Although the new rulers adopted many of the Roman administrative forms and functions, communities missed the stability the empire had provided.

The beginning of the Islamic era in the 7th century led to dramatic changes in the East. Muhammad (C.E. 570–632), the founder of Islam, was inspired by Christianity, Judaism, and an abhorrence of the moral decadence of Mecca. Islam offered a comprehensive system of law and precepts for good government that have influenced millions of people around the globe down to this day. One of every five human beings is a Muslim, the Islamic world today extending from Morocco in the west to Indonesia and some of the Philippine islands in the east. While Europe wallowed in backwardness and superstition in the Middle Ages, Muslim scholarship drew on the philosophical and scientific heritage of Persia, ancient Greece, India, and China, and expressed little interest in the barbarians to the north.

The East Asian Sphere

Further to the east we find in China and Japan ancient civilizations marked culturally by Confucian, Taoist, Buddhist, and in the Japanese experience, Shinto traditions that survive into the present period. With a written history extending over five millennia, China has had substantial influence over peoples in Korea, Japan, and those in southeast and central Asia on the borders of China's frontier. The emperors of China saw themselves as presiding over the middle kingdom—the world-center toward which others always would (and should) turn.

As in the West, empires emerged in ancient China and Japan, the imperial type of system surviving into the 20th century. Although Buddhist influence moved from India to China in the 3rd century B.C.E. and subsequently to Korea and Japan, there was virtually no direct contact between the European and Eastern spheres until the Venetian trader, Marco Polo (about C.E. 1254–1324) made his famous 24-year trip to China in 1369 at about 15 years of age, returning to Venice just before turning 40 some 24 years later. Tales of this great exploratory adventure awakened Europeans to life on the other side of the world, which contributed to enthusiasm a century later to explorations conducted to the Americas by Christopher Columbus, who thought he had discovered a passage to India. Ferdinand Magellan was the first to sail from the Atlantic westward to the Pacific, his crews completing the first voyage around the world (C.E. 1519–1522).

Some scholars trace the origins of globalization to these early explorations that were followed by European colonial and imperial ventures in Africa, the Americas, and Asia, carrying with them mercantile and later capitalist forms of political economy as well as the idea of dividing the world into a system of sovereign states—a construct that had distinctly European roots that emerged from feudalism in the late Middle Ages. But we've gotten a bit ahead of our story!

Medieval Europe and the Feudal System

The decline and fall of the Roman Empire and the resulting decentralization of authority produced a high degree of diversity in Western Europe. The final collapse of Rome in the 5th century C.E. was followed by some thousand years that came to be known by later scholars as the Middle Ages or the medieval period. Its end point is generally marked by the Renaissance and the Reformation of the 15th and 16th centuries. This period is of particular interest to students of international relations because it encompasses the period immediately prior to the onset of the current state system. As we will see, the organization of the world into territorially based states was not an inevitable outcome of the Middle Ages; other possibilities existed.

During the Middle Ages the major purveyor of the notion of the unity of humankind was the Christian Church, the teachings of which became the religion of the Roman Empire after Constantine's conversion in C.E. 312 or 313 or, as some historians argue, Constantine co-opted Christian leaders to provide an imperial religion to help unify an empire of many diverse peoples. Christianity offered a religious-cultural frame consistent with earlier Stoic philosophical roots. As Rome's empire collapsed in the following century, however, Christian leaders realized that they would need to develop their own sources of worldly power to support their evangelical mission. Thus the Church became an increasingly wealthy and privileged organization with much to lose from invasions and general chaos. Even later, as more and more "barbarians" came under the influence of Christianity, the Church continued in self-defense to strengthen its organization and centralized authority through the **papacy** in Rome. Despite the sometimes corrupt and hypocritical behavior of many members of the Church hierarchy, Christianity was the framework within which medieval life, private as well as public, was conducted.

papacy ■ the office held by the pope as head of the Catholic Church

Although the Church in Western Europe proclaimed the universality of its message in the sacred realm, political power in the secular or temporal realm was greatly fragmented with a wide variety of different types of actors claiming legitimacy. The Holy Roman Empire, founded by Charlemagne in the early 9th century, was centered in Germany and, as the philosopher Voltaire wryly noted, was not very holy, Roman, or much of an empire, compared to that of the Caesars or even that of Byzantium (present-day Turkey) to the east. Yet Charlemagne's successors provided a limited secular counterweight to the growing power of the Church. Indeed, Christian doctrine initially allowed for two separate but essentially equal papal and imperial powers.

The Holy Roman Empire effectively collapsed, however, because of internal weaknesses and invasions by the Saracens, Magyars, and Norsemen. Constituent kingdoms still existed, but administratively they lacked efficient bureaucracies and permanent military forces. As a result, kings often had little power over local barons. Thus there developed a contradiction between the actual diversity of medieval institutions and the religious and philosophical emphasis on greater unity as provided by emperor or pope.

The power of local barons was reflected in feudalism, the preeminent form of authority that emerged earlier and became prominent by the 10th century. A defining characteristic of feudalism is public authority placed in private hands. As a result of the chaos of late-9th-century Europe—a time in which the stability provided by Roman law and legions had faded from memory—public authority came to be treated as the private possession of local lords who controlled territory known as fiefs. The lords held their authority at the expense of kings, who were often distant and weak. For example, courts of justice were viewed as a private possession of individual lords who passed judgment as they saw fit. Similarly a vassal's loyalty and obligation to a lord was of a personal nature; it was not owed to some distant and abstract entity called "the state." In sum, this privatization of public authority in the hands of local nobles was a cause and consequence of the predominance of local government over the claims of kings and the general fragmentation of political authority throughout Europe.

Political authority during feudal times was therefore claimed by a diverse collection of institutions and individuals, including local barons, bishops, kings, and popes. For students of international politics, it is interesting to note that, depending on their status, any one of these entities could be granted or denied diplomatic status or right of embassy. This medieval system has been characterized by historians as "a patchwork of overlapping and incomplete rights of government" that were "inextricably superimposed and tangled."[7]

Can we speak of this motley collection of polities during the latter half of the Middle Ages as an international system? Perhaps, even though it does not have the elegant simplicity of an international system composed of sovereign states. The present-day distinction between internal and external political realms with rigid territorial demarcations, a centralized bureaucratic structure claiming to exercise public authority, and the claim to a right to act independently in the world would have seemed odd to the medieval mind.

But during the Middle Ages, diplomacy still existed. The papacy and the imperial leadership adopted certain Roman principles and established new ones that have become part of international law: the safe conduct of ambassadors, secrecy in diplomatic negotiations, and condemnation of treaty violations. In terms of secular contributions, personal relationships were a key to diplomacy. Royal marriages were particularly important. Territorial borders were fluid, and relations between kingdoms were a function of dynastic marital connections.

One did not speak of the national interest, but rather the interest of particular rulers or dynasties. The high Middle Ages were a much more cosmopolitan era for the elites of the time than anything we have seen since: Political courtships

---

[7]John Gerard Ruggie, "Continuity and Transformation in the World Polity," in Robert O. Keohane (ed.), *Neorealism and Its Critics* (New York: Columbia University Press, 1986), 142, citing, respectively, J. R. Strayer and D. C. Munro, *The Middle Ages*, 4th ed. (New York: Appleton-Century-Crofts, 1959), 115, and Perry Anderson, *Lineages of the Absolutist State* (London: New Left Books, 1974), 37–38.

and marriages could result in a prince of Hungary becoming heir to the throne in Naples or an English prince legitimately claiming the throne of Castile in present-day Spain. This web of dynastic interdependencies, characterized by royal mobility and a sense of common identity, was paralleled in the rising merchant or bourgeois, middle classes—precursors to the emergence of capitalism—whose interest in commerce also made for a more cosmopolitan view of the world.

THE RISE OF THE EUROPEAN INDEPENDENT STATE SYSTEM

3.3 Explain the key developments that led to the rise of the European independent state system and how it eventually became globalized as a form of international politics.

✳ Explore the **"Integration: You Are a Citizen of Europe"** at **mypoliscilab.com**

By the 12th century, there was some reconcentration of political power in the hands of kings. Invasions around Europe's periphery ceased, allowing kings and nobles to devote more attention and resources to internal affairs and expand the size of their bureaucracies. Peace on the periphery also helped to account for the dramatic increase in the size of the European population. A larger population helped to revive towns, increase the size of the artisan class, and encourage greater trade. With expanded economic activity, taxation reappeared and was levied against churches, towns, and nobles. This required the establishment of a salaried officialdom. Greater royal income encouraged the payment of troops as opposed to relying on the "vassalic" contract based on mutual obligation between lord and vassal. Kings, therefore, began to acquire two of the key elements associated with effective rule—financial resources and coercive power.

The 12th and 13th centuries were also an era in which major strides were made in education. It is impossible to underestimate the importance of the growth of literacy to the rise of the state. As literacy expanded, the idea of written contracts gained currency, and ideals, norms of behavior, and laws could more easily be passed from one generation to another. Aquinas drew inspiration from the ancient Greek writers, universities were established (Paris, Padua, Bologna, Naples, Oxford, Cambridge), Roger Bacon engaged in experimental science, Dante wrote in the language of the common person, and Giotto raised art to a higher level. With the rise of educated bureaucrats, states formed archives that were essential to the continuity of government.[8]

This was also an era, however, in which there were major clashes between the sacred and secular or temporal realms over learning, commerce, and politics. In terms of learning, the clash between scholars with their emphasis on reason and the Church with its claims to authority based on what they believed was the revealed word of God would continue through the centuries.

In the realm of commerce, the growth of capitalism led to a clash between the Church's emphasis on religious man and the emerging capitalist view of economic man. The medieval Christian attitude toward commerce was that those engaged in business should expect only a fair return for their labor efforts; earning interest on the loan of money (usury) and even making profits on sales were considered sinful. Gradually the feudal notion that the ownership of property was conditional

---

[8]Marc Bloch, *Feudal Society*, v. 2 (Chicago: University of Chicago Press, 1964), 421–422.

on explicit social obligations was replaced by the modern notion that property is private, to be disposed of as the individual sees fit.

Politically the clash between the sacred and secular realms resulted in a breakdown in the balance of power between the pope and the emperor. This contributed to the breakup of the unity of Christendom, weakened the empire and the papacy, and hence assisted the rise of national states.

Two immensely important developments during the one hundred years commencing with the mid-15th century were the Renaissance and the Reformation. Taken together, they have been viewed by historians as the twin cradles of modernity. The Renaissance, generally associated with Western Europe's cultural rebirth in learning, the arts, exploration and commerce, was an ethical and humanistic movement that also elevated the individual and individual accomplishments. The Reformation, closely associated with the German religious leader Martin Luther (1483–1546) and his personal struggle for a right relationship with God, was a religious movement that eventually undercut papal authority and any hope for a unified Christendom. Luther and fellow Protestant John Calvin (1509–1564), a native Frenchman who emigrated to Geneva to escape religious persecution, believed that secular and religious authority should be separate. As the Protestant movement spawned greater religious pluralism, national monarchies grew in strength, and religious differences among the ruling houses exacerbated political problems.

Conflict over religion, religious authority, and the power of the Holy Roman Empire touched off civil war in 1618 in Bohemia (the present-day Czech Republic), eventually expanding throughout Europe into what has come to be known as the Thirty Years' War. Although religion was an important factor, the underlying cause of war was arguably the shifting balance of power among the major states, harkening back to Thucydides' description of the origins of the Peloponnesian War—the rise of Athenian power and the fear this inspired in Sparta.

The Thirty Years' War had a number of important results. First, the Peace of Prague in 1635 addressed the religious problem in the empire, providing a basis for dealing with the issue in the Peace of Westphalia, which ended the war in 1648. The ruler of a state would determine the religion of the inhabitants of that state. As a result, secular leaders of Catholic countries could ignore the papacy's call for a militant counter-reformation policy. Second, a new balance of power emerged that led to the rise of Brandenburg-Prussia (in the eastern part of present-day Germany), Sweden, and France as the most powerful states in Europe. The chance, therefore, of a secularly or temporally based empire was now as distant as the pope's hope for the unity of Christendom under papal guidance. The writings of Englishman Thomas Hobbes (1588–1679)—particularly his book *Leviathan* (published in 1651)—captured the essence of the modern state (whether ruled by a monarchy or parliament) and the new international system of independent states of which it was a part. As realists who draw from Hobbes argue (see Chapter 2), order in international relations depends upon state power and the balance of power among states.

A contemporary of Hobbes, the Dutch writer Grotius (his full name, Hugo de Groot, 1583–1645) provided a rule-based order for commerce and the conduct of war and peace—earning himself the title "father of international law," an honor he retains to the present day. If order were to be maintained within the newly emerging system of states, the balance of power alone was not sufficient. States (or more

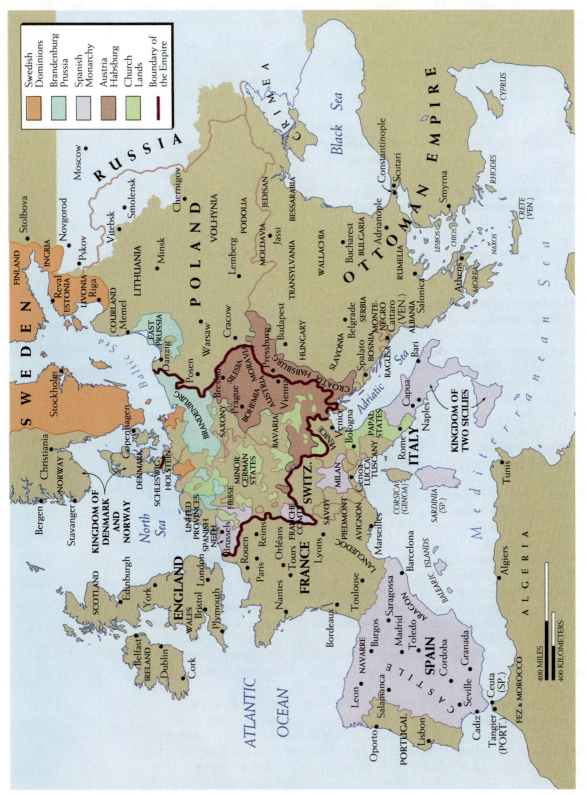

FIGURE 3.3

Europe after the 1648 Peace of Westphalia

Westphalia is viewed as marking the birth of the modern state system and the principle of sovereign territoriality. Note, however, the legacy of feudalism as exemplified by the fragmented nature of what is now unified Germany. The Ottoman Empire was also at its peak and threatened the security of Europe until its defeat at the battle

precisely, their monarchs and other leaders) would find security in the mutual acceptance of a set of agreed, legally binding rules to be in their enlightened self-interest. As also discussed in the previous chapter, it is this argument upon which English School "rationalism" rests—that states may choose to rely on rules, many of which have the binding character of law, as a source of order among them.

By 1660 the territorial state was the primary political unit in Europe, so we can begin to speak of an independent state system. The peace agreement at Westphalia in 1648 helped to solidify the trend of increasing power to the modern state at the expense of the other political forms. Not only were rulers put in the position of determining the religion of the inhabitants of their states, but the virtually complete authority of these princes in matters of state was recognized. With the realignment of territorial borders, the notion of the sovereignty of the state gradually became accepted—a new construction tied to the state.

Sovereignty involves political authority based on the territory and autonomy of states. Territoriality means that there is a right claimed by states to exclusive political authority over a defined geographic space—sometimes referred to as the internal dimension of sovereignty. Autonomy means that no external actor—such as another state—enjoys authority within the borders of the state. For example, by agreeing to recognize each ruler as the final and absolute authority within his kingdom, rulers also essentially agreed not to support internal subversion in neighboring states, stir up religious discontent, or otherwise interfere in their domestic affairs.

sovereignty ■ a claim to political authority to make policy or take actions domestically or abroad; based on territory and autonomy, historically associated with the modern state

Notwithstanding claims by princes to a right to be independent or autonomous in their foreign relations—the external dimension of sovereignty—the Peace of Westphalia established a system that did little to curtail the drive for territorial conquests. In fact, the relative military equality of the major states seems to have stimulated war, as many rulers thought they might be able to turn a system of independent states into an imperial system. As a result, anti-hegemonic coalitions arose whenever a would-be emperor such as Louis XIV or Napoleon Bonaparte tried to conquer Europe. The balance of power, in other words, became a key aspect of the European independent state system, a system severely lacking in collective governing principles or conflict resolution norms or procedures.

Another equally important trend occurred along with the rise of the independent state system. Over time, people began to identify with a particular state to the point that in some countries the nation and the state merged into the concept of nation-state. Leaders could draw on their public's nationalism to gain popular support for national defense and wars fought against foreign enemies. Wars no longer would be fought by mercenaries. Instead citizens provided the troops for imperial conquest or national defense. This trend further restricted movement toward the effective regulation of relations among states. The pursuit of narrow national interests was the order of the day.

nationalism ■ a mind-set glorifying the national identity, usually to the exclusion of other possible identities, infused with a political content

The rise of the state and the independent state system was seen not only in the political, diplomatic, and military spheres, but also in the economic realm. Indeed, economic developments were critical in contributing to the ultimate victory of the state system over other contenders. For example, the seventeenth century was the heyday of large trading companies. But while in earlier years these companies were associated with families, now the companies were chartered by monarchs in the name of the state: the East India Company in England (1600), the Dutch East India Company (1602), the Hamburg Company in north Germany (1611). As these state-backed firms increased in power, private city-based firms and trading associations declined.

The development of state trading companies and banks was part of the dominant economic doctrine of the 17th century known as mercantilism. Proponents of **mercantilism** preached that the state should play a major role in the economy, seeking to accumulate domestic capital or treasure by running continual trade surpluses in relation to other states. This was not in pursuit of some lofty moral aim or simply for the benefit of private entrepreneurs; the ultimate objective was to provide resources that could be used for war or conquest. In the name of regulating and protecting commerce, authoritarian state bureaucracies emerged, contrasting dramatically with the primary economic units of the late Middle Ages, the autonomous and self-regulating guilds. These national bureaucracies viewed competition in zero-sum terms: Whatever one state gained came at the expense of another.

In retrospect, all of these developments may seem to have led inexorably to the rise of a system of independent, belligerent states. This was certainly the view of such realists as Niccolò Machiavelli (1469–1527) and later Thomas Hobbes. But there were also developments working to counteract or, at least, mitigate this trend. They included developments of a transnational character: the impetus to commerce resulting from the discovery of America and new routes to the Indies, a common intellectual background resulting from the flowering of the Renaissance, a sympathy bond between coreligionists in different states that transcended national borders, and a common revulsion toward armed conflicts due to the horrifying cost of earlier religious wars. As one author argues, such "causes co-operated to make it certain that the separate state could never be accepted as the final and perfect form of human association, and that in the modern world as in the medieval world it would be necessary to recognize the existence of a wider unity."[9]

Such recognition was evident in the development of **international law**. Hugo Grotius and other writers abandoned the medieval ideal of a world-state and accepted the existence of the modern, secular, sovereign state. But they denied the absolute separateness of these states and the extreme version of international anarchy as propounded by Thomas Hobbes. However limited it might be, the idea of community or an international society of states could be applied, they argued, to the modern European independent state system. Even the recognition of sovereignty's external aspects—the claimed right of all states to be independent or autonomous in their international relations as a commonly accepted norm—even if not always followed, expressed a certain degree of community. This is the same perspective—viewing international relations as occurring within a community or society of states—that is core to present-day scholars who identify themselves with what has come to be called the English School of thought discussed in Chapter 2.

mercantilism ■
a theory of early capitalism that saw the wealth of nations as a function of the gold and other treasure it could accumulate

international law ■
laws that transcend borders and apply to states and in some cases individuals and corporations

---

[9]J. L. Brierly, *The Law of Nations: An Introduction to the International Law of Peace,* 6th ed. (New York and London: Oxford University Press, 1963), 6–7.

The Emergence of Collective Hegemony

It was in the 17th century that we find the beginnings of what could be termed a society of European states. Despite political differences, all of the major European powers from the time of the Peace of Westphalia in 1648 to the start of the 20th century worked gradually to regulate, delegitimize, and eventually eliminate the practices of such nonstate actors as mercenaries and pirates. If force were to be used, armies organized by states and only states would carry it out.

The rise of Napoleon after the French Revolution that began in 1789 upset the European order as France moved eastward beyond its borders, invading other countries and establishing a French empire. The subsequent defeat of Napoleon was followed by the Congress of Vienna (1814–1815), which created a collective hegemonic (or multipolar) system. Certain rules, values, and expectations developed by the major powers influenced relations not only among these states, but also among the lesser powers as well.

The major powers formed the core membership of what has been termed the **Concert of Europe**. This was an attempt to devise international rules of conduct and maintain the balance of power that would prevent situations that had arisen in the past, such as Napoleonic France attempting to turn an independent state

Concert of Europe
■ early 19th-century effort by policymakers in Great Britain, Austria, Russia, Prussia, and France to create a society of states

---

ARGUMENT-COUNTERARGUMENT | Thucydides and Power Transition

The Greek historian Thucydides (c. 460–406 B.C.E.) is the author of the untitled history of the Peloponnesian War. His is the foremost ancient work on international relations, for Thucydides was interested in examining current events in order to shed light on underlying patterns of politics that transcend any particular age.

ARGUMENT   The Peloponnesian War was inevitable, given the increase in Athenian military power and the fear this caused in Sparta.

Thucydides is credited with being the father of what has come to be known as *power transition theory*. Power transition theorists see the international system as hierarchically ordered with the most powerful state dominating the rest, which are classified as satisfied or dissatisfied with the ordering of the system. His explanation, therefore, focused on the changing distribution of power in the Greek system of city-states and how this shift generated suspicion and distrust among Sparta and its allies. Thucydides' argument has

been applied to numerous cases throughout history, whether the rise of France under Louis XIV, Germany in the late 19th century and again in the 1930s, or the Soviet Union after 1945.

COUNTERARGUMENT   The nature of the state or society dictates militaristic actions. Other international relations scholars—realist as well as liberal—point to a complementary, yet what they consider to be a more important explanation: the nature of the state or society. Some states are status-quo powers, while others are revolutionary and seek to dominate the international system. Revolutionary France before and during the reign of Napoleon and Nazi Germany in the 1930s and 1940s are both examples of the nature of the state approach.

APPLICATION   China epitomizes a rising economic and military power. What would be possible policy prescriptions for dealing with China based upon the two different historical and theoretical approaches? ▲

system into an empire. Conflicts of interest would continue, but it was hoped that disagreements also could be worked out in a pragmatic fashion.

Furthermore, the major players (Great Britain, Austria, Russia, Prussia, and France) realized that nationalist and democratic sentiments could conceivably threaten all of them, and in this sense their interests were broadly compatible. Europe, therefore, was viewed as a unique international society—not merely an international system. Such a vision was at odds with Thomas Hobbes's view of an anarchic world of states and more in line with that of Hugo Grotius (more discussion on Hobbes and Grotius can be found in Chapter 2).

Pragmatism was evident in European diplomatic practices. Between 1830 and 1884, twenty-five meetings were held among the representatives of the major powers. Though not formally promulgated, the underlying practices and norms that served in practice as the bases for these meetings included the following:

1. The Concert powers have a common responsibility for maintaining the Vienna settlement.
2. No unilateral changes to the settlement are allowed.
3. No changes should be made that significantly disadvantage any one power or upset the balance of power in general.
4. Changes are to be made by consent.
5. Consent means consensus, but formal voting does not occur.[10]

Despite revolutionary outbursts in a number of countries in 1848, the Crimean War of 1853–1856, and the Franco-Prussian War of 1870–1871, during the rest of the 19th century Europe experienced its longest period of stability since the rise of the modern state system. It is important to note that no single crisis or conflict in this period ever threatened to erupt into a continental war. Not until 1914 with the outbreak of World War I—some ninety-nine years after the Congress of Vienna— was Europe to experience the awful consequences of a return to major or general warfare now made even more destructive by technological advances and mass production of weaponry—state capabilities born of the Industrial Revolution.

The collective hegemony of the great powers in the 19th century and the relatively peaceful period that resulted was apparent in the way they decided the fate of the smaller powers. The Concert sanctioned the independence of Belgium, Romania, Serbia, and Montenegro and prevented war between Luxembourg and Belgium and between Holland and Belgium. Aside from a common interest in European stability, the Concert powers were also able to make the system work because of their generally flexible approach to balance-of-power politics. Permanent coalitions or alliances did not develop. This situation was also encouraged by the British desire to keep continental Europe divided.

The Globalization of the European System

The European system of independent states did not confine territorial and economic competition to Europe. Over the centuries, the European system spread over

---

[10]Kalevi J. Holsti, *Peace and War: Armed Conflicts and International Order, 1648–1989* (Cambridge: Cambridge University Press, 1991), 167.

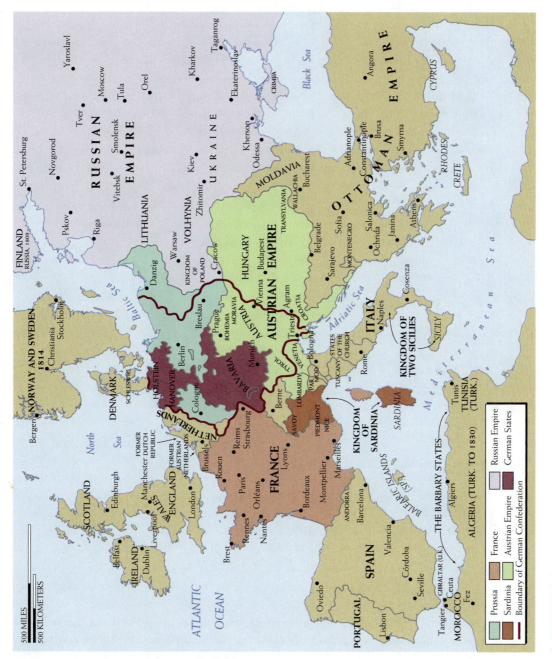

FIGURE 3.4

Europe after the Peace Settlement at the Congress of Vienna (1815)

Following the Napoleonic wars, diplomats at the Congress of Vienna attempted to rebalance power in Europe by, among other decisions, increasing the territory of Prussia and Austria. Compare this figure to Figure 3.3. Note not only the expansion of the Austrian empire, but the reduction of the Ottoman Empire and the consolidation of many minor German states into what would eventually become Germany.

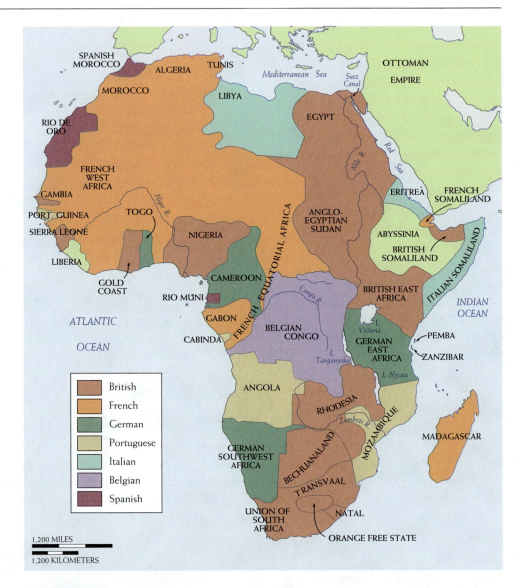

FIGURE 3.5

Africa after the 1880–1914 Partition

Almost all of the African continent was divided among European powers except for Liberia and Abyssinia. Little regard was made for ethnic or tribal lines.

the world. Following Europe's stunning realization in 1492 that a much larger world existed than was previously thought, the Spanish and Portuguese agreed to spheres of influence. They treated the Americas as they treated the lands that fell under their dominion in the Iberian Peninsula—as integral parts of their kingdoms bound by their laws, administration, and Catholicism. Indigenous civilizations

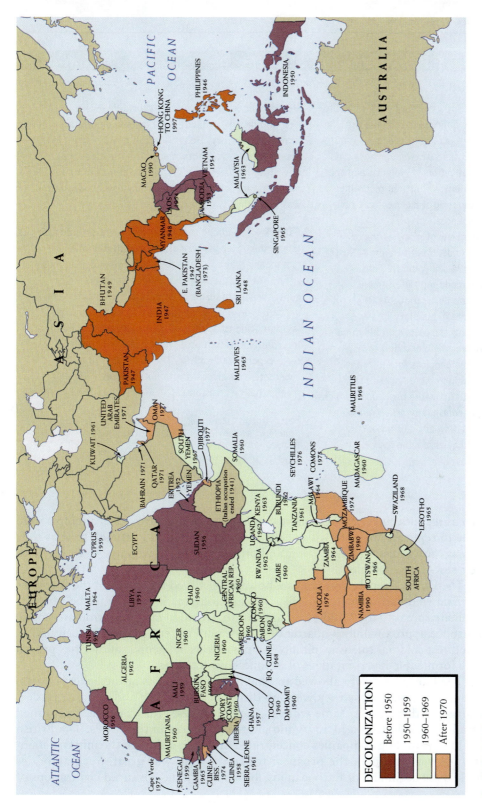

FIGURE 3.6

Decolonization in Africa and Asia

The collapse of Europe's modern colonial empires began in 1947 on the Indian subcontinent with the creation of the states of Pakistan and India. Compare this figure with Figure 3.5. For an overview of the entire process, go to Wikipedia and search for "Decolonization." You'll find a discussion of the emergence of the less-developed world, differing perspectives on decolonization, and a table listing every state that received independence from the 18th century (beginning with the United States) to today.

CASE & POINT | Politicians and Strategy

CASE In almost any country military leaders would understandably prefer for politicians to make the decision to go to war, but once that decision is made, turn the actual running of the war over to those who are the experts in the application of violence and the designing of military strategy. "Political meddling" by politicians once the shooting starts can only have negative military consequences.

This was certainly the view of many of the generals and admirals who dealt with Prime Minister Winston Churchill during World War II. These professionals found his "meddling" in military matters to be annoying and frustrating. As Churchill's military chief of staff wrote in his diary in 1944, Churchill "has only got half the picture in his mind, talks absurdities and makes my blood boil to listen to his nonsense." What the generals found irritating was that Churchill had an incredible appetite for information and wanted to know the basis upon which decisions were made. He continually asked questions about military plans, excelling at pointing out unstated assumptions and questionable logic.

He brought to the conduct of World War II a rich and detailed knowledge, however vicarious, of military history. He echoed Clausewitz with his cautions that history makes it quite clear that uncertainties were inherent in war and faith in an absolute, unchanging blueprint for a successful war was an absurdity.

POINT The cliché that "war is too important to be left to the generals" is right. After all, the military is a means that can be used to achieve political ends. All military actions can have important strategic consequences in terms of affecting the outcome and hence the original strategic objectives a statesman is attempting to achieve. Potential practitioners of international relations do not necessarily have to have experienced military life to be able to make substantive contributions to national security and foreign policy decisions.

*Quote is from Elliot Cohen, *Supreme Command: Soldiers, Statesmen, and Leadership in Wartime* (New York: Anchor Books, 2002), p. 98.

---

such as the Inca in Peru and the Aztec in Mexico were destroyed as attempts were made to replicate the authority of the kings in Spain and Portugal, bent as they were on accumulating gold, silver, and other economic advantage to be found in their new-found colonies.

The Dutch, French, and English, however, believed the riches of the Americas and Asia were fair game for all. Few inroads were made initially in the Muslim-dominated areas of the Middle East and North Africa. In fact, the Ottoman Empire controlled approximately a quarter of Europe until the end of the 17th century. In Asia direct colonial rule was initially not possible as indigenous authorities proved to be formidable representatives of advanced civilizations.

The Europeans were allowed to establish trading posts at the behest of local rulers, but in this sense they were no different from Arab and Chinese traders who sailed through the same waters. The Portuguese, for example, established a trading post in China in 1516 and another in Japan in the 1540s. The British and French trading companies concentrated on India; although the initial amount of trade was minimal, the prospect for future gain was great. Such activities marked the beginning of European involvement with the advanced civilizations of

Asia as well as the beginning of conflict among European states for commercial advantage there.

The pattern of dependent states in the Americas and mutually beneficial commercial operations in Asia continued until the end of the 1700s. Toward the end of the century, Britain lost North American colonies, but European leaders continued to believe that colonies and their commodities were important sources of state power. The 18th and well into the 19th centuries, therefore, witnessed an increase in the ultimate expression of economic exploitation—the capture or purchase of African slaves destined to provide backbreaking labor in the colonies of the Caribbean and North and South America.

European rule continued to be established where indigenous authority was weak or divided. The advance of British rule in India was initially aided by the collapse of the Mogul imperial system into numerous warring states, just as the Dutch managed to spread their influence gradually throughout the East Indies (present-day Indonesia). But in the 19th century, Britain worked hard for the independence of Latin American colonies. A primary reason was that, following the Napoleonic war, Great Britain aggressively pursued international trade. By opening up heretofore closed markets, British industry rapidly expanded, leading to dramatic gains in economic growth and wealth that could be translated into state power. The British navy, in conjunction with the Monroe Doctrine of the United States, discouraged the European powers from attempting to reassert control over the newly independent states of Latin America.

European imperial expansion in the 19th century, therefore, was directed toward the Middle East, Africa, and Asia. As the Ottoman Empire, which included the Balkans and Greece, began to weaken, both Russia and Austria saw an opportunity for imperial expansion. But with both Britain and France concerned about the implications of a slow disintegration of the Ottoman Empire, diplomatic compromises kept the Concert powers from military confrontation except during the Crimean War (1853–1856). A similar process of compromise was evident in the Congress of Berlin in 1884, during which the major powers carved up the remaining territory of Africa, the slave trade having long since ended. In Asia, great-power cooperation was also evident during the collapse of the Manchu dynasty in China. With the outbreak in China of the Boxer Rebellion in 1900 and the attacks against foreign traders and diplomatic legations, the European powers, along with the United States and Japan, worked together in joint policing and military operations.

By the early part of the 20th century, the areas of the world outside Europe and North America consisted of a variety of states with differing degrees of political, economic, and cultural dependence. None, however, could avoid the influence of the emerging global capitalist economy, and all took on at least some of the formal trappings of the modern state as defined by the European experience. This meant, at a minimum, acceptance of Western economic practices, commercial standards, and international law. Especially in colonial situations, locals who were hired to assist in administrative matters also were influenced by Western values. This was especially true for those few—the elites from the colonies or dominions—who studied in France, Britain, or elsewhere in Europe, then returned to their native lands.

TABLE 3.1

Selected Wars and Peace Settlements in Modern European History

As historians and political scientists have observed, peace settlements at the end of wars often go beyond cessation of hostilities to establish major principles or alterations in the structure of power relations:

- The Peace of Westphalia (1648) ended the Thirty Years' War and established more formally the sovereignty or right of princes to exercise authority over the people in territories within their jurisdictions and to be autonomous in the conduct of foreign relations. The prince or sovereign authority could even determine the religion of the inhabitants of a state.

- The Peace of Utrecht (1713) provided for an end to the War of the Spanish Succession (1701–1714), curbing French expansionism and Spanish power in Europe and the New World to the advantage of Britain.

- The Congress of Vienna (1815) ended the Napoleonic Wars that followed in the aftermath of the French Revolution that began in 1789. These negotiations established a new balance of power and provided for diplomatic arrangements known as the Concert of Europe among Britain, Austria, Prussia, Russia, France, and other European states. Although the Bourbons were restored to the French throne and the territorial boundaries of France were drawn comparable to those that had existed in 1789, French power was again constrained by these formal agreements.

- The Crimean War (1853–1856) and the Treaty of Paris ended a relatively minor armed conflict (although one with substantial casualties), curtailing Russian power in southeastern Europe through the opposition of Britain, France, Sardinia, and the Ottoman Turks. The war was fought primarily to prevent the Russians from establishing military positions in the Crimea on the Black Sea.

- The Franco-Prussian War (1870–1871) once again curbed French power and was followed by a Prussian-led unification of German states into a newly formed German empire, or Reich. The dispute began with protests by France over efforts to assume the Spanish crown by a branch of the ruling Hohenzollern dynasty in Prussia.

- World War I (1914–1918) set a unified German empire allied with the Austro-Hungarian and Turkish empires as central powers against British, French, Russian, and, by 1917, American allies. The war contributed substantially to undermining the Romanov dynasty in Russia, leading to its overthrow by Bolshevik revolutionaries in 1917. The new regime in Russia under Vladimir Lenin quickly made peace with Germany in the Peace of Brest-Litovsk (1918); however, the western allies continued to fight until they defeated Germany in 1918. The Peace of Versailles (1919) established a League of Nations (and World Court) for a new postwar order but also imposed harsh terms on Germany. Most historians believe these terms contributed to the failure of democracy in Germany and the subsequent rise in the 1930s of nationalist revanchism that led to World War II.

- World War II (1939–1945) set a German-Austrian and Italian Axis, joined later by Japan, against the same World War I Allies—the United Kingdom, France, Russia (which had become the communist Soviet Union), and, by 1941, the United States. The defeat of Axis powers by the Allies was followed by three peace conferences in 1945 at Yalta in the Crimea, Potsdam just outside of Berlin, and San Francisco, where the United Nations Charter was signed, laying a basis for a postwar world order.

TWENTIETH-CENTURY HEGEMONIC SYSTEMS IN A GLOBAL CONTEXT

At the same time European values and economic practices were creating a web of global interdependencies, increasing political separatism was occurring among the major powers in Europe. Perhaps the single most important factor accounting for the collapse of the Concert of Europe was the inability of Europe to adjust to the political, military, and economic rise of Germany (a favorite case study for the application of power transition theory). When World War I finally broke out in August 1914, its viciousness and degree of devastation were shocking. As noted above, this was due partly to the Industrial Revolution, which had helped to produce weapons of tremendous destructiveness. The other important factor was inflamed nationalism, which spurred the development of mass armies and a political-ethnic consciousness coterminous with state boundaries. Karl Marx's hope that workers of the industrial world would unite to overthrow existing governments and institute an international system of peaceful socialist states was not achieved since workers tended to identify nationally or patriotically more with their own countries than with fellow workers in other countries.

At the end of World War I in 1918, an attempt was made to create an international organization that would prevent the outbreak of future wars. The key legal concept underlying the League of Nations was faith in **collective security**, the idea that if one state behaved aggressively, other states had a legal right to enforce international law against aggression by taking collective action to stop it. In other words, the League of Nations hoped to institutionalize legally the historical phenomenon of anti-hegemonic coalitions. The League, however, failed to keep the peace, as evidenced by its inability to halt German, Italian, and Japanese aggression, which resulted in the outbreak of World War II (1939–1945). International law alone was not enough to stop Germany in Europe or Japan in the Far East from using force in acts of aggression against other countries in their respective regions.

A second attempt to institutionalize global collective security was the United Nations, created at the end of World War II. But with rare exceptions—Korea in 1950, Congo in 1960, and peacekeeping missions in places as diverse as the Mediterranean island of Cyprus and the Sinai desert—Cold War politics and ideology prevented the United Nations from playing the major collective-security or law-enforcement role originally intended for it in 1945. On the other hand, the UN Charter did permit the formation of alliances as states pursued individual and **collective defense** through the formation of defensive alliances permitted under Article 51 (for example, NATO and the Warsaw Pact).

While East and West were locked into a conflictual situation of strategic interdependence—particularly because of the development of nuclear weapons capable of devastating much of the globe—economic, ideological, and political independence between the blocs was the norm. Within the blocs, economic, social, and political interdependence dramatically expanded. A political disjuncture, however, was occurring between the so-called First World of the West and the newly emerging states and developing societies of the Third World. The victorious allies had fought Germany, Japan, and Italy in the name of freedom and independence. Now the leaders of the independence movements asked the embarrassing question: "Why

3.4 Evaluate and explain the relative success and failure of attempts by states to develop collective security arrangements.

Watch the Video "The Cuban Missle Crisis" at mypoliscilab.com

collective security
■ the idea that if one state behaved aggressively, other states had a legal right to enforce international law by taking collective action

collective defense ■
a strategy relied upon by states that pool capabilities to balance the power of rivals or enemies

did the West not apply the same logic to its colonies?" In some cases, such as the British in India, Palestine, and Yemen, the colonial power grudgingly disengaged. In other cases, particularly the French in Vietnam and Algeria, insurgencies came to power violently and eliminated direct foreign rule. This process continued through the 1970s as the Portuguese disengaged from Angola and Mozambique in Africa and reached its logical conclusion in South Africa in 1990 when the indigenous white elite finally recognized the impossibility of maintaining a monopoly on political power in the face of the political and economic demands of the black majority.

Dual Hegemony during the Cold War

Given the fact that we continue to sort out the implications of the end of the Cold War on present-day international relations, it is worthwhile to examine this era more closely. When did the Cold War actually begin? It could be argued it began in 1939 when two dictators, Joseph Stalin of the Soviet Union and Adolf Hitler of Germany, agreed to divide Poland. Stalin's broader European goals were consistent with those of his Kremlin predecessors: dominate the states bordering the Soviet Union and gain control over the Baltic region and the Turkish Straits that connect the Black Sea to the Mediterranean. Beyond that, Stalin hoped to influence strongly events in Eastern Europe and Germany.

With the German invasion of the Soviet Union in 1941, the Soviets joined the Western alliance in the battle against fascist Germany, Italy, and Japan. Moscow's ultimate goals, however, remained the same. This was apparent at the Yalta Conference (in Soviet Crimea on the Black Sea) where Stalin, U.S. President Franklin Roosevelt, and Prime Minister Winston Churchill of the United Kingdom met to discuss the postwar future of Europe. The Soviet Union had suffered more than twenty million dead and vast destruction of property as well. It was not surprising, therefore, that Stalin argued Eastern Europe should fall within Moscow's sphere of influence.

containment ■ the grand strategy of the United States to deal with the Soviet Union during the Cold War

With defeated Germany under four-power control (United States, United Kingdom, France, and Soviet Union), Berlin became a symbol of the Cold War as relations between Moscow and the West rapidly deteriorated after World War II. The United States response was to be a policy of global **containment** of the Soviet Union specifically and communism in general. This doctrine was crafted by one of the "Wise Men," diplomat George Kennan, both in a classified long telegram he sent to Washington in February 1946 from the U.S. Embassy in Moscow where he was then Deputy Chief of Mission (DCM) and, later, in an anonymous article signed "X" published in the July 1947 issue of *Foreign Affairs,* journal of the Council on Foreign Relations in New York.

The U.S.-sponsored Marshall Plan, designed to revive economically war-torn Europe, was viewed with suspicion by Stalin. An ominous sign was the creation of the Communist Information Bureau (Cominform) in September 1947. At its inaugural meeting, a close aide to Stalin announced to the assembled delegates that Europe and the world in general were divided into two hostile camps, capitalist and communist. Then in February 1948 the Czech government was overthrown, and soon after the Soviets began harassment of western trains into Berlin. By mid-June the blockade of the three western sectors of Berlin had begun. Road and rail access across East Germany were denied to the Western allies. The blockade was broken only by a dramatic eleven-month airlift resupply effort. The West, believing it could not work out a deal with the Soviets on a unified Germany, proceeded in its preparations for a West German government and the creation of the North Atlantic Treaty Organization (NATO) in 1949.

Events in Asia also alarmed the West. In China, communist forces led by Mao Zedong came to power in 1949. Then in June 1950 the North Korean communist regime invaded South Korea. The invasion galvanized the United States and led to a dramatic increase in the defense budget, a decision also influenced by the Soviet Union's successful test of an atomic bomb in 1949. In September 1950 the administration of President Harry Truman adopted a new national security document, NSC 68, a document that essentially laid out the U.S. view of its Soviet adversary throughout the Cold War. The Soviet Union, it was stated, aimed at nothing less than the destruction of the free world. The Chinese intervention in the Korean War in November 1950 only reinforced this view, and officials in Western capitals discussed the danger of a major East-West war. The prescription in NSC 68 for the West to match the Soviet Union in conventional arms in Europe was never implemented in large part because of the enormous cost of doing so, particularly with a war on in Korea. Instead, following doctrine articulated by the Eisenhower administration, the United States and its NATO allies relied more on nuclear weapons to balance the conventional and nuclear forces of the Soviet Union and its Eastern European satellite countries.

With the death of Stalin in 1953, there was cautious hope that a new Soviet leadership would be more accommodating in trying to settle East-West differences. A summit meeting in Geneva in 1955 left political leaders and outsiders with the feeling that although the Cold War would continue in Europe and Asia, it would not turn into a "hot" or shooting war. But even as the summit was taking place, a Soviet ship was unloading Czech-manufactured weapons in Egypt, marking the expansion of the Cold War into other areas of the developing world. In the same year, the Soviet Union formed the Warsaw Pact with its Eastern European satellites in opposition to NATO. Europe in general, Germany in particular, remained deeply divided between East and West throughout the remaining decades of the Cold War.

Throughout the 1950s and 1960s a number of other crises occurred: the defeat of the French in Vietnam in 1954, the U.S.-Communist China dispute over the Taiwan Straits in 1955 and afterward, the Warsaw Pact invasion of Hungary in 1956, and another Berlin crisis in 1960 during which the Soviets constructed the Berlin Wall, dividing the occupied city into separate eastern (Soviet) and western (American, British, and French) sectors and restricting movement of people across the barrier. Soviet support for national liberation movements in the less-developed world was matched by U.S. support for pro-Western regimes with attempts made to overthrow a number of nationalist and pro-Soviet or left-leaning leaders in these countries.

The most dangerous crisis, however, focused on Cuba during thirteen days in October 1962. It was then that President Kennedy learned the Soviets were constructing sites for nuclear-armed, intermediate-range ballistic missiles in Fidel Castro's Cuba. The president and his key advisers at the time saw Soviet leader Nikita Khrushchev's actions as an intolerable provocation. Kennedy, therefore, in his view had no choice but to compel the Soviets to withdraw the missiles to reduce

The Peloponnesian War pitted two city-states—Athens and Sparta—and their respective alliances against each other. It is an early example of a bipolar hegemonic state system. In this scene, Sparta's ally, Syracuse, defeats the Athenian fleet in the harbor at Syracuse, Sicily.

Hannibal's troops are depicted during the Second Punic War against Rome, 218–201 B.C.E, which was one of the titanic historical struggles between two empires. The war was marked by Hannibal's invasion of Italy and his initial victory, but his ultimate failure occurred here at the battle of Zama.

The Congress of Vienna (1814–1815) helped to establish an underlying order and prevent a general war until 1914. It epitomized the concept of a hegemonic state system characterized by multipolarity or collective hegemony of the major powers.

Checkpoint Charlie was the best-known crossing point of the Berlin Wall during the Cold War (1946–1991). Communist East Berlin was on one side and West Berlin, controlled by the three Allied powers (Great Britain, France, the United States), on the other. The checkpoint symbolized the Cold War divide.

the likelihood of surprise attack on the United States, maintain the balance of power vis-à-vis the USSR, preserve NATO, and illustrate the United States' continuing resolve to do whatever it deemed necessary for the security of itself and its allies.

The key political-military decision was to establish a naval blockade of Cuba as opposed to launching an invasion or air strikes on the missile batteries. Although the tactic was successful, the president later stated that the probability of a nuclear disaster had been "between one out of three and even." A second major crisis occurred in 1973 during the Arab-Israeli War when Moscow raised the possibility of armed intervention in the conflict. The United States responded quickly by putting its nuclear forces on alert, thus signaling its resolve to oppose any such action.

After the Cuban missile crisis passed, the two superpowers did agree in 1963 on two important arms control agreements—one a test ban on nuclear tests in the atmosphere or oceans and the other a hotline between Washington and Moscow to allow leaders in the two capitals to talk directly in the event of any future crisis. At the same time, however, the two sides continued their strategic nuclear arms buildup that further strained East-West relations. Armed intervention by the United States in Vietnam and support for the South Vietnamese government that escalated dramatically in 1965 and 1966 were also countered by Soviet aid to North Vietnam and its communist (Viet Cong) allies in the South, actions that added to tensions between the superpowers.

Another major development was the Chinese-Soviet split apparent in the early 1960s, leading ultimately to armed clashes along the Sino-Soviet border in 1969. This opened the way for the United States to play the so-called China card, epitomized by national security adviser Henry Kissinger's secret trip to Beijing in July 1971. President Nixon made a formal visit in February 1972 and the Shanghai Communiqué signed there set in motion a path to normalization of diplomatic relations between the two countries, continued in President Ford's administration, finally completed in 1979 during the Carter administration.

détente ■ an easing of tensions among states as in the late 1960s and 1970s between the United States and the Soviet Union and their respective allies

The 1971 Sino-U.S. summit and other factors persuaded Leonid Brezhnev and the Soviet leadership that a relaxation of tensions, or *détente*, with the West was a viable option and, in any event, better than strategic isolation. The first set of Strategic Arms Limitation Talks (SALT) resulted in arms control agreements signed in Moscow by Nixon and Brezhnev in May 1972. Further progress in arms control was made by the subsequent U.S. administrations of Presidents Gerald Ford and Jimmy Carter and their Soviet counterparts.

Détente suffered a major setback with the Soviet invasion of Afghanistan in late 1979. This event and the inability of the United States to do very much about it aided the election of Ronald Reagan, who continued and expanded substantially the massive U.S. military buildup begun under his predecessor. The imposition of martial law in Poland (December 1981), designed to squash a reformist labor movement (and thought to be due at least in part to Soviet pressure), further soured East-West relations. The Soviet experience in Afghanistan resulted over several years in enormous human and material losses, proving to be a disaster. This was one reason Mikhail Gorbachev (who termed Afghanistan "a bleeding wound") came to power in the Kremlin in March 1985, at a time when it was obvious to all that the Soviet economy was failing.

▶ **ARGUMENT-COUNTERARGUMENT |**   **Why a Cold War and Not a Hot War?**

ARGUMENT   Bipolarity and international system stability helped maintain the "long peace."

Some theorists argue that the replacement of a multipolar world with a bipolar structure of power after World War II contributed to international system stability. The supposed advantage of a bipolar distribution of power over multipolarity is that the responsibility for maintaining the system is concentrated, not dispersed. Calculations between two principal competitors are also simpler than in a multipolar balance when the calculations and interactions of several states are at issue. A superpower can even tolerate an occasional defection from an alliance because the overall distribution of power would not be affected dramatically.

COUNTERARGUMENT #1   Nuclear weapons acted as a deterrent to the outbreak of World War III.

Once nuclear weapons were available to both the Soviet Union and the United States, neither side was willing to run the risks required to achieve its objectives by force as major states had routinely done throughout history. The consequences of a nuclear war could easily be imagined by leaders on both sides; hence, these leaders were self-deterred from using their nuclear arsenals.

COUNTERARGUMENT #2   Obsolescence of major war deterred the outbreak of a Third World War.

This view argues that the two previous explanations are essentially irrelevant to explaining the long peace. Recognition of the escalating costs of war for advanced industrial societies is the key, and this was evident to all in World War I. It took the evil genius of Hitler, the bumbling of Mussolini, and a handful of Japanese militarists to start World War II. This war simply confirmed the catastrophic results of war in the industrial age; hence, from this perspective, the long peace after 1945 would have ensued even if nuclear weapons had never existed. Given the cataclysmic effects of two world wars that took place within just three decades in the first half of the 20th century, national authorities finally had learned to avoid stumbling yet again into general war.

APPLICATION   Make an argument that these three competing explanations are actually complementary. How could the levels of analysis framework be applied? ▶

Gorbachev revived the policy of *détente* with the United States and the West with an eye to providing some relief from ruinous spending on the arms race. Lacking an economic base comparable to that of the United States, the Soviet Union found matching American efforts to expand its conventional and nuclear arsenals extraordinarily expensive. Put another way, the United States during the early years of the Reagan administration was better able to afford outspending the Soviets on defense, although doing so contributed to trebling the U.S. national debt during the twelve Reagan-Bush years.

In any event, Soviet spending sustained at high levels in the 1970s and 1980s had had adverse effects on the country's economy with a disproportionate share of GDP allocated to defense.[11] Under his economic policy of *perestroika*

---

[11]One of the co-authors of this volume met in the summer of 1992 with senior RAND Corporation analyst Charles Wolfe, who had returned from a research trip to Moscow. Economists he met there estimated at the time that about a third of Russian GDP had been spent on defense—as much as 50 percent in Ukraine. If true, it is no wonder that the economy collapsed, precipitating the demise of the Soviet Union and the end of the Cold War.

(restructuring), Gorbachev's goal was to introduce limited economic incentives into the country's socialist economy, reallocating some resources away from the military to other sectors of the Soviet economy. Gorbachev neither desired nor expected that his shifts in domestic and foreign policy would set in motion events that ultimately led to the collapse of the Soviet empire and the end of the Cold War.

Arms control efforts begun in 1981 at the outset of the Reagan-Bush administrations became more successful from the mid-1980s onward as the Soviet leadership under Gorbachev agreed to eliminate short- and intermediate-range nuclear missiles in Europe and later with mutually agreed reductions in strategic nuclear arsenals of both superpowers. The Clinton administration continued to pursue arms control with the Russian Federation throughout the 1990s—further strategic nuclear arms reductions, a multilateral Chemical Weapon Convention, a comprehensive nuclear test ban treaty (CTBT), and other efforts.

President George W. Bush's administration that took office in 2001, noting the end of the Cold War a decade earlier and less enamored of arms control as the security centerpiece of its relations with Russia or other countries, abrogated the earlier Anti-Ballistic Missile (ABM) Treaty, which it deemed obsolete, opposed ratification of the CTBT, and did not pursue arms control with the same priority given it by previous administrations. The Barack Obama administration that took office in 2009 also has been somewhat reserved in advancing arms control agendas, but did secure U.S. Senate ratification of a follow-on strategic arms reductions treaty with Russia that, when fully implemented later in this decade, will reduce strategic nuclear weapons on both sides to just under 90 percent of their Cold War levels.

RISING POWERS

3.5 Evaluate the impact of the rising economic strength of the European Union and the four rising BRIC powers on future international developments.

Use your favorite search engine and type in "rising power." You'll be surprised at the number of institutes, conferences, research projects, and books devoted to this topic. Speculation on which states would eventually challenge the United States as the sole superpower began immediately after the fall of the Soviet Union and the end of the bipolar world in 1991. No one is suggesting that there is currently a peer rival. Athough there are dissenters, many argue that the *relative* power position and thus influence of the United States is gradually diminishing, if not eroding. It is not so much that the country is losing its absolute amount of so-called hard power (military and economic clout), but rather that other countries are rising in comparison.

👁 **Watch** the **Video** "China's New Rich" at mypoliscilab.com

The European Union has become more integrated in an economic and monetary union with its own currency, the euro, used by most EU members in lieu of national currencies. The aggregate size of the U.S. economy and that of the EU taken as a whole are both over $14 trillion. An important motive for this deeper level of economic integration is a European concern voiced in the 1980s and afterward that in order to compete globally Europe would have to come together, realizing the economies of scale and free movement of resources, capital, and labor enjoyed in the U.S. economy. Recent financial crises put this goal in jeopardy.

Apart from the EU, the four countries usually mentioned as rising powers are Brazil, Russia, India, and China—all four together known by the acronym BRIC. Estimates hold that these four countries by 2020 will account for a third of the global economy and be the locations of a continually expanding middle class.[12] We will briefly examine each in turn, taking them in reverse order. We will first make the case for their increase in power and then note limitations to this line of argument. The conceptual framework is what has come to be known as Thucydides' power transition theory.

BRIC ■ refers to Brazil, Russia, India, and China as rising economic political powers

China

If there is one country that figures prominently in the speculation of what international relations and world politics will look like in the next few years, it is China. Despite unprecedented access to China in the past three decades by scholars, businesspeople, journalists, diplomats, Olympic athletes, and tourists, the country conjures up many different and conflicting images. For some, China is epitomized by its economic miracle and the skyscrapers of Shanghai, the spread of cell phones, and dusty construction sites. Others point to the suppression of pro-democracy demonstrators in Tiananmen Square in 1989 and the continual repression of dissidents as evidence of the real China. The diversity and complexity of this giant country provide evidence to support almost any point of view.

The United States and its allies in East Asia, Japan, and South Korea—not to mention some Southeast Asian states—cast a wary eye on China's military modernization. This modernization includes the building of several aircraft carriers, modern submarines, and new destroyers. Carriers in particular are usually viewed as expressing the goal of creating a "blue water navy," meaning the ability to project power far from one's shoreline. China also has dramatically expanded its land-based ballistic and cruise missile capabilities. Over a thousand short-range missiles are aimed at Taiwan, the independent island country off the coast of the Chinese mainland, which Beijing has claimed since 1949 is a part of its People's Republic. China's submarines, missiles, and anti-ship cruise missiles could threaten U.S. aircraft-carrier battle groups operating in the East Asian area. China's military also has worked assiduously to improve its capabilities to act as one integrated force while, at the same time, allegedly has taken a major role in cyber espionage in an attempt to gain Western technological and military secrets. The United States military has stated publicly that China has the greatest potential to compete militarily with the United States on a global scale.

Critics of this alarming view, however, note that as a share of gross domestic product (GDP), China spends less than half the American figure on military budgets. Others doubt the quality of China's equipment and the manpower that operate these new systems, essentially arguing that pessimists overestimate the Chinese threat and underestimate America's power.[13] Some also criticize some American

---

[12]Goldman Sachs, "Is This the BRIC's Decade?" Global Economic Paper No. 134, May 2010. www2.goldmansachs.com/ideas/brics.

[13]"Friend or Foe? A Special Report on China's Place in the World," *The Economist*, December 4, 2010, p. 9.

analysts who see China as an inevitable threat instead of cultivating the nation as a partner with shared interests in economic gains as well as regional and global stability essential to the security of both countries. From this perspective, painting China as an inevitable adversary will lead the United States to pursue militant policies likely to produce that outcome—a self-fulfilling policy.

There are also mixed feelings concerning China's spectacular economic growth over recent years. As a result of its continual double-digit annual growth, it is now the world's second largest economy and perhaps the most dynamic. Eventually some project China to overtake the United States. Yet China has a population approaching 1.4 billion people compared to more than 307 million in the United States. China will have to grow to far more than parity in aggregate economic size with the United States to approach, much less match, its per capita national income and wealth.

Instead of seeing China's economic growth as a threat to the United States, an alternative take is that China can now play a greater role to promote the domestic and regional stability that is clearly in the country's economic and security interests. Observers give major credit to the Chinese government for its investment in state-owned industries and economic infrastructure from roads and bridges to power plants and dams. It also has facilitated the acquisition of foreign intellectual property and has pursued an astonishing number of economic deals in Africa and South America to secure long-term access to natural resources required to keep the economic engine running. But China has also developed a thriving entrepreneurial class that exists outside the powerful state-controlled companies.

There is uneasiness in North America and Europe over the vast pool of Chinese savings that is today largely invested in these countries' government bonds. Such capital could be used to buy foreign companies, but this uneasiness is tempered by the fact many businesspeople in the West see China simply as a vast market, its huge population potential customers for a wide variety of consumer goods. International businesses, the United States, the European Union, and other advanced industrial countries lobbied for China's admittance to the World Trade Organization (WTO), which finally occurred in 2001. Bipartisan U.S. political support had already resulted in Congress granting permanent normal trading relations (PNTR) status to China in May 2000. Both China and its trading partners, it was claimed, would benefit in economic terms from the tariff-reduction and market-widening proposals, but so would purchasers of Chinese products in other countries.

There was an important political argument as well—by being brought into the global trading system, China no longer is the self-isolated Middle Kingdom, but rather a vested partner in a stable global economic system. This follows the logic of economic liberalism and arguments for the pacifying effects of economic globalization. Although not all are so optimistic, many in the West hope that economic development ultimately will lead to a transition from authoritarianism to a regime in Beijing more supportive of human rights. To these observers more optimistic about prospects for liberalization in China, trade with foreigners will add needed pressure for the further development of the rule of law. Hence supporters of PNTR status for China have managed to combine economic self-interest with claims of being supportive of human and political rights in China.

Some realist critics dismiss the economic liberalism argument as historically unfounded and empirically incorrect. The simple proposition that the benefits of economic exchange make war too costly to pursue seems intuitively plausible, yet in an anarchic world fear will be ever-present, and hence so will be the possibility of war. Moreover, trade with China has resulted in enormous deficits paid for with dollars and other currencies held by the Chinese central bank at levels well in excess of reserve requirements. To realists, trade with China has made the United States and other countries dependent on Chinese willingness to buy American and other countries' bonds—in effect, loans by China. Such vulnerability to possible shifts in China's (or any other country's) policy is what realists seek to avoid.

Other critics, however, take a different tack, arguing that in the pursuit of trade benefits the world is too willing to overlook China's human rights abuses. By granting PNTR and admitting China to the World Trade Organization, advanced industrial states were, in effect, placing their seal of approval on the regime. Why, it was asked, should the advanced industrial democracies so readily have given up a carrot (admittance to the WTO and PNTR) that could have been used more effectively as leverage to improve human rights in China?

What most observers would probably agree on, however, is that the single biggest challenge for the current Chinese leadership is the need to deliver continual economic growth or risk political turmoil. The economic reforms that began in the late 1970s generated catch-up growth—gains from disbanding agricultural communes and the resultant influx of cheap labor to low-end manufacturing firms made for double-digit economic growth. Those days are gone, as growth rates in the manufacturing sector have slowed and agricultural productivity has reached its limits due, in part, to a severe shortage of water in some areas. The gap in the standard or level of living between the city and the countryside remains a serious problem, as is the growth in corruption and widespread environmental degradation. The Chinese government may well find that domestic challenges—economic, social, as well as political—will preoccupy their attention and temper any possible shift to a more aggressive foreign and national security policy.

India

With over 1.2 billion persons, India ranks only behind China in terms of population and work force and, in terms of number of citizens, is the world's largest democracy. It is the eleventh largest economy based on gross domestic product (GDP). In the late 1980s its economy was as large as China's, but the latter soared ahead due to the introduction of economic reforms and the availability of capital from direct foreign investment and sustained export surpluses with the outside world. In recent years India's own economic prospects dramatically expanded since market reforms were instituted beginning in the early 1990s. Furthermore, in some ways India's economic future is even brighter than China's as it has a younger working-age population and a critical mass of English-speaking workers. As a result it is on track to pass Japan to become the world's third largest economic power. Once known to poorly informed foreigners as essentially the location of call centers, India has become a major player in high-tech industries, pharmaceuticals, and biotechnology.

Despite apparent economic and demographic similarities to China, India is not viewed by powers outside South Asia as a political or military threat. The United

States has worked assiduously to maintain and even expand cordial relations. Despite the fact India detonated nuclear test devices in 1974 and 1998, the United States decided to assist India in its development of its domestic nuclear power program and, in return, India placed the program under International Atomic Energy Agency (IAEA) safeguards and inspections. This agreement is unique in that India is the only country with nuclear weapons that is not a signatory to the Nuclear Non-Proliferation Treaty and yet can engage in international nuclear commerce with the United States and others.

India's 1998 nuclear test spurred India's next door neighbor and rival, Pakistan, also to seek a nuclear device. The resultant tense situation is a major potential flashpoint in world politics. The two rivals have fought three conventional wars and numerous border skirmishes since the breakup of British colonial India and the creation of India and Pakistan in 1947. The ongoing dispute over the Kashmir region along the northwest India-Pakistan border, which dates back to 1947, could once again spark a military confrontation, but this time both states would have nuclear weapons at their disposal. On the other hand, fear lest conflicts ever escalate to the nuclear level, which would be so devastating for both sides, has induced some degree of caution in relations between the two countries.

India also has difficult relations with China. There has long been a dispute between the two countries over areas along the Indian and Tibetan (controlled by China) border. In 1962, a shooting war broke out in which some three thousand Indian troops were killed. China has blocked India's attempt to get a permanent seat on the United Nations Security Council. China also has close relations with Pakistan in a classic example of balance-of-power politics—the enemy of my enemy can be my ally. In fact India cited the China threat to justify its decision to test a nuclear bomb in 1998.

Despite India's booming economy and the resultant growing confidence on the international scene, it still is faced with a number of significant domestic challenges. Although generally known as a Hindu nation, it is in fact the second largest state in terms of the number of Muslims. Its ethnic, religious, and cultural diversity is extraordinary. Tens of millions of its citizens struggle to maintain the most basic level of living. Despite its international reputation as a center for IT innovation, within India there exists a tremendous literacy and digital divide between those who have these skills and electronic access and those who do not.

Russia

As the core of the former Soviet Union, Russia has an impressive imperial past whether under the czars or the Communists. It is the largest country in the world in terms of land mass, spanning nine time zones from East Asia to Europe. In the decade following the collapse of the Soviet Union and the independence of constituent republics and former satellite states in Eastern Europe, Russia entered a troubled decade. The privatization of state agencies to well-connected individuals led to a flight of capital to foreign countries and widespread corruption. Criminal violence skyrocketed. Steep economic decline was accompanied by dramatic increases in such social problems as crime and overall declining health conditions as well as further environmental degradation.

Politically alienated from the West and resentful of the United States' unchallenged role as the world's sole remaining superpower, a nationalist backlash occurred. This was most evident in the presidency of Vladimir Putin who was elected in 2000. His presidency began at a time when high oil prices and increased domestic consumer demand contributed to a decade of improved level of living (wages increased by 10 percent a year) and the creation of not only new millionaires but also an ever-expanding middle class. Putin inherited the problem of restive ethnic movements in the Northern Caucasus in such regions as Chechnya where a brutal war broke out between separatists (termed terrorists by the Putin government) and Russian security forces. The heavy-handed military approach led to international condemnation over human rights, but Putin replied Russia was merely engaged in its own war against Islamist extremism.

The single most important factor that has fueled Russia's economic resurgence and designation as a rising power is the fact it contains the world's largest reserves of natural gas, is eighth in oil, second in coal, and also contains a treasure trove of minerals. The result has been an amazing increase in Russian financial reserves from $3 billion in 1991 to $430 billion in 2009.[14] Western Europe has become dependent on Russian natural gas exports, and there is speculation as to the circumstances under which such exports could be used for political leverage.

Russia in recent years has reasserted its claim as a major international player whose interests and views on any number of international issues must be taken into account. Putin, even in his postpresidential period, has been unapologetic about this. His confidence made him a popular figure among Russians of many different backgrounds and classes even as recent years have witnessed a reduction in political freedoms and increasing recentralization of power in Putin's United Russia party. In the last several years, however, some of the steam has gone out of the Russia economic engine. The country was particularly hard-hit by the global financial crisis that began in 2008. What this means in terms of Russia's foreign policy and national security objectives remains to be seen. What we can say, however, is that a resurgent Russia is reassuming a prominent role in Eurasian and global politics.

Brazil

In May of 2010, Brazil and Turkey surprised the world by announcing a diplomatic mission to break the stalemate between Iran and the West over Iran's nuclear research and development program. This foray into international diplomacy was not well received by the United States and its European allies—nor was Brazil's voting against a UN resolution to tighten sanctions against Iran's nuclear program—but it represents the growing confidence Brazil has in terms of its place and role in the world. At a time when the United States was not only dealing with Iran, North Korea, wars in Iraq and Afghanistan, as well as an ongoing financial crisis and sluggish economy, Brazil believed it had something to offer as a truly international and not simply regional player.

Originally a Portuguese colony and hence the only country in South America where the official language is Portuguese, it is the world's fifth largest country in both land mass and population. Economically Brazil is eighth in the world in terms of GDP, but the economic trend lines are for the most part moving upward. It is the largest economy in South America and has a booming agricultural sector,

---

[14]"Dimitry Medvedev's Building Project," *The Economist*, November 26, 2009. www.economist.com.

diversified industrial base, and untapped natural resources including newly discovered oil fields in 2007. It is a leading producer of ethanol. Trade is the centerpiece of its foreign policy, and in 2008 it passed China in an index measuring emerging markets. Investment from China and India is significant, and Brazil's upper and middle classes continue to expand, resulting in a consumption boom that helps to keep the economy moving forward. The gap between rich and poor has shrunk in recent years more than in any other South American country.

At peace with its neighbors, Brazilians took great pride in Rio de Janeiro being awarded the 2016 Olympic Games, beating out, among other cities, Chicago. Brazil is represented not only in the Organization of Economic Cooperation and Development (OECD) in Paris—the so-called rich-countries' club—but also in the Group of 20 that claims to represent the interests of less-developed countries.

Such pride, however, is tempered by the reality that there is still a great deal of poverty and crime, particularly involving violent gangs in the slums of Rio. The country has a history of political volatility and short tenure of democratic rule. Nevertheless, as one report noted: "In some ways Brazil is the steadiest of the BRICs. Unlike China and Russia it is a full-blooded democracy; unlike India it has no serious disputes with its neighbors. It is the only BRIC without a nuclear bomb."[15]

The rise of the BRICs leads to the question of the possible policy responses of the United States. Following the end of World War II in 1945, the United States took the lead in working to establish the United Nations and associated economic institutions such as the World Bank, International Monetary Fund (IMF), and General Agreement on Trade and Tariffs (GATT). While the basic motivation might have been the self-interest of the United States, the resulting web of international organizations certainly helped to stabilize at least the economic world order in the aftermath of the most devastating war in history.

As realists claim, international order historically has been a function of the distribution of power among major states. This was evident, for example, with the Concert of Europe following the Napoleonic wars in the 19th century and the role of the United States following World War II. With the rise of the BRICs, it is not clear that the United States will be able to play a similar dominant role. This might, as we will discuss in subsequent chapters, open the door for an enhanced role for multilateral institutions such as the Group of 20, the United Nations and its affiliated organizations, and the creation of issue-specific international regimes essential to 21st-century global governance arrangements for dealing with a seemingly ever-expanding worldwide agenda of issues.

CONCLUSION

The so-called "Wise Men" referred to at the outset of this chapter were Americans faced with a broad range of interrelated challenges ranging from the containment of Soviet power and influence to the political and economic rehabilitation of Western Europe. All were well read in history and aware of the challenges faced by their predecessors in earlier times when the international power structure had been

---

[15]"A Land of Promise," *The Economist*, April 12, 2007. www.economist.com.

rearranged. None were strangers to Thucydides' pessimistic analysis of the implications of a rising power challenging a dominant state.

These statesmen would have been well acquainted with the reasons for devoting this toolbox chapter to a discussion of historical international systems. It is hard to discern what may be unique about the current global system unless we know what it has in common with (or how it differs from) earlier international systems. The history of constant competition and conflict among diverse political entities should make us cautious about expecting global peace and harmony to break out any time soon. War or the threat of war has been constant down through the centuries no matter the time period, the region, the civilization, or the types of political units (city-states, empires, or modern states). On the other hand, we have noted how international systems come and go, and it is shortsighted to assume the planet's future must necessarily replay the past. A look into the past also teaches us that other peoples have experienced dramatic changes in the international systems of their day. They, too, no doubt looked to the future with a mixture of consternation and hope.

While historical analogies and comparisons have their place, there is always the danger of applying inappropriate historical comparisons to the current international environment. As noted at the outset of this chapter, rarely are circumstances exactly the same and hence it is dangerous to assume that the "lessons of history" are always clear-cut. A discussion of historical international systems reveals the conceptual contribution of a number of historians and scholars beginning with Thucydides. This chapter offered the would-be practitioner a conceptual and theoretical understanding of international relations in world politics beyond historical facts and figures. In other words, to think historically and conceptually is to be prepared better to anticipate future international developments such as challenges to integration in the EU alongside the current rise of China, India, Brazil, and a resurgent Russia. By placing our historical overview in the framework of the rise, fall, and evolution of various types of international systems, we encourage the reader to think conceptually. In the following chapters, we continue to introduce different concepts associated with globalization, international relations, and world politics, but they all start with an appreciation of the historical roots of many of the challenges facing us today.

✓—[Study and **Review** the **Post-Test & Chapter Exam** at **mypoliscilab.com**

LEARNING OBJECTIVES REVIEW

3.1 Compare and contrast the four types of international systems we identify—independent, hegemonic, imperial, feudal—and explain the benefits of applying this conceptual understanding to the history of international relations.

International systems are limited in geographic scope compared to a global system which, as the term implies, encompasses the entire world. An international system is defined as an aggregation of diverse entities linked by regular interaction that sets them apart from other systems. The four types of international systems are the independent state system (no superior power is acknowledged), hegemonic system (one or more states dominate), imperialist system (a dominant state tends to manage the affairs of subject colonies), and feudal system (a highly diverse group of governmental entities and the decentralization of power).

KEY TERMS

International system 55
Structure 55
Global system 55
Independent state system 56
Hegemonic state system 56
Imperial system 57
Feudal system 58

ADDITIONAL READING

Adam Watson, *The Evolution of International Society* (London: Routledge, 1992). If we were to recommend a single book on historical international systems and how to define them, it would be this work. Our debt to this superb work is evident throughout this chapter.

3.2 Apply the four categories or types of international systems to the cases of ancient Persia, Greece, India, Rome, and feudal Europe.

The examination of select historical international systems utilizing the concept of system allows for the ability to compare and contrast how political authority was organized in different times and geographic regions. We can also compare and contrast past systems to world politics today. The Persian, Roman, and late Indian empires all controlled and governed what were at the time vast geographic spaces. Persuasion and cooperation versus coercion were the preferred method of political control. The classical Greece independent state system evolved into a hegemonic system dominated by Athens and Sparta. Costly and recurrent wars ended up weakening both states and made them susceptible to the rule of Macedonia. The feudal system of medieval Europe is a fascinating example of how an international system can be characterized by a decentralization of power among a very diverse set of actors (kings, popes, merchants, barons).

KEY TERMS

Satraps 60
Delian League 61
Papacy 66

ADDITIONAL READINGS

S. N. Eisenstadt, *Political Systems of Empires* (New York: The Free Press, 1963). A focus on different historical empires including ones discussed in this chapter.
Michael W. Doyle, *Empires* (Ithaca, NY: Cornell University Press, 1986). This book offers an excellent combination of history, IR theory, and normative considerations. An in-depth discussion of the Greek international system is particularly noteworthy.

3.3 Explain the key developments that led to the rise of the European independent state system and how it eventually became globalized as a form of international politics.

The 12th century witnessed the beginning of the gradual reconcentration of political power in the hands of kings. Relative peace, larger populations, expanded economic activity, and an increase in literacy among the upper classes all contributed to the rise of the state. With the Peace of Westphalia (1648) the concept of sovereignty began to take hold and contributed to the idea of the nation-state as the focus of loyalty. The rise of Napoleon in France upset the European political and military balance, and his defeat was followed by the Congress of Vienna (1814–1815), which created a collective hegemony of the major states. This European system of states spread to areas outside Europe in the form of colonies.

KEY TERMS

Sovereignty 71
Nationalism 71
Mercantilism 72
International law 72
Concert of Europe 73

ADDITIONAL READINGS

Paul Kennedy, *The Rise and Fall of the Great Powers* (New York: Random House, 1987). The book that has generated years of debate on the question "Is the United States headed for decline?"

Adam Hochschild, *King Leopold's Ghost* (Boston: Houghton Mifflin, 1998). A very disturbing yet engrossing examination of the impact of colonialism in Africa, in this case the Belgian Congo.

3.4 Evaluate and explain the relative success and failure of attempts by states to develop collective security arrangements.

By the end of the 19th century tension rose in Europe, particularly due to the rise in power of Germany. Following World War I (1914–1918) an attempt at collective security via the creation of the League of Nations ended in failure. A second attempt to institutionalize global collective security was after World War II (1939–1945) and the creation of the United Nations—collective security augmented with provisions allowing for collective defense (i.e., defensive alliances). Conflict between East and West—particularly the Soviet Union and the United States, which were the two hegemonic powers—made for a series of crises and the expansion of competition to areas of the developing world. U.S. policy was focused on containing Soviet influence. Improved relations in the 1970s were evident by a general relaxation of tensions (*détente*) and a number of arms control agreements such as SALT I. With the collapse of the Soviet Union in 1991 the result was a unipolar system of U.S. dominance.

KEY TERMS

Collective security 81
Collective defense 81
Containment 82
Détente 86

ADDITIONAL READINGS

Stephen Ambrose, *Rise to Globalism* (Penguin Books, multiple editions). A thorough and eminently readable overview of the rise to prominence of the United States in the 20th century.

Michael J. Hogan (ed.), *The End of the Cold War: Its Meaning and Implications* (Cambridge: Cambridge University Press, 1992). An anthology containing a wide variety of views on how and why the Cold War ended.

3.5 Evaluate the impact of the rising economic strength of the European Union and the four rising BRIC powers on future international developments.

The past decade has seen the rise in power of a number of states. In addition to greater economic integration in the EU, the four most often mentioned rising powers are Brazil, Russia, India, and China (the BRIC countries). The single most important indicator of their power is not military capability, but rather economic prowess. China is known for its manufacturing and export revolution; India for its overall economic development and expanding technological industries; Russia for its oil, mineral, and natural gas reserves that have fueled rises in levels of living; and Brazil for its natural resources that have spurred a dramatic increase in international trade. Domestic challenges, however, could have a major impact on the ability of these countries to continue their economic expansion. It is also not clear the extent to which these countries harbor larger international political and military ambitions or whether they will see themselves as having common interests with others in regional and global stability.

KEY TERM

BRIC 89

ADDITIONAL READINGS

Fareed Zakeria, *The Post-American World* (New York: Norton, 2008). The most cited book noting the continual rise of China, India, Russia, and Brazil, written by one of the most recurrent guests on Jon Stewart's *The Daily Show*.

Ye Sang, *China Candid: The People on the People's Republic of China* (Berkeley: University of California Press, 2006). Sang is a journalist who provides an alternative history of China from its founding as a socialist state in 1949 up to the present. He does not interview top party officials, but rather gives voice to people who have lived in the maelstrom of China's economic reforms—artists, businessmen, women, former Revolutionary Red Guards, migrant workers, teachers, computer geeks, hustlers, and other citizens. All speak with candor about the realities of China as the rising power of East Asia, and the human costs involved.

CHAPTER REVIEW

1. The earliest period to which the concepts of globalization and global politics can be applied is
   a. villages, clans, and tribes throughout history.
   b. ancient civilizations.
   c. the rise of the modern state.
   d. none of the above.

2. Which of the following are types of international systems?
   a. Independent state system
   b. Hegemonic state system
   c. Feudal system
   d. All of the above

3. Which of the following statements concerning international systems are not accurate?
   a. All actual historical systems must match up with one of the four discussed.
   b. None of these systems can overlap in terms of characteristics or time period.
   c. Ideas and concepts have little impact on history compared to economics.
   d. None of the above is true.

4. Which of the following are best described as imperial systems?
   a. Persian
   b. Indian
   c. Roman
   d. All of the above

5. Under the regime of Chandragupta Maurya, India
   a. was isolated from the rest of the world.
   b. was influenced by Persians and Greeks.
   c. became Buddhist.
   d. became a bipolar system of states.

6. The classical Greek independent state system evolved into
   a. a hegemonic system dominated by Athens and Sparta.
   b. an Athenian empire.
   c. a Spartan empire.
   d. a Persian-Athenian hegemonic system after the defeat of Sparta.

7. Which of the following international systems is best characterized as extremely decentralized in terms of authority?
   a. Athens and Sparta before the outbreak of the Peloponnesian War
   b. India prior to its development into an imperial system
   c. The Roman empire due to its willingness to allow regional political independence
   d. Medieval Europe

8. During the 12th and 13th centuries
   a. literacy expanded and universities were established.
   b. the idea of written contracts was relatively unknown.
   c. there was hardly any economic activity of any kind.
   d. the sacred and temporal authorities were always in agreement.

9. The rise of an independent state system in Europe was associated with all of the following EXCEPT
   a. an increase in the religious authority of the Pope.
   b. the decline of feudalism and the rise of market capitalism.
   c. an increase in the power of kings.
   d. increasing trade.

10. By the late 17th century, the primary political unit in Europe had become the
    a. church.
    b. territorial state.
    c. feudal kingdom.
    d. Concert of Europe.

11. The Concert of Europe refers to
    a. a treaty signed in 1648 to end thirty years of warfare in Europe.
    b. the collective hegemony of the five major European powers that emerged after the defeat of Napoleon in 1815.
    c. the leaders of the major European countries subsequent to World War I.
    d. a musical event in 1750 that marked the high point of Bourbon rule in France.

12. The European system of independent states
    a. confined territorial competition to Europe.
    b. confined economic competition to Europe and the United States.
    c. eventually spread throughout the world.
    d. collapsed in the Great Depression of the 1930s.

13. The idea that states have a legal right to enforce international law against aggression by taking collective action to stop it is called
    a. alliance systems.
    b. international cooperation.
    c. collective sanctions.
    d. collective security.

14. Dual hegemony during the Cold War refers to
    a. China and the Soviet Union (USSR).
    b. United States and the Soviet Union (USSR).
    c. China and the United States.
    d. the League of Nations and the United Nations.

15. The containment policy of the United States was principally directed against
    a. the Soviet Union.
    b. communism in general.
    c. communist parties in Europe and the United States.
    d. a and b.

16. The Cold War ended
    a. with the Russian civil war.
    b. with the collapse of communist China.
    c. with the rise of NATO and the European Union.
    d. None of the above.

17. *Détente* refers to
    a. relaxation of tensions between East and West in the 1970s.
    b. containment of the Soviet Union (USSR) in the 1950s through the early 1990s.
    c. Napoleon's military campaign plans for Europe.
    d. the French colonial strategy.

18. BRIC stands for
    a. Burundi, Rwanda, Indonesia, and the Congo.
    b. Brazil, Russia, India, and China.
    c. Brazil, Russia, Indonesia, and China.
    d. Britain, Russia, India, and China.

19. The two BRICs with the greatest natural resources are
    a. Brazil and Russia.
    b. Indonesia and the Congo.
    c. China and India.
    d. Brazil and China.

20. The common factor that may decide the role of the BRICs in the international system is
    a. the response of the United States.
    b. the role of the United Nations.
    c. the response of the European Union.
    d. domestic developments.

Geography

"Geography has made us neighbors. History has made us friends. Economics has made us partners, and necessity has made us allies. Those whom God has so joined together, let no man put asunder." —President John F. Kennedy, Former President of the United States

LEARNING OBJECTIVES

4.1 Explain the differences between physical and human geography and why a basic understanding of both is necessary when studying international relations and world politics.

4.2 Evaluate the impact of religion in global politics, particularly with regard to conflict.

4.3 Compare and contrast the concepts of nation, nation-state, and nationalism, and explain how they can be a source of conflict in global politics.

4.4 Identify the different policy approaches to dealing with nationalism and ethnicity and identify their limitations.

Read and **Listen** to **Chapter 4** at **mypoliscilab.com**

Study and **Review** the **Pre-Test & Flashcards** at **mypoliscilab.com**

Mahmud is a graduate student studying business at a college on the East Coast of the United States. His hometown of Mumbai, India, is eleven time zones and some 8,000 miles away on the other side of the world. Modern communications such as Skype, however, have allowed him to stay in touch with family and friends. He is somewhat bemused at the stereotypes of India held by a number of his classmates: "They assume I'm a follower of the Hindu faith and expect me to be wearing a turban. In fact, I was raised as a Muslim and it is my Sikh friends who wear turbans." While Hindis in fact total over 80 percent of the Indian population, Muslims account for some 13 percent of the population, making India the country with the third largest Muslim population in the world. "People also expect me to be some sort of expert on all of India, which is a huge and incredibly diverse country. Trying to generalize about India in a few sentences is like saying New York City, New Orleans, and Los Angeles are all alike. What I do hear from my business classmates is a lot of talk about India as a rising economic power." Part of the reason for this is that while India is geographically one-third the size of the United States, it has 1.15 billion persons compared to the U.S. population of 310 million persons.

Any serious student of international relations and world politics is required to have a basic understanding of geography. Whether we are viewing the world through the lenses of politics, economics, history, or theory, all human actions must be played out on land, sea, air, or, in some cases, space. It is tempting to believe that globalization has reduced the importance of physical geography, at least, as the far side of the globe doesn't seem too far away given modern transportation and communication. But if anything, the perception that the world is becoming a more interconnected place means we should be all the more aware of how divergent political, religious, and ethnic entities can have an impact on our own lives.

PHYSICAL AND HUMAN GEOGRAPHY

4.1 Explain the difference between physical and human geography and why a basic understanding of both is necessary when studying international relations and world politics.

There are two basic types of geography: *physical* and *human*. Most people think of **physical geography** in terms of the use of maps to depict material manifestations of terrain: continents, mountains, rivers, lakes, and oceans. **Human geography** (or cultural geography), on the other hand, involves the visual depiction of human activities overlaid on physical terrain maps. A diagram depicting population density on the European continent would be an example, with each dot representing 10,000 persons. Other examples would include a map depicting locations and extent of religions, languages, and even current locations and levels of political violence around the world. What both have in common is a graphic representation of spatial concepts. Without such basic understanding, it would obviously be difficult to understand political and economic trends in international relations and world politics, let alone make sense of day-to-day events. Let's further discuss both types of geography and their importance to understanding international relations and world politics by reference to several historical and current examples.

👁 **Watch** the **Video** **"America's Oil Addiction"** at **mypoliscilab.com**

physical geography ■ material manifestations of terrain such as continents, mountains, rivers, lakes, and oceans

human geography ■ the visual depiction of human activities overlaid on physical terrain maps, which include, cultural, religious, and other factors related to the world's peoples

Physical Geography

As a practitioner, you will find that maps will always be important tools. Some tasks may require getting a particular map or set of maps in hard copy or electronic form. Other maps are in our heads. When someone mentions a problem or issue in North Africa, for example, do you immediately see the desert region along the Mediterranean coast divided into states following independence movements from European colonial powers? From west to east (left to right in our mind's eye) these countries are the Maghreb countries of Morocco, Algeria, and Tunisia influenced earlier by French colonialism; Libya, which was an Italian colony; and Egypt, which was under British influence.

If someone says northeast Asia, do you immediately see China, two Korean states, and Russia on the Asian mainland with the Japanese islands offshore, Taiwan further south? How about southeast Asia? Do Vietnam, Laos, Cambodia, the Philippines, Brunei, the Indonesian archipelago, Singapore, Malaysia, and Myanmar come to mind, and, if so, what can you say about them—their history, colonial experiences, present relations within regional or international organizations like ASEAN (the Association of Southeast Asian Nations)?

What countries come to mind and where are they located in relation to each other when one thinks of the Pacific Islands? Down Under in the Australian subcontinent, the two main islands of New Zealand offshore? Antarctica? South Asia and the Indian Ocean? Central Asia? The Persian (or, as it is sometime called, Arab) Gulf? Europe and the North Atlantic including the Arctic region, Greenland, and Iceland? Sub-Saharan Africa? North and South America? Our purpose here is that we all no doubt have locational-geography homework to do if we are to be effective as practitioners.

Understanding physical geography didn't particularly matter thousands of years ago when human communities were essentially localized. But as communities grew in size and expanded outward, they came into contact with other communities. Territoriality, the attachment to a particular geographic area under the administrative control of an overriding authority, became important not just in terms of political and military competition, but also in terms of commercial competition as trade routes developed and expanded. Growing communities desired control over their expanding physical geography.

territoriality ■
geographic area under
the administrative
control of an
overriding authority

Seaports   Seaports and natural or humanly developed harbors were particularly important assets historically and politically, and indeed, they remain so today. Although aviation has become an increasingly important means for transporting people and cargo, global trade of goods still depends very heavily on sealift, accompanied on land by both road and rail connections. Great powers have always depended upon navies to secure trade routes and to deploy armed forces abroad—warships and army or marine units. Indeed, water covers more than 70 percent of the earth's surface—a fact not overlooked by naval advocates. Command of ports helped and continues to facilitate a state's exercise of territorial authority over a geographic region.

Transportation Routes   Transportation at sea, on land, and in the air depends heavily on infrastructure—not just seaports and harbors, but also airports and both road and rail lines that must cross geographical challenges posed by mountains, lakes, and rivers. Since the 19th century technological advances in transportation truly have been breathtaking—from wind power driving sailing ships to steam engines powered by wood or coal, combustion engines fueled by petroleum, and now some naval ships and submarines powered with nuclear energy. Civil and military aviation made the transition after World War II from piston-engine to turboprop and later to jet engines, the latter becoming prominent not only in combat applications, but also making possible greater airlift capacity for both passengers and cargo. High-speed rail in many countries is displacing 19th- and 20th-century technologies in train travel. Automobiles and trucks are moving finally to more efficient engines; cars to hybrid, electric, and other alternatives to gasoline or diesel-combustion engines. The net effect of all these technological advances in transportation is to make the world figuratively a smaller place, physical geography no longer the obstacle it once was to crossing oceans and continents. Who maintains control of the transportation routes, however, does impact access.

Mapping the Physical World   Cartography, the art and science of making maps, dates back in the West to Babylonian clay tablets from about 2,300 B.C.E. and has always had military and economic implications. The ancient Greeks and Romans made serious efforts to chart their spheres of influence and empires, and the Middle Ages witnessed an increase in interest in cartography in Europe and even earlier in Arab lands. With the Renaissance and the age of exploration, maps became essential as trade routes were charted and eventually reproduced for wider dissemination with the invention of the printing press. Gerardus Mercator of Flanders (Belgium) famously developed a cylindrical projection of the world that assisted

cartography ■ the
drawing of maps

navigation and exploration. The scientific revolution continually improved the accuracy and quality of maps.

Beyond trade and exploration, maps were obviously useful when it came to engaging in wars of conquest and planning military campaigns. Military theorists and practitioners such as Antoine Henri de Jomini discussed in great detail military lines of operations, while Carl von Clausewitz noted the importance of logistics for any army that hoped to be successful in foreign military campaign.

Maps were essential in depicting physical geographic obstacles to conquest. Island nations such as Great Britain benefited from the protection of the English Channel. The Pyrenees mountain chain of southwestern Europe formed a natural border wall between France and Spain. The United States had an entire ocean between itself and the political competition and wars of Europe and Asia. Lack of mountains, major rivers, and other geographic barriers helps to explain the troubled history of Poland, a land of plains from the Baltic Sea in the north to the Carpathian Mountains in the south, continually invaded from both east (Russia) and west (Germany)—not to mention historic invasions by Sweden entering from the Baltic Sea in the north and Austrian imperial encroachment from the south. Also a country largely composed of flat plains and itself a creation resulting from historic conflict among great powers, Belgium was quickly invaded and occupied by Germany in both of the 20th century's two world wars.

Natural Resources   Physical geography is also important in drawing our attention to the location of natural resources that can be critical components of state power. Oil is the obvious example and helps to explain the Western interest in Arab lands such as Saudi Arabia where the first concession for oil exploration was signed in 1923. Minerals such as tin and tungsten from war-torn Congo in Africa are essential to the world's laptops, GPSs, and PDAs. Congo has seen upwards of five million persons killed in civil war and violence over the past ten years, often fueled by violent competition to control these mineral resources.

Modes of Communication   Advances in communications have also made the world ever more interconnected. Mail transit by horse-driven carriage was replaced in the 20th century by trucks and aircraft. Nineteenth-century telegraph communications, followed by the introduction of the telephone, gradually removed geographical barriers to rapid communications within countries and across national borders. Transcontinental and oceanic cables were laid, but development of Earth satellites in the last half century coupled with the digital transformation and advances in both fiber-optic and wireless transmission have so increased global reach that we now take for granted how easy and relatively inexpensive communicating globally has become. The rapid pace by which transportation, telecommunications, and digital technologies are all still moving not only removes the geographical obstacles that were so foreboding in the past, but also facilitates transnational connections in this increasingly globalized world. The removal of the physical barriers makes communication much harder to regulate, as seen with China's and other countries' attempts to control their citizens' internet access.

Today much is made of the process of globalization and the supposed shrinking of the world caused, among other things, by the virtually instantaneous dissemination of ideas via the internet, the dramatic expansion of global air freight and parcel delivery services, cost-free communications such as Skype, and the ability of individuals to board planes and be on the other side of the world in less than twenty-four hours.

But physical geography still matters. Consider the following:

- One reason for U.S. concern over the North Korean missile program is the fact that the North Koreans have apparently developed a missile capable of reaching Hawaii, Alaska, and perhaps the West Coast of the United States and Canada.
- The United States' geographically contiguous border with Mexico of over 1,900 miles running through the U.S. states of California, Arizona, New Mexico, and Texas, much of it open plains and desert separated by no more than identification markers, helps to explain why so much of the illegal immigration debate revolves around that portion of the hemisphere.
- The Suez Canal in Egypt connects the Red Sea with the Mediterranean Sea. The canal accounts for 7.5 percent of world trade. Should the canal be blocked as it was after the 1967 Arab-Israeli War (Egypt did not reopen the canal until 1975), ships would have to travel around the Cape of Good Hope at the tip of Africa, significantly adding time and expense to the transport of goods.
- The fact that Israel is geographically located in the heart of the Arab Middle East and that Hutus and Tutsis are geographically located in the same region of central Africa obviously contributes to our basic understanding of the outbreak of wars between Israel and its neighbors beginning in 1948 and the genocide in Rwanda in the mid-1990s.

In recent years there has been a renewal of interest in physical geography. For example, Georgetown University's undergraduates in the School of Foreign Service, which accounts for most of the students who major in international politics, are required to pass a rigorous geography exam before they are allowed to graduate. For graduates to be taken seriously in government, business, or nongovernmental organizations that deal with international relations, they must know map locations and physical geography (climate, terrain, bodies of water, and waterways) in order to make sense of our globalized world. The days of knowing only the geography of your own country are history.

The early literature on international relations used to devote a great deal of time to physical geography under the heading of geopolitics. This is exemplified by the work of Sir Halford Mackinder (1861–1947), who presented a paper entitled "The Geographical Pivot Point of History" to the Royal Geographical Society in London in 1904. He argued: "As we consider this rapid review of the broader currents of history, does not a certain persistence of geographical relationship become evident? Is not the pivot region of the world's politics that vast area of Euro-Asia which is inaccessible to ships?" This is the "Heartland" of the world, and Mackinder then presented his famous, if not slightly bizarre, thesis: "Who rules east Europe commands the Heartland; who rules the Heartland commands the World-Island [Europe, Asia, Africa]; who rules the World-Island commands the World." Such geographical determinism is frowned upon nowadays by most historians and writers on international relations. Yet Mackinder's thesis certainly

geopolitics ■ an attempt to understand the issue of national power almost exclusively in terms of physical geography

resonated throughout the Cold War as presidents and prime ministers worked to contain the Heartland-occupying Soviet Union.

Mackinder popularized the concept of geopolitics, which, at its simplest, concerns the impact of geography on politics. But it also has policy implications when it suggests strategic prescriptions when dealing with such topics as the relative importance of land and sea power or where a state should engage in strategic planning to deal with a rising power.

Human Geography

A basic appreciation for the international landscape of human (or cultural) geography is also essential for students of world politics. While charts and tables can list data concerning such topics as arms expenditures, numbers of nuclear weapons, or the gross domestic product (GDP) of various states, such data have a greater impact if graphically presented or overlaid on maps. An outstanding example of this approach is the *Penguin State of the World Atlas*, now in its eighth edition. This book creatively uses color-coding to depict visually the geographic location and size of such figures as casualties of war, ethnicity, religion, peacekeeping missions, refugees, warlords, militias, human trafficking, sex tourism, and international terrorism hotspots. In some cases the data are configured to depict the relative size of state populations, economies, and energy use.

demography ■
collection and study
of data on populations

Demography   Demography is a part of human geography that focuses on populations, providing, for example, statistics on the number of people in close to 200 states (and their respective societies). These may be aggregated by regions: Africa, Europe, the Middle East, South and Central Asia, East Asia and Pacific, and the Western Hemisphere—North, South and Central America and the Caribbean islands. Using the same global, regional, and state-and-society categories we can find data on human conditions—literacy, life expectancy, health, population growth, per capita income, economic growth, production by sector (agricultural, manufacturing, and service), and the like. Demographic data of this kind can be extremely important in identifying trends and the relation between one or another of these factors.

For example, China's one-child policy—limiting families, particularly in urban areas, to having only one daughter or son—is a government policy designed to bring population growth into line with expected economic growth. Were Chinese authorities to allow population size to grow faster than the economy, the already difficult conditions in peasant villages would grow even worse than they already are for some 75–80 percent of the country's population. Critics, particularly outside of China, not only object to the loss of freedom to determine the size of one's family, but also to the draconian measures including abortion—not to mention infanticide—that result from such a policy. Although there has been some loosening of the policy in recent years (it has never been completely enforced), the government's response is always that restraints on population growth in a country approaching 1.4 billion people are essential for China's economic growth. Keeping population growth within bounds is also part of the country's pursuit of an improved regional and global position in world politics.

Global Civilizations   With the end of the Cold War in 1991, a number of ambitious works developed provocative theses that reflected a view of the world in terms of human geography. Francis Fukuyama in *The End of History* argued that democracy was the logical political outcome of the evolution of international society. Indeed, democratic movements came to the fore in a number of the states of the former Soviet empire. A very different view, however, was expressed by Samuel Huntington initially in his influential article, "The Clash of Civilizations?" in the journal *Foreign Affairs* (1993) and later in his full-length book *The Clash of Civilizations and the Remaking of World Order* (1996). His thesis was that post–Cold War conflict most likely would be due to clashes among civilizations marked by major cultural differences as opposed to the ideological clash between communism (e.g., the Soviet Union and the communist bloc) and democracy (e.g., the capitalist West led by the United States) during the Cold War. As he argued:

> The rivalry of the superpowers is replaced by the clash of civilizations. In this new world the most pervasive, important, and dangerous conflicts will not be between social classes, rich and poor, or other economically defined groups, but between peoples belonging to different cultural entities."[1]

The world's major civilizations were identified by Huntington as (1) Western, (2) Latin American, (3) Islamic, (4) Sinic (Chinese), (5) Hindu, (6) Orthodox, (7) Japanese, and (8) African. All more or less have a geographic focal point. This use of *civilization* as the principal unit of analysis contrasts with the usual international relations emphasis on the classical notion of sovereign states as the key unit of analysis. His policy prescription and warning was that Western nations, collectively constituting a *civilization*, would lose out to other civilizations if they failed to recognize the irreconcilable nature of this new global competition.

Huntington's thesis drew a fair amount of criticism to include the charge that his list of civilizations was simplistic, monolithic, and failed to take sufficient account of the tensions within "civilizations." Most of these critics (to include the authors of this book) prefer to speak of *state* and *society* as units of analysis, focusing not on alleged clashes between or among *civilizations*, but rather on cultural, economic, social, political, and other similarities and differences. Our purpose is simply to note that viewing world politics from a human-geography perspective is useful, but this requires an understanding of some of the major transnational trends that involve what we call identity politics.

identity politics
■ the political implications of individuals identifying with religious, national, ethnic, tribal, or clan values

Identities   Questions relating to religious, national, ethnic, tribal, clan, or other human identities are universal. Human beings are social creatures, as Aristotle observed, a fact that has both up and down sides. For the most part, we live and work together cooperatively, divided only by relatively small differences or conflicts. The great achievements of humankind have depended on our ability to pool talents and resources in social groups of one kind or another. At the same time, however, human beings who are organized into separate, conflicting groups can be the source of mutually destructive activities, as has been evident in recent years in parts of Africa and Asia.

[1]Samuel P. Huntington, *The Clash of World Civilizations and the Remaking of World Order* (New York: Simon and Schuster, 1996), p. 28.

social constructivism
■ identities are not essential or given attributes but rather are constructed by individuals and groups

An ongoing debate revolves around the question of whether identities are essentially primordial in origin, passed down through generations and a given almost as much as our genetics. Conversely, social constructivists argue that identities are formed, created, malleable, and subject to change and self-definition. Where one comes down on this issue has a dramatic impact on whether one is pessimistic or optimistic about the ability of groupings of individuals to live in relative harmony. From the perspective of international relations and world politics, the world is conventionally divided into single nation-states, multinational states, and nations dispersed in two or more states. Individuals may derive a sense of security or other value from having a particular national or ethnic identity, but this ethnic identification may make others, particularly minority groups, feel insecure. Mutually exclusive communities within, between, or across state boundaries appear to be the source of conflict based on these national, ethnic, religious, historical and cultural, racial and physical, or other differences. Conflicts may smolder for decades and even centuries, breaking out as interstate or civil wars, insurgencies, terrorism, or other forms of revolutionary violence.

One of the most vexing and important issues in world politics at the beginning of the 21st century involves conflicts relating to state sovereignty and national identity. Two interrelated questions involving physical and human geography arise:

■ In the name of upholding the concept of state sovereignty, should the aspirations of a minority ethnic group for an independent country be ignored?
■ On the other hand, if national self-determination is embraced across the board, then will the world witness increasing geographic fragmentation of the international state system? If so, is this such a bad thing in the age of globalization?

Such questions are not part of an abstract academic enterprise. For example, should all ethnic minorities within the boundaries of the current Russian state be granted independence? What about African tribes, which number literally in the thousands and whose communities cross many sovereign-state borders?

We devote the rest of this chapter to key aspects of human geography—religion followed by a discussion of nationality and ethnicity. We illustrate the obvious fact that the world is replete with conflicts and controversies related to religion, nationality, and ethnicity. These are all played out on the geographic terrain. We then turn to a discussion of approaches designed to foster peace among differing religions and nationalities.

WORLDWIDE RELIGIOUS TRADITIONS

4.2 Evaluate the impact of religion in global politics, particularly with regard to conflict.

One impact of the Cold War was to overshadow the role of religion in global politics. Although from the perspective of some in the West the Cold War was a battle between Christianity and other religions against "godless communism," most people saw it in nonreligious terms as a battle between two visions of the appropriate political and economic forms of governance—Western-style democracy and market capitalism versus centrally directed, state-socialist or communist economies.

Historically, however, religion has at times played a major role in international politics. Christian crusaders attempted to "liberate" the Holy Land in the Middle

Ages and dominate that geographic region. Conversely, Muslims fought to repel the "infidels" and retain sovereignty over the territory. The 17th-century Thirty Years' War on the continent and the English civil war also concerned significant religious issues involving Protestants versus Catholics as well as various countries' desires to improve their political positions by expanding their geographic reach. Not confined to Europe, religious conflict spread to the western hemisphere and later to Africa, Asia, and the Pacific, as Protestant and Catholic missionaries competed with each other in a quest to "save the souls" of indigenous peoples they regarded rather uncharitably as "heathens."

In more recent times, the Iranian revolution of 1978–1979 and the coming to power of Shiite Muslim religious leaders were seen as harbingers of things to come. But observers of international relations almost universally failed to foresee the significant challenge to modern, secular regimes posed by a global resurgence at the end of the 20th century of religious ideas and movements. What is fascinating about this global phenomenon is that it has occurred within diverse cultures, different types of political systems, and in countries with varying levels of economic development. In this regard, Figure 4.1 graphs the relative numbers of people who identify with one of the major religions with worldwide following.

Watch the Video "The Iran-Iraq War" at mypoliscilab.com

religion ■ a system of belief in a divine or superhuman powers(s) with accompanying practices and values

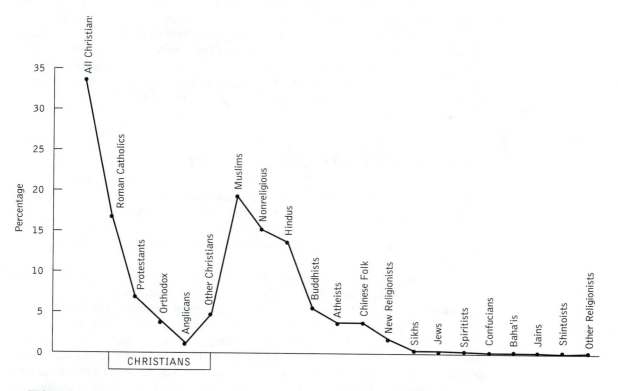

FIGURE 4.1
Religions of the World

Source: Based on data in the 1997 *Britannica Book of the Year* (Chicago: 1997), 311.

The global rediscovery of religion has some obvious and some contradictory implications. First, transnational organizations such as the Roman Catholic Church, the World Council of Churches, and the Society for the Propagation of Islam presumably would assume more important roles. The pronouncements of various religious organizations over the years, of course, supposedly have had universal application, no matter where the flock may reside. But thanks to the internet, Skype, and other modern telecommunications technologies, religious organizations have found it even easier to communicate their messages. Their global religious networks reach out across and beyond the more confining physical borders of states. It seems, however, that it is not the mainstream religions that have benefited most from the communications revolution, but rather some of the smaller, more extreme elements who preach religious intolerance, if not hate, toward adherents of other religious faiths.

Second, transnational religious movements and beliefs also strengthen the development of transnational identities not constrained either by state borders or secular, nonreligious forms of nationalism. For some, religious identity is more important than any particular national identity. To these people, loyalty to their faith comes first with the state a more distant second or third.

Third, if such a trend continues, its implications for global conflict are uncertain. On the one hand, some religious movements have spearheaded peace movements and crusades for human rights and justice. On the other hand, as discussed above, Samuel Huntington suggested that religious identity could be a key component of a broader clash of civilizations with the fault lines of conflict, for example, between civilizations or cultures influenced by Judeo-Christian religious traditions on the one hand and those influenced by Islam on the other—not to mention periods of intercommunal strife between peoples of Buddhist and Hindu identities that have occurred in Sri Lanka.

Religion and International Relations Theory

In this section we explore briefly and apply the images or understandings in international relations theory discussed in Chapter 2 to religion as a factor in domestic or international politics. We start with realism, liberalism, the English School, and economic structuralism as images and then add some of the interpretive understandings offered by constructivists, feminists, postmodernists, and critical theorists.

From a realist perspective, religion remains less important than other factors in relations among states. While religious groups will undoubtedly continue to influence government policies around the globe, most realists argue that the governments themselves will continue to operate in international politics primarily on the basis of national interests and security. Even the Iranian and the now defunct Afghani Taliban governments, for all their Islamist pronouncements, have used religion not as the exclusive road map for foreign policy, but rather as a means to legitimate among their followers the pursuit of power linked to both domestic and foreign policy objectives. Thus, to realists, power and national interest remain the dominant factors—essentially secular objectives cast in religious garb in order to make them more appealing to peoples whose support they seek.

Religious diversity can be a positive element not inevitably associated with conflict, as liberals are prone to point out. It is one of the defining elements of an emerging global civil society. To liberals, national or other common identities that transcend religious or ethnic differences already exist in many countries and, over time, can be constructed in others. Moreover, international, transnational, and nongovernmental organizations can facilitate development over time of greater understanding, tolerance, and even acceptance of religious diversity within and across national boundaries. Indeed, to liberals increasing globalization may reduce or ameliorate conflict among religious groups professing different faiths.

A synthesis of these realist and liberal understandings can be found in the English School that combines the insights of Hobbes on power and balance of power as core factors in international politics with the rule-oriented approach offered by Grotius as a remedy to the ongoing problem of finding order in international society. These rules, compatible as they are with the essentially secular, enlightened self-interests of states, often have religious or moral underpinnings, which Grotius and scholars following in his path have explored. That said, secular factors are most prominent in international society, although some in the English School, following Kant, see the global norms with morally binding content accompanying the transition from an international to what will become a world society. Religion as such is not explicitly part of this construction, but the idea of a world society built on observance of morally binding norms (as opposed merely to agreed rules based on interest) is expressed in secular terms, but is not without its religious underpinnings. Critics within the English School, wedded as they are to the idea of international society, are prone to see those anticipating the emergence of world society as idealistic—religious utopianism expressed in secular terms.

For economic structuralists influenced by Karl Marx, economic class identities are what dominate in both domestic and international politics. Marxists have always recognized (and bemoaned) the pervasive power of religion as an "opiate" to induce "false consciousness" on the part of the working class, effectively subordinating them to the will of the owners (and managers) of capital who use state power and authority to secure their dominance. More often than not, churches usually side with the ruling powers and thus legitimize their dominance over mass publics.

Social constructivists see religious identity as something socially constructed, not a given. It is acquired, not present at birth. There is nothing inherently violent and warlike or pacifist and peace-oriented about any particular religion apart from the meanings those who construct these understandings give them. These meanings do matter, of course, since religious and cultural understandings are ideational factors that impact the ways and means by which both domestic and international politics are conducted.

Skeptical of churches or organized religions that relegate women to the generally submissive, supportive roles customarily assigned to women, many feminists see even mainstream religions reinforcing the already militant, masculinist tendencies found cross-culturally among political leaders—a perspective that contributes to exacerbating intercommunal strife and acceptance of war as somehow the answer to human conflicts. Instead of settling matters through force of arms, religious understandings that favor peaceful remedies are more likely to inspire leaders to pursue conflict resolution or, at least, management of these differences short of resorting to violent means.

Finally, postmodernists and critical theorists see religion—embedded as it is in culture—as worthy of research precisely because written and spoken religious words and phrases contain important meanings we need to unpack if we are to grasp their political significance. It is the critical theorist who takes this inquiry to the next step—examining the extent to which religious pronouncements and the beliefs they foster among their followers are cover stories for underlying political realities of power and dominance. Like Marx to whom many acknowledge an intellectual debt, many critical theorists tend to see religion advanced institutionally by churches or other religious forms of organization as legitimating the status quo among their followers, thus sustaining the various forms human exploitation takes, whether within a particular state and society or among them in their international relations.

Overview of the Major Religious Traditions

The five major religious traditions representing over 4.5 billion people are comprised of the Eastern religions of Hinduism and Buddhism, with more than 2 billion people influenced by their teachings from India to China, Korea, and Japan; and the Western religions of Judaism, Christianity, and Islam, with more than 2.5 billion in their ranks or directly influenced by them worldwide. The remaining human population on Earth fall outside these five traditions, their spiritual identities found in polytheistic or other naturalist understandings grounded deeply in the human experience over the millennia.

Hinduism is itself a complex aggregation of many different sects with different theological understandings that have developed over several millennia. Likewise, Buddhism has divided into different strains: Theravada and Mahayana, the two major branches—the former in Sri Lanka and much of southeast Asia, and the latter in most of northeast Asia. Buddhism in China is mixed culturally with Confucian and Taoist understandings, also influenced by the secularism of the communist revolutionary period. Japan alone is home to four schools of Buddhism. Moreover, these Japanese Buddhist divisions are overlaid not only with the same Confucian and Taoist philosophies that spread historically from China to Japan, but also with indigenous Shinto religious understandings.

The Shinto religion was impacted by political ambition when, in the late 1800s, Emperor Meiji declared Shinto the state religion and himself its divine leader. His imperialistic perspectives set Japan on a militaristic path and eventually led to the dismantling of the State Shinto religion by the Allied Forces after World War II. Only now is the Shinto religion reemerging in Japan. When one considers cultural differences among followers in many countries, different theological understandings, and other political factors, it is not surprising that all of the five major religions (not to mention those with smaller followings) split into many, sometimes competing denominations or sects.

Sometimes we easily jump to wrong conclusions about particular religions being more or less warlike. In fact, human conflict and warfare can be found in peoples of all faiths. Both biblical history and current events makes clear that security of the Jewish people has been an elusive quest over the millennia. More blood was shed in the three decades between the outbreak of World War I in 1914 and the end of World War II in 1945 in predominantly Christian Europe (either in actual numbers or in proportion to population size) than ever occurred before then or since. For its part, the Islamic world has its own set of experiences, caught historically between imperial struggles of the Ottoman and Russian empires, later European colonial competition for spheres of influence, and in recent decades conflicts among themselves and wars or the threat of war with Israel.

Interstate conflict between India, a predominantly Hindu country, and Muslim Pakistan has continued since the end of the British imperial presence in 1948 when the country was partitioned at independence, creating separate Muslim areas in the west (Pakistan) and the east (now Bangladesh). Conflict between Buddhists and Hindus in Sri Lanka makes clear the universality of intercommunal strife that can occur within and across all of the five major religious identities. Put another way, the thesis that some religions are more warlike than others doesn't stand the empirical test. Human beings seemingly engage in conflicts and use force—sometimes even leading to genocide—against one another regardless of religious identity or theological conviction.

Culture and Religious Beliefs

Religions are deeply embedded in cultures and, as such, influence both believers and nonbelievers. The place of religion as part of culture in society has been compared metaphorically to the cat in Lewis Carroll's *Alice in Wonderland*. Sometimes you see the cat, sometimes the cat seems to dissolve to only its smile, but the cat is always there! Even in more secular societies where religion is separated from politics or the affairs of state, the values people hold often have deep religious underpinnings.

Reflecting different interpretations that developed historically, each of these religions has deep divisions among adherents who identify with particular denominations or sects. Judaism, for example, is divided into orthodox, conservative, and reformed (as well as more secular) communities. From its earliest days, Christianity included many different sets of interpretations. The first major split occurred in Europe in 1054 C.E. between the church in Constantinople (present-day Istanbul) and the pre-Reformation church in Rome. Some four centuries later, the Reformation quickly spread in the northern states of western Europe. The Reformation began in Germany when, in 1520, Luther posted his theses and in England, in 1533, when Henry VIII separated the English church from Rome. Henry VIII's separation may have had as much to do with power and land ownership as it did with his desire to divorce his wife, a right he claimed that was denied by the papacy in Rome. Before the split, the Roman Catholic Church owned the majority of land within Henry's kingdom. Henry separated from the Church and the Pope, seized the Church's assets, formed the Church of England, and declared himself the head of his new church. The outcome of these divisions in England and Germany was a further split in Christianity between a post-Reformation Roman Catholicism and various Protestant denominations that appeared throughout Europe and America, splitting further over time into many other sects.

If we are to understand the culturally diverse people with whom we deal in a globalized world—whether in business, government, or socially—knowing and respecting the beliefs of others are essential components of the professional's toolkit. We each have a right to our own religious beliefs or, alternatively, to choose not to follow any of these traditions. As professionals, however, if we are to navigate successfully in a world of religious diversity, all of us can develop tolerance and acceptance of religious diversity in the world around us. Fuller understanding of these religions, of course, goes well beyond the space we can allocate here to this important topic. We apologize that we are only able to present a short overview of four of these culturally rich religious traditions.

Given the misunderstandings about the Islamic religion that are rampant in other parts of the world, we've given more attention to it here. With one out of every five human beings identifying as Muslim, international relations practitioners need to know and understand the extraordinarily important role Islam plays both at the surface and subsurface of politics, economics, and other social matters in societies from Morocco in the West to western China, Malaysia, Indonesia, and even some islands in the Philippine archipelago in the East. With ongoing globalization, the numbers of Muslims in Europe, the Americas, and other countries also have increased substantially. We encourage readers to be like the authors—still seeking to know more about not only all of these world religions and the denominations or sects that divide them, but also the many other religious or philosophical currents present in and across the societies in which we live. As both professionals and fellow human beings, we need to know how other people think.

Eastern Religious Traditions

Hinduism is, perhaps, the oldest of the major religious traditions with ancient roots in prehistoric India more than five millennia B.C.E. This ancient Indian foundational religion also saw the emergence of Buddhism half a millennium before the birth of Jesus. Deeply set in the cultures of non-Islamic India, Hinduism does not have the degree of codification of beliefs one finds in a generally accepted creed or formal teachings from religious authorities.

Hinduism is to many, however, more a "way of life" with both cultural and philosophical roots. As such, the religious tradition is also more open to multiple interpretations on metaphysical questions relating to one's soul or spirit (*Atman*) to God (referred to by some as *Vishnu*) and other heavenly figures. Many Hindus take a more **polytheistic** view—multiple gods or God in many forms, perhaps linking *Vishnu* to two other gods—Brahma and Shiva. In this three-part formulation are *Brahma,* the god of creation, *Vishnu,* the great global spirit, and *Shiva,* a complex figure seen in one or another interpretation as purifier, transformer, or, perhaps, destroyer of ignorance—the three god-figures referred to as a triad or *Trimurti.* Different Hindu sects elevate one or another of these gods over the others.

polytheism ■ belief in more than one god

More important for our purposes here, however, are the principles that define the Hindu way of life. *Dharma* refers in effect to the ethics of right conduct—the duties, for example, one has in relationships with others; *artha,* the search in life to prosper and achieve economic well-being; *kama,* satisfying the sensual needs in life; and *moksha*—freedom or liberation from suffering in the successive process

CASE & POINT | Religious Intolerance

CASE Religious intolerance, of course, is not restricted to Muslim *jihadists*. It is a global, human problem involving peoples identified with all (or, in some cases, none) of these religious traditions. In this regard, murder, rape, torture, and other forms of injustice are contrary theologically to all five religious traditions. Nevertheless, contrary to religious teachings:

- In 2002 we witnessed Hindus in Gujarat, India, killing several hundred Muslims with the collaboration of local officials.
- Muslims and Hindus have attacked each other in the disputed Kashmir region between India and Pakistan over more than half a century since the partition of India at independence from Britain in 1948.
- Apparently with government backing, Sinhalese of Buddhist identity, the majority in Sri Lanka, conducted genocide against Hindus as a response to terrorist and other violent actions by the "Tamil Tigers"—a decades-long insurgency reacting against discrimination perpetrated against the Hindu minority in the small island state.

- Genocide in the former Yugoslavia in World War II and, more recently, in the 1990s, cost the lives of both Muslims and Christians.
- Semitic peoples—both Jews and Arabs, Muslim or Christian—all too often have been the victims of discrimination that sometimes takes lethal form.
  1. The Holocaust (or *Shoah*) killed more than six million Jews in the late 1930s and early 1940s during World War II.
  2. Many Palestinian Arabs were dispossessed of their lands upon creation of Israel as a Jewish state, settlement of this issue along with Israeli settlements in lands taken by force in the 1967 Arab-Israeli war remaining major obstacles in the peace process between the two communities.
- Many in Western countries have a dangerous tendency to equate all of Islam with terrorism when, in fact, only a very small number of Muslims engage in such activity, usually for political or other purposes.

POINT It is not religion or religious teachings per se, but rather the use of them by people to serve their own purposes that has been so corrosive of the human condition worldwide. ▲

of reincarnation from one life to the next. One achieves through spiritual development, which for many Hindu believers brings the soul into an identity with the godliness of *brahma*—a heavenly state of *nirvana*. The term *karma* captures cause-effect relations linking one's deeds to bearing the consequences of one's actions. In this regard, the religion also provides guidance or suggested methods (*yogas*) for attaining these lofty ends in one's life—right conduct in relationships with others, knowledge or wisdom, meditation that develops the mind, and devoted love that links a person to a supreme being.

Born in this Hindu cultural context, Siddhārtha Gautama (perhaps 566–483 B.C.E.) became the Buddha—the enlightened or awakened one who set aside human concerns for material things, discovering in his meditations the ways to get beyond human suffering that begins at birth and continues throughout our lives. He found the origin of suffering in our cravings that, if set aside, can get us beyond this human travail. Buddhists thus focus more on how human beings deal with life's processes than on questions of God and eternity that often are central concerns in other religions. We seek enlightenment, *nirvana*—becoming a Buddha means achieving perfect enlightenment that typically occurs over the course of several lifetimes. We carry marks of our past lives as we proceed—one on the way to becoming a Buddha is referred to as *bodhisattva*.

From the Buddha's meditations, he offered eight very practical prescriptions—the Noble Eightfold Path that helps followers put suffering behind them:

a. WISDOM
1. A correct understanding—seeing things as they really are, not as they may appear to be
2. Acting with the right intention
b. ETHICAL BEHAVIOR
1. Truthful speech
2. Right actions that avoid harm
3. Everyday work—a livelihood that causes no harm
c. CONCENTRATION—DEVELOPING THE MIND
1. Genuine effort to improve
2. Mindfulness—paying attention and looking within oneself
3. Meditation—right concentration

Western Religious Traditions

monotheism ■ belief that there is only one god

Monotheism—belief in a single god or creator—is essentially a Western idea found in Egypt during the seventeen-year reign of the pharaoh Akhenaten, who died about 1334 or 1336 B.C.E. This radical departure from Egypt's polytheistic tradition was reversed after Akhenaten's death, but the idea was not lost. Indeed, it was fully developed in the Judaic tradition that preceded both Christianity and Islam.

Jews, Christians, and Muslims constitute the grouping of three Western religions that share belief in a single creator. Most historians see Judaism as a recognizable religion three millennia ago, although it is difficult to specify precisely when Judaism emerged. A matrilineal passing of the Jewish identity is core to the Judaic tradition—regardless of whatever a father's religious identity might be, one is a Jew if one's mother is a Jew. Unlike both Christians and Muslims, Jews generally do not proselytize or try to convert followers. They believe Abraham made a covenant with God, who identified them as "chosen" people. In this covenant, Abraham concurred that henceforth all males would be circumcised as a mark of their select standing before God.

Jesus lived just over two millennia ago. As a monotheistic religion, Christianity initially was a sect of Judaism in the 1st century after the death of Jesus. Sacred books of the Judaic tradition were retained as an "Old" Testament, but new ones were selected from many that were written to constitute what became a "New" Testament—the new covenant that identified believers and followers of Jesus, displacing the earlier Abrahamic covenant with God. The new Christian theology articulated in the Nicene Creed was not finally agreed upon until the 4th century. The document affirmed monotheistic belief in a single God, but one in three divine persons—Father, Son, and Holy Spirit. This most significant departure from the Judaic tradition was the belief in the divinity of Jesus as an integral part of a godly Trinity.

This belief so central to Christians marked a permanent theological breach between Judaism and Christianity. In this respect, Islam shares with Judaism an understanding of Jesus as a holy man—to Muslims he is a prophet or messenger of Allah, not God himself. These three Western religions are all monotheistic, but each defined its monotheism separately as each historically took its place on the world stage.

Seeing itself as something of a capstone of the three Western religions—Muhammad the last of Allah's messengers—Islam accepts the holy scriptures of both Judaism and Christianity. The *Bible* is foundational to the *Qur'an* and other Islamic scriptures. As such, the biblical prophets recognized by Islam start with Adam and end with Jesus and Muhammad. In the Islamic tradition, both Jews and Christians are also "people of the Book," accorded mutual respect for being so.

Of the ancient prophets it is Abraham and his son, Ishmael, who have a particular place of distinction among Muslims, particularly those with Arab identity. In the tradition accepted by Jews, Christians, and Muslims, one of Abraham's wives, Hagar, gave birth to Ishmael, who led his Arab brothers and sisters into the desert where they live to the present day—many in large cities, of course. Ishmael's half brother, Isaac, was born of Abraham's first wife, Sarah. Isaac and, later, his son, Jacob, were the early Jewish patriarchs in a long line of descent from Abraham. As constructivists remind us, human identities often stand on traditions we internalize. If one accepts this tradition, Jews and Arabs could see themselves as cousins.

The *Koran* (in some transliterations from Arabic, the *Qur'an*) is at the core of Islam, understood to be the word of God passed by the angel Gabriel to the

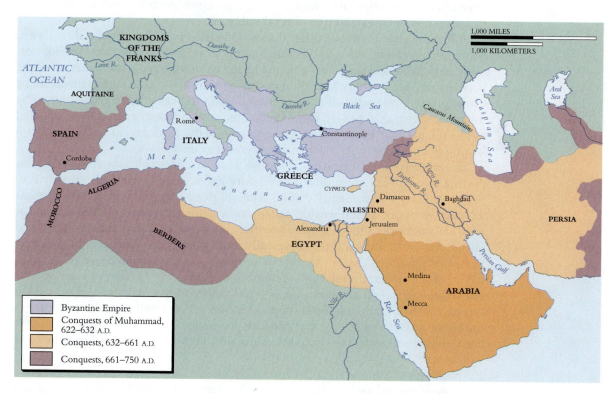

FIGURE 4.2

Muslim Expansion around the Mediterranean

prophet Muhammad. Muslims annually celebrate this enlightenment of Muhammad in the holy days of Ramadan. Written in Arabic, the Koran is the most sacred of texts to Muslims. Anyone able to read Arabic can experience the poetry and prose of the *Koran* as a work of great literary art.

To Muslims, Muhammad is the last of the prophets. The belief that there is only one God named *Allah* (the name in Arabic for God) was an Islamic reaction not only to polytheistic religions then prominent in the Middle East, but also to the Christian belief of God as a trinity of three divine persons. Accordingly, among their obligations the first is that all Muslims are to recite the *Shahadah*—a clear, unambiguous statement of faith: "I bear witness that there is no God but Allah and Muhammad is His Prophet." Indeed, reciting this statement is the most important obligation in Islam.

Even in ordinary conversation, when Muslims say they are hoping or planning for something to happen, they frequently add the word *Insha'llah*—"if it is God's will," or more simply "God willing." Another common expression in everyday Arabic is *Alhumdulillah*, or "Praise God." Acknowledging God's supremacy over human beings or seeing oneself, correctly or otherwise, as carrying out God's will may lead one to assert "*Allah Akhbar!*"—"God the Almighty!" Of course, such phrases—"God willing, praise be to God, and Almighty God"—are by no means foreign to many devout or practicing Christians and Jews. The three religions are, after all, cut from the same Western religious cloth deeply grounded in Middle East traditions that extend over several millennia.

Muslims also have four other duties. One is to pray five times a day (dawn, noon, midafternoon, dusk, and before midnight but after darkness has set in), normally with head covered, shoes off, and kneeling on a carpet in the direction of the holy city of Mecca where Muhammad was born in 570 c.e. In earlier times, many Christians did much the same thing—in addition to prayer upon rising and going to bed at night, they prayed the *Angelus*, the call to prayer customarily signaled by the ringing of church bells at the beginning of the workday, at noon, and upon leaving the fields or other place of employment at dusk.

Another Islamic obligation is to give alms or charitable contributions, thus putting more abstract notions of generosity and humanitarianism routinely into practice. For those financially able, contributions should be at least 1/40th or 2.5 percent of one's total wealth; using total wealth rather than annual income as a base often means a much greater sacrifice by the truly wealthy than a tithe based on 10 percent of annual income typically required in some Christian or other religious communities. Moreover, one is to fast in daytime (from dawn to dusk) as an act of self-denial during the holy month of Ramadan. Finally, at least once in one's life, one should make the *Hajj*—a pilgrimage to Mecca in Saudia Arabia—if one can. The *Kaabah* is located there—a sanctuary or small cubelike structure in the Great Mosque of Mecca that contains the sacred black stone believed to have been given by God to the patriarch Abraham, father to both the Arabs and the Israelites.

God's guidance and the rules by which one is to live one's life are to be found not only in the *Koran* but also the life of Muhammad in the *Hadith* (sayings) and *Sunnah* (deeds) of the Prophet. Upon these sources rests the *Shariah*, or Islamic law, that extends beyond the mosque in many Muslim countries to society as a

Shariah ■ Islamic law

whole. To be a Muslim is to be "one who submits"—the meaning of *Muslim*—to the will of God. As with other religions, culture often matters in defining how Muslims actually practice their religion in daily life. How the *Shariah* is interpreted is also subject to cultural variations with some interpretations differing across the vast Islamic world.

Islam not only allows but also encourages trade and commerce so long as transactions between buyer and seller are just or equitable. Indeed, along with conquest, trade was a most important vehicle for the rapid spread of Islam to the far reaches of the world in the 7th, 8th, and subsequent centuries. In this understanding, so long as one is honest or just, to become wealthy through commerce is a good thing, pleasing to God. That said, much as in pre-Reformation Christian communities, making money through lending and charging interest is contrary to Islamic teaching. Mobilizing capital for investment through equity shares, joint ventures, or other creative approaches thus avoids direct loans for which interest would have to be paid.

The *Koran*'s opening command that one should read and thus educate the mind exemplifies the very down-to-earth nature of the religion. Islam is concerned with the affairs of day-to-day living, including both work and commercial activities. This interest in practicality underscores Islam's deep, religiously based commitment to knowledge and explains why Euclidian geometry and the writings of Plato, Aristotle, and other Greeks were retained throughout the Muslim period in Egypt and elsewhere in the Arab world long after the fall of the Roman Empire and the European "dark ages" that followed.

This created a favorable academic environment that no doubt contributed to discovering algebra and the concept of zero in mathematics; perfecting an ability to perform cataract removal and other delicate surgeries unheard of in Europe during the late Middle Ages; developing a medical art and science that understood details of human anatomy—skeletal, nervous, and circulatory systems. By the early 11th century Islamic scholars already had found fault with the ancient Greek Ptolemaic view of Earth as the universe's center, an understanding held long before formulations of a solar system offered by the Polish astronomer Nicholas Copernicus (1473–1543) and his later Italian counterpart Galileo Galilei (1564–1642). Consistent with this commitment to knowledge, great universities were established in Damascus, Baghdad, Bukhara, Seville and Cordoba in Spain, and Cairo (which became the intellectual center for Islam).

As with Hinduism, Christianity, and Judaism, Islam also has its sectarian divisions. Most Muslims are **Sunni**; however, most in Iran are **Shiah**, a division that dates from a dispute on succession to the Prophet in the century after Muhammad's death. Shiah Islam holds that Ali was selected by Muhammad as his successor, a claim disputed by Sunnis. Ali was succeeded in the line of the Prophet by other *imams* (leaders), the twelfth being Muhammad al Mahdi, whom Shiites believe disappeared but never died; his immanent presence is understood as a source of guidance to the present-day religious leadership.

Indeed, the Islamic clergy plays an important role, particularly in the Shiite understanding of Islam. The Shiites believe Mahdi eventually shall reappear one day to establish a new Islamic golden age. Although different in details, this belief is similar in some respects to the Judaic belief in the coming of a messiah or the

Sunni ■ largest of the two great divisions of Islam

Shiah ■ second largest of the two great divisions of Islam

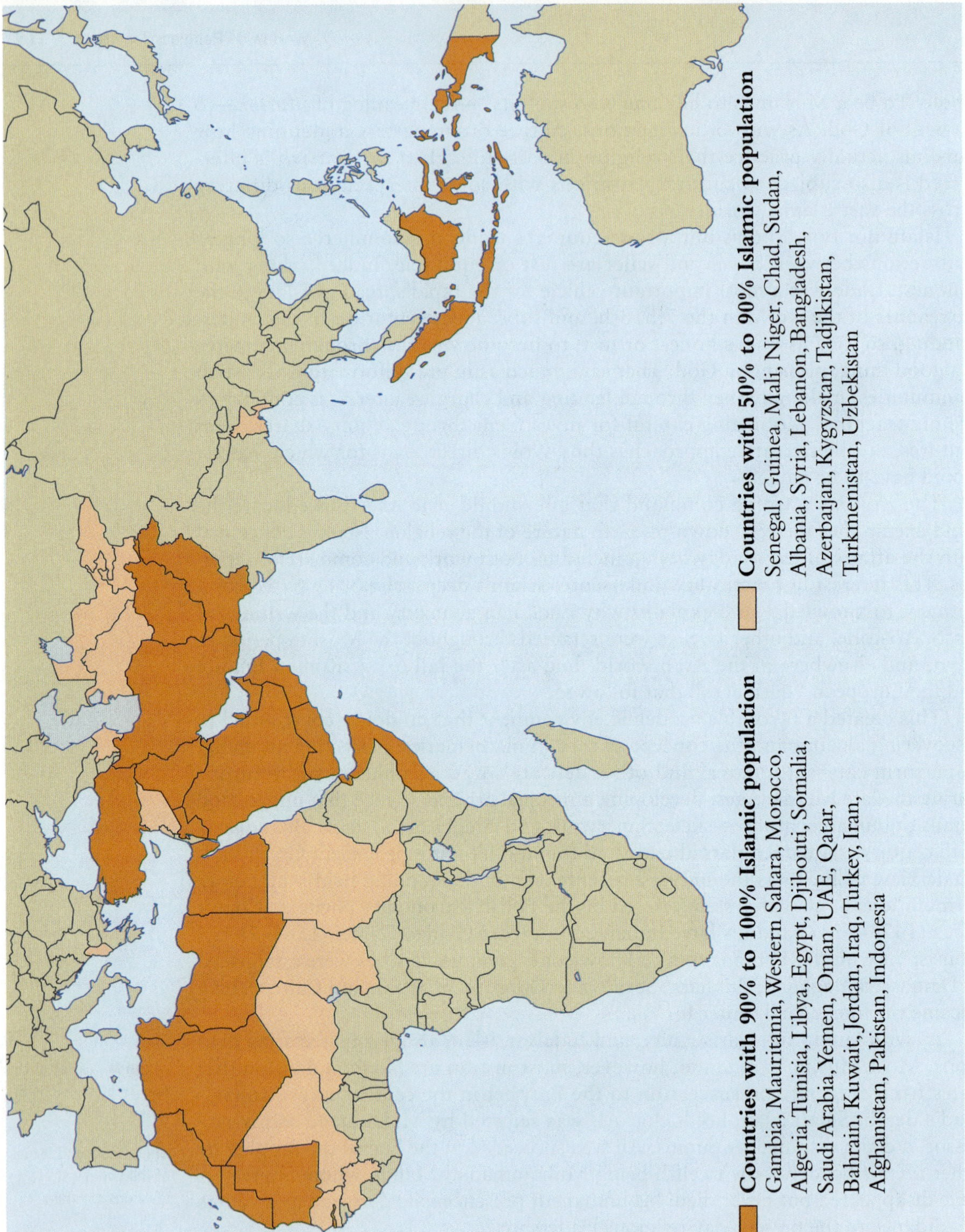

Countries with 90% to 100% Islamic population
Gambia, Mauritania, Western Sahara, Morocco, Algeria, Tunisia, Libya, Egypt, Djibouti, Somalia, Saudi Arabia, Yemen, Oman, UAE, Qatar, Bahrain, Kuwait, Jordan, Iraq, Turkey, Iran, Afghanistan, Pakistan, Indonesia

Countries with 50% to 90% Islamic population
Senegal, Guinea, Mali, Niger, Chad, Sudan, Albania, Syria, Lebanon, Bangladesh, Azerbaijan, Kyrgyzstan, Tadjikistan, Turkmenistan, Uzbekistan

FIGURE 4.3
The Islamic World

Christian belief in the second coming of Jesus (also accepted by Muslims). Most Sunnis, although they accept the second coming of Jesus, reject the Shiah belief in the immanent presence of Mahdi as heretical. With a few exceptions, Sunnis also place much less emphasis on the clerical role in daily life.

The **Wahhabi** sect in Saudi Arabia takes a very strict Sunni Islamic fundamentalist view and disagrees with the Shiah and Sufi (a more mystical approach) interpretations of Islam. Influences from other cultures and what they perceive to be false interpretations of the *Koran* are to be eliminated. Particularly in rural areas of the desert kingdom, clergy educate the populace religiously and enforce compliance with the *Shariah,* informed as it is by this particular interpretation of the *Koran, Hadith*, and *Sunnah*. Religious leaders authorized to do so from time to time when circumstances dictate may issue a decree (or *fatwah*) for religious guidance on various topics to include calling for *jihad* or holy struggle as against infidels, whether non-Muslims or Muslims who have strayed from their religious obligations.

Wahhabi ■ conservative Muslim group found mostly in Saudi Arabia

The establishment of *madrassas,* or religious schools, is seen by many faithful as a blessing. A large number are funded by Saudi Wahhabists in countries such as Pakistan where public schools are often poor or nonexistent, and the *madrassas* provide meals for the young boys who attend. The curriculum, however, essentially emphasizes the rote memorization of the *Koran* and only educates men. It was out of such *madrassas* that the leader of the Taliban, Mullah Omar, and a number of his associates emerged. While much is made of the potential of conflict between Islam and other faiths, of equal concern should be the internal struggle within Islam. Muslim fanatics, or *jihadists* like al-Qaeda, have carried out fearful acts of violence in the name of Islam, and voices have been raised that such persons are threatening to hijack Islam and use it to justify their extreme worldview.

NATIONS AND STATES

While the role of religion in international politics seemingly only recently has been rediscovered, the concepts of nation and state have been at the forefront of studies of global politics for years. These are examples of human geography: religion, nation and state—all social constructions. A certain amount of confusion, however, continues to exist over their meanings and the meanings of related terms.

4.3 Compare and contrast the concepts of nation, nation-state, and nationalism, and explain how they can be a source of conflict in global politics.

The terms *nation* and *state* are frequently used interchangeably as if they were synonyms. To use the terms this way, however, is to miss important differences. The term *state* is a legal concept that refers to a population administered by a government or other administrative authority on a given territory with a claim to sovereignty recognized by other sovereign states. Therefore a state is depicted as a geographical entity on a map and is an example of physical geography. When a particular state is composed of a single **nation** or people with a common identity, we enter the realm of human geography. We call it a **nation-state** because the people who compose the "nation" live on the geographic territory of that "state." Nation and state may be coterminous or overlapping, as in the United States where most of the people consider themselves to be American, notwithstanding the diversity of racial, ethnic, and cultural differences among them.

◉—Watch the **Video "Germany's Anschluss of Austria"** at **mypoliscilab.com**

nation ■ people with a common identity based on certain characteristics that distinguish them from other social groups

SLIDESHOW | Physical and Human Geography

This slideshow depicts two types of geography—physical and human. Oil, critical to the world economy, was discovered in Saudi Arabia in 1938. Until recent claims by Venezuela, the Saudi reserves were the largest in the world, accounting for one-fifth of the world's total.

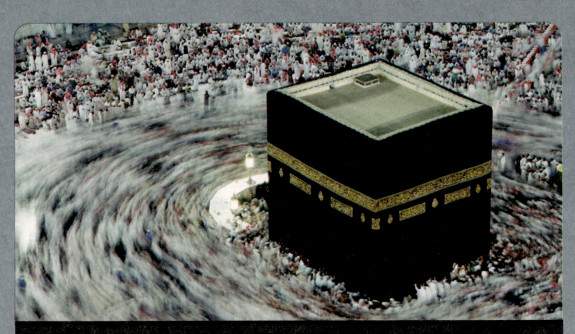

The Kaabah in Mecca, Saudi Arabia, is the most sacred site in Islam. The Koran states it was constructed by Abraham and his son Ishmael. A visit to it is part of the hajj or pilgrimage for Muslims. The concentration of Muslims in various parts of the world such as Indonesia, South Asia, and the Middle East is an example of human geography.

Geography plays an important role in a state's security. The development of long-range missiles by North Korea is of concern to neighbors such as Japan, but also the United States as North Korea continues to develop its missile capabilities.

War is the most destructive of all human activities. Whether a civil war or a war among states, its ravages can be depicted on a map of the world. In this photo an anti-Kaddafi rebel examines a military aircraft destroyed by NATO forces prior to Kaddafi's death.

Race refers to identifiable physical differences used to categorize people, whether or not individuals share a common identity. Although race can be a basis for identity, it is also a very problematic basis for establishing unity. Racial distinctions that are used to justify divisiveness, discrimination, or unequal treatment are common enough. In the extreme, racism can also lead to genocide—the mass murder of people because of their race or other identity. Because of this, many prefer not to draw racial distinctions among peoples at all; it is better from this perspective to identify only with the human race. Focusing on a common humanity avoids the scourge of racism that may come from accentuating separate identities based on physical or other differences.

The distinction between a nation and an ethnic group is often difficult to make. One reason is that the terms are subjective; people themselves are the ones who make the choice when they define their identities in either national or ethnic terms. Adding to the confusion, the two terms are frequently used interchangeably. In the United States, people tend to identify nationally as Americans while at the same time holding other ethnic identities that define them as individuals or groups within society.

Nationality involves a significant degree of self-definition and refers to a people with a sense of common identity, if not destiny. In other words, a nation is whatever a group of people says it is. This common identity may be the result of such diverse factors as race, ethnicity, religion, culture, shared historical experiences, or some combination of these. When this common identity has political consequences and serves as a basis for national mobilization, the result is **nationalism**.

Constructivists remind us that when we consider race, ethnicity, national, or other forms of identity, we are talking about social constructions. These distinctions do not exist in nature, but have become part of a human narrative. When we deconstruct these narratives, as postmodernists are prone to do, we find that physical or other differences are not decisive in drawing discriminatory distinctions. More often than not, they amount to establishing a community's own identity by defining an "other" as being somehow different.

Matters get even worse, of course, when this "other" community is described not only as different, but also inferior to one's own community—all of which has been constructed. Unfortunately, this is not just abstract, but as discussed below, becomes dangerous when different communities view themselves as mutually exclusive—having few, if any, links that would bring them together as fellow human beings. Intercommunal violence is often the expected outcome when policymakers foster these mutually exclusive constructions or allow them to simmer for years, perhaps decades or longer.

Nationalism

The birth of modern nationalism is generally traced back to the 18th century. More than a mere change of political regime and authorities, the French Revolution that began in 1789 was a watershed of political ideas and ideologies—some democratic and others authoritarian—that would take root throughout Europe and later spread primarily through colonialism throughout the rest of the world. The mobilization of the masses in politics, which had previously been the exclusive domain of upper classes or elites, was one important legacy; nationalism was another.

Local and even national identities were not new to Europe. In the 15th century, Machiavelli had written in *The Prince* that the ruler of the city of Florence, Lorenzo de Medici, needed to use his resources to unify Italy and thus avoid continual warfare among Italian city-states and invasion or other intrusions by France and Spain. Because they were without unity, Machiavelli observed rather emotionally that Italians had been "more enslaved than the Hebrews, more oppressed than the Persians, and more scattered than the Athenians." They were "without a head, without order, beaten, despoiled, lacerated, and overrun," having "suffered ruin of every kind."[2] Machiavelli is honored in present-day Florence for having been among the first advocates of Italian unity.

In fact, however, unification of Italy would have to wait until the 1880s. It was the French in their revolution and its aftermath who first put to practical use the notion of nationalism to inspire an entire nation of people to act as a unit. This idea dominated much of the 19th and 20th centuries.

In past centuries, French and English kings had raised armies to fight one another, but they had relied heavily on professionals or mercenaries in their employ. Departing from this tradition, Oliver Cromwell's "new model army" was raised from the general population during the 1640s to fight the king's forces in the English civil war. This very successful approach was used to fill the ranks of Napoleon's mass armies as they set forth on military campaigns across the European continent. The French employed a draft—conscription for national service (the *levée en masse*)—as an effective means to raise popular armies galvanized in their fervor by nationalism and nationalist appeals. It was a model followed in Europe and elsewhere, often with disastrous consequences, throughout the 19th and 20th centuries.

Nationalism can be a benign force or even make a contribution to peace, as when fostering a common national identity within a geographically bounded state, and is used to overcome conflicts in an ethnically or racially diverse population. Nationalism can be a basis for improving the welfare of the people within a state and society. It has also been used to unify a people and lead to the formation of a single nation-state, as was true in Germany and Italy in the 1870s and 1880s and Israel in 1948.

The Italian patriot and revolutionary Giuseppe Mazzini (1805–1872) and the Hungarian Jewish newspaper correspondent Theodor Herzl (1860–1904) are representative of writers in the 19th-century nationalist genre.[3] Mazzini argued that God had "divided humanity into distinct groups upon the face of our globe, and thus planted the seeds of nations." He wrote that Italians were a people "speaking the same language, endowed with the same tendencies, and educated by the same historic tradition" and Italy "the home that God has given us, placing therein a numerous family we love and are loved by, and with which we have a more intimate and quicker communion of feeling and thought than with others."

---

[2] Niccolò Machiavelli, *The Prince* (London: Penguin Books, 1961), Ch. xxvi.

[3] Quotes from Mazzini's *The Duties of Man* and Herzl's *The Jewish State*, as reprinted in Michael Curtis, ed., *The Great Political Theories*, vol. 2 (New York: Avon Books, 1962, 1981), pp. 237–248.

In a similar line of argumentation, Herzl asserted that Jews throughout the world "are a people—*one* people." He and fellow Jewish nationalists, or Zionists, referring to ancient biblical lands that were home to the Israelites, called for "restoration of the Jewish State." Observing that "no nation on earth has endured such struggles and sufferings," he saw "the distinctive nationality of the Jews" as best preserved within a Jewish state.

Early 19th-century nationalism in Latin America took the form of independence movements that ended Spanish and Portuguese empires there. Nationalist political movements in the 1940s, 1950s, and 1960s also succeeded in ending European colonial rule in most of Africa and Asia, thus creating new states in these geographic regions.

Nationalism, however, also can serve darker purposes when it is used at the expense of others and contributes to civil strife and warfare. In these circumstances, there is a mutual exclusivity or intolerance of differing national and ethnic groups. Extreme nationalism, often expressed by those feeling that their people have been oppressed, usually fosters an intolerance of others, particularly if they are seen as the oppressors.

In some cases, as in Germany during the 1930s, the extreme-nationalist appeal may take the illusory form that the oppressed are actually a superior people who have been downtrodden unjustly by so-called inferiors. Adolf Hitler's 20th-century ultranationalist and racist supremacy arguments went well beyond those of Johann Fichte (1762–1814) and other 18th- and 19th-century German nationalist writers. Hitler (1889–1945) and his National Socialist movement portrayed Jews, Slavs, Gypsies, and other non-Germanic peoples as racially and culturally inferior. Germans were said to be Aryans—a "master race"—who deserved to be treated as such and given the territory needed to expand and grow. In certain regions, this geographic expansion led to the elimination of the indigenous population. Nationalism pushed to this racist extreme was the rationale used in an attempt to "justify" Germany's aggression against non-German nation-states in World War II and the Holocaust, in which more than six million Jews as well as approximately five million Slavs, Gypsies, ethnic Poles, homosexuals, disabled, mentally ill, and others were murdered or worked to death.

Other ethnic groups have suffered from genocide as well. Beginning in 1894, nearly 200,000 Armenians were slain in two years by Turkish soldiers and police. In 1909 the renewed massacre of Armenians began again and ended only because of the intervention of outside powers, including the United States. Armenian support for the Allied cause in World War I led to the estimated elimination of one million Armenians. More recently, ethnic conflict in the African state of Rwanda resulted in the massacre of at least 500,000 Tutsi at the hands of the Hutus. Genocide in the former Yugoslavia has also claimed large numbers of Muslims, Croats, Serbs, and Kosovars as victims.

Countries that enjoy a relatively strong sense of unity, as is true for most Americans in the United States, tend to characterize additional identities among peoples as *ethnic* distinctions rather than seeing them as differences in nationality. Thus Native Americans, Hispanics, Jews, and other Americans of European, African, or Asian origin are referred to customarily as ethnic groups, although some Native Americans see themselves as "nations" within the United States. Whatever their differences, they still identify themselves as Americans.

In this usage, ethnic groups retain a separate identity within the larger, more ethnically diverse nation. Members of ethnic groups may speak the same language, share cultural values, or even have physical similarities; however, all of these groups still maintain an overarching or common national identity.

Although most French are of European origin, many of African or Asian derivation (often from local elites in 19th- and 20th-century French colonial populations) consider themselves as French nationals despite racial differences compared with those of European origins. More homogeneous as a nation-state than either the United States or France is Japan. Indeed, with the exception of a small proportion of Korean or other origin, most of Japan's population share a common language, history, culture, physical characteristics, and national identity.

Things get more confusing when we talk of a state made up of several "countries," as in the United Kingdom (U.K.), which is composed of England, Scotland, Wales, and Northern Ireland. States are countries, but not all countries are states. Although the Irish, Welsh, and Scottish communities are separate from each other, their Celtic identity differentiates them collectively from the English who descended from Angles and Saxons. Of course, these different identities are examples of what we've been discussing—social constructions that have come down over the centuries, in some cases millennia, to the present time (see Figure 4.4).

Scotland and England, which already had established dominance in earlier centuries over Wales and Ireland, did not unite as a single state until they finally became a united kingdom in 1707. English and Scottish monarchs were almost always at odds and had often been at war with each other. Although the United Kingdom is a single state, frictions and conflicts among the different national or ethnic groups continue to the present day. Scottish nationalists, a minority within Scotland, certainly see "Scottishness" as much more than a mere ethnic distinction. If they had their way, their country would again become a separate state. It remains to be seen whether the creation of Scottish and Welsh parliaments at the end of the 1990s as well as an Irish Assembly in Belfast to handle many regional affairs will satisfy nationalist sentiment or simply spur demands for even greater autonomy, if not complete independence.

Binational States

Very often two or more nations exist within the borders of a single state. After World War I, the victorious allied powers created a single Czechoslovak state from some of the territory that had been part of the just-defeated Austro-Hungarian empire. Physically the same people, Czechs and Slovaks shared the same language and, although there were some Protestants and Jews in the population, most were Catholics.

Of course this focus on physical, linguistic, and religious similarities overlooked significant cultural differences related to their separate development over some 500 years. Among other factors, for example, Czechs were subject more to Austrian and Slovaks more to Hungarian influences. Complicating reconciliation of these Czech-Slovak cultural differences were ethnic (at times "national") differences between Bohemian Czechs in the western part and Moravian Czechs in the eastern part of the present-day Czech Republic.

Separate identities between Czechs and Slovaks proved to be more than just ethnic differences, leading in 1993 to the formal breakup of Czechoslovakia into

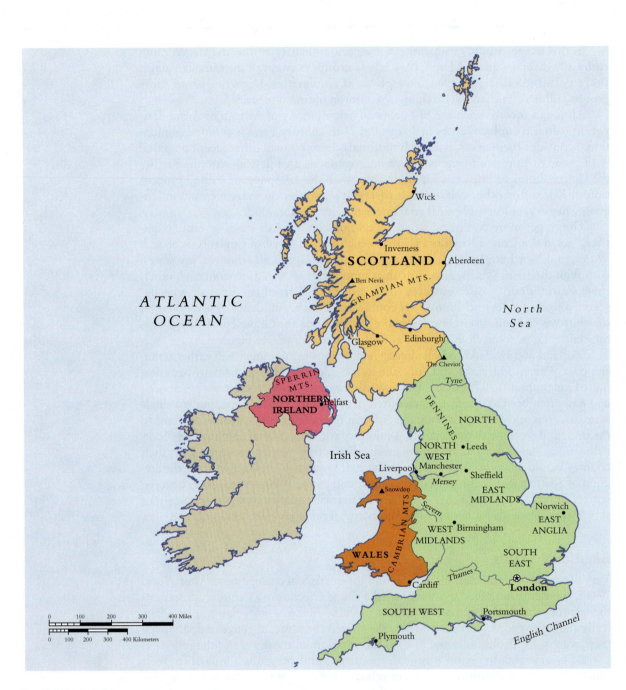

FIGURE 4.4

The United Kingdom and Ireland

Many people think when they use the term "England" they are referring to Great Britain or the United Kingdom. Actually, Great Britain is composed of England, Wales, and Scotland. The United Kingdom is composed of Great Britain plus Northern Ireland.

separate Czech and Slovak states. Czechoslovakia is thus an example of a *binational state* that has become separate Czech and Slovak nation-states.

There are other binational states, by contrast, that thus far have stayed together. One example is Belgium, with its separate Flemish- and French-speaking national groups. Some see the Belgian state as being composed of two separate countries or nations—Flanders to the north with its Flemish-speaking Flemings and Wallonia to the south with its French-speaking Walloons. Different language groups in a particular country usually are an indicator of diverse cultures with different histories and, as a result, separate national identities that tend to be reinforced by being concentrated in different geographic locations as in the case of Belgium.

Keeping Belgium together as a single state has been a formidable challenge for more than a century and a half. A common religious affiliation (most Belgians are Catholics) has not been enough. Indeed, the church in Belgium has come to reflect Flemish-Wallonian cultural differences. In such circumstances, choosing a common form of governance proved to be as difficult in the 20th century as in the 19th. In the winter of 1830–1831, the great powers meeting in London brought in a king from one of the German states (Leopold of Saxe-Coburg) in an effort to keep the country together. The monarchy of Belgium continues its efforts (as it has for over 170 years) to perform the same national-unity function. To accommodate aspirations of the different communities, the Belgian government has separate institutions that deal with education, labor, and other issues of importance to Flemings and Walloons.

Canada is yet another example of a binational state with its separate English- and French-speaking national groups. Some Canadians say "binational" is inaccurate because it excludes Canada's Inuit, the Arctic peoples, or other Native Americans referred to by many Canadian ethnologists as First Nations. In any event, the extent to which these peoples identify themselves as Canadians or choose instead to have separate national identities is a crucial distinction if we are to understand the complexity of the Canadian society. Of course, a feeling of national unity as Canadians, notwithstanding considerable national diversity, contributes to keeping the country together. In other words, as the Canadian example demonstrates, it is possible to have different levels of national identity. Thus one can be Canadian first and English- or French-speaking Canadian second. More troublesome for national unity, however, is when French- or English-speakers see themselves as separate (and separable) nations. In 1995, for example, a referendum in Quebec to create an independent state was barely defeated.

Multinational, Multitribal, and Multiethnic States

Switzerland is an example of a relatively successful multinational state composed of German, French-, Italian-, and Romansch-speaking Swiss. (Romansch, a language closely related to Latin, the language of the Roman Empire, survives among a minority of Swiss, mainly in the very mountainous area in the southeast part of the country.) The Swiss confederation allows a considerable degree of local autonomy, while still allowing broad Swiss identification.

In fact, Swiss citizenship is not established by the central government in Bern; it is determined instead by the canton (the state or provincial level) and more specifically by the local *Gemeinde* (to use the German word) or community of one's family at birth. Key to keeping the country together over centuries has been de-centralization of as many matters as possible. Over time, however, there has been agreement to collaborate in such matters as establishing a common currency and to cooperate centrally in other ways to promote commerce, maintain common defenses (although with considerable local authority), and conduct a common foreign policy.

Unsuccessful examples of multinational states include the former Soviet Union and the former Yugoslavia, both of which have broken apart into separate states since 1991. Given a changed international climate and much domestic turmoil after the end of the Cold War, national groups in both countries found that most of the obstacles to separatism had been either removed or weakened substantially. Use of coercive means to maintain unity—actions by the police and armed forces—failed in both countries.

FIGURE 4.5
The Ethnic Composition of the Former Yugoslavia

The rapid changes in Eastern Europe during the close of the 1980s intensified long-standing ethnic tensions in the former Yugoslavia. This figure shows where Yugoslavia's ethnic population lived in 1991 before internal conflicts escalated.

The boundaries of states in much of Africa, Asia, and Latin America were determined by divisions agreed upon by the former colonial or imperial powers for reasons often having very little to do with respecting national, tribal, ethnic, or other local identities. In fact, containing peoples with diverse identities within the same borders and establishing geographic boundaries that countered the homogeneity of groups allowed colonial powers to maintain control by capitalizing on these differences, thus making national unity against their rule more difficult to achieve. This was particularly true in Africa where in Nigeria, for example, boundaries of this former British colony include three separate tribal groups (Ibo, Yoruba, and Hausa-Fulani) that outnumber the populations of many countries. After independence and the departure of British administrators and security forces from Nigeria, civil war broke out there with fighting among tribal groups continuing into the 1970s. "Nigerian" as a national identity has proven to be elusive at best. People continue to identify by tribal group and resent advantages taken by some groups over others.

While one could call Nigeria a multinational state, it is referred to more commonly as a multiethnic or multitribal state. It is interesting to note that in the case of Africa, it is common to use the terms *tribes* and *tribalism* rather than nations and nationalism. For some observers tribalism carries negative (if not pejorative) connotations, while nationalism has more positive overtones. Hence the massacres that occurred in Rwanda in 1994 were ascribed to tribalism, whereas much of the slaughter occurring in the former Yugoslavia in the 1990s was generally attributed to Serbian or Croatian nationalism. Whether the different use of terms is an accurate reflection of regional or local preferences or instead is indicative of bias or ignorance on the part of the observer is often unclear.

tribalism ■ people with a common identity but often reserved for Africans

By no means are Nigeria and Rwanda isolated cases in Africa or elsewhere, especially in less-developed areas of the world. Divisions by tribe or clan in Africa are often much stronger than any pretense of national unity. To avoid civil war and other forms of ethnic strife as have occurred in places as diverse as Nigeria, Rwanda, Burundi, Ethiopia, Somalia, Chad, Liberia, and Sudan, postcolonial governments have tried with varying degrees of success to build working arrangements to manage this diversity.

While tribalism is associated with Africa, group identities in many countries throughout the rest of the developing world are often characterized in terms of ethnicity. Hence civil strife occurs involving Sikh, Tamil, and other religious and ethnic minorities in India and in Sri Lanka (the island state we've discussed above, known as Ceylon when it was part of British India). The potential for (or reality of) ethnic strife persists in Indonesia, Malaysia, and other multiethnic societies in South and Southeast Asia, as elsewhere in the developing world. Again, what is characterized as nationalism in Europe is often termed tribalism or ethnicity in other regions.

Neocolonialism refers to foreign influence by the former colonial power that persists despite an end to its physical, controlling presence. Although neocolonialism is sometimes criticized, some unity among elites has been found through their linguistic, cultural, and commercial ties with the former colonial powers, particularly in Africa and Asia. Quite apart from local identities along tribal, familial, or

neocolonialism ■ relations of economic, social, cultural, and even political dominance by a former colonial ruler of a now independent state

other ethnic affiliation, elites who initially came to power in these countries had developed strong European associations. To varying degrees they acquired either British, French, Belgian, Dutch, or Portuguese linkages that have been retained in the postcolonial period to the present day. As a practical matter, the European colonial language provided a means of communication across tribal and linguistic groups, particularly by elites. In addition, aspects of European social and political values were either blended with or grafted onto local cultures and customs.

English, for example, is the common language of the political, social, and commercial elites in both Indian and Pakistani societies. After World War II, when the British and local nationalists negotiated independence in India in 1947–1948, a decision was made to divide India and Pakistan along Hindu-Muslim lines as separate countries. This division did not accommodate the Sikhs' desire for a separate Punjab nation. Partition into different states did not prevent war, continuing tensions, and more recently, a nuclear weapons development competition between India and Pakistan. Moreover, partition still left India itself as a very heterogeneous society with many religious and ethnic divisions.

Nation-States and Nations without States

As noted earlier, it is possible for a nation to exist without being associated with a particular state. The Irish were a nation without a state until 1922, when nationalists finally were successful in establishing a separate state after several centuries of British rule. Omitted from the new Irish Republic, however, were six of the nine counties in the northern region known as Ulster. Protestant majorities in Ulster with their historical ties to Scotland and the English crown remained under British protection as part of the United Kingdom.

Although the strife in Northern Ireland is commonly understood as being strife between Catholics and Protestants, the conflict is really not about religion *per se*. Religious difference between the two communities is only a surface-level indicator of much deeper historical, cultural, and political cleavages underlying recurrent intercommunal strife. Great strides have been made toward peaceful relations between the communities in recent years. As an indicator of how much better things are, the political climate between London and Dublin made it possible for Queen Elizabeth to make a state visit to Dublin in 2011—a symbolic gesture of goodwill on both sides that would not have occurred just a few years ago. Still, some minority factions identified with the Irish Republican Army (IRA) remain discontent with any settlement that leaves a British presence in Ulster and, from time to time, still resort to violence.

Until the creation of Israel in 1948, Jews were dispersed in any number of countries (as they still are). The late 19th- and 20th-century Zionist movement sought a state, or at least a homeland, for Jews in the ancient biblical lands. The horror of the Holocaust of the 1930s and 1940s in which some six million Jews died in concentration camps primarily in Germany and occupied Poland contributed to the international decision to create a Jewish state in Israel. Although many ethnic Jews have chosen to retain American or other national identities, those who wish to make their homes in Israel have been able to emigrate there and formally become Israeli nationals.

ARGUMENT David A. Lake and Donald Rothchild argue that many popular explanations for ethnic conflict are incomplete or simply wrong.

A tremendous amount of literature has been produced on nationalism. Typologies abound, and numerous hypotheses, frameworks, and theories have been advanced to explain the origin of nationalism and the conditions under which it contributes to international conflict. David A. Lake and Donald Rothchild have developed an interesting framework and argument concerning the circumstances under which ethnic conflict arises within a state, which may result in civil wars and genocide.

Ethnic conflict is not caused directly by intergroup differences, ancient hatreds, or the stresses of modern life caused by a global economy. For them, intense ethnic conflict is most often caused by collective fears of the future. This occurs when states lose their ability to arbitrate between groups or provide credible guarantees of protection for groups. In other words, a crisis of confidence in the state or the actual specter of state failure is the key underlying factor they identify for the rise in ethnic conflict. The effects of international anarchy—fear and a feeling that self-help is the only option—take effect at the societal level of analysis. Groups may arm out of a sense of fear, but the result is to stimulate competition among groups, raising the collective fear factor even higher. Groups become suspicious of the intentions of other ethnic groups—the security dilemma is at work. State weakness, therefore, is a precondition for violent ethnic conflict within states, just as the absence of a superordinate authority in the international system of world politics is a permissive cause of war.

Once groups begin to fear for their safety, other factors come to the fore. Of particular importance is the rise of ethnic activists and political entrepreneurs who build on group fears. Political memories and historical symbols are stirred and utilized to whip up nationalist feeling and gain broader support. Once political minorities realize they cannot rely on the state for their protection, they usually look outward

to the international community for protection. The international response has been, in the minds of Lake and Rothchild, feeble and unconvincing; states are reluctant to intervene to end systematic, state-sanctioned ethnic killing. When they do, as in Rwanda in the mid-1990s, it is often after hundreds of thousands of people have already died.

COUNTERARGUMENT Stephen Van Evera has suggested that four primary attributes of a nationalist movement determine the potential to produce violence. First is the movement's political status: Is statehood attained or not? If national self-determination is denied, he argues this raises the risks of war in the international system. A struggle for national freedom can produce wars of secession, risking the conflict spilling over into the international arena. For example, at the time of his writing 15 of the 104 nationalities of the former Soviet Union had achieved statehood, but the other 89 had not. Chechnya is one example. Such stateless nationalities total approximately 25.6 million people, or 10 percent of the former USSR's total population. Furthermore, even if a nationalist movement successfully creates a new state, the seeds of future conflict may be planted if other groups are displaced. For example, Zionism's displacement of the Palestinian Arabs in 1948 set the stage for later Arab-Israeli wars as well as terrorist activities. Finally, successful nationalist leaders may reject the old "rules of the game" of interstate politics, creating regional instability.

The second factor that determines the potential of a national movement producing violence is the movement's stance toward its national diaspora (the dispersion or scattering of persons across different lands): If the movement has a national state, will it try to incorporate its nationals via territorial expansion or by encouraging immigration? The latter policy has been pursued after World War II by both German and Israeli governments. The territorial expansion route was pursued by pre-1914 pan-Germanism and by pan-Serbianism in the 1990s.

(continued)

The third factor is the movement's attitude toward other independent nationalities: Is it one of tolerance or hegemony? In other words, does the nationalist ideology respect the freedom of other nationalities or does it assume a right or duty to rule them? Hegemonic nationalism is the rarest and most dangerous variety. The obvious examples are interwar Nazi nationalism in Germany, fascist nationalism in Mussolini's Italy, and militarist nationalism in imperial Japan.

Fourth is the nationalist movement's treatment of its own minorities: Are the rights of minorities respected or abused? The nationalism of many immigrant nations (such as the United States and Canada) tend to be more likely to respect minorities. By contrast, nonimmigrant nationalisms tend to discriminate against or even suppress or oppress their minorities; for example, Iraqi and Turkish policy against the Kurds, China's actions in Tibet, and Serbian oppression of Slavic Muslim and Albanian (Kosovar) minorities, which contributed to the wars in the former Yugoslavia in the 1990s.

According to Van Evera, these four attributes constitute a "danger scale," highlighting the level of danger posed by any given nationalism. If all four attributes are positive or benign, such nationalisms may actually dampen the risk of war. Conversely, if all four attributes are negative or malign, the nationalism at issue is bound to clash with others, increasing the risk of war.

APPLICATION   For practical tips on how to actually go about facilitating compromise and—hopefully—eventually peace among parties in conflict, reference the material provided by the United States Institute of Peace (www.usip.org) Many of its pamphlets and practical toolkits are written by practitioners skilled in the art of diplomacy, prevention, mediation, and conflict resolution. What new ideas for facilitating compromise emerge from your reading? On this website you also can sign up for numerous eNewsletters and access relevant podcasts. ▶

Sources: David A. Lake and Donald Rothchild, "Containing Fear: The Origins and Management of Ethnic Conflict," *International Security*, vol. 21, no. 2 (Fall 1996): 41–75; Stephen Van Evera, "Hypotheses on Nationalism and War," *International Security*, vol. 18, no. 4 (Spring 1994): 5–39.

Palestinians and Kurds are two national groups, many of the latter having distinct tribal identities as well, without single states to call their own. The Kurds were promised a state in the peace settlements after World War I, but have remained dispersed in and near mountainous areas of Iran, Iraq, Syria, Turkey, Azerbaijan, and elsewhere in the trans-Caucasus region of the former Soviet Union.

Palestinians, a population with many highly educated people, live in a number of countries including Israel, Jordan, southern Lebanon, Syria, and the Gulf states. Palestinians also remain in the Israeli-occupied territories taken in the June 1967 war, primarily in and around Jerusalem and territory on the West Bank of the Jordan River, which is referred to by those Israelis laying ancient claim to the area as the biblical lands of Judea and Samaria. One also finds Palestinians in many cities throughout the Middle East, where they often hold highly skilled positions as well as providing clerical, information technology, and other commercial services.

Palestinians and Kurds, as minorities in the countries in which they live, have suffered from severe forms of discrimination. Turkish government policy at one time was to deny the very existence of Kurds as a separate national group, referring to them instead as "mountain Turks." As noted above, many Palestinians felt dispossessed of their homes and homeland in Palestine when Israel was established as a Jewish state in 1948. Aside from routine forms of discrimination, governments have conducted military campaigns and other attacks against Kurdish and Palestinian groups.

For their part, involvement in insurgent or terrorist activities by Kurds and Palestinians have added to hostilities, promoting further discord and no doubt encouraging further recriminations against them. At least in the Palestinian case, the 1990s witnessed a move toward a degree of political autonomy in the West Bank and Gaza strip. Terrorism, however, was continued by Palestinian factions such as Hamas. Most Palestinians hope that self-rule in areas of the West Bank will eventually lead to an independent Palestinian state with worldwide recognition of its sovereignty.

NATIONALISM AND ETHNICITY

The principle of national self-determination as a policy option asserts nations have the right to choose their political status, whether that be an autonomous unit within an existing state or a new state based on this common identity. This obviously entails some degree of political control over a geographic area. The principle, advocated by American President Woodrow Wilson and other leaders after World War I, was used as a criterion for determining the geographic boundaries of states in their efforts to redraw the map of Europe. The aim was to create new nation-states to take the place of the defeated German, Austro-Hungarian, and Turkish empires that had dominated East-Central Europe.

However well intentioned the principle was at its inception, national-self-determination has been abused. Hitler, for example, claimed in 1938 that the Sudetenland—that part of Bohemia in Czechoslovakia that was added to that nation's borders after World War I, which had a predominantly German population—should be a part of Germany. Hitler got his way at a 1938 summit conference held in Munich. After all, and quite apart from German aggressive designs on the territory of Czechoslovakia, supporters of the Munich concession could point to the arrangement merely as a line-drawing adjustment to post–World War I maps, an exercise consistent with the principle of national self-determination.

In recent years, with the seeming explosion of ethnic conflict within some states, the international community has been forced to come to terms with two conflicting principles: respect for territorial sovereignty of the state and the right of national self-determination. During the Cold War this was less of a problem. When political independence movements in the Third World struggled to end colonialism, they were not calling for the partition of a state but rather its complete independence from foreign rule. Leaders in emerging less-developed states agreed to respect colonial borders. There were exceptions: Tibetans in China, the Ibos in Nigeria, and Kashmir in India. Still, the one major successful breakup of an existing state during the Cold War occurred in 1971 when Bangladesh (then East Pakistan), with India's help, shattered the unity of Pakistan at the cost of tens of thousands of deaths and the flight of ten million refugees to India. The British formula in 1948 of creating alongside predominantly Hindu India two Islamic Pakistans—one "East" and the other "West" Pakistan—had now become two sovereign states, Bangladesh and Pakistan, respectively.

Limiting self-determination was actually endorsed unanimously by the U.N. General Assembly in the 1970 Declaration of Principles of International Law Concerning

4.4 Identify the different policy approaches to dealing with nationalism and ethnicity and identify their limitations.

✷ **Explore** the "Using Theory: You Are the New Prime Minister" at **mypoliscilab.com**

national self-determination ■ the assertion that nations have the right to choose their political status, which in practice often means the creation of a new state

Friendly Relations among States. This resolution sought to sustain the international stability resulting from reaffirmation of the primacy of the sovereign state over people on its own territory. The years since end of the Cold War, however, have seen substantial erosion of this idea. The outbreak of nationalist sentiment, particularly the unraveling of the Soviet Union with the recognition of the independence of the Baltic states and other republics in central Asia, set a different precedent: Self-determination could be achieved even at the expense of the unity of an existing state.

What was largely a voluntary and peaceful development in the former Soviet Union, however, played out quite differently as the former Yugoslavia broke apart in the early 1990s, spawning a series of Balkan wars accompanied by widespread civil strife. In the case of sub-Saharan Africa, during the Cold War both Moscow and Washington as well as former European colonial powers worked to keep their favorite strongmen in control as the two superpowers engaged in fierce global competition. In the 1960s and 1970s, China also competed for favor in Africa and elsewhere in the developing world. With the end of this political and military competition on the African continent, countries such as Zaire or Congo were no longer strategic battlegrounds, and outside powers seemed to lose interest in the fate of many of these ethnically diverse states. The exceptions were those states that contained valuable minerals within their geographic borders.

Maintaining Unity in Binational, Multinational, and Multiethnic States

With varying degrees of success or failure, several different strategies or approaches have been adopted to manage two or more nations within a given state. Keeping binational and multinational states together in intercommunal peace and mutual acceptance has proven to be a formidable task wherever it has been tried. What can be done to stem a potential tide of ethno-nationalist conflicts that threaten to undermine regional if not international stability?

Partition   Partition or formal separation can be used to stop or reduce national and ethnic strife, at least for a limited time. Separating national and ethnic groups into distinct, mutually exclusive communities—drawing solid-line boundaries around them—is at best a short-term approach or coping mechanism as long as they remain within a single state. It is not by any means a long-term solution to the problem of national and ethnic or racial strife.

Intercommunal fighting in Lebanon in the 1970s and 1980s, for example, could be stopped only by creating what amounted to strict territorial zones for different religious and cultural groups, policed by Syrian and other troops as well as multinational peacekeepers. At best, such informal or de facto partition could produce only a very fragile peace, which easily could (and did) break down again into intercommunal warfare. Similarly, *de jure* or formal, legal division into separate Pakistani and Indian states in 1948 did not resolve differences between Muslim and Hindu communities either. As already noted, hostilities (actual warfare or continual threat of warfare) have remained a fairly constant condition in Pakistani-Indian relations. These conflictual relations, moreover, have contributed substantially to efforts by both countries to acquire nuclear-weapons capabilities, which poses a threat to security in South Asia that goes well beyond differences between India and Pakistan.

Similarly, dividing peoples by national and ethnic identity into separate states in the former Yugoslavia did not promote peace. Civil strife became international war as each new state sought to expand or defend its territorial base. Not surprisingly, some of the worst fighting occurred in Bosnia, the state that was most ethnically diverse. These examples should give one pause when considering whether partition along religious-sectarian lines in Iraq will bring stability to the country. Furthermore, some of the most vicious fighting is among competing groups within the Shiah community.

One of the most severe examples of separation policies was racial division of blacks and whites in South Africa. Universally criticized for its injustice, South African **apartheid**, a policy of strict racial segregation, allowed a white minority to maintain a dominant position over the black majority. Moreover, as a white-dominated state, South Africa became isolated from neighboring black African states, giving the latter ample incentive to support antigovernment, black-nationalist groups in South Africa. Ending formal apartheid by the early 1990s, of course, did not resolve black-white problems, much less tribal and other differences within the black majority. Efforts were in fact taken in the 1990s to expose abuses by all parties during the apartheid period in an attempt to achieve reconciliation. As elsewhere, prospects for a long-term peace in South Africa rest instead on improved economic well-being and greater social tolerance or acceptance across ethnic communities, aspirations always much more easily stated than achieved.

apartheid ■ a state policy of discrimination and strict racial segregation in a society

Assimilation   Another strategy or approach, sometimes a very oppressive one, is **assimilation** of diverse populations into a single national grouping. This may entail denying that national differences exist at all or, if they do, denying their legitimacy as separate identities. Assimilationist policies were adopted in the Soviet Union during Stalin's time in an effort to "Russify" non-Russian peoples. The Iraqi government under Saddam Hussein conducted military campaigns to suppress or maintain control over the non-Arab Kurdish population in the northern part of the country. Turkish policies mentioned previously that denied Kurds a separate identity, referring to them merely as "mountain Turks," are another example of assimilationist policy.

assimilation ■ a strategy, often oppressive, to create a common identity among diverse peoples

The United States has also tried to assimilate diverse populations, establishing "American" as a common national identity. Earlier in its history, particularly in the 19th century, military campaigns were conducted to gain control over Native American populations, later placing them on reservations. This policy of formal exclusion gradually changed, as many Native Americans were encouraged to leave the reservations and become part of the larger American society.

Slavery in the United States lasted until the 1860s and effectively denied African Americans in slave states any degree of autonomy. Racial segregation policies that formally separated blacks from whites, particularly in the American South, survived into the 1960s. Segregationists did not intend that blacks should ever see themselves as a separate nation as many American Indians did; the goal of segregationist policies was to impose on blacks a separate (and lower) status within American society. Similarly, mainstream civil rights reformers opposed the few who advocated separation into different, racially distinct states or societies. The aim instead was racial integration, a view perfectly consistent with assimilationist strategy.

Consistent with the assimilationist idea, Indians are referred to in present-day parlance as Native Americans and blacks as African-Americans, in much the same way as European and Asian populations came to be identified as Polish-Americans, Irish-Americans, Italian-Americans, Norwegian-Americans, Japanese-Americans, Chinese-Americans, and so forth. There are those, of course, who object to any such hyphenation of the American nationality, preferring the complete assimilation or unity implied by the single term *American*. But those who want to retain ethnic identities as part of the American fabric, particularly those living in and identifying as part of ethnic communities, tend not to object to hyphenation or ethnic labels in which they take pride. Thus from this perspective to acknowledge explicitly that one is of Japanese, Finnish, Hispanic (or Latino) origin, for example, is still to be very much an American.

Wherever assimilationist policies have been relatively successful, adopting a common national identity has not necessarily meant dropping all other identities. There can still be unity in diversity. Separate ethnic and racial identities have survived, if not flourished, in the United States. The important point, however, is that almost all members of these groups still commonly identify themselves as "Americans." The common bond is a commitment to the idea of being an American or to the democratic ideals expressed in the national Constitution, not to any single or separate ethnic identity.

A commitment to multiculturalism allows for the richness of cultural diversity while still retaining an overarching national identity. It is when cultural diversity is interpreted as separatism that controversy ensues. One sees this in the United States in the debate over national language. Most assimilationists in the United States, for example, acknowledge that different ethnic and cultural groups have a right to speak Spanish, Mandarin or one of the other Chinese dialects, Italian, Vietnamese, or whatever. On the other hand, they voice opposition to giving other languages equal status with English. To be bilingual or multilingual is a matter of choice, not a requirement for other Americans who choose to communicate only in English. They refer to English as the traditional, spoken language in the United States that cuts across—and thus contributes to uniting—different ethnic, cultural, or other identities. The controversy is particularly acute in major cities such as New York and Miami or in the American Southwest where large numbers, in some cases approaching a majority, of people speak languages other than English.

Consociationalism in Multinational Unitary States

In a unitary state, all political power and authority come to rest in the institutions of a central government. Although almost all countries have at least one or more ethnic minorities in their societies, those coming closest to being single nation-states—states with one common or overarching national identity and lacking deep national and ethnic divisions—may choose to vest central government institutions with significant political power and authority. This is the case in France, Japan, the Scandinavian countries, the Republic of Korea, and most nation-states throughout the world.

On the other hand, when unitary states are composed of two or more nations or strong ethnic communities, a **consociational model** may be the means for maintaining peace and keeping the state together. Through agreements and formal rules that share or divide the powers and positions of government among different national and ethnic groups, consociationalism typically allows a maximum of local autonomy for the different communities within binational and multinational states.

consociational model
■ formal division of power among different national or ethnic groups

Prior to its breakdown into civil war in the 1970s, Lebanon was viewed by many as a model of consociational arrangements among different cultural communities. Strict rules were followed for several decades that allocated positions of political authority and representation among the different Christian and Muslim communities. It proved extraordinarily difficult to renegotiate these arrangements, partly because any such alteration was seen by many Christian Lebanese as undermining their position in favor of increasing the representation of one or another of the Muslim communities. Differences among familial and other factions vying for power in the different communities contributed to the complexity of recasting political relationships. The interests of outside states as diverse as Syria, Iran, and Israel made an already difficult problem next to impossible to resolve. Intercommunal bloodshed, direct and indirect interventions by outside powers, and *de facto* partition of the different communities ensued. Although consociationalism can contribute to unity and civility among diverse peoples within a state, the Lebanese example underscores how fragile these arrangements can be.

Belgian accommodation of different Flemish and Wallonian interests has required continual attention. Establishing duplicate governmental ministries, political parties, and even universities for the separate Flemish- and French-speaking communities is an approach consistent with the consociational model. A central government has remained in Brussels even as there has been considerable decentralization of political authority to the separate communities.

If diverse communities are to stay together within a single state, considerable efforts are required continually over time to refine, modify, correct, and legitimize these power-sharing and power-dividing arrangements. For this to work, political elites must be dedicated to maintaining the system as opposed to exacerbating ethnic tensions to their particular advantage.

Federal and Confederal Approaches As noted, unitary states establish single, centralized governments. By contrast, a federal state is one composed of separate state or provincial governments that have important functions to perform independently, but must coexist with a strong central government that may well take the upper hand on many matters. The United States is an example of a federation, although the reasons for Americans choosing federalism were not related to problems of nationality and ethnicity. The American rationale for establishing a federated state had more to do with distrust of unchallenged centralized power, geographic distances that were significant in the 18th century when the U.S. Constitution was written, and a desire to provide for security as well as some degree of local autonomy to states that had developed historically as separate colonies.

federalism ■ division of powers between states or provinces and the central government

In Canada, on the other hand, the rationale for federalism goes beyond such geographic and other concerns to provide a vehicle for managing differences between separate French-speaking and English-speaking communities. Thus francophone Quebec has a separate distinction and some local authority even as it remains part of the Canadian federation. Separatists, thus far still a minority, find present arrangements unsatisfactory. Efforts have been made, however, to accommodate the national and ethnic concerns they represent. Agreements have been made protecting separate language and cultural identities and allocating additional funds and more local authority over issues of importance to the different provinces. These agreements have served a similar function to the consociational arrangements discussed above, which is to keep different peoples together within a single (in this case, federal) state.

The terms perhaps can be best understood as different points on a continuum. The distinction between federation and confederation is not always clear-cut. Federations and confederations are both composed of states, republics, provinces, cantons, or other political units with their own separate governments. Confederations, however, have much weaker central governance than federations and put relatively more political authority at local levels. In short, **confederalism** takes a major step further in the direction of greater local autonomy through decentralization.

confederalism ■ weak central governments and strong political authority at state and local levels

Decentralized governance, for example, has been a key ingredient in Switzerland's success in keeping its Italian-, French-, German-, and Romansch-speaking peoples together in a single state—a confederation. Cantons the size of many American counties retain considerable authority over education, health care, law enforcement, and even the conveying of citizenship. Important functions are entrusted to central authorities—making a common foreign policy, planning for defense against invasion by outside powers, and maintaining the country's economic and monetary systems. Even these are subject to scrutiny by authorities representing local interests.

Rather than having a single president of the Swiss Confederation, for example, there is a seven-person presidency that (similar to consociational arrangements in some unitary states) assures representation in national councils of diverse interests among the different cantons. This is in addition to a national legislature constituted to bring representatives together to deal with issues that cannot be dealt with at the local (or cantonal) level. Important questions are frequently given to the people to vote on directly in a referendum. Such direct democracy is consistent with a "town meeting" tradition still practiced, particularly in smaller Swiss cantons.

The former USSR, or Union of Soviet Socialist Republics, formally had been a federation, even though in practice political authority always was concentrated within the central leadership of the Communist Party. Given this experience, breakaway national republics found even confederation too strong a set of ties for their political taste. With the collapse of the Soviet Union, the most that could be worked out at the time was agreement on establishing a commonwealth—a very loose association of sovereign states.

Outside Intervention, Social, and Economic Approaches

How can intercommunal conflicts be halted? Over a half century of experience in United Nations and other multilateral efforts to establish and maintain peace in places as diverse as Cyprus, the Sinai, and the Balkans, three functions have been identified. A first step is to establish peace. Diplomatic efforts to end fighting among the groups is the peacemaking function. An alternative or supplement to diplomatic efforts is peace enforcement—the threat or actual use of force by local or multilateral authorities as when actions are taken under U.N. auspices designed to stop the fighting and halt or at least reduce bloodshed among national or ethnic groups. This may be followed by peacekeeping, a maintenance function that typically involves monitoring or enforcing in a neutral fashion a cease-fire or peace already agreed to by the contending parties. The problem with all three, however, is that they are stopgap or short-term measures and do little to address the underlying causes of intercommunal strife.

As noted above, when the social orientation of human beings takes a turn toward the mutual exclusivity of different national, ethnic, or other group identities, we are usually observing a problem with deep psychological or social-psychological roots. From peace theory we learn that prospects for peace are greatest if there at least can be an acceptance or tolerance of people with diverse identities. Some degree of intercommunal tolerance or acceptance is a minimal condition for maintaining peace over time.

Of course, no easy remedy can be found to solve problems of national, ethnic, or racial strife. In the short term, we may need to draw lines on maps to partition or separate people just to keep them from fighting. Peace theorists do look, however, to a longer-run transformation of these solid lines that divide peoples (dividing them from one another in mutually exclusive categories) into dotted or permeable lines that allow for passage across intercommunal boundaries of people, their ideas, and economic resources. This prescription for peace is based on liberal principles. The idea is hardly new.

That there can be tolerance or acceptance of diverse peoples has roots in the 17th- and 18th-century Enlightenment, in the cosmopolitan sense of unity among peoples that prevailed in the Middle Ages, and in the ancient Greco-Roman Stoic idea that whatever our differences, it is common humanity that unites us. Such tolerance or acceptance of cultural diversity and different identities within, between, and across societies is a minimum condition for a durable domestic peace. Difficult as it may be to achieve, this intercommunal peace can be strengthened still further when social relationships go beyond mere tolerance to a higher level of mutual respect for diverse cultures.

A durable peace, of course, cannot rest on mere assertion, however pleasing or enlightened cosmopolitanism may sound. When it has been achieved it is the outcome of policies pursued patiently over time. Although peacemaking, peace enforcement, and peacekeeping provide security in the short term by stopping the violence and bloodshed of intercommunal strife, it is not enough merely to establish law and order through the use of force or otherwise. Two kinds of development—social and economic—are necessary to provide a firm, long-term basis for lasting peace among diverse peoples.

Social development means establishing over time a greater degree of mutual acceptance or tolerance among different peoples. It involves education, cultural exchanges, communications, and other constructive efforts that over decades tend to bring diverse peoples together. Commercial and professional ties, friendships, and marriages that cross intercommunal lines are indicative of a relatively high level of social development.

Social development involves values that are usually slow to change. Education of younger generations, reeducation of older generations, and building new human associations across communal lines are core tasks in social-developmental efforts. This is central to the social-constructivist perspective on identity, which is equally applicable to societal relations as it is to international relations. Social constructivism emphasizes the ability of people to redefine how they look at the world and hence their conception of how they relate to others. One's identity is not something one is simply born with, but is the result of interactions with society. As the term suggests, identity is a matter of social—that is, shared—construction.

Even so, measures intended to promote greater tolerance or acceptance proceed at a glacial pace, with progress measured only over decades. Older generations are least likely to change their outlook, particularly if they have experienced the human costs of civil strife or intercommunal warfare. Memories are long. Such memories often block the best-designed reconciliation efforts.

In such circumstances, peace practitioners adopt a patient stance, waiting for the eventual passing of older generations while, at the same time, hoping to foster cosmopolitan values among younger generations. To a considerable degree, this has been the approach followed in Western Europe after World War II. Even though old antagonisms have not been eliminated entirely, there is today an extraordinarily higher degree of tolerance or mutual acceptance than many would have thought possible among the Germans, French, British, Belgians, Dutch, Danes and other Scandinavians, Spaniards, Italians, Greeks, and others.

This Western European achievement did not just happen; it was the result of a decided effort to change the mutual exclusivity of national and ethnic mind-sets. European international organizations were established and expanded into what is now the European Union (EU). In addition to the specific purposes of particular organizations or channels of communication across national borders, the attempt was to go beyond the national and ethnic divisions that had contributed to the bloodshed of two major world wars in the first half of the 20th century.

Economic development that reduces disparities in levels of living among different communities is also an essential ingredient. It is difficult to have open frontiers when disparate economic levels on different sides of borders result in migration of large numbers of people from poorer countries or areas to richer ones.

Even the better-off economies of advanced industrial countries have limits on how many immigrants they can absorb before suffering real economic costs. This is as true in North America as in Europe. Thus attempts have been made to restrict the flow of labor from Mexico into the United States. In Europe during the early post–Cold War years, limits were placed on flows of people from Eastern countries moving to Germany and other highly developed Western countries. Only when levels of economic development become somewhat less disparate (if not equalized) is it conducive to open borders fully with unrestricted movements of peoples. In the case of Europe, there is no doubt that immigration from the developing world has exacerbated tensions at a time when many economies are in difficulty. No one expects many African states, for example, to achieve a level of economic development sufficient to encourage those without economic prospects to stay home.

The problem is that we are talking, in some cases, of no less than a long-term international endeavor and commitment to save failed states and their peoples. In this regard, some advocates favor an international "conservatorship" to administer critical government functions of "failed states" until the country can govern itself. But how long might that take if ethnic war has destroyed the social and economic infrastructure? How patient would outside powers be? Even if basic state functions are reestablished, how can the memories of ethnic violence be muted in the case of those who have witnessed atrocities perpetrated on their communities?

Some may think, therefore, that relying on social and economic development over time is simply a utopian approach to countries ravaged by ethnic conflict. It may be. On the other hand, to proceed as if national and ethnic strife are insoluble problems becomes a self-fulfilling prophecy. Although there is no certainty that social and economic development conducted in a physically secure environment will put national and ethnic strife to rest, the degree of civility among nations that has been achieved in Western Europe supports the view that such social and economic development policies can be fruitful.

CONCLUSION

Without a basic understanding of the earth's physical and human geography, it is difficult to understand the significance of current international events. This is why this is designated a toolbox chapter. Mahmud is like many students who have studied overseas in that they develop a much better grasp of the physical and cultural diversity of the world. How can one understand what is unique about one's country or culture unless one has some basis of comparison?

The growing importance of religion and the continual relevancy of nationalism are essential aspects of the cultural geography of world politics, yet are also associated with geographic locations. Witness, for example, the importance of Saudi Arabian oil fields and the important role that Islam plays in that region. While Islam tends to grab the headlines in the West, the reality is that aside from Europe many parts of the world have seen an increasing relevancy of religion in the realm of both domestic and international politics. Any student who aspires to work in government, business, or international and nongovernmental organizations must grasp at least the basic dynamics of these phenomena.

From the perspective of many realists, nationalism, or serving the national interest, is perhaps the single biggest reason the state will continue into the indefinite future. Crises of authority may cause a state to be torn in two, but the result will be the seceding territory joining a neighboring state or the creation of a newly independent state. Similarly, if a state motivated by extreme nationalism and an expansionist ideology successfully conquers a neighbor, the result is simply a larger state. The point is that whether nationalism helps to keep a current state together or tears it apart, the end result is the same—a state. Nationalists are not interested in transferring power and sovereignty upward to an international organization, let alone a world government. They also are suspicious of regional associations among states, which helps to account for the fact that even in the European Union people still tend to call themselves Germans, French, or English first, not "European." Younger generations, however, have been somewhat more prone than their parents and grandparents to adopt a European identity first.

Liberals also recognize that nationalism is a primary cause of conflict in the world. But they tend to be more optimistic about the possibility of taming nationalism. This will not happen by either avoiding or somehow transcending politics; it will happen *through* politics. Following the logic of the social constructivists, people can learn from the past and from past mistakes and internalize new norms. International organizations and regimes can facilitate the more orderly conduct of interstate relations. Nongovernmental organizations and the growing global civil society provide other voices for moderation in the relations among peoples. The state will not wither away, as predicted by orthodox Marxists and idealistic world federalists. The state and the people it encompasses within its borders likely will continue to be a major focus of identity. But that does not

✓—[Study and **Review**
the **Post-Test & Chapter
Exam** at mypoliscilab.com

mean necessarily that the state's function is to be the vehicle for expressing national prejudices against other states and peoples.

Nationalism and religion, therefore, are two of the most significant phenomena in world politics. Perhaps the ideological competition between East and West after World War II obscured the ongoing relevancy of religion in other parts of the world. Certainly with the end of the Cold War after the events of 1989, the suppressed nationalisms of Central and Eastern Europe (to include the former Soviet Union) burst forth. On the one hand, nationalism can be a force for unity and solidarity and be supportive of democracy. On the other hand, it can also tear a society apart. Nationalism can buttress existing political authority or be the rallying cry of those who wish to overthrow it. It can be a progressive as well as a repressive force, fostering at the same time unity at home and wars of aggression abroad. As we have seen, the constitutive elements of nationalism vary from case to case. Despite its importance and the amount of research and thought conducted on the subject, it remains complex, elusive, and often difficult to grasp.

LEARNING OBJECTIVES REVIEW

4.1 Explain the differences between physical and human geography and why a basic understanding of both is necessary when studying international relations and world politics.

Physical geography involves the depiction of material manifestations of terrain such as continents, mountains, rivers, lakes, and oceans. Human geography, on the other hand, involves the visual depiction of human activities overlaid on physical maps. What both have in common is a graphic representation of spatial concepts. Without such basic understanding, it would obviously be difficult to understand political and economic trends in international relations and world politics, let alone make sense of day-to-day events.

KEY TERMS
Physical geography 102
Human geography 102
Territoriality 103

Cartography 103
Geopolitics 105
Demography 106
Identity politics 107
Social constructivism 108

ADDITIONAL READINGS
Dan Smith, *The Penguin State of the World Atlas*, 8th ed. (New York: Penguin Books, 2008).
  The visual depiction of data includes population, religion, wealth, wars, military spending, refugees, human rights abuses, women's rights, health, and the environment.
Andrew Boyd and Joshua Comenetz, *An Atlas of World Affairs* (New York: Routledge: 2007). International issues and conflicts since the end of World War II (1945) are placed in their geographical contexts through the integration of over one hundred maps.

4.2 Evaluate the impact of religion in global politics, particularly with regard to conflict.

Observers of international relations almost universally failed to foresee the significant challenge to modern, secular regimes posed by a global resurgence of religious ideas and movements at the end of the 20th century. Established transnational religious organizations but also the more extreme elements that preach religious intolerance have taken advantage of modern means of communications, strengthening the development of transnational identities not constrained either by state borders or secular nationalism. If such a trend continues, its implications for global conflict are uncertain. Realists, liberals, English School theorists, and economic structuralists take different positions on the role of religion in domestic and international politics from constructivists, feminists, postmodernists and critical theorists, who see religion through different interpretive lenses.

KEY TERMS
Religion 108
Polytheism 114
Monotheism 116
Shariah 118
Sunni 119
Shiah 119
Wahhabi 121

ADDITIONAL READINGS
Joanne O'Brien and Martin Palmer, *The Atlas of Religion* (Berkeley and Los Angeles: University of California Press, 2007). Maps the nature, extent, and influence of each of the major religions and shows, country by country, how religions are spread, how they relate to government, laws, and world hunger, and the role they play in wars. It also locates the origin and the sacred places of each of the major religions and provides essential background with a valuable table showing the fundamental beliefs of Buddhism, Christianity, Hinduism, Islam, Judaism, Sikhism, and Taoism.

Karen Armstrong, *Islam: An Introduction* (New York: Modern History, 2000). Traces the development of Islam from the 6th-century days of the Prophet Muhammad to the present, arguing that the picture of Islam as a violent, backward, and insular tradition should be laid to rest. Maps show the geographic ebb and flow of Islam, and there is also a useful historical timeline and a guide to the key figures.

4.3 Compare and contrast the concepts of nation, nation-state, and nationalism, and explain how they can be a source of conflict in global politics.

The separate identities peoples construct result in nations coterminous with states of which they are a part—nation-states, binational or multinational states, and, in some cases, nations without states. The liberal idea of national self-determination, if pursued to its logical extreme, would produce a world composed of many more states than exist today, but creating ever-smaller entities is not always in the interests of the populations who may have more to gain from greater national diversity, larger markets, and greater economic and other resources available in larger states.

KEY TERMS
Nation 121
Nation-state 121
Race 124
Nationalism 124
Tribalism 131
Neocolonialism 131

ADDITIONAL READINGS
Elie Kedourie, *Nationalism*, 4th ed. (Oxford, UK: Blackwell, 1993). One of the best resources for a historical overview of the rise of nationalism.

Walker Connor, *Ethnonationalism: The Quest for Understanding* (Princeton, NJ: Princeton University Press, 1994). Despite its publication date, this anthology remains one of the best in unraveling the complexities of nationalism and ethnicity.

4.4 Identify the different policy approaches to dealing with nationalism and ethnicity and identify their limitations.

The concept of national self-determination refers to the principle that nations have the right to determine their own political status, which might include the creation of a new nation-state. This principle has clashed with the concept of state sovereignty and can thus potentially result in political violence and even civil wars. Approaches to maintaining unity within existing multinational states include political ones (partition, assimilation, consociationalism, federalism, confederalism, outside intervention to include peacekeeping missions) as well as social and economic programs. All have their limitations, but pursued effectively in tandem may succeed in reducing intercommunal strife.

KEY TERMS

National self-determination 135
Apartheid 137
Assimilation 137
Consociational model 138

Federalism 139
Confederalism 140

ADDITIONAL READING

Chester A. Crocker, Fen Osler Hampson, and Pamela Aall, eds. *Leashing the Dogs of War: Conflict Management in a Divided World* (Washington, DC: US Institute of Peace, 2007). An excellent overview of the sources of contemporary conflict and multiple perspectives on how best to prevent, manage, or resolve conflicts around the world.

CHAPTER REVIEW

1. Physical geography can deal with the graphic representation of
   a. mountains.
   b. rivers.
   c. oceans.
   d. all of the above.

2. Human geography can deal with the graphic representation of
   a. populations.
   b. religions.
   c. size of economies.
   d. all of the above.
   e. none of the above.

3. Geopolitics involves
   a. the politics of geothermal energy.
   b. understanding the national power almost exclusively in terms of physical geography.
   c. how politics influences our understanding of geography.
   d. none of the above.

4. Religious conflicts tend for the most part to be about
   a. religious doctrine.
   b. quarrels among religious leaders.
   c. different religious identities and politics.
   d. theological differences.

5. At the beginning of the 21st century, religious ideas and movements
   a. take second place to political ideology.
   b. are basically irrelevant in modern materialistic societies.
   c. are constrained by international organizations.
   d. have seen a general global resurgence.

6. According to Samuel P. Huntington, the clash of states will be replaced by
   a. clash of NGOs and the state
   b. clash of IOs and the state
   c. clash of civilizations
   d. none of the above

7. All of the following are considered to be duties for Muslims EXCEPT:
   a. pray five times a day and, if one can, make a pilgrimage to Mecca once in one's lifetime.
   b. recite the Sunna once a month.
   c. give charitable contributions—one-fortieth of one's wealth each year.
   d. fast (not eat) during the day in the holy month of Ramadan.

8. Terms used to describe the way the world is conventionally divided include all of the following categories EXCEPT:
   a. nation-states.
   b. multinational states.
   c. nations.
   d. ethnic groups.

9. The term "ethnic group" is often used to refer to a
   a. tribe.
   b. clan or extended family.
   c. people with a separate identity within the nation or society.
   d. church organization.

10. Nationalism is
    a. an ideology that mobilizes national identity.
    b. the same as ethnicity.
    c. inherently dangerous.
    d. patriotism.

11. Binational states include all of the following EXCEPT:
    a. Germany.
    b. Belgium.
    c. Canada.
    d. the former Czechoslovakia.

12. An unsuccessful multinational state that has broken apart is each of the following EXCEPT:
    a. the Soviet Union.
    b. Yugoslavia.
    c. Czechoslovakia.
    d. Belgium.

13. Nations without states
    a. are banned under the Charter of the United Nations.
    b. are given voting status in the U.N. General Assembly.
    c. are only represented in the European Union.
    d. at times have achieved statehood.

14. Neocolonialism is associated with all of the following EXCEPT:
    a. influence of former colonial rulers.
    b. maintaining elite ties between European countries and their former colonies.
    c. compensating former colonies for previous injustices committed by Europeans.
    d. sustaining European social and political values among former colonial elites.

15. Nationalities or nations without a state include all of the following EXCEPT:
    a. Basques.
    b. Armenians.
    c. Kurds.
    d. Palestinians.

16. Donald Rothchild and David Lake feel that the main cause of ethnic conflict is
    a. fear of the future.
    b. intergroup differences.
    c. ancient hatreds.
    d. economic differences.

17. The social process whereby various ethnic groups are merged under a new identity is called
    a. integration.
    b. assimilation.
    c. consociationalism.
    d. cultural genocide.

18. Another term for a state in which all political power and authority come to rest in the institutions of a central government is
    a. communism.
    b. totalitarianism.
    c. dictatorship.
    d. unitary state.

19. States composed of two or more nationalities and which through agreements and formal rules share or divide powers and positions of government are said to be
    a. mixed.
    b. consociational.
    c. confederations.
    d. decentralized governments.

20. States in which separate state or provincial governments have important functions to perform independently or share with a central government are called
    a. mixed political-economy states.
    b. consociational states.
    c. federal or confederal states.
    d. decentralized states.

Globalization

"A world-economy, capitalist in form, has been in existence in at least part
of the globe since the sixteenth century. Today, the entire globe is operating
within the framework of this singular social division of labor we are calling
the capitalist world-economy." —Immanuel Wallerstein, Social Scientist

LEARNING OBJECTIVES

5.1 Identify the key economic, social, and cultural aspects of the globalization, the role of technology, and assess both positive and negative implications for the human condition.

5.2 Trace the historical emergence and development of capitalism as a worldwide form of political economy,

identifying its principal attributes and progressive globalization.

5.3 Explain attempts at global governance in the post–World War II era to deal with trade, finance, and investment resulting from rapid globalization.

Read and Listen to **Chapter 5** at **mypoliscilab.com**

Study and Review the **Pre-Test & Flashcards** at **mypoliscilab.com**

The World Economic Forum is an independent international organization committed to improving the state of the world by engaging business, political, academic, and other leaders of society to shape global, regional, and industry agendas. Each year a different theme is emphasized as participants gather in Davos, Switzerland, a splendid mountain resort tucked away in the Alps. Even entertainers like Bono of U-2 fame have addressed participants on issues of burning concern to them—in his case the plight of the poor and the deprivations they suffer—hunger, disease, and short life spans.

While the principal theme may vary, the ongoing agenda deals with key global challenges such as building sustained economic growth, mitigating global risks, promoting health for all, improving social welfare, and fostering environmental sustainability. The theme of the 2011 meeting was "Shared Norms for the New Reality." This topic was selected to acknowledge that we are living in an increasingly complex and interconnected world in which an erosion of common values and principles have come to undermine public trust in leadership, future economic growth, and political stability.

Speakers included the prime minister of Japan, the chancellor of Germany, the presidents of France and Russia, and the Secretary-General of the United Nations. But private citizens and NGOs were also well represented. There were speakers from Transparency International, an anti-corruption NGO; a taped message from human rights advocate Aung San Suu Kyi of Burma; philanthropists Bill and Melinda Gates, who pledged $100 million to wipe out polio; and even the former goalkeeper of the German national soccer team. The debates are carried on YouTube, the photos on Flickr, and key quotes on Twitter.

The World Economic Forum also has drawn strong criticism from antiglobalization protestors who see the gathering as little more than blather, pomp, platitudes, and the opportunity for the rich and famous to hobnob with one another and feel good about their expressed concern for global issues.

globalization ■ The continual increase in transnational and worldwide economic, social, and cultural interactions that transcend the boundaries of states and the resultant political implications. These interactions are aided by advances in technology.

5.1 Identify the key economic, social, and cultural aspects of the globalization, the role of technology, and assess both positive and negative implications for the human condition.

👁—⎡Watch the **Video "Zimbabwe's Economic Crisis"** at **mypoliscilab.com**

The World Economic Forum perfectly captures the diversity of reactions to **globalization**. This last toolbox chapter takes up this important topic. Its key aspects will be discussed in turn—economic, social, cultural, the impact of technology, and political ramifications. This will be followed by an in-depth look at the historical development of what most observers consider to be the hallmark characteristic of globalization—the development and expansion of a capitalist global economy. We then examine attempts by policymakers and practitioners to develop mechanisms of global governance to deal with globalization in the areas of trade, finance, and investment. We end with an overview of globalization and the developing world.

CURRENT DYNAMICS IN GLOBALIZATION

Globalization is a shorthand term for a multifaceted phenomenon. Given its complexity, its component elements have to be examined sequentially. We begin with technology as this tends to permeate the economic, social, and cultural aspects of globalization.

Technology

Globalization owes much to great advances in technology, especially in transportation, communications, and related technologies. Widespread application of these technologies has already transformed the ways in which we do business and interact with each other. In trade we now engage in global marketing, sales, and delivery of goods and services; in finance we transfer large amounts of money instantaneously across the globe. According to "Moore's law," the number of transistors that can be put on a single computer chip doubles roughly every eighteen months.

This expansion of computing capacity has enhanced substantially human capability to process and store data, making it available to government, business, and households. Instead of each user having to maintain its own information technology (IT) infrastructure, a shift to "cloud services" (Amazon's AWS Cloud, Microsoft's Azure, Google, Rackspace, Apple's iCloud) is underway, making access to computing power more cost-effective and efficient.

Accessing stored data in a cloud through internet-enabled applications such as Apple iTunes or Amazon eBooks can be accomplished by almost any desktop or mobile device anywhere in the world. These facilities are moving well beyond limited access, expanding the numbers and kinds of applications and data stored, as it were, in cyberspace. Such clouds—business or personal document and data archives that can be accessed online—are actually located in data centers filled with hundreds of thousands of servers. As their processing power has soared, cost has plunged, with availability even to small, private users expanding dramatically. Although files stored in a cloud are secured to some degree, the activities of sophisticated hackers create important security and privacy challenges for government, proprietary, and other sensitive data.

For the individual, an investor no longer needs to utilize a broker to buy or sell his or her mutual funds, but can engage in financial transactions via the internet from the comfort of home. We can even be thousands of miles away and use our local bank's debit card to get cash from an ATM in Bangkok or use our smartphone to pay the fare on London's Underground. We can now download to our computers and mobile device "apps" such as those from the Apple Store, which offers more than 300,000 of them. Users of Facebook install such apps at the rate of twenty million a day. Individual entrepreneurs can try out new ideas for online businesses without worrying about brick-and-mortar start-up costs—building or paying rent for large commercial work spaces when home or other relatively small offices may suffice, much less showrooms for the display of merchandise now marketed online.

We use computers (and supercomputers) in analysis of data and exchange information globally through the internet and other media. Free software called Hadoop allows ordinary PCs to analyze huge quantities of data that before required a supercomputer. Data are parceled out to numerous computers, which saves time and money. The *New York Times*, for example, used Hadoop and cloud computing to convert over 400,000 scanned images from its archives dating from 1851 to 1922. Companies such as Wal-Mart can now handle more than one million customer transactions every hour, feeding databases estimated at more than 2.5 petabytes. This is equivalent to 167 times the number of books in America's Library of Congress. The company's inventory management system enables suppliers to see the exact number of their products on every shelf of every store, and the rate of sale by hour, by day, and over the past year. The manipulation of large data sets has other uses, such as predicting when machines may break down, allowing for preventive maintenance, and hence saving dollars or Chinese yuan.[1]

Video teleconferencing has been a staple of major business corporations for years, allowing meetings to be held that include executives and marketing managers located all over the world. But as the quality of video transmission has advanced, we have reached the point where video teleconferencing also allows buyers and manufacturers located on opposite sides of the globe to examine the color of a cloth and even the stitching on a garment.

The gradual development of new communications technologies began in the mid-19th and early 20th centuries with the development of the telegraph and then the telephone (carried by above- and below-surface wires and even undersea cables linking continents); radio and radar; and, by the late 1930s and 1940s, the development and marketing of black-and-white television. Color television and vacuum-tube, mainframe computers emerged in the 1950s and 1960s, enhanced by the development in the 1960s and 1970s of transistors and solid-state technologies that largely replaced reliance on vacuum tubes in computers and most communications applications. Use of Earth satellites developed since the late 1950s for military and commercial purposes was enhanced by new semiconductor, microchip, and related microelectronic technologies in the 1980s and 1990s, pushing computers and telecommunications to ever-higher levels.

Advances in wireless technology went well beyond earlier walkie-talkies and limited-range field telephones to mass marketing in the 1990s of portable, handheld

---

[1] "Data, Data, Everywhere: A Special Report on Managing Information," *The Economist*, February 27, 2010, pp. 3, 8.

cellular telephones for routine domestic and limited transnational use—satellites even allowing global communications for those able to afford this extended, world-wide coverage. These new technologies, of course, also have found their way into vehicles of every sort as well as the navigation and communications machinery of transportation systems on land, at sea, and in the air. A far cry from using sextants and other mechanical means, radio, radar, or electronic-based devices for measuring the location of a ship or airplane, Earth satellites can now be used with extraordinary accuracy in determining precise geographic position at any point in time.

Transmission via satellite of telephone, radio, television, and other electronic signals has literally made routine a diverse variety of worldwide links of human beings that outside of science fiction were inconceivable to most people just two or three decades ago. Sometimes portrayed as an "information superhighway," the internet or World Wide Web emerged for widespread use in the 1980s and 1990s. It is amazing to realize that the first truly user-friendly operating system hit the market in 1990, allowing people to use a dial-up modem, connect their 64K computer to their telephones, and send e-mails around the world.

This development allows a great deal of work to be parceled out anywhere in the world, rendering geographical distances irrelevant. Two professors, for example, can work on an international relations textbook with one living in Washington, DC, and one in Colorado and Hawaii. We can expect that most of the limitations on the technology's bandwidth and speed will be overcome in the next five to ten years, substantially enhancing information transit in all modes.

CASE & POINT | Five Forces That Flattened the World

CASE The past thirty years have seen almost unimaginable technological and political changes that have spurred the globalization process:

1. *Late 1980s:* common Web-based standards are developed allowing software applications to communicate with one another
2. *Fall of 1989 and collapse of communist regimes:* tipped the balance of power across the world to those advocating democratic, free-market-oriented capitalism and encouraged expansion of Microsoft's Windows operating system
3. *August 1995:* Netscape, developer of the browser, goes public as a company
4. *1990s:* free open-source software such as Apache aids online collaboration; example: Wikipedia
5. *1990s:* technological developments in telecommunications allow for information outsourcing to call centers in India and elsewhere

POINT The *spread* of these technologies had little, if anything, to do with states. It was companies in the private sector who took many of the technologies developed by states (World Wide Web, telecommunication satellites) and developed applications and enhancements to become drivers of much of the economic and social developments in the current era of globalization. ▲

Source: (*New York Times* journalist Thomas Friedman discusses these forces of globalization and others in his book *The World Is Flat: A Brief History of the Twenty-First Century* (New York: Farrar, Straus and Giroux, 2005).

Economic Impact

For some academics, pundits, and analysts of international relations and world politics, globalization is a relatively recent phenomenon. After all, the concept of globalization did not even exist in mainstream literature on international relations and world politics until after the end of the Cold War in 1991. Prior to that time the popular term in the 1970s and 1980s was interdependence. For others it is the expansion of the capitalist world economy that is the critical dynamic of the process known as globalization, tracing its origins back to the 16th century.

We take this historical perspective when discussing globalization. To us the term *globalization* may be new, but the development of technology and the construction of a capitalist global economy are multicentury projects that have had, and still continue to have, enormous political, social, and cultural implications worldwide. Indeed, globalization has done much to blur the distinction between international and domestic contexts and raises the issue of the salience of territorial borders. In the economic realm, which deals with the production, exchange, and consumption of goods and services, several examples will help make the point:

- Multinational corporations (MNCs) are tied more closely to stockholders and other interested parties—whatever their nationality—than to any one state. It has become increasingly difficult to determine what is meant by an "American" or "French" company when the firm has a global market and strategy and a truly multinational workforce including top-level managers. What matters when it comes to hiring is not one's nationality but rather one's talents and skills. As a result Americans are competing for jobs with individuals from around the world.
- Trade integration—the level of a country's participation in world markets through trade—has continued to increase steadily over the past several decades from 30 percent or less to more than 40 or 50 percent. Multilateral trade liberalization has been a major contributor to the world economy's unprecedented growth over the past half century. At the same time, regional trade agreements such as the North American Free Trade Agreement (NAFTA) have also expanded. These are trade arrangements under which member-countries grant one another preferential treatment in trade—reducing or eliminating tariffs or quotas on imports and other barriers to trade.
- Global financial linkages continue to grow rapidly. More than a trillion dollars a day enter and leave the world's financial institutions. Upward or downward shifts in one stock market have ripple effects with comparable swings in other markets.
- Foreign direct investment—money invested in countries aside from one's own—totaled over $1.2 trillion in 2010. The United States was the number one destination for investment at $186 billion, while China was number two at $100 billion. This was also the first year in which wealthy countries received less than half of the investment.[2]

interdependence ■ a situation in which actions and events in one state affect people in other states and assumes some degree of reciprocal effect

trade integration ■ the level of a country's participation in world markets through trade

foreign direct investment ■ money invested in countries aside from one's own

---

[2]"Foreign Direct Investment," *The Economist*, January 20, 2011.

- Financial difficulties in one country can send tremors throughout a region or world due to increased levels of economic integration. European countries, for example, found it difficult to insulate themselves from the financial crises of fellow **European Union** (EU) members Greece, Spain, and Ireland in 2010 and 2011.

European Union
- an economic and political partnership between 27 European countries designed to ensure peace, stability, and prosperity by helping to raise living standards and progressively building a single Europe-wide market

Multinational corporations have a long history of being major players in global economics. During the 1600s, Europe began exploring the world and placing its finances on a sounder footing, establishing corporations whose stocks traded in the world's three financial centers—London, Amsterdam, and Paris. After the great financial crash of 1720, there was not much international activity in stocks for the next 100 years. When the Napoleonic wars ended in 1815, however, the capital used to fund the wars was allocated to canals, railroads, and governments in Europe and South America. Private corporations made a resurgence.

Oil companies were considered the first major global corporations. In 1933, the Saudi government signed a concessionary agreement with Standard Oil of

---

ARGUMENT-COUNTERARGUMENT | Globalization or Americanization?

ARGUMENT Many see the terrorist attacks on the World Trade Center and the Pentagon on September 11, 2001, as at least in part a violent reaction against what some view as the ultimate purveyor of globalization—the United States. Indeed, to some, globalization is just another word for Americanization—an effort by Washington to impose not only its will, but also its values on other parts of the world. Whether in the economic realm—firms that invest or sell abroad (e.g., General Motors or Ford, Microsoft or Apple, Coca-Cola, McDonald's, Starbucks, Kentucky Fried Chicken) or in the cultural realm (e.g., pop music, salacious Hollywood movies, or provocative television series, and websites of all kinds), such critics are prone to view the United States, the lone superpower (or hyperpower), as not only militarily but also economic, socially, and culturally imperialistic.

COUNTERARGUMENT The United States does not seek to hold territory as was the case in the 19th- and 20th-century British, French, Belgian, Dutch, German, Spanish, and Portuguese empires. When the United States does intervene abroad, it does not seek to stay for long, occupying foreign territory only as

long as it takes to accomplish humanitarian, security, or other purposes. After all, other countries call upon the United States to help for such purposes. Thus, words like *imperial* or *empire* to describe present-day American foreign policy or societal influence present a distorted view of what is happening.

Moreover, the democratic or liberal values being advanced globally are not uniquely American, but rather are the outcome of the 17th- and 18th-century Enlightenment period in European history and thus are shared by many countries. Finally, if large segments of other societies embrace American pop culture and cuisine (if sodas and hamburgers qualify as cuisine), that speaks well of America and says something about what is lacking in other societies. American firms market goods and services globally, but it is *they* (foreign purchasers) who buy them.

APPLICATION The term *globalization* is a classic example of what is termed in the social sciences a "contested concept." Even if people can agree on its definition, there are contentious differences as to the positive or negative effects of globalization. What is your own opinion on the pervasive influence of American pop culture among youth around the world? Why? ◢

California allowing the company to begin exploration. It was not until 1938 that the first major oil reserves were discovered, but after that the rush was on as the world entered the modern age of oil-dependency and oil-fueled economic growth. Since that point, global commerce and the economic power of multinational corporations have expanded enormously. Corporate revenues now exceed or are comparable to the size of national economies. In 2010, for example, Wal-Mart generated revenues of $405 billion and ExxonMobil $383 billion. By way of comparison, in the same year the gross domestic product (GDP) of Sweden was $444 billion and that of Saudi Arabia $434 billion.

Especially in the high-technology sectors in advanced economies, corporate production has become dependent on alloys containing "rare-earth" metals used in such diverse products as computers, cell phones, rechargeable batteries, fluorescent lighting, and catalytic converters—some 97 percent of which are mined in China, mostly in inner Mongolia (although there are other sources). Another precious mineral, columbite-tantalite, which is found principally in Australia but also in the war-torn African Democratic Republic of the Congo, once refined, becomes a highly heat-resistant metal powder called tantalum.

For the high-tech industry, tantalum is a key component in everything from mobile phones made by Nokia and Ericsson, computer chips manufactured by Intel, to Sony stereos, games, and DVD players. Violent competition for this ore has helped fuel the war in Congo, where 5.4 million deaths have occurred since 1998. This makes the conflict the deadliest since World War II. Mining of rare earth and other precious minerals also has adverse environmental impacts, particularly when rules for extracting these materials are nonexistent or not enforced.

Social-Cultural Impact

For some observers of international relations and world politics, it is not the economic but rather the social-cultural dimension of globalization that is most important. Just as the amount and velocity of economic transactions have increased over the years, so, too, has there been an intensification of worldwide social relations. World markets and world communications have both expanded, and both have been facilitated by the technological developments outlined above.

The most obvious example of social-cultural impact is Facebook, the social networking website. It is home to more than 800 million active users and forty billion photos. As noted on the Facebook statistical page:

- 50 percent of active users log on to Facebook in any given day.
- Each average user has 130 "friends" linked to the account.
- On average, more than 250 million photos are uploaded per day.
- An average user is connected to 80 community pages, groups, and events.
- About 75 percent of Facebook users are outside the United States.
- Over 300,000 users helped translate the site through the translations application.
- More than 7 million apps and websites are integrated with Facebook.

The power of Facebook and other applications such as Skype, live video feed that connects people around the world, was unimaginable to earlier generations of students who went off to college or studied overseas. To minimize postage cost, letters from Europe or elsewhere abroad were often sent in lightweight, blue-papered aerogrammes. If you were hitchhiking or traveling by train, one of the few places to receive mail was at an American Express office where you also could exchange dollars (cash or traveler's checks) to buy needed local currency. If you had an AMEX card, you could cash a hometown check for currency—debit cards and cash machines had not yet been introduced. To call home was prohibitively expensive and required the assistance of an overseas operator. Staying in touch with new foreign friends upon completion of overseas study required dedication to putting pen to paper and spending money for overseas postage.

The economic impact of foreign products is easy to address if one has access to corporate annual financial reports. McDonald's, for example, has over 32,000 restaurants in 117 countries around the globe. In 2010 there were 64 million customers and sales totaled over $16 billion. More difficult to assess is the impact of accompanying corporate values on local social and cultural values.

In fact, the term "McDonaldization" has been viewed by critics of globalization as a synonym for "Americanization." The idea is that American consumer culture, including dietary habits, has come to undermine local societal and cultural traditions and values. For its part, McDonald's does try to accommodate some local preferences—for example, offering beer with burgers in Germany, red wine in France, rice and other local specialties in many Asian restaurants. Still, its mainline offerings—classically the Big Mac—can be purchased worldwide in the corporation's customary style of fast-food, standardized fare.

The transmission of cultures is, of course, nothing new in history. Greek culture, for example, is considered to be the wellspring of values that have spread first throughout the Western world and then on to other areas of the globe. Under colonialism, Western values were spread in a limited manner in the capital or major city of a colony. These Western values were generally restricted to privileged native elites who studied at the London School of Economics or the Sorbonne University in Paris or received other cultural tutelage. Technological developments have since made cultural transmission more rapid and direct to most individuals around the globe.

The supposedly pernicious effect of Western values has been a constant refrain, especially of religious leaders and intellectuals in the developing world. Western materialism in particular is seen as undermining religious faith and turning young people away from the mosque, church, and temple.

Just as U.S. goods flooded world markets in the post–World War II era, U.S. culture is now penetrating every continent through the dramatic growth of mass communications such as music, television, films, and the internet. Hollywood, the music industry, and the power of advertising have resulted in young people adopting at least the outward trappings of American pop culture. Of course, Europe has made its own contributions—reality television, music, and fashion, to name a few.

To visualize the impact of Western consumer culture globally, study the photos within newspapers such as the *New York Times* or the *Times* of London in their coverage of unrest in the developing world. Whether in Somalia, Egypt, Pakistan, Brasilia, or Burma, it is astonishing to see the number of youth wearing New York Yankees baseball caps and T-shirts emblazoned with Western sports apparel logos such as Nike and Adidas.

A more specific example involves China, still officially a communist state. Since 2008, China has had more internet users than any other country. Although the Chinese government aggressively censors political content online, it's more lax about cultural matters. More than 200 million Chinese now have online access to American television. Downloading has become so popular that it's even cutting into the profits of vendors who sell pirated DVDs!

Yao Jun is one young man who prefers to get his entertainment on the internet. In a den on the second floor of his apartment outside Beijing sits Yao's desktop computer with a high-speed internet connection. He's a big *Lost* fan and he prefers American TV to Chinese television. "I like that kind of [American] culture, and I like that kind of lifestyle better," Yao says as he excitedly watches the opening scenes. "I don't like the Chinese shows. They are often pretentious. They don't look real."[3]

The interesting question is whether globalization is making people around the world more similar or different. The immense global popularity of American films, music, sitcoms, and dramas is a fact, but does that necessarily mean a rejection of local culture? Or can foreign and domestic cultures coexist? Stated differently, does an affinity for American culture result in a shift in one's personal identity? Does drinking a Coke make one any less a dedicated Muslim or Hindu? Put another way, don't we carry multiple identities—new ones not necessarily canceling or eliminating already established ones?

Political Impact

Profound disagreement exists over the implications of the economic component of globalization and particularly who benefits or is hurt by it. For some college students, the development of a truly global economy offers the tantalizing prospect of working for a multinational corporation, bank, or other nongovernmental organization, whether at home or abroad. For workers in manufacturing industries, the global economy is as much a threat as an opportunity, depending on the industry and country.

With the growth of the global economy, states increasingly believe they are unable to exert effective influence—let alone control—over their domestic economies. This has resulted in domestic political consequences within states as well a source of political tension and conflict among states. Global competition has led to the collapse of certain industries as cheaper labor is available elsewhere or as companies simply move their production facilities to lower-cost countries. The American steel industry lost much of its market to Japan, which, in turn, lost much of its market to South Korea. White-collar computer jobs in North America continue to migrate to Asia. The resultant anger or discontent of displaced workers is often directed not only at business executives, but also at government leaders, who are judged to have failed to protect domestic jobs from foreign competition.

Particularly in less-developed countries, such as those in Africa where the source of foreign income is often limited to a few basic commodities, the power

---

[3]Laura Sydell, "Chinese Fans Follow American TV Online — for Free," *National Public Radio*, June 24, 2008.

of the global economy can have a devastating effect. If there is a drop in copper, tin, or rubber prices, for example, the resultant unemployment is not cushioned by such state-supported unemployment programs as exist in many advanced, industrial, high-income countries. The problem is compounded in those less-developed countries with high birthrates and a limited capacity to absorb the youth population into the workforce. Such conditions are ripe for political and social discontent and a loss of governmental authority.

The use of social networking technology has also had profound political impact in recent years. Facebook and Twitter were used by young people in Egypt and Tunisia in 2011 to disseminate information on antiregime protests, and cell phone photos were instantly sent around the world. Anyone with a high-speed computer can download or upload video clips of political demonstrations on YouTube. Even easier than setting up one's own website, any of us can create a blog on sites such as blogspot.com that allows others to read whatever we post and view photos and videos we upload. For governments there is a difficult trade-off: Though such media as the internet help transmit scientific and business information essential to economic development, such networks also allow political dissidents to communicate with the outside world. On the other hand, access to and use of the internet and other media for communications locally or globally are a realization of a liberal idea core to civil society.

Some governments have fought back. China, for example, has constructed a "great firewall" that imposes tight controls on internet links with the outside world as well as allows the government to monitor traffic and make many sites and services unavailable to their populace. Similar efforts have been made by Iran, Cuba, Saudi Arabia, and Vietnam. Governments have also monitored Facebook pages of known and suspected dissidents in order to target them for harassment and arrest, sometimes punishment, even torturing some "enemies" of the state.

An interesting example involves the use of Twitter and Facebook by young members of Iran's Green Movement during the 2009 antiregime protests. Among other things they uploaded videos of police brutality and announced planned demonstrations. Authorities cracked heads and also computers to trace users, block services, and close websites. Such actions inspired a 26-year-old hacker in Ohio by the name of Austin Heap to develop anticensorship software. He named the program Haystack and in early 2010 began to distribute it to Iranian opposition leaders. He was named "innovator of the year" by the British newspaper the *Guardian* and received praise from U.S. Secretary of State Hillary Clinton. But computer experts raised doubts, and, upon investigation, it turned out Haystack suffered from a high level of insecurity. Not all messages would encrypt properly, but skilled Iranian government computer experts could also locate some users' identities and locations. The software was withdrawn in September 2010, but even this failed attempt demonstrated popular solidarity across national borders and cultures indicative of a still-emerging global civil society.

cyber-war ■
politically motivated computer network hacking designed to conduct sabotage and espionage

In the political-military realm, a new concern for many states is what has been called **cyber-war**. Instead of bombs, the concern is that a "worm"—a piece of software that infects industrial control systems—may work its way into computer networks. The goal could be to steal information, manipulate the information, or destroy it and render computers useless. Military command and control systems are potential targets, but also banks and the banking system, electrical grids, and nuclear power stations. The alarmists refer to the possibility of a "digital Pearl Harbor"—a surprise, highly destructive attack. Moreover, should such a cyber attack occur, we may not even know the identity of the perpetrators for some time, if at all. By contrast to conventional war, attackers in cyber-war may not readily be identifiable.

Modern technology has also contributed to the development of computer programs that engage in what is termed social network analysis (SNA) that has economic as well as political implications. SNA involves crunching large quantities of data that place individuals in the context of their social networks to determine their patterns of life. This is used in business for marketing or, for example, as a way to keep customers from defecting from a cell phone plan. But it is also used to map the influences among larger segments of society to aid in political and social forecasting. One program, for example, analyzes a wide range of information about the politics, business, and society of Lebanon to predict rocket attacks by the Lebanese Hezbollah militia against Israel. Mapping large social networks may facilitate the spread of democracy by identifying tipping points when ideas go mainstream despite government repression and censorship. Other work is designed to enable aid workers and diplomats to understand better which locals are most likely to cooperate with Westerners. Data that inform these analyses include such diverse, seemingly unrelated factors as weather, land and water disputes, cabinet reshuffles, reactions to corruption, court cases, economic activity, and changes in tribal geographic maps.[4]

social network analysis ■ software designed to place individuals in the context of their social network and hence discern personal ties and relationships

patterns of life ■ repeated human behavior and tendencies

capitalism ■ an economic system, form of political economy, or mode of production that emphasizes money, market-oriented trade, capital investment for further production, and a set of values or culture legitimating investment and market-oriented behaviors

CAPITALISM AS A WORLDWIDE FORM OF POLITICAL ECONOMY

Capitalism as a mode of production or form of political economy gradually emerged in Europe during the late Middle Ages into the Renaissance, eventually displacing feudalism. Feudal political economy concentrated agricultural and other production in small communities, carried out by peasants under the protection of lords or aristocratic landholders on whose estates they worked. These communities were largely self-sufficient economically. Relatively little need for trade existed in a feudal society, other than for a few spices, silks, or other commodities not produced locally. Feudal markets for exchange of goods and services therefore were marginal or relatively unimportant compared to those that arose under capitalism.

Markets emerged as towns sprang up near the castles or estates that had been the centers of feudal life. Townsmen (or *burghers*, as they were called in the German-speaking states) traded the goods and services that they and others produced. They would become the core of a new middle class between the land-owning aristocracy and the peasantry or farm people tied to landed estates in the countryside. This new middle class of townsmen or burghers was labeled in French the *bourgeoisie* or more commonly in English the "capitalist class."

5.2 Trace the historical emergence and development of capitalism as a worldwide form of political economy, identifying its principal attributes and progressive globalization.

◉─Watch the **Video "Deforestation in the Brazilian Amazon"** at mypoliscilab.com

---

[4]"Untangling the Social Web," *The Economist*, September 4, 2010, p. 17.

The impact of globalization evokes a wide variety of responses, but its economic impact in particular is undeniable. A trader in Kuwait City reacts to economic news and data being delivered instantaneously to the electronic market boards.

In fall 2011, protestors expressed their anger at economic inequality and the power of global financial institutions by occupying Zucotti Park in New York City. The movement spread to cities throughout the United States and other parts of the world.

A block away from Zucotti Park, a trader contemplates the ups and downs of the Wall Street stock exchange at a time of financial crisis in Europe. No financial instrument on any global exchange seemed to be a good place for one's investments.

The epicenter of this financial crisis that threatens the future of the European Union was in Greece. As the Greek government was faced with defaulting on its loans unless willing to make drastic cuts in government spending, protestors gathered outside the parliament in Athens.

mode of production
■ the form of political economy associated with the production of goods and services at different historical periods—a term used in Marxist understanding of ancient slavery, feudalism, and capitalism as different modes of production

Trade among towns and cities increased substantially as markets became more important throughout Europe. Examples of early urban centers of market activity, including banking, are such 14th- and 15th-century trading cities as Venice and Bruges, in modern-day Italy and Belgium, respectively. Printing presses and other tools and hand-operated machines were the new technologies that contributed to production in towns and urban settings, even as agricultural production remained centered in the great landed estates of the passing feudal era. We can see evidence of these feudal and early capitalist political economies in the castles and usually well-preserved or restored old centers of late medieval and Renaissance towns and cities throughout modern-day Europe.

Identifying the Attributes of Capitalist Political Economy

political economy
■ the intersection of politics (or authoritative choice), particularly in relation to trade, money, finance, and investment—the flows of capital across national boundaries

Attributes of emerging capitalism included markets and money, but these were not new. Markets and money were the bedrock of ancient forms of political economy to be found, for example, among Phoenicians, Egyptians, Greeks, Persians, and Romans. Money provided a standard of value for buying and selling in markets and a store of value that could be held until needed for spending at a later time. These functions were essential to commerce in ancient market economies that relied so heavily for production on human, including slave, labor. Even the technologies for harnessing animal labor, especially for agricultural production, were late in coming and would not be fully developed until the feudal period of the Middle Ages.

capital ■ savings that can be used for investment in the means for producing goods and services

Investment as an Attribute of Capitalism   What distinguishes capitalism from feudal and ancient political economies is its greater need for investment of **capital**. Advancing technologies that produced the machinery and tools of early preindustrial capitalism would be followed by a late 18th- and 19th-century Industrial Revolution that began in the United Kingdom. This soon spread to France, the German states, and elsewhere on the European continent and the Americas, particularly the United States. The tools and hand-operated machines of early capitalism, the heavy machinery of industrial capitalism, and the high-technology machinery and computers or artificial intelligence of advanced or postindustrial capitalism all require that substantial amounts of capital resulting from savings be put aside for investment in these tools and machinery that are essential to production.

If we consumed all that we were capable of producing, there would be nothing left for investment or for the purchase of new plants and machinery. An airline that as a service industry provides transportation of passengers or cargo needs to invest in new airplanes and airport facilities, not only to expand its present business but also to maintain and eventually replace aging equipment or facilities. An industry producing goods—automobiles, personal computers, other manufactured and agricultural products—faces the same need to invest in new factories or plants and machinery. So it was in preindustrial capitalism, when some time, effort, and resources or savings had to be put into crafting, purchasing, and maintaining the tools and hand-operated machines used in the production of goods and services.

The plants, tools, and machinery that are essential to the production of *other* goods and services are referred to by economists as capital goods. Capital goods have no value to us in themselves other than their contribution to the production of other goods or services we do value or want to produce for consumption. A lathe used in cutting or shaping metal or wood in manufacturing, an airplane used to carry passengers or move cargo, a printing press used by a publisher of books or newspapers, and a computer and software used by a writer for word processing are examples of capital goods. We do not consume everything we produce but put our profits from sales, salary, or other income from earlier production into new investments in capital goods for further or future production.

Two important components of gross national product (GNP)—a measure of the aggregate size of a national economy—are annual consumption and investment. Measured in dollars or other currency, how much has been spent on goods and services and how much has been saved or set aside for capital investment—the purchase or acquisition of capital goods for future production? Capitalist economies that do not invest sufficiently tend to decline or experience a drop in production, consumption, and standard or level of living. To maintain or expand present levels of production, consumption, and living standards, capitalist economies require sufficient capital formation—new and continuing investment in capital goods for production and consumption. The box on the following page examines in greater detail gross national product (GNP) and two related terms: gross domestic product (GDP) and gross national income (GNI).

A Commercial Culture as an Attribute of Capitalism

The late 19th- and early 20th-century German political sociologist Max Weber observed how the emergence of capitalism was also accompanied by a new set of social values supportive not only of market-oriented trade and monetary activities but also of the savings and investment function so essential to capitalism. Given this emphasis on the development of new values and the power of ideas, constructivists can lay claim to Weber as an intellectual precursor. Church teachings in the Middle Ages had held that the righteous did not commit the sin of usury, which was defined as earning interest from loans or by making profit on sales.

Religion is so deeply embedded in a society's culture or set of values that it is often difficult to distinguish between values that have a religious grounding and those that do not. The anti-market religious orientation of church authorities was perfectly consistent with the feudal political economy, which did not rely heavily on markets anyway. Weber observed how the rise of capitalism was encouraged by a revolution in religious thought on economic matters. This was a product of the Reformation that he referred to as a "Protestant ethic" or "spirit of capitalism."[5]

The importance of the individual in Lutheran thought, for example, was a liberal idea consistent with the new capitalist political economy that would come to rely so heavily on individual initiative in the marketplace. Calvinist or puritanical ideas held that hard work was good, and that one ought to lead a productive but

capital goods ■ refers to goods used in the production of other goods or services, e.g., the machinery and tools in a factory

GNP ■ gross national product—a country's annual output of goods and services, calculated as the sum of consumption, investment, government spending, and exports minus imports

capital formation ■ new and continuing investment in capital goods for production and consumption

GDP ■ gross domestic product—GNP minus return on foreign investment since the latter is a measure of *foreign*, rather than *domestic* production

GNI ■ gross national income—GNP minus indirect (like sales and excise) business taxes

---

[5]Max Weber, *The Protestant Ethic and the Spirit of Capitalism* (New York: Charles Scribner's Sons, 1958, 1976).

The Wealth of a Nation and Its Productive Capacity: Gross National Product and Gross Domestic Product

ARGUMENT-COUNTERARGUMENT

ARGUMENT Mercantilism was a theory of early capitalism that the wealth of a nation was a function of the amount of gold and other treasure that it could accumulate. Accordingly, running trade surpluses (more exports than imports), while finding new gold in mines or accepting it in payment for goods or services became national economic policy. Imperial Spain is an example.

COUNTERARGUMENT Adam Smith observed that the wealth of a nation was not to be found in its stock of gold and other treasure; it was to be found instead in the productive capacity of its economy—that is, the total of goods and services that could be produced. Gross national product (GNP) is now a commonly used annual measure that captures the essence of Smith's idea.

GNP is the total or aggregate of goods and services produced in a state in a given year. We can compute it by summing the dollar amounts of the following:

1. Domestic consumption of goods and services (C)
2. Investment (I) of surplus or savings—additions to the capital stock used for future production
3. Government spending to purchase goods and services (G)
4. Exports of domestic production (X) minus imports of foreign production (M)—a subtraction that also takes account of the contribution of foreign-produced goods and services to domestic production and consumption levels

Gross domestic product (GDP) is a more refined measure that subtracts national earnings from foreign investments in other countries. After all, domestically owned capital invested abroad contributes to foreign, not domestic, production. GNP counts returns from such investments; GDP does not:

$$GDP = GNP - \text{returns on foreign investments}$$

In addition to statistical problems in counting accurately the sum of commercial transactions, neither GNP nor GDP accurately captures production of goods and services not traded in the marketplace. Because goods and services produced and consumed in a household cannot be measured directly, GNP and GDP are criticized for understating aggregate or total domestic production. This is particularly acute in developing world economies that typically have a higher proportion of household production and consumption.

GNP	=	C	+	I	+	G	+	X-M
Demonstrated National Productive Capacity		Consumption		Investment		Government Spending		Trade Balance

APPLICATION Consistent with Smith's focus on the wealth of nations, GNP and GDP are aggregate measures at the state and society level. Yet we live in an interdependent and interconnected global economy. What do you think of the argument that measures of demonstrated productive capacity at regional, global, or other levels of aggregation may well be more appropriate? After all, globalization trends that accelerated in the 20th century have continued into the 21st century.

prudent life. Further, it was held that one ought not to consume all that one produced but should invest the savings of money originally earned from hard work (thus putting one's money to work as well). Earning a fair profit or a fair return on loans and investments was now legitimate in the new religious teachings.

Weber observed that eventually the religious underpinnings of these new market-oriented values in an emerging capitalist culture would be forgotten. The important point for us, however, is to recognize that as a form of political economy, capitalism has its own "culture" or set of supporting values, just as European feudalism had. Capitalism legitimizes profit-making enterprises and allows for interest on loans and returns on investment that are essential to its functioning. Indeed, worldly success was believed by some Protestant sects to be a mark of one's membership in the "elect," who were predestined to enjoy eternity in heaven. Poverty was not seen as a sign of God's favor.

Setting religious underpinnings aside, the new commercial ethic oriented members of society in a deeper sense to produce above consumption needs and to accumulate savings, thus increasing wealth available for investment. In the secular European and American commercial cultures, the religious sources of these ideas may have been forgotten, but the ideas spawned by these religious understandings decidedly were not lost. Indeed, these ideas related to work, savings, and investment were retained in a commercial culture accepted by people of diverse religious identities as well as by those claiming no religious preference.

After all, investment is the "fuel" that drives the capitalist "engine." If capitalist economies are to be maintained and grow, there is a continuing and seemingly never-ending need for more investment in capital goods. Indeed, one of Weber's principal insights was to identify capitalism's dependency on a commercial culture that treats market-oriented activities as legitimate, encourages hard work, and promotes a propensity to save and invest. This was as true in preindustrial capitalism as it is in the more advanced forms of industrial and postindustrial capitalism that continue to require enormous amounts of investment in capital goods.

The Passing of Feudalism and the New Politics of Capitalism, Mercantilism, and Liberalism

As capitalism gradually displaced feudalism, states were also emerging as a new political unit. Notwithstanding divisions leading to an 11th-century schism between the Christian Church in the West at Rome and the Orthodox Christian Church in the East at Constantinople (Istanbul in present-day Turkey), the Western European feudal idea of unity in Christendom survived throughout the Middle Ages. The 15th- and 16th-century Protestant Reformation, however, split Christendom in Western Europe along the new state lines as warring princes chose either Protestant or Catholic professions of faith.

The 1648 Peace of Westphalia that ended the Thirty Years' War concluded that the religion of the inhabitants would be determined by the prince or temporal authority in any given realm—in Latin, *cujus regio ejus religio* (the religion of the inhabitants of the realm as being determined by the ruler) captured this new idea. The authority of princes in these new political units called states was indeed supreme if even religious choice could be determined by them.

States thus displaced the landed estate or feudal community in the new European political and economic order that emerged. The monarchs in these new states gradually accumulated more and more central authority within their realms. As a matter of state policy, kings and queens favored international trade that enriched them and their governments. If one visits the churches and other well-preserved buildings in Toledo, the imperial capital of Spain, one can see in the altars and other artworks vast amounts of gold, precious gems, and other treasure acquired primarily by 16th-, 17th-, and 18th-century Spanish monarchs.

mercantilism ■ the concept that national wealth is a function of the amount of gold and other accumulated treasure—present-day neomercantilist policies pursued by some states trying to maximize trade surpluses, accumulating large monetary-reserve balances

In addition to acquiring new gold from mines in New World colonies, mercantilism as an economic policy involved states acquiring gold from running a favorable balance of trade and storing it in national treasuries. Hoards of gold, silver, and other precious metals accrued in national treasuries from the profits or royalties from commercial transactions conducted by state-chartered corporations and other traders. Sometimes such treasures were retained by these national firms as a store of value to finance future purchases required in their business ventures. The ideal in mercantilism was for traders to sell more than they bought, requiring others to pay for their purchases with gold or silver, which then could be added to the national treasure.

Adam Smith   The Scottish political economist Adam Smith (1723–1790) took issue with the mercantilist view in *An Inquiry into the Nature and Causes of the Wealth of Nations* or, more simply, *The Wealth of Nations*, which he published in 1776. Smith argued that national wealth in capitalism was not to be found in the treasure that accrued in treasury vaults; rather, wealth was to be found in the productive capacity of economies. This was increasingly to be found in their capital stock along with labor and land (or natural resources), collectively termed factors of production.

factors of production ■ land (including natural resources), labor, and capital as components essential to the production of goods and services

Smith understood the importance of producing tools, machinery, or other capital goods but still relied on a labor theory of value—that is, the value of what is produced is the result of labor put into the production process. Indeed, Smith argued that efficiency can be enhanced significantly with specialization and a division of labor. His was also a liberal view of capitalist political economy, emphasizing free markets in which governments took a hands-off or *laissez-faire* approach, allowing nongovernmental, private firms and individuals to buy and sell in the marketplace without interference by state authorities.

After all, state authority or government in European feudalism had been in the hands of land-owning aristocrats. In many instances, state authority had been used against the bourgeois or commercial interests of the new middle class. Consistent with the political liberalism of John Locke, Smith's economic liberalism supported the interests of the new middle class by holding that free-market enterprises were far more likely to increase national wealth.

In serving their own interests, capitalists would have to compete with other self-oriented buyers and sellers in the marketplace. Competition among free traders would force firms and individuals wanting to stay in business to be more efficient without government interference, thus supplying the market with quality goods and services at lower, more competitive prices. Instead of government direction, an invisible hand of market competition would force these efficiencies, resulting in greater productivity and thus wealth for the nation as a whole than could be acquired under mercantilism.

David Ricardo   Following Smith's lead as a classical political economist in the economic liberal tradition, the early 19th-century English writer David Ricardo

(1772–1823) was even more explicit in favoring the new commercial middle-class or bourgeois interests against those of the aristocracy. He complained that land-owning aristocrats contributed virtually nothing to capitalist production in exchange for the rents they collected as mere owners of land used by others for productive enterprise. As such, aristocrats were a drag on capitalist economies.

Ricardo extended Smith's analysis, criticizing aristocratic or other landholding interests not only for putting an unwarranted cost on production, but also for restraining international trade through tariffs and other protectionist measures that favored their agricultural interests. Arguing that **free trade** allowed for national specialization in accordance with **comparative advantage**, Ricardo saw that great gains in overall or aggregate production would come from allowing international markets to operate without government interference favoring particular class interests. With this international focus, Ricardo became an intellectual forefather of the idea of globalization.

For Ricardo, **protectionism** (typically in the form of tariffs or taxes on imports) favored agricultural interests and denied firms and individuals the freedom to buy and sell at market prices without restriction across national frontiers. Tariffs and other barriers to free trade both protected and encouraged inefficient producers. Pushing Adam Smith's economic liberalism beyond the borders of the state, Ricardo argued that international trade free of such government interference would have the same positive effect on productivity as free trade in domestic political economies. Of course, Ricardo's free-trade prescription favored the newly emergent capital-owning class, which put its capital to work in manufacturing and would benefit from free markets in which to sell its products.

Consistent with both Smith's and Ricardo's analyses, Karl Marx (1818–1883) accepted the same labor theory of value but focused on what he understood to be the exploitative character of class relations. Smith had referred to classes as various "orders" in society, understanding as did Marx later that classes had played a historic role in the political economy. Marx expanded Ricardo's criticisms of the aristocracy to include capitalist and other classes that have been dominant over the course of human history. Marx also understood capitalism as a worldwide form of economy with commercial implications on a global scale.

free trade ◼
commerce unobstructed by tariffs, quotas, or other barriers to trade

comparative advantage ◼
free-trade principle that countries tend to specialize in producing those goods and services for export in which they are most efficient, leading to a global specialization or division of labor that maximizes aggregate productivity

protectionism
◼ policies favoring a country's industries, agriculture, or other producers by imposing tariffs or quotas on imports, subsidizing production, and erecting other barriers to free trade

The Progressive Globalization of Capitalism

The 17th and 18th centuries marked the first wave of imperial expansion from Europe, focusing on acquiring colonies in the New World of the Americas. The British, French, Dutch, Spanish, and Portuguese were the key players. Mercantilist policies dominated in this early stage of capitalism as colonial powers sought trade and commercial advantages over each other.

In the process of acquiring and maintaining these colonies, settlers and successive generations brought with them European political and economic ideas that took root in the new world. As colonies gained their independence in the late 18th and early 19th centuries, new states formed with claims to sovereignty following the European or "Westphalia" model. Along with the state, the elements of market capitalism were also transferred. The political economy of states and societies in the Western Hemisphere resembled those of the European countries that had organized and cultivated them.

imperialism ■ a position or policy of preeminence or dominance vis-à-vis foreign elements as in the establishment of colonies or by virtue of the capabilities a great power has over less powerful states, perhaps in the form of economic, social, or cultural imperialism

The second wave of 19th- and 20th-century **imperialism** effectively spread capitalist political economy throughout the globe to distant parts of Africa, Asia, and the Pacific. The same European powers, along with Germany, Belgium, and the United States, were the key players that established new colonies or other territorial holdings. Corporations and banks from imperial countries were transnational actors, which operated globally just as state-chartered firms had done in the first wave of imperial expansion.

One does not have to be an economic structuralist to recognize the fact that motivated primarily by mercantilist policies, colonial empires were constructed to serve the commercial advantage of the colonial power. At the same time, European and American administrations and firms transferred their ideas about capitalist political economy throughout the world. As colonies in Africa, Asia, and the Pacific became independent, particularly in the first quarter-century after World War II, their capitalist political economies were often linked by **neocolonial** ties with the former colonial power.

neocolonialism ■ relations of economic, social, cultural, and even political dominance by a former colonial ruler of a now independent state

Nevertheless, the effect of the second wave of imperialism and the decolonization that followed was to complete the globalization of capitalism and capitalist political economy. Multinational corporations (MNCs), firms that own and manage economic units in two or more countries, and multinational banks headquartered in the world's largest economies operated alongside firms in the markets of these new states.

Even communist or socialist states in Central and Eastern Europe, China, Cuba, and elsewhere that experienced revolutions led by those seeking to overthrow capitalism were forced to adopt what some political economists refer to as a particular and sometimes brutal form of state capitalism. Instead of privately owned capital being at the core of the domestic political economies of these countries, capital was expropriated in the name of the people from private owners. It was concentrated in the hands of state authorities in centrally planned or controlled economies following a Leninist political design of democratic centralism within a ruling-party apparatus.

Most people accepted the claims by these regimes that they had rejected capitalism, establishing socialism as an intermediate step en route to communism. By contrast, many economic structuralists and other political economists have disagreed, noting that in fact these Leninist regimes had succeeded only in overthrowing free-market capitalism in which capital was privately owned, the most common form of capitalism. To them, the centrally planned and directed political economies of these Leninist regimes still remained part of a worldwide capitalist political economy and retained in their domestic political economies a capitalist reliance on markets, money, and investment subject to state direction or control with a supporting commercial culture expressed in a Marxist-Leninist, materialist ideology. *State* capitalism is not *free-market* capitalism, but it bears the marks of capitalism all the same.

The end of the Cold War resulted in the abandonment of Leninist and state-capitalist forms of political economy by most of these states and societies. The logic of the world-capitalist system seems to be playing out. Experiments, some not always very successful, were undertaken with different forms of free-market capitalism. Some of these included a strong social-democratic component with some state ownership of industries, utilities, or other means of production. Others have had little or no government ownership and a much less generous provision for the kind of social security taken for granted in the more advanced Western welfare states. The underlying cultures in these different societies are decisive in determining the degree to which regimes in these states will privatize their economies and the emphasis they will place on achieving social-democratic or welfare-state goals.

The globalization of capitalism in the present-day world is one in which money, markets, and investment are central attributes. As Max Weber understood, an orientation to work, productivity, and a propensity to save and invest remain key cultural values essential to the effective functioning of capitalist political economies anywhere. At the same time, beneath the surface of global capitalism is a world of great diversity. Capitalist political economies do differ substantially from country to country. There are differences in commercial and political values that affect the way business is conducted and the political, social, and economic choices that are made.

For example, the United States probably has (by choice) the least generous and Switzerland and Sweden, also by choice, have among the most generous welfare states of any of the advanced capitalist political economies. On the issue of privatization versus socialization or public ownership of the means of production, Switzerland is much closer to the United States, with most production capital in private hands. Sweden also has widespread private ownership of both small and well-known, large firms such as Saab and Volvo—the former sold to General Motors (later sold back to a Swedish firm, Koenigsegg Automotive) and the latter internationalized in a passenger-car merger with Ford (which later sold it to Geely, a Chinese firm). On the other hand, state subsidies of private industries and outright public ownership of other firms has been more prevalent in Sweden, as it is in other northern European countries with strong social-democratic expectations.

To illustrate how commercial culture and the structure of government–private sector relations can vary, we can compare the United States with Japan. As in the United States, most of the Japanese economy is in private hands, but the relation between Japanese firms and their government is close-knit, with direct coordination and state subsidies widely accepted as perfectly legitimate within the Japanese commercial culture. In this regard, the Ministry of International Trade and Industry (MITI) has been widely studied for the role it has played in advancing the global competitiveness of Japanese industry.

Although there are U.S. government subsidies and government-industry partnerships for research and development as well as other contracts with private-sector firms, the underlying American commercial culture generally views government intervention in the market with skepticism. As a result, no U.S. equivalent institution to MITI for coordinating government-industry relations exists. Suggestions that the United States emulate or copy the Japanese (or, for that matter, French) government-industry, joint-planning approach to market competitiveness have been strongly resisted by many in the United States. Nevertheless, by contrast, almost all other advanced industrial countries have ministries or agencies concerned with advancing the global competitiveness of their national industries. Quite apart from balance-of-payments considerations, government involvement in these countries typically tries to optimize employment of the national labor force as well as assure sufficient returns to domestic owners of capital invested in these enterprises.

Although there are similarities, the ways in which multinational corporations and banks operate and interact on a global basis also reflect the diversity of the underlying commercial cultures they represent. Some will be more likely to form alliances or even cartels with other firms, much as they are accustomed to doing in their domestic markets. Other firms, reflecting fiercely competitive and free-market-oriented values in their domestic commercial cultures, are likely to act in the same way abroad.

On the other hand, there can also be convergence of multinational corporate orientations across cultures on such issues over time. Globalization has also meant an increasing concentration of capital as competition for market share has driven some firms to seek strategic alliances or mergers and acquisitions. For example, in reaching out to global markets, American multinationals like United Airlines, now merged with Continental, have organized strategic alliances with other non-U.S. airlines—Air Canada, Japan's All Nippon Airways (ANA), Air China, Asiana (South Korea), Thai Airways International, Singapore Airlines, Austrian Air, Croatia Airlines, Swiss International, British Midland International, Germany's Lufthansa, SAS (Denmark, Norway, and Sweden), Brussels Airlines (Belgium), Blue1 (Finland), Spanair (Spain), TAP (Portugal), Adria (Slovenia), Aegean (Greece), LOT (Poland), Turkish, Egypt Air, South African Airways, and TAM (Brazilian) as well as regional alliances with still other carriers. Delta, American and other major carriers have done much the same thing.

In the automotive industry, U.S. multinational Chrysler merged with German Daimler-Benz to form Daimler Chrysler, but the two later split—Chrysler then taken over by Fiat, the Italian automaker. As noted above, Swedish Saab and Volvo (passenger) were purchased respectively by General Motors and Ford, but later were sold to Swedish and Chinese automakers. Although adaptation can be difficult, these alliances and mergers have forced often very diverse corporate cultures to grapple with the challenges of building fully collaborative alliances and organizations compatible with their diversity in national perspectives and corporate cultures.

cartel ■ an association among financial, commodity-producing, or industrial interests, including states, for establishing a national or international market control, setting production levels, and increasing or stabilizing the prices of such diverse products as oil, tin, and coffee

THE ONGOING, TWENTIETH-CENTURY DEBATE ON GLOBAL COMMERCE

5.3 Explain attempts at global governance in the post–World War II era to deal with trade, finance, and investment resulting from rapid globalization.

A knowledge of historical background on the emergence and globalization of capitalism is essential to understanding 20th-century and present-day arguments among economic liberals, mercantilists, post–World War II neomercantilists, and world-system theorists. After the heyday of economic liberalism in the late 19th and early 20th centuries, the period between the two world wars was marked by a revival of mercantilist ideas. As a result, the economic dimension of the globalization process dramatically slowed. Countries erected high tariffs and other barriers to trade to protect domestic industries and agricultural sectors from foreign competition. They also devalued their currencies in an effort to secure a price advantage for domestic industries, making exports cheaper to foreign buyers while making imports more expensive to domestic buyers. It was a game all countries could play, and most did as they engaged in successive rounds of competitive devaluations.

The aim was to run a favorable balance of trade—exporting or selling more than was imported or bought from abroad, regardless of the effects of such policies on foreign producers. As in the mercantilist period, relatively more successful players could be identified by the amount of gold or other monetary assets they accrued from positive trade balances. Referred to by economic liberals as "beggar-thy-neighbor" policies, protectionism and competitive-devaluation policies resulted in an enormous reduction in the volume of trade during the 1930s as each country strove to avoid purchasing other countries' exports. No country really won in this game; all experienced economic depression and the loss of productivity. Indeed, as Adam Smith had observed a century and a half before, the wealth of nations was not to be found in their gold stocks, but rather in their productive capacities.

Any trade that did go on tended to occur in mutually exclusive trade blocs—for example, Germany at the core of Central European trade, Britain within its empire and commonwealth, the United States in North America and the Caribbean, and Japan in its East Asian co-prosperity sphere. Many historians have identified the breakdown of economic liberalism and the formation of political-economic blocs in the 1930s as contributory causes of World War II. In any case this was widely believed, particularly among British and American policymakers who were charged with constructing a post–World War II global economy based on liberal, free-trade principles—over time eliminating or, at least, reducing tariffs and other barriers to trade.

Their objective was to establish an open trading and commercial environment on a global basis, rather than to repeat the experience of the interwar period. International economic regimes or sets of rules governing commerce were established, as were international organizations charged with implementing the three-part grand design, which included free or open trade, monetary means for maintaining the currency exchange essential to commerce, and capital investment for economic development.

By any standard, the almost seven decades following World War II were a remarkable period for economic growth, although marked by a number of recessions—the most serious beginning in 2008. A number of newly industrializing countries made remarkable economic gains in the last quarter of the 20th century, a trend continuing into the 21st century. Emerging alongside South Korea, Taiwan, Singapore, and other Asian "tigers" are regional economic giants in several continental locations—Brazil in South America, Russia in Eurasia, India in South Asia, China in East Asia (the "BRIC" countries)—joined in some analyses by South Africa, Indonesia, Argentina, and Chile.

But these same years also witnessed periods of inflation, high unemployment, and productivity slowdowns in the industrialized countries. For the West Europeans, the end of the Cold War marked an opportunity to integrate the economies in the east within an expanding European Union. We will briefly provide an overview of key developments in post–World War II trade, monetary, and investment issues and provide more detail in later chapters.

Explore the "International Development: You Are the Minister of Trade and Finance" at mypoliscilab.com

competitive devaluation ■ since devaluations reduce the export price of goods and services to purchases in foreign currencies, some countries may devalue their currencies merely to gain an unfair competitive advantage, a tactic often matched by devaluations in other countries

Global Governance—The Export-Import Trade Regime

regimes ■ sets of rules and associated international organizations that have been constructed by states to coordinate, manage, or regulate relations in a particular issue area

Global governance of trade depends upon coordination and collaboration by governments and private-sector interests that cross national borders. Regimes are sets of rules the players in their enlightened self-interest agree to follow. Sustaining and expanding trade and other forms of commerce require generally accepted rules governing buying and selling, importing and exporting. In the absence of such rules and both international and nongovernmental organizations that apply and follow them, the overall volume of trade would shrink dramatically with adverse effects on all parties.

Attempts after World War II to establish an International Trade Organization (ITO) as a key institution for a free- or open-trade regime failed when opposition at the time, particularly in the United States, described such a plan as "too socialistic." There was the possibility that an ITO would become too strong and intervene against corporate or national interests. Although the ITO idea failed, a General Agreement on Tariffs and Trade (GATT) was established in 1947. In succeeding decades, GATT negotiation rounds worked painstakingly to reduce tariffs and other barriers to trade.

GATT ■ General Agreement on Trade and Tariffs, signed in 1947 and lasted until 1993 when it was replaced by the WTO

tariffs ■ taxes placed by governments on imported goods from other countries

WTO ■ World Trade Organization, created in 1995, whose mission is to reduce barriers to trade

In turn, the GATT has been succeeded in 1995 by the World Trade Organization (WTO), an institution incorporating the GATT arrangements and finally given the task the ITO would have had—continuing the work of reducing barriers to trade and fostering as open a trading environment on a global basis as possible. It is an incredibly important task since the multilateral trading system developed since World War II has underpinned global prosperity. Further liberalization will not be easy, as evidenced by the collapse of trade talks. In 2001 in Doha, the capital of Qatar, meetings began seeking to lower trade barriers where freer trade would help poor countries the most, particularly in agriculture. Meetings toward this end have been held throughout the world and have been highly contentious. Given both small-farm and corporate agribusiness interests at stake, agricultural issues often prove to be the most difficult. There is substantial pressure to reach some agreement and thus bring the Doha Round of negotiations finally to a close.

With 153 members, the WTO is the only trade forum where all countries—no matter how poor—have veto power. In no other world forum do poor countries have such influence. Even the wealthiest countries can be held accountable in the WTO for violations of trade rules—for example, subsidizing certain industries or firms in order to get an unfair trade advantage, making the price of their exports less expensive and thus more competitive than they otherwise would be. Some political economists see the failures to reach agreement as reinforcing growing tendencies to form competing European, American, and Japan–East Asian trade areas. Trade areas are not inherently bad for simple geographic reasons. Although Chinese and other Asian exports to Europe, Canada, and the United States are massive, internal trade within North America and within Europe tends to be greater than their external trade with other areas. Enhancing such trade within regional areas can be beneficial, but free-trade advocates worry lest these trade areas eventually become mutually exclusive trade blocs, as they were in the 1930s.

The challenge for the WTO and other organizations will be to maintain global trade across regions on as open a basis as possible, even as efforts are made to enhance intraregional trade. At the same time (and responding to public pressures), the WTO and other international organizations concerned with global commerce will be called on to accommodate, to a greater degree than in the past, demands from both labor and environmental interests, often supported by nongovernmental organizations, adversely affected by the increasing globalization of capital and commercial transactions.

Global Governance—The International Monetary Regime

Trade and investment across national borders depends on the ability to exchange money from one currency to another—another focus of global-governance arrangements. Creating an international monetary regime and an **International Monetary Fund (IMF)** for the post–World War II period was much easier than constructing a trade regime. Competitive devaluations, such as those that had occurred during the interwar period, were forbidden, and exchange rates of one currency for another were to be stable. This was set forth by the Bretton Woods regime, named for the New Hampshire location where the international agreement was reached in 1944.

The IMF was to maintain **international liquidity**, helping states with insufficient foreign cash reserves by making short-term loans, enabling them to balance their books in the event of a shortfall in foreign currency reserves or other monetary assets. In the absence of IMF lending or other sources of credit from abroad (national treasuries, central banks, and privately owned banks or other sources of capital), a state might be forced to put up trade barriers against further imports, thus cutting off trade to the disadvantage of other countries. The IMF serves the financial needs of states, namely their treasuries and central banks, and, if necessary, is the lender of last resort to keep countries from going into bankruptcy. Of course, such loans usually come with strings attached—commitments to get economic matters in order with particular attention to fiscal matters (tax and spend) and monetary policy (interest rates and the money supply).

The international monetary regime changed in the 1970s from relatively **fixed exchange rates** under Bretton Woods to a regime of "managed flexibility"—floating exchange rates subject to currency-market interventions by central banks. The IMF, however, remained in place as a monetary lending agency with the purpose and capacity to maintain international liquidity. In a regime in which exchange rates are set in currency markets, central banks and national treasuries may choose to intervene in these markets unilaterally or, more likely, in concerted, multilateral actions. They intervene in order to buy and sell national currencies so as to affect their price or exchange rate, in turn affecting prices of goods and services. To intervene effectively in these money markets may require borrowing foreign currencies from other countries or from the IMF.

The prices of a country's exports—what they can be sold for in foreign markets—is directly affected by even small changes in exchange rates. For example, at a euro-dollar exchange rate of €1.0 = US$1.46 a Mercedes sedan manufactured at the plant in Böblingen in Baden-Württemberg, Germany, and priced at €100,000 costs $146,000. If the dollar gets stronger so that it only takes $1.40 to purchase a euro—a six-cent difference—the cost of the same automobile drops $6,000!

IMF ■ International Monetary Fund, created in 1944, charged with overseeing the international monetary system to ensure exchange rate stability and encouraging members to eliminate exchange restrictions that hinder trade

international liquidity
■ in monetary affairs, the ease with which foreign currencies are available to countries so they can settle their accounts with other countries

fixed exchange rates ■ a system in which the value of a country's currency, in relation to the value of other currencies, is maintained at a fixed conversion rate through government intervention

The same sensitivity in relation to changes in exchange rates is true for both the costs of investments and the amount of profits or return on these investments that can be repatriated or taken home. Thus, at €1.0 = US$1.40 a European firm that invests €100 million in the United States can buy plant and equipment amounting to $140 million. If the dollar weakens by ten cents so that €1.0 = US$1.50, the same €100 million now buys $150 million in the United States—a far more attractive investment opportunity. At the same time, the firm may be less inclined to take its profits out of the United States than before since a $100,000 profit or return on investment at €1.0 = US$1.40 converts to €71,429 ($100,000 divided by 1.4), but at €1.0 = US$1.50 the same profit is worth only €66,667 ($100,000 divided by 1.5)—some €4,762 less!

Put another way, whether for investment, trade, or merely the cost of traveling abroad next summer, exchange rates matter. Because they do, there are those who win and those who lose on any exchange-rate change. We need not be too surprised that something as important as money—what it can and cannot buy—quickly becomes an essential part of global governance: the construction, maintenance, and change of rules and institutions related to international monetary regimes.

Global Governance—The Investment-and-Development Regime

World Bank ■ an IO created in 1944, currently designed to be a source of financial and technical assistance to developing countries around the world

Finally, a multilateral capital-investment regime was established after World War II with the World Bank as its principal agency. The formal and original title of the World Bank—International Bank for Reconstruction and Development (IBRD)—reflects its original purpose, which was to rebuild post–World War II war-torn economies in Europe and Asia. Capital invested from foreign aid and multilateral lending coupled with loans from investment and other private-sector banks resulted in extraordinary success for these previously war-torn countries.

The Organization for European Economic Cooperation (OEEC) was formed in 1948 in Paris in the aftermath of World War II to facilitate capital-investment flows (U.S. assistance under the Marshall Plan as well as Canadian aid) to rebuild European economies. Aims at the time were to promote trade and monetary cooperation among member countries, fostering production and the economic reconstruction of Europe, promoting trade by reducing tariffs and other barriers, considering formation of a customs union or free-trade area, and exploring arrangements for regional monetary payments on a multilateral basis.

Immediate postwar economic reconstruction in Europe largely completed, an expansion of scope took place in 1961 with the formation of the Organization for Economic Cooperation and Development (OECD) to replace the OEEC. At its origins the OECD had eighteen European members plus the United States and Canada. Admissions no longer confined to Europe, there are now thirty-four member states from around the world committed to market economy, pluralist democracy, and respect for human rights. Often referred to now as the rich countries' club, the OECD works to expand free or open trade and contribute to economic development not only in advanced-industrial and postindustrial countries but also in developing countries.

The World Bank's task in more recent decades, however, has been to lend capital for development purposes to capital-poor, developing or Third World countries with an eye to integrating them more effectively in an open and global political economy. The extraordinarily large gap in technology, capital, and levels of living between advanced-industrial and postindustrial countries of the North and those in the South (where most people live) is a striking characteristic of the present-day global political economy.

French socialists first started using the expression *Third World* in the 1960s to denote the most populous category of the world's peoples, in much the same way as the term *third estate* in French history and culture refers to the masses of people who at the time of the French Revolution in 1789 were decidedly less well off than those in the upper classes—the clergy and aristocrats or nobility in the first two estates. This original usage of *Third World* thus had a positive connotation because it carried the implication that improvement in life conditions for the world's masses was still possible, whether by revolution or other means. In more recent years, however, the term has fallen into disfavor among those who feel the term devalues or puts lower-income countries in a third-rate position.

In any event, in this chapter and throughout this volume we use these terms descriptively without any intended connotation. **First World** and **North** are used interchangeably to refer to high-income, capital-richer countries that with a few exceptions lie in the Northern Hemisphere. Third World or **South** are also interchangeable terms that reflect that most middle- and low-income, capital-poorer countries are in the Southern Hemisphere. As a practical matter, the term *Second World*, which during the Cold War referred to the Soviet Union and other centrally planned, Marxist-Leninist political economies, has much less usage today.

Efforts by the World Bank are supplemented by regional development lending banks, such as the Inter-American Development Bank (IADB) and Asian Development bank (ADB), as well as bilateral loans from capital-rich to capital-poor countries. As with the now capital-rich countries reconstructed after World War II, the best way for capital-poor countries to borrow for investment purposes, if possible, is at concessionary rates of interest, that is, below market rates from long-term lenders such as the World Bank, other international lending institutions, or foreign governments. Loans at concessionary rates for development purposes are really a form of grant or foreign aid. If they are prudent, borrowing countries will set aside a portion of the concessionary loan, investing it at higher market rates and allowing compound interest over time to produce the funds needed to pay off the loan when due.

Heavy borrowing in the 1970s and 1980s by capital-poor countries—often at market interest rates from privately owned multinational banks and foreign governments—left many of these less-developed countries of the South deeply in debt. The heavy interest payments were burdens on their domestic political economies. Moreover, much of the money borrowed was not spent for development or, when it was, was not always allocated to sound projects. As a result, many of the expected economic gains for which the loans were originally requested were not realized either. Although many lenders offered refinancing and debt relief to borrowers so they could avoid default, the burden was reduced and crisis avoided primarily by the gradual reduction in global interest rates in the 1980s and 1990s.

Significant economic growth in the highly developed, capital-rich, industrial, and postindustrial economies of the North did have positive effects contributing to

First-Third Worlds
■ *First World*: capital-rich countries of the North; *Third World*: capital-poor countries of the South

North-South ■ *North*: advanced-industrial or postindustrial, high-income countries and societies generally in the northern hemisphere; *South*: less industrially developed, lower-income countries and societies generally in the southern hemisphere

economic development in the South. Good economic times for capital-rich countries usually mean increased purchases to include imports from developing countries. A rising tide raises all ships. At the same time, of course, recessions in the North typically result in reduced imports with adverse impact in the South. The phenomenal economic growth in China and India—linked so closely as their economies are to Europe and North America—still continued throughout the global recession, particularly given high demand for imports of both manufacturers and services.

Beyond the WTO, IMF, World Bank, and OECD, the principal UN organization responsible for global economic matters is the UN Economic and Social Council (ECOSOC). Other UN organs and specialized agencies linked to ECOSOC or other UN organs also deal with economic or commercial matters on a global basis. For example, the UN Development Programme (UNDP) in New York, the Food and Agricultural Organization (FAO) in Rome, the UN Industrial Development Organization (UNIDO) in Vienna, the UN Conference on Trade and Development (UNCTAD) and World Intellectual Property Organization (WIPO) in Geneva, and the International Atomic Energy Agency (IAEA) in Vienna address, respectively, different aspects of economic and commercial development and production, copyrights and patents, and electrical energy through nuclear power.

A world profile using UN Development Programme (UNDP) data (see Table 5.1) divides countries by level of development into very high-, high-, middle-, and low-human development categories. Take a close look at this table. As is immediately apparent, the disparities are enormous, which shows dramatically how human conditions vary. Real per capita income in very high-development countries, for example, is still about 18.5 times the average in middle-income countries, and more than 52 times the average in low-income countries (most of which are in Africa). Other indicators of level of living show literacy at close to 100 percent in high-income countries but only about three-fifths of that in low-development countries, the middle-development countries splitting the difference. Given disease and shortfalls in nutrition as well as high infant mortality, it is hardly surprising that life expectancy declines from just over 80 years in very high-development countries to just under 70 and 56 years, respectively, in middle- and low-development countries.

High-income countries have remained highly urbanized even as high-technology, capital-intensive, information-based services have displaced many labor-intensive industries. Low- and middle-income countries have also experienced a substantial shift in recent decades from agriculture to urban-centered industry and services. In pursuit of a better life and responding to the labor demands of new industries, people in low- and middle-income countries have become more urbanized, many leaving the countryside and their rural way of life behind. But many, if not most, have not found a better life in the cities as the rapid urban in-migration has overloaded the capacity of many governments to provide even such essential services as clean water and sanitation.

Historically, when we think of international cooperation, we think of cooperation among states: Consider the post–World War II creation of the IMF, the World Bank, the GATT and, finally, the WTO. The dominant paradigm or image among political leaders traditionally has been one of national economies facing

TABLE 5.1

Levels of Human Development

Compare the statistics in the right- and left-hand columns. Across virtually all dimensions there is a staggering gap between the low- (essentially developing world) and high-level (essentially the West and Japan) countries. Particularly striking is the huge difference in per capita income (GDP per person in US$). Whatever one may think of the economic structuralist critique, which lays much of the blame at the feet of the North or developed capitalist countries, the challenging questions are: What can and should be done? In a globalized world with so many interconnections, events and trends on the far side of the globe are not so easily dismissed as simply irrelevant to our safety, security, and economic well-being.

	Low	Middle	High / Very High
Number of countries in category	42	42	43 / 42
Gross domestic product (GDP) in US$ billions	$771	$7,636	$8,552 / $42,600
Average annual GDP growth rate (1970–2008)	−0.4%	2.7%	1.1% / 2.3%
Population (millions): 2010	1,099	3,597	1,052 / 1,056
Per capita income (GDP per person in US$)	781	2,200	8,937 / 40,748
Life expectancy: age in years	56.0	69.3	72.6 / 80.3
Literacy	61.2%	80.7%	92.3% / —
Population growth rate (annual average 2010–2015)	2.1%	1.1%	0.7% / 0.5%
Estimated output by economic sector (% of GDP)			
Agriculture	22%	9%	2%
Industry	28%	38%	28%
Services	50%	53%	70%

Source: UNDP, *UN Development Report,* 2010.

the outside world, paralleling the realist perspective of states as the key unit of international relations. This distinction between national and international economies does seem outdated given the remarkable globalization of trade and financial markets that erodes the ability of states to control their own national economies. Similarly, in terms of production, it becomes difficult to determine exactly what is an American product since parts frequently come from other countries, or even those components manufactured in the United States may be assembled as final products in China, Korea, India, or elsewhere.

We may also witness further political fallout from the increase in economic globalization. First, now that economic barriers among the advanced capitalist states have been reduced significantly, differences in domestic economic structures—government policies and patterns of private-sector industrial organization—may become more important. The best example involves U.S. criticism of China's domestic economic structure and policies, which aggressively push Chinese exports and make it difficult to import foreign goods and services. A key aspect of support for the postwar international economic order has been a domestic social compact between state and society. In many countries this means support for an open international market is balanced by domestic programs designed to support workers with unemployment compensation, retraining, and other benefits as part of a social safety net. High and increasing costs have made it increasingly difficult for governments to live up to their end of the domestic bargain. As a result, political criticism of free trade continues to mount.

Second, even if unilateral protectionism does not come about, regional trade and other economic arrangements run the risk of becoming mutually exclusive camps if members turn inward and away from interdependent relations within broader global markets. Such blocs could evolve in North America, Europe, and East Asia.

The growing North–South economic divide is not only a challenge to a truly global economy, but also a threat to an emerging global civil society. Economic and social inequality continues to be an important feature of world politics. If populations continue to grow so rapidly, capitalist political economy will be put to the test as resource and environmental constraints make sustainable development extraordinarily difficult in many areas of the world. Domestic, regional, and international political repercussions could be significant.

In sum, maintaining an open global financial and trading environment consistent with liberal or openness principles remains a substantial challenge in coming decades in a world that could just as easily move in the opposite direction.

CONCLUSION

We have examined in this toolbox chapter the key components of the globalization phenomenon. Technology was given a prominent place in our discussion as it has had a dramatic impact on the social, cultural, and economic aspects of globalization. Technology, of course, has impacted these realms throughout history, whether we're talking about the development of the wheel and lever or modern electronic circuitry. What is different over the past century, however, is the speed with which the globalization process has occurred and, as the term implies, its worldwide or global sweep. Globalization has often been equated with "Americanization." This equation for many has negative connotations and perhaps has some validity in terms of the spread of American popular culture. But it is also factually incorrect to the extent it underplays the contribution of technological contributions made by scientists and engineers in other countries. As for its political impact, globalization is neither simply good nor bad. It can help authoritarian regimes keep track of dissidents, but also provide these individuals with a means to rally support and maintain contact with the outside world.

The impact of technology on the development of a global political economy is striking. When people speak of the expansion of globalization, very often they are referring to economic globalization. Particularly since the end of World War II, the world has been increasingly caught up in a web of economic relations, the full extent and density of which were heretofore unknown. Furthermore, economic globalization has progressively worked to undermine the claims of governments that they have the ability to protect national economies from the effects of the larger, global political economy. The lines between global and state economies are becoming blurry as international economic issues become domestic political issues and vice versa.

As we have also noted, the benefits of economic globalization are uneven, a point made for years by economic structuralists, liberals interested in international economic cooperation, and protestors at the annual World Economic Forum. Some states prosper more than others. As in earlier decades, much of the South continues to be trapped in poverty. Already beset by problems of political legitimacy, many such regimes see their authority further eroded by an unforgiving global economy that rewards those with highly trained and adaptable workforces with access to the most modern technology.

Effective global governance—coordination, if not always full collaboration of state and nonstate actors—may help sustain gains, reducing when possible the adverse effects of globalization. Adapting trade, monetary, and investment-for-development regimes to changing circumstances—even transforming them, if necessary, in a major overhaul—is the ongoing task before us as we seek to better the human condition both nationally and on a global scale. Twenty-first-century challenges for global and national governance include maintaining environmentally sustainable economic growth, distributing at least some of the gains toward providing shelter and eliminating the crushing weight of poverty, starvation and malnutrition, and diseases that continue to afflict humankind. Even basic economic needs—food, clothing, and shelter—have yet to be met adequately for more than a billion people in more than forty of the least-developed countries at the bottom of the global heap, where per capita income is less than $800 per year. There is much yet to be done. . . .

✔●—Study and Review the Post-Test & Chapter Exam at mypoliscilab.com

LEARNING OBJECTIVES REVIEW

5.1 Identify the key economic, social, and cultural aspects of the globalization, the role of technology, and assess both positive and negative implications for the human condition.

The dramatic increase in worldwide economic, social, and cultural interactions are facilitated by the development of modern communication technologies. This section notes the uneven, asymmetric distribution of gains as well as the resultant political implications of globalization.

KEY TERMS

Globalization 150
Interdependence 153
Trade integration 153
Foreign direct investment 153
European Union 154
Cyber-war 158
Social network analysis 159
Patterns of life 159

ADDITIONAL READINGS

Robert Gilpin and Jean M. Gilpin, *Global Political Economy: Understanding the International Economic Order* (Princeton, NJ: Princeton University Press, 2001). An in-depth, historically grounded examination of how markets and the policies of states determine the way the world economy functions.

Joseph E. Stiglitz, *Making Globalization Work* (New York: W.W. Norton, 2007). The author addresses both the ups and downs of globalization with consideration of remedies for the latter.

Thomas L. Friedman, *The World Is Flat 3.0: A Brief History of the Twenty-first Century* (London: Macmillan/Picador, 2007). Friedman analyzes key drivers and technological developments that exemplify and reflect globalization.

5.2 Trace the historical emergence and development of capitalism as a worldwide form of political economy, identifying its principal attributes and progressive globalization.

The economic dimension of globalization is generally recognized as the most salient characteristic. This section provides a historical overview of the development of the global political economy. Markets, money, a set of values, and the prominence of capital as one factor of production over the others—land or resources such as labor—are key elements that help define capitalism as a mode of production or form of political economy. The importance of writers such as David Ricardo and Adam Smith are highlighted.

KEY TERMS

Capitalism 159
Mode of production 159
Political economy 159
Capital 162
Capital goods 163
GNP 163
Capital formation 163
GDP 163
GNI 163
Mercantilism 166
Factors of production 166
Free trade 167
Comparative advantage 167
Protectionism 167
Imperialism 168
Neocolonialism 168
Cartels 170

ADDITIONAL READINGS

Adam Smith, *The Wealth of Nations* (1776). Many editions—a foundational reading in classical economics worth pursuing in serious study. The first three of the five "books" or parts are the most important; however, his classic reference to the invisible hand is to be found in the fourth book. Smith's earlier *Theory of Moral Sentiments* (1759 and 1761) presents his understandings about how moral values relate to political economy in society.

Max Weber, *The Protestant Ethic and the Spirit of Capitalism* (New York: Charles Scribner's Sons, 1958, 1976), written as a challenge to Marx's more material explanation for the emergence of capitalism, formulates the hypothesis that religious ideas that eventually became secularized in modern commercial culture were at least as important as material factors, if not more so. See also Weber's classic *Economy and Society* (Berkeley: University of California Press, 1968, 1978).

Karl Polanyi, *The Great Transformation* (Boston: Beacon Press, 1944, 1957) depicts major changes in international relations and world politics stemming from the spread of global capitalism in the industrial age.

Joseph A. Schumpeter, *Capitalism, Socialism, and Democracy* (New York: Harper and Row, 1942, 1976) assesses different forms of capitalist political economy—ideas and practical realities in relation to public versus private ownership of the means of production.

5.3 Explain attempts at global governance in the post–World War II era to deal with trade, finance, and investment resulting from rapid globalization.

Global governance—coordination or collaboration among state and nonstate actors—takes practical form in the construction, maintenance, and transformation of international trade, monetary, and investment-for-development regimes (sets of agreed rules and associated multilateral institutions). Associated international organizations and regimes are noted, with further discussion reserved for later chapters. The extraordinarily uneven distribution of gains and losses of globalization become crystal-clear when one examines the profound difference in the human condition across the spectrum from low to very high levels of development between developing and developed countries. Statistical table make the point clear.

KEY TERMS

Competitive devaluation 171
Regimes 172
GATT 172
Tariffs 172
WTO 172
IMF 173
International liquidity 173
Fixed exchange rates 173
World Bank 174
Third World 174
First-Third World 175
North-South 175

ADDITIONAL READINGS

Robert O. Keohane, *After Hegemony: Cooperation and Discord in the World Political Economy* (Princeton, NJ: Princeton University Press, 2005). This liberal-institutionalist scholar known for his work on international organizations focuses here on cooperation so essential to effective global governance.

Margaret P. Karns and Karen A. Mingst, *International Organizations: The Politics and Processes of Global Governance* (Boulder, CO: Lynne Rienner, 2010). The authors examine global governance from the liberalism perspective, focusing on international organizations broadly conceived, NGOs, and global civil society.

Jeffrey Sachs, *The End of Poverty: Economic Possibilities for Our Time* (London: Penguin, 2006). This well-known economist sets his sights high, taking on the global scourge of poverty and possible ways to ameliorate it.

Amartya Sen, *Development as Freedom* (Harpswell, ME: Anchor Publishing, 2000). This Nobel Prize–winning economist relates development to enhancement of individual freedom, viewing the latter as both a basic constituent of development in itself and an enabling key to other aspects. No knowledge of economics is assumed.

CHAPTER REVIEW

1. What is the critical dynamic of globalization?
   a. The expansion of the capitalist world economy
   b. The expansion of the world labor movement
   c. The expansion of communication technologies
   d. The expansion of international banking

2. The field of international political economy tries to explain what?
   a. The intersection between domestic and international economies
   b. The intersection between national and international governments
   c. The intersection between politics and economics either domestically or globally
   d. The intersection between economics and human behavior on the international stage

3. The term *internationalization* refers to what?
   a. The increase of international identities in a globalized world
   b. The decrease of sovereign states within the international system
   c. The increase of international labor movement between societies
   d. The increase of trade, commerce, investment, and other interactions between states

4. Economic structuralists agree with which of the following statements?
   a. Laissez-faire policies are the most productive.
   b. All politics can be reduced to economics when viewing international relations.
   c. Economic issues can occupy extremely high places on international agendas.
   d. Economic issues are to be considered "low" politics.

5. Measurements of state-to-state economic or commercial activities will _____ as globalization continues.
   a. increase in importance
   b. retain their importance
   c. be replaced by new measures
   d. tend to lose their significance

6. Feudal political economy concentrated what resources and methods of production in small communities?
   a. Agriculture
   b. Manufacturing
   c. Shipping
   d. Steel works

7. In the European feudal period, markets began to develop outside the walls of
   a. banks.
   b. government buildings.
   c. castles or estates.
   d. prisons.

8. Money plays what two important roles in markets?
   a. Provides a standard of value for buying and selling and acts as a store of value
   b. Provides wealth and barterability between commodities
   c. Provides a store of value and easily convertible commodity prices
   d. Provides a standard of value for buying and selling and acts as a wealth distributor

9. David Ricardo argued what about international trade?
   a. Decreased government interference would have the same positive effects in international trade as in domestic trade.
   b. Increasing government interference would create the same positive effects in international trade as in domestic trade.
   c. International trade should be conducted between friendly states in order to be successful.
   d. War makes international trade unproductive.

10. What is a decisive factor in determining the degree of privatization in a particular state?
    a. The amount of capital
    b. The amount of labor
    c. The underlying cultural values
    d. The underlying norms of capital construction

11. Competitive devaluation refers to the process of
    a. states devaluing their currency in order to secure price advantages for domestic producers.
    b. states competing with other states to devalue their currency more quickly to receive cheaper imports.
    c. creating a global compact against currency devaluations.
    d. states devaluing their currency in order to secure price advantages for foreign exporters.

12. GATT negotiation rounds were primarily designed to reduce
    a. competitive devaluations.
    b. tariffs.
    c. export quotas.
    d. currency controls.

13. The WTO is distinct from most other international organizations for what reason?
    a. All countries of the world are members regardless of political orientation.
    b. It has a dispute resolution mechanism.
    c. Decisions are reached by consensus.
    d. No country has a veto power.

14. The main purpose of the IMF is to
    a. foster development in developing countries
    b. maintain international liquidity.
    c. act as a capital investment regime.
    d. maintain international price stability.

15. The primary purpose of the World Bank is to
    a. act a lender of last resort for states.
    b. maintain international liquidity.
    c. act as a provider of capital invested for development.
    d. be the bank of international travelers.

16. Regional trading blocs pose what risk to the international trade effort?
    a. They can become mutually exclusive trading camps.
    b. States will not participate in the WTO.
    c. They can become mutually inclusive trading camps.
    d. States will begin to go to war more often.

17. According to the UNDP data, high-development countries have a per-capita income _____ times higher than low-income countries.
    a. 5
    b. 10
    c. 20
    d. more than 50

18. Rapid in-migration of labor to cities has had what effect on Third World governments?
    a. Overloaded their service delivery capacities
    b. Provided a usable labor force
    c. Caused riots to break out
    d. Improved the infrastructure in cities

19. What may become more important as a factor affecting further economic globalization?
    a. Differences in domestic political systems
    b. Differences in political parties
    c. Differences in the ways domestic economies are structured and operate
    d. Differences in preferential trading arrangements

20. The continuation of the North-South capital divide will have what effect on further globalization of the world economy?
    a. Speed up the process of expanding it
    b. Be a challenge in the process of expanding it
    c. Have no effect on expanding it further
    d. Stop further expansion of it due to actions taken by states

Power

"We assume that statesmen think and act in terms of interest defined as power, and the evidence of history bears that assumption out." —Hans J. Morgenthau, Realist Scholar

LEARNING OBJECTIVES

6.1 Grasp how power and national interest (or objectives consistent with interest) are core to national security and foreign policy.

6.2 Differentiate between the conflicts and dilemmas policymakers must address when establishing a national security framework.

6.3 Classify the types of capabilities that comprise power.

6.4 Illustrate how the diversity of capabilities impacts the way in which power is measured.

The Obama administration's National Security Strategy explicitly provides an assessment of the overall strategic environment. According to the document, the key challenge is to determine "how to advance American interests in a world that has changed—a world in which the international architecture of the 20th century is buckling under the weight of new threats." Indeed, "wars over ideology have given way to wars over religious, ethnic, and tribal identity; nuclear dangers have proliferated; inequality and economic instability have intensified; damage to our environment, food insecurity, and dangers to public health are increasingly shared; and the same tools that empower individuals to build enable them to destroy."[1]

Beyond merely countering threats, a strategy also takes advantage of opportunities. In President Barack Obama's much anticipated Cairo Speech in June 2009, for example, he promised a "new beginning" in relations between the United States and the Muslim world. Rather than viewing Muslims almost exclusively through the prism of Islamic extremism and terrorism, the administration sought a strategy of global engagement that would encompass such areas of common interest as education, the environment, and the economy.

Read and Listen to Chapter 6 at mypoliscilab.com

Study and Review the Pre-Test & Flashcards at mypoliscilab.com

This chapter takes up both national power and the interests states pursue or, more concretely, the objectives they wish to achieve that governmental authorities understand to be consistent with those interests. Some states may seek to maximize their power either absolutely or relative to other states as a national objective, thus attaining or sustaining superiority over others either regionally or globally. Another, less competitive way to view power, however, is to see it as the set of capabilities by which to serve the national interest using it both to counter threats and to take advantage of opportunities both domestically and internationally.

[1]www.whitehouse.gov

As such power becomes more a *means* political authorities use than an *end,* as they seek merely to improve the relative position in the regional or global "pecking order" among states.

We see national power exercised diplomatically, militarily, economically, and culturally as states and their societies interact in an increasingly globalized world. Although globalization has elevated the role of nonstate actors—international and nongovernmental organizations, individuals and groups—states are still key players and the national power they wield, though challenged, more often than not is decisive, particularly when national interests are at stake. Countering threats and achieving objectives through the exercise of national power—sometimes in coalitions or alliances with other states—remains an essential part of 21st-century international relations and world politics.

HOW TO THINK ABOUT NATIONAL SECURITY

6.1 Grasp how power and national interest (or objectives consistent with interest) are core to national security and foreign policy.

As noted in Chapter 2, "Theory," the realist perspective on international relations and world politics closely matches that of many, if not most, policymakers. Whether a dictator or democrat, leaders of states pursue objectives understood to be consistent with their separate national interests. For example, a basic or core interest is protection of the physical integrity of a state. A more specific objective is to defend against any invasion a neighboring state might launch. Within the global system, opportunities present themselves that, if handled properly, can help to achieve specific objectives. Similarly, threats emanating from other states have to be dealt with, particularly if they interfere with the achievement of national objectives. To exploit these opportunities and to handle these threats, leaders devise specific policies that employ various elements of national power at their disposal. They mobilize national capabilities to exert power constructively to achieve objectives and protect their interests. If there is one concept most closely associated with international relations and world politics, it is power. As noted by Hans Morgenthau in his *Politics Among Nations*: "Whatever the ultimate aims of international politics, power is always the immediate aim." In fact, for Morgenthau, "interest [is] defined in terms of power."[2] Whatever the specific objectives policymakers may pursue to achieve and defend a state's interests, power is required.

Figure 6.1 depicts a national security policy conceptual framework. This framework is important for two reasons: (1) Policymakers explicitly or implicitly think in terms of interests, objectives, threats, and opportunities when conceiving and implementing their policies; and (2) the framework has utility not only for policymakers of states, but also for practitioners at international organizations, multinational corporations, and transnational nongovernmental organizations. Although realists are most explicit in elaborating this power-and-interest formulation, it is also part of a liberal framework, and also finds a place in English School and economic-structuralist theorizing. Beyond survival of the state and other national security–related objectives, however, liberals are more likely

---

[2]Hans J. Morgenthau, *Politics Among Nations*, 4th ed. (New York: Knopf, 1967), 25.

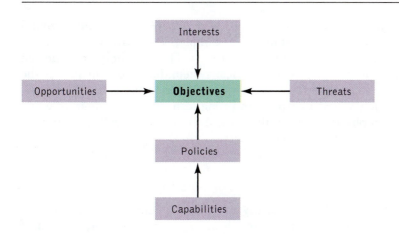

FIGURE 6.1
Understanding State Behavior

to include human rights and socioeconomic, welfare-oriented goals as part of the agenda of objectives they see as part of the national interest.

Interests

A skeptic would claim that the **national interest** of any state is simply what political leaders say it is—merely a rhetorical device designed to justify the pursuit of a controversial policy. There is certainly an element of truth to this—all leaders claim they act in the selfless pursuit of the national interest whether dictator, democrat, or demagogue. It is fair to say, however, that there are a few basic national interests that transcend any single type of political leader.

national interest
 a state's core security interests and values

Survival   First, there is no disagreement among policymakers that national survival as a state is the minimum objective—sometimes referred to as a core or vital interest common to all states. Survival as a state implies maintenance of its sovereign status. The exercise of **sovereignty** is a right claimed by a state to exercise complete jurisdiction, power, or authority internally or within its territory and externally to act independently or autonomously in the conduct of its foreign affairs. For all their differences, leaders in the United States, Israel, Iran, and North Korea all are first and foremost concerned with national survival.

sovereignty ■
a claim to political authority to make policy or take actions domestically or abroad; based on territory and autonomy, historically associated with the modern state

Economic Vitality   A second core interest for states is economic vitality and prosperity. Economic prosperity is not only sought on behalf of citizens of a society, but also it can be an important source of power in international affairs. Granted, there are despots who assiduously work to plunder their own societies and have little concern for their subjects, but such instances are exceptions to the rule. Even those dictators bent on expansionism realize that without the engine of economic growth their dreams of imperial glory are unlikely to be realized. The international economic crisis—the Great Recession that began in 2007 and 2008—raised this core interest to the status of front-page news.

Core Values   Finally, the preservation of a society's core values is often a vital interest in itself. In many Western states, for example, democratic values are key elements of national identity. So are human rights. They not only are reflected in the structure and functioning of the political system, but also help answer the questions: "Who are we, and for what do we stand?" On the other hand, some Islamic states and societies view European and American liberal consumer-oriented cultures with their emphasis on materialism and overt sexuality as threats to basic religious and moral values they wish to preserve.

Objectives

objectives ■
specific goals of a state, international organization, or transnational organization

Interests are so general that they are usually an inadequate guide for policymakers. They do, however, inform more specific goals or **objectives**. The core interest of survival for a landlocked state like Poland or Zimbabwe, for example, is defined more specifically as defense against invasion by neighboring states. Similarly, a state with long coastlines such as the United States and Brazil that is dependent on foreign trade might see the protection of sea lanes as an important national objective in order to maintain economic prosperity.

Beyond defensive concerns, policymakers may also opt for a broad range of other objectives. Some states may wish to conquer others or take territory by force, as occurred, for example, in both of the 20th century's world wars, the Korean War in 1950, the Vietnam War in the 1960s and 1970s, and Iraq's invasion of Kuwait in 1990.

As a practical matter, however, most national objectives pursued by policymakers are usually more modest than conquest or defense against invasion. The scope of these other objectives is really quite broad, covering a wide range of political, social, and economic issues. For example, policymakers in the United States, Canada, Japan, or some European states may seek to achieve long-range objectives in order to advance human rights, put a cap on the arms race and reduce the likelihood of war, reduce poverty and increase agricultural and industrial productivity in developing countries, and slow environmental degradation by putting limits on deforestation and pollution of the oceans and the atmosphere. Some foreign policy objectives may be more immediate—short term or short range—such as stabilizing the chaotic situation in Afghanistan or handling the latest crisis reported by the news media. Table 6.1 provides some examples of short-term, middle-range, and long-term objectives.

Threats

States do not decide to pursue specific objectives in a vacuum. Objectives are critically influenced by perceived threats emanating from the global system. Prior to 1992, Western European states paid relatively little attention to events in Yugoslavia. When the country divided and wars and ethnic cleansing erupted among the Croats, Serbs, and Bosnians, a prime European objective became preventing the spread of the conflict beyond the borders of the former Yugoslavia.

Currently, policymakers in the United States and Europe are understandably concerned about the political stability of Pakistan given its possession of nuclear

> ▶ **TABLE 6.1**
>
> **Categorizing the Foreign Policy Objectives of States**
>
> The challenge for policymakers is that at any one point in time, a state could be pursuing short-, medium-, and long-term objectives in all three categories at the same time. For example, in 2010, the United States was engaged militarily with Libya in an attempt to unseat Colonel Kaddafi (short-term goal). But it was also working to avoid conflict between India and Pakistan (middle-range goal) and to achieve a durable peace among Israel and its Arab neighbors (long-term goal).
>
> **Objectives**
>
> | Issues | Short-Term (Often High Urgency) | Middle-Range (Not Urgent, Somewhat Important) | Long-Term (Not Urgent, Usually of Greater Importance) |
> |---|---|---|---|
> | warfare (survival) | Militarily defeat an enemy; negotiate a cease-fire; separate the warring parties | Maintain effective peacekeeping; manage unresolved conflicts to avoid escalation to warfare | Achieve a durable or lasting peace; resolve conflicts and reconcile the parties |
> | commerce (economic vitality) | Persuade the other party to make a trade concession such as lowering a tariff or trade barrier | Establish a good climate conducive to expanding trade relations | Assure global open trading orders will flourish |
> | human rights (core values) | Secure the release of particular political prisoners; halt human rights abuse in another country | Establish and foster legitimacy for human rights in as many countries as possible | Achieve the societal and political elements essential to durable democratic regimes in other states |

weapons and the existence of multiple Islamic jihadist and other extremist groups within its borders dedicated to expelling India from neighboring Kashmir, attacking North Atlantic Treaty Organization (NATO) forces in Afghanistan, and threatening terrorist attacks on the West. As the most recent U.S. National Security Strategy states: "This Administration has no greater responsibility than the safety and security of the American people. And there is no greater threat to the American people than weapons of mass destruction, particularly the danger posed by the pursuit of nuclear weapons by violent extremists and their proliferation to additional states."

When threats are assessed, avoidance of engaging in threat inflation is crucial. The key question to ask is basic, but hard to answer: To what extent is the threat truly a danger to national security? Was the threat of Saddam Hussein's possession or potential for acquiring weapons of mass destruction sufficient to justify the United States and allied invasion of Iraq in March 2003? Would continuing the containment and deterrent policy have been more effective? Similarly, was the threat of a resurgent Taliban such that the Obama administration was correct in authorizing additional troops to support a counterinsurgency campaign in Afghanistan? North Korea has a nuclear capability. What, if anything, do they intend to do with it? Iran, as assessed by many intelligence services, is interested in developing a similar nuclear capability. To what extent do these countries represent a threat to their neighbors and to the world at large?

Such questions are obviously easier to answer in hindsight. Some analysts prefer to limit themselves to detailing the capabilities adversaries and others may have without engaging in assessments of intentions—a highly subjective enterprise. On the other hand, others argue that intentions also need to be considered lest the focus on capabilities alone lead to exaggeration of the threat posed by other states. Thus, they prefer to combine both intentions and capabilities (particularly military assets) possessed by adversaries, basing their overall threat assessment on the best intelligence available. Put simply, analysts in government agencies and think tanks can assess the extent of a threat by the following multiplicative formula:

$$\text{Intentions} \times \text{Capabilities} = \text{THREAT}$$

Thus, for example, Germany has the *capability* to invade France, but nowadays has no *intent* to do so. Thus, the German threat to France today is virtually zero—quite different from threat analysis in 1938 and 1939 just before the outbreak of World War II when German military capabilities were strong and its intentions vis-à-vis France hostile.

Threats, then, are really social constructions—understandings held by those in power and in the populations that follow them. The effort to find out what is threatening and what is not is highly subjective. As such, the threat analysis formula becomes:

$$\text{Perceived Intentions} \times \text{Perceived Capabilities} = \text{THREAT PERCEPTION}$$

Moreover, as constructivists argue, if the authorities in one country see another country as threatening, conduct of the threatened party—such as defense preparations—also may be perceived as threatening.

This intersubjective sharing of threat perceptions can spiral, each party feeling increasingly vulnerable. Arms races may be one by-product, rising tensions leading to armed conflict another. The security dilemma, as John Herz once observed, lies in one party's increased defense preparations perceived and understood by the other as threatening. As each takes even legitimate "defense" measures, both respond by matching or surpassing steps taken by the other—the net effect being that both parties actually undermine their own and the other's security.

Another present-day example is threat analysis on the Korean peninsula. Government authorities in Seoul (the capital of South Korea) keep close tabs on what is going on in Pyongyang (the capital of North Korea). Given the commitment of some 25,000 U.S. military forces to the defense of South Korea, the two allies share intelligence each collects on both capabilities and intentions, particularly the former. Thus a high state of readiness by both South Korean and U.S. military forces rises to an even higher state of alert when the regime in Pyongyang speaks more aggressively than usual or provokes the South by attacking naval or ground units.

The simplest way to think about threats, then, is to answer the following question: "What are the intentions and capabilities of a rival state?" If a state has the intent to do harm but has no capability, then the threat is low. Similarly, a state might have the capability, but if intelligence indicates there is little or no intent to attack, then the threat is also low. As those who prefer to focus on capabilities are quick to comment, however, threat analysis can be wrong—intelligence may not have as good a handle on enemy intentions as political authorities would like.

capabilities ■
material and nonmaterial resources that can serve as the basis for power

Thus, there is always a chance of surprise attack. To these more conservative analysts, that's precisely what happened before the Japanese attack on Pearl Harbor and other U.S. locations on December 7, 1941. U.S. intelligence analysts were well aware of Japanese naval capabilities including aircraft carriers and other ships deployed in the Pacific, but the prevailing view was that the Japanese High Command would not risk attacking the United States territories so far from the Japanese home waters.

A final point to keep in mind is that a completely threat-based national security strategy is unsustainable over the long haul. Coming up with a laundry list of potential threats is easy. But what is their relative priority? No country has the economic capability to lavish untold amounts of their budget on both legitimate threats as well as what could best be called international irritants. How is Cuba an actual threat to the United States? Is Hugo Chavez of Bolivia with his control of vast oil reserves a threat or an irritant? Devising a national security strategy

▶ CASE & POINT | Key Drivers of National Security Policy

CASE Merely assessing the capabilities of other states is an inadequate approach to designing a national security policy. If political authorities do not take intentions into account, they will be fearful of even close allies or coalition partners. For example, the British and French both have a nuclear capability. Does the United States fear this situation? No. In fact, since the 1950s, U.S. administrations have correctly assessed that neither country has an intention to use these weapons against American targets. Hence the threat from the British and the French militaries is virtually nonexistent.

But focusing only on assessed intentions of other states is also too limiting. For example, the communist government of Cuba may have nothing but negative intentions and feelings toward the United States, but its military capability to act on these intentions is essentially nil. Hence Cuba's military threat to the United States—as is the case with the United Kingdom and France—is also low.

POINT The real concern and the driver of national security priorities are those cases where an adversary has not only intentions to harm, but also a capability to do so. This was the situation between the United States and the Soviet Union during the Cold War (1945–1991). The result of this situation during the Cold War was that billions of dollars were spent by both countries and their allies to deter, defend, and enhance their respective interests. ◀

with multiple ambitious international goals increases the potential for economic bankruptcy. The former Soviet Union based its Cold War strategy on a model that did not provide the sound economy needed to finance extraordinarily high rates of defense spending seemingly in perpetuity. Spending by some estimates 35 percent or more of GDP in the country's military-industrial sector distorted the allocation of capital, labor, and other resources and contributed to economic collapse. Economic failures evident in the last years of the Cold War were followed by the unraveling of the Warsaw Pact alliance and the Soviet Union itself in 1991—a territorially truncated Russian Federation and Commonwealth of Independent States (former Soviet republics) emerging in January 1992. The Cold War had ended, Western economies and their militaries having prevailed without firing a shot!

Opportunities

The global system presents policymakers not only with threats to national interests, but also with opportunities that may influence the formulation of foreign policy objectives. As with threats, determining what is an "opportunity" worth pursuing is also highly subjective. Moreover, pursuit by one country of what its governing authorities think is an opportunity may be taken as a threat by others. Again, what is or is not a threat or opportunity is always subject to interpretation.

The decision by former Soviet leader Mikhail Gorbachev to lift the heavy hand of repression from Eastern European client states in the late 1980s created an opportunity for the Federal Republic of Germany (West Germany) to reunite with the German Democratic Republic (formerly communist East Germany). China's decision to create foreign trade zones in its eastern coastal provinces in the 1980s provided an opportunity for other states to pursue the objective of expanded trade and economic investment with the world's most populous country. Even the aftermath of bloody wars provides opportunities for policymakers of the victorious states to reconfigure the international system. This occurred in 19th-century Europe after the defeat of Napoleon and also after World War II when the United States led the way promoting international trade and investment and creating such international organizations as the United Nations, the World Bank, and the International Monetary Fund.

POLICYMAKING CONFLICTS AND DILEMMAS

6.2 Differentiate between the conflicts and dilemmas policymakers must address when establishing a national security framework.

The previous discussion may leave the impression that the formulation of a state's national security or foreign policy objectives is a straightforward task that can be reduced to a formula of national objectives seen as a function of (or in relation to) perceived interests that, in turn, are based on assessments of perceived threats and perceived opportunities:

$$\text{OBJECTIVES} = f \text{ perceived interests (based upon perceived threats and opportunities)}$$

Policymakers, however, must contend with at least three challenges: qualifying the nature of interests and objectives, prioritizing objectives, and balancing competing domestic and foreign policy objectives.

ARGUMENT Hans J. Morgenthau has explained the utility of the rational, unitary actor assumption in terms of policymakers defining and achieving objectives:

> We put ourselves in the position of a statesman who must meet a certain problem of foreign policy under certain circumstances, and we ask ourselves what the rational alternatives are from which a statesman may choose ... and which of these rational alternatives this particular statesman, acting under these circumstances, is likely to choose. It is the testing of this rational hypothesis against the actual facts and their consequences that gives meaning to the facts of international politics and makes a theory of politics possible.*

For example, Western policymakers were not privy to either the calculations made or the thinking done by the former Iraqi dictator Saddam Hussein when he pursued weapons of mass destruction. But it was assumed that he had aggressive intent, particularly after Iraqi's invasion of neighboring Kuwait in 1991, an act of aggression thwarted by a U.S.-led military coalition. It is assumed that he believed such weapons would deter the West from attempting to remove him from power as well as deter Iran from reigniting the bloody war between Iran and Iraq that raged from 1980 to 1988 and resulted in over a million casualties.

COUNTERARGUMENT Liberal theorists would offer different, yet potentially complementary explanations. Those who emphasize the role of personality and perception would suggest Saddam Hussein's behavior was the result of a paranoid personality. Others would point to his fear of internal unrest or a military coup. The possession of such weapons would help to solidify his domestic political position. Such explanations are based on factors operating at the individual and domestic level of analysis and have less to do with the international environment.

APPLICATION North Korea is appropriately known as the Hermit Kingdom. Since the end of actual combat in the Korean War in 1952, the country has been ruled by a bizarre and elaborate cult of personality revolving around the Kim family. With an appalling human rights record and a devastated economy that has caused death by starvation of an estimated hundreds of thousands of its citizens in the 1990s alone, North Korea has one of the worst human rights records of any state, is the most militarized nation on earth in terms of percentage of its population under arms, and has developed a nuclear capability. Very few outsiders are allowed to visit the country, so information is limited on the current dictator, Kim Jong-un, who assumed his position in December 2011 upon the death of his father, Kim Jong-il. A full general at the age of 28, Kim Jong-un depends upon Army support to sustain his regime.

Using this limited information, apply the rational actor assumption to explain the following incident: On March 26, 2010, an explosion tore through the hull of a South Korean naval vessel that was operating in waters near North Korean territory. Forty-six sailors were killed. The South Korean government accused the North Korean Navy of deliberately attacking its ship. North Korea responded that the charge was pure fabrication, "orchestrated by the group of traitors in a deliberate and brigandish manner to achieve certain political and military aims." Was it merely "a very unfortunate incident" as the Chinese government observed, with the implication it might have been an accident? If it was a deliberate act, what possible rationale could the North Korean government have had? Even if you lack knowledge of North Korea, what possible hypotheses can you assert utilizing the levels of analysis framework—role of the individual, group decision making, nature of the state or society, or international (concern for security and external threats)? ▶

*Hans J. Morgenthau, *Politics among Nations*, 4th ed. (New York: Knopf, 1967), 5.

✴ Explore the
"Conflict: You Are a
Strategic Analyst" at
mypoliscilab.com

Qualifying the Nature of Interests and Objectives

Even if policymakers can agree on basic interests, they may disagree on what constitutes a threat, an opportunity, or a worthwhile foreign policy objective. For example, in the mid-1980s Western political leaders across the board viewed Mikhail Gorbachev as simply the latest in a long line of Soviet leaders hostile to the West. Hence, he was viewed as a threat. In the early 1990s, however, then German Chancellor Helmut Kohl and British Prime Minister Margaret Thatcher came to view Gorbachev as an opportunity to be seized to achieve a dramatic improvement in East-West relations, a position only belatedly accepted by the Reagan administration. Nevertheless, some members of the U.S. government continued to treat Gorbachev as a threat, believing that his reassuring words concerning East-West rapprochement and nuclear disarmament were little more than a sophisticated deception campaign.

Moreover, these controversies are not always confined to government officials. If we shift the analysis to the societal level, to democracies in particular, interest groups and the general public may hold quite different points of view. In 2011, for example, the weakening of Europe's economic and financial position and debt crises in Portugal, Spain, Greece, and Ireland even triggered public discussion of moving away from the euro as the European Union's (EU's) currency. Notwithstanding these difficulties, governmental authorities often use the national interest to legitimize their more specific foreign policy objectives. Indeed, they customarily speak and act as if they were serving precisely defined state objectives or goals deemed to be in the national interest. As with threats and opportunities, constructivists remind us that national objectives and the interests they serve are not objective truths government officials discover, but rather are *subjectively* understood, constructions determined typically by those in authority to do so—presidents or prime ministers, foreign and defense ministers or secretaries, and the like.

Is defining objectives easier in dictatorships and other authoritarian regimes than in democracies? Certainly not. Both regime types have difficulties setting objectives and then holding to their agendas. Although sometimes suffering retaliation for their outspokenness, a few officials dared to disagree with Adolf Hitler of Nazi Germany (1933–1945), Joseph Stalin of the Soviet Union (1930–1953), and Robert Mugabe of Zimbabwe (1980–present). Similarly, elites in or out of power and the general public can have a substantial impact in democracies. Thus, the American public's disenchantment with the situation in Vietnam in the late 1960s and early 1970s and, more recently, in Iraq and Afghanistan contributed to shifts in policy and in election outcomes.

Although democracies are constituted to take popular views or public opinion into account, the distinction between democracies and authoritarian regimes in terms of popular influences is often overdrawn. Authoritarian regimes also can be influenced by popular sentiments. The authoritarian shah of Iran, an important U.S. and Western ally, was overthrown in 1979 by an Islamic and student revolution. Similarly, once East European communist regimes lost the security guarantee of the former Soviet Union, they found they could not deal with public demands from their emerging civil societies, and beginning in 1989 they collapsed like dominos. More recently authoritarian leaders were overthrown in early 2011 in Tunisia and Egypt, the crisis of authority and challenge to political leadership also experienced in Libya, Syria, Yemen, Bahrain, and elsewhere across the Middle East.

Resolving controversies on interests and objectives by governmental decision is common in democracies as well, particularly those with a strong cultural tradition in their politics of deference to authorities in matters of state like foreign policy. By contrast, given the strong American political tradition that allows for challenges to all policies, domestic or foreign, mandates of this kind are difficult to sustain in the United States for very long without public support. Moreover, in the U.S. style of **presidential government**, although the executive branch has the lead in foreign policy matters, **separation of powers** also gives substantial authority in such matters to the legislature, both houses but particularly the Senate.

Indeed, the U.S. president and members of the Congress are often at loggerheads in determining interests, objectives, and appropriate actions. By contrast, in the more common **parliamentary government**, the head of government is also the leader of the majority party or coalition in the legislature, which somewhat simplifies the consensus-building task. Difficult as it still may be, parliamentary regimes such as those in the United Kingdom, Germany, and Japan need to reach consensus only within the majority party or governing coalition, not across separate, independent branches of government. Still, their foreign policies will encounter opposition if there is not sufficient support from or deference by the general public.

Prioritizing Objectives

Let us assume the leaders of a state have agreed on the objectives they wish to pursue. The next problem they face is that the foreign policy objectives of any given state, or international and transnational organization, for that matter, may conflict and, thus, not be entirely compatible. For example, a state's objective of promoting human rights may well conflict with the objective of maintaining good relations or reduced tensions with countries thought to be in violation of human rights. A corporation may want to get early returns on investments in various countries but not be as aggressive or exploitative as to expose itself to foreign complaints that would put its longer-term business position in jeopardy.

Needless to say, such rank ordering is often extremely difficult to accomplish. Sometimes objectives conflict, which makes it even more difficult to rank order. Consider, for example, Western relations with two rising powers, Russia and China. The United States and Europe are critical of Moscow's shutting down much of the independent press in Russia and violating human rights in the bloody war in the Republic of Chechnya. Yet European countries are heavily dependent on Russian natural gas and oil for industrial purposes as well as to heat homes and fuel cars—factors that constrain them from being too critical of Moscow. As Russia has risen from the depths of economic collapse at the end of the Cold War, there is also interest in Western capitals to cultivate Moscow, assuring if they can that Russia will remain nonthreatening and more connected to political, economic, and cultural life in the West than was possible during the Soviet period.

Similarly, to what extent should Western states criticize China's human rights abuses, given the objective of wishing to maintain good commercial and other relations with an economic dynamo and growing military power? Moreover, not

presidential government ■ a form of government in which the executive branch is separate from the legislature

separation of powers ■ a political system in which power is distributed between two or more branches of government

parliamentary government ■ a form of government in which the executive (the prime minister and cabinet) are part of the legislative branch

only does China hold a substantial share of American debt, but Beijing also has more direct influence over North Korea than any other country—a linkage Washington taps from time to time as efforts are made to keep the peace on the Korean peninsula. For its part, the United States also seeks to maintain good relations with both China and Taiwan—an effort both to keep Taipei from provoking Beijing unnecessarily and the latter from threatening Taiwan.

Competing Domestic and Foreign Policy Objectives

Accept that policymakers have decided upon basic foreign policy objectives, but find it difficult to establish their relative priority. Next, as noted above, foreign policy objectives may be consistent with some, but conflict with other objectives also sought by policymakers.

A real-world example involves the United States and its important relations with Japan since the end of World War II. By allowing U.S. military bases on its soil, Japan has gained defense support and facilitated projection of U.S. forces in the region, provided inexpensive imports until the 1960s, and has been welcomed as a member of the "club" of fellow democratic states. The United States, being a major trading nation itself, also has been a leading proponent of an open international trading system, which has made the reduction of tariffs on imports a key foreign policy objective. Over the years, however, U.S.–Japanese relations have had their ups and downs, principally due to Japan's tremendous economic success and the consequent competitive challenge to American producers.

Until overtaken by concerns with China, the U.S.-Japanese trade imbalance—heavily favoring Japan—had been a U.S. domestic political issue as presidents, Congress, and the public worried about Japanese imports putting U.S. manufacturers out of business. How do policymakers balance the domestic objective to save American jobs, the commitment to an open international trading system, and the foreign policy objective of maintaining good relations with a valued ally such as Japan? It is not an easy task. Similar concerns, of course, are also evident in U.S.–China relations.

Even if senior policymakers are able to sort out conflicting foreign and domestic objectives and prioritize them, there is usually considerable disagreement among individuals, interest groups, corporate leaders, and agency officials as to what foreign policy objectives should be, not to mention in what rank order or priority they should be placed. For example, the U.S. Department of Agriculture and privately owned agribusinesses may favor increasing grain exports because increased sales are beneficial to American farmers. The State Department may agree, but for a different reason: They want to maintain or improve relations with countries wanting to import American wheat. For their parts, the Department of Commerce and the Treasury Department may both be inclined to favor such sales because of the favorable impact increased exports will have on the American trade and payments balances.

On the other hand, consumer groups may fear that grain exports will reduce the domestic supplies of wheat, driving up prices of bread and other products made from grain. During the Cold War years, some interest groups and government officials in the United States saw increased agricultural (and technological) exports

The concept of balance of power is very important to realists, particularly those who emphasize the critical role of the systemic or international level of analysis to explain patterns of state behavior in the international system. Three questions of considerable debate among scholars are:

1. How is the term defined?
2. Do balances of power automatically occur or are they created by political leaders?
3. Which balance of power—bipolar or multipolar—is more likely to maintain international stability?

ARGUMENT   Hans Morgenthau, a realist, stated there are least four meanings of the balance of power: (1) a policy aimed at a certain state of affairs; (2) an objective or actual state of affairs; (3) an approximately equal distribution of power among states; (4) any distribution of power among states, including a preponderance of power by one over the others.

COUNTERARGUMENT   One critic of realism, Ernst Haas, found at least seven meanings of the term: (1) distribution of power; (2) equilibrium; (3) hegemony; (4) stability and peace; (5) instability and war; (6) power politics generally; (7) a universal law of history. Balance of power has also been criticized for leading to war as opposed to preventing it, serving as a poor guide to political leaders, and functioning as a propaganda tool to justify defense spending and foreign adventures. Given these diverse usages and meanings, does balance of power really mean anything? Despite criticism and reformulations of its meaning, balance of power remains a central part of the realist vocabulary. This is true for academic theorists, policymakers, and practitioners.

Do Balances of Power Automatically Occur or Are They Created by Political Leaders?

ARGUMENT   Former U.S. Secretary of State Henry Kissinger emphasizes a voluntarism perspective to the question of whether balances of power are automatic or created. The balance of power is a foreign policy creation or construction of political leaders; it doesn't just occur automatically. Makers of foreign policy do not act as prisoners severely constrained by the balance of power. Rather, they are its creators charged with maintaining it.

COUNTERARGUMENT   Kenneth Waltz sees the balance of power as an attribute of the system of states that will occur whether it is willed or not. Given the realist assumptions that the state is a rational and unitary actor that will use its capabilities to accomplish objectives, states inevitably interact and conflict in the competitive environment of international politics. The outcome of state actions and interactions is a tendency toward equilibrium or balance of power. From this point of view, balance of power is a systemic tendency that occurs whether or not states seek to establish it.

Which Balance of Power—Bipolar or Multipolar—Is More Likely to Maintain International Stability?

ARGUMENT   J. David Singer and Karl Deutsch argue that in a multipolar system, war is less likely to occur because as the number of major actors increases, decision makers must deal with more information and hence greater uncertainty. They believe that uncertainty breeds caution in the making of policy, and therefore a multipolar world is more conducive to stability.

COUNTERARGUMENT   Kenneth Waltz, however, believes that greater uncertainty makes it more likely a decision maker will misjudge the intentions and actions of a potential foe. Hence a multipolar system, given its association with higher levels of uncertainty, is less desirable than a bipolar system because uncertainty is at a low level when each state can focus its attention on only one rival.

APPLICATION   As discussed extensively in Chapter 3, "History," does the increasing clout of the European Union's economic and monetary union and the rise of China, India, Russia, and Brazil change the pecking order among states in international politics? Applying this discussion of balance of power, how would Kissinger and Waltz differ on what policymakers can actually do about such changes? How do you think Singer and Deutsch would answer? How much does such a question actually matter? ◤

For many people military capabilities are the critical element of national power, whether one is talking about the size of armed forces or fighter aircraft, naval vessels, rockets, or tanks. These Abram tanks saw service in the U.S. and coalition wars against Iraq in 1991 and 2003.

Underpinning military power and national power in general, however, are economic capabilities. Oil continues to be a key driver of the modern economy with oil exploration being conducted in what once were difficult locations and circumstances. The Cook Inlet in Alaska is one example.

What often differentiates the powerful from the most powerful, however, are technological capabilities. The information revolution has driven not only innovation in consumer electronics, but also in other applications. Here the ERS-1 satellite is mapping the earth's atmosphere and surface. Military applications are also important.

A country's political culture and values can also be a source of strength or weakness domestically as well as internationally. Despite its relatively small geographic size, the United Kingdom was able to project global power for several centuries. The opening of Parliament is an occasion for pomp and circumstance.

balance of power ■
a key concept among
realists that is often
defined as a condition
of equilibrium among
states

voluntarism ■
the philosophical
position that humans
can influence,
if not control,
outcomes such as in
international relations

power ■ means
by which a state
or other actor
wields or can assert
actual or potential
influence or coercion
relative to other
states and nonstate
actors because
of the political,
geographic, economic
and financial,
technological,
military, social,
cultural, or other
capabilities it
possesses

6.3 Classify
the types of
capabilities that
comprise power.

👁 Watch the **Video**
**"Chamberlain's
Appeasement"** at
mypoliscilab.com

to the Soviet Union as helping the other side in a global, competitive struggle with significant security implications for the United States. Private interests, members of Congress, and various executive-branch departments and agencies thus weigh in on the different sides of what may have seemed to be a relatively simple issue.

In short, for policymakers selecting and rank ordering foreign policy objectives is not as easy as it might first seem, particularly when domestic goals are taken into account. Determining foreign policy objectives is a rather complex matter when one understands that a country's foreign and domestic objectives often conflict.

In the final analysis, of course, these conflicting interests and competing objectives are usually resolved either through some form of compromise, concession by one or more interested parties, or decision by the chief executive or other authorities. At this point a government may move from debating *what* is hoped to be achieved—the objectives—to specifically *how* they are to be attained—the policies pursued. It is all well and good, for example, to proclaim that the United States is interested in achieving a lasting and just Middle East peace settlement or stable relations between nuclear-armed neighbors India and Pakistan, but then specific policies have to be devised and implemented. Similarly, other countries may wish to freeze or roll back Iranian and North Korean nuclear programs, but what should be the mix of carrots—incentives—and sticks—threats? Can the parties find common ground—shared interests—or is compromise the best that can be achieved? What is the role in this process, if any, of allied countries, the United Nations, and other international organizations?

In sum, policymakers may disagree among themselves about what are appropriate objectives to pursue and what their relative priority should be. There also may be conflicts between foreign policy and domestic objectives. Finally, states must contend with other international actors that have their own set of objectives that might conflict with those of any particular state. What may help decide the outcome of such a confrontation, however, is the relative power of the actors involved.

CAPABILITIES AND POWER

Policymakers can talk all they want about the need to formulate and rank order specific foreign policy objectives based upon fundamental national interests and threats and opportunities emanating from abroad. But such an exercise is academic unless a state has the capabilities or power to pursue those objectives. This last part of the policymaking framework is, therefore, perhaps the most important. The relation between capabilities and power, however, is difficult to specify because little consensus on the precise meanings of the terms exists in the social sciences, let alone the literature on international relations.

For some policymakers power is equated with capabilities; the terms are used interchangeably. They see, for example, a country with a large military and great economic wealth and pronounce: "Country X is a great power." A second view is that "large military" and "great economic wealth" mean something only if one asks, "Large or great compared to what?" France has a large military compared to Switzerland, but a small one compared to the United States.

A third and related perspective is that the power of a state is evident only when placed in the broader context of multiple states. This concept of relative power as the distribution of capabilities can be viewed from a global perspective. The emphasis is on different polarities or power distributions—unipolar where one state dominates, bipolar in which two states dominate (to economists a "duopoly" in which two firms are dominant), and multipolar whereby three or more major states dominate (to economists, an "oligopoly" or small number of competitors). Academic proponents of this perspective believe that simply knowing the distribution of capabilities allows us to predict basic patterns of behavior in international politics. For example, in a bipolar system as in the Cold War, alliances will coalesce around the two major states; such alliances tend to be stable, in equilibrium, with few member-state defections. Conversely, in a multipolar system such as in the 19th and 20th centuries before World War II, different combinations of states can ally with one another at different times.

Many observers see the 21st century moving from unipolarity with the United States as single dominant power (to economists, a "monopoly") to multipolarity—the United States, Japan, perhaps a more united Europe, and the "BRIC" countries—Brazil, Russia, India, and China. There will no doubt be a lot of jockeying for position now and in forthcoming decades. Power transition theorists tell us to watch out as historically such shifts have been dangerous times marked by war and other disturbances. The authors join you in waiting to see what actually happens—whether we've learned anything from the past and can navigate successfully through what may be very troubled waters. Maybe as a practitioner (or policy-oriented theorist) you'll be able to participate and add constructively in the process of transition, assuming that's what's happening.

The overall distribution of capabilities will also influence other states that are not major players. Even if a major state is not directly attempting to exert influence on such states, the mere existence of its large, imposing capabilities will influence how states with modest capabilities will act or react. For example, the Cold War era was a bipolar system—a "duopoly," economists might say—between the United States and the Soviet Union, then termed superpowers. Even if less powerful states like Sweden or India were ignored by Moscow and Washington, the former did not have the luxury of similar indifference—the political fallout of Soviet-American competition could affect them directly. As an African proverb notes: "When two elephants fight, the grass gets trampled."

As noted earlier by Hans Morgenthau, power can be viewed as a means to an end, however different those ultimate objectives may be from the perspective of political leaders. States accumulate capabilities in an absolute sense that at some point can be brought to bear on other states or actors. As such, power is a potential means of influence, not an end in itself. Although all actors may not be so motivated, it may be that a state will seek as a national objective to increase or sustain its influence internationally by accumulating more power—enhancing its power position relative to other countries or other actors. This makes power more of an end or objective states may pursue. The typical reason for taking such measures, however, is the knowledge that power is necessary in an anarchic world without central authority if a state is to achieve its ends—its diverse purposes. Put another way, even when enhancing or sustaining a state's power position is the objective, the power or power position a state achieves ultimately remains means to other ends or objectives on the national agenda.

People, however, are puzzled when a state with superior capabilities cannot influence an obviously much weaker state. The United States and its inability to curb North Korean and Iranian nuclear ambitions comes to mind. Even the most powerful states are constrained by limits to what their capabilities can accomplish. Moreover, the power of a state or other actor depends not just on the apparent reality of having certain capabilities, but also on the perception held by other actors of the state's willingness to employ its capabilities for various purposes. Unless a state can make others believe in its willingness to use its capabilities, its actual influence will tend to diminish. In short, credibility is an important element in power calculations—yet another social construction determined as much by the understandings others may have in relation to what one says or does.

This leads us to the final perspective: Power can be viewed as an effect, meaning that influence is actually achieved in a particular situation. Consider, for example, two mechanisms through which military capabilities are transformed into effective or actualized military power—victory in war and a change in state behavior due to threats. Victory in war involves taking one's capabilities and actually applying them in a coercive manner either single-handedly (unilaterally) or in coalition with other states (multilaterally) so that a rival is physically defeated or punished to the point at which it surrenders. But an effective threat of force may also be sufficient to change the behavior of another state. In either case power has been achieved over a rival—the net effect is to the advantage of one party or side over the other.

Thus, the United States and its allies achieved victory over Germany and Japan at the end of World War II in 1945 and presided over the reconstruction and reconstitution of its defeated enemies. During the Cold War, the power of the NATO alliance kept the Soviet Union and its allies from invading or encroaching further on Western Europe. For their part (and their perspective), the threat of force—the power of the Warsaw Pact allies—kept the West from rolling back post–World War II gains made by the Soviet Union in its Eastern European sphere of influence. More recently, after Iraq invaded Kuwait in 1991, the United States-led coalition of some 40 countries defeated Iraq militarily and forced it to withdraw its forces back to its own country.

For our purposes, then, power is defined as the means by which a state or other actor wields or can assert actual or potential influence or coercion relative to other states and nonstate actors because of the political, geographic, economic and financial, technological, military, social, cultural, or other capabilities it possesses. Power is essentially a means; even if its enhancement is pursued as an end, the state does so instrumentally as a means to enable or facilitate its attainment of other ends. This definition views capabilities as the underpinnings of power. Once capabilities are mobilized, their utilization is expressed in the attempt or actual ability to influence, such as by diplomacy, or to coerce, such as by the use of military force, the behavior of another state, coalition, alliance, or nonstate actor. We will now discuss key capabilities that policymakers may wish to create or enhance. The particular mix of capabilities will vary depending on the state.

Political Capabilities

When we discuss political capabilities as a contribution to or constraint on national power, our focus is on states and their societies. At least four factors are involved in defining a country's political capabilities: human resources, technology, reputation, and the nature of its political system and political culture. Some or all of these factors can dramatically influence the effectiveness of the application of material capabilities.

Human Resources   First, human resources are obviously important. Some states, due to their larger population size and higher education levels, have greater diplomatic and bureaucratic resources that contribute to their political capabilities. Experienced diplomats and other representatives of the state, backed up by competent bureaucratic staffs at home and abroad, certainly enhance the capacity of decision makers to establish policies that exercise influence in international affairs.

Some states, by contrast, are unable to find, recruit, train, and assign enough people competent to carry out diplomatic, bureaucratic, and other governmental tasks effectively. Of course this is often the case with lower-income, developing countries where bureaucracies are often bloated and staffed with individuals whose loyalty is to the current ruler. Leaders in developing countries, therefore, often have to conduct their foreign policies with diminished political capabilities compared to those states and societies having a larger pool of educated individuals and adequate money and institutions to train them.

Communications Technology   Second, one should not ignore technology's contribution to political capabilities, particularly communications technology. Not all states can afford the advantages provided by advanced telecommunications and related technologies that can be used to coordinate and direct the efforts of diplomats and other representatives around the world. These resources also facilitate the communication of a country's point of view and justification for its policies to the public at home and abroad. Most countries have propaganda ministries or information services, but some are more effective than others in targeting and reaching their intended audiences.

Policymakers' access to intelligence also varies considerably. Some states have better technology at their disposal in addition to their human resources. Although all states engage in intelligence collection, only a few have the necessary means to collect and analyze such information adequately on even a regional, much less a global, scale. Even if technologies are available, widespread use of aircraft, ships, electronic ground stations, satellites, and other technical devices is prohibitively expensive for most countries. Diplomats with access to top-notch intelligence that can be disseminated to them rapidly have an obvious advantage when engaging or negotiating with their counterparts.

Reputation   Third, the reputation and prestige of a state should not be underestimated as a capability. If a state, for example, has a reputation of meeting its security commitments in terms of its allies, other states may hesitate to engage in any action that may be viewed as a threat to those allies. Similarly, a state's reputation might convince another state to join with it in an alliance, knowing security guarantees made to it will be met. This is undoubtedly why after the Cold War so many former Eastern European states were desirous of joining the U.S-led NATO alliance as a hedge against possible Russian aggression. Conversely, a state with a reputation for failing to meet its commitments will find its promises and proposals viewed with skepticism. Particularly in the minds of policymakers, reputation is seen as vital to an effective foreign policy.

Government Systems

The political capabilities available to policymakers are also related to the nature of the state's political culture, how its political system is structured, and how it functions. The processes of politics—how domestic and foreign policies are made and how well they serve or respond to national interests or objectives—are influenced or constrained by both cultural and structural aspects of a given political system. The ability of policymakers to reach decisions that can be implemented effectively in a timely fashion thus varies from country to country.

Niccolò Machiavelli's argument that the power of the state rests in part on popular consent holds as true today as it did in his time during the early 16th century. When governing officials or the regime lose **legitimacy**—their "right to rule" in the eyes of the citizenry based on custom or consent—the ability of these policymakers to carry out either domestic or foreign policy is markedly weakened.

In this respect, democracies by their very nature sometimes enjoy greater popular support than authoritarian regimes. Democracies may also be more responsive to public opposition to certain policies, changing course or modifying them consistent with public opinion. This is often frustrating to policymakers and other "experts" who have their own views on what are usually very complex issues, not always well understood by the general public. Nevertheless, treating public opinion as an important consideration may pay off in the long run. Political capabilities are enhanced when policies, domestic or foreign, enjoy widespread support.

Building a broad consensus through public discussion of issues can be a source of enormous strength in democracies. Speed and relative efficiency of decision making are sacrificed in exchange for policies informed by a greater number of alternative views and accompanied by greater prospects for forging a consensus. Foreign policies are easier to carry out when the people support them. Of course, maintaining a public-support base for policies over time is a continuing challenge for political leaders.

Democracies such as Japan and most European countries have a parliamentary government in a **unitary state**. Political authority is more concentrated than in the United States, which has separation of powers between legislative and executive branches within a **federal state** (see Table 6.2). Thus, in the United Kingdom the executives—prime minister, foreign secretary, defense secretary, chancellor of the exchequer (treasury), and other cabinet ministers—are themselves members of parliament. In the United Kingdom and other countries with parliamentary governments, executive and legislative authority is effectively fused instead of being separated into distinct legislative and executive branches, each with its different bases for authority and power, as in the American form of presidential government.

Considerable debate and compromise still remain both within and outside the majority party or coalition in states with parliamentary governments, but not usually to the same degree as in states with presidential governments, in which political power and authority are dispersed or more fragmented. Compromises on foreign policy as in other political matters in parliamentary governments need only be made among legislators within the majority party or coalition of governing parties. Although concurrence by opposition parties can be helpful by providing a

legitimacy ■ a right to govern and exercise power based on popular acceptance

unitary state ■ a system of government in which most powers are reserved for the national-level government

federal state ■ a system of government in which power is apportioned between a national-level government and states or regions

TABLE 6.2

Structural Types of States and Democratic Governments

An ongoing debate has been whether presidential or parliamentary forms of government are more efficient in making national security and foreign policy decisions. But the real question is not efficiency, but rather effectiveness in terms of achieving national objectives and safeguarding interests. The evidence is inconclusive in this matter.

Types of States	Characteristics	Examples
Unitary states	Those that *concentrate* all political authority or power in one government in its capital city; most states are of this kind.	Japan, United Kingdom, France, Italy, Argentina, China
Federal states	Those that *divide* all political authority or power between a central government and additional state or provincial governments; although less common than unitary states, many are of this kind.	United States, Canada, Germany, Russia, Australia

Types of Democratic Governments	Characteristics	Examples
Parliamentary governments	Those that fuse in particular the executive and legislative functions into a single branch of government; this is the most common form of democratic governance.	Japan, Germany, United Kingdom, Italy, Sweden
	The judiciary is usually independent, in some cases with authority to exercise judicial review to assure the constitutionality of governmental acts.	Germany
	In some there is no political authority higher than an act of parliament.	United Kingdom
Presidential Governments	Those that separate the executive, legislative, and judicial function into separate branches of government; the relative strength of branches varies, with the executive clearly stronger in some countries.	France, Indonesia
	In others there may be more of a contest between the legislature and the executive. In some countries authority for judicial review to interpret and assure constitutionality of laws and executive acts is common.	United States

broader base of support for a parliamentary government's foreign policy, there is no formal requirement for such a consensus. Moreover, there is no need to compromise in the consensus-building process across branches of government because the executive is in fact part of the legislature in parliamentary regimes. As a result, states with parliamentary governments tend to be somewhat more decisive and often have more comprehensive and coherent foreign policies than those with presidential governments.

division of powers ■
power is distributed among a central and constituent state or provincial governments as in a federal republic

By contrast, compared to most other countries, there are many more potentially influential voices on foreign policy matters and many more points of access for the exercise of such influence in the United States. Given a federal division of powers between central and state and local governments and the aforementioned separation of powers between executive and legislature in all of these governments, there is a fragmentation of authority and a proliferation of points of access for individuals and interest groups. With so many incremental compromises required before decisions are taken, these governments tend to be slower in reaching decisions. When decisions are made, they tend to be step-by-step, incremental choices in which short-term factors often dominate. Although not impossible—given the fragmentation of power and authority under both federalism and separation of powers—it is much more difficult in the United States to develop comprehensive, logically coherent policies that take midrange and long-term considerations seriously into account. However, this does not necessarily mean U.S. policy is less effective in defending its interests and achieving its objectives compared to a parliamentary system.

political culture ■
those norms, values, and orientations of a society's culture that are politically relevant

Culture   The political capabilities policymakers can draw upon are also affected by political culture—those norms, values, and orientations of a society's culture that are politically relevant. Many societies have a tradition of deferring, for the most part, to political authorities in such matters of state as foreign policy. In some societies, by contrast, there is a greater tendency for people to become involved. Although government officials in the United States often may have greater latitude in foreign policy matters than on domestic issues, Americans are not prone to defer entirely to political authorities on either domestic or foreign policy and readily let their views be known, whether the issue is U.S. involvement in Iraq or some other country.

In some democracies with consensus-oriented political cultures, such as Japan, Switzerland, or Sweden, there may be a greater tendency to seek a broader basis of support for policies than is constitutionally or legally required. In other democracies, such as the United Kingdom, Germany, or the United States, where conflict-oriented politics prevail as part of their political cultures, a narrow, simple majority of 50 percent plus one vote will do. Wider margins may be desirable but are by no means required in such countries either by law or by expectation within the prevailing political culture.

Social and Cultural Capabilities

The social cohesion of a society has a direct impact on its power position. States suffering from crises of authority and being torn apart by economic, ideological, religious, ethnic, racial, language, or other cultural differences can hardly allow policymakers to act effectively in the international arena. Witness the ongoing precarious political stability in Iraq or Afghanistan. Culturally and socially homogeneous states like Japan or the Scandinavian countries, by contrast, tend to be less divided at home and thus are usually more effective at pursuing their international objectives than countries torn by internal divisions.

Another important aspect of cultural capabilities is the extent to which countries are able to maintain influence over other countries through common language, religion, ethnic or racial identity, or legal and political tradition. The French and the British, for example, have maintained fairly close ties with the elites of many of their former colonies. In spite of political differences, elites in these former colonies typically speak the language and often adopt many of the ways of the former colonial power. In some instances, these cultural ties have been buttressed or reinforced by continuing military, trade, financial, and other commercial relations. Critics refer to such ties as a manifestation of neocolonialism—a new form of long-established patterns of dominance by former colonial powers.

neocolonialism ■ relations of economic, social, cultural, and even political dominance by a former colonial ruler of a now independent state

The education levels, distribution of skills, and value systems that characterize different societies often have substantial impact on the roles countries play in world politics. Economic strength, for example, depends directly on such factors. Market-oriented cultures, in which entrepreneurial skills are valued, provide an environment within which individuals and businesses can thrive. A highly skilled and educated population oriented toward productivity makes economic success possible. Societies lacking sufficient numbers of such human resources are hard-pressed to compete successfully in global markets, however committed the country's leadership may be to achieving economic gains and sustaining development.

Social and cultural appeal from the perspective of the rest of the world can also be a significant source of a state's power. For example, U.S. military capabilities are a source of "hard" power. But the cultural appeal of the United States in terms of movies, music, fashion, and most importantly its professed political ideals could be viewed as a form of soft power. However resented the United States may be by some peoples abroad due to its exercise of military power, American culture and ideals are appealing to many individuals in foreign lands, even though leaders of certain regimes see these values as a threat. Iran is a good example. American popular culture is embraced by large segments of the expanding younger population while it is viewed as a threat to the religious and political authorities who run the regime.

soft power ■ non-material capabilities such as reputation, culture, and value appeal that can aid the attainment of a state's objectives

Geographic and Economic Capabilities

As noted in Chapter 4, geographic location can affect the capabilities of states. Geography, defined in terms of natural resources, obviously has an important impact on state capabilities. Whatever power the petroleum-producing countries may have stems in large part from the fact that most industrial countries remain so dependent on them for oil and natural gas supplies. In cases such as Iran and Saudi Arabia, petrodollars from the West help keep authoritarian leaders in power as they can provide goods and services for the local populations. Although the United States is somewhat less dependent than Japan and most European countries, more than half of American consumption is from foreign sources. The United States also has vast supplies of lumber, coal, iron, and other raw materials, but the country imports the bulk of its tin, bauxite, chromium, cobalt, manganese, nickel, and zinc.

Compared to most countries, however, the United States is still very rich in natural resources. By contrast, Japan is at the other extreme and remains dependent on foreign sources for most of its raw materials. Putting this into perspective, however, the comparative advantage of the resource-rich United States is reduced somewhat by the fact that the country is also the world's largest consumer of natural resources.

gross national income (GNI) ■
GNP minus indirect (like sales and excise) business taxes

The United States also has the world's largest economy as measured, for example, by its **gross national income (GNI)**. These are measures of the total dollar value of all goods and services produced in a given year. Economic productivity stems from the efficient use of capital as well as human and natural resources. Third after the United States and China in national economic output is natural resource–poor Japan, which nevertheless has demonstrated its capability to organize its economy into one of the most productive in the world. Beyond the industriousness of Japan's labor force, considerable capital investment in new and advanced technologies has made possible that phenomenal economic growth over almost seven decades since the end of World War II.

The leading industrial countries with the largest economies in terms of sheer size include the United States, China, Japan, Germany, France, the United Kingdom, Italy, Russia, and Canada (see Table 6.3). A number of other advanced industrial countries have smaller economies but often higher standards or levels of living than some of the countries with larger economies. Switzerland immediately comes to mind. Taiwan, Singapore, South Korea, and other relatively newly industrializing countries (NICs) have made impressive economic gains in recent decades; these countries have educated and skilled populations with market orientations, but economic capabilities in all of these countries are a function more directly of such factors as labor productivity, the effectiveness of management, the extent and quality of capital investment, the degree of technological innovation, and the condition of the economic infrastructure—such production-support factors as roads, sea- and airports, public transportation, and telecommunications. Others have joined (or are in the process of joining) the pack—Vietnam, Indonesia, and South Africa prominent among them.

By contrast, agrarian societies with less developed industrial economies like Ukraine are heavily dependent on agricultural production both for their own domestic consumption and in some cases for export. Because these countries rely more heavily on labor to sustain their economies, they are usually less efficient even in agricultural production than advanced industrial countries such as the United States. Advanced industrial countries that are also endowed with good soil and a favorable climate have made very heavy capital investments in machinery used by the large agribusinesses and smaller, cooperative farm arrangements. Technology-intensive agriculture in the United States, for example, has made it the world's largest exporter of food products.

Vulnerability to price fluctuations in the international market is most severe for those countries that are dependent on export of one or a few crops, minerals, or other raw materials. With the notable exception of the oil-exporting countries, attempts to form producer cartels for other minerals and for agricultural products have not been very successful. In part this is because consumers of these products can more easily substitute other minerals or agricultural products or increase their

TABLE 6.3

GNI as Indicator of Relative Capabilities or Power Position: Comparing the Size of Selected Economies (2009)

What is striking about these numbers is how easily the United States outpaces all other countries. Much is justifiably made of the dramatic economic expansion of China in recent years, but it still lags far behind the United States in terms of gross national income (GNI).

Country	Gross National Income (U.S. $ Millions)	Country	Gross National Income (U.S. $ Millions)
Group of Seven		**Others**	
United States	14,052,600	China	4,778,270
Japan	4,830,310	Brazil	1,557,240
Germany	3,484,690	India	1,368,710
France	2,754,610	Russia	1,329,670
United Kingdom	2,567,480	South Korea	966,600
Italy	2,112,490	Iran	330,619
Canada	1,442,980	South Africa	284,499

Source: World Bank

own domestic production of these products. By contrast, large-scale substitution of other energy sources for oil in the oil-dependent industrial countries is not easily accomplished, at least not in the short run.

Military Capabilities

Particularly for many realists and certainly for policymakers of whatever stripe, the military is another important capability or component of a state's power. In some countries the armed forces perform a domestic order maintenance function similar to that performed by police. Indeed, in some authoritarian regimes the military's primary function is not to protect the country, but to protect the regime from its own citizens. Examples of government use of military forces against its own people occurred in Libya, Bahrain, Yemen, and Syria. Although the ability to maintain stability or order within the state has an important impact on the state's relative power position, the external capacity of its military forces is perhaps even more important.

The continued development of nuclear weapons since World War II added a new dimension to military capabilities, but conventional or nonnuclear military forces remain a vital part of the calculus of a state's military capabilities.

Policymakers have the challenging task of determining what size and kinds of force a state can deploy, where, and for how long, variables that have a significant impact on a state's relative power position. The United States is clearly the world's biggest military spender with a worldwide military capability greater than that of any other country. Its corporations also have the world's largest market share in arms exports to other countries.

Paradoxically, the rapid advancement of military technology, particularly in nuclear weaponry, has served to constrain those states possessing such capabilities. Indeed, use of such weapons can invite retaliation by one's adversary with unacceptable destructive consequences. Often states not possessing such weapons have been able to assert far more leverage than one would expect, given their apparently inferior military capabilities. As a practical matter, since the end of World War II, the world's nuclear powers have been reluctant to use such weapons to achieve objectives at the expense of nonnuclear states. Nevertheless, states tend to believe that the possession of nuclear weapons enhances the state's international reputation and prestige. India and Pakistan are recent examples, although both also had security-based reasons for acquiring them—Pakistan seeing India as a threat and India seeing both Pakistan and China as threats.

It is easy to overstate the importance of the military component of national power relative to other factors. Prudent decision makers will take seriously any existing or potential military capability that could be threatening in order to assure that they have enough military capability of their own, or alliances with capable partners, to offset potential threats. Yet, military capabilities do depend on the strength of the underlying economy as a source of personnel and for the economic means to procure military equipment and supplies. In this regard, economic capabilities may define the limits of the military capabilities policymakers may choose to develop.

MEASURING POWER

6.4 Illustrate how the diversity of capabilities impacts the way in which power is measured.

Given the diversity of capabilities affecting states, it is exceedingly difficult to produce a single measure for ranking them in order of their power positions. Most would agree that the United States is currently the world's sole superpower or strongest great power, but who comes next: China? Japan? Germany? France? The United Kingdom? Russia? Not only is there no agreement on the weighting or relative importance of the capabilities outlined, but also it is virtually impossible to quantify such factors as cultural and social capabilities in any meaningful fashion. They are nonadditive—like trying to add apples and oranges. At best, one can only construct indicators—indirect measures—of these diverse capabilities that collectively, we say, define the power a state has at its disposal.

Moreover, some realists, as well as scholars working in the liberal tradition, claim that to talk of power as an integrated concept is not particularly useful. They argue that in different **issue areas** different capabilities have different degrees of importance. From this point of view, military capabilities have considerable salience in strategic or security matters, but do not have great weight in trade, investment, and other economic issues. How useful, for example, are American military capabilities when it comes to trade disputes with China?

issue area ■ military, economic, and political issues in which different types of power are most relevant

On the other hand, most realists argue that one cannot talk of such economic issues as trade and investment relations among the countries belonging to, or associated with, the EU strictly in terms of economic capabilities. From this perspective, especially during the Cold War, the European states benefited from the security umbrella provided by the United States. Thus, one can argue that military capabilities are at least as important as economic capabilities in determining the power of states in economic issue areas. Certainly the United States derives some **economic leverage** in its relations with EU members and other European states that have depended to some degree on America's contribution to the NATO alliance and overall European security.

Similarly, realists note that in the 1970s a great deal of attention was given to OPEC, the Organization of Petroleum Exporting Countries. With headquarters in Vienna, this international organization is composed of both Arab and non-Arab oil-exporting countries. Though OPEC was a relatively inconsequential organization in the 1960s, its members had considerable success in the 1970s raising the world price of petroleum, thus markedly improving their collective power position. The oil-exporting countries were, in effect, displacing the multinational oil companies from the price-setting role, a task the MNCs had previously performed. OPEC assumed this price-setting function by regulating the supply of oil to world markets. For the first time, these industrially less developed countries were able to assert very real financial leverage on the industrialized countries. Almost overnight, some observers proclaimed, the OPEC member nations had become major international players.

The price increase "oil shocks" of the 1970s, however, led industrialized countries to take domestic measures with varying levels of success in an attempt to reduce their dependence on oil and natural gas. Beyond conservation measures designed to reduce energy waste, these countries also sought to substitute other energy sources such as coal or nuclear power and have invested in longer-term research and development projects in nuclear, solar, wind, geothermal, and other energy sources.

Divisions within the OPEC cartel and decisions by Saudi Arabia and other major producers to maintain an adequate supply of petroleum to world markets until recently precluded major price increases comparable to those in the 1970s. In particular, the United States took measures designed to assure the security of the principal oil supplier, Saudi Arabia, in exchange for at least a tacit assurance of continuing flow of oil to the global market. The point is that from a realist perspective Saudi Arabia proved to be a one-dimensional power as evidenced by its reliance on the military prowess of the United States and other powers, such as France and the United Kingdom, to deter Iraqi aggression following the 1990 invasion of Kuwait.

In short, little or no consensus exists among analysts as to whether one should treat power as a single, integrated concept or whether one should disaggregate the concept into its separate component capabilities. Perhaps one can differentiate between "hard" power—military and economic capabilities—and "soft" power, the other components we've discussed. "Smart" power, then, is the ideal combination of the two applied to the particular issue with which policymakers are grappling.[3]

> **Watch** the **Video**
> "Normalizing Sino-Japanese Relations" at
> **mypoliscilab.com**

economic leverage
■ the ability to use economic power to extract political concessions

---

[3]We credit this insight to Joseph S. Nye, Jr. at Harvard. In similar fashion, Stanley Hoffmann also disaggregated power into component units, some more applicable to some issues than others—different "chessboards," the metaphor he used to capture this diversity of issues policymakers face.

Contemporary practitioners identifying themselves with this realist perspective on international relations seek to enhance military and economic hard power as well as other, "softer" components of state power—political or bureaucratic, diplomatic, intelligence, social, and cultural. They may do this through domestic or internal measures, such as taking actions designed to strengthen the national economy or to improve the capabilities of the armed forces. External measures designed to increase state power include forming alliances, influencing members of already existing alliances to increase their contributions, and directly arming allies, thus improving their capabilities.

CONCLUSION

It was noted at the outset of this chapter that each American administration issues a National Security Strategy document. While it may appear to be rather straightforward in terms of the described interests, objectives, threats, and opportunities, our discussion has pointed out the difficulties, complexities, and trade-offs required for its actual implementation.

Policymakers may disagree among themselves or with opposition politicians and the media about what is an opportunity or a threat as well as the prioritization of agreed-upon foreign policy objectives. To complicate matters, foreign policy objectives may be undercut by domestic events. In the summer of 2010, for example, a Florida Christian minister threatened to burn the Koran (and later did so) to protest the establishment of an Islamic religious and cultural community center near the site of Ground Zero where the World Trade Center Twin Towers were destroyed by Islamic terrorists on 9/11. The expected reaction from throughout the Islamic world only made White House global engagement efforts that much more difficult, particularly in the Arab and Muslim worlds.

Merely possessing capabilities or power potential does not make a state effective in world politics unless it has the will to use these capabilities in pursuing its objectives. It will face opposition from both states and nonstate actors forwarding their own interests, objectives, and agendas. A country's sensitivity to public opinion, international legal considerations, and domestic politics as well as perceptions of its resolve and its degree of international prestige also may constrain the use of its capabilities. There is no agreement on whether power should be treated as a single, integrated concept, or whether it should be disaggregated into separate components. Military capabilities are obviously important in times of war, but the salience of economic capabilities is of equal importance in day-to-day interstate relations. In addition to these "hard power" assets are the political or bureaucratic, diplomatic, intelligence, social, and cultural components that collectively constitute the "soft power" policymakers may use to implement the policies they are pursuing.

✓•─[**Study** and **Review**
the **Post-Test & Chapter**
Exam at **mypoliscilab.com**

In the following chapter we turn to statecraft and foreign policy—how policymakers actually put power or capabilities to work through diplomacy, the use of force, and other mechanisms available to achieve objectives and serve interests. While the objectives, capabilities, and power of international and transnational organizations remain important, we continue our focus on state policymakers in this section of the book.

LEARNING OBJECTIVES REVIEW

6.1 Grasp how power and national interest (or objectives consistent with interest) are core to national security and foreign policy.

For practitioners to navigate through international relations and world politics, a basic roadmap is essential. In this chapter we propose that it is necessary for policymakers to take into account the basic national interests to be defended, the threats to those interests, opportunities sought, and the capabilities or power available to defend or secure interests. Interests as they are understood by policymakers typically take the form of specific objectives on the national agenda.

KEY TERMS

National interest 187
Sovereignty 187
Objectives 188
Capabilities 191

ADDITIONAL READINGS

E. H. Carr, *The Twenty Years' Crisis: 1919–1939* (New York: Macmillan, 1939). The classic work on power and interest on the one hand and ideals or moral values on the other.

Hedley Bull, *The Anarchical Society: A Study of Order in World Politics* (New York: Columbia University Press, 1977, 1995). A foundational work in the English School.

Martin Wight, *International Theory: The Three Traditions,* ed. Gabriele Wight and Brian Porter (London: Leicester University Press, 1991). Another classic of the English school.

Hans J. Morgenthau, *Politics Among Nations* (New York: Knopf). First published in 1948 and reprinted or revised in subsequent editions, this is the most famous American realist work on power from the 1950s through the 1970s.

Kenneth Waltz, *Theory of International Politics* (Reading, MA: Addison-Wesley, 1979). Responding to Morgenthau, Waltz moves the argument to a more systemic level, portraying the influence of the distribution of capabilities or power among states as directly influencing the behavior or conduct of states.

6.2 Differentiate between the conflicts and dilemmas policymakers must address when establishing a national security framework.

Even if policymakers can agree on basic interests, they may disagree on what constitutes a threat, an opportunity, or a worthwhile foreign policy objective. This is further complicated if interest groups and the general public have different views. Even the distinction between democracies and authoritarian regimes in terms of popular influences on policy decisions is often overdrawn. Separation of powers in such countries as the United States can limit unilateral actions by policymakers. This is less of a problem in parliamentary forms of government where the head of the government is also the leader of the majority party or coalition in the legislature. Prioritizing foreign policy objectives can be difficult. Domestic and foreign policy objectives also may conflict.

KEY TERMS

Presidential government 195
Separation of powers 195
Parliamentary government 195

ADDITIONAL READINGS

Klaus Knorr, *The Power of Nations: The Political Economy of International Relations* (New York: Basic Books, 1975). Knorr provides an excellent discussion of the elements of power from a classical realist perspective.

Joseph S. Nye, Jr., *Power in the Global Information Age: From Realism to Globalization* (London and New York: Routledge, 2004). A more recent overview of the role of power in the age of globalization.

Kenneth N. Waltz, *Foreign Policy and Democratic Politics: The American and British Experience* (Boston: Little, Brown, 1967). A classic study on how power plays out in democracies.

6.3 Classify the types of capabilities that comprise power.

Capabilities and power are essential in order for policymakers to protect state interests and achieve their objectives. The relation between capabilities and power, however, is subject to debate. For some observers, they have the same meaning. For others, power is best expressed as the relative distribution of capabilities among states—a comparative or relational perspective. We conclude that power is the means by which a state or other actor wields or can assert actual or potential influence or coercion relative to other states and nonstate actors because of the political, geographic, economic and financial, technological, military, social, cultural, or other capabilities it possesses.

KEY TERMS
Balance of power 197
Power 200

Voluntarism 197
Legitimacy 204
Unitary state 204
Federal state 204
Division of powers 206
Political culture 206
Neocolonialism 207
Soft power 207
Gross national income(GNI) 208

ADDITIONAL READING
Joseph Nye's books *Bound to Lead* (New York: Basic Books, 1990) and *The Paradox of American Power* (New York: Oxford University Press, 2002) underscore the importance of what he calls "soft" power, which often is overlooked by those who focus only on military and economic capabilities that he defines as "hard" power.

6.4 Illustrate how the diversity of capabilities impacts the way in which power is measured.

Given the diversity of possible capabilities a state may have at its disposal, it is exceedingly difficult to produce a single measure for rank ordering states' power positions relative to one another. This is because it is hard to determine how much weight should be given to any one type of capability. Should military capabilities in all cases be considered most important in determining outcomes? Or are economic capabilities more important at other times? That is why some scholars believe that we should talk about the varying importance of different types of capabilities based upon the issue area under discussion.

KEY TERMS
Issue area 210
Economic leverage 211

ADDITIONAL READING
Robert O. Keohane and Joseph S. Nye, *Power and Interdependence: World Politics in Transition* (New York: Longman, 1977, 2001). This book is an influential work within the field written by two scholars who integrate the concepts of power and interdependence and popularized the concept of issue areas. As noted above, Nye's hard-soft power distinction appears in several of his works, including *Soft Power: The Means to Success in World Politics* (Cambridge, MA: Perseus Books, Public Affairs, 2004).

CHAPTER REVIEW

1. The conceptual framework discussed in this chapter best reflects which perspective on international relations?
   a. Realist
   b. Liberal
   c. Economic structuralist
   d. Social constructivist

2. The term that best refers to the types of resources a state may have in order to serve its interests and achieve its objectives is
   a. threats.
   b. capabilities.
   c. opportunities.
   d. economic assets.

3. The right of a state to exercise complete jurisdiction, power, or authority internally or within its borders and to act independently or autonomously externally in the conduct of foreign affairs defines its
   a. legitimacy.
   b. national interest.
   c. power.
   d. sovereignty.

4. Compared to national interests, national objectives are
   a. more broadly defined.
   b. more narrowly defined.
   c. always identical with national interests.
   d. less important.

5. Policymakers need to consider
   a. short-range objectives.
   b. middle-range objectives.
   c. long-term objectives.
   d. all of the above.

6. Policymakers are faced with the challenge of
   a. determining what actually constitutes a threat or opportunity.
   b. prioritizing objectives once decided upon.
   c. balancing competing domestic and foreign policy objectives.
   d. all of the above.

7. Public opinion most likely influences
   a. authoritarian regimes.
   b. democratic republics.
   c. monarchies.
   d. dictatorships.

8. Parliamentary governments are more likely than presidential governments to
   a. fail to devise coherent foreign policies.
   b. choose their leader by the popular vote of the public.
   c. have the head of government also leader of the majority party.
   d. none of the above.

9. Power is
   a. often referred to as the same as capabilities.
   b. evident when compared to other states or nonstate actors.
   c. has an effect on outcomes.
   d. all of the above.

10. Which of the following is *not* an indicator of a state's capabilities?
    a. Social, cultural, and political arrangements
    b. Economic and financial strength
    c. Number of years established as a sovereign state
    d. Technological and military resources

11. The political capabilities of a state are least affected by:
    a. the human factor.
    b. communications technologies.
    c. natural resources.
    d. regime type.

12. A state's political culture is its
    a. tradition of patronage of the arts.
    b. specific social and cultural heritage, which support the identity of the nation-state.
    c. norms, values, and orientations that are politically relevant.
    d. all of the above.

13. A single measure of power capturing all of the capabilities discussed above is
 a. the goal of most realist theorists.
 b. the goal of most liberal theorists.
 c. the goal of both realists and liberals.
 d. none of the above.

14. The best single measure of power in international relations and world politics is
 a. bureaucratic capabilities.
 b. social capabilities.
 c. political capabilitites.
 d. none of the above.

15. The idea of applying power to issue areas is applicable to
 a. military competition among states.
 b. economic competition among states.
 c. political competition among states.
 d. all of the above.

Diplomacy and Foreign Policy

"*A Foreign Secretary is always faced with this cruel dilemma. Nothing he [she] can say can do very much good, and almost anything he may say may do a great deal of harm. Anything he says that is not obvious is dangerous; whatever is not trite is risky. He is forever poised between the cliché and the indiscretion.*"

— *Harold Macmillan, Former Secretary of State for Foreign Affairs and later Prime Minister of the United Kingdom, 1955*

LEARNING OBJECTIVES

7.1 Explain the relation between foreign policy and diplomacy by identifying the roles played by both state and non-state actors in the foreign policy decision-making process.

7.2 Identify the high points of the Congress of Vienna and explain how it helped shape the customary practices of present-day communications among governments of states.

7.3 Outline how diplomacy works: recognition of states and governments, diplomatic immunities and protections, the organization of diplomatic missions, diplomatic carrots and sticks.

7.4 Illustrate the potential benefits of diplomatic negotiations focused on arms control and disarmament, types of agreements, and ongoing proliferation concerns in terms of nuclear, radiological, chemical, biological, ballistic missiles, and advanced conventional weapons.

Read and Listen to Chapter 7 at mypoliscilab.com

Study and Review the Pre-Test & Flashcards at mypoliscilab.com

In March 2011 Secretary of State Hillary Clinton emerged as a principal advocate of decisive military action in Libya to protect populations under fire in a civil war between rebel forces and those loyal to Muammar Kaddafi's regime in Tripoli, the country's capital. Defense Secretary Robert Gates initially indicated reluctance to intervene (a view also shared by the president's national security adviser, Thomas Donilon), particularly given ongoing commitments to wars in Iraq and Afghanistan. Secretary Gates also received cautionary counsel from his personal adviser, General Brent Scowcroft, former national security adviser to presidents Gerald Ford and George H. W. Bush.

President Obama initially was reluctant to commit to yet another intervention, but indicated that if he did decide finally to do so that it must be a multilateral event in which other countries assumed leading, not just symbolic roles. A foreign policy debate at the highest levels of the Obama administration also took French, British, Arab, and other countries' positions into account. The secretary of state, diplomats in the State Department, at the UN, and in American embassies in these countries worked toward an international consensus on what to do and why.

For their part, the French recognized the anti-Kaddafi forces located in and around the city of Benghazi in eastern Libya as constituting the legitimate government of Libya. Indeed, displacing the al-Kaddafi regime was an aspiration held in common by many, but the international consensus ultimately supported intervention only on humanitarian grounds—protecting civilians put in jeopardy by Kaddafi's forces. Diplomats bargained at the UN on the text of a resolution—a process that moved forward more rapidly when the Arab League finally endorsed establishment of a "no-fly" zone over Libya intended to preclude further bombing raids and thus blunt advances by Kaddafi's forces against rebel strongholds. Intense negotiations among ambassadors and staffs at the UN Security Council finally produced a resolution authorizing the use of force that passed unanimously 10–0, albeit with five abstentions—truly a major diplomatic achievement, quite apart from the final outcome of the intervention—the toppling of the Kaddafi regime

Diplomacy is an essential tool in the foreign policymaker's and practitioner's tool kit. Achieving goals and serving the national interest require communicating not only with allies and coalition partners, but also with adversaries and those charting a more independent course between these two friend-or-foe categories. Presidents or prime ministers, secretaries of state or foreign ministers, and their ambassadors and other diplomats have the principal responsibility for the foreign policies of the countries they represent. In the United States the president—often referred to as commander-in-chief of the armed forces—is also the nation's chief diplomat. If you take a look at Article II of the U.S. Constitution (readily available online), you'll find the president designated as principal for both security and foreign policy.

diplomacy ■ the management of international relations by communications, including negotiations at times leading to a bargain or agreement

treaty ■ a written agreement or contract between two or more states pledging adherence to any number of commitments

We take up in this chapter how foreign policy decisions are made and diplomatic actions are taken to advance what government leaders understand to be in their national interest. Sometimes the approach involves persuasion and accommodation, as is evident in arms control negotiations, which we will examine in this chapter. At other times the use of force, or the threat of doing so, may be the form diplomacy takes. On a day-to-day basis the task of maintaining or building good relations with other countries may not receive much publicity, but it is an important part of diplomatic practice.

executive agreement ■ agreement made between leaders of two or more states that does not have the more formal characteristics of treaties

DIPLOMACY AND FOREIGN POLICY

A useful definition of the term **diplomacy** is the management of international relations by communications, including negotiations at times leading to a bargain or agreement. Indeed, the emphasis on negotiation is viewed by most people as the essence of diplomacy—negotiating a **treaty**, reaching an **executive agreement**, or bargaining with another state over the terms of a proposed agreement. The emphasis on the state as key diplomatic actor—whether acting on its own or within international organizations, alliances, and other coalitions—is consistent with a realist perspective on diplomacy. Liberals also understand the importance of states, of course, but they are prone to considering officials and staffs of both international and nongovernmental organizations as important players that ought not to be overlooked.

7.1 Explain the relation between foreign policy and diplomacy by identifying the roles played by both state and non-state actors in the foreign policy decision-making process.

Less publicized is day-to-day diplomacy—more commonplace interactions aimed simply at maintaining or improving relations between countries and the diplomats that represent them. One former U.S. secretary of state, George Shultz (1982–1989), described this kind of diplomacy as tending to the garden, keeping relations on track. Put another way, sustaining and improving the communications process in international relations may be as (or even more) important than

👁 Watch the Video
**"Conflict Diamonds
and the Kimberley
Process"** at
mypoliscilab.com

the particular issues being discussed or negotiated. Anyone interested in the day-to-day work of American diplomats could consult the infamous WikiLeaks documents published beginning in 2010—hundreds of diplomatic cables that were part of some 250,000 communications from 274 American embassies and consulates taken from U.S. State Department classified systems and copied to computer disks by a U.S. Army private.

In ordinary conversation, the words *diplomacy* and *diplomat* usually have a positive connotation. To say someone was "very diplomatic in dealing with the problem" is a compliment that implies that the person is a good communicator—one who possesses understanding, sensitivity, and effective interpersonal skills. Professional diplomats who have developed this ability to communicate effectively often become respected members of their foreign policy establishments. They are able to represent their governments or international organizations quite well even when the messages they convey are not always positive.

démarche ■
a diplomatic
representation,
request, or protest
from one government
to another

As diplomats, they are the advocates of national or international organizational interests and positions on any number of issues. Diplomats may craft a *démarche*, for example, which is a statement to a foreign government, usually making a formal proposal in the expectation of a formal response. Proposals to foreign governments can be expressed in positive, cooperative language or on other occasions in more forceful language. Even when a country wishes to make an *ultimatum*—"do this or else"—it normally uses language that customarily conforms to diplomatic standards for such communications.

Whether the diplomat personally agrees with or opposes a particular foreign policy position, it is the diplomat's task to represent it as well as he or she can. Lawyers for plaintiff and defense in a civil court case are by necessity in opposition to one another, but each can at the same time respect the competency and honesty of the other. So it is with diplomats, who develop international reputations for the degree of competency or trustworthiness they exhibit in representing their countries or international organizations.

Such work is not restricted to a state's ambassador assigned and accredited to a foreign country or an international organization such as the United Nations. Diplomacy may be done by heads of state during a summit meeting, foreign ministers and other government officials, or by a specially designated diplomat or envoy as in one who seeks to secure peace between warring parties. Examples of such diplomacy include:

- President George W. Bush's meetings with Prime Minister Tony Blair to assure and maintain British partnership during and after the invasion of Iraq in 2003
- President Barack Obama's person-to-person discussions with Russian president Medvedev in 2010 on his efforts to secure ratification by the U.S. Senate of the new Strategic Arms Reductions Treaty (New START)

Examples of interstate diplomacy below the head-of-government level include:

- Assistant Secretary of State Christopher Hill's involvement with negotiations with North Korea over its nuclear program, particularly in 2006–2007
- Special Envoy Richard Holbrooke's efforts in 2009 and 2010 to coordinate U.S. foreign policy with governments in Afghanistan and Pakistan

Diplomacy can involve formal or informal negotiations. These negotiations can be conducted with the full knowledge of the world or in secret. Negotiations can be conducted on a bilateral basis, between two states, or on a multilateral basis, involving three or more states. The secretary-general and other diplomats of the United Nations and other international organizations are often in a position to play a constructive role in managing conflicts and assisting parties in the negotiations process.

Diplomacy among states includes a wide range of both positive and negative approaches—both incentives and disincentives, including the use of force. In Chapter 9, we focus more specifically on the actual use of force in international politics. Diplomacy can be viewed more broadly, however, as a means by which states attempt to harness their capabilities—military, economic, and other forms of power—for the purpose of achieving their objectives and securing their interests. Realists generally share this power-based understanding of how diplomacy best serves national interests pursued by those who make foreign policy.

In those situations in which states' preferences or interests are close enough to be reconciled and the parties involved desire to achieve a mutually beneficial accommodation, noncoercive diplomacy will play a major role in achieving such an outcome. One example is the development of the European Union (EU) over recent decades—daily collaboration on many issues to include creating and sustaining economic growth through trade and investment. Another is the North American Free Trade Agreement (NAFTA) that brings the United States, Mexico, and Canada to the task of reducing tariffs and other barriers to trade among them. Although, on a number of indexes, the capabilities will differ among the states involved, all governments believe they have a common interest in seeing an agreement reached.

In those situations in which states' preferences or interests sharply diverge or are viewed as incompatible, policymakers and diplomats may resort to more forceful measures:

- *The active use of physical force* is the most basic of means to assert power. This characterized the situation involving the major European states in the late 1930s and Japan and the United States commencing with the attack on Pearl Harbor in December 1941. At the risk of oversimplifying, diplomats are often in the forefront of negotiations to prevent war. If they fail, the military takes over and does what it is trained to do—fight wars. Once force has defeated or demoralized one of the participants, diplomacy plays an important role in any peace negotiations or settlement.
- *Threatening to use force* is a prevalent aspect of diplomacy. Some threats are designed to get another state or states to do what they would not otherwise do—to compel them to take particular actions. This is often referred to as *coercive diplomacy* (or *compellence*) and may include the selective application of actual military force to get a foe to accede to one's wishes. Alternatively, threats of force can be an aspect of *deterrence*—a way to persuade states from doing what they intend or might like to do. This demonstrates a more passive use of force.

  For example, the United States initially utilized more positive diplomatic measures in early 1990 to try to persuade Saddam Hussein of Iraq to resolve peacefully his grievances with neighboring Kuwait, including the organization of an international coalition. Following Iraq's invasion of Kuwait in June 1990, however, Iraq was threatened not only with economic sanctions, but also with military action unless it withdrew its forces—a prime example of the use of coercive diplomacy.

■ *Economic threats or sanctions* represent another set of options or disincentives that can be used for the same purposes. For example, UN economic sanctions were imposed on Libya in an effort to coerce that country into turning over two Libyan intelligence agents charged with the bombing of Pan Am Flight 103 in December 1988. The Libyan agents were tried at an international court in The Hague, Netherlands, and one was convicted. International economic sanctions were also imposed for many years against South Africa in an attempt to change its racial apartheid or segregation policies.

Interstate relations can be played out anywhere along this continuum, moving back and forth depending on the countries involved, the issues in dispute, and the time period. In the next section, we define and provide a brief overview of what is meant by diplomacy. Second, we discuss the historical development of diplomacy, drawing on examples from the international systems outlined in Chapter 3. Finally, we examine in some detail diplomatic structure and process—the nuts and bolts of how states actually use diplomacy to further their interests and objectives. We also discuss how in recent years nongovernmental organizations (NGOs) have come to play diplomatic roles.

Diplomacy has traditionally been the almost exclusive domain of official representatives of states and international organizations composed of states. Indeed, the term *diplomacy* has traditionally referred to authoritative communications in international relations. Modern diplomacy, by contrast, is often less restrictive, sometimes including private citizens and nongovernmental organizations. Individuals acting in their private capacities have certainly made a difference, particularly when their diplomatic initiatives were sanctioned by a government. During the 1962 Cuban missile crisis, for example, President Kennedy sent private citizen and former secretary of state Dean Acheson to represent American policy to the president of France, Charles de Gaulle. He was selected in large part because of his positive reputation as a former secretary of state and diplomat. As a result, he was more likely than most others to be able to convey the rationale for American policy to the French, thus securing their support. Similarly, former president Jimmy Carter has been asked as a private citizen to perform diplomatic functions in the Middle East, Africa, and Latin America— contributing to bringing contending parties together or using his center's resources to help assure fair elections. On some of these occasions he engaged in diplomatic activities as a formal representative of the United States. Subsequently, former secretary of state James Baker was enlisted by the George W. Bush administration to encourage a number of states to forgive the debt incurred by Iraq after the former regime was overthrown in 2003 as a consequence of the U.S.-led invasion.

At other times, individuals have entered the diplomatic world without invitation. Much to the dismay of state officials, these private actors sometimes have worked at cross-purposes with policies advocated even by their own governments. Sometimes they have performed supportive though still independent roles. Although as a practical matter most diplomacy is conducted by government-employed diplomats, the roles that individuals as private citizens play from time to time can be significant.

The official positions taken by diplomats are the result of a state's foreign policy decision-making process. Scholars engaged in studying foreign policy decision-making processes from a liberal perspective emphasize that entities known, for example, as the "United States" or "Canada" do not make decisions; decisions are made by individuals. Similarly, a particular bureaucratic entity termed the "State Department" or "Foreign Office" is composed of individuals. It is therefore not surprising that the study of individuals and small groups has been a primary focus of analysis for a number of scholars.

ARGUMENT Scholars focus on how psychological stress arising out of difficult, emotion-laden situations affects rational calculations. One example of this perspective is the work of Irving L. Janis, who has examined the tendency for social pressure to enforce conformity and consensus in cohesive decision-making groups. He calls this tendency *groupthink*, a mode of thinking that people engage in when they are deeply involved in a cohesive in-group, when the members' strivings for unanimity override their motivation to appraise alternative courses of action realistically. He has applied this concept to a number of case studies, including the 1962 Cuban missile crisis.

A number of international relations scholars also have conducted case studies to determine better how psychological processes influence decision making during times of crisis—a situation between peace and war. The tendency for individuals to strive for *cognitive* consistency—interpreting information so that it confirms one's bias or view—and for groups to enforce consensus among their members is particularly evident in crisis situations characterized by high stress, surprise, exhausting around-the-clock work schedules, and complex, ambiguous environments. As a result, there is a general erosion of cognitive capabilities. Tolerance for ambiguity is reduced, policy options are restricted, opposing actors and their motives are stereotyped.

By the mid-1980s there was an evident decline in the amount of literature devoted to the role of cognition in international relations. Indeed, it was seemingly not as fashionable at the time to study the broader role of ideas in international relations. The late 1980s, however, witnessed a revival of interest in the role and causal importance of ideas, a focus that continued throughout the 1990s and into the present period as constructivist perspectives on international relations became more popular. On the importance of ideas on policymaking, Judith Goldstein argues that in order to understand U.S. trade policies over the years, considering only system-level factors or domestic economic interests is insufficient. Rather, one must also take into account actors' causal beliefs as to which economic policies can best achieve preferred interests. She and Robert Keohane see worldviews, principled beliefs, and causal understandings as ideas that become embedded in institutions and impact diplomacy and the making of foreign policy by acting as cognitive road maps.

COUNTERARGUMENT No one would deny that the study of individuals is important if we wish to improve our understanding of international relations. The important question, however, is: "How much emphasis should be placed on the individual level of analysis as opposed to other levels?" The realist Hans Morgenthau observed that in order to understand how a political leader reached a particular decision, we speculate how we would respond in similar circumstances. In other words, by keeping the decision-making environment constant, we could hypothesize that any rational individual would have acted in the same manner. Despite a diversity of backgrounds or temperaments, the structure of the situation encourages diplomats and decision makers to respond in a similar fashion.

APPLICATION When you watch foreign policy in the making—interviews and presentations by decision makers in videos on TV or the internet, look out for

(continued)

evidence of psychological or social-psychological factors that may be affecting the way decisions are made. Studies applying the concept of groupthink and other social-psychological concepts rely heavily on memoirs and interviews with participants. What do you think are the limitations of using such approaches?

To read more about psychosocial factors and the role of ideas in policymaking, see, for example, Irving L. Janis's *Victims of Groupthink* (Boston: Houghton-Mifflin, 1972); Robert Jervis, *Perception and* *Misperception in International Politics* (Princeton, NJ: Princeton University Press, 1976); Ole Holsti on theories of crisis decision making in Paul Gordon Lauren (ed.), *Diplomacy: New Approaches in History, Theory and Policy* (New York: 1979); Judith Goldstein and Robert O. Keohane (eds.), *Ideas and Foreign Policy: Beliefs, Institutions, and Political Change* (Ithaca, NY: Cornell University Press, 1993); and Valerie M. Hudson, Derek H. Chollet, and James M. Goldgeier, *Foreign Policy Decision-Making Revisited* (New York: Palgrave, 2002). ▲

nongovernmental organizations (NGOs)
■ transnational organizations with a standing independent of governments, often with a diverse membership that works to fulfill specific political, social, or economic objectives

International conferences addressing economic and social issues are often accompanied by parallel discussions among interested nongovernmental actors who try to influence the process during the months or years of the planning phase and in the international conference itself. Building a consensus for agreements that goes beyond governments is an increasingly important diplomatic function performed by nongovernmental organizations and key individuals. At least since the 1995 conference held in China on the global state of women, for example, official delegations were joined by unofficial delegations that came to influence the conference as well as public debate. Scientists in 2007 negotiated with government representatives on the final statements published by the Intergovernmental Panel on Climate Change (IPCC), and in 2011 telecommunications experts began renegotiating the distribution and use of frequencies, an issue of enormous importance in a world in which there is an ever-growing volume of transmissions as well as technological advances that improve our abilities to communicate globally.

This active role for **nongovernmental organizations (NGOs)** has become commonplace, particularly in association with UN-sponsored conferences. Annual and other periodic meetings of specialized agencies such as the World Bank, International Monetary Fund, and the World Trade Organization have also become opportunities for diverse interest groups and advocates of policy change on such issues as economic development, equity for labor, and concern for the environment. This focus on the importance of nonstate actors is consistent with a liberal or pluralist perspective on world politics.

7.2 Identify the high points of the Congress of Vienna and explain how it helped shape the customary practices of present-day communications among governments of states.

THE HISTORICAL DEVELOPMENT OF DIPLOMACY

In a world of increasing complexity, diplomacy in all of its manifestations will continue to play an important role. The formalization of diplomatic practices, however, has taken centuries.[1] From the realist perspective, self-interest will lead political entities to develop mechanisms to deal with rivals or allies. Even before

[1]Sir Harold Nicholson, *Diplomacy,* 3rd ed. (London: Oxford University Press, 1963), 7–14.

▶ CASE & POINT | NGOs and Diplomacy in the Field

CASE With the end of the Cold War, the increase in ethnic conflict within states, and the often-resultant humanitarian crises, NGOs and international organizations are playing a new and increasingly important role. Operational NGOs serve in the field, working directly with the recipients of humanitarian aid and economic development projects. Traditionally, humanitarian-relief NGOs have worked assiduously to maintain a strict policy of neutrality and leave the diplomacy and conflict-resolution functions to government diplomats. This policy is changing and has caused a great deal of discussion and debate as to whether NGOs should do more than provide medical care, food, and water to populations suffering from the ravages of war.

In response to the question of roles, there are certain conditions that must be met before NGOs engage in conflict management activities:

- The NGO knows the country and the regional institutions involved in the conflict resolution effort.
- The NGO has indigenous partners.
- The NGO staff has a good knowledge of conflict mediation skills.
- The NGO's field staff members fully understand the personal risks they are assuming.

Equally important is the development of further coordination among the different types of operational NGOs and between the NGO community and other actors involved in complex emergency interventions.

It is more than apparent that NGOs of all varieties are seriously grappling with issues raised by working in situations of conflict in Darfur and elsewhere in Africa, the Middle East, Central Asia, and other parts of the world. On the one hand, there is widespread recognition that NGOs might unwittingly become a party to conflict in the course of their humanitarian relief work. This would understandably increase the likelihood of physical harm to employees. On the other hand, NGO actions could be part of a concerted, coordinated effort involving governments, international and regional organizations, and private groups to avert or resolve conflict. They also have the ability both to provide early warning and to shore up the political will of governments to act. Finally, they can give guidance to policymakers in their own countries and encourage community building and the development of civil societies in countries decimated by war.

POINT The work of NGOs forms an important part of the entire repertoire of intervention strategies for dealing with conflict in the post–Cold War era. Whether due to circumstances or design, NGOs are playing increasingly important diplomatic roles in global politics. Would-be practitioners may want to check out the website of the United States Institute of Peace, which offers a professional training program to improve the conflict management skills of U.S. and foreign diplomats, military personnel, law enforcement professionals, and leaders of NGOs, as well as activists and tribal and other leaders in conflict zones. ▲

recorded history, warring clans and tribes must have found it useful to negotiate with one another, even if this was simply to recover their dead after a battle. In the self-interest of all the warring parties, such envoys were undoubtedly granted different treatment from warriors and hence had a special status that allowed them to return unharmed to their own people to convey the demands or requests of the enemy. From the social constructivist perspective, the modalities of diplomacy epitomize the process of the purposeful creation of language, norms, and rules of behavior, which in turn become part of the structure of international relations and hence influence future diplomatic interactions.

In ancient Greece, each city chose a herald to communicate with foreigners. Heralds required a good memory and a strong voice so they could accurately repeat the views of their leaders. The heralds were placed under the tutelage of the god Hermes—perhaps an unfortunate choice from the point of view of future diplomats, as Hermes symbolized charm, cunning, and trickery. Beginning in the sixth century B.C.E, however, the Greek independent state system experienced increased commercial interdependence, and political relations became more complex. As a result, the city-states chose their finest orators to plead their city's case before foreign assemblies.

The Romans acquired the Greek diplomatic traditions, but an expanding empire has scant need for negotiating talents when it is crushing all those before it. Roman contributions to international law, however, certainly had diplomatic implications. The Roman emphasis on the fulfillment of contracts, for example, applied to their view of treaties. Their work on *jus gentium*, law applied not just to Romans, but to all peoples whether citizens or foreigners, and *jus naturale*, law whose principles are discovered by reason and thus are common to all humanity no matter one's race, creed, or color, had foreign policy implications that extended beyond administrative law for an empire; that is, that certain universal principles should govern relations among political units. Finally, the Romans developed trained archivists who became specialists in diplomatic procedures.

jus gentium ■ laws applicable to all humanity, states, and individuals

jus naturale ■ natural law or the laws of nature that some writers see as superseding man-made law

During the latter years of the Roman Empire, however, a need arose for trained negotiators. The Eastern Byzantine hub of the empire in Constantinople realized force alone could not keep the barbarians at bay. Diplomats, therefore, were critical players in a three-part diplomatic strategy to foster rivalry among the "barbarians," secure the friendship of frontier tribes and peoples by flattery and money, and convert as many of the "heathens" to Christianity as possible. Such a strategy helps to account for Emperor Justinian's ability to extend Byzantine influence as far south as Sudan and keep at arm's length the warrior tribes of the Black Sea and Caucasus. In order to implement the strategy, however, the emperor's diplomats had to be more than heralds or orators; they also needed to be perceptive political observers who could accurately assess the strengths and weaknesses of neighboring despots and warriors. This emphasis on astute observations and sound judgment has become a hallmark of the best professional diplomats down through history.

The collapse of the western half of the Roman Empire led in the Middle Ages to an end of the political and administrative rationality imposed by Rome. Political authority was fragmented among a wide variety of local and regional rulers and the Church in Rome, which claimed universal moral authority. As communication and civil authority broke down, commerce suffered, as did contact throughout feudal Europe. Indeed, it was often extremely dangerous to pass from town to town or castle to castle. As a result, no established system of international contacts existed, resulting in little advancement in diplomatic practices and conventions.

Modern diplomacy arose in the 13th and 14th centuries in Italy. Essentially standing outside the rest of feudal Europe, the Italian city-states resembled the Greek independent state system—common cultural and commercial interests racked by intense political and military competition. It is not surprising that out of this turmoil came such ambassador-scholars as Dante, Petrarch, and Machiavelli. The first recorded diplomatic mission was established in Genoa in 1455 by the Duke of Milan.

The Congress of Vienna (1814–1815) is of greatest historical importance. Three reasons stand out. First, the era of the Concert of Europe could be characterized as a multipolar (more than two) state system. It is not an exaggeration to observe that ministers, political leaders, and diplomats of the day deserved credit for establishing an international system that successfully mitigated the worst aspects of anarchy among states. France was restored and diplomats constructed a balance among the European great powers—Britain offshore and, on the European continent, France in the west, Russia in the east, and Austria and Prussia in between the two in central Europe. Periodic international conferences were held in succeeding decades (referred to by historians as the Concert of Europe) to make necessary adjustments to the European order—the balance of interests and power supportive of stability that also contributed to the avoidance of general war. Small wars occurred over the next half century, but each was contained, and none posed a substantial challenge to the overall order that had been established. Although the Concert of Europe as a formal diplomatic mechanism fell apart after several decades, the underlying order and expectations established by diplomacy at Vienna in 1815 contributed to preserving Europe from another outbreak of general war until 1914. Indeed, scholars in the English School of thought often speak of a society of states in Europe existing through much of the 19th century.

Second, it was not until the Congress of Vienna that a truly organized system of diplomatic practices and norms emerged. The follow-on Congress of Aix-la-Chapelle, for example, agreed on a hierarchy of diplomatic representation. Within each category diplomatic precedence and status were not a function of who represented the most powerful country, but rather who had held the diplomatic post the longest. By 1815 diplomatic services came to be viewed as distinct branches of each government. Diplomacy was increasingly professionalized, with common rules, norms, and expectations.

A certain etiquette, for example, is maintained even between enemies preparing for war. After the Japanese bombed Pearl Harbor on December 7, 1941, the United States declared war on Japan, and diplomatic relations were terminated. Consistent with international law, diplomats were quickly given safe passage out of both countries. The rules of diplomatic immunity long established in customary international law were formally codified in the Vienna Conventions on Diplomatic and Consular Relations in 1961.

Finally, the Congress of Vienna is worth studying because it is a classic example of successful **multilateral diplomacy**—a number of countries communicating and negotiating, often over the most contentious of issues. Successful multilateral diplomacy depends on accommodating the interests and specific objectives of not only two states, as in **bilateral diplomacy**, but rather a number of participants. International organizations and settlements or agreements that prove to be durable over time derive from a broad consensus and can be modified or adapted as conditions and objectives change. Bureaucratic rigidity or an inability to adapt to changing circumstances will reduce the utility or functionality of international institutions in multilateral diplomacy, leading perhaps to their ultimate collapse.

The Versailles Treaty and other multilateral settlements following World War I (1914–1918) pale in comparison to the successes of the Congress of Vienna. The Versailles peace lasted only two decades. World War II (1939–1945) repeated the

multilateral diplomacy ■ negotiations involving three or more states

bilateral diplomacy ■ negotiations involving two states

mass destruction of lives and property of World War I but at even higher levels made possible by technological advances in military weaponry. Consistent with the obliteration of urban areas through bombing that had become the norm, dropping atomic bombs on two Japanese cities was the cataclysmic finale of World War II.

Perhaps as a result of learning from earlier experiences, multilateral diplomacy following World War II did prove to be somewhat more successful, although the succeeding half century was also marked by periods of high tension that threatened mass destruction on a truly global scale, thanks to East-West competition during the Cold War. Nevertheless, multilateral diplomacy in international conferences and within international organizations has assumed an increasingly important role in world politics since 1945. More recent examples of multilateral diplomacy dealing with demographic, environmental, economic development, and humanitarian issues are discussed elsewhere in the book.

DIPLOMATIC PROCESSES

7.3 Outline how diplomacy works: recognition of states and governments, diplomatic immunities and protections, the organization of diplomatic missions, diplomatic carrots and sticks.

In order to grasp how governments implement foreign policy, we explore in this section the ways and means of diplomatic practice. Ambassadors, their country teams, and other emissaries relate to the leaders and ministries or offices of other governments, their embassies and consulates, and international and nongovernmental organizations.

Recognition of States and Governments

sovereignty ■ a claim to political authority to make policy or take actions domestically or abroad; based on territory and autonomy, historically associated with the modern state

A sovereign state comes into existence under international law when a population living in a defined territory that is administered by a government is recognized by other sovereign states. Recognition of a state's **sovereignty** amounts to an acceptance of its present and future claims to two rights—one internal and the other external. The internal claim is to a right as a sovereign state to exercise complete jurisdiction over its own territory free of interference by other states in its domestic affairs. At the same time, there is an external claim to a right to be independent or autonomous in its foreign affairs, not subordinated to any other state in the conduct of its international relations.

As a practical matter, of course, states do not always respect the sovereign claims of other states. When they choose to interfere in the domestic affairs of another state, the response may well be a diplomatic protest note or public declaration to the same effect. Thus, during the Cold War, the United States privately and on occasion publicly condemned Soviet policies that violated the human rights of its citizens, particularly Jews, who were not permitted to leave the country. The typical Soviet response at the time was to condemn the United States for unlawful interference in its domestic affairs: Soviet emigration policy, in Moscow's view, was a domestic matter and not the business of the United States. The American position was that the Soviet Union had obligations under international law to respect the human rights of all peoples, including its own citizens, and should not try to exempt itself from international scrutiny just because it was a sovereign state.

More serious, of course, is when a state commits aggression against another state. For example, Germany's invasion of neutral Holland in World War II and neutral Belgium in both world wars clearly violated the sovereignty of these states. They claimed rights to their neutrality in foreign policy and to their continued administration of their own countries. As a factual matter, of course, the European states that were successfully invaded ceased exercising their sovereignty over their territories for several years; nevertheless, violation of sovereignty did not extinguish their legal claims to sovereignty. Indeed, invaded states maintained governments in exile located in other friendly countries such as the United Kingdom that were willing to recognize them as the legitimate governments of their invaded countries then under foreign occupation. These governments in exile maintained their claims to sovereignty throughout the war. Upon liberation of their territories, they were able to reestablish actual control.

When the invading power establishes a so-called puppet government, diplomatic recognition is sometimes withheld. A good example involves the Vichy regime installed in France following the German invasion in 1940. International recognition went to the French government in exile based in London. Even if no government in exile exists, recognition of a regime perceived as illegitimate might still be withheld. This was the case with the former German Democratic Republic (communist East Germany), which was isolated by other states for many years as well as being denied seats in such international organizations as the United Nations and its affiliated agencies.

In some cases decades may pass before diplomatic recognition is fully achieved. The United States and many other states, for example, did not recognize the Soviet annexation in 1940 of the Baltic republics. Estonian, Latvian, and Lithuanian claims to sovereignty were kept alive for half a century through governments in exile that maintained diplomatic ties with foreign governments. At the end of the Cold War, when for political reasons Moscow was willing to relinquish control of the Baltic republics, they reemerged on the world stage as independent and sovereign states.

States continue to be recognized as legitimate entities even when governments change. After the communist takeover in China in 1949, the United States and other like-minded countries chose to deny recognition to the new government in Beijing under Mao Zedong even though, as a factual matter, it had control of all of mainland China. Instead, these countries continued to recognize the nationalist, noncommunist government under Chiang Kai-shek on the island of Taiwan. Chiang's government maintained that it would one day regain control of all of China.

Because they saw it in their interest to do so, for more than two decades the United States and other foreign governments that were friendly to Taiwan and opposed to communism supported the legal fiction of Taiwanese legitimacy as the government of all of China. In 1971 and 1972, however, the United States finally reversed its long-standing policy and recognized the Beijing government as the legitimate government of China. Consistent with the new policy, U.S. diplomats were withdrawn from Taiwan, and diplomatic relations were established between Beijing and Washington. Diplomats from Beijing replaced those from Taiwan in the Chinese embassy in Washington.

Commercial, cultural, and other nongovernmental ties with Taiwan were maintained as Taiwan remained formally part of the same Chinese state. Government recognition changed, but all the territories recognized as part of China were the same. On this, governments in both Beijing and Taipei always agreed: Taiwan

✹ Explore the "Foreign Policy: You Are the President" at mypoliscilab.com

is part of China. As a practical matter, the government on Taiwan has remained in control there, although without much of the international recognition it had depended on for its legitimacy. For its part, the government in Beijing continues to refer to Taiwan as a renegade province, but still an integral part of the People's Republic of China.

Recognition is at times a function of how outside powers view a particular conflict—as a war between states or a civil war. Consider the United States and the Vietnam War in the early 1960s. The U.S. government argued that it was aiding the Republic of Vietnam (South Vietnam) in its defense against aggression from the communist Democratic Republic of Vietnam (North Vietnam). Coming to the aid of a state victimized by aggression by request of the legitimate government is allowable under international law, and the United States presented itself merely as helping a victimized state against communist aggression, as it had been asked to do.

Critics of the American policy in Vietnam, however, claimed that there were not two Vietnamese states, one committing aggression against the other. Rather, these critics argued, the Vietnam War was a civil war between contending governments in the same state. If so, then no outside state had a right to intervene militarily or otherwise in what was really a domestic matter within Vietnam.

Because the U.S. government under presidents Eisenhower, Kennedy, Johnson, Nixon, and Ford (covering the years 1953–1976) recognized the government in Saigon as the legitimate government of a South Vietnamese state under attack by North Vietnam and its Vietcong insurgents, it rejected the notion that the conflict was a civil war. Pressed on the issue, Henry Kissinger, national security adviser and later secretary of state in the Nixon and Ford administrations, admitted that the Vietnam War really had aspects of both a war between states and a civil war; however, the United States used the former understanding to justify its intervention policy.

Gaining acceptance in the international community through recognition of state and government is an important prize to those seeking such status. Recognition of Israel as a new state was granted in 1948 by many countries, including the Soviet Union, but to this day many Middle Eastern states continue to withhold recognition. Palestinians also seek the same recognition of a territorial state of their own, many having been dispossessed of their homes and property in the newly created Israeli state. Although progress toward a peaceful solution was made in the 1990s, for more than six decades Palestinians have been confronted by Israeli security forces, particularly in territories occupied by Israel since 1967.

Aspirations of Palestinians and many other national groups for the creation of new nation-states remain unfulfilled. Suppression of these nationalist movements by existing state authorities is common. Historical claims to a separate national identity by Chechens in the Transcaucasus region of the Russian Federation has been resisted by Russian authorities. A Chechen secessionist uprising has faced confrontation by the military since the mid-1990s, with large numbers of casualties on both sides. Significantly, outside states for the most part accepted Russian claims to sovereignty in the region, effectively treating the Chechen uprising as an internal matter within the Russian Federation.

In the final analysis, recognition of governments and states is a political choice left to other sovereign states and their governments. Some favor a policy that bases recognition of a particular government, for example, on the facts of the case as sole criterion: Does a particular government actually have control over the territory over which it claims jurisdiction? If it does, then it warrants recognition. Another approach is to grant recognition based on a second criterion, which is the perceived desirability of a particular state or government. Thus, the United States denied recognition of the Soviet Union and its government from 1917 until 1934, when diplomatic relations finally were established. As discussed earlier, recognition of the Chinese government in Beijing was denied from 1949 until the 1970s, when normalization of relations began to take place.

Diplomatic Immunities and Protections

While living and doing business in the host country, all diplomats on the diplomatic list are immune from arrest or prosecution by local authorities. Diplomats cannot even be prosecuted for traffic and parking violations, which is very frustrating to national or local governments. Nevertheless, diplomatic immunity is a reciprocal privilege that extends to all diplomats in all of their activities. Private citizens traveling abroad do not have this privilege of immunity from local laws and law-enforcement measures.

diplomatic immunity ■ a reciprocal privilege among states by which diplomats are not subject to arrest, prosecution, or penalty in the foreign state to which they are assigned

The reciprocity that assures the mutual safety of diplomats is absolutely essential if countries are to maintain contact and conduct business with one another. Not only would it be unseemly to arrest the diplomats of other countries, it could lead to reprisals against one's own diplomats. The only legal remedies for the host country for unacceptable conduct on the part of a foreign diplomat are to ignore or overlook such transgressions, to protest these activities to the host government, or to declare the diplomat unwelcome (persona non grata, or PNG for short), forcing his or her removal from the country.

Depending on the circumstances, misconduct can ruin a diplomatic career when it causes one to be declared persona non grata. On the other hand, some diplomats may face expulsion for reasons unrelated to their personal behavior. If relations sour between the diplomat's country and the host country, he or she may be subject to recall by his or her own country or alternatively to expulsion through the persona non grata declaration. Recalling one's own diplomats or expelling the diplomats of foreign countries is one way of signaling displeasure with the policies of those countries and may have nothing to do with the actual conduct of individual diplomats.

Diplomatic conventions, although legally binding as treaties, do not always assure in practice that diplomats will be treated correctly. In 1979, for example, Iranian revolutionaries held American diplomats as hostages. The revolutionaries' takeover of the American embassy and confiscation of its files also violated the same Vienna diplomatic convention as well as customary international law that protects embassy property even in wartime.

When countries break diplomatic relations, the embassy and its grounds are placed in caretaker status, sometimes under the daily control of a third country mutually acceptable to both disputing countries. This is because of the legal fiction of extraterritoriality, which assumes that an embassy and the ground it stands on are part of the sovereign territory and property of the foreign country. Because states are required under international law to respect the sovereignty of other states, embassies and their diplomats are given privileged, protected status.

extraterritoriality ■ the legal fiction that an embassy or consulate and the ground it stands on are part of the sovereign territory of the foreign country

Even the violation of these rules in Iran did not give the United States or any other country a right to do the same thing to Iranian diplomats or the Iranian embassy and grounds in Washington. The urge to take reprisals in kind is understandable, but any such action was avoided.

Because embassies are viewed as the property of the foreign country and thus not legally subject to host-country intrusion, they provide for their own security. The U.S. Marine Corps has traditionally been assigned the task of guarding American embassies in conjunction with State Department security officers. Host-country police or other security personnel also have the responsibility of protecting embassies by supplementing efforts of the embassy itself.

Embassies sometimes serve as places of asylum for host-country citizens or others seeking protection. The political decision to grant asylum is up to embassy officials and usually is limited or reserved as a humanitarian gesture to those whose political or other rights have been (or likely will be) violated. For example, Roman Catholic cardinal Mindzenty, an opponent of the communist takeover in Hungary after World War II, was one of the more celebrated recipients of American asylum at the U.S. embassy in Budapest. The host country may protest the granting of asylum or even try to prevent individuals from entering embassy grounds; but once asylum has been granted, host-country officials may not legally force entry to the embassy or its grounds to remove those who have found shelter there.

The Organization of Diplomatic Missions

ambassador ■
a state's highest-ranking representative assigned to an embassy in a foreign country

Emissaries of states bear different titles. Ambassador is the highest-ranking position and chief of mission in any given mission. *Mission* is a term that refers to an embassy, including a consular section in the same embassy, consulates located elsewhere in a foreign country, a diplomatic mission to an international organization, or a delegation to an international conference. In the absence of an ambassador as chief of mission, the mission may be left under another person in charge—a *chargé d'affaires* or, more simply, a *chargé*. The *chargé* is often the second-ranking person, also known as the deputy chief of mission or DCM.

Consul or consul general is usually the title of the official in charge of a consulate in the capital and in one or another of the major cities outside of the host country's capital. These consuls or consuls general work directly for the ambassador, whose residence is in the capital city near or on the embassy grounds. A consulate (or consular section in an embassy) coordinates the issue of passports to its own citizens, issues visas to citizens in the local country, and performs related administrative tasks. Consulates are also a focal point for promoting trade and cultural exchange in areas of the host country outside of the capital city. They report to the embassy or home country directly on political, economic, and other developments they observe.

The level of representation that a state sends to a host country is politically significant. When relations are fully developed or "normal," countries typically are represented at the ambassadorial level. When conflict has resulted in a breach of diplomatic relations between two countries, restoration of these relations is sometimes implemented in a gradual normalization process. The first step in normalizing relations often entails establishing an interest section in a mutually friendly

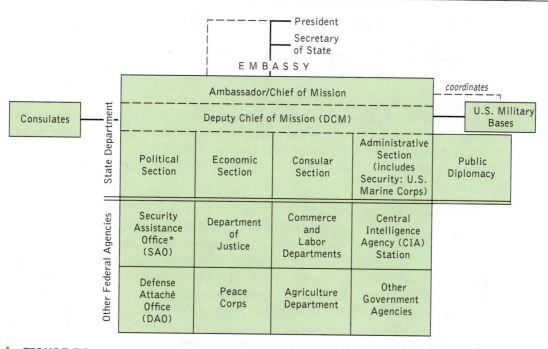

FIGURE 7.1

Organization of a U.S. Diplomatic Mission*

*Also known as Office of Defense Cooperation (ODC), Office of Military Cooperation (OMC), or Military Assistance and Advisory group (MAAG).

country's embassy. Later the embassy may be reopened with a lower-ranking diplomat serving as *chargé d'affaires*. Eventually a full embassy with a serving ambassador is established, perhaps with consulates in other important cities.

A typical embassy, headed by an ambassador as chief of mission and a DCM as second in charge, is divided into a number of functional sections. Most countries staff their embassies to perform various political, economic and commercial, consular, administrative, military, and intelligence functions. Missions to international organizations or international negotiations usually have specific tasks to perform and are staffed accordingly. Not surprisingly, embassies and other missions usually mirror the structural and cultural approaches to policy of their home countries.

Coordinating the diverse work of an American embassy is no easy task for any chief of mission. As Figure 7.1 indicates, only part of the embassy is State Department turf, the remainder containing offices from multiple U.S. government departments and agencies. The country team concept is one approach to integrating these efforts. Members of the country team—usually the chiefs or deputies of the different sections within the embassy—meet as a group at least once a week to review the embassy's collective work. Sometimes, particularly in smaller missions, personalities can be brought together under an effective ambassador or DCM to make a country team that can work together well, ironing out differences as they arise. In many cases, however, disputes go well beyond embassy personalities, reflecting conflicts among agencies in the national government that are not easily resolved.

American embassy officials thus are often as divided among themselves as are their respective agencies and agency heads in Washington. The reality is that, just as any president of the United States has difficulty controlling government agencies, whether engaged in domestic or foreign policy, an ambassador and the DCM face comparable challenges on a much smaller scale. Countries with a less fragmented political structure and less pluralism in political processes domestically than the United States no doubt have embassies that are far less fragmented and more deferential to the central authority of the ambassador and DCM.

Diplomatic Incentives and Disincentives

Whether in bilateral or multilateral settings, diplomats depend on the leverage they can bring to their negotiations and less formal discussions and interactions. Depending on the issue involved, economic or military resources may play an important role. Foreign aid may take the form of grants for social, economic, or military purposes; loans, particularly at concessionary interest rates (reduced below market levels by the donor country as a form of assistance); trade preferences (as in reducing tariffs on imports from a foreign country or guaranteeing purchase at a favorable price of one or another of the exporting country's products); or military assistance (the transfer of weapons free of charge or at reduced prices or the provision of military training). Such incentives or carrots may be very helpful, but one should always understand them for what they are—incentives. The firmer foundation on which lasting agreements are based is one in which the mutual interests and objectives of the parties are also accommodated.

An example of the use of diplomatic carrots is the 1978 accord reached at Camp David, Maryland, between Egyptian President Anwar Sadat and Israeli Prime Minister Menachem Begin that normalized relations between Israel and Egypt. The Sinai Desert land taken forcibly from Egypt by Israel in 1967 was returned in exchange for recognition by Egypt of Israel's sovereignty or right to exist as a state. In addition to the positive influence he was able to assert because of personal skills and the high stature of his office, President Carter was able to cement the agreement with promises of substantial military and economic aid to both negotiating parties.

Effective diplomacy is markedly easier to achieve when the parties have an established record of positive accomplishments over decades or longer. Mutual trust is a very important asset in diplomatic exchanges of any kind. Lack of trust, by contrast—perhaps due to a record of broken obligations or other conflicts—poses a significant obstacle or challenge to diplomats. The Camp David Accords proved to be only the first major step in a continuing peace process filled with some gains but also setbacks and disappointments.

Diplomacy, of course, is not simply about such positive inducements as economic and military aid. Diplomacy, as we have noted, can also be coercive—a stick forcing another country to do what it would not otherwise do. In adversarial relations, veiled or explicit threats of economic sanctions or military action can influence or coerce diplomats and policymakers in other states.

One country can punish or exercise economic leverage over another by threatening or actually imposing economic sanctions. Actually imposing sanctions amounts to economic warfare. If the punishing state has been giving aid or other assistance, it can be reduced or cut off entirely. A boycott against the other country's exports or an embargo or prohibition against selling or engaging in other commercial transactions can be imposed. These are legal restrictions preventing the sale or purchase of any goods or services to or from that country. The aim is to get the embargoed state to change its policy or comply with the wishes of the state imposing the embargo.

Economic sanctions are not always very effective in achieving their purposes. When a state's exports are boycotted by one country, it may simply find other markets for its goods. Notwithstanding legal prohibitions, it may also find other states willing to avoid or evade an embargo, which will continue to sell their products to the embargoed state or engage in other commercial activities. A multilateral boycott or embargo imposed by a coalition of states may be more effective by bringing greater collective pressure. Even so, ways are often found to circumvent these restrictions. The multilateral embargo against South Africa, for example, took many years to have noticeable effect. But eventually, in the early 1990s, the apartheid policy that had segregated the races was abandoned, and a regime led by Nelson Mandela finally was put into place.

A more serious stick is a blockade, a more intense form of economic warfare, in which warships or ground forces are used physically to prevent commerce going into or coming out of a country. Imposition of a blockade is an act of war that can escalate into an armed conflict.

If two states have a perceived conflict of interest and neither backs down, events can produce a crisis. Once a crisis begins, there is a basic policy dilemma: Each side feels it must do whatever is needed to advance or protect its interests but at the same time recognizes that it must avoid taking actions that could escalate the crisis to the point that it gets out of control.

Crisis diplomacy usually entails objectives that are both urgent and extremely important. It requires the greatest care in finding common ground as well as the appropriate combination of carrots and sticks. The Cuban missile crisis of 1962 is one such case. When American intelligence sources discovered in October 1962 that Soviet offensive missiles with nuclear warheads had been deployed to Cuba, American decision makers sought to have the missiles removed while, at the same time, attempting to avoid an escalation of the conflict into a major war. A keen awareness of the importance and urgency of accomplishing both of these short-term objectives clearly influenced deliberations on the various policy options open to the United States.

How the Soviets would respond to U.S. military actions was a matter of grave concern to President Kennedy and his advisers. Although American decision makers did not know it then, Soviet commanders in Cuba already had authority from Moscow to use battlefield nuclear weapons in the event of an American invasion. Had the American response been any more provocative than it was, nuclear war might well have occurred.

Fortunately, President Kennedy and his advisers decided upon a naval blockade of Cuba rather than a ground invasion or air strikes, while continuing to exercise

economic sanctions
■ coercive means to influence a state's behavior such as by a boycott, embargo, freezing bank assets, or blockade

crisis ■ a situation characterized by surprise, high threat to a state's values or interest, and short decision time

diplomatic and other channels of communication with the Soviets. Trying to soften somewhat the diplomatic impact of the blockade, some officials in the U.S. administration preferred to call it a quarantine of Cuba, which seemed to them a less provocative term. Using the metaphor "quarantine" cast the blockade less as an act of war and more as a temporary measure that would be lifted as soon as "health" was restored. Choosing a less provocative term was a war-avoidance measure, one calculated to allow an adversary to seek a peaceful resolution of the dispute.

Although even this course of action was highly risky, it proved to be successful in getting the Soviets to withdraw the missiles without armed conflict between the two states. But Kennedy wisely provided a carrot to the Soviet premier, Nikita Khrushchev, which was to promise to remove U.S. Jupiter missiles based in Turkey and aimed at the Soviet Union. Significantly, the security interests of both sides were accommodated. Recognition of how close the United States and the Soviet Union had come to the brink of nuclear war led, however, to setting an arms control agenda aimed at reducing tensions and building a foundation for better communications between the two, particularly in times of crisis.

Perceptions concerning the credibility of threats matter a great deal. If threats are not credible, a threatened state may choose to ignore them. Alternatively, the other state may make threats of its own: Saber rattling is common enough in diplomacy. States on a collision course may well wind up in armed conflict, particularly in a crisis in which high stakes and time pressure may undercut a reasoned, rational discussion of policy options. Paradoxically, when communications are most necessary, traditional practice is to sever diplomatic relations entirely. As the 19th-century Prussian writer Clausewitz observed, war is merely state policy conducted by other means. Inevitably, if cease-fires are to be arranged and peaceful settlements made, diplomacy must play a primary role.

There is also a place for diplomatic communications in wartime, sometimes facilitated by the good offices of third parties who assist in getting the parties to communicate and cease hostilities. This is the diplomatic peacemaking role as in the Middle East and elsewhere that aims toward a settlement through direct or indirect negotiations, mediation or arbitration, judicial settlement, or other means. In most cases, the conflicts that led parties to war in the first place are extraordinarily difficult to resolve. Divisions deepen as each party suffers the scourge that is the human cost of war.

Of course, if one side wins or prevails on the battlefield, it may be in a position to dictate the terms of the settlement. The losing party in such circumstances can take some solace in the outcome of the Congress of Vienna. Even without military or economic leverage, a losing party—France—was able to contribute to constructing a settlement that accommodated the diverse and often conflicting interests of the parties. Unfortunately, diplomatic miracles of this sort are usually few and far between, with vindictive and punishing terms for the loser of a war—such as Germany after World War I—a distinct possibility.

Diplomatic Communications

Diplomacy as a means of communications between or among governments has many sides. As noted, in the extreme one can play hardball and issue threats or an ultimatum to one's adversary. Ultimata of this sort, however, are not the usual,

Graham Allison and his colleagues in the late 1960s engaged in a now-classic study of U.S.-Soviet crisis diplomacy when the two countries came to the brink of nuclear war in 1962 over Soviet missiles secretly deployed in Cuba. Both the unitary and rational assumptions associated with realism are relaxed from the organizational process and bureaucratic politics perspectives adopted by Allison.

ARGUMENT The *organizational-process* model of foreign policy decision making views organizational routines and procedures as determining some and influencing other foreign policy decisions and outcomes. Organizational ethos and worldview are also relevant considerations. In an often-cited statement, Allison notes that where a given bureaucratic actor or diplomat stands on a given issue is often determined by where he or she sits; that is, one's view of alternative courses of action is highly colored by the perspective of the organization to which one belongs or the role one plays.

Allison's *bureaucratic politics* model of foreign policy decision making involves forming coalitions and countercoalitions among diverse bureaucratic actors in a competitive environment. The focus is on specific individuals in positions at the top of organizations and on the pulling and hauling among them. This is in contrast to the more routine, preprogrammed activity of the organizational-process model. Hence, foreign policy decisions at times may be the result of which individual or which coalition of individuals can muster the most political power. What may be best for an individual or his or her bureaucracy in terms of increased prestige and relative standing within the government may lead, however, to less than the best foreign policy for the state as a whole. Parochial, personal, and bureaucratic interests may reign over any expressed concern for the national interest.

Robert Keohane, Joseph S. Nye, Jr., and others have taken the liberal image of foreign policy a major step forward, arguing that the state may not be able to confine bureaucratic actors operating in its name. Organizations, whether private or governmental, may transcend the boundaries of states, forming coalitions with their foreign counterparts. Such transnational actors even may be working at cross-purposes with government leaders in their home states who possess the formal authority to make binding decisions. For example, the British Foreign Office may see a given issue similarly to its American State Department counterpart. On the other hand, the British Defence Ministry and the U.S. Defense Department may share a common view contrary to that of both diplomatic organizations. Moreover, nongovernmental interest groups in both countries may form coalitions supportive of one or another transgovernmental coalition.

If it is typically the way foreign policy is made, then the focus by realists on the state as the principal, rational, purposive actor would seem to be misdirected. From the liberal perspective, more attention should be given to organizational process and bureaucratic politics as well as to the entire range of transnational actors and their interactions.

COUNTERARGUMENT Realists argue that the disaggregation of the state into its component parts or players overlooks the fact that when all is said and done, a state still speaks authoritatively with one voice. This is especially the case in a crisis situation, and indeed, this is what occurred in the Cuban missile crisis; bureaucratic actors and organizational interests still resulted in the *president*—not anyone else—making the final decision on the "quarantine" or naval blockade that was imposed on the Soviet fleet sailing toward Cuba. From the realist perspective, the state retains its prerogatives when important foreign policy interests are at stake, precluding circumvention by bureaucratic or transnational actors. It is more likely that in cases where national security is not at stake—issues of less importance to realists—that the liberal perspective provides the more convincing explanation.

(continued)

APPLICATION Liberal models on foreign policy decision making were developed almost exclusively with Western states and political leaders in mind. How relevant are such approaches to dictatorial or authoritarian states in which a small number of individuals make the critical foreign policy decisions? For more detail, including access to Soviet data that became available to Western scholars in the post–Cold War period, see Graham Allison and Philip Zelikow, *Essence of Decision*, 2nd ed. (New York: Longman, 1999); James G. Blight and David A. Welch, *On the Brink: Americans and Soviets Reexamine the Cuban Missile Crisis* (New York: Hill and Wang, 1989); and James A. Nathan (ed.), *The Cuban Missile Crisis Revisited* (New York: St. Martin's Press, 1992). On the role of transnational (and transgovernmental) actors in world politics, the now-classic study is Robert O. Keohane and Joseph Nye (eds.), *Transnational Relations and World Politics* (Cambridge, MA: Harvard University Press, 1972) ▶

day-to-day stuff of diplomacy as is evident in the so-called WikiLeaks diplomatic cables. We will discuss three other kinds of diplomatic communications: informational transfers, symbolic messages, and negotiations designed to avoid or defer conflict.

Informational Transfers First, some communications are merely informational transfers not designed to produce any particular outcome. Such governmental agencies as departments (or ministries) of foreign affairs, defense, commerce, or their diplomatic representatives in embassies throughout the world let local governments and interested individuals and groups know about newsworthy events or other happenings. For example, the U.S. National Aeronautics and Space Administration (NASA), its Jet Propulsion Laboratory (JPL), or its other centers inform governmental counterparts, scientists, and the general public about shuttle launches into space, photographs of space retrieved from the orbiting Hubble telescope, and missions to Mars or past other planets and moons.

Other informational communications may have a purpose that goes beyond merely transmitting facts. Government agencies may communicate directly to foreign publics or work through centralized agencies or ministries of information. For example, the State Department wants to convey to foreign publics the rationale for U.S. policies and explain U.S. understanding of and approaches to world events. Most countries have similar information ministries with established press contacts for access to radio, television, and print media. Mailing lists and government sites on the internet are also used to present a country's point of view—information with a decided purpose. More recently, countries have enlisted Facebook pages and Twitter feeds. Because such communications are expected by design to be one-sided advocacy of a country's policy positions (not necessarily balanced presentations with all sides of an argument considered), information ministries in democratic countries may well be restricted from disseminating their communications to citizens residing within their own countries. Lest they be accused of propagandizing their own citizens, the target audience of information ministries in democratic countries is foreign publics.

Symbolic Other communications are symbolic, usually designed to reinforce positive aspects of relations between two countries. Thus, French foreign ministry and other government officials attend a Fourth of July celebration hosted by the U.S. embassy in Paris. Naturally, U.S. officials reciprocate by attending a similar Bastille Day (July 14) celebration hosted by the French embassy in the Georgetown section of Washington. On such occasions symbolic references are often made to 18th-century French help in the American Revolution, the fact that neither country has ever gone to war with the other, and that both countries share long-established commitments to democratic values.

Another example of symbolic communications is to demonstrate respect by presidents and senior government officials or their representatives, ambassadors, and other diplomats attending important state events such as the coronation of a monarch, inauguration of a president, royal family or other state weddings or funerals, and other state events. The level of representation at such events is carefully considered, usually to avoid any insult to the host country. Thus, the funerals following the deaths of U.S. President Kennedy in 1963, Egyptian President Sadat in 1981, the Jordanian King Hussein in 1999, and U.S. President Ronald Reagan in 2004 brought presidents and prime ministers from all over the world. The wedding of Prince William, heir to the British throne, to Kate Middleton in 2011, however, resulted in a much lower level of foreign representation.

Conflict Avoidance   Political statements can also be made by not negotiating. Indeed, one approach to a conflict is to sidestep, avoid, or ignore it. Sometimes the issues dividing the parties are inconsequential or relatively unimportant and thus not worth any bother, particularly when raising such issues may worsen relations without accomplishing much, if anything. At other times, however, there may be important issues at stake that one or more of the parties may wish to defer to a later time, perhaps realizing that the issues are not likely to be resolved satisfactorily any time soon. This may require some fancy diplomatic footwork, leaving matters to rest as they are, unresolved, and without yielding anything in principle to the other side.

No Expectation of Agreement   The real challenges in diplomatic negotiations occur when the parties are deeply in conflict. Sometimes one or both parties do not really want to reach agreement at all but see some value in the negotiating process, at least in appearing to negotiate. The objective may be merely to delay taking any action on the conflict at issue. In this mode, one or both sides may set forth a maximum position that neither expects the other side to accept.

From the perspective of the West, this is what the Iranian government has been doing for years in terms of negotiations over its nuclear development program. Similar doubts about the sincerity of the North Korean regime in terms of nuclear arms negotiations have also been expressed.

Negotiation Strategies

The mentality in negotiations is often that what one side gains, the other loses. Game theorists refer to this as zero-sum—the pluses one side gains come at the expense of the minuses the other side loses. As discussed earlier, incentives, "carrots," and disincentives or threats, "sticks," may be used by the parties, although

zero-sum ■ concept in game theory that one side's gain amounts to the other side's loss

such methods are rather blunt instruments. Give and take, pulling and hauling by opposing parties, and formation of coalitions and countercoalitions in multilateral negotiations are tactics often employed to forge compromise agreements when interests and related objectives are in conflict. Sometimes this is the best that can be achieved—a compromise in which typically each side gains something but also gives up something. Each side achieves some points of satisfaction but is also left with some disappointments—points it may have had to give up in order to get some concessions from the other side or perhaps to get any agreement at all.

A potentially far more productive approach to durable agreements is to use negotiations as a means to search for common ground among the parties, forging a positive-sum outcome based on mutual gains. Such agreements may involve some compromises but rest more fundamentally on satisfying the parties' multiple interests—some shared, some not. The Harvard negotiation project has identified several principles or guidelines for "getting to yes"—an essentially positive-sum approach to use when parties are in conflict. The methodology was developed for diverse negotiation settings, but for our purposes it has direct application to diplomatic communications aimed at achieving win-win outcomes.

Although personalities and orientations matter in how negotiators relate to one another, negotiations are about issues, not personalities. In focusing on issues, the parties avoid digging in their heels and taking hard-and-fast positions. Instead, they pay attention to the interests of all of the parties in a search for common ground. Interests are of two kinds, those related to the substance of what is being negotiated and those related to preserving and improving relationships in the negotiations among the parties and the countries they represent. There also needs to be room for creative approaches to finding common ground—at times inventing options for mutual gain. Finally, they should not be content to rest agreements merely on the will of the parties; objective criteria or standards for measuring what has been agreed, accompanied by fair procedures, are essential to effective implementation of any agreement. In point-by-point summary form, the getting-to-yes method is (1) don't bargain over positions; (2) separate the people from the problem; (3) focus on interests, not positions; (4) invent options for mutual gain; and (5) insist on using objective criteria. Focusing on the interests of all of the parties is not just confined to the substantive issues at hand, but also extends to the relationships among those engaging in the negotiations. Maintaining respectful, professional (even friendly) relationships may contribute to getting to yes.

We turn now to a discussion of arms control and disarmament negotiations, focusing on those that have taken place over more than half a century. We use this important national security issue—how much, what kinds, and where a country's armaments should be deployed—to illustrate how diplomacy in both bilateral and multilateral negotiations can lead to important disarmament and arms control outcomes. Getting to yes has been far more than a matter of carrots and sticks or compromises. Satisfying the interests of the negotiating parties has been the key ingredient to successful, positive-sum outcomes. Durable agreements are grounded in the interests the parties secure—even when some gain more than others.

DISARMAMENT AND ARMS CONTROL

Destroying and prohibiting the instruments of violence in national arsenals remains on the international and foreign policy agenda and have proven to be a major focus of diplomats and political leaders. However distant achievement of such a goal may seem, we often hear presidents, prime ministers, and other national leaders calling for **disarmament** or, at least, the ongoing pursuit of **arms control** as remedies for interstate warfare. Critics claim that the focus ought to be on conflicts and ways of resolving or managing them—not on weaponry, as if that were the cause of the problem.

Dealing with weapons in national arsenals is hardly a new problem confronting humanity in the 21st century. There have been efforts to promote general and complete disarmament of all weapons of a particular type (as in the elimination of nuclear, biological, or chemical weapons). How elusive has been the biblical challenge to turn all "swords into plowshares," instruments of productivity rather than of human destruction! Nevertheless, over the years people have joined together to protest the development and use of all types of weapons. It is assumed that the elimination of major weapons systems would, if not eliminate war, at least reduce its destructive capacity.

Rarely is a state willing to disarm unilaterally (i.e., on its own initiative and being the only state to disarm). Although great schemes have been drawn up for general and complete disarmament, this approach appears to have been too ambitious. As a practical matter, diplomatic attempts to achieve disarmament have succeeded only (and even then not completely) when directed toward particular categories of weaponry such as agreed prohibitions against chemical and biological agents. An example is the 1987 U.S.-Soviet Intermediate-Range Nuclear Forces (INF) treaty, which removed from Europe and destroyed an entire category of weaponry—all intermediate-range missiles capable of carrying nuclear weapons.

The elimination of certain categories of weapons has become a central focus of nongovernmental organizations (NGOs) as well. Land mines placed during wars, for example, not only kill and wound soldiers but also maim children and adult noncombatants who happen to stumble on these explosive devices long after wars have ended. Given this continuing danger, a concrete example of global civil society at work involved the more than one thousand local and international NGOs in more than seventy-five countries that joined forces in the 1990s in an international campaign to ban land mines. The rallying cry was not "state security," but rather "human security."

British princess Diana was among the many individual advocates of a treaty banning land mines. After much work by such public-spirited individuals and NGOs, 122 governments signed the Land-Mines Treaty in 1997. The treaty went into force in 1999; however, the United States and Russia are among the countries not signing the accord because of their continuing reliance on these weapons. If signed and ratified, the treaty requires signatories to destroy all mines in national arsenals within four years, removing and destroying all of those already in the ground within ten years.

Statecraft based on possessing weaponry and fielding armed forces, however, historically has been the more common norm. Far from viewing weapons as a cause of war, they can serve a positive function in terms of not only protecting a state's national security but also maintaining the peace. *Si vis pacem, para bellum* ("if you wish peace, then prepare for war") reflects the realist understanding that

7.4 Illustrate the potential benefits of diplomatic negotiations focused on arms control and disarmament, types of agreements, and ongoing proliferation concerns in terms of nuclear, radiological, chemical, biological, ballistic missiles, and advanced conventional weapons.

Watch the **Video** "Iran's Nuclear Ambitions" at mypoliscilab.com

disarmament ■ reducing to zero either all weapons in national arsenals (as in general or complete disarmament) or all weapons of a particular type (as in biological weapons)

arms control ■ a negotiation process aimed at producing agreements on weapons and their use

Diplomatic efforts to curb weapons proliferation led to the 1972 SALT agreement. As was usually the case with such major agreements, the U.S. president and the head of the Soviet Union signed the agreements. Here President Richard Nixon shakes hands with Soviet leader Leonid Brezhnev.

While some agreements capped the number of warheads or missiles, other types of systems were often still being deployed. During discussion to introduce U.S. middle-range missiles in Germany and the United Kingdom in the early 1980s, mass protests occurred in both countries to put pressure on the allied governments. One such demonstration occurred in Trafalgar Square, London.

Conventional weapons, however, are found in the arsenals of all countries. During the deadly Iran-Iraq war (1980–1988), for example, conventional weapons and also the use of chemical weapons on the part of Iraq led to a half million civilian and military deaths and untold numbers of maimed and injured.

Gas centrifuges are required for uranium enrichment. In 2004 A.Q. Khan, a Pakistani scientist, admitted to being involved in an international proliferation network that smuggled nuclear technology to Libya, Iran, and North Korea.

peace with neighboring and other states is best assured by a position or posture of military strength. If a state is relatively strong militarily, such strength in principle will deter or dissuade others who might be prone to attack. Hence weapons, some argue, are actually necessary to maintain peace.

Disarmament advocates are quick to point out, however, that such thinking, coupled with technological advances in weaponry, is in fact responsible for the carnage in two world wars that alone made the 20th the bloodiest century in human history. Moreover, advances in nuclear, chemical, and biological weaponry also threaten global destruction, particularly if in the hands of transnational terrorist organizations—a key concern on the 21st century's global agenda. From this perspective, military strength is hardly a reliable source of security. Arms races in which states compete to achieve security through acquisition of armaments and strengthened armed forces only worsen the global security problem, particularly if such weapons escape their control. That more spending on weapons may actually worsen or undermine security is thus at the core of the security dilemma facing states and international and nongovernmental organizations concerned with such matters.

If complete global disarmament is viewed as an unrealistic diplomatic goal, if not a fantasy, and the complete elimination of a type of weapon is also exceedingly difficult to achieve, what about a more modest goal of placing restrictions on the number and types of weapons and curtailing their spread? Thus we enter the realm of arms control.

Once instituted after intensive diplomatic negotiation, multilateral arms control agreements constitute international security regimes. Somewhat more modest in scope than general and complete disarmament, these measures still offer rules and thus some degree of structure to the development, acquisition, deployment, and use of armaments. Such agreements are typically aimed at one or more of the following: (1) Curb arms-race competition; (2) achieve economic savings from reduced military expenditures; (3) lessen the risk of war; (4) reduce damage should war occur; and (5) enhance regional and global security. Put another way, when it comes to enhanced security through arms control, diplomats can and do make a difference.

Critics note that states and coalitions of states may also see arms control as a way of gaining some strategic advantage over other states by getting them to agree to provisions that disadvantage them in the arms-race competition. Arms-control regimes can also provide rules states voluntarily agree to follow in their security relations with each other, lending some degree of order and providing greater security to an otherwise anarchical world lacking central authority or governance.

Ways to Conceptualize Arms Control

Given the large number of arms-control agreements reached since the late 1950s, understanding the meaning and significance of what has been accomplished to date can be difficult. One way to cut through this thicket is to classify the provisions of arms-control treaties and other agreements as those dealing with the following:

1. Quantitative and qualitative limitations on armaments and armed forces (Table 7.1)
2. Geographic or spatial limitations (Table 7.2)
3. Functional mechanisms—communications and other confidence- and security-building measures (Table 7.3)

TABLE 7.1

Armaments—Qualitative and Quantitative Controls

Treaty or Agreement	Principal Quantitative and Qualitative Restrictions, Limitations, and Other Provisions: Numbers, Types, Locations, Research, Development, Testing, and Use
Biological and Chemical Weaponry	
Chemical and Bacteriological Use (1925)	Prohibits use of asphyxiating, poisonous, or other chemical and bacteriological (biological) weapons
Production and Stockpiling	
Biological Weapons (1972)	Prohibits development, production, stockpiling, otherwise acquiring, or transferring biological weapons; requires destruction of existing stocks
Chemical Weapons (1993)	Prohibits development, production, stockpiling, transfer, acquisition, and use of chemical weapons; requires destruction of existing stocks; permits on-site inspections
Nuclear Weaponry: Testing and Transfer Restraints	
Test Bans	
Limited Test Ban (1963)	Prohibits nuclear weapons tests or other nuclear explosions in the atmosphere, outer space, or underwater (e.g., oceanic)
Threshold Test Ban (1974)	Prohibits underground nuclear weapons tests with yields greater than 150 kilotons; national, technical means of verification expanded by 1990 protocol to require advance notice and allow on-site inspections and measurement for tests greater than 35 kilotons
"Peaceful" Nuclear Explosions (1976)	Reaffirmed 150-kilotons limit on yield for nonweapons or "peaceful" nuclear explosions (PNE)
Comprehensive Test Ban (1996)	Proposes to eliminate all nuclear testing
Nuclear Non-Proliferation and Safeguards (1968)	Nuclear weapons states agree not to transfer and nonnuclear weapons states agree not to receive nuclear weapons or weapons-related technologies; all parties agree to work toward nuclear disarmament
Protection of Nuclear Material (1980)	Holds states responsible for secure transit of nuclear materials used for peaceful purposes, providing standards and remedies.
SALT I (U.S.-USSR Strategic Arms Limitation Talks: 1969–1972)	
Defensive Forces	
Anti-Ballistic Missiles (ABM) 1972 Treaty and 1974 Protocol	When in force, it prohibited deployment by the United States and the Soviet Union (later the Russian Federation) of ABM systems for territorial defense, allowing only limited ABM deployments for defense of a state's national capital or one ICBM-launcher complex; development, testing, or deployment of sea-based, air-based, space-based, or mobile land-based ABM systems; transfer of ABM systems or components to other states; provided for national technical means of verification while prohibiting concealment measures

(continued)

TABLE 7.1 | Continued

Treaty or Agreement	Principal Quantitative and Qualitative Restrictions, Limitations, and Other Provisions: Numbers, Types, Locations, Research, Development, Testing, and Use
Offensive Forces	
Offensive Arms Limitations: Interim Agreement (1972)	Prohibits construction of additional fixed, land-based intercontinental ballistic missile (ICBM) and submarine-launched ballistic missile (SLBM) launchers or ballistic missile submarines; conversion of existing ICBM launchers from light to heavy types; provides for national technical means of verification (while prohibiting deliberate concealment measures); and relies on a Standing Consultative Commission to deal with compliance issues
SALT II (U.S.-USSR Strategic Arms Limitation Talks: 1972–1979)	Not ratified as a treaty, but treated as an executive agreement that put quantitative limits on ICBMs and SLBMs, heavy bombers, and air-to-surface and cruise missiles and qualitative restraints on modernization and conversion, testing, and deployment of new systems (including limits on numbers of reentry vehicles on ICBMs and SLBMs); advance notification of ICBM launches; allowing for national technical means of verification (while prohibiting deliberate concealment measures) and providing for the Standing Consultative Commission
Intermediate-Range Nuclear Forces (INF): U.S.-USSR (1987)	Eliminates all intermediate-range (1,000–5,500 km) and shorter-range (500–1,000 km) ballistic and ground-launched cruise missiles and launchers
Strategic Arms Reduction Talks (START I): U.S.-USSR, 1982–1991	Reduces substantially strategic offensive armaments (ICBM, SLBM, and heavy bombers) to 1,600 each with associated warheads limited to 6,000 each (down from more than 12,000 nuclear warheads in U.S. and Soviet inventories); warhead limits reduced subsequently to some 3,000; in 1992 Belarus, Kazakhstan, and Ukraine joined the Russian Federation and the United States in acceding to the treaty
(START II): U.S.-Russia, 1993 and 1997	Strategic warheads to be reduced to 3,500 or fewer on each side
Moscow Treaty (2002)	By 2012 arsenals reduced to 1,700–2,200 strategic warheads each
New START (2010)	By 2018 arsenals reduced to about 1,550 strategic warheads each
Missile Technology Control Regime (MTCR) (1987 and 1993)	Establishes common export control policy and list of controlled items with intent to stop spread to other countries of ballistic and cruise missiles and technologies capable of delivering a 500-kilogram nuclear payload (1987) as well as chemical and biological weapons (1993) to a range of 300 kilometers or more (32 state participants)
Nunn–Lugar Cooperative Threat Reduction (1991)	U.S. assistance to Russian Federation in reducing weapons of mass destruction
Conventional Armed Forces in Europe (CFE) (1990)	Limits numbers, types, and locations in Europe of tanks, artillery pieces, armored combat vehicles, combat aircraft, and attack helicopters of all countries

(continued)

	Principal Quantitative and Qualitative Restrictions, Limitations, and Other Provisions: Numbers, Types, Locations, Research, Development, Testing, and Use
TABLE 7.1 *Continued*	
Treaty or Agreement	
U.N. Registry on Conventional Arms Exports (1991)	Compiles information provided by members on conventional arms transfers (exports and imports)
Wassenaar Arrangement (1996–1997)	Requires arms-exporting state participants to exchange information on arms sales and denials, working to minimize adverse impact on international and regional security and stability (33 state participants)
Land Mines (1997–1998)	Requires signatories to destroy all mines in national arsenals within four years, removing and destroying all of those already in the ground within ten years
Strategic Offensive Reductions Treaty (May 2002)	Russia and United States would eventually reduce the number of "operationally deployed" strategic nuclear weapons from about 6,000 in each country to between 1,700 and 2,200

The majority of agreements deal with quantitative or qualitative restrictions on armed forces and armaments—aircraft, tanks, artillery pieces, and the like; however, a particular treaty or agreement may also have provisions that include one or both of the other two categories: (1) geographic or special limitations—for example, the numbers, types, and locations of military deployments in Europe, Latin America, or other regions; and (2) functional mechanisms—hotlines, risk-reduction centers, and other confidence- and security-building measures (CSBMs).

Functional approaches to controlling or managing conflicts include establishing and sustaining CSBMs that increase trust and reduce threat perceptions as well as maintaining effective communications even between adversaries in wartime. Multilateral peacekeeping missions under UN or other auspices may also contribute functionally as controls on the use of armed forces and armaments in conflict situations.

Communications as an arms-control function has been a major focus of arms-control efforts, particularly since the 1962 Cuban missile crisis that brought the United States and the Soviet Union to the brink of nuclear war. Clear, direct communications would have been helpful at such a dangerous time. Government leaders in Washington and Moscow had to rely instead on exchanging notes delivered by cable, with many hours lost in the process of transmission and translation. Even at that time, telecommunications technology had more to offer than the systems governments were then using. The hotline agreement reached in the following year established a direct communications link between the White House and the Kremlin, a system that would be expanded and modernized over the years as new telecommunications technologies became available.

Approaching arms and conflict control through communications and agreed procedures for managing crises to avoid their escalation to armed conflict have also been the inspiration for a set of nuclear accidents, incidents at sea, and prevention

TABLE 7.2

Controlling Armaments and Conflicts: Locational or Geographic Limitations and Restrictions

Treaty or Agreement	General Terms
Antarctica (1959)	Allows only peaceful, scientific, or other nonmilitary use of Antarctica; direct inspection by states of all facilities or aerial observation anywhere at any time; provides for open exchange of information from scientific investigation of Antarctica; requires advance notice to other parties of expeditions to and within Antarctica, stations in Antarctica occupied by its nationals, any military personnel or equipment intended to be sent (which are allowed only for scientific research or other peaceful purposes); promotes preservation and conservation of living resources; prohibits new territorial claims, nuclear explosions, or storage of radioactive waste materials
Outer Space (1967)	Prohibits orbiting nuclear or other weapons of mass destruction; military bases or maneuvers on (or national, sovereign appropriation of) celestial bodies; provides for damage claims and recovery of astronauts and objects launched into outer space
Latin America Nuclear (1967)	Latin America defined as a nuclear weapons–free zone, prohibiting Free Zone testing, use, manufacture, production, acquisition, or any other form of possession of nuclear weapons by Latin American states or anyone on their behalf
Seabed Arms Control (1971)	Prohibits nuclear or other weapons of mass destruction in the seabed or ocean floor and subsoil; provides for nondisruptive inspection of suspect facilities
Environmental Modification (1977)	Prohibits military or any other hostile use of environmental modification techniques having widespread, long-lasting, or severe effects as the means of destruction, damage, or injury to any other state
Conference on Security and Cooperation in Europe (1975 Helsinki Final Act); subsequent conference accords in Stockholm (1985) and Vienna (1991)	Specific to the Atlantic-to-Urals European area, conventional arms reductions are combined with a regime of confidence- and security-building measures

TABLE 7.3

Communications and Confidence- and Security-Building Measures: Functional Approaches to Controlling or Managing Conflict

Treaty or Agreement	General Description of Terms
U.S.-USSR "Hotline" Agreement (1963); modernized (1971); expanded (1984)	Established in the wake of the 1962 Cuban missile crisis, the U.S. and USSR established and subsequently maintained and expanded direct communications links between Washington and Moscow
Nuclear Accidents: U.S.-USSR (1971)	Requires organizational and technical arrangements to reduce risk of accidental or unauthorized use of nuclear weapons; advance notice of missile launches extending beyond national territory; communications in the event of accidents
Incidents at Sea: U.S.-USSR (1972)	Provides cautionary measures to avoid collisions or other incidents at sea; prohibits simulated attacks on each other's ships; requires advance notification of actions on the high seas that are dangerous to navigation or to aircraft in flight
Prevention of Nuclear War: U.S.-USSR (1973)	Requires parties to refrain from the threat or use of force against each other or each other's allies that would endanger international peace and security, act to avoid military confrontations and the outbreak of nuclear war, and engage in urgent consultations if relations are in risk of nuclear conflict
Confidence- and Security-Building Measures (CSBMs): Atlantic-to-Urals	Specific to the Atlantic-to-Urals European area, confidence- and security-building measures established in 1975 and 1986 in European Area were expanded substantially (1991), requiring notifications of military exercises and allowing for observers; providing for exchange of information to include numbers, types, and locations of armaments, aerial reconnaissance, and announced and unannounced on-site inspections of military installations (measures when combined with limits on armaments effectively establish "transparency" or military openness, increased warning time should any party prepare to attack any other, and overall reduction in the risk of war)
Nuclear Risk Reduction Centers: U.S.-USSR (1987)	Establishes Nuclear Risk Reduction Centers in Washington and Moscow with communications links between the two and regular meetings between representatives of the centers at least once a year
Ballistic Missile Launch Notification: U.S.-USSR (1988)	Requires notification through the Nuclear Risk Reduction Centers at least twenty-four hours in advance of the planned date and launch and impact areas of any strategic ballistic missile launch; in the event of launch postponement, notice is good for four days
Open Skies (1992)	Consistent with negotiated annual quotas, NATO and former Warsaw Pact countries agreed that in the European Atlantic-to-Urals area each has the right to conduct and the obligation to receive aerial reconnaissance flights by other parties

of nuclear war measures adopted in the early 1970s. The United States and the Soviet Union established risk reduction centers in 1987 in each other's capitals, staffed by officials from both countries, and agreed in 1988 on procedures for mutual notification of ballistic missile launches, both of which were efforts to strengthen communications mechanisms between the two principal nuclear powers—examples of confidence- and security-building measures depicted in Table 7.3.

We deal in this chapter with arms control as an example of how states have used bilateral and multilateral diplomacy as a means to achieving national security and other objectives. In Chapter 9 we examine how arms control relates to theories of deterrence and the use of force.

Arms Control, Verification, and Compliance

verification ■ finding out whether another party to a treaty or other agreement is living up to its obligations

Treaties may be signed, but what do they matter if one party can get away with cheating? Many arms-control treaties and agreements therefore address questions of **verification** and compliance. It's one thing to make agreements; it's another to live up to them, as evident by international concern over the North Korean attempts to deceive international inspectors concerning their development of nuclear material in violation of the Non-Proliferation Treaty. Verification of compliance with (or violation of) treaties or agreements is achieved in a number of ways, such as open admission of violations, on-site inspection by other parties, reports by reliable human-intelligence sources, or through national technical means (NTM) of verification. These means include advanced technical-intelligence capabilities on ground stations, aircraft, ships, and satellites or other space vehicles.

Alleged violations are presented in diplomatic exchanges in the expectation of bringing violators into compliance. As such, verification or knowing what other countries are actually doing can be understood as the first phase, to be followed by what amounts to an enforcement phase in which compliance is sought, if any of the parties is thought to be in violation of a treaty or agreement. Even during the height of the Cold War, adversaries met formally to discuss and debate allegations of non-compliance. The Standing Consultative Commission (SCC, a U.S.–Soviet bilateral forum located in Geneva) was an important mechanism for airing differences, if not always working them out very quickly. As such, the SCC was a means for managing superpower disputes and maintaining the strategic-arms security regime.

weapons proliferation ■ the spread of weapons and weapon systems to countries not previously possessing them (horizontal proliferation) or the stockpiling of weapons or weapons systems by particular countries (vertical proliferation)

ballistic missiles ■ missiles that when launched follow a trajectory to the ground subject to gravitational forces; as their range and warhead explosives increase, so does the perceived threat to other countries

Weapons Proliferation

One topic that has dominated every international arms-control diplomatic agenda in the post–Cold War era is the issue of **weapons proliferation**. There are five major areas of concern: nuclear or radiological weapons, chemical weapons, biological weapons, **ballistic missiles**, and advanced conventional weapons systems. Nuclear weapons and *matériel*, however, have dominated international debate and discussion.

The startling collapse in 1991 of the Soviet Union with its 33,000 nuclear warheads set governments, think tanks, and academe scrambling. There was concern over the future of the nuclear arsenals and related technologies possessed by the Russian Federation and former Soviet republics. Indeed, some 3,000 of these weapons were located in the former Soviet republics of Ukraine, Kazakhstan, and Belarus. Although Ukraine initially demonstrated some reluctance, all three finally did agree to relinquish control over nuclear warheads on their respective territories to Russia—diplomats from the United States and other countries working closely with Russia and the three republics to make this happen. The physical security of the weapons in Russia and the former republics continues to be a problem, raising the frightening specter of weapons and matériel being stolen and perhaps sold for private gain on the black market to terrorist groups and states such as Iran.

The linchpin of the international nonproliferation regime is the 1967 Nuclear Non-Proliferation Treaty (NPT), in which the five declared nuclear powers at the time (the United States, the United Kingdom, the Soviet Union, France, and China) pledged not to export to nonnuclear states either nuclear weapons or nuclear weapons components or technologies. Other signatories agreed, as nonnuclear states, not to try to acquire a nuclear weapons capability in exchange for a commitment by the nuclear powers to negotiate in good faith on cessation of the nuclear arms race and the pursuit of nuclear disarmament. All parties that have signed the treaty agreed to safeguards and inspections by the Vienna-based International Atomic Energy Agency (IAEA) of nuclear power plants and other nuclear facilities used for peaceful purposes. The goal of these provisions, of course, is to reassure states that their neighbors are not secretly building nuclear weapons capabilities and thus persuading states to forgo pursuing weapons programs of their own.

Testing of nuclear weapons by India and Pakistan in 1998 added two more members to the nuclear club. It is assumed that Israel also has nuclear weapons capabilities. South Africa developed these capabilities but chose to disarm itself of them after a significant change of regime took place in the 1990s. Likewise, Brazil and Argentina have moved away from developing nuclear weapons capabilities.

As possession of nuclear weapons spreads, the possibility of inadvertent use increases because new nuclear states are not likely to have as secure command and control over these weapons as did the major powers during the height of the Cold War. In a crisis, a state may be more likely to launch nuclear weapons against a neighbor, believing it must get in the first strike before its rival—a preemptive strike.

What can be done about the nuclear proliferation threat? One approach is on the *supply side*—prevention of the further spread of nuclear weapons or nuclear weapons technologies by prohibiting such exports by states already possessing these capabilities. On the *demand side*, the aim is to improve regional security conditions so that states will be less likely to feel a need to acquire such weapons. Diplomatic efforts to persuade would-be nuclear powers from pursuing the acquisition of nuclear weapons or weapons technologies are demand-side measures. Thus, in arms control usage, the term *supply side* refers to countries already in possession of a particular weapon, weapons system, or related technologies, whereas *demand side* refers to countries wishing to acquire any of these weapons, weapons systems, or technologies.

No doubt signaling their future intentions, India and Pakistan never signed the Nuclear Non-Proliferation Treaty, resulting in unilateral efforts by other states to deny certain technologies to these countries. At most, the treaty merely slowed India's and Pakistan's drive for nuclear weapons capability. Then, in 2003, it was revealed that Pakistan's top nuclear scientist, Dr. A. Q. Khan, had been part of a large-scale operation designed to export nuclear know-how and technology to other states, including Iran and North Korea.

The NPT does not prohibit a state from conducting research and development of civilian nuclear-power programs intended for peaceful, electric power–generation purposes, which is what the Iranians claim they are doing. The obvious problem with this, however, is that such a program also can be used not only in developing expertise that can then be applied toward a weapons development program, but also in generating plutonium and other products that can be used in constructing nuclear weapons.

Efforts by North Korea to develop its own nuclear weapons became apparent when it announced in 1993 its intent to withdraw from the NPT regime in order to avoid an impending IAEA inspection of a suspect site. International pressure and subsequent negotiations kept North Korea formally within the NPT regime for several years. In 2002, however, North Korea announced it was withdrawing from the NPT regime, resumed its nuclear weapons program, and announced some four years later its detonation of a nuclear weapon, its second test occurring in 2009. Coupled with its development of both ballistic and "air-breathing" cruise missiles as a means of delivering these weapons to overseas targets, North Korea's growing arsenal is threatening to Japan, other countries in the region, and, given the increasing range of its ballistic missiles, even to the United States—Alaska and Hawaii in particular.

Diplomatic efforts by the United States and other countries to bring North Korea back into the NPT regime have been highly problematic, often accompanied by North Korean military threats and hostile actions directed primarily toward South Korea. Multilateral six-party talks with the United States, China, Japan, Russia, and both North and South Korea finally resumed in 2007, and in the fall of that year, North Korea did agree to allow technical teams to survey some of its nuclear facilities. The U.S. envoy, Ambassador Christopher Hill, then an assistant secretary of state, was a central player in the six-party talks. He also met bilaterally with authorities in both North Korea and China, the latter potentially having the most influence of the five on the political leadership in North Korea.

Bilateral diplomacy typically accompanies multilateral efforts but, given their distrust of North Korea's leaders, the Bush administration initially opposed direct contact between the United States and the North Korean regime outside of the forum provided by the multilateral, six-party talks. After the first nuclear weapon detonation, however, Ambassador Hill was finally given a green light to meet one-on-one with North Korea as, indeed, the Clinton administration had done in the 1990s.

Beyond immediate concerns about proliferation of nuclear weapons are concerns about the vast global armaments market. Both legal and illegal sales of armaments by and to states and nonstate actors continue on a truly massive scale. Critics observe that arms purchases deplete national resources that might otherwise be spent more productively on investment for economic development or other purposes. Moreover, acquiring armaments beyond realistic defense needs fuels arms races that diminish (rather than enhance) the security of states and societies in a region.

Because the arms trade is a profitable business for many who engage in it, agreeing on rules to limit or constrain it has proven to be extremely difficult. There is probably no more difficult challenge than to try to reduce, if not eliminate, a money-making enterprise. Critics in World War I and after referred to arms sellers as "merchants of death." On the other hand, from their perspective, suppliers of arms are merely responding to legitimate national security needs for weaponry.

Indeed, demand for weaponry continues to be very strong, and there is no shortage of suppliers willing and able to meet it. Moreover, arms-producing corporations and states can realize greater economies of scale when they have large export markets, which reduce the per-unit cost to producers of tanks, aircraft, or other expensive military hardware. In short, the interests that favor a continuing and expanding global arms trade have proven far stronger politically than those arms controllers who seek construction of regimes that put limits on the kinds of arms that are traded globally and regionally.

CONCLUSION

It was noted at the outset of this chapter that diplomats have to take into account allies as well as domestic audiences when engaged in diplomacy. Contemporary diplomatic practices, however, seem to be increasingly subject to various trends associated with globalization. First, there has been an erosion of diplomatic norms. Consider, for example, the sanctity of diplomatic missions. Over the years, missions certainly have been attacked by mobs, but the takeover of the American embassy in Tehran in November 1979 by radical students established a dangerous precedent because the revolutionary Islamic regime sanctioned the action. In the 1980 Venice Declaration, the seven participating heads of state from Europe, North America, and Japan noted they were "gravely concerned by recent incidents of terrorism involving the taking of hostages and attacks on diplomatic and consular premises and personnel." They had good reason to be, because by 1980 diplomats had become major targets for terrorism. Furthermore, the Iranian and Libyan regimes used their overseas missions to plan and support terrorist acts on foreign soil. Add to this the rise in crime in urban areas throughout the world, significant health risks, and increasing social anarchy in a number of developing countries, and it is clear that life for diplomats and their families is a long way from the popular image of champagne-and-caviar embassy parties.

Second, the nature of diplomatic communication between governments has evolved. Historically the resident ambassador has been the key communications link with the host government, presenting his or her state's views and reporting back those of the host government. Now regular summits among leaders, backchannel contacts that skirt the embassy, and direct, secure telephone and electronic lines between political leaders all reduce the relevancy of the ambassador. Even in those situations in which the ambassador has direct access to top host government officials, the result can be to bypass the professional diplomatic circuit.

Third, the end of the Cold War reduced the importance of Western embassies in the former Eastern bloc as sources of information for policymakers. Particularly during the Cold War, Western journalists had little access to Eastern bloc countries, so official political reporting from embassies was critical. As East-West tensions eased, however, journalists were granted entry to previously remote parts of the Soviet Union and Eastern Europe and also found it easier to cultivate their own sources of information in various foreign policy bureaucracies. It is not unusual for policymakers to find important insights in quality online newspapers and magazines, blogs, and research institutes with a focus on international relations.

Fourth, the worldwide communications revolution has also reduced the importance of diplomatic reporting. Thanks to satellites, the first sources of information on breaking events are often television networks, the internet, and radio reports, with diplomatic and intelligence reporting lagging behind. Indeed, key offices throughout the State Department feature television sets that are tuned to news channels throughout the day. CNN and other networks are also a staple for twenty-four-hour operations centers located in various government agencies that deal with foreign policy and national security issues. Satellite transmissions allow government intelligence analysts as well as regular citizens to watch live news broadcasts from foreign television stations covering local events. Facebook, Twitter, and other social networks have enabled citizens to organize themselves politically from rallies during election campaigns to movements seeking regime change. Not surprisingly, governments and their intelligence agencies also follow these social networks closely.

One drawback to relying on live broadcasts and internet postings is that the information viewers receive does not provide the broader, interpretive context that characterizes diplomatic and intelligence reporting. Furthermore, social network postings and live broadcasts to millions of people may force the pace of events or sensationalize issues, putting pressure on policymakers to make a decision before diplomats can meet to negotiate a mutually acceptable solution.

Fifth, in an increasingly globalized and interdependent world, members of the diplomatic corps of today and tomorrow have to be more than familiar with complex social, technological, and environmental trends. As Secretary of State Hillary Clinton remarked during the upheaval in the Middle East and North Africa in early 2011 that witnessed the overthrow of a number of authoritarian regimes, U.S. diplomats have to engage not just foreign governments, but also foreign civil societies. While the young protestors were adept at utilizing Facebook and Twitter, the same could not be said for the U.S. foreign policy establishment. Furthermore, diplomats have to be informed on a wide variety of issues of international concern, including the impact of ozone depletion and the cutting down of the Amazon rain forests, the social and environmental impact of exploding birth rates, the threat of viral pandemics, and the challenge of helping to resolve disputes between states on conflicting claims to natural resources such as water. It is highly debatable whether the diplomatic corps of most countries are adequately recruiting, training, and retaining persons with expertise in such areas. Yet without such personnel, who must also be skilled in negotiating, it is unlikely that a state will be able to resolve the sorts of challenges and conflicts that are discussed later in this book.

Sixth, particularly in the case of humanitarian disasters and civil wars, "field diplomacy" on the part of nongovernmental relief and aid organizations may become increasingly the norm. Often attuned to local politics and knowledge of key players, these nonstate actors may play a key or supporting role in conflict mitigation or even conflict resolution.

Finally, diplomacy conducted over decades on particular foreign policy issues like the arms control example we have dealt with at length in this chapter

✓•─ **Study** and **Review**
the **Post-Test & Chapter**
Exam at **mypoliscilab.com**

(or human rights, the environment, and other issues addressed in other chapters) can have a substantial impact on how both state and nonstate actors operate. As we continue to experience the impact of globalization, diplomacy as a means by which foreign policy is implemented continues to play an enormously important role. By no means has the diplomat become obsolete!

LEARNING OBJECTIVES REVIEW

7.1 Explain the relation between foreign policy and diplomacy by identifying the roles played by both state and non-state actors in the foreign policy decision-making process.

Diplomacy in the broadest sense captures the full range of interstate communication that is core to the making and implementation of foreign policy. Diplomacy can be conducted not only by diplomats, but also heads of state and special envoys who may be private citizens. Nongovernmental organizations (NGOs) have played an increasingly important role, especially in United Nations–sponsored conferences. In support of foreign policy goals, diplomacy includes formal and informal negotiations, but diplomatic strategies run the spectrum from positive inducements to threats as well as the search ideally for common ground or overlapping interests, sometimes settling on compromise.

KEY TERMS
Diplomacy 219
Treaty 219
Executive agreement 219
Démarche 220
Nongovernmental organizations (NGOs) 224

ADDITIONAL READINGS
Henry Kissinger, *Diplomacy* (New York: Simon & Schuster, 1994). A major summary of his thoughts on diplomacy by a former U.S. secretary of state.

Valerie M. Hudson, Derek H. Chollet, and James M. Goldgeier, *Foreign Policy Decision-Making Revisited* (New York: Palgrave, 2002). A conceptual framework to understand the factors that account for foreign policy decisions.

Geoffrey R. Berridge, Maurice Keens-Soper, and Thomas G. Otte (eds.), *Diplomatic Theory from Machiavelli to Kissinger* (New York: Palgrave, 2001). As suggested by the title, a historical overview of the development of diplomatic practices.

Paul R. Viotti, *American Foreign Policy* (Cambridge, UK: Polity, 2010). A short introduction on how what policymakers think affects the making and implementation of American foreign policy.

7.2 Identify the high points of the Congress of Vienna and explain how it helped shape the customary practices of present-day communications among governments of states.

Diplomacy and foreign policy (externally directed decisions and actions) have a long history over the millennia, well before states were constructed and became principal actors in international relations. The ancient Greeks engaged in what we would call diplomatic practices, and the Romans expanded upon these traditions. Roman contributions to international law expanded diplomatic norms and protocols. Modern diplomacy, however, dates from the 13th and 14th centuries in Italy, with the Congress of Vienna (1814–1815) a high point that exhibited the importance of diplomatic skills. The ensuing era of the Concert of Europe was a multipolar state system. The Congress accelerated the organization of diplomatic practices and norms, and it is a prime example of successful multilateral diplomacy. The onset of World War I and World War II exhibited the limitations of diplomatic efforts to maintain the peace. Although a Cold War emerged after post–World War II settlements, there was no return to general war waged on a global scale.

KEY TERMS

Jus gentium 226
Jus naturale 226
Multilateral diplomacy 227
Bilateral diplomacy 227

ADDITIONAL READINGS

George Kennan, *American Diplomacy* (New York: New American Library/Mentor Books, 1951). A classic work by one of America's foremost Cold War diplomats and historians.

Paul Kennedy, *The Rise and Fall of the Great Powers* (New York: Random House, 1987). A magisterial overview of modern history, reminding us that no one power maintains supremacy forever.

Henry Kissinger, *A World Restored* (New York: Grosset & Dunlap, 1964). An analysis of the personalities and factors that made the Congress of Vienna a diplomatic success.

Harold Nicholson, *Diplomacy*, 3rd ed. (London: University Press, 1963). The best short primer on the history and ways and means of diplomacy.

Dean Acheson, *Present at the Creation* (New York: W. W. Norton, 1969). A memoir by a former secretary of state who witnessed and participated in momentous events at the end of World War II and the beginning of the Cold War.

7.3 Outline how diplomacy works: recognition of states and governments, diplomatic immunities and protections, the organization of diplomatic missions, diplomatic carrots and sticks.

For a state to engage in diplomacy it must be recognized as a sovereign entity by other states. Widespread recognition of a state's sovereignty does not, however, preclude a state being invaded, destroyed, or even denied sovereign status by some other states. Diplomatic reciprocity and immunities are justified as necessary for diplomats to represent their countries in foreign lands. An embassy is headed by an ambassador and usually consists of representatives from varying government agencies concerned with foreign policy matters. Effective diplomacy requires a judicious mix of carrots and sticks combined with a search for settlements that satisfy the interests of the negotiating parties.

KEY TERMS

Sovereignty 228
Diplomatic immunity 231
Extraterritoriality 231
Ambassador 232
Economic sanctions 235
Crisis 235
Zero-sum 239

ADDITIONAL READINGS

Fred C. Iklé, *How Nations Negotiate* (New York: Harper & Row, 1964). A short primer on negotiation.

Gary R. Hess, *Presidential Decisions for War*: Korea, Vietnam, the Persian Gulf, and Iraq, 2nd ed. (Baltimore: Johns Hopkins University Press, 2001, 2009). Case studies on how presidents have handled crises and decisions to take their country into war.

Jeanne A. K. Hey (ed.), *Small States in World Politics: Explaining Foreign Policy Behavior* (Boulder, CO: Lynne Rienner, 2003). A useful collection of essays that take small countries and their foreign policies as the center of analysis.

Paul R. Viotti (ed.), *American Foreign Policy and National Security: A Documentary Record* (Upper Saddle River, NJ: Prentice Hall, 2005). A useful collection of often hard-to-find documents of U.S. foreign policy that identifies the conceptual and historical underpinnings of American foreign policy.

7.4 Illustrate the potential benefits of diplomatic negotiations focused on arms control and disarmament, types of agreements, and ongoing proliferation concerns in terms of nuclear, radiological, chemical, biological, ballistic missiles, and advanced conventional weapons.

A major focus of foreign policy for many states has been the disarmament or elimination of certain types of weapons. Failing that, a much more realistic approach has been arms control. Agreements seek to curb arms-race competition, achieve economic savings, lessen the risk of war, reduce damage should war occur, and enhance regional and global security. Specific agreements have placed quantitative and qualitative limitations on armaments and armed forces, geographical and spatial deployment, and improved communication and confidence-building measures. Verification is an important element of many agreements, but is often difficult to achieve. Ongoing concerns include nuclear and radiological, chemical, biological, ballistic missile, and advanced conventional weapons proliferation.

KEY TERMS

Disarmament 241
Arms control 241
Verification 250
Weapons proliferation 250
Ballistic missiles 250

ADDITIONAL READINGS

Richard Dean Burns, *The Evolution of Arms Control: From Antiquity to the Nuclear Age* (New York: Praeger, now Santa Barbara, CA: Praeger/ABC-Clio), 2009. The title says it all.

Jeffrey A. Larsen and James J. Wirtz (eds.), *Arms Control and Cooperative Security* (Boulder, CO: Lynne Rienner, 2009). Essays on how arms control can facilitate and reflect cooperative security relations among states.

Robert Williams and Paul R. Viotti (ed.), *Arms Control: History, Theory, and Policy.* 2 vols. (Santa Barbara, CA: Praeger/ABC-Clio, 2011). A collection of essays covering all aspects of arms control.

Paul R. Viotti (ed.), *Arms Control and Global Security: A Document Guide* (Santa Barbara, CA: Praeger/ABC-Clio, 2010). A useful compendium of documents relating to the historical evolution of arms control.

CHAPTER REVIEW

1. All of the following describe diplomacy EXCEPT
   a. for the most part it is noncoercive.
   b. it may include use of threats and other forms of coercion.
   c. it is extremely dangerous work, particularly since diplomats legally may be arrested by the host country.
   d. it involves communications even with enemies or adversaries.

2. Economic sanctions are considered
   a. highly coercive.
   b. moderately coercive.
   c. noncoercive.
   d. collaborative.

3. Diplomacy may be accomplished by
   a. heads of state.
   b. accredited diplomats.
   c. private citizens sent as emissaries.
   d. all of the above.

4. The establishment of the first recorded diplomatic mission was by the
   a. Greeks.
   b. Romans.
   c. Italians.
   d. French.

5. The Byzantines used diplomats to
   a. foster rivalry among the barbarians.
   b. secure friendship of frontier tribes.
   c. convert the "heathens."
   d. all of the above.

6. A truly organized system of diplomatic practices and norms emerged from the
   a. Roman legal system.
   b. Byzantine Empire.
   c. Congress of Vienna.
   d. Treaty of Paris.

7. A classic example of successful multilateral diplomacy that endured for decades was
   a. the Athens-Sparta agreement of 404 B.C.E.
   b. the Congress of Vienna.
   c. the Versailles Treaty.
   d. all of the above.

8. The highest ranking position in a diplomatic mission is that of
   a. ambassador.
   b. consul.
   c. consul general.
   d. chief of mission.

9. The idea that an embassy and the ground it stands on are a part of the sovereign territory of the foreign country is that of
   a. asylum.
   b. extraterritoriality.
   c. sovereign extension.
   d. diplomatic immunity.

10. When the relations between two countries are considered normal, they are each represented at the level of
    a. ambassador.
    b. consul general.
    c. *chargé d'affaires.*
    d. first secretary.

11. Diplomatic incentives, or carrots, may take the form of all of the following EXCEPT
    a. foreign aid.
    b. trade preferences.
    c. increased compensation for diplomats.
    d. debt forgiveness.

12. If two states have a perceived conflict of interest about an important security matter and neither backs down, events may produce an immediate
    a. stalemate.
    b. crisis.
    c. diplomatic incident.
    d. negotiated settlement.

13. International security regimes include all of the following EXCEPT
    a. arms reductions agreements.
    b. quantitative and qualitative limits on armaments.
    c. geographic prohibitions on where arms may be deployed or used.
    d. efforts to reduce poverty, thus improving human security.

14. *Qualitative* restrictions as part of arms control regimes include all of the following EXCEPT
    a. the numbers of weapons systems in a country's military arsenal.
    b. limitations on research and development, testing and evaluation of weapons systems.
    c. prohibitions on weapons testing.
    d. location—where weapons systems are deployed.

15. _____ and _____ are two of the major difficulties in combating any weapons proliferation issue.
    a. Implementation and enforcement
    b. Agreement and procedures
    c. Capabilities and political will
    d. Size and scope

16. Two approaches can be taken to combat nuclear proliferation and weapons proliferation in general. What are they?
    a. supply side and political pressure
    b. supply side and demand side
    c. demand side and political pressure
    d. demand side and military pressure

17. The problem of determining whether states live up to what they have promised is the problem of
    a. certification.
    b. treaty commitment.
    c. verification.
    d. transparency.

18. Problems associated with arms transfers include all of the following EXCEPT
    a. inability to control end use.
    b. the money spent on arms thus cannot be spent on national development.
    c. they contribute to regional arms races.
    d. they reduce profits to defense-industry arms exporters.

19. A major concern continues to be proliferation to nonnuclear states and disaffected groups of nuclear weapons or weapons technologies from
    a. the Republic of South Africa.
    b. the Russian Federation and the former Soviet republics.
    c. Sweden.
    d. Serbia.

20. The Nuclear Non-Proliferation Treaty has NOT been signed by
    a. the United States.
    b. Israel.
    c. North Korea.
    d. Iran.

International Law and International Organization

"States remain the most powerful actors in world politics, but it is no longer even a reasonable simplification to think of world politics simply as politics among states. A larger variety of other organizations, from multinational corporations to nongovernmental organizations, exercise authority and engage in political action

LEARNING OBJECTIVES

8.1 Identify the multi-century construction and sources of international law and critique the norms and rules developed in global civil society.

8.2 Describe how the development of international law in global civil society was and is impacted by matters of war and peace, economics, human rights, the environment, and criminal accountability.

8.3 Evaluate how international law and organizations influence decisions by state authorities to use force.

8.4 Evaluate the reasons why state authorities seek allies or coalition partners to enhance the security of their states and societies.

The jurists sitting on the International Court of Justice (ICJ) at The Hague in the Netherlands were perplexed by the question before them—the legality of nuclear weapons, a case first brought by the World Health Organization (WHO) in 1993. The ICJ did not take the case, ruling that the WHO—a nonstate actor—did not have the standing to bring such a case of import primarily to states.

As with most courts, justices on the ICJ tend to avoid getting in the middle of political controversies among the governmental parties unless requested or required by a clear mandate to do so. That mandate came a year later in 1994, when member states of the UN General Assembly requested a judgment on the question. The ICJ accepted the case in January 1995. A year and a half later the Court finally delivered its ruling.

Disappointing those on both sides of the question, the ICJ split in a 7-to-7 vote on whether "the threat or use of nuclear weapons would generally be contrary to the rules of international law applicable in armed conflict." The Court also could not agree on "whether the threat or use of nuclear weapons would be lawful or unlawful in an extreme circumstance of self-defence." In many respects this indecisiveness reflected very real political and legal quarrels among the parties themselves—divided as they were between states seeing these weapons of mass destruction as contrary to their security interests, on the one hand, and those possessing these weapons (or dependent upon nuclear-capable allies for their own security) on the other.

Deciding such questions is by no means an easy matter. The ICJ did agree unanimously in its July 1996 ruling that any use of nuclear (as with other) weapons must be compatible with provisions of the UN Charter on the use of force and other legal requirements in both the law of war and humanitarian law. That said, the legality of using or threatening to use nuclear weapons remains an open question.

Read and Listen to **Chapter 8** at **mypoliscilab.com**

Study and Review the **Pre-Test & Flashcards** at **mypoliscilab.com**

global civil society ■ the gradual worldwide emergence of the rule of law and networks or relationships among people in a world composed of both states and nonstate actors

We use this opening example to underscore that constructing a global civil society—one based on the rule of law among both state and nonstate actors—is still very much a work in progress. So are the international organizations (IOs) that perform substantial political, military, economic, commercial, and other social roles in global civil society. Though IOs were created by and for states, liberals in particular note the degree to which they have become significant actors in their own right. To what extent do they influence states' interests, preferences, and objectives? Or do IOs merely reflect member states' interests and, at most, provide a forum for debate or discussion?

INTERNATIONAL LAW AND THE EMERGENCE OF GLOBAL CIVIL SOCIETY

8.1 Identify the multi-century construction and sources of international law and critique the norms and rules developed in global civil society.

To focus only on violence, wars, and instances of fragile governmental authority is to miss out on a remarkable development in international relations and world politics over the past several hundred years—the gradual evolution of an international global civil society. We fully recognize that such a process is far from complete, has developed at a painfully slow pace, and is fragile and subject to setbacks. Yet such changes must be highlighted to provide a complete and balanced picture of international relations and world politics.

Use of the term *civil society* in "domestic" societies within states implies that behavior of people within these societies is subject to the rule of law. So it is with a still-emergent global civil society. We examine here the emergence in the last five hundred years of developments that not only contributed to the rise of states—the traditional focus of international relations and world politics—but also developments that have provided early glimpses of a still-emerging global civil society. As much an aspiration as a reality, the slow development of global civil society—as well as the rise of states—is in part a function of the multicentury, gradual globalization of international relations and world politics.

international organization (IO) ■ an institution composed of states as members (for example, the United Nations [UN], European Union [EU], and the North Atlantic Treaty Organization [NATO])

In essence, global society becomes a truly civil society to the extent that values or norms gain legitimacy and become widely accepted, some even acquiring the force of international law. This doesn't mean, of course, that the rules—legally binding or not—always will be followed. Means available for international law enforcement of international law are weak compared to the power and authority that governments usually have for such purposes on the territories within their states over which they have jurisdiction.

norms ■ values that states or people take seriously and that influence behavior, such as concern for human rights

Nevertheless, breaking laws and agreed rules or norms that have legitimacy—acceptance as binding—may result in costs for those who break them. For example, when a state invades another without just cause or legal basis or its authorities orchestrate genocide—the killing of people of a particular identity—such acts are likely to draw not only condemnation by other states and wider publics, but also economic sanctions and, perhaps, the use of force by other states acting to counter the aggression or genocide. The authorities responsible for such conduct also may be held to account in domestic courts or in the International Criminal Court (ICC).

international law ■ binding rules or law that transcend borders and apply to states as well as to individuals (natural persons) and organizations or corporations (legal persons)

ARGUMENT-COUNTERARGUMENT | Ideas and the Social Construction of Global Civil Society

Norms that become established in the form of either tacitly accepted understandings or explicitly agreed-upon rules (some of which have the binding quality of international law) lie at the foundation of international regimes: voluntarily agreed-upon sets of principles, norms, rules, and procedures concerning diverse issues such as human rights, war and peace, commercial transactions and their servicing institutions.

ARGUMENT These regimes and institutions evolved or are the outcome of human design efforts intended to provide an authoritative basis for regulating or at least influencing the behavior of both state and nonstate actors. So understood, the development of global society is a constructivist enterprise. Social constructivists portray self-help, power politics, and similar concepts as having been socially constructed under the anarchy of international relations and world politics; they are not inevitable or essential attributes of international politics. The key point is that international relations and world politics do not have an independent existence; they are what people make (or have made) of them. Ideas, culture, and norms matter and can influence behavior, including the creation of multilateral institutions.

COUNTERARGUMENT The ideational focus in constructivist accounts—ideas, culture, and norms—gives less attention to, if it does not ignore, power—the material realities that drive international politics. This essentially is the realist response—that, as always, liberals and others who think like them have discounted or minimized the importance of power (as if ideas alone could drive political and social outcomes).

APPLICATION Which helps explain better the decision of western European powers and the United States to intervene militarily against the Kaddafi regime in early 2011—power and interest calculations or value considerations like human rights? How about other interventions? Is there a tension between power and interest on the one hand and values or ideals on the other? If so, how can policymakers and other practitioners reconcile these factors?

The Emergence of International Law

By the 15th and 16th centuries, increased commerce associated with advancing transportation technologies at sea raised questions concerning rights of navigation through the coastal waters of different states as well as the modalities by which goods would be bought and sold—imported and exported across territorial boundaries. Although territorially a rather small state, Holland had already emerged as a major sea-based commercial center by the 16th and 17th centuries. With its "head" turned toward the sea and its "back" toward the rest of Europe, it is not surprising that the idea of international law or law among nations would gain prominence in Holland.

Hugo Grotius (1583–1645), both a scholar and a very practical man living in the Dutch commercial town of Delft, turned his attention to these concerns of governments, trading companies, and businesses of newly formed states in his day—commercial issues and matters of war and peace. Writing in the wake of the

International Criminal Court ■ tribunal located in The Hague, Netherlands, for prosecution of war crimes, genocide, and other crimes against humanity

international regime ■ voluntarily agreed-upon sets of principles, norms, rules, and procedures constructed by states to coordinate, manage, or regulate their relations in a particular issue area

horrors of the Thirty Years' War (1618–1648), Grotius offered formulations of law drawn from several sources. One can see the influence on Grotius of the philosophical and historical legacy of a Roman imperial *jus gentium*, a law to govern relations among diverse peoples in the ancient Roman empire, as well as natural law thinking.

Natural law is a philosophical view that claims there are laws inherent in nature that transcend any laws made by mere mortals. Such thinking is closely tied to the writings of Augustine, Aquinas, and other Christian writers of the late Roman Empire and Middle Ages. Grotius also knew how to make general principles and customary practice central to his constructions of legal rules of the road for states in a newly emerging, state-based European society. Thanks to the colonial and imperial extension of European states in the 18th, 19th, and 20th centuries, this would eventually move closer toward a global society of peoples within states.

Aided by new transportation and communications technologies, territorial states became the principal actors in this new international societal order. Following Grotius and other writers, international law developed rapidly in two principal areas—economic (mainly trade and commerce) and security matters of war and peace (including diplomacy). For example, following Grotius, the territorial sea came to be defined by a three-mile limit extending from the shoreline of the coastal state. The reason three miles was chosen was that artillery technology of the time limited the range of a cannonball to about three miles, the practical distance that any country could expect to defend from the shore without actually going to sea.

Principles of just war, limits on conduct of and in warfare developed by Cicero, Augustine, Aquinas, Gentili, Suarez, and other philosophers over more than 1,500 years of Western civilization, now became matters of international law, not just moral preachings. Ideas concerning mutual respect for the welfare of foreign diplomats and their embassies and consulates also became legal obligations based on the customary practice of states.

Sources of International Law

As certain values and norms of proper conduct have gained legitimacy and acceptance on a global scale, many of these have also acquired legal status. For example, understanding, acceptance, and growing commitment since World War II to such ethical principles as respect for life, human dignity, and justice or fairness as global norms have motivated efforts to construct and expand international law on human rights.

Treaties or conventions are the most concrete forms of international law. Governments, as agents of the sovereign states they represent, contract when they sign and ratify treaties or international conventions to be bound by mutual agreement to the terms of these documents. The ancient idea from Roman times that treaties are binding, *pacta sunt servanda* in Latin, finds practical application in global civil society in the construction of international law on human rights, defining civil and criminal jurisdictions of legal accountability, managing the global environment, and reducing environmental degradation. As a result, security has come to be viewed by a number of scholars and international activists not only in terms of national security and the use of force, but also human security. At the same time,

natural law ■ obligations and rights that exist in nature, discoverable through reason

just war ■ specific conditions must be met both to establish the right to use force (*jus ad bellum*) and to assure right conduct while engaged in warfare (*jus in bello*)

Watch the Video "The Crisis in Darfur" at mypoliscilab.com

pacta sunt servanda ■ Latin term for treaties or conventions that are binding on states party to these agreements

the more traditional domains of international law on matters of security in war and peace as well as commerce are expanding in an increasingly global economy.

Another important source of international law is customary practice. Over time such **customary international law** often becomes codified later in treaties or conventions. General principles inform our understandings of international law, particularly for those who turn to a natural law tradition that sees universal principles of law as discoverable by applying human reason.

customary international law
■ law found in the common practice of states established over time

Finally, we rely on the writings of jurists—justices and judges—whose legal opinions in cases before international as well as domestic courts bring all of these sources into sharper focus. Legal precedents are important in establishing wider legitimacy and acceptance of the rule of law on an ever-increasing number and diversity of issues in international relations and world politics.

Some ideas or norms in global civil society over time may become institutionalized as the legitimate and accepted ways and means of conduct in international relations and world politics. For example, **multilateralism** has become the preferred way of dealing with many issues on the global agenda. Rather than resorting to unilateral actions by individual states, these issues are thought to be addressed more properly in the international organizations to which states belong and in other multilateral settings. These settings are increasingly open not only to states but also to nongovernmental organizations, groups, and even individuals. The idea of global civil society is thus an ever-more cosmopolitan vision of the ways and means of conducting international relations and world politics.

multilateralism
■ working on international issues jointly rather than unilaterally by a single state—often a means to achieve mutual gains

Not only do ideas become institutionalized—accepted as the appropriate or legitimate ways in which states and nonstate actors expect (or are expected) to behave—but these ideas often become embedded in both international and nongovernmental organizations in which states or their citizens participate and interact with one another. For example, the UN organization or any of its specialized agencies provide a multilateral forum, procedures, and processes for dealing with the wide range of issues in which states and nonstate actors engage.

THE EXPANDING SCOPE OF INTERNATIONAL LAW IN GLOBAL CIVIL SOCIETY

The two oldest fields in the construction of the rule of law in global civil society are (1) security or war and peace issues and (2) economic or commercial matters. The newest and much less developed fields are (3) human rights, (4) the environment, and (5) international accountability for criminal acts. We will briefly examine each in turn.

8.2 Describe how the development of international law in global civil society was and is impacted by matters of war and peace, economics, human rights, the environment, and criminal accountability.

Diplomacy and Security: Matters of War and Peace

The emergence of sovereign states in 15th-, 16th- and 17th-century Europe resulted in an outpouring of speculation as to the implications of this development, not unlike the literature addressing globalization today. Attention was focused on the ways and means of diplomacy or communications among states, their security concerns, and the conduct of relations among them in both war and peace. Consistent with the writings of Jean Bodin (1530–1596), Hugo Grotius (1583–1645),

✷─Explore the
"Transnational Issues:
You Are an
Environmental
Consultant" at
mypoliscilab.com

and other legal scholars, international law came to define the sovereignty of a state as conveying a right to exercise complete jurisdiction on its own territory as well as a right to be independent or autonomous in conducting foreign policy or international relations. Although they are unequal in power and position in international relations, sovereign states enjoy legal equality as members of the United Nations and other international organizations. Indeed, Article 2, Section 1 of the UN Charter states clearly and unequivocally that the "organization is based on the principle of the sovereign equality of all its Members."

Routines and procedures for diplomatic representation became established practice over time and thus served as a customary basis for international law. States came to accept as a matter of international law the immunity from arrest or prosecution of foreign diplomats and the extraterritorial idea or legal fiction that the small parcel of land on which an embassy, consulate, or other diplomatic mission was located was to be secured and respected as subject to the sovereign prerogatives of the foreign country as if it were its own territory. Although long established as customary international law, these and other rules governing diplomacy finally were specified formally as treaty obligations in the Vienna Conventions on Diplomatic and Consular Relations in 1961 and 1963, respectively.

Nongovernmental organizations, other groups, and individuals in their private capacities can influence decision making and implementation of foreign and national security policies, but diplomacy and war and peace matters are primarily the domain of states and international organizations made up of states. Grotius also wrote about war and peace, drawing from the moral tradition in Western thought. That use of force in war must be justified (*jus ad bellum*), and that states engaged in warfare are obligated to observe limits and practice right conduct (*jus in bello*) thus acquired legal in addition to moral standing through the work of Grotius and other writers.

jus ad bellum ■
Latin term for moral criteria establishing the right to go to war

jus in bello ■ Latin term for moral criteria establishing right conduct in war

Efforts began in the late 19th century to codify and expand upon these principles, which resulted initially in The Hague Conventions of 1899 and 1907 that specified certain legal obligations as well as illegal conduct in warfare. Reacting to the enormous carnage of World War I that had devastated Europe between 1914 and 1918, signatories of the Covenant of the League of Nations tried to find alternatives to war and the use of force in international relations. Pooling state resources to take appropriate action against any lawbreaking aggressor state was one suggestion. The Pact of Paris or General Treaty for the Renunciation of War (more commonly referred to as the Kellogg-Briand Pact) took matters a substantial step further in 1928 by declaring that resorting to war was an illegal activity.

However well intended, this legal approach to security and matters of war and peace failed to prevent acts of aggression in the 1920s and 1930s, as well as the onset of a second world war in 1939. After World War II, the UN Charter retained collective law enforcement but supplemented it by recognizing the inherent right of sovereign states to use force to provide for their individual or (joining with other states in alliances or coalitions) their collective self-defense.

Geneva Conventions
■ prescribing right conduct toward both combatants and noncombatants in warfare and defining war crimes, crimes against the peace, and related offenses

On the conduct of warfare itself, the tradition of The Hague Conventions was revived in the formulation by treaty of obligations and limits in the **Geneva Conventions** on the Laws of War (1949). These laws of war were formulated with interstate wars in mind but fell short in addressing civil wars and other armed conflicts that may occur within or across boundaries of states. Accordingly, two protocols to these conventions signed in 1977 extended coverage of laws of warfare to cases of "armed conflict not of an international [i.e., interstate] character." Security issues have also been a major growth area in global civil society since World War II, as indicated by the extraordinary proliferation of arms control agreements and treaties emerging from exhaustive diplomatic efforts over the last half of the 20th century and continuing to the present day.

Economic and Commercial Matters

A culture in global society dealing with economic or commercial matters also has deep roots. Certainly Grotius and other contributors made commerce a core focus in developing rules to govern trade. Early rules that acquired legal standing under international law were that ships carrying cargoes were free to transit the high seas without interference. Moreover, piracy threatening international commerce was understood as a crime against the law of nations, punishable by any state. Rules that emerged in customary practice governing the responsibilities of exporters to deliver and importers to pay for the goods they buy reduced to a routine how commercial traders would conduct their business. Also contributing to the expansion of trade was developing **most-favored nation (MFN)** status as a diplomatic measure, granting other countries and their firms a right to sell their products at the same low level of tariff or tax as was imposed on imports from their most-favored trading partners.

Similarly, international law came to require nondiscriminatory treatment of foreign investments. Such properties may be expropriated or taken by a host country's government only for some legitimate public purpose. Let's say, for example, that as part of its economic development plan the Ecuadoran government has decided to put in a new highway directly across Guayaquil, one of the country's coastal cities. This will require the government to nationalize or take for public use all private properties in the path of the proposed highway, giving the owners monetary compensation for their losses, typically the market values of properties seized. It is not enough just to compensate domestic property owners: International law also requires the government to give fair or just compensation to foreign property owners as well.

Since the end of World War II, international law on economic and commercial issues has continued to grow. States belonging to the General Agreement on Tariffs and Trade (GATT)—now the **World Trade Organization (WTO)**—located in Geneva have reduced taxes and quotas or limitations on imports as well as other barriers to trade in treaties or other agreements that effectively have the force of international law. Other international organizations and UN specialized agencies such as the World Bank and International Monetary Fund, both located in Washington, DC, follow legal procedures and processes in lending capital respectively for economic development or for maintenance of international **liquidity**—cash needed from time to time by national treasuries and their central banks to settle financial obligations owed to the central banks or national treasuries of other countries. This procedure maintains the viability and facilitates the exchange of national currencies used in international commerce.

most-favored nation (MFN) ■ status given by one state to another state as in setting tariffs at the lowest level charged on imports from any other country

World Trade Organization (WTO) ■ Geneva-based international organization that seeks to lower, if not eliminate, tariffs and other barriers to international trade

liquidity ■ availability of cash—in international monetary affairs, the ease with which foreign currencies are available to countries so they can settle their accounts with other countries

International transportation is subject to rules with the effect of law made by member states and staffs in UN specialized agencies—the International Civil Aviation Organization (ICAO) in Montreal and the International Maritime Organization (IMO) in London. Similarly, another UN specialized agency, the International Telecommunication Union (ITU) in Geneva, has regulatory authority on international use of telecommunications frequencies. A more recent example of continued growth in international law concerning economic or commercial matters is the Anti-Bribery Treaty negotiated within the Organization for Economic Cooperation and Development (OECD)—an international organization composed of First World, "rich," advanced industrial countries. The treaty obligates its signatories to pass laws prohibiting corporations seeking contracts from paying bribes to government officials.

Intellectual property law—legal obligations to respect copyrights and patents across national borders—is yet another expanding area of international law in the economic and commercial sector, particularly given the development of ever-new technologies needing such protection.

Human Rights and the Environment

Prior to World War II, international law dealt primarily with security, diplomatic, and economic or commercial matters. As indicated in the previous two sections, these domains have continued to expand substantially since 1945. Human rights and the environment, however, are the new growth areas for extending international law within global civil society. These topics will be discussed in greater detail in later chapters, but some basic background is appropriate at this point.

The Holocaust in Germany and other areas in Europe under the National Socialist (Nazi) regime's influence or control in the 1930s and 1940s cost some six million Jews their lives and forced millions more to flee their homes, leave their property behind, suffer extreme trauma, and sustain enormous psychological damage. Additional millions of Slavs, Gypsies, homosexuals, regime opponents, and others deemed undesirable by the regime were also sent to labor or concentration camps where many were exterminated. Also stirring the human conscience were reports of atrocities in Asia and the Pacific, particularly those conducted by the Japanese military against Chinese and other Asian peoples. Moreover, all of these losses were in addition to the tens of millions killed in the war itself. Reflection on these horrific human losses led to calls for action to preclude any such occurrence from ever happening again.

One immediate response was to hold perpetrators accountable in the Nuremberg and Tokyo war crimes trials held in 1945 and 1946. In addition to crimes against the laws of war, two other categories were delineated in 1945 by the United States, the United Kingdom, France, and the Soviet Union: crimes against the peace (as in planning and waging a war of aggression) and crimes against humanity (such inhumane acts against civilian populations as murder, extermination, enslavement, and deportation). Though criticized by some as merely a case of the victorious holding the vanquished accountable, the trials did set an important precedent by holding individuals internationally accountable for criminal acts.

The trials were followed in 1948 by two important agreements: (1) a UN Genocide Convention that defined this crime against the law of nations as being one committed "with intent to destroy in whole or in part, a national, ethnic, racial or religious group, as such," and (2) a UN General Assembly Universal Declaration of Human Rights, discussed in greater detail in Chapter 13, "Human Rights."

These initiatives in effect set a human rights train in motion, leading over several decades to international agreement in the UN General Assembly on a number of important treaties:

International Convention on the Elimination of All Forms of Racial
   Discrimination (1965)
Covenant on Civil and Political Rights (1966)
Covenant on Economic, Social, and Cultural Rights (1966)
International Convention on the Suppression and the Punishment of the Crime
   of Apartheid (1973)
Convention on the Elimination of All Forms of Discrimination against
   Women (1979)
Convention against Torture and Other Cruel, Inhuman, or Degrading
   Treatment (1984)
Convention on the Rights of the Child (1989)
The Act of Helsinki (1975) within what is now the Organization for
   Security and Cooperation in Europe

Universal acceptance of these sweeping provisions as international law, of course, is a decades-long process requiring both signature and ratification of these treaties. What they do represent, however, is a growing consensus in global civil society on the universal norms that should guide human conduct and protect human rights no matter where one resides or travels.

A growth area in the construction of international law for global civil society is the physical environment within which human beings, plants, and animals live. Pollution and other forms of environmental degradation as well as depletion of nonrenewable resources and global warming are global concerns on a planet of more than six billion people, many of whom suffer from poverty, malnutrition, and little or no access to adequate health care. At the same time, populations continue to grow, and demands for better levels of living continue to rise. Pressures on the environment are enormous as we try to sustain the economic development that is so necessary for improving the welfare of human beings and other forms of life on Earth.

Notwithstanding the high aspirations of environmental advocates, efforts to construct international law on such matters have been extremely difficult. For one thing, uneven development and distribution of wealth and income around the world create diverse interests and purposes. Poorer countries understandably want to be able to pursue their economic development plans with as few environmental obstacles as possible. For their part, richer countries already consume a disproportionate share of resources, the high levels of production they sustain contributing substantially to resource depletion and environmental degradation.

Not only are interests divergent, but scientific efforts to find remedies or viable approaches to reducing environmental degradation have been clouded by uncertainties as to both cause and effect. Nevertheless, relatively modest agreements have been reached on such matters as ozone-layer depletion and global warming or climate change. For example, understanding that such chlorofluorocarbon (CFC) uses as freon in refrigerators and aerosol propellants in spray cans are causes of ozone-layer depletion, negotiators finally reached an initial agreement in 1987 in the Montreal Protocol to put limits on CFC emissions in an effort to phase them out. The parties have continued to address the matter, updating the protocol by amendments agreed at multilateral meetings throughout the world. Although many countries have yet to ratify all of these amendments, the original 1987 protocol now enjoys universal ratification—all UN members subscribing, the last adherents finally joining in 2009. Indeed, the consensus on curbing CFC emissions is an important, foundational norm for the legally binding requirements to which state authorities have agreed.

global warming ■ an increase in the volume of carbon dioxide in the atmosphere contributing to a green-house effect that traps heat from the sun's rays and raises the average temperature around the world

There is now scientific consensus that a principal cause of global warming is continued emissions of carbon dioxide and other greenhouse gases produced in particular by industrial and other burning of fossil fuels—coal, petroleum products, and natural gas. These greenhouse gases work in effect as an atmospheric blanket that retains heat from the sun's rays. Even an increase of a degree or two in the Earth's temperature has substantial climatic effects indicated, for example, by increased turbulence and severity of storms, melting icecaps in Arctic regions, and rising sea levels. Naysayers who challenge the global-warming thesis may be particularly vocal when experiencing an extremely cold winter, but defenders of the global-warming claim are quick to point out that temperature extremes outside of the norm in any season are precisely what one can expect from global warming, not to mention other adverse effects.

Signatories of the Kyoto Protocol (1997) pledged to reduce their production of such gases by the year 2012 by 5.2 percent compared to 1990 emissions levels. The Kyoto Protocol is the product of a continuing process of negotiations within the UN Framework Convention on Climate Change (1992). The United States is among the few countries that chose not to be bound by these restrictions on the use of fossil fuels. Nevertheless, the 2007 reports from the Intergovernmental Panel on Climate Change (IPCC) solidified the international consensus that not only is global warming a real and growing threat to the planet, but also that we need at least to take actions to slow, if not stop, the rate of global warming.

The December 2009 "Copenhagen Summit"—formally the United Nations Climate Change Conference—was unable to break the logjam on specifying further reductions of CO_2 emissions. Less-developed countries wanting to increase industrial production have relied on burning more carbon-based fossil fuels like oil, gas, and coal as core to reaching their economic-development goals. Advanced industrial and postindustrial countries with highly developed economies also find reductions difficult, the transition to nonfossil fuels likely taking decades to accomplish.

The Copenhagen Summit did produce a statement that specified the desire to keep the average global temperature from increasing by any more than 2 °C, but did not specify how this would be accomplished other than acknowledging the importance of continuing reductions in CO_2 emissions. Even if this goal were reached somehow, atmospheric scientists warn, substantial climatic and environmental changes will occur. What we need, they say, is time to adapt to changes by markedly slowing the increase in global temperatures. More easily said than done, particularly given the lack of consensus on allowable CO_2 emissions.

Doing little or nothing and thus allowing average temperature to rise much above this modest threshold risks even cataclysmic climate change with rising sea levels, loss of seacoast land and harbors, converting some agriculturally fertile areas into deserts while flooding others, perhaps making Europe a colder place were the customarily warm Gulf Stream flows disrupted, putting whole countries like the sea-level Maldives underwater, and inundating others. Since no one country can resolve the global-warming issue single-handedly, it is clearly a challenge that can only be dealt with effectively multilaterally. International organizations and the conferences they sponsor, followed closely and supported by NGOs, become pivotal in dealing with this 21st–century challenge.

International Criminal Accountability

States seeking judicial settlement of their conflicts can turn to the International Court of Justice (ICJ), a principal organ of the UN and successor to the World Court in the League of Nations formed after World War I. When states try to enforce the law against persons within their territorial jurisdictions, they typically use their own courts for such purposes. The United States, for example, has done this in trials of alleged terrorists at its base at Guantánamo Bay in Cuba, establishing special military commissions there as a alternative venue to federal civilian courts or military courts martial within the United States.

International Court of Justice (ICJ) ■ a United Nations judicial body

On other occasions states have employed international tribunals for holding individuals accountable for the most serious criminal offenses—most notably the Nuremberg trials after World War II. Genocide in recent decades occurring in places as far apart as Cambodia, central Africa, Yugoslavia, and elsewhere underscored the absence of international mechanisms for holding perpetrators to account for war crimes, genocide, and other crimes against humanity. An international conference in Rome took a major step forward in 1998 when it formulated as a treaty for signature and ratification a new statute for an International Criminal Court (ICC) with global jurisdiction, complementary to national courts, for such crimes. Unlike previous war crimes courts with jurisdiction limited to specific conflicts, the ICC is a permanent institution.

Unlike the ICJ, it is not an organ of the United Nations. Although the Clinton administration favored its creation, the Bush administration that followed shifted the U.S. course and opposed it. Three countries openly stated they would not vote for the establishment of the ICC—the United States, Israel, and China. U.S. negotiators claimed they feared American soldiers and peacekeepers abroad could be brought before the court on politically motivated charges. The "global war on terror" only exacerbated these concerns.

In May 2002, a month after the ICC formally came into existence, President George W. Bush informed the United Nations that the United States would not ratify the agreement, raising questions about the court's legitimacy. Gains in criminal accountability before international courts have not been matched, however, by expansion of international jurisdiction for civil cases (as when individuals or corporations sue each other for violations of contracts, torts, and other offenses, or when allowed by domestic law, try to sue or petition governments for redress of grievances). For the most part, civil law remains the domain of states exercising jurisdiction within their territorial boundaries.

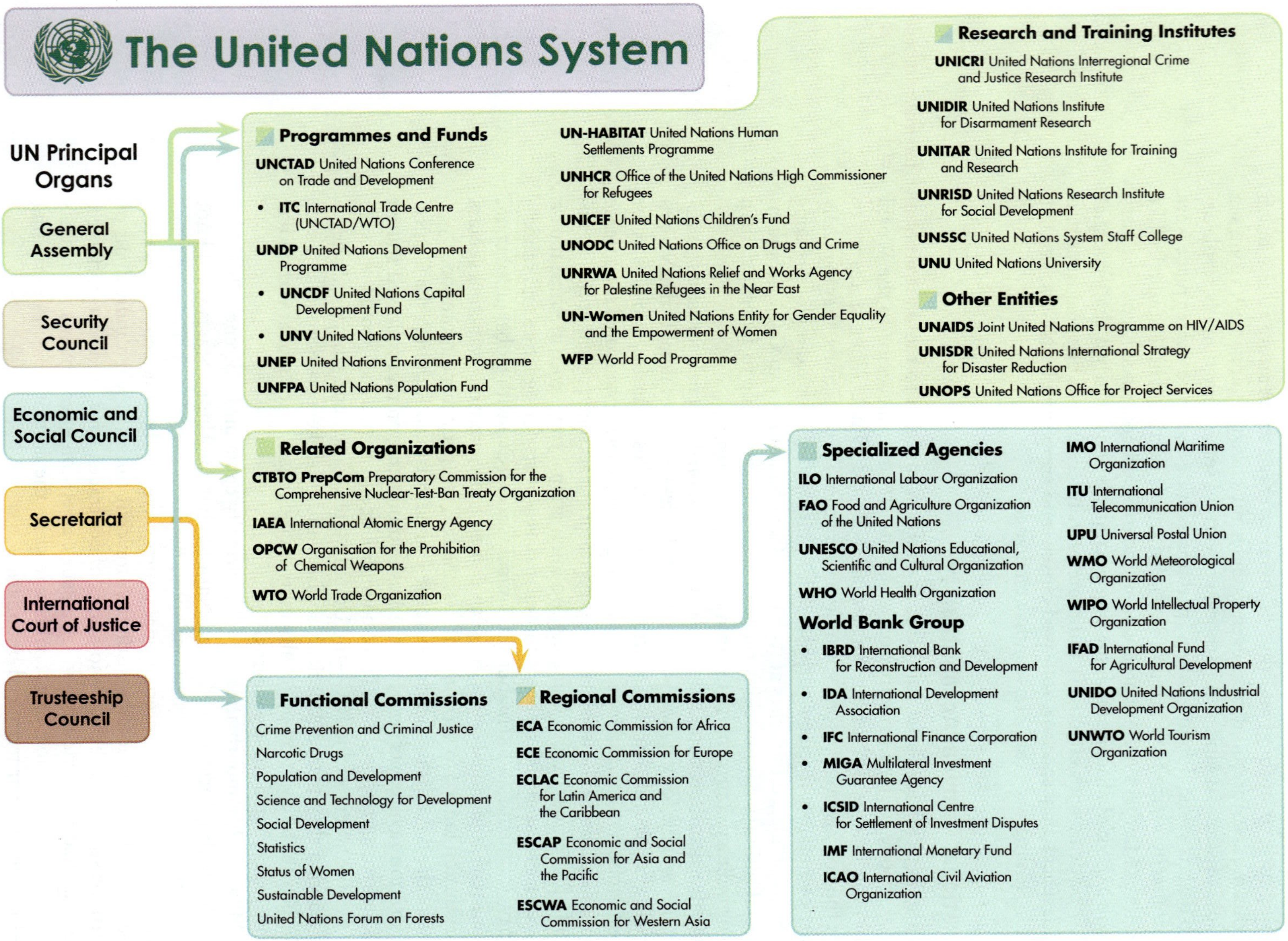

The United Nations System

UN Principal Organs

- General Assembly
- Security Council
- Economic and Social Council
- Secretariat
- International Court of Justice
- Trusteeship Council

Programmes and Funds

UNCTAD United Nations Conference on Trade and Development

- **ITC** International Trade Centre (UNCTAD/WTO)

UNDP United Nations Development Programme

- **UNCDF** United Nations Capital Development Fund
- **UNV** United Nations Volunteers

UNEP United Nations Environment Programme

UNFPA United Nations Population Fund

UN-HABITAT United Nations Human Settlements Programme

UNHCR Office of the United Nations High Commissioner for Refugees

UNICEF United Nations Children's Fund

UNODC United Nations Office on Drugs and Crime

UNRWA United Nations Relief and Works Agency for Palestine Refugees in the Near East

UN-Women United Nations Entity for Gender Equality and the Empowerment of Women

WFP World Food Programme

Research and Training Institutes

UNICRI United Nations Interregional Crime and Justice Research Institute

UNIDIR United Nations Institute for Disarmament Research

UNITAR United Nations Institute for Training and Research

UNRISD United Nations Research Institute for Social Development

UNSSC United Nations System Staff College

UNU United Nations University

Other Entities

UNAIDS Joint United Nations Programme on HIV/AIDS

UNISDR United Nations International Strategy for Disaster Reduction

UNOPS United Nations Office for Project Services

Related Organizations

CTBTO PrepCom Preparatory Commission for the Comprehensive Nuclear-Test-Ban Treaty Organization

IAEA International Atomic Energy Agency

OPCW Organisation for the Prohibition of Chemical Weapons

WTO World Trade Organization

Functional Commissions

Crime Prevention and Criminal Justice
Narcotic Drugs
Population and Development
Science and Technology for Development
Social Development
Statistics
Status of Women
Sustainable Development
United Nations Forum on Forests

Regional Commissions

ECA Economic Commission for Africa

ECE Economic Commission for Europe

ECLAC Economic Commission for Latin America and the Caribbean

ESCAP Economic and Social Commission for Asia and the Pacific

ESCWA Economic and Social Commission for Western Asia

Specialized Agencies

ILO International Labour Organization

FAO Food and Agriculture Organization of the United Nations

UNESCO United Nations Educational, Scientific and Cultural Organization

WHO World Health Organization

World Bank Group

- **IBRD** International Bank for Reconstruction and Development
- **IDA** International Development Association
- **IFC** International Finance Corporation
- **MIGA** Multilateral Investment Guarantee Agency
- **ICSID** International Centre for Settlement of Investment Disputes

IMF International Monetary Fund

ICAO International Civil Aviation Organization

IMO International Maritime Organization

ITU International Telecommunication Union

UPU Universal Postal Union

WMO World Meteorological Organization

WIPO World Intellectual Property Organization

IFAD International Fund for Agricultural Development

UNIDO United Nations Industrial Development Organization

UNWTO World Tourism Organization

FIGURE 8.1

The U.N. System is composed of the principal organs plus other international organizations or agencies affiliated or linked to one of these organs.

The United Nations (UN): Objectives and Structure

When states become members of the United Nations, they agree to accept the obligations of the UN Charter, an international treaty. According to the Charter, the United Nations has four basic principles: (1) to maintain international peace and security, (2) to develop friendly relations among nations, (3) to cooperate in solving international problems and in promoting human rights, and (4) to be a center for harmonizing the actions of nations. Some critics charge the United Nations has done a poor job in achieving these aims, whereas others charge the United Nations is doing too much and is a threat to the sovereign power of member states.

The United Nations organization (UN or UNO) has six principal organs: the General Assembly, Security Council, Economic and Social Council, Trusteeship Council, International Court of Justice (ICJ), and Secretariat. All are located in New York except the ICJ, successor to the earlier World Court, which remains at The Hague in the Netherlands. The UNO is at the core of a worldwide network or system of international organizations linked to one or another of these principal UN organs. For an institutional map of this complex United Nations system of international organizations, refer to Figure 8.1.

The *General Assembly* consists of all member states. It meets as a deliberative body to consider pressing global problems. Each state has one vote. If the decision involves important matters involving peace and security, admitting new members, the UN budget, or the budget for peacekeeping, a two-thirds majority is required. Other issues require a simple majority. The Assembly cannot force any state to take an action, but the United Nations views Assembly recommendations as an indication of world opinion. The Assembly meets from September to December. When it is not meeting, its work is carried out by its six main committees and the UN Secretariat.

The *Security Council* is given the main responsibility for maintaining international peace and security and hence may meet at any time. There are fifteen Council members, with five—China, France, the Russian Federation, the United Kingdom, and the United States—permanent members. The other ten are elected by the General Assembly for two-year terms. In recent years there have been discussions about changing the composition of the Security Council. Decisions of the Council require nine yes votes. Each of the five permanent members, however, has veto power. When there is a threat to international peace, the Council generally first explores ways to settle the dispute peacefully, such as undertaking mediation efforts. If fighting has broken out, the Council may try to secure a cease-fire. If a truce or cessation of hostilities occurs, the Council may send in an international peacekeeping force to keep the opposing forces apart. The Council can also take measures to enforce its decisions, such as imposing economic sanctions or ordering an arms embargo.

As its title suggests, the *Economic and Social Council* coordinates the economic and social work of the United Nations. It is the central forum for discussing international economic and social issues and formulating policy recommendations. The Council receives input from numerous nongovernmental organizations that engage in lobbying and informational efforts.

(continued)

The United Nations (UN): Objectives and Structure | *Continued*

The *Trusteeship Council* was originally established to provide international supervision of eleven trust territories administered by seven member states. The Council's goal was to help these territories prepare for self-government or independence. By 1994 all of the trust territories had achieved this goal.

The *International Court of Justice* (known before 1945 as the World Court) is located in The Hague, Netherlands, and is the main judicial organ of the United Nations. It consists of fifteen judges elected by the General Assembly and the Security Council. The Court decides disputes among member states, but participation in the proceedings is voluntary. If, however, a state agrees to participate, it is obligated to comply with the Court's decision.

The *Secretariat* carries out the substantive and administrative work of the United Nations as authorized or directed by the General Assembly, the Security Council, and other organs. The head official is the Secretary General. The UN staff totals some 8,700 persons drawn from 160 countries. Aside from the headquarters in New York, personnel are assigned to UN offices in Geneva, Vienna, and Nairobi. ▲

ARMED INTERVENTION, INTERNATIONAL ORGANIZATIONS, AND INTERNATIONAL LAW

8.3 Evaluate how international law and organizations influence decisions by state authorities to use force.

The 1928 Pact of Paris (or Kellogg-Briand Pact) was an unsuccessful attempt to eliminate the use of force in international relations, outlawing "recourse to war for the solution of international controversies." Hope was placed in world peace through law in a system of collective security under the League of Nations. As such, collective security is different from collective defense—alliances or coalitions that rely ultimately on armed defense or military power rather than law.

The League of Nations tried to substitute law-abiding behavior for individual and collective-defense relations based on power, balance of power, and military might. Law-abiding states under collective-security arrangements enforce international law against law-breaking states. But the League of Nations seemed powerless to counter such aggressive actions as French intervention in Germany and the Italian capture of the Mediterranean island of Corfu (1923), the outbreak of the China-Japan War (1931), the Bolivia–Paraguay Chaco War (1932–1935), Italy's invasion of Ethiopia (1935), Germany's annexation of Austria and part of Czechoslovakia (1938), and finally the outbreak of World War II in 1939.

In an attempt to put the lessons of the interwar period to practical effect, the United Nations Charter (1945) does specify conditions under which force may legally be used:

1. Unilaterally in self-defense
2. Multilaterally when authorized by the UN Security Council "to maintain or restore international peace and security"
3. Multilaterally by regional collective defense action

Watch the **Video** "Toppling Hussein" at mypoliscilab.com

collective security
■ the idea that if one state behaved aggressively, other states had a legal right to enforce international law by taking collective action

the capabilities of law-abiding states against aggressors and other international lawbreakers.

The actual scope of collective security cooperation varies along a continuum. At one end are arrangements involving all states and covering all regions of the globe—universal arrangements. Members agree to respond collectively to aggression wherever it occurs. At the other end of the continuum is a concert of the great powers of the day. Their interest in peace may be global in scope or limited to particular regions. Unlike many alliances, there is no binding, ironclad commitment to collective action. Decisions are often made through negotiations and the emergence of a consensus. Although a concert requires that its members share essentially compatible views on the desired nature of the international order, power politics and competition among member states still occur. Such competition, however, falls short of overt hostility. In order to make the distinctions between the universal and concert approaches to collective security clearer, we will discuss several historical examples.

The Concert of Europe   As we noted in earlier chapters, the Concert of Europe effectively lasted to a greater or lesser degree from the Congress of Vienna (1815), which was convened to put Europe back together after the defeat of Napoleon, until the Crimean War (1854). In 1815, the major players were the remaining great powers of the day: Great Britain, Russia, Austria, and Prussia (with territory in parts of present-day Germany, Poland, and Russia). France was admitted in 1818. In keeping with the Concert approach, minor states were not members of this select circle, and the geographic interest of the members was limited to Europe. Disputes outside Europe stemmed from the often competing colonial ambitions of the major powers.

The critical, underlying consensus was that all members would abide by the territorial settlement of 1815. The status quo was to be changed only by consensus. If collective action were to be taken, it would be done through informal diplomatic negotiations, not by some formal mechanism such as those stipulated by the League of Nations Covenant or UN Charter. Some observers believe this informality accounts for the nearly four decades of peace among the major European powers in the first half of the 19th century.

Collective management of relations, as under the European Concert system, could be accomplished, some thought, by invoking universally accepted legal principles and norms. As such, Concert diplomacy can be understood as an early expression of collective security. That there are lawbreaking states that commit aggression or otherwise infringe on the sovereign prerogatives of other states was well understood. Law-abiding states, faced by aggression against any one of them, could band together to stop the violation. Any state could find security in the collective assurance that other states would come to its rescue. In sum, the Concert of Europe is an example of an international regime—one with rules of organization and norms of behavior.

League of Nations
■ international organization established after World War I—forerunner to the UN

The League of Nations   The idea of collective security was a cornerstone of the new League of Nations established in 1920 after World War I (1914–1918). The League was an attempt to institutionalize multilateral efforts toward maintenance of peace and prevention of the awful carnage that had just been experienced.

CASE Napoleon had lost the war, and France had good reason to fear the results of the peace conference held in Vienna beginning in 1814. The French emissary, Count Talleyrand, faced a seemingly impossible task—to rescue his country from the vengeance of its wartime adversaries. During Napoleon's wars, French armies had moved deliberately across Europe, forcibly conscripting troops along the way, overthrowing uncooperative princes, and leaving a trail of devastation in their wake. The anger and bitterness they left behind them promised little chance for a charitable outcome now that the tables were turned.

As a bishop of the Catholic Church, Talleyrand had been part of the *ancien régime,* the old order under the Bourbon dynasty that had been overthrown in the revolution that began in 1789. Always a political survivor, Talleyrand was extraordinarily flexible, jettisoning his clerical identity and navigating through the revolutionary turmoil virtually unscathed. He emerged in 1815 as part of a restoration movement designed to reestablish the prerevolutionary order in Europe as a whole and France in particular.

Talleyrand had to face France's now-formidable adversaries without any military or economic leverage to support his negotiating position. The victims of French aggression now had the opportunity to carve up France, dividing it among themselves or at least separating the country into such small pieces that it could no longer be a threat.

The most important delegations at Vienna were those representing the interests of the four great powers that prevailed following the defeat of France. Prince Metternich of Austria was the leading figure, known historically for his intelligence, cleverness, and diplomatic acumen—a man extremely adept at serving Austria's imperial interests. Playing lesser but still very important roles in constructing the settlement at Vienna were Tsar Alexander of Russia, Viscount Castlereagh of Britain, and Prince von Hardenberg of Prussia.

In the final analysis, Talleyrand was able to save France, but not through any charity felt by its erstwhile enemies. Instead, France was restored (territorially even slightly larger than it had been in 1789) only because it was in the interest of all of the great powers to do so. The French Revolution not only had transformed politics in France; it had also threatened the institution of monarchy in continental countries that had never previously experienced such challenges. From this perspective, strengthening European monarchies as legitimate institutions in the post-Napoleonic period meant returning the Bourbons to their "rightful" positions in France as well.

Beyond these considerations, a restored France contributed substantially to maintaining what the British had long favored as a centerpiece of foreign policy—a balance of power on the European continent to keep any one country from becoming too strong. For Austria, a restored France kept growing Prussian power at bay. Finally, the settlement also served Russian interests by maintaining a balance to its west, not just between Prussia and Austria, but also between both of them and France.

For France, it was a badly needed diplomatic triumph. Even though he lacked the military and other tangible resources to strengthen his negotiating position, Talleyrand accomplished his short-term goal. He restored France to legitimate standing in Europe as a great power, much as it had been for centuries preceding the defeat of Napoleon's empire. He was able to accomplish this because, in the course of negotiations, a restored France came to be understood as being in the interest of all of the great powers. More important for Europe as a whole, however, was the lasting influence of the Vienna settlement. It was the basis for a long peace that (with a few interruptions) would last for some ninety-nine years.

POINT Maintaining peace and security required international organization—bringing the parties together in a "concert"—a loose, but effective institutional arrangement based on generally accepted principles—the realist balance of power coupled with a liberal commitment to diplomatic engagement. Not just power, but ideas also mattered. ◢

Great hopes were placed in the League. It was meant to include all countries and to resist aggression everywhere; it was meant to be universal in scope. Thirty-two states attended the initial meeting that established the League. By 1938, there were fifty-seven members. All states were represented in the General Assembly, but the League Council was an inner circle consisting of great-power permanent members and several smaller powers that served on a rotating basis.

According to Article 16 of the League Covenant, its charter, states that engage in an act of aggression shall "*ipso facto* be deemed to have committed an act of war against all other Members of the League." All states were required to impose collective economic and diplomatic sanctions against the aggressor. The use of military action, however, was to be decided upon by the Council, which would recommend what each member should contribute to the military force. As a practical matter, however, there were technical difficulties in defining aggression with sufficient legal precision or clarity to be sufficient grounds for collective action in particular cases. Furthermore, all Council recommendations had to be agreed on unanimously, so both temporary as well as permanent members in effect had veto power. States unwilling or unable for one reason or another to take collective action could (and did) hide behind these legal ambiguities. Genuine commitment by League members to collective security fell short. The League's inability to deal with the aggression of the Axis powers (Germany, Italy, and Japan) in the 1930s led ultimately to the demise of the League of Nations and the outbreak of World War II in 1939.

The United States must also share a portion of the blame. The United States did not even join the League and was not a participant in the collective security system. President Woodrow Wilson had asserted extraordinary influence in the post–World War I settlements that led to enshrining collective security within the new League of Nations, but the U.S. Senate failed to ratify the League Covenant. As events would finally demonstrate, the League and its collective security system failed to keep the peace. World war began again in 1939, some twenty years after the first world war had ended.

The United Nations   During World War II, diplomats charged with constructing a postwar international system drew lessons from earlier failures. The term *United Nations* was used by President Franklin D. Roosevelt in 1942 when twenty-six states pledged their governments to continue fighting together against the Axis powers (Germany, Italy, and Japan). The UN Charter was drawn up by representatives of fifty countries at the United Nations Conference on International Organizations, which met in San Francisco in 1945. Delegates deliberated on the proposals worked out by representatives of China, the Soviet Union, the United Kingdom, and the United States at Dumbarton Oaks, in Washington, DC, from August to October in 1944. The charter was signed on June 26, 1945. The United Nations officially came into existence on October 24, 1945, when the charter had been ratified by the United States, China, France, the Soviet Union, the United Kingdom, and by a majority of other signatories.

As with the League, UN membership was to be universal in scope, all states participating in the General Assembly. Once again, however, the major powers at the time—the United States, the United Kingdom, France, the Soviet Union, and China (the victors in World War II over Germany and Japan)—became permanent

United Nations
■ an international organization created in 1945 with universal membership, dominated by the major powers in the Security Council

members of the Security Council. Article 42 of the UN Charter granted the Security Council the power to initiate collective military action. Veto power was also retained by the five permanent members. As a practical matter, then, military force or other sanctions could never be directed under UN Security Council auspices against any of these five major powers because any resolution to that effect certainly would be vetoed by the major power affected.

While the United Nations did not abandon collective security as a concept, it was supplemented by both **preventive diplomacy** and collective defense. Preventive diplomacy seeks to prevent fighting from occurring in the first place. Accordingly, the UN Security Council was granted legal and political authority to facilitate dialogue and negotiation between disputants.

As a form of international law enforcement, collective security seeks to dissuade states from committing aggression, which may entail taking offensive military operations against the designated aggressor; however, collective defense, supported by a legal framework allowed under Article 51 in the UN Charter, rests primarily on power and balance of power considerations. Alliances are formed to assure defense through mutual or collective efforts. If collective security and respect for international law fail to prevent aggression, states can still rely on their own power and that of their allies to provide defense. The central point is that the new United Nations retained the League's collective security or collective law-enforcement commitment but did not place exclusive reliance on it for assuring international security. States also would retain their sovereign rights to individual or collective defense in collaboration with other states in alliances or other power-based coalitions.

UN supporters contend that this significant modification of the League system has contributed substantially to the absence of world war since 1945. In times of high tension during the Cold War, the Security Council could not reach consensus on many issues. In these circumstances, states could still rely on their respective collective defense alliances.

One major UN-sponsored military operation occurred during the Korean War (1950–1953). This came about only because the Soviet delegation walked out of the meeting and was not present to veto a U.S.-sponsored resolution that committed troops to turning back the communist forces that had entered southern Korea in June 1950. Even in the most difficult Cold War times, however, there was at least sufficient consensus in the Security Council to authorize a number of peacekeeping missions to the Middle East, the Mediterranean (Cyprus), Africa, and Asia, where core interests of Security Council members were typically not at stake.

Nothing in the UN Charter forbids a state to help itself when Security Council measures fail to have the desired effect. Its inherent right as a sovereign state to defend itself either by its own means or in collaboration with others remains intact.

Limitations to Collective Security   Why has more not been accomplished by organizations concerned with collective security? Universal and concert approaches to collective security suffer from at least six problems.[1]

preventive diplomacy ■ efforts taken to address international problems with constructive approaches, avoiding if possible the deterioration of relations that could lead to armed conflict

---

[1]Mark T. Clark, "The Trouble with Collective Security," *Orbis*, vol. 39, no. 2 (Spring 1995): 241 *et passim*.

First is confusion about what is cause and what is effect in the relation between collective security and peace. Does collective security encourage peace, or does peace have to exist in order for collective security arrangements to be instituted? In other words, both the League of Nations and the United Nations were created after exhausting, devastating wars. These times of postwar positive expectations did not last very long, and the usefulness of such organizations should be judged on how they perform in difficult (not just in good) times. When fascism reared its ugly head in the 1930s in Europe and Asia, the League ultimately failed. When the Cold War began in the late 1940s, many realists subsequently argued that the United Nations had become more of an arena for Soviet–American competition than an ameliorating factor in reducing East-West tensions.

Second is a gap between states' expressed commitments to collective security and their actions. For a number of reasons, states are sometimes reluctant to fulfill their international commitments even when the act of aggression seems blatant. Consider, for example, the international reaction to Iraq's invasion of neighboring Kuwait in 1991. This would seem to have been an easy test for the efficacy of collective security—flagrant aggression by a dictatorial state against a country with significant oil reserves. Yet there was a great deal of hand-wringing in capitals around the world, and it took U.S. leadership and some arm-twisting to put the coalition together.

Third, timing is often a problem. Unlike an alliance, which traditionally has an identified enemy, war plans, and joint training, collective security efforts do not have these established elements. Consider again the first Gulf War against Iraq, which required six months of training and planning before Operation Desert Storm was launched. Even Operation Enduring Freedom, the second war against Iraq, which was launched in 2003, took months of planning and preparation. The point is that putting together a coalition, deciding on who contributes what, and devising a strategy take time, which may lead in some cases to a belated military response.

Fourth, by relying on collective security's multilateralist response, there is always the possibility that the virtues of unilateralism (actions taken by one state) will be overlooked. While a collective security effort offers the greatest amount of pooled or collective power, it does so at the expense of flexibility. Numerous states will doubtless want to influence policy decisions. A unilateral response may provide less power but greater flexibility in terms of planning and implementation.

Perhaps the best combination was evident in the 1991 Gulf War, in which an international coalition was formed under the leadership of the United States. The United States put the powerful coalition together and was in the driver's seat in planning the military strategy for the campaign and actual deployment of coalition forces. By 2003, however, U.S. efforts to re-create a large international coalition to overthrow Saddam Hussein were stymied by contending assessments of the degree of threat posed by Iraq, the status of its weapons of mass destruction program, and differing assessments as to the potential for success on the part of UN weapons inspectors.

Given the tremendous gap in military power between the United States and other countries that widened even further during the 1990s, the United States had, from its point of view, the best of all worlds—supreme military power plus flexibility in terms of planning and implementing the invasion of Iraq. But while the

U.S.-led invasion was a military success in terms of overthrowing the Iraqi regime, the alienation of important NATO allies found the United States scrambling for support in postinvasion efforts to stabilize Iraq.

Fifth, as collective-security obligations typically call for some response, it is possible that a minor war could escalate into a major war. For example, a small war between two states in Africa might not draw a great deal of international attention. On the other hand, if there were an automatic collective-security mechanism in operation that demanded a response to any breach of the peace, the possibility exists that with greater international involvement a small brushfire war might expand or escalate to become a larger regional or even global conflict.

Finally, collective security can imply a commitment to the status quo. The Gulf War aside, concern for threats to the peace are paramount. Issues of justice tend to be secondary concerns. When questions of justice are ignored and blame is not assigned, there is a good chance that the collective security mechanism might break down due to disagreements among states on the legitimacy of the cause.

Peacekeeping: Managing and Controlling Conflicts

Peacekeeping can be understood as an extension of collective security thinking to cover conflicts that threaten international peace and security, particularly in the regions where these conflicts are being played out. Resolving conflicts involving states and nongovernmental parties are often decades-long projects at best, particularly when territorial issues are linked to competing national, ethnic, or tribal claims. Sometimes the most that can be achieved is to manage these conflicts—to contain and keep them from becoming violent as constructive steps are taken to address the difficult, divisive issues involved.

peacekeeping ■ task performed by UN or other multilateral forces in an effort to keep conflicting parties from resorting (or returning) to armed hostilities

Since the end of World War II, even at the height of Cold War tensions, important efforts have been undertaken to keep the peace by stationing multinational UN forces, so-called Blue Helmets, or other national and multinational contingents on patrol in territorial border areas. The goal is to provide a buffer or separation between conflicting parties and perform other functions necessary for the security and welfare of populations and the conflicting parties. At various times and often for extended periods, one could find peacekeepers in such diverse places as the Mediterranean island of Cyprus, the Sinai desert, sub-Saharan Africa, the Balkan area of southeastern Europe, central Asia and Cambodia, and East Timor in Southeast Asia.

UN peacekeeping forces have never been intended to fight wars. Accordingly, they have usually been relatively small, lightly armed contingents, capable militarily only of modest defense of their own positions if they come under attack by any party. During the Cold War, peacekeepers were drawn from the national militaries of neutral or nonaligned states, often with equal representation of NATO and Warsaw Pact members as well. Their purpose was to capitalize on the moral authority drawn from their position as peacekeepers accepted in principle by all contending parties. As such, they were not to intervene in these conflicts, much less take sides. They were only to monitor the peace and to provide a necessary presence to dissuade the parties from resorting to force against each other.

Though never without problems, peacekeeping has worked best in these circumstances. A vexing problem, however, is what to do when a government

collapses, civil war breaks out, no one is in charge, or widespread famine occurs. In such cases there are no parties to agree to a UN presence. This occurred in Somalia in 1993 when the regime collapsed and domestic disorder broke out. An international operation organized by the United States was initially dispatched to ensure the delivery of food supplies. Permission was not requested as Somalia was not a unified state but rather a collection of warring clans. What is known as mission creep subsequently occurred: The relief effort gave way to an attempt to enforce peace—a substantial expansion of the original humanitarian mission.

Long-term civil unrest in East Timor came to a head in 1999 when residents of this former Portuguese colony taken by Indonesia in 1975 voted to become independent of Indonesia in a referendum watched by UN observers. Opposed to the outcome, elements of the Indonesian security forces cracked down on the East Timorese population, murdering residents and committing other human rights violations. With UN backing and concurrence of the Indonesian government in Jakarta, a multinational coalition led by Australia ultimately intervened to restore order.

The Somalia and East Timor cases typify the sorts of challenges the international community continues to face. Efforts have thus been undertaken to expand beyond the more limited peacekeeping or peace-monitoring roles to include peace enforcement and even peacemaking. These UN Blue Helmets lacked the military capability to perform these latter tasks, which are less peace-oriented than they sound; they really amount to using force to "make the peace" or enforce it. Pressed by compelling circumstances, performance of these collective security tasks has evolved well beyond both the original, more limited understanding of peacekeeping and the forces detailed for that purpose. Indeed, the great powers in the UN Security Council have been late to respond or reluctant to authorize or provide necessary resources for humanitarian interventions in places as diverse as Rwanda in central Africa and Darfur in Sudan.

ALLIANCES AND COALITIONS

8.4 Evaluate the reasons why state authorities seek allies or coalition partners to enhance the security of their states and societies.

Policymakers in a formal alliance or less formal coalition with like-minded states may decide to participate in multilateral collective security or peacekeeping actions under UN auspices or, alternatively in collective-defense actions. **Alliances** are coalitions of states, usually involving formal, long-term commitments; however, not all **coalitions** are alliances, at least not in the formal usage of the term. In 1991 President George H. W. Bush organized a coalition of some 40 states under UN auspices to drive Iraq's military forces out of Kuwait and to deter any further Iraqi aggression against other states in the region, particularly Saudi Arabia.

NATO is an example of an alliance that has been around for more than 60 years. More than an alliance, NATO is also an international or intergovernmental organization with established institutions, bureaucratic processes and routines, and command structures that facilitate the performance of its activities.

Alliances or coalitions can be offensive in character, as in World War II when Germany (then including Austria and other territories in central Europe) allied with Italy and Japan to form the Axis powers. Most alliances now, however, are defensive in orientation, pooling military forces and other resources for collective

alliance ■ a formal agreement between two (bilateral) or more (multilateral) states to cooperate in security matters—a formal security coalition of states with specified commitments

defense. Offensive alliances seek to upset the existing order or balance of power, whereas defensive alliances typically aim to maintain it, usually opting for the status quo—keeping things more or less the way they are.

This pooling of resources has the obvious advantage of spreading the burden of the costs of defense. According to realists, if states confront each other with relatively equal military capability, a balance of power exists, and aggression is less likely to occur. This was the logic behind NATO, created in 1949 both to deter Soviet aggression during what had become a "cold" war and to incorporate the new Federal Republic of Germany into a security framework so that past aggressive behavior by Germany in two 20th-century world wars would not be repeated.

Although allies and friendly states frequently have differences among themselves, the alliances and other coalitions they form do provide arenas or forums for both cooperative and collaborative activities. Even major disputes between allies, as between Greece and Turkey, both members of NATO, are usually better managed within an alliance framework that allows other alliance members to participate in helping find mutually acceptable approaches to the problems at hand. Cooperation even in assisting allies to manage or settle conflicts, therefore, is to be found primarily within an alliance or other coalition. Allies or coalition partners work together to strengthen their individual and collective positions in competition with other states and opposing alliances or coalitions. In other words, cooperation within an alliance and competition between an alliance or coalition and its adversaries typically characterize these relations.

Less formal coalitions may not have alliance status. The close relations that the United States has maintained with Israel, for example, include an agreement to cooperate on security matters that stops short of being a formal alliance. In large part, it is the United States that has avoided formally allying with Israel, in fear that doing so would undercut U.S. ability to work with and influence Arab states. Although strains in U.S.-Israeli relations have shown themselves from time to time, Israeli need for U.S. support and American commitment to the survival of Israel have kept the bilateral coalition intact.

Other coalitions formed to exercise security functions under the UN Charter do not qualify as formal alliances. The multinational coalition formed in 1990 and 1991 to liberate Kuwait from occupation by Iraqi forces is an example. Although balance-of-power, collective-defense considerations played a central role, the purpose was also to enforce a legal, collective security mandate under UN Security Council auspices. Once Kuwait was liberated, the coalition dissolved. The much less robust coalition led by the United States in 2003 to overthrow the Saddam Hussein regime was also blessed by a UN Security Council resolution, although there was dispute on the Council on its interpretation.

coalition ◼ formal or informal grouping of actors that share some common purpose or purposes

NATO—The North Atlantic Treaty Organization

NATO now has twenty-eight members. Sixteen are from Western Europe and North America: the United States, the Federal Republic of Germany, the United Kingdom, France, Italy, Canada, Belgium, Netherlands, Luxembourg, Denmark, Norway, Iceland, Greece, Turkey, Portugal, and Spain. Additions from the Cold War–Soviet sphere of influence include former Warsaw Pact (1955–1991)

members—Hungary, Poland, Bulgaria, Romania; Slovakia and the Czech Republic (a single country, Czechoslovakia, from 1918 until 1993 when the two separated); Croatia and Slovenia in the former Yugoslav republics; Albania (Warsaw Pact member, 1955–1968); and the Baltic republics—Estonia, Latvia, and Lithuania—*de facto* part of the Soviet Union until 1992. This geographic expansion eastward by NATO was originally quite controversial to the extent that such extensions were seen as threatening by the Russian Federation or other successor republics to the Soviet Union, which broke up at the end of 1991.

As one British diplomat somewhat undiplomatically asserted at the time NATO was formed in 1949, the alliance was established with three purposes in mind: (1) to keep the Americans "in" (i.e., U.S. participation in assuring European security), (2) to keep the Russians "out" (i.e., containing the Soviet Union from further expansion of its sphere of influence into Western Europe), and (3) to keep the Germans "down" (i.e., from rising yet again as a threat to other countries in Europe). Undiplomatic as they sounded, these three phrases did capture three key security concerns among the charter members of NATO.

A regional international organization that performs collective defense functions consistent with Article 51 of the UN Charter, NATO's geographic scope was originally limited to the European and North Atlantic area. For its part, the United States in 1949 did not want to be placed in the position of defending against attacks on British, French, Dutch, Portuguese, or Belgian colonies in Asia, Africa, or Latin America. As European empires were dismantled in the 1960s and subsequent decades, the United States tried to get NATO countries to support American efforts in such places as Vietnam and the Gulf; however, European countries (reluctant to engage in conflicts beyond the geographic scope authorized by the North Atlantic Treaty for NATO involvement) chose not to participate, identifying such contingencies as "out of area."

An attack against any NATO member is considered an attack against all. Although the North Atlantic Treaty provides for consultation by the allies if any member is threatened, in the event of such an attack, there is no provision for an automatic use of force. Force may be used, but the alliance is pledged under Article 5 only to take "such action as it deems necessary . . . to restore and maintain the security of the North Atlantic area." Nevertheless, the NATO alliance proved to be a substantial bulwark for maintaining peace in Europe during and after the Cold War, routinizing collaboration among its members on security matters. Indeed, Article 5 was invoked after the terrorist attack on the United States on September 11, 2001.

As a practical matter, NATO's principal adversary during the Cold War was the Soviet Union and the Soviet-led Warsaw Pact—an alliance formed in 1955 and composed of the Soviet Union, the German Democratic Republic (East Germany), Poland, Czechoslovakia, Hungary, Romania, and Bulgaria. The long Cold War struggle over more than four decades was marked by crises and years of high tension interspersed with periods of *détente* or reduced tensions. At the end of the Cold War, the Warsaw Pact was dismantled as the Soviet Union itself dissolved into the Russian Federation and other new states formed from its component republics; but NATO survived.

Questions were raised in the 1990s concerning NATO's post–Cold War future, but the alliance proved useful as a means to secure continuing American

Nationalism and Civil Conflict | SLIDESHOW

The year 1992 marked the beginning of direct international organization involvement in the civil wars. Initially a small **UN** Protection Force (**UNPROFOR**) was deployed. But as mass killings continued and **UN** forces came under attack, **NATO** carried out bombing missions against Serbian targets. In this photo the commander of **UN** forces in Bosnia greets local inhabitants.

Aside from **UN** peacekeepers, diplomatic efforts, and the use of **NATO** military power, international organizations played an important role once the wars ended in late 1995. Here former Yugoslav president Slobodan Milosevic appears at the International Criminal Tribunal for the former Yugoslavia. The five-year-long trial ended without a verdict, but Milosevic died in prison in 2006.

ARGUMENT-COUNTERARGUMENT | Security as a Collective Good

The free-rider concept is an idea in public- or collective-goods theory—that others who make no payment or contributions themselves to providing the public or collective good are able to benefit from the contributions of one or a few who single-handedly or jointly provide the public good.

ARGUMENT In the classic case of those who finance or build a lighthouse on a seacoast, the lighthouse provides a benefit to ships or ship companies that have not paid for the light they are using to guide themselves at night. Access to the light from a lighthouse cannot effectively be limited only to those who have paid for it; access is universal to any ship or boat passing by. So it is with providers of security who pay the costs for security that benefits others who pay nothing (free riders) or pay less than they otherwise would have to pay (referred to here as reduced-fare riders) for this public- or collective-goods benefit. In principle, all members should pay a share of the costs proportionate to their economic capabilities as measured, perhaps, by GDP. This would avoid the free-rider problem and reduce resentment on the part of the state that feels it is bearing an excessive amount of the cost.

COUNTERARGUMENT In practical terms, some countries such as the United States pay far more than others (some "reduced-fare" riders, others not paying anything at all) for the security that an alliance such as NATO provides. Although leaders in these organizations are instrumental in providing security as a collective good, they are actually doing so in their own self-interest—not out of charity for others. Thus, these leader states may try to have others contribute more, but they need not expect all to comply with these demands. Such an asymmetric distribution of costs is typical in most forms of multilateral cooperation, whether in an alliance or other international organization. As such, leadership has its own rewards for states assuming this role.

APPLICATION Let's take the above logic one step further. In the case of an alliance in which one state pays a disproportionate cost, what do you think would logically happen to the alliance if the threat it is designed to counter went away? This scenario and question arose in the early 1990s with the collapse of the Soviet Union and the disintegration of its Warsaw Pact alliance. Why should NATO continue to exist? But it does, so how do you think this state of affairs came about?

commitment to European security. In the last half of the decade, NATO's well-developed organizational infrastructure facilitated carrying out military operations in the Balkans, both in Bosnia-Herzegovina and in Kosovo. In the post-9/11 era, NATO established a new precedent in 2003 by taking command of the international peacekeeping force in Afghanistan.

NATO's headquarters is in Brussels, and its military arm is located near Mons in the French-speaking part of Belgium, south of Brussels. The military arm is headed by an American four-star general who holds the title of Supreme Allied Commander Europe (SACEUR) and also is the senior commander of U.S. forces in Europe. By contrast, the position of secretary general at NATO headquarters in Brussels is a civilian post held historically by European members of the alliance. In addition to serving as a collective defense alliance, NATO may also be called on under UN mandate to perform collective security and other security and peacekeeping tasks.

Alliances as Collective Goods

When alliances are successful, security is the **collective good** (or public good, as it is sometimes called) they produce. Canada and the United States formed a bilateral alliance in the 1950s known as the North American Air (now Aerospace) Defense Command (NORAD). For its part, the United States maintains important bilateral alliances with a number of countries, including Japan and the Republic of Korea. Both Canada and the United States also belong to NATO, with its twenty-eight member states.

A key political question in alliances is who will pay—and how much—for the collective good. Because member countries of alliances differ in capabilities, their contributions cannot be equal. Quite apart from their greater economic capability to pay more, countries such as the United States, which assume leading roles in alliances such as NATO, often pay proportionately more than countries playing less of a leading role. Some member countries pay a premium—more than their fair share—while others pay less, a reduced-fare price for the security provided by an alliance or other coalition. Politics within alliances such as NATO and other coalitions have often focused on burden sharing and the **free-rider** problem, adjusting the distribution of costs among members in the interest of greater equity.

For some observers, the very success of NATO spells its ultimate doom. The conditions that gave rise to NATO and sustained it for forty Cold War years—the Soviet or communist threat—no longer exist. The Soviet Union collapsed in 1991, and its own military alliance involving Eastern European states, the Warsaw Pact, also dissolved. Cold War fears had encouraged cooperation in the West and prompted the European members of NATO to defer to broader U.S. foreign policy objectives. Furthermore, it was under the umbrella of U.S. security guarantees that Western European economic recovery and development occurred. Without the Soviet threat, NATO was in search of a new role.

Did NATO need a new threat or new set of risks to provide it a renewed sense of purpose and unity? It was initially thought that "political instability" might be an appropriate rallying cry. But, for some observers, NATO's inability to come to grips initially with the war in the former Yugoslavia was disappointing. Notwithstanding differences among the NATO allies, the organization eventually launched combined operations in the last half of the 1990s, first in Bosnia-Herzegovina, then in Kosovo near the Albanian border. Others have been wary about the future of democracy in Russia, believing NATO must continue in effect as an insurance policy against any significant change of regime or orientation in Russia that in the future might pose new threats to other states in Europe and the North Atlantic area.

NATO's importance was apparent after the terrorist attacks on the World Trade Center in New York and the Pentagon outside Washington, DC, on September 11, 2001. U.S. allies in NATO rallied quickly, invoking Article 5 for the first time in NATO's history and supporting the U.S. war effort in Afghanistan against terrorist bases and the Taliban regime. Support for the United States took various forms, including Germany's assumption of some U.S. air patrol responsibilities in North Atlantic air space, which then allowed the U.S. Air Force to reallocate these aircraft to the war effort. NATO members have also played an important role in providing peacekeeping forces in Afghanistan. The alliance was hurt, however, when divisions arose over how to deal with Saddam Hussein's Iraq in 2002–2003. The British, Spanish, and Italian governments were among those that supported the U.S. decision to go to war against Iraq, while the French, Germans, and others were adamant that strengthening the UN weapons inspection teams was the way to go.

National positions within alliances and in other coalitions shift, of course, in different times and in different contingencies. In 2011, for example, the French, British, and American allies coalesced once again to advance a common interest—as indeed they had many times in the past during and after World War II. Citing the threat to people in Libya posed by Muammar Kaddafi's regime, the UN Security Council concurred in a unanimous 10–0 vote (albeit with five abstentions including Russia, China, Germany, India, and Brazil) to authorize the use of force by the coalition to relieve pressure on Libyans under siege by Kaddafi's air and ground units. The French already having recognized the rebels in eastern Libya as the legitimate government of the entire country, the three coalition partners diplomatically worked out differences among them as to what should be done by whom, when, and how. Working together, the three Cold War "western allies" found common ground and successfully persuaded naysayers on the Security Council not to vote against (much less veto in the case of Russia and China) the resolution authorizing the use of force.

CONCLUSION

We noted at the beginning of this chapter that the International Court of Justice (ICJ) will only accept cases referred to it by states. Even when it accepts a case, the verdict could be nonconclusive, perhaps reflecting divisions among states themselves. This was evident in the question of whether the threat or use of nuclear weapons is contrary to the rules of international law.

This example makes the point that the expansion of global civil society—based in part on the rule of law and the role of international organizations—remains a work in progress. It is important to remember that international law and international organizations were created by and for states as noted in the case of commercial interests explaining the 16th-century expansion of international law. Similarly, the concept of just war was developed in part because it was in the interest of states. The same logic has been applied in more recent years to the growth in international law as applied to human rights and the environment.

The best example, however, of state interests driving the establishment of international organizations involves collective security arrangements such as NATO, an alliance originally designed to protect the most basic core security interests of its member states. At times, such alliances may also become the basis for peacekeeping missions with justification based upon a combination of security interests and international legal norms.

It is to be expected, therefore, that state interests will limit the extent to which international law and international organizations are able to place constraints on state actions. But the interesting question is how the continual expansion of globalization may force states in their own self-interest to place greater reliance on international law and international organizations.

✔•[Study and Review the Post-Test & Chapter Exam at mypoliscilab.com

LEARNING OBJECTIVES REVIEW

8.1 Identify the multi-century construction and sources of international law and critique the norms and rules developed in global civil society.

The globalization project, facilitated by telecommunications, transportation, and other technologies, has reached the far corners of the Earth. The growth of international law and less-formal rules or customary practices intended to serve the enlightened self-interests of both state and nonstate actors has accompanied this ever-expanding globalization and global governance of matters occurring outside of state boundaries.

KEY TERMS

Global civil society 262
International organizations (IOs) 262
Norms 262
International law 262
International Criminal Court 262
International regimes 263
Natural law 264
Just war 264
Pacta sunt servanda 264

Customary international law 265
Multilateralism 265

ADDITIONAL READINGS

Paul F. Diehl and Brian Frederking (eds.), *The Politics of Global Governance: International Organizations in an Interdependent World*, 4th ed. (Boulder: Lynne Rienner, 2010). On global governance and the roles international and nongovernmental organizations play.

John Rawls, *The Law of Peoples* (Cambridge, MA: Harvard University Press, 1999). Rawls revisits the idea of public reason that underlies law.

Don Eberly, *The Rise of Global Civil Society: Building Communities and Nations from the Bottom Up* (New York: Encounter Books, 2008). On global civil society as a communitarian idea.

William A. Schabas, *An Introduction to the International Criminal Court* (Cambridge, UK: Cambridge University Press, 2011). The author addresses international criminal accountability of individuals responsible for genocide, war crimes, and other crimes against humanity.

8.2 Describe how the development of international law in global civil society was and is impacted by matters of war and peace, economics, human rights, the environment, and criminal accountability.

Earlier development of legal rules for diplomacy, war, and international commerce have continued, but now have expanded to cover human rights, the environment, and individual accountability before international tribunals. The rule of law is central to global governance and the idea of a global civil society.

KEY TERMS

Jus ad bellum 266
Jus in bello 266
Geneva Conventions 266
Most-favored nation (MFN) 267

World Trade Organization (WTO) 267
Liquidity 267
Global warming 270
International Court of Justice (ICJ) 271

ADDITIONAL READINGS

Michael Walzer, *Just and Unjust Wars* (New York: Basic Books, 1977, 2006). A must-read on moral questions related to warfare.

David Fisher, *Morality and War: Can War Be Just in the Twenty-First Century?* (Oxford, UK: Oxford University Press, 2011). More recent coverage of law and warfare in the current period.

William A. Schabas, *International Law*, 6th ed. (Cambridge, UK: Cambridge University Press, 2008). One of a large number of books providing an overview of international law.

8.3 Evaluate how international law and organizations influence decisions by state authorities to use force.

Global governance related to interstate conflict includes relying on preventive diplomacy, collective security, and collective-defense arrangements—states coming together multilaterally in international organizations if possible to keep war from occurring or at least to minimize the adverse effects on lives and property that accompany the use of force. When wars have ended, international and nongovernmental organizations participate alongside states in postwar reconstruction and development efforts.

KEY TERMS

Collective security 274
Collective defense 275
League of Nations 278

United Nations 280
Preventive diplomacy 281
Peacekeeping 283

ADDITIONAL READINGS

Ramesh Thakur, *The United Nations, Peace and Security: From Collective Security to the Responsibility to Protect* (Cambridge, UK: Cambridge University Press, 2006) and Peter G. Danchin and Horst Fischer (eds.), *United Nations Reform and the New Collective Security* (Cambridge, UK: Cambridge University Press, 2010). Both volumes cover the role of the UN in maintaining international peace and security.

Inis L. Claude, Jr., *Power and International Relations* (New York: Random House, 1962). Still one of the best, now classic discussions that contrasts the balance of power (and collective defense) with the rule of law and law enforcement against aggression (collective security).

8.4 Evaluate the reasons why state authorities seek allies or coalition partners to enhance the security of their states and societies.

The power of a state acting alone rarely is sufficient to provide security. As a result, states frequently look to other states in coalitions or alliances to provide assurances, give their support, and share their capabilities.

KEY TERMS

Alliance 284
Coalition 284
Collective good 288
Free rider 288

ADDITIONAL READINGS

Gulnur Aybet and Rebecca R. Moore (eds.), *NATO: In Search of a Vision* (Washington, D.C.: Georgetown University Press, 2010), and Rebecca R. Moore, *NATO's New Mission: Projecting Stability in a Post-Cold War World* (Santa Barbara, CA: Praeger, 2007). On the present and future of the NATO alliance.

Mancur Olson's *The Logic of Collective Action* (Cambridge, MA: Harvard University Press, 1965, 1971). The classic source on collective goods theory.

CHAPTER REVIEW

1. International law began gaining prominence in Holland because of _____.
   a. increased international commerce associated with advancing sea transportation technologies.
   b. increased military tension between Holland and Denmark.
   c. increased political interaction between Holland, Russia, and England.
   d. decreased transaction costs associated with sea transportation.

2. _____ and _____ are the most concrete forms of international law.
   a. Norms and Customary Law
   b. Judicial Briefs and Treaties
   c. Conventions and Norms
   d. Treaties and Conventions

3. Customary law is a form of international law in which a practice has not yet been _____ but is considered law by its widespread practice.
   a. written
   b. signed
   c. codified
   d. interpreted

4. International legal precedents play what role in shaping international law and society?
   a. establishing wider acceptance and legitimacy of the rule of law
   b. allowing judges to expand their opinions to a wider audience
   c. establishing the ICC as a purveyor of international norms
   d. creating legitimacy for the ICC

5. _____ is an example of the institutionalization of a norm that shapes global society and the behavior of states.
   a. Unilateralism
   b. Multilateralism
   c. Customary practices
   d. Human rights

6. The 1949 Geneva Conventions on the Laws of War had what shortcoming? They
   a. failed to address intrastate war (civil war).
   b. were not signed by the United States.
   c. were never codified.
   d. did not protect soldiers in prison camps.

7. Which of the following is an example of a recent development in the economic and commercial sector of international law?
   a. Anti-Bribery Treaty
   b. Anti-Lobbying Treaty
   c. non-negotiable trade compacts
   d. Most Favored Nation (MFN) inclusive trading pacts

8. According to the text, what is one important human rights convention that immediately followed the Tokyo and Nuremburg war crimes trials?
   a. International Convention on the Suppression and the Punishment of the Crime of Apartheid
   b. UN Genocide Convention
   c. Convention on the Elimination of All Forms of Discrimination
   d. Convention Against Torture and Other Cruel, Inhuman or Degrading Treatment

9. According to the authors, what protocol represents the first major international attempt to control environmental damage collectively?
   a. 1900 Nairobi Protocol
   b. 2010 Copenhagen Protocol
   c. 1987 Montreal Protocol
   d. 1997 Kyoto Protocol

10. The 1998 Rome Treaty was designed to establish a new statute for what international body?
    a. The Hague
    b. The UN Security Council
    c. The International Criminal Court
    d. The European Court of Human Rights

11. Article 2 of the UN Charter commits UN member states to _____.
    a. refrain . . . from the threat or use of force [toward] any state.
    b. participate collectively in all UN programs.
    c. protect collectively the headquarters of the UN [and its member states].
    d. provide logistical support [for any and all] UN peacekeeping missions.

12. _____ is the essential idea of collective security.
    a. Every nation for itself
    b. All against one
    c. All against all
    d. Peace at all costs

13. Collective security is understood as an alternative to what type of general security system?
    a. collective action pacts
    b. the Vienna Treaty of 1815
    c. the Geneva Accords
    d. balance-of-power mechanisms

14. The main difference between the UN collective security system and that of the League of Nations was what?
    a. The UN placed more of the burden on individual states to maintain order within their territorial boundaries.
    b. The UN did not place exclusive reliance on collective security as the sole mechanism to maintain international peace.
    c. The UN included members states that were fundamentally opposed to the idea of war.
    d. The UN excluded any and all states that were hostile to the great powers of the time.

15. What is one potential problem of collective security arrangements?
    a. A potential exists for them to create larger conflicts.
    b. States will not get along and end up going to war with each other.
    c. They will compete with the UN.
    d. The UN will make it difficult for individual states to create their own national armies.

16. Offensive security alliances are primarily used for what purpose?
    a. to engage in military training exercises
    b. to seek advantage, upsetting the existing order or balance of power
    c. to create close military relations between or among states
    d. to pursue arms control and thus reduce defense expenditures

17. What collective good do military alliances seek to produce?
    a. security
    b. power
    c. military capabilities
    d. peace

18. The text defines which of the following as a key political question for military alliances to consider?
    a. Who will contribute the most troops?
    b. Where will the headquarters be located?
    c. Who will lead the alliance?
    d. Who will pay for the alliance and how much?

19. Which of the following agreements qualifies as a formal alliance, as defined in the text?
    a. the 2003 Iraq War coalition
    b. the 1991 Gulf War coalition
    c. the North Atlantic Treaty Organization (NATO)
    d. the U.S.-Israeli military partnership

20. The example of NATO illustrates which of the following ideas concerning military alliances?
    a. The purpose of alliances can shift over time.
    b. Once the purpose of an alliance is accomplished, it should be dissolved.
    c. Only large alliances are valuable.
    d. Military alliances should always act in a unanimous manner or risk dissolving.

Interstate Conflict

"War is a matter of vital importance to the state; the province of life or death; the road to survival or ruin. It is mandatory that it be thoroughly studied."
—Sun Tzu, The Art of War, c. 500 B.C.E.

"War is the last of all things to go according to plan."—Thucydides,
The Peloponnesian War, c. 404 B.C.E.

LEARNING OBJECTIVES

9.1 Explain how international relations practitioners use the rationality assumption to determine when it is in their interest to use force.

9.2 Illustrate how the international system, the individual and group, and the state and societal levels of analysis help to understand the causes of interstate conflicts.

9.3 Evaluate the concept of war as an instrument of policy by linking military and other capabilities to the national goals or objectives policymakers seek to achieve.

9.4 Illustrate how military force-employment doctrines of deterrence, defense, and warfighting apply not only to great-power strategic nuclear arsenals, but also to states with smaller arsenals.

9.5 Apply moral or ethical and legal considerations to both the decision to use force or go to war (*jus ad bellum*) and conduct in the war itself (*jus in bello*).

9.6 Describe the diverse purposes that motivate states and the criteria state authorities use to decide whether or not to intervene militarily in another country.

With the peaceful overthrow of authoritarian leaders in Tunisia and then Egypt in early 2011, many citizens of another north African country, Libya, hoped for the same outcome. But the country's dictator for the past thirty years, Colonel Muammar Kaddafi, had other ideas. His response was to try to crush the uprising militarily. As he moved ever closer to achieving this goal while, at the same time, vowing brutal retribution against those who rose up against him, leaders from Western Europe and North America were unsure how to respond. The last thing the Obama administration wanted was to become engaged in a war involving another Muslim country at a time when it was trying to extricate itself from Iraq and Afghanistan. The French president, Nicolas Sarkozy, however, was adamant that the West needed to respond militarily to support the rebels once threats directed at the Libyan leader failed to work. While the United States had the firepower, it also wanted diplomatic cover, and hence U.S. secretary of state Hillary Clinton assiduously worked to get at least a few African and Middle Eastern states to publicly support the use of NATO military forces.

The hope of the Western diplomats was that the limited use of force against Kaddafi's military would not only provide protection for the rebels, who lacked training and weapons, but encourage Kaddafi to leave the country. U.S. drone attacks and NATO airstrikes on military targets were followed by the introduction of small teams of Special Forces to train the ragtag rebel army, and eventually laser-guided missiles were employed as the extent of NATO engagement expanded.

Read and **Listen** to **Chapter 9** at **mypoliscilab.com**

Study and **Review** the **Pre-Test & Flashcards** at **mypoliscilab.com**

The Libyan case seemed to be the classic challenge faced by practitioners who decide to engage in interstate conflict—what types and how much force is required to achieve one's political objectives? Ideally, the mere threat of force would be all that is required. That failed, and hence the allied discussion became one on the application of force. The fear of the Obama administration was that even limited military action was the beginning of a slippery slope that ultimately could result in a military stalemate on the ground, the partition of Libya, and a dictator remaining in power who in the past conducted and supported acts of international terrorism as well as engaged in efforts to develop nuclear weapons. The challenge for policymakers, as noted by Thucydides, is that it is impossible to clearly foresee how what might begin as a relatively small-scale interstate conflict with the limited application of military force could evolve into a full-scale interstate war. In this case, following an October 20th, 2011 attack on his convoy by NATO warplanes, Kaddafi was taken alive, beaten, and then killed by opposition Libyan forces.

Wars are the most destructive of human activities. The enormous human costs of war have not prevented countless repetitions of the phenomenon throughout human history in all parts of the world. An estimated two million people lost their lives on the battlefields during Europe's Thirty Years' War (1618–1648), 2.5 million during the French Revolution and Napoleonic Wars (1792–1815), 7.7 million in World War I (1914–1918), and 13 million in World War II (1939–1945). Such estimates do not even include the death and injury of civilian populations, nor do they adequately reflect the devastation caused by civil wars (wars within a state). The great American Civil War of 1861–1865, for example, resulted in more American deaths—600,000—than all other wars fought by Americans from 1776 to the present, combined.

It is not surprising, therefore, that over the centuries observers of international relations have been primarily interested in understanding patterns of conflict and cooperation among various types of political units and have studied their history from the ancient Greek city-states of the fifth century B.C.E. to modern nation-states. The question "Why do wars occur?" is not all that different from the question "What factors account for peace?" and international relations practitioners apply various theories to make predictions of future patterns or trends in interstate conflict. Indeed, war and peace can be viewed as opposite sides of the same coin.

interstate conflict ■
use of armed force in conflict between two or more states

In this chapter the focus is primarily on interstate conflicts. The term could be applied to interstate disputes on such matters as trade or monetary policy. For our purposes, however, interstate conflict ranges from the threat of use of force to its actual application. Threats could involve the potential use of conventional weapons all the way up to nuclear weapons. The application of force could be, as indicated in the case of Libya, limited to armed intervention. Or it could involve a full-scale war between states such as occurred in World Wars I and II. The reality is that the use of force has proven to be an important option in the practitioner's toolbox. For all the death and destruction caused by wars and the apparent irrationalities of warfare notwithstanding, the actual decision to go to war is often the result of rational choice—a weighing of costs and benefits in relation to objectives sought.

rational choice ■
decisions based on maximizing benefits or minimizing costs of alternative courses of action directed toward attaining one or more objectives

THE RATIONALITIES AND IRRATIONALITIES OF INTERSTATE CONFLICT

Although interstate conflicts may not occur as frequently today as they have in the past, they have proven difficult to eliminate precisely because rationally motivated policymakers may see war, or other uses of force resulting in war, as serving their national objectives or purposes. The devastation caused by interstate conflicts and the very real human and economic costs involved may well be viewed as irrational by outside observers, but the decisions to use force or go to war rarely are—at least not in the minds of those who make them. In fact, they are usually made based on maximizing expected gains or minimizing expected losses consistent with the objectives and the interests of the parties making the decision. Simply because policymakers decide to go to war, which then ends in disaster and defeat, does not necessarily mean the original decision was irrational. This perspective on war as rational choice is most closely associated with realists, but the rationality assumption is also key to much work in the liberal perspective on world politics.

In practice, rationality is highly subjective. Deciding which objectives (or expected gains) to pursue and which losses (or expected costs) are acceptable may vary depending on who is making the decision. Adolf Hitler's decision to invade the Soviet Union in 1940, for example, might not have been taken had a different leader been in power in Germany at the time. A disinterested observer may estimate costs and benefits but cannot be sure that those actually making the decisions will see them this way. The value or weight they place on various criteria may be influenced by past experiences and highly subjective perspectives or points of view. Moreover, decisions may have to be made without complete information under conditions of uncertainty or under time and other pressures. Misperceptions and miscalculations further complicate the decision-making process. As a result, decisions in practice may be suboptimal—less than the best—in the process of being made as well as in hindsight.

The use of force as part of the policymaker's tool kit—not just an adjunct to diplomacy, but an integral part of it—is an understanding that gives legitimacy to going to war. Outside of law and norms, states have agreed or come to accept, in the final analysis, that there is nothing to stop states bent on using force except other states willing and able to employ diplomatic, economic, and, if necessary, military means. It is not surprising, then, that interstate conflict remains part of international politics, however devastating its consequences for humankind.

9.1 Explain how international relations practitioners use the rationality assumption to determine when it is in their interest to use force.

THE CAUSES OF INTERSTATE CONFLICT

Policymakers need an understanding of the causes of war if they are to be effective in discovering and applying remedies to reduce the use of force and the incidence of interstate conflict. If proposing, for example, that states pursue arms control as an alternative to an arms race that might lead to war, it would be helpful to the policymaker if a connection can be drawn between this proposal and the underlying or proximate causes of the conflict it seeks to remedy. In this section we examine some of the most important causes of war, which shape the ultimate decision to resort to the use of force.

9.2 Illustrate how the international system, the individual and group, and the state and societal levels of analysis help to understand the causes of interstate conflicts.

◉─[Watch the Video
"The South
Ossetia Crisis" at
mypoliscilab.com

Although we have argued the decision to go to war may be viewed as rational from a policymaker's perspective, various factors may influence the calculation. For our purposes, these causes can be categorized according to our four basic levels of analysis—the international system, state and society, group, and the individual.

International System Level of Analysis

anarchy ■
The absence of
political authority.
International politics
or the international
system is said to be
anarchic as there is no
world government—
no central or
superordinate
authority over states,
which retain their
sovereign rights.

Many observers, particularly realists, argue that interstate conflicts start because there is nothing to stop them.[1] In a world characterized by **anarchy**, there is no world government or central authority, much less one with the necessary power to constrain states or other organized groups from using force or engaging in warfare. In such a world, some states may choose to use force to achieve their objectives. When these actions confront other states, armed conflict may be the result.

Realists note there was no central authority, for example, among city-states in ancient Greece. In these uncertain circumstances, according to the writer Thucydides, it was fear in Sparta about the rising power of Athens that was the underlying cause of the Peloponnesian War. The Spartans' perception of a change in the distribution of power upset existing security calculations, making them more fearful. Sparta took measures to counter Athenian power before it became too strong; these steps contributed to the onset of war. Above all, there was no authority higher than these city-states to intervene, assure both sides of their security, and preclude them from going to war.

For realists, it is this anarchy or absence of any central authority or government in the ancient world, or in the present one, for that matter, that is the underlying or permissive cause of war. It is a self-help system in which states seek to attain their objectives or serve their own interests. International relations have a permissive quality, posing no governmental or other authoritative obstacles to countries wishing to use force to achieve their objectives by such means.

A number of constructivists, however, have taken issue with this perspective. They argue that while anarchy may exist, the response does not have to be self-help or power politics. The supposed imperative of self-help is not a given or a fact of nature, but rather a human convention. International systems do not have an independent existence, but are what states make of them—they are socially constructed.[2]

civil war ■ war
within a state and
society as two or more
factions compete for
governmental power
and authority

The lack of effective governing authorities with power or capability to keep a society together is perhaps most evident in the case of **civil wars**—armed conflicts within a given state and society—such as the American Civil War or the one between the Hutu and Tutsi in Rwanda in the mid-1990s that led to widespread genocide. Even when a central government exists, a civil war may break out if the regime lacks legitimacy, which is acceptance by its population as a whole that

---

[1] The analysis in this section draws from Kenneth N. Waltz, *Man, the State and War* (New York: Columbia University Press, 1959).

[2] Alexander Wendt, "Anarchy Is What States Make of It: The Social Construction of Power Politics," *International Organization*, vol. 46, no. 2 (Spring 1992): 391–425.

it has the right to exercise political authority. In any event, the government also lacks the necessary coercive power (military and police capabilities) to maintain domestic law and order.

Competing governments in the same state and society may emerge, perhaps identified with different national, ethnic, or other identities. In such circumstances, outside states may intervene to support one side or another, creating the possibility of a civil war turning into an interstate war. Intervention can take a number of forms—diplomatic action, aid to one or another of the parties, or other forms of interference, including the use of armed force or **armed intervention**.

armed intervention ■ use of force by a state in another country

Other systemic-level hypotheses or explanations of war involve such phenomena as conflicts between alliances or global security competitions that produce arms races. Alliances and counteralliances were said to have caused World War I. Secret treaties and war clauses committing states to defend one another if injured or attacked resulted in a chain reaction; as one party mobilized for war, others followed suit. The 1914 assassination in Sarajevo of the Austrian archduke Franz Ferdinand by a Serbian anarchist was merely the spark or catalyst that set into motion a series of actions and reactions among alliance members that resulted in world war.

Many of those who accepted this explanation for World War I argued strenuously for a world in which the use of force for aggressive purposes was outlawed. Rather than the power and balance-of-power politics of alliances, a **collective-security** system of "law-abiding" states was finally established after the war in the League of Nations. President Woodrow Wilson was a principal advocate of such a league and also argued for a world of open (rather than secret) covenants or treaties among states.

collective security ■ the idea that if one state behaved aggressively, other states had a legal right to enforce international law by taking collective action

If alliances with secretive clauses in their agreements were a contributory cause of World War I, paradoxically it was the absence of alliances, posing no obstacle to a resurgent Germany, that may have contributed to World War II. As a legal system of obligations, collective security within the League of Nations failed to stop aggression or eliminate the use of force by states acting unilaterally.

That arms races contribute to the onset of war is another systemic-level hypothesis. Richardson's arms-race differential equations are sometimes used to explain the relations among variables affecting arms race behaviors that can lead to war. Was it the late-19th and early-20th-century naval and ground-force competition between Britain and France against Germany that was one cause of World War I? If so, could the mid- to late-20th-century U.S.–Soviet Cold War arms competition have resulted in the same outcome? What kept the peace? Quantitative and other studies have tried to answer such questions, determining how militarized disputes contribute to the occurrence of war.

Individual and Group Levels of Analysis

If anarchy, the absence of effective central authority, is an underlying or permissive cause of all wars, then a particular war may be influenced by perceptions or misperceptions in a leadership group (if not in the society as a whole) of the intentions and capabilities of an adversary. Psychological and social-psychological factors of individuals or small groups may affect such calculations.

In addition to focusing on perception or misperception, explanations at the individual or small-group levels examine individual psychologies and group dynamics. Thus, some argue that human beings are by nature aggressive, or that the personality of an individual leader is a critical factor in a country's decision to go to war. For example, would it have made any difference if Al Gore were president rather than George W. Bush when it came to the decision to go to war against Iraq in 2003? Do you think a leader's orientation toward the efficacy of using force matters? Is the outbreak of war more or less likely when a leader, or the group of advisers she or he depends upon, see force as having practical value in efforts to achieve national purposes?

Rather than focusing just on individual leaders, some argue that the mind-set or even the frustration of groups or individuals in group settings can lead to aggressive behavior that, in turn, can lead to conflict. Particularly in cohesive small groups, there is the danger of members reinforcing each other's mutual biases, leading to a phenomenon known as **groupthink**. The result is that information that contradicts the group's devoutly held beliefs and prejudices is ignored. Critics of the U.S. decision to invade Iraq in 2003, for example, noted the prevalence of high-level officials who had served together in the earlier Bush administration (1989–1993) and also shared more militant, neoconservative orientations in terms of U.S. national security policy.

groupthink ■
tendency over time for members of a group to think alike; screening out ideas or perspectives that contradict what has become their commonly accepted wisdom

State and Societal Levels of Analysis

For others, it is the nature of a state or society that is critical in explaining the outbreak of war and the propensity of a country to use force. In his administration (1913–1921), President Woodrow Wilson and those who shared his views argued that dictators and those within their ruling elite are more prone to choose war than those democratically elected to office and held responsible to the people. In his war address to the U.S. Congress on April 3, 1917, Wilson blamed the war on those who "provoked and waged" it "in the interest of dynasties or of little groups of ambitious men." Wilson saw the 1914–1918 world war as "the war to end all wars," defeating dictatorship in Germany and the other central European powers and making the world "safe for democracy." In short, the Wilsonian hypothesis was that dictatorships like "the Prussian autocracy" in Germany produce war, but democracies produce peace.

The Russian revolutionary leader Vladimir Ilyich Lenin, who came to power in 1917, expressed a different view on what type of state or society was more likely to encourage international peace. Socialist states, supposedly representing the interests of the working classes traditionally forced to do the fighting and dying in wars, would be inclined to avoid war. In leading the revolution that overthrew the tsarist regime in Russia, Lenin argued that capitalist states and societies tend to become imperialist as they compete with each other for markets throughout the world. Lenin viewed World War I as a war among imperial powers, and the new socialist workers regime he headed would have no part of it. Peace was made soon after he and the Communist Party came to power; Russia pulled out of the war.

Or was the economist Joseph Schumpeter right when he argued, contrary to Lenin, that capitalism would be more conducive to peace?[3] Although arms producers and sellers, "the merchants of death" as they were derisively called, might register some short-term gains, the net effect of war is to destroy capital—the productive capacity of economies. Because it is the capitalists who own this productive capacity, their real interest is in protecting and expanding capital, not destroying it. According to this reasoning, peace is served by the spread of capitalism and commercial values that displace heroism, gallantry, glory, and other obsolete, war-oriented values of an earlier precapitalist or feudal period.

Although Wilson, Lenin, and Schumpeter differed respectively over whether democracy, socialism, or capitalism is more conducive to peace, all of these arguments have one thing in common: It is the nature of state and society or the political and economic regime that is responsible for increasing or decreasing the likelihood of war. We can apply the observations of Wilson, Lenin, or Schumpeter in broader terms than merely describing the relative likelihood of one or another kind of state or society to engage in war. Worldwide democracy as in a universal concert or partnership of democratic regimes, worldwide socialism, or worldwide capitalism are alternative, international system-level outcomes that, if achieved, might affect the likelihood of war.

The key point is that a combination of causes at the individual and small-group, state and society, and international system levels undoubtedly accounts for the outbreak of any particular war. The difficult challenge is to determine which ones are salient in any given case. Realist observers of world politics and war, however, would claim that it is the underlying anarchy of the system that allows wars to happen regardless of the specific cause or set of causes of a particular war. Other observers agree.

Consistent with this logic, those who want to eliminate war need to change the underlying world order. The most ambitious world federalists, for example, would replace international anarchy with some form of world government. They would vest a central authority with enough power (including armed forces and police units) to keep component states and societies from going to war.

Responding to plans to end war in Europe by constructing a confederation of states, 18th-century philosopher Jean-Jacques Rousseau did not fault the logic of such schemes (eliminating the anarchy of international relations through world governance) so much as their impracticality. World federalists are quick to respond that the very act of defining world government as an impossibility makes it so. It is a self-fulfilling prophecy. We are not likely to achieve or even try to achieve what we have defined as an impossibility.

Even if world government were the solution to interstate conflict, many would find it undesirable. Different peoples in different societies value their independence in a world of sovereign states and prefer to hold on to a national identity. For those with this view, implementing world government as a remedy for war would be worse than continuing to live with armed conflicts and the use of force.

world federalists
■ those seeking international order or peace through the rule of law as in constructing federations or confederations of states

---

[3]See Schumpeter's *Capitalism, Socialism and Democracy* (New York: Harper and Row, 1942, 1962).

How do we explain the decision for launching a particular war? Why did the United States decide to go to war against Iraq in 2003?

ARGUMENT   One explanation is that it was essentially a rational choice on the part of the Bush administration—a calculation of expected costs and benefits related to achieving national (or international) objectives through the use of force. Some of the reasons offered at the time by President Bush: (1) Iraq was said to be a threat to national and international security as it possessed chemical and biological weapons capabilities. (2) Iraq also was understood to be developing nuclear weapons of mass destruction. After all, Iraq was controlled by a dictator who in the 1980s used chemical weapons against Iraqi Kurds and against Iranians in the Iran–Iraq War, 1980–1988. (3) Added to this was deep suspicion by some, later understood not to be the case, that Saddam Hussein's regime was somehow tied in with the 9/11 terrorist attacks against the World Trade Center in New York and the Pentagon in Washington, DC. In short, removing Saddam Hussein from power—changing the political regime in Iraq—would eliminate the threat his regime posed to the United States and to international peace and stability.

COUNTERARGUMENT   The levels of analysis emphasizes different factors. First, one may focus on the individual roles and personalities of President George W. Bush, Vice President Richard Cheney, Secretary of Defense Donald Rumsfeld, Undersecretary of Defense Paul Wolfowitz, Secretary of State Colin Powell, and National Security Adviser Condoleezza Rice, among others. Underneath the publicly stated view that Iraq was a threat, some saw President Bush as personally holding the same ideological worldview or neoconservative perspective of some of his key advisers—Cheney, Rumsfeld, and Wolfowitz, who argued for striking first by taking preemptive military action against countries posing significant threats to the United States. Still others

speculate that the plot instigated by Saddam Hussein in 1992 to assassinate the president's father, former President George H. W. Bush, on his tour of liberated Kuwait may also have been part of President Bush's calculation to go to war in 2003. Even if not decisive, some see it as contributory to other arguments for going to war. In any event, documentary evidence for this "revenge" hypothesis is slim at best. On the other hand, that the president and his advisers apparently did perceive Saddam Hussein as unsavory, if not diabolical, is easier to document. To the extent that perception influenced the way "facts" were interpreted by decision makers and meanings drawn from what they observed, we see the importance of psychological factors.

A second level of analysis emphasizes the decisive, collective role of this relatively small group of policymakers and their trusted advisers and subordinates in the White House and the Office of the Secretary of Defense (OSD)—a neoconservative decision-making elite—that constituted a coalition favoring preemptive military intervention against Iraq as the best way to serve U.S. national security interests. Neoconservatives also saw American purposes served by spreading democracy to "rogue states" such as Iraq—transforming Iraq into a democratic model for all of the Middle East to emulate. By changing the regime in Iraq, a major threat to Israel also would be removed.

A third level of analysis emphasizes the overall power structure of the international system of states. The United States was the most important power in a unipolar international system in which just one superpower holds so dominant a position. With no effective balance to block its power, the United States was able to act at will against Iraq. Indeed, however reluctant member states of the United Nations might have been, the organization (to include members of the Security Council) ended up acquiescing to the U.S. invasion of Iraq. Some say that quite apart from particular causes or justifications offered, the way the

(continued)

ARGUMENT-COUNTERARGUMENT | *Continued*

United States acted was to be expected in a world in which the strong do what they will and the weak do what they must—an echo of the ancient Greek writer Thucydides who recounted the Athenian conquest of the small island of Melos in the Aegean Sea. Great powers facing no effective obstacles tend to act this way—doing whatever they want (or see as being in their interest) to do.

APPLICATION   Choose any recent article from the weekly news magazine, *The Economist,* or an online newspaper such as *The New York Times, Times of London,* or *The Washington Post* that deals with a foreign policy pronouncement from any state. Apply the rational choice model and the levels of analysis to develop hypotheses that might help us answer the question, "Why was the decision made?" ▶

NATIONAL STRATEGY AND THE USE OF FORCE

The Prussian general and writer Carl von Clausewitz (1780–1831) worked for years on a theory of war and the use of force. He had practical experience, serving both Russia and his native Prussia in wars against the French that ended with the defeat of Napoleon in 1815. Clausewitz accepted an important position in 1818 as director of the German War School, which allowed him time to think, research, and write. His incomplete work *On War* was published in 1832, a year after his death.

The book has had an enormous influence on how states use force to achieve their purposes. To Clausewitz, war was merely one means states might employ to achieve objectives set by political authorities. As such, wars (and the armed forces called upon to fight them) were merely rational means to accomplish objectives, not ends in themselves. War was not glorified as something good in itself. The only legitimate purpose of war, according to Clausewitz, was to serve political objectives; it is diplomacy by other means: "an instrument of policy"—"the sword in place of the pen."[4]

On War presents chapters on the nature and theory of war, strategy and plans for fighting a war, and leadership and tactics or methods of combat operations. After establishing that war should be a rational instrument of state policy and, as such, the armed forces are subordinated to the political authorities of the state, Clausewitz specifies the way in which any battle or war is won. He elaborates what constitutes military necessity in war.

The military aim is always the same—to destroy or substantially weaken an enemy's warfighting or warmaking capability. Clausewitz observes that "if War is an act of violence to compel the enemy to fulfil our will, then in every case all depends

9.3 Evaluate the concept of war as an instrument of policy by linking military and other capabilities to the national goals or objectives policymakers seek to achieve.

Explore the "Military Force: You Are a Military Commander" at mypoliscilab.com

strategy ■ plan that connects capabilities (or means) to ends or objectives sought

tactics ■ the methods or way in which one takes actions or conducts operations

---

[4]Carl von Clausewitz, *On War*, Book V, Ch. 6 (B). Originally published as *Vom Kriege* (Berlin: Ferdinand Duemmler, 1832). Readily available English editions include one edited by Anatol Rapoport (New York: Penguin Books, 1968) and one edited and translated by Michael Howard and Peter Paret (Princeton, NJ: Princeton University Press, 1976). Citations in this chapter are taken from the Penguin edition. Clausewitz defines tactics as "the theory of the use of military forces in combat" and strategy as "the theory of the use of combats for the object of the War." He elaborates that "Strategy forms the plan of the War" and "is the employment of the battle to gain the end [or objective] of the War." Strategy has its "moral, physical, mathematical, geographical, and statistical elements." See ibid., Book I, Ch. 1, and Book III, Chs. 1 and 2.

These four slides represent different perspectives and levels of analysis on how to explain war. Adolf Hitler exemplifies the power of individuals to contribute to the outbreak of wars. Here he addresses the opening of the German parliament or Reichstag.

Vladimir Lenin, first leader of the Soviet Union, argued that capitalist production and war profiteers of the capitalist class were the major cause of interstate wars. This represents the Marxist-Leninist argument that capitalism as a condition of a society is the cause of war—the state/societal level of analysis.

Joseph Schumpeter, however, while he agreed on the contribution of war profiteers and elements of the upper classes to the outbreak of war, argued that capitalism as a mode of production was actually conducive to international peace—also the state/societal level of analysis.

IR theorists who utilize rational choice theory would argue that war and particular applications of the use or threat of force are often carefully calculated decisions. One popular case study to illustrate this perspective is the Cuban missile crisis of October 1962 involving the United States and the Soviet Union. Determined not to allow the Soviets to deploy missiles that could reach the United States, the Kennedy administration "rationally" considered the pros and cons of attacking Cuba via air and sea, but ultimately settled on a naval "quarantine" of Cuba.

on our overthrowing the enemy, that is, disarming him, and on that alone." More to the point, he asserts: "The military power [of an enemy] must be destroyed, that is, reduced to such a state as not to be able to prosecute the War." Actions taken in war for this purpose, and this purpose alone, constitute military necessity.

In order to defeat the enemy it is necessary to direct and "proportion our efforts to his powers of resistance." The commander searches for, finds, and attacks the enemy's **center of gravity** or focal point, which, if successful, disrupts the enemy's forces, facilitating their destruction. Clausewitz identifies a physical factor—military capabilities (C)—and a moral factor—will to use these means (W)—as two critical and related variables responsible for battlefield effectiveness (E). E is expressed as a "product of two factors which cannot be separated, namely, the sum of available means [or capabilities] and the strength of the Will." Expressed symbolically this is

$$E = C \times W$$

If either factor C or W declines or approaches zero, so does E. One can lose a battle or an entire war if either military capabilities or will to fight decline, particularly if the enemy has kept up its capabilities and will.

Although Clausewitz does not develop or use the concept of **deterrence**, there is a suggestion of it in his observation that if there is a balance or equilibrium in conflict relations between two states, we can expect peace to be maintained for the time being, at least until one side gains an advantage over the other, thus upsetting the balance. Capabilities and will (or strength of motive to fight) are again key variables: "[T]he equation is made up by the product of the motive and the power."

In its modern formulation, which owes much to Clausewitz, deterrence is a psychological concept. One state makes a credible threat to use military capabilities if another state commits aggression or undertakes some other action the deterring state considers undesirable. The deterred state perceives the deterring state's military capabilities and will to use them in armed conflict and is dissuaded from committing aggression or other offense. Expressed symbolically, deterrence (D) is similar in form to battlefield effectiveness (E). It is the product of perceived capabilities (C) and credibility or will (W) to use them:

$$D = C \times W$$

It is, as Clausewitz had it, a multiplicative function: the product of power and motive or will, expressed nowadays more commonly as military capabilities times credibility. If either of these two factors weakens, deterrence becomes unstable or tends to break down. In the extreme cases when either capabilities or credibility approaches zero, deterrence also goes to zero—it fails.

Among the principles of war that have resonated down through the years, Clausewitz identifies mass or concentration of forces (when "the greatest possible number of troops" is "brought into action at the decisive point"), surprise (achieving military successes through "secrecy and rapidity"), and economy of force (a conservative approach that avoids "waste of forces, which is even worse than their employment to no purpose").

Success in war also depends on military leadership with strong mental and organizational capabilities. He calls for officers with strong mental "power of discrimination" and "good judgment." This is particularly important because of the complexities and uncertainties commanders face in war.

center of gravity
■ metaphor from mechanics that captures the idea that an adversary's military may have a focal point that is critical in holding that structure together

deterrence ■ keeping an opponent from doing something by threat of punishment or by possessing capabilities the adversary knows will block or deny any such attempt

Things in war, of course, often do not go according to even the best-laid and rationally calculated plans. Clausewitz refers to the accumulated effect as friction. In physics or mechanics, we calculate the forces we expect will operate on an object in an ideal situation. We try to predict its motion—its velocity or speed and direction—perhaps drawing a diagram specifying the forces with vectors or arrows. As a practical matter, of course, we learn that in the real world the motion of objects is impeded or slowed by friction, which is often difficult to measure in advance. We can get a sense of how much friction is involved through experimental trials, and we may decide to take corrective measures to reduce friction by lubricating the surface or streamlining the object. One may reduce friction, but it cannot be eliminated entirely.

So it is with plans for war drawn up in peacetime or in an office setting. According to Clausewitz, a great gap exists between the conception of war and its execution. As he puts it: "Everything is very simple in War, but the simplest thing is difficult. These difficulties accumulate and produce a friction which no one can imagine exactly who has not seen War." He adds that incidents take place in war, changes in weather, for example, that are virtually "impossible to calculate, their chief origin being chance." At best one can conduct military exercises or experimental trials to try to identify and correct major sources of friction.

Through such measures one may be able to reduce the friction that comes from taking war plans off the shelf and putting them into practice, but one cannot eliminate the effect entirely. Compounding the effects of friction and contributing to it is what Clausewitz called the fog of war—the sum of all uncertainties and unpredictable occurrences that can happen so rapidly in war.

Clausewitz understood war as a zero-sum phenomenon. One side's gain is the other's loss: "In a battle both sides strive to conquer. . . . The victory of one side destroys that of the other." But Clausewitz was never an advocate of war for war's own sake. Given his own participation in the wars against Napoleon's armies, Clausewitz had observed the awful consequences of armed conflict and worried about its character as it "approaches the form of absolute War." More than a century before the nuclear age, Clausewitz expressed his concerns about circumstances when general or total war is the expected outcome. He counseled how necessary it is "not to take the first step" into such a war "without thinking what may be the last."

This remains good advice today. Whether a state's initial military objectives are achieved or not, leaders must be prepared to answer ahead of time the question "And then what?"

DETERRENCE, DEFENSE, AND WARFIGHTING

During World War II, American-British collaboration and the gathering of other European physicists in Los Alamos, New Mexico, contributed in the Manhattan Project to the development of nuclear weapons used by the United States in 1945 to bomb two Japanese cities, Hiroshima and Nagasaki. The Japanese surrender that followed put an end to the war. The Cold War soon underway, the Soviet Union conducted its first nuclear weapon test in 1949. Succeeding decades witnessed efforts to increase the size of American, British, and Soviet nuclear arsenals—an arms race joined in the 1960s by two new members of the nuclear "club"—France and China.

friction ■ metaphor from mechanics that captures the idea that implementation of a plan likely will face impediments or obstacles

fog of war ■ metaphor that captures the uncertainties in warfare—factors not considered or, quite simply, that bad luck may have adverse effects

zero-sum ■ concept in game theory that one side's gain amounts to the other side's loss

9.4 Illustrate how military force-employment doctrines of deterrence, defense, and warfighting apply not only to great-power strategic nuclear arsenals, but also to states with smaller arsenals.

The proliferation of nuclear weapons and weapons-related technologies among these five former World War II allies produced fear that conflicts among them (mainly the Western allies—the United States, United Kingdom, and France—arrayed against the Soviet Union or China—then both communist or state-socialist countries) could escalate into a devastating nuclear war. Preventing the outbreak of such a war by threatening to retaliate and thus punish any enemy that tried to do such a thing (or dissuading them from attacking on the ground that there would be nothing to gain and so much to lose from doing so) quickly became the focus of Cold War strategic theory and force-employment doctrines.

Put another way, strategists committed to national security in the nuclear age focused on theories of deterrence, defense, and warfighting. Deterrence relations among the great powers that possess nuclear weapons seem relatively less important these days compared to during the Cold War. An improved climate of great-power relations and a wide array of strategic arms-control achievements in the last half of the 20th century have contributed substantially to international security and a reduced risk of general war in the 21st century, now in its second decade.

At the same time, however, great-power strategic nuclear arsenals remain intact, even though in 1992 the United States and the Russian Federation agreed to reduce strategic nuclear warheads by some 75 percent to about 3,000 each (from their Cold War highs of more than 12,000 warheads apiece). Although by 2002 the parties had some 6,000 warheads each, both agreed to continue reductions to some 1,700 to 2,200 warheads each by the year 2012. As the United States and Russia continue the nuclear disarmament process, the new START agreement that entered into force in 2011 drops the maximum number of strategic warheads to 1,550—the drawdown over a seven-year period beginning in 2011. Nevertheless, arms controllers still have a significant challenge to find ways to reduce nuclear arms below these still high levels without destabilizing deterrence relations and endangering international peace and security.

Deterrence, defense, and warfighting theories or doctrines dominated U.S.-Soviet security concerns during the Cold War. The continuing 21st-century importance of the topic is not only due to nuclear weapons remaining on the arms-control agendas of the major powers possessing them, but also because India, Pakistan, Israel, North Korea, and other countries have acquired (or may yet acquire in the case of Iran) nuclear weapons capabilities, not to mention chemical or biological weapons of mass destruction. Notwithstanding extensive, well-intended efforts to avoid further spread of nuclear and other weapons of mass destruction (see the arms control discussion in Chapter 7), proliferation of such weapons and weapons-related technologies seems likely to continue.

Military doctrine attempts to apply rational analysis to answer two key questions: (1) What military means shall be employed to protect a country? and (2) How shall they be employed? Doctrines concerning deterrence, defense, and warfighting involve either the threat or actual use of force. In deterrence, the effort is merely to dissuade another state, through the threat of force, from doing something it has not yet undertaken; it is not actually required to change a course of action. This also may involve extended deterrence—threats designed to protect allies. If deterrence fails, defense involves the use of military force to repel an attack. Warfighting is thus an active use of force for defense or to achieve other political-military goals.

defense ■ programs and capabilities designed to repel or deter an enemy attack

warfighting ■ the application of violence to achieve one's political and military objectives

extended deterrence ■ threats designed to deter and protect other countries from an attack by a common enemy

The military forces (i.e., such force posture considerations as numbers, types, and locations of forces) required to deter, defend, or engage in warfighting depend heavily upon force-employment doctrines and related national security strategies. (See Table 9.1 that relates different offensive and defensive force postures to particular strategic doctrines.) In the absence of change in doctrinal and strategic understandings and commitments, these national requirements also effectively define the needs and limits of concessions that realistically can be made by negotiators in any arms control talks. (For details on diplomacy and arms control, see Chapter 7, Diplomacy and Foreign Policy.)

force posture ■ numbers, types, locations, and other qualitative factors concerning a state's military forces

Minimum or Finite Deterrence

The least-demanding alternative in terms of numbers of nuclear forces is minimum or finite deterrence, which requires only a relatively small number of nuclear weapons that can be used against an adversary. With only a few nuclear weapons (say one or more, but perhaps fewer than 100), a country cannot realistically choose to engage in actual nuclear warfighting against another nuclear power, which would require a much larger arsenal with a full array of nuclear and nonnuclear offensive and defensive capabilities.

minimum or finite deterrence ■ a doctrine in which a state maintains a relatively small number of nuclear or other weapons of mass destruction for use in making deterrence threats

Understanding minimum or finite deterrence is particularly relevant in the present period of nuclear proliferation when a larger number of countries may acquire relatively small nuclear arsenals. Because a minimum-deterrence country has only a relatively few nuclear weapons, its nuclear forces can be used effectively only to threaten attack against an adversary, typically against population centers or so-called countervalue targets. In a minimum-deterrence situation, there are not enough weapons to direct attacks at a large number of military or counterforce targets that would need to be struck if a country were trying to destroy or substantially weaken an enemy's warfighting capability. Hence, minimum or finite deterrence can realistically be based only on a threat of punishment primarily to enemy populations should another country undertake aggression or other undesirable action as specified by the deterring state. Even if the genuine purpose is to deter war by such threats, aiming weaponry at population centers raises obvious moral questions.

A moral paradox is thus inherent in the sincere effort of arms-control negotiators to reduce nuclear arsenals to minimum levels. A breakdown of deterrence in these circumstances could maximize the human cost of nuclear war. By contrast, larger arsenals do allow for counterforce targeting as a way of reducing unnecessary death and destruction. The irony, then, is that fewer weapons, as in a minimum-deterrence posture, may be even more problematic morally than larger nuclear arsenals that can be directed more effectively against the larger number of military or counterforce targets, thus avoiding population centers whenever possible.

Critics are quick to point out, however, that such distinctions have little if any meaning when weapons of mass destruction are involved—that the distinction between civilian (countervalue) and military (counterforce) targets is difficult, if not impossible, to make when the destructiveness of such weapons can so easily spill over from military targets to adjacent or nearby cities, towns, or other settlements. Beyond direct losses of human life and property, severe damage to the environment, including massive loss of animal and plant life, are additional

TABLE 9.1

Implications for Strategic Arms Control Regimes of Alternative Deterrence or Defense Doctrines and Force Postures

The key conclusions to be drawn from this table are to be seen by comparing the top and the bottom— different strategic doctrines have different implications for the possibility of achieving arms control agreements. What makes matters doubly difficult is if states have different strategic nuclear doctrines, which might be a function of technological capabilities, perception of the threat, national security objectives, and geography.

	Strategic Nuclear Doctrines			
	Minimum or Finite Deterrence	**Deterrence by Assured (or Mutual Assured) Destruction (No Real Warfighting Capabilities Intended; Deterrence Only through Threat of Punishment)**	**Defense by Damage Limitation (Some War-Fighting Capabilities)**	**Deterrence or Defense by Denial (Robust War-Fighting Capabilities)**
Implications for Force Posture				
Offensive (bombers and other aircraft and missiles)	Perhaps 100 or fewer nuclear weapons	Large numbers of nuclear weapons	Very large numbers of nuclear weapons	Largest number and diversity of nuclear weapons
Defensive				
A. **Active** (artillery, fighter-interceptors, surface-to-air and antiballistic missiles, space-based systems, etc.)	None required	None required	Some	Robust, fully developed
B. **Passive** (radars, communications, civil defense, etc.)	Minimal needs (for early warning)	Minimal needs (for early warning)	Substantial need (for civil defense and early warning)	Robust, fully developed
Implications for Deterrence Stability	Potentially unstable	Usually considered the most stable	Potentially unstable	Usually considered the most unstable
Implications for Arms Control	Most conducive to arms control limits or restrictions	Caps possible on offenses; effort to block development of defenses	Somewhat compatible with arms control efforts	Least compatible with arms control limits

adverse consequences of using any weapons of mass destruction. The horrendous blast, radiation, and thermal (i.e., heat) effects of nuclear weapons thus blur the distinction between counterforce and countervalue targets. Even if a state focuses on using nuclear weapons only against military or counterforce targets, massive collateral damage (death and destruction) to civil populations and property still cannot be avoided.

Compared to the enormous size of U.S. and Soviet nuclear arsenals during the Cold War (and the thousands of strategic nuclear weapons that still remain in U.S. and Russian inventories), those belonging to the United Kingdom, France, and China then and now seem minimal indeed. Strategists have raised serious questions concerning the viability of such small national-deterrent capabilities and the stability of deterrence relations based on them. These problems are compounded for India, Pakistan, North Korea, and other countries newly acquiring nuclear weapons and related technologies because of the serious interstate conflicts in which they typically have been involved. Iran is the latest concern.

If nuclear weapons continue to proliferate in coming years, the countries acquiring them likely will have only relatively small arsenals to which minimum-deterrence concepts apply. Possible implications include the following:

- New nuclear weapons states likely will come to rely primarily on the threat of retaliation as the basis of their deterrent, with relatively few, if any active defenses (fighter-interceptors, surface-to-air missiles, and antiaircraft artillery to shoot down enemy aircraft carrying these weapons). Nor is an effective antiballistic missile system (much less space-based or other strategic defenses) either attainable or affordable.
- A viable command-and-control mechanism that can make and implement nuclear weapons decisions in a timely manner is problematic.
- A smaller number of weapons is more vulnerable to a comprehensive enemy attack aimed at destroying them before they can ever be used to retaliate.
- Decision makers under pressure in a country with just a few nuclear weapons who believe their country is (or could be) under attack might launch their few forces even before confirming that the attack was real. Fearing that virtually all of the country's retaliatory forces might be destroyed by an enemy before they can be launched in retaliation may lead a minimum-deterrence country to launch on warning without having (or taking) the time to verify that an attack is actually underway.
- Stable deterrence depends on both capability and credibility. Some critics of minimum deterrence argue that smaller numbers not only undermine an adversary's perception that a deterring country could deliver a retaliatory strike, but also raise questions as to a minimum-deterrent state's will to resort to nuclear strikes.

In short, critics worry about the stability of minimum deterrence when both capability and credibility can so easily be drawn into question. This is another reason that arms control advocates feel so strongly about maintaining and expanding the nuclear nonproliferation security regime that forbids the transfer or acquisition of nuclear weapons and weapons technologies to nonnuclear countries.

Deterrence through Assured Destruction and Defensive Efforts

Assured (and mutual assured) destruction and defensive efforts to limit damage were dominant ways of thinking about deterrence between superpowers during the Cold War. For reasons presented in the previous section, many critics of minimum deterrence then and now have preferred a larger number of offensive nuclear-deterrence forces. Accompanied by hardening, mobility, dispersion, and diversification of these forces to enhance their survivability, the superpowers established and maintained a capability for second-strike assured destruction. In these circumstances, neither side would be foolish enough to attack first. Mutual assured destruction (MAD) exists if both parties in a bilateral deterrence relation have a second-strike, assured-destruction capability against the other. If they do, the threat of punishment or destruction presumably is enough to deter both parties from launching (or even considering) a first strike. Even at reduced levels of strategic nuclear weapons in the Russian and U.S. inventories, there still are sufficient numbers to maintain second-strike capabilities for both sides.

mutual assured destruction (MAD)
■ a nuclear deterrence doctrine that aims to avoid war by reciprocal threat of punishment through an unacceptable level of destruction

Deterrence based strictly on assured destruction (or mutual assured destruction) requires a strong offense accompanied, as in minimum deterrence, by passive defenses for the earliest possible warning of attack and a viable command-and-control system able to make and implement nuclear-employment decisions in a timely fashion. A stable deterrence under these circumstances depends, paradoxically, on maintaining a condition of mutual vulnerability to a first strike, coupled with the assurance that comes from having sufficient survivable second-strike forces. The logic is that neither party would undertake a first strike against the other with the knowledge that doing so would invite unwanted retaliatory destruction.

The SALT accords in the 1970s between the United States and the Soviet Union were based, at least from the American point of view, on deterrence by this threat of mutual assured destruction. Caps were placed on strategic offense, specifying maximum numbers and types of missiles and bombers each side could have. At the same time, severe restrictions were placed on strategic defenses, quantitatively limiting deployment of antiballistic missiles (ABMs) and qualitatively prohibiting space-based testing of strategic-defense components. Limitations on strategic defense were intended not only to curb the arms race but also to maintain the mutual vulnerability central to deterrence by mutual, assured destruction.

Termination of the ABM Treaty in 2002, at the time a controversial decision taken by the Bush administration, cleared away a substantial obstacle to deployment of missile defenses. Arguing that the end of the Cold War and good relations with Russia made the ABM Treaty obsolete, President Bush carried forward the defensive program begun under President Clinton, seeing missile defenses as important lest the United States (or its allies) be attacked by smaller nuclear powers in a period of increased proliferation of nuclear weapons and related technologies. Developing missile defenses is still on the national agenda as a means of countering potential threats from North Korea that already has nuclear weapons (and Iran, should it acquire them) as well as missiles, aircraft, or other means of carrying them to targets in the region or beyond.

Defense

The distinction between deterrence and defense became abundantly clear in the 1950s and 1960s. If deterrence broke down, what defenses would a society be able to muster? Hardened blast and fallout shelters could be part of a passive civil-defense plan. Active defenses that could destroy incoming bombers and missiles would be used to reduce or limit damage. Damage limitation could also be achieved by striking enemy missiles before they were launched (or by developing technologies to destroy them in the middle or terminal phases of their trajectories en route to targets). Of course, the discussion of using active defenses or even offensive forces to limit damage made defense sound more and more like nuclear warfighting.

In fact, damage limitation involved acquiring effective area and point defenses offered by antiballistic missile or space-based systems, as well as robust offensive systems with sufficient accuracy to take out enemy air bases and missile sites. There is a danger that one side may think its offensive and defensive damage limitation forces are strong enough to make a first strike against the other a feasible option. A credible **first-strike capability** includes not only a capacity to strike first but also an ability to nullify or reduce to "acceptable levels" the ability of an adversary to retaliate in kind. To be able to absorb a first-strike attack and still launch a counterattack means a state has a **second-strike capability.**

Even if neither side in fact has such a credible first-strike capability, if either side perceived the other were on the verge of acquiring one, it might lead the disadvantaged party to act preemptively, starting a war before the other side achieved any strategic advantage. In short, pursuing the development of damage-limitation forces is seen by many as potentially destabilizing. Even extensive civil-defense networks honestly designed to protect or defend populations in the event of war can be misinterpreted by an adversary as an indication of secret plans to develop a credible first-strike or warfighting capability. Thus, developing or extending even passive defenses can be destabilizing, particularly when such actions are accompanied by existing active defenses and strong offensive capabilities.

In the SALT negotiations, arms control was used as one means of preventing the development of effective strategic defenses that, beyond their defensive value, also could be seen by an adversary as part of an effective warfighting arsenal. A good offense, after all, depends on having good defenses as well. Arms-control agreements that limited nuclear warfighting capabilities by constraining defenses were understood as contributing to the stability of deterrence relations.

first-strike capability ■ the ability to launch an attack against an enemy so that its ability to retaliate is severely degraded

second-strike capability ■ the ability to absorb a nuclear first strike with sufficient retaliatory forces surviving to launch a counterattack

Warfighting

In the late 1970s and 1980s, talk turned more directly to developing nuclear warfighting forces that could win or at least prevail if deterrence broke down and nuclear war broke out. Credible nuclear warfighting capabilities were seen by some as another form of deterrence or, more generally, dissuasion. Although punishment would no doubt be involved, the primary focus would instead be on denial. From this perspective no would-be adversary would ever take on a country with nuclear superiority or at least an ability to fight and prevail in nuclear warfighting. Because adversaries in effect would be denied any rational purpose for engaging in nuclear war, they would be dissuaded from undertaking it in the first place. Hence, another paradox of deterrence: The point of talking credibly about fighting and prevailing in a nuclear war is the belief that in so doing, that particular horrible possibility will never come about. Although we call this *deterrence by denial* of anything to be gained by escalating to nuclear warfare, some prefer to call this *dissuasion* so as not to confuse it with *deterrence by threat of punishment*. Indeed, French nuclear forces were introduced in 1958 as a *force de dissuasion* to capture the idea that even though these forces necessarily were substantially less in numbers and capabilities than the United States and the Soviet Union had already deployed, any country that might consider attacking France with nuclear weapons would suffer great losses with little, if anything gained through such a venture.

Force posture for effective nuclear warfighting capabilities is the least conducive to constructing arms-control regimes. As in all warfighting, the aim of such a denial doctrine is to destroy or substantially weaken an enemy's warmaking capability. Arms-control restraints on numbers, types, and locations, as well as on research, development, test, and evaluation (RDT&E) of weapons, weapons systems, and other factors are an impediment to developing and deploying large numbers of offensive forces able to penetrate enemy territory and air space (as in employing "stealth" technologies that reduce or disguise the appearance on enemy radars of incoming aircraft and missiles) and destroy even the most hardened targets. This requires high accuracy in delivering bombs to target. Strategic offenses must also be accompanied by well-developed and extensive active and passive defenses—objectives incompatible with most arms-control agendas.

Moreover, research, development, test, and evaluation, as well as acquisition of substantial offensive and defensive nuclear warfighting capabilities, were upsetting to the general population. The public suffered understandably from Cold War nuclear anxieties, made worse by saber rattling and other strong rhetoric between the United States and the Soviet Union. Perhaps even more important were anxieties in the Soviet military high command that the United States was trying to achieve a credible first-strike capability and had the technological superiority to do so.

If this were so, Soviet second-strike forces were now potentially in jeopardy. Soviet command-and-control authorities considered shifting to a posture of launch on warning rather than waiting to confirm an attack until it was too late to retaliate. "Launch on warning" is a highly unstable readiness posture compared to "launch after attack." The danger of false alarm (due to radar, computer, or other equipment malfunction), other accident, or miscalculation causing war to break out is less when time for command-and-control decisions is increased.

The Post–Cold War Period

The attitudes of Soviet leader Mikhail Gorbachev and Russian leader Boris Yeltsin in the late 1980s and 1990s and the willingness of American leaders to trust them signaled a change for the better, making the international climate more conducive to arms-control agreements of all kinds. Such agreements had implications for both defense and warfighting doctrines. Agreement under the Strategic Arms Reduction Talks (START) to reduce strategic nuclear weapons by about 75 percent, as well as dramatically scaling back strategic defense plans, also meant that both sides were, in effect, abandoning notions of deterrence or dissuasion that involved maintaining robust nuclear warfighting capabilities. New arms-control limitations and a U.S. decision at the time to accept a strict interpretation of the ABM treaty that prohibited space-based testing of strategic defense components effectively put a lid on the nuclear arms race; however, proponents of deploying an effective national missile defense called for renegotiating and amending the ABM treaty or, failing that, abrogating it. Indeed, the Bush administration consulted with Russia and gave the required six-month notice for treaty termination in 2002.

The move away from planning to fight and prevail in nuclear warfare was a notable shift back to an earlier force posture compatible with the mutual assured destruction deterrence doctrine. In a period of lower threat and risk of war, both the Russian Federation and United States agreed to put their strategic nuclear forces on less of a war footing, reducing alert and readiness levels. Under heavy diplomatic pressures, the former Soviet republics also agreed to disarm themselves of the nuclear weaponry they inherited after the formal breakup of the Soviet Union in 1992. With a strategic regime of quantitative and qualitative restrictions in place, deterrence relations among the major powers are more stable, the overall climate of post–Cold War international relations is much improved, and the risk of general war among great powers has remained relatively low. The nuclear weapons reduction process continues between the two countries. Renewal of the Strategic Arms Reduction Treaty in December 2010 will bring projected numbers of American and

CASE & POINT | Technology and the Future of Warfare

CASE   The information revolution is not only a result of advances in computerized information and telecommunications technologies, but also innovations in how to organize and utilize the technology. Not surprisingly, the United States, in shifting from an industrial to an information-based society, has been the leader in developing theoretical and operational concepts related to the revolution in military affairs (RMA). A flood of books about the use of high-technology weapons have been written since the early 1990s with such titles as *The Transformation of War, War Made New: Technology, Warfare, and the Course of History, The New Face of War: How War Will Be Fought in the 21st Century*, and *Wired for War: The Robotics Revolution and Conflict in the 21st Century*.

In *Wired for War*, P. W. Singer demonstrates how science fiction has come to the battlefield—remote-controlled Predator drones flown by armchair pilots in Las Vegas, Nevada, bomb terrorists in Afghanistan and Pakistan while the number of unmanned systems on the ground in Iraq has gone from zero to 12,000 over the last five years. This technological revolution promises only to increase in speed and innovation. There is even the distinct possibility that weapons systems will develop to the point where the decision calculus as to whether a target is a friend or foe will be made by a machine and not a human being. This raises an interesting question in terms of law and ethics—who would be held liable for the death of an innocent person? The robot? The official who sent the robot out on a mission? The software programmer? The builders of the robots? The government that ordered the research and development of the robot?

POINT   The development and deployment of advanced technologies is not just a military issue but also raises important questions concerning the laws of war, morality, ethics, and accountability.

Russian strategic weapons to some 1,550 on each side—reductions to occur over a seven-year period.

Concerns with Deterrence Theory

Reading military doctrinal statements can be a chilling experience for many people. Often written in a straightforward, technical manner, they are unsettling, particularly when they describe, often in matter-of-fact fashion, a possible nuclear exchange between states. Some feminists characterize all this talk about deterrence by threatening mass destruction as no more than yet another masculinist construction masquerading as if it were a "theory." Other critics of deterrence, defense, and warfighting theories or doctrines make several salient points.

First, what is known as the usability paradox lies at the heart of U.S. nuclear weapons policy. Two key objectives of U.S. policy—(1) to deter aggression against the United States and its allies, and (2) to prevent accidental war—require that U.S. nuclear forces be usable, but not *too* usable. In other words, for deterrence to work, nuclear forces must be usable enough that an adversary is convinced that a U.S. nuclear response would be forthcoming if the United States or its vital interests were attacked. On the other hand, to prevent an accidental nuclear war, U.S. weapons must not be so usable that they could conceivably be launched by computer error or insane missile silo operators or used in such a way that they provoke a fearful adversary to launch a preemptive attack. Second, and perhaps even more disturbing, studies of two of the most dangerous crises in the Cold War—Cuba (1962) and the Middle East (1973)—suggest that leaders in both Moscow and Washington misperceived each other's motivations and intentions, making for much more dangerous situations than we had realized previously. Theories of deterrence, it is argued, may give leaders a false confidence that they can calibrate carefully their actions to those of an adversary, thus effectively communicating their intentions.

Third, there are major areas of concern involving nuclear weapons and the developing world. The key question is the extent to which the logic of deterrence as outlined here (essentially devised by American scholars and political leaders in relation to their Cold War, then-Soviet counterparts) is equally applicable, for example, to Indian–Pakistani relations or to present-day U.S.–Russian relations. There is also concern over China's views on limited deterrence and the fact that Beijing is bent on expanding and modernizing its nuclear arsenal in the years ahead. Without China as a full player, both the nuclear nonproliferation and comprehensive test ban regimes are decidedly of less value. Although the United States continues to endorse obligations under the Non-Proliferation Treaty, failure by the U.S. Senate to ratify the Comprehensive Test Ban Treaty and talk from time to time of nuclear modernization make it more difficult to keep these (and potentially other) parties in compliance with arms-control regimes.

Fourth, there has been growing recognition that the mass destruction likely to be suffered from use of nuclear, chemical, or biological weapons makes them of very limited, if any, value outside of their use as a deterrent to warfare. Much more useful are conventional, non-nuclear weapons and weapons systems that can be deployed and used, if doing so is compatible with national interests. It's hard to imagine what advantage would come from battlefield use of nuclear or other weapons of mass destruction, which accounts for the continued push by even military authorities, if not to eliminate them altogether, then at least to reduce the numbers of them remaining in national arsenals.

Finally, urging other countries like North Korea and Iran not to acquire nuclear weapons has been an extremely hard sell in much the same way as Israel, India, and Pakistan were not dissuaded from acquiring them. Battlefield use of such weapons would be as much or even more devastating to them as members of the original nuclear "club" of great powers that emerged in the 1950s and 1960s (the United States, United Kingdom, Russia, France, and China) would experience were they to use them in armed conflict. Still, nuclear weapons for those who seek them do raise a country's "status" and the degree to which it must be taken more seriously not only by its adversaries, but also by other countries around the world.

Fortunately, however, since 1945 countries that acquire these weapons have so far avoided using them in armed conflicts. Doing so risks a devastating retaliatory response whether with nuclear or conventional attacks—a strong antidote to reckless behavior. The fear of retaliatory attack or invasion tends to induce an even greater degree of caution after acquiring these weapons than typically might have been the case beforehand. Indeed, acquiring weapons and using them against other countries is potentially suicidal—hardly an enhancement of the country's security. This security dilemma remains—acquiring nuclear weapons actually tends to undermine, rather than enhance, a country's security.

MORAL PRINCIPLE AND THE USE OF FORCE

Pacifism is a philosophical position that in its purest sense rejects all forms of war and any use of force as legitimate means for attaining objectives, resolving conflicts, or any other purpose. Its opposite—a bellicose orientation or **bellicism**— either sees value in war itself or at least understands war as so essential a part of world politics that it cannot be avoided.

Bellicists tend to discount the human costs of armed conflict, observing that war also produces people willing to make sacrifices, who exhibit courage and outright bravery in the face of danger, industriousness, loyalty, obedience, and other martial values a society may wish to cultivate. Taken to the absurd extreme, war is seen to be a "purifying bath of blood and iron,"[5] presumably a therapeutic effect for society as a whole.

Pacifism or commitment to nonviolence is a perfectly defensible philosophical or moral position. The same cannot be said for bellicism, which sees positive value in violence and the use of force. Just because we live in a world prone to violence does not mean that violence is morally right or good in itself, particularly not in an age when war can lead to mass destruction on an unprecedented scale. The principal challenge to pacifism, of course, is also the question of its practicality in an anarchic world, in which states and even nonstate actors may use force to attain their objectives.

9.5 Apply moral or ethical and legal considerations to both the decision to use force or go to war (*jus ad bellum*) and conduct in the war itself (*jus in bello*).

👁 **Watch** the **Video "The Uncertain Status of Enemy Combatants"** at mypoliscilab.com

pacifism ■ commitment to peaceful, nonviolent approaches to conflict

---

[5]The quote is sometimes attributed to Georg Hegel, although the attribution may be apocryphal.

ARGUMENT-COUNTERARGUMENT | A Democratic Peace?

ARGUMENT　Immanuel Kant, the 18th-century philosopher, argued that the best way to ensure progress toward peace is to encourage the growth of democratic republics, as those types of political systems are more peaceful than authoritarian states. President Woodrow Wilson represented World War I as the war to end all wars—by eliminating dictatorships to make the world safe for democracy. Echoing Kant, if countries became republics—representative democracies—war in principle could be eliminated. After all, it is people who fight and die in wars so, if allowed to have a democratic political voice, there would be little, if any, enthusiasm for the use of armed force.

COUNTERARGUMENT　Particularly with the end of the Cold War in the early 1990s, scholars have attempted empirically to test the proposition that democracies are more peaceful in their foreign relations. Among others, Michael Doyle has observed that democracies, while quite capable of using force or going to war, tend not to go to war with each other. Not everyone agrees with Doyle (or, for that matter, Kant and Wilson). Beyond the problem of how one defines or identifies a democracy, to many realists it is national interest and cost-benefit calculations in relation to using force to achieve their objectives that matters—not the type of regime.

APPLICATION　The answer to the question of whether democracies are more peaceful in relation to one another is not merely of academic interest; it has significant foreign policy implications. On the one hand, state support of democratic movements around the world can be justified on the grounds of enhancing the prospects of peaceful relations among states.

The George W. Bush administration made this argument in 2003, claiming a peaceful and democratic Iraq would be a model and thus have a positive ripple effect on authoritarian regimes in the Middle East, transforming them over time into democracies. On the other hand, some are highly suspicious of such pronouncements, reasoning that the idea of a democratic peace can be used (or misused) to justify interventions in the domestic affairs of other states or merely as an excuse to dismiss past acts of aggression by democracies.

In 2011, popular challenges to authoritarian regimes occurred across the Arab world—initially in Tunisia and Egypt, later in Bahrain, Yemen, Libya, and Syria. Although these antiregime movements enjoyed widespread support, there was no assurance that new, democratic regimes would emerge throughout the region, much less that this would be conducive to peace in our time. Based on your knowledge of the current political situation in the Middle East (include non-Arab countries like Iran and Pakistan), what obstacles exist to making this peaceful vision a reality? ◣

bellicism ■ idea that war and war preparations have positive value to state and society

just-war theory ■ arguments as to the accepted circumstances in which states can go to war and conduct warfare

Just-War Theory

Just-war theory (sometimes called just-war doctrine) is an example of normative theory that prescribes right conduct—how states and their agents ought to act. International law concerning war—the law of armed conflicts—rests on treaty obligations, customary practice, the writings of jurists, and general principles closely linked to just-war theory. This theory adopts a position between the pacifist and bellicist positions, but it is somewhat closer to the pacifist pole because it seeks to avoid war or, failing that, to limit its destructive consequences. Every effort is made to avoid armed conflict in the first place:

←——————— *Pacifism*　　　　*Just-War Theory*　　　　　　　　*Bellicism* ——————→

Just-war theory, encompassing both *jus ad bellum* (Latin term for the right to go to war) and *jus in bello* (Latin term for right conduct in war), comes from a long tradition in Western thought that can be traced to Plato (427–347 B.C.E.). The first explicit reference to the just-war concept is from Plato's Roman follower Cicero (106–43 B.C.E.), who stated that "just wars should be fought justly."[6] The ideas elaborated by Cicero in a non-Judaic, pre-Christian context were developed further by St. Augustine, who presented it as an alternative to pacifism that had been dominant in the early Christian Church. Aquinas (1225–1274), Vitoria (1480–1546), Suarez (1548–1617), Gentili (1552–1608), and other writers contributed further to establishing just-war concepts as a more formal philosophical or moral foundation upon which international law concerning war would come to rest.

Building on the work of Suarez and Gentili, who had dealt with legal aspects of just-war theory, the Dutch policy-oriented scholar Hugo Grotius (1583–1645) incorporated much of just-war thinking in his writings on international law. His *Law of War and Peace* (first published in Latin in 1625 as *De Bellum ac Pacis*) took just-war theory from its moral or theological base to develop what would become legally binding principles. As with other international law, the law of war has been drawn from general principles, customary practice, formal treaties, court cases, and the writings of jurists. The Hague Conventions and Regulations (1899 and 1907) and Geneva Conventions and Protocols (1949 and 1977) represent a formalization or codification of the modern-day law of war.

The *jus ad bellum,* or right to go to war, depends first and foremost upon having a just cause, such as when a country comes under attack by an aggressor state. Second, the decision to go to war cannot be made by anyone; it must be made by the legitimate authority within the state. Determining which is the legitimate authority is not always an easy matter, of course, particularly not in civil wars within a state when each side contends that it is the legitimate authority. Third, just-war theory dictates that resort to armed force as an option must first of all be proportionate to the provocation, not a disproportionate response to a relatively minor cause. Fourth, there also must be some chance of success, or resort to war would be a futile enterprise wasting lives and property unnecessarily. Finally, war is the last resort. The decision to use armed force should be delayed whenever possible until every reasonable peaceful means for settling the dispute has been exhausted.

Satisfying all of these criteria depends heavily on right intention. If decision makers are not committed to doing the right thing, no set of moral or legal principles can be effective. Clever political leaders and diplomats can always find ways to skirt any set of rules, perhaps even manipulating them in an elaborate rationalization of their conduct. Critics of just-war theory make precisely this point. The historical record suggests to them that more often than not the practitioners of statecraft have manipulated just-war principles to justify some rather unjust causes. Even if this is so, of course, it is more a criticism of the orientation and conduct of many leaders and diplomats than it is an effective assault on the logic of the just-war position. Defenders of just-war theory use this same evidence to underscore the need for greater compliance with a practical mechanism for avoiding war, especially in an age when the mass-destructive consequences of war are so great. Given

jus ad bellum ■ Latin term for moral criteria establishing the right to go to war

jus in bello ■ Latin term for moral criteria establishing right conduct in war

---

[6]See Cicero, *The Republic*, II: xxvii; III: xxiii, xxiv, and xxix; and *The Laws*, II: ix, xiv; and III: iii, xviii.

these criteria, some have contested the decision of the United States to invade Iraq in 2003 as meeting the standards of a just war. What do you think? Why?

These conditions for a just war are very demanding. They clearly are skewed in the direction of avoiding war if at all possible. As such, they stand much closer to the pacifist than to the bellicist pole. War is not to be sought.

Conduct during War

Just-war theory does not confine itself merely to whether one has a right to use armed force or resort to war in international relations. It goes beyond the *jus ad bellum* to raise questions of right conduct in war once armed conflict breaks out. Another set of principles governs right conduct in war *(jus in bello)*, whether or not the decision to go to war was just. Very real limits are set in an effort to limit or confine the death and destruction of warfare to what is militarily necessary, thus reducing war's barbarity.

The principle of military necessity can be construed so broadly as to allow almost any conduct in war, if political authorities or military commanders do not approach the use of force with a spirit consistent with the human-cost-reduction purpose of just-war theory. It is a narrow construction of military necessity that is

---

▶ CASE & POINT | Mark Twain's War Prayer

CASE   Reflecting on the American experience of mass casualties and destruction of property that occurred in the Civil War (1860–1865), Mark Twain—more commonly known for such novels as *Tom Sawyer, Huckleberry Finn, A Connecticut Yankee in King Arthur's Court*—provides a case against war in a fictional account of a prayer delivered by a holy man addressing a church congregation. It is a bitter, satiric critique of war as an instrument of policy.

O Lord our Father, our young patriots, idols of our hearts, go forth to battle—be Thou near them! With them, in spirit, we also go forth from the sweet peace of our beloved firesides to smite the foe. O Lord our God, help us to tear their soldiers to bloody shreds with our shells; help us to cover their smiling fields with the pale forms of their patriot dead; help us to drown the thunder of the guns with the shrieks of their wounded, writhing in pain; help us to lay waste their humble homes with a hurricane of fire; help us to wring the hearts of their unoffending widows with unavailing grief; help us to turn them out roofless with their little children to wander unfriended the wastes

of their desolated land in rags and hunger and thirst, sports of the sun flames of summer and the icy winds of winter, broken in spirit, worn with travail, imploring Thee for the refuge of the grave and denied it—for our sakes who adore Thee, Lord, blast their hopes, blight their lives, protract their bitter pilgrimage, make heavy their steps, water their way with their tears, stain the white snow with the blood of their wounded feet! We ask it, in the spirit of love, of Him Who is the Source of Love, and Who is the ever-faithful refuge and friend of all that are sore beset and seek His aid with humble and contrite hearts. Amen.

POINT   War is highly destructive, barbaric in its implications for the human condition. Yet, it still has legitimacy among people (including religious leaders) who see it as a legitimate remedy for resolving human conflicts. To Twain (and certainly to pacifists), war is not the answer. What do you think? Do you agree or disagree with Twain? Why or why not? ▶

Source: *Mark Twain*, Europe and Elsewhere. *Copyright 1923, 1951 by* The Mark Twain Company.

prescribed by just-war theory. Consistent with the earlier discussion of Clausewitz's theory of war, armed force is used only to destroy or substantially weaken an enemy's warmaking capability.

Destroying an enemy's warmaking capability focuses destructive efforts on an adversary's armed forces and only those parts of the society's infrastructure that directly contribute to its warmaking effort. It is not a call to destroy an entire society, its population, or anything else of material or cultural value. People will still be killed and property destroyed, but probably far less collateral damage will be sustained when the principle of military necessity is narrowly interpreted to limit the destructiveness of war to what is absolutely necessary for military purposes.

Obliteration bombing of cities or other population centers was widely practiced by both sides in World War II. At the time, many defenders of this strategy saw these raids as undermining societal morale in enemy countries, thus weakening an enemy's will to resist. But postwar evaluation of strategic bombing and other uses of air power raised a serious challenge to this rationale. Rage among survivors contributed in many cases to an increased will to resist rather than to submit. If so, then obliteration bombing proved to be counterproductive or dysfunctional, even militarily speaking.

With the benefit of hindsight, obliteration bombing of population centers has been discredited both militarily and morally in the years since World War II. Put another way, there can be no moral justification under just-war doctrine for such mass death and destruction, particularly because these military actions did not serve legitimate military purposes. Just because military purposes are served, of course, is not enough to justify any conduct in war. Additional conditions need to be met to satisfy *jus in bello* obligations.

Noncombatants   An effort must be made to spare noncombatants and other defenseless persons. Guilty or not, noncombatants—civilian populations—are not the proper object of warfare. Even captured enemy soldiers are now defenseless persons who may be taken prisoner but may not be executed just because they are prisoners. Prisoners of war (sometimes called PWs or POWs) have rights, and these have been made part of international law. This is why the establishment of the prison at Guantanamo Bay, Cuba, by the United States has been so controversial. The prison was established following the overthrow of the Taliban in Afghanistan in the fall of 2001 to hold suspected terrorists. The U.S. government, relying on laws dating back to the Civil War and World War II, declared that these individuals were not prisoners of war, but rather "enemy combatants" held as "detainees." As a result, they could not invoke the international legal rights associated with prisoners of war—a perspective disputed by critics of American prison policies in Cuba and elsewhere.

A distinction is often drawn between counterforce and countervalue targets. Counterforce targets include military headquarters, troop or tank formations, combat aircraft, ships, maintenance facilities, and other military installations, the destruction of which would directly weaken an enemy's warmaking capability. Countervalue targets are factories, rail junctions, civilian airports, and power plants in or near cities that contribute to an enemy's warmaking capability or overall war effort. Even if people are not the intended victims, the bombing of countervalue targets usually produces more civilian, noncombatant casualties than counterforce targeting.

Moreover, the means used to accomplish military purposes need to be proportional to the goal. If a 300-pound bomb can be used to destroy a particular military target, a 10,000-pound bomb ought not to be used, particularly if doing so increases the collateral damage or destruction of lives and property. In the same spirit, navy warships may choose to avoid sinking an enemy merchant ship by disabling the propeller, so they can board and search the cargo instead. Just-war theory aims to reduce unnecessary death or other damage.

dual or double effect principle ■ a single act that may have more than one effect, perhaps some good and others not.

Some just-war theorists invoke the **dual or double-effect principle** in dealing with the moral problem of killing noncombatants and producing collateral damage in warfare. Any action may have two or more effects or consequences. If the intent is to destroy a legitimate target that contributes to an enemy's warmaking capability or overall war effort, then every reasonable effort must be made to avoid unnecessary casualties or other destruction. The "good effect" is destroying the legitimate military target. Dropping bombs, sending missiles, landing artillery shells, or firing on such a target may also have unintended human and material consequences—the bad effect.

Following double-effect logic and assuming proportionality—that the target is worth destroying in light of its military value when weighed against the expected consequences—just-war theorists argue that killing noncombatants or destroying civilian property may be morally justifiable when both effects occur simultaneously or the good effect precedes the bad. For example, in targeting an armaments factory at night when most workers were expected to be at home, it is accepted that a few workers may still be killed when the factory is destroyed. Or a bomb may go astray and kill some people in a residential area next to the factory, even though efforts were made to avoid this unfortunate outcome. That is the misfortune of war. Bad things happen in war, which is why just-war theory puts so much emphasis on avoiding war in the first place. Principles by which wars need to be examined in order to be deemed just are outlined in Table 9.2.

If warriors intend the bad effect or if it precedes the good, such conduct does not satisfy the principle of double effect and is therefore morally wrong. Bombing workers at their homes next to the armaments factory (the bad effect) will likely reduce or eliminate the production capacity of the factory (the good effect, militarily speaking). The problem is that this good effect depends upon achieving the bad effect first. However good one's objectives or purposes may be, just-war theorists argue that good ends cannot justify evil means: The ends do not justify the means. It would be wrong to bomb the village. If factory production must be halted, then the factory itself should be targeted, preferably at a time when as many workers as possible can be spared.

Any weapon can be used immorally, but some could not be used morally even if one intended to do so. Immoral weapons are those that are indiscriminate or cause needless suffering. A rifle is not immoral in itself; if used properly it can be used with discrimination, sparing noncombatants. If used improperly to murder noncombatants, for example, it is the action and not the weapon that is immoral.

The same is true for most conventional bombs delivered accurately by airplanes or missiles. They can be used morally or immorally, depending for the most part

▸ **TABLE 9.2**

Just-War Principles

In recent years there has been interest in a third category of just-war principles—*jus post bellum,* or what should be done after the shooting stops to create a just and stable peace. One suggestion is "no witch hunts" or stripping the vanquished of all their rights. This seems to be increasingly important in those cases where a Western power stays on for a number of years after major combat operations have ended, such as the United States in Iraq.

Jus ad Bellum	*Jus in Bello*
1. Just cause	1. Military necessity
2. Legitimate authority	2. Spare noncombatants and other defenseless persons
3. Proportionality of war	3. Proportional means
4. Chance of success	4. Means not immoral *per se*: not indiscriminate or causing needless suffering
5. War as last resort; exhaust peaceful means to resolve dispute	

Note: Application of all principles assumes right intention.

on the target selected and how it is to be destroyed. The more accurate the better is true from both a military and a moral position. Indeed, destruction of a legitimate military target is more likely, and collateral or unnecessary death and destruction, if not eliminated, can at least be minimized if accurate weapons are employed.

Chemical and Biological Weapons   By contrast, wildly inaccurate weapons—including chemical or biological agents as in gas or germ warfare—by their very nature eliminate the distinction between combatant and noncombatant. Such weapons usually are not useful militarily, as winds disperse chemical agents indiscriminately, and diseases can spread to both sides of the battlefield. Such weapons are immoral in themselves and have been declared illegal.

Treaties prohibit use of chemical and biological weapons. The international consensus that led to these chemical and biological conventions rests on this moral argument. Not only are these weapons indiscriminate, they fail another moral test by causing needless suffering. Rifle bullets or other antipersonnel weapons designed to prolong or otherwise increase agony also fail this moral test. Killing in war is supposed to be as humane as possible. Most categories of weapons that are intended to enhance rather than reduce human suffering have also been defined in treaties as illegal.

Nuclear Weapons   Nuclear weapons are a more controversial case. The two atomic bombs that the United States dropped on the Japanese cities of Hiroshima and Nagasaki in 1945 were justified by many on the utilitarian grounds that the bombings would shorten the war. Those who made this argument saw the loss of life at Hiroshima and Nagasaki as precluding an even greater loss of life that would have resulted from an Allied invasion of the Japanese home islands. The Japanese had fought tenaciously to defend islands in the Pacific such as Iwo Jima and Guam; it was believed they would fight with even greater determination to defend their homeland. Others questioned the morality of bombing people even for this purpose, suggesting that if the bombs were to be used at all, they should have been directed toward strictly military targets, not population centers interspersed with military targets. Decision makers responded that the Japanese leaders could take the blame, as they made the decision to locate military-related plants where they did.

Each of the weapons dropped on Japan was less than 20 kilotons (20,000 tons) in yield. Many nuclear weapons today have a much larger megaton (million tons) or multimegaton yield, with such heat, blast, and radiation effects that they cannot be used with discrimination, so these weapons fail on human-suffering grounds as well. On the other hand, some have argued that lower-yield, tactical nuclear weapons (perhaps as small as one kiloton or less, with reduced-radiation effects) can be used with discrimination and need not cause unnecessary suffering.

Critics are skeptical of this claim. They also counter that using any nuclear weapons at all "opens Pandora's box," legitimating this category of weaponry and increasing the likelihood that even larger nuclear weapons will be employed by one or another of the parties. Indicative of the lack of consensus on these issues, and unlike chemical and biological agents, nuclear weapons have not yet been declared illegal, however ill advised or immoral their use might be.

ARMED INTERVENTION AND NATIONAL SECURITY

9.6 Describe the diverse purposes that motivate states and the criteria state authorities use to decide whether or not to intervene militarily in another country.

●─ Watch the Video "Western Arm Sales and the Rwandan Genocide" at mypoliscilab.com

raison d'état ■
literally "reason of state," which is seen as the realist rationale for foreign and national security policies pursued by state authorities

Quite apart from legal considerations, the question of *when* to use force in armed interventions is an important national security matter. Some argue that the sole criterion should be national interest, particularly if a vital interest is at stake. Domestic critics challenged post–Cold War interventions by the United States in Somalia, Rwanda, and Haiti and the contribution of U.S. troops to the NATO peacekeeping operation in Bosnia. U.S. and NATO intervention in Libya in 2011 raised similar concerns. These critics questioned whether sufficient U.S. interests were involved to bear the costs or risks involved, however worthy any of these ventures might have seemed to advocates justifying them on purely humanitarian grounds.

When national interests or objectives are compelling, legal restrictions are often overlooked—or stretched to justify national purposes. The French term *raison d'état* (or, in German, *Staatsräson*) refers to the rationale of justifying state policy only by the state's own security interests or objectives. In 1914 Germany justified its invasion of Belgium on precisely these grounds. Germany had no particular quarrel with Belgium, which claimed a right to be neutral in the dispute between France and Germany. In a rare diplomatic admission in such circumstances, the German chancellor apologized for having to violate Belgian neutrality and thus its sovereignty, but claimed that this was necessary in order to protect Germany from an attack by France across Belgium.

The Belgian experience is reminiscent of the plight of the people on the Aegean island of Melos off the Greek coast when confronted by Athens. Melos had claimed a right to be neutral in the Peloponnesian War (431–404 B.C.E.) between Athens and Sparta. Recounting the events, Thucydides tells us how Athens tried to force

Melos to join in an alliance against Sparta and its allies. When the Melians resisted, claiming the right to remain neutral, the Athenians responded that, in the real world, *might makes right*: "The strong do what they will and the weak do what they must." Even though we dispute the Athenian claim to any right based on its power position, they nevertheless had the capabilities to force the Melians into subjection, which they proceeded to do. Athenian might trampled Melian right.

Humanitarian Intervention

In the absence of an invitation from the legitimate government of a state, even humanitarian intervention—using force to stop the fighting among competing groups, provide the necessary security to feed starving people, or halt ethnic cleansing—legally violates the principle of nonintervention in the domestic affairs of a state. The UN Charter does not give the Security Council authority to use force for humanitarian purposes *per se*. Armed intervention under UN auspices in the internal affairs of a state, however justifiable the humanitarian purpose might seem, is legitimate in this strict interpretation only if the problem cannot likely be contained, thus posing a threat to international peace and security. Some argue that interventions to stop genocide or other serious human rights violations do have a humanitarian basis or grounding in customary international law, but not everyone agrees. There is a consensus, however, that the UN Charter does allow intervention for these purposes when genocide or other human rights violations rise to the level of being a threat to international peace and security—the Article 42 criterion the Security Council uses to authorize such actions.

humanitarian intervention ■ application of force within another country in order to stop the fighting among competing groups, provide the necessary security to feed starving people, or halt ethnic cleansing

The case of Kosovo in 1999 illustrates the issue. No one denied that Kosovo was a province of Yugoslavia. The Serbs stated that whatever actions they took in the province were therefore an internal matter, and outside intervention was a violation of Yugoslavian sovereignty. The Serbian policy of systematic ethnic cleansing, however, led to NATO military action on the grounds of humanitarian intervention and the claim that Serbian actions were a threat to regional peace and security. It is significant that NATO did not ask for the blessing of the United Nations for NATO's air campaign, given opposition within the UN Security Council on both political and legal grounds.

Humanitarian motives may genuinely accompany actions taken primarily for national-interest reasons. In other cases, however, humanitarian motives are presented as a pretext used by political leaders and diplomats in an effort to justify armed interventions done exclusively (or almost entirely) for national-interest reasons. Propagandists like to present humanitarian purposes for armed intervention to make the behavior seem less self-serving.

Because states usually intervene to serve their interests does not mean that they always do so for only self-serving purposes. They may wish to intervene quite genuinely for humanitarian purposes or, consistent with their broad interests, to contribute to restoration of international peace and security. This seems to have been the case when NATO intervened in Kosovo. Or they may wish to use military force in efforts against drug smugglers. In such cases states may weigh the costs and benefits of armed intervention or in terms of how well they serve the human condition.

In some cases the use of force for humanitarian purposes may cause even more bloodshed than if no intervention had taken place. In other cases the reverse is true: Armed intervention at relatively low cost may succeed in providing greater security and meeting human needs. The difficulty, of course, is that expected net costs or benefits to human beings are not always easy to estimate accurately.

Competing Criteria for Decisions on Armed Intervention

Events in 1989 brought an end to the Cold War but not to armed intervention. Subsequent years have been marked by a continuation of armed intervention by outside states and multilateral coalitions of states, as in responses to Iraq's armed takeover of Kuwait; post-9/11 interventions in Afghanistan and Iraq; civil strife in Somalia and Haiti; and genocide in the Balkan states, the Rwanda-Burundi-Congo area in central Africa, and Darfur in Sudan. Sometimes interventions for humanitarian purposes seem too little or too late to stop the bloodshed, as was true in central Africa in the 1990s and Darfur in the first decade of the 21st century—efforts in Sudan confined primarily to diplomatic and peacekeeping efforts, the latter under the auspices of the African Union.

Policymakers face difficult decisions about whether or not to intervene with armed force to respond to aggression, prevent or stop genocide, restore order, or maintain the peace. We can identify seven, often competing, criteria typically part of the decision-making calculus—factors weighed by policymakers considering armed intervention: (1) estimate of domestic political support for (or opposition to) the proposed intervention, which is often expressed in "pro or con" terms using one or more of the other six criteria; (2) assessment of economic, military, and other capabilities needed to carry out an armed intervention; (3) determination of whether the intervention is permissible because the legitimate government of the targeted sovereign state has invited the action or, if not, whether respect by policymakers for the sovereignty claimed by the targeted state precludes such action; (4) assessment or understanding of national interest (and related national objectives); (5) consideration of whether defending human rights warrants armed intervention; (6) estimate of the net expected effect on the human condition of the proposed intervention—whether doing so will help or just make matters worse; and (7) assessment of the degree to which sufficient international support can be garnered to multilateralize the intervention instead of unilaterally going it alone with few, if any, other countries participating.

Popular Support (or Opposition)   Armed interventions prove difficult (if not destined for failure) if they proceed without domestic political support. This is particularly true in democracies, but even authoritarian regimes find it easier to intervene militarily when their publics support such action. A problem for policymakers is how fickle popular support often can be—perhaps enthusiastic at the outset, shifting over time to opposition, particularly as the human and material costs mount. Even in the absence of popular support, policymakers may choose to intervene or sustain their military presence in other countries when they understand important interests are at stake.

Economic and Military Capabilities   Not all countries have the economic and military capabilities they need to intervene, particularly if such contingencies are far away, well beyond their borders. Even when they have these capabilities—as is usually the case for the United States—there may be real limits on the number of such interventions that can be conducted simultaneously. Thus, contingencies in Iraq and Afghanistan—not to mention standing commitments in Europe, Japan, South Korea, and elsewhere—make additional interventions problematic even when humanitarian or other factors might warrant doing so.

Sovereignty   Under international law, states are normally prohibited from intervention in the domestic affairs of other sovereign states unless requested by the legitimate government of the state subject to such intervention; however, use of force (including armed intervention) is allowed under the UN Charter:

- For collective security, as when the Security Council authorizes using force in response to a contingency endangering international peace and security (Chapter VII, particularly Article 42)
- For self-defense or collective defense by alliances or coalitions of states, as in responding to aggression against a sovereign state (Chapter VII, Article 51)

National Interest   Armed intervention is an option often weighed against considerations of national interest and related national objectives. Some argue that armed intervention should be pursued only if there is a *vital* national interest to be served. Even if one considers this criterion to be decisive, as many realists do, there is no escaping the practical difficulty in trying to define precisely what the national interest (much less *vital* national interest) might be in a particular case. The national interest is subject to multiple interpretations, but even with this ambiguity, it remains part of the decision-making calculus.

Human Rights   A consensus has been forming, mainly in the last half of the 20th century that continues to the present and holds that human beings have rights that may supersede those claimed by sovereign states. This human rights consensus rests on increasing understanding and acceptance of respect for life, human dignity, and justice or fairness as universal ethical or moral principles that have global application to individuals, groups, and other categories or classes of human beings. Voluntary assistance for relief in natural disasters is one manifestation of these principles in action. The enormous human and material cost suffered by the victims of mass destruction and atrocities throughout the 20th century resulted in substantial growth in international law (codified by numerous treaties coming into force after World War II), which has come to (1) define certain civil or political, social, and economic rights, and (2) prohibit certain acts defined as war crimes, genocide, and other crimes against peace and humanity. When such human rights violations are also understood to endanger international peace and security, there is clearer legal ground for humanitarian, armed intervention under UN Security Council auspices, following Chapter VII of the UN Charter.

Net Effect on the Human Condition   Armed intervention has very real costs not just to people and property in states and societies subject to intervention, but also to the armed forces conducting such interventions. The extent of these costs usually cannot be known with certainty, but policymakers nevertheless try to estimate what they are likely to be. It is extraordinarily difficult, if not impossible, to quantify with precision the net effect (benefits minus costs) on the human condition even after an armed intervention has occurred. Deaths and other casualties can be counted and property losses estimated, but some human costs (for example, psychological damage) may not be known for many years, if then. The problem is compounded when one tries to estimate what these costs might be in advance of an armed intervention. Nevertheless, this criterion typically plays on the minds of policymakers who contemplate whether armed intervention will improve or worsen the human condition. At the very least, expected net effect on the human condition can influence how an armed intervention is implemented. Using this criterion, policymakers may select options expected to minimize or reduce adverse consequences to both armed forces and the peoples subject to their actions.

Degree of Multilateralism   As unilateral armed intervention, regardless of motivation or justification, has come increasingly into disfavor, policymakers have been more prone to look for multilateral support and cooperation in conducting armed interventions. UN Security Council mandates, for example, provide political and legal grounds for proceeding. In the absence of such Security Council action, proceeding multilaterally under Article 51 as a collective-defense response is still viewed by most policymakers as politically preferable to unilateral action. This helps explain why the George W. Bush administration, despite a generally dismissive attitude toward the United Nations, sought a UN Security Council resolution in the fall of 2002 requiring Iraq to readmit weapons inspectors. This effort included an elaborate oral and visual presentation by Colin Powell, the secretary of state. The UN Security Council previously authorized intervention in Afghanistan (2001) and later in Libya (2011).

These seven criteria often compete with one another, and choices concerning how much weight to give to one over another have to be made sooner or later. That said, we are left with an analytical framework that specifies factors that typically are part of decisions to engage in armed intervention.

CONCLUSION

So many trees have been sacrificed to provide the paper for scholars and political leaders to pontificate on the causes of interstate conflict and the use of force that many people believe these are the defining issues in the study of international relations and world politics. Current policymakers dealing with dictators and authoritarian leaders in such countries as North Korea and Iran would probably agree. The situation in Libya exemplified the complexities of deciding to actually engage in military action against other regimes. Despite U.S. and NATO intervention, the war dragged on for months until Kaddafi's death in October 2011. Following Clausewitz, war should be viewed as an instrument of policy, but this requires thinking very carefully about what objectives are being sought, what capabilities can be brought to bear, and what should be done if the original plan does not result in the anticipated success. Even such considerations do not guarantee a desired outcome. Furthermore, in the modern age a series of questions also arise once the shooting stops. In the case of Libya, what responsibility, if any, will outside powers have in repairing the damage in the post–civil war period? Is foreign aid to be provided? Do the outside state powers have any role to play in the domestic political scene?

    If it is any comfort, however, the world today has changed in at least one basic aspect—interstate wars have become rare. Over the centuries, certain norms, laws, and rules of the game have been devised by clashing kings, prime ministers, chancellors, and presidents to influence, if not govern, their international contests. Certainly, using force is often seen by decision makers as a rational instrument of policy or means to attain their national objectives or serve their national interests. In our world of such increasing dangers as nuclear proliferation and recurrent crises of authority that tempt external armed intervention, we can only hope that most states will see the logic behind the need in collectively abiding by a common set of rules to guide the conduct of their international relations even as they make their strategic and tactical calculations in pursuit of their national interests.

✔— Study and Review the Post-Test & Chapter Exam at mypoliscilab.com

LEARNING OBJECTIVES REVIEW

9.1 Explain how international relations practitioners use the rationality assumption to determine when it is in their interest to use force.

Wars don't just happen. Although they may miscalculate, policymakers may see the use of force as necessary or as a cost-effective way to achieve their objectives. However desirable it may be to eliminate interstate conflict, the use of force still has legitimacy among policymakers in many countries, particularly when peaceful remedies have been exhausted.

KEY TERMS

Interstate conflict 296
Rational choice 296

ADDITIONAL READING

Bruce Bueno de Mesquita, *The War Trap* (New Haven, CT: Yale University Press, 2009). A rigorous application of logic and math to aid in understanding why wars occur.

9.2 Illustrate how the international system, the individual and group, and the state and societal levels of analysis help to understand the causes of interstate conflicts.

Using the levels of analysis is an excellent way to formulate hypotheses (educated guesses) as to why a conflict has occurred. Factors or explanations may involve individuals, small groups, the nature of state and society, or the structure of the international system—the distribution of power among states. An example provided was explanations as to why the United States invaded Iraq in 2003.

KEY TERMS

Anarchy 298
Civil war 298

Armed intervention 299
Collective security 299
Groupthink 300
World federalists 301

ADDITIONAL READING

Kenneth N. Waltz, *Man, the State and War* (New York: Columbia University Press, 1959). The classic statement on war utilizing the levels of analysis: *individual and group*: human nature, the psyche, cognition, and human relationships and associations; *state and society*: the type of state or government, culture, social structure, and the economy; and *system*: the role of anarchy—the absence of a central authority in international politics.

9.3 Evaluate the concept of war as an instrument of policy by linking military and other capabilities to the national goals or objectives policymakers seek to achieve.

The 19th-century Prussian writer and military officer Carl von Clausewitz argued that war should only be pursued as an instrument of national policy or goals, not for glory or personal satisfaction. Although policymakers should plan as rationally as possible—weighing, for example, the appropriate means to achieve the desired ends—such factors as friction and the fog of war often cause the best-laid plans to go awry.

KEY TERMS

Strategy 303
Tactics 303
Center of gravity 306
Deterrence 306
Friction 307
Fog of war 307
Zero-sum 307

ADDITIONAL READING

The Book of War: Sun-Tzu's "The Art of War" & Carl Von Clausewitz's "On War" (New York: Modern Library, 2000). Two classic books on the nature and conduct of war.

9.4 Illustrate how military force-employment doctrines of deterrence, defense, and warfighting apply not only to great-power strategic nuclear arsenals, but also to states with smaller arsenals.

Deterrence doctrines attempt to prevent an adversary from attacking, defense is designed to mitigate the effects of an attack if deterrence fails, and warfighting can be employed for offensive reasons or in retaliation for being attacked.

KEY TERMS

Defense 308
Warfighting 308
Extended deterrence 308
Force posture 309
Minimum (or finite) deterrence 309
Mutual assured destruction (MAD) 312

First-strike capability 313
Second-strike capability 313

ADDITIONAL READINGS

Lawrence Freedman, *Evolution of Nuclear Strategy*, 3rd ed. (NY: Palgrave Macmillan, 2003). The best historical overview of nuclear strategy and the individuals associated with various doctrines.

Thomas Schelling, *The Strategy of Conflict* (Cambridge, MA: Harvard University Press, 1960, 1981). A highly influential work that utilizes game theory to produce insights on conflict and nuclear bargaining.

P. W. Singer, *Wired for War: The Robotics Revolution and Conflict in the 21st Century* (New York: Penguin Press, 2009). The best volume on where war might be headed. Science fiction meets current and future technological developments.

9.5 Apply moral or ethical and legal considerations to both the decision to use force or go to war (*jus ad bellum*) and conduct in the war itself (*jus in bello*).

Pacifism rejects any use of force. Bellicism sees value in war in and of itself. Just-war theory (sometimes called just-war doctrine) is an example of normative theory that prescribes right conduct—how states and their agents *ought* to act. International law concerning war—the law of armed conflicts—rests on treaty obligations, customary practice, the writings of jurists, and general principles closely linked to just-war theory. Both *jus ad bellum* (the right to go to war) and *jus in bello* (right conduct in war) have a tradition dating back to Plato, Cicero, Augustine, and Aquinas.

KEY TERMS
Pacifism 317
Bellicism 317
Just-war theory 318
Jus ad bellum 319

Jus in bello 319
Dual or double effect principle 322

ADDITIONAL READING
Michael Walzer, *Just and Unjust Wars*: *A Moral Argument with Historical Illustrations,* 4th ed. (NY: Basic Books, 2006). The preeminent book on the topic.

9.6 Describe the diverse purposes that motivate states and the criteria state authorities use to decide whether or not to intervene militarily in another country.

Key factors include (1) degree of domestic political support for (or opposition to) intervention; (2) assessment of economic, military, and other capabilities needed to carry out an armed intervention; (3) determination of whether the intervention is permissible because the legitimate government of the targeted sovereign state has invited the action or, if not, whether respect by policymakers for the sovereignty claimed by the targeted state precludes such action; (4) assessment or understanding of national interest (and related national objectives); (5) consideration of whether defending human rights warrants armed intervention; (6) estimate of the net expected effect on the human condition of the proposed intervention—whether doing so will help or just make matters worse; and (7) assessment of the degree to which sufficient international support can be garnered to multilateralize the intervention instead of unilaterally going it alone with few, if any, other countries participating.

KEY TERMS
Raison d'état 324
Humanitarian intervention 325

ADDITIONAL READINGS
Richard N. Haass, *War of Necessity, War of Choice*: *A Memoir of Two Iraq Wars* (New York: Simon & Schuster, 2009) and *Intervention*: *The Use of American Military Force in the Post–Cold War World,* rev. ed. (Washington, DC: Carnegie Endowment for International Peace, 1999). Thoughtful reflections on war and peace by a scholar and practitioner.
Stephen Kinzer, *Overthrow: America's Century of Regime Change from Hawaii to Iraq* (New York: Times, 2007). A sobering overview of the repeated use of U.S. military force to change regimes and the unintended consequences that usually result.

CHAPTER REVIEW

1. According to the text, which of the following is an example of a rational choice to go to war?
   a. To defend the territory of the state
   b. To settle personal disputes
   c. To loot another territory
   d. To demonstrate military prowess

2. Why is it so difficult for outsiders to analyze the rationality of any decision to go to war?
   a. Rationality is intersubjective between two states.
   b. Rationality is objective.
   c. Rationality is subjective.
   d. Rationality is based on misperceptions.

3. The use of force is _____ to diplomacy.
   a. adjunct
   b. integral
   c. legitimate
   d. necessary

4. Why does war continue to exist in international politics despite its devastating consequences?
   a. There are vested interests in continuing war.
   b. Politicians secretly enjoy war.
   c. Militaries need something to do.
   d. There is nothing to stop one state from attacking another state.

5. Which of the following is *not* used as a level of analysis when analyzing the causes of war?
   a. The United Nations
   b. The international system
   c. Group
   d. State and society

6. Explaining a civil war as being caused by a lack of regime legitimacy is an example of using what level of analysis?
   a. International system
   b. State and society
   c. Group
   d. Individual

7. Explaining a war as being caused by an arms race is an example of using what level of analysis?
   a. International system
   b. State and society
   c. Group
   d. Individual

8. The state and society level of analysis might suggest that _____ are responsible for increasing or decreasing the likelihood of war.
   a. heads of states and heads of societies
   b. political regimes and economic systems
   c. democrats and Republicans
   d. terrorists and armies

9. World federalists seek to eliminate war by what specific means?
   a. Strengthening international anarchy
   b. Creating multiple regional security organizations
   c. Replacing international anarchy with world government
   d. Eliminating national identities

10. According to Clausewitz, what is the ultimate strategic purpose in conducting war?
    a. To destroy or substantially weaken an enemy's warfighting or warmaking capability
    b. To destroy or substantially weaken an enemy's political will
    c. To destroy or substantially weaken an enemy's economic capital
    d. To destroy or substantially weaken an enemy's underlying civilian productive capacities

11. Battlefield effectiveness is linked to what two variables?
    a. Political capabilities and military will
    b. Military capabilities and will to use them
    c. Military capabilities and economic strength
    d. Will to use means and political capabilities

12. What two strategic variables must a national leader account for when judging threats from another state?
    a. The threatening state's perceived capabilities and their credibility
    b. The threatening state's perceived weaknesses and their capabilities
    c. The threatening state's political and economic capital
    d. The threatening state's propensity to use force and the battle readiness of their forces

13. What is the core strategic question policymakers should be prepared to answer prior to any use of force?
    a. How will we win?
    b. Why are we fighting?
    c. And then what?
    d. How many lives will be lost?

14. Minimum or finite deterrence requires:
    a. only the same number of nuclear weapons as any potential adversary.
    b. a relatively small number of nuclear weapons.
    c. at least ten nuclear weapons.
    d. none of the above.

15. Which of the following are examples of military doctrines?
    a. Deterrence
    b. Defense
    c. Warfighting
    d. All of the above

16. Concerns over new nuclear weapon states include
    a. heavy reliance on the threat of retaliation as the basis for deterrence.
    b. the command and control system.
    c. that a small number of nuclear weapons in a country's arsenal might tempt another state to launch a first strike.
    d. all of the above.

17. Once a war breaks out, just-war theory seeks to
    a. end the war.
    b. limit its destructive consequences.
    c. create total destruction regardless of the consequences.
    d. force one side to surrender unconditionally.

18. According to the principle of *jus ad bellum* a state must have what in order to go to war?
    a. A just cause
    b. A large military
    c. A charismatic leader
    d. Nuclear weapons

19. According to the principle of *jus in bello* an army need only _____
    a. employ the least destructive weapons.
    b. target an enemy's political leaders.
    c. bomb civilian targets indiscriminately.
    d. destroy or substantially weaken an enemy's warmaking capability.

20. Just-war theorists argue that killing noncombatants or destroying civilian targets may be morally justifiable under what conditions?
    a. When bad effects of an action precede the good
    b. When the good effects of an action precede the bad effects
    c. When an enemy did it first
    d. Never

21. Immoral weapons are defined in the following manner:
    a. weapons that are indiscriminate or cause needless suffering.
    b. weapons that are too destructive.
    c. weapons that could possibly destroy civilians.
    d. any weapon with a larger than 20,000 ton yield.

22. Under a strict interpretation of the UN Charter, humanitarian intervention is only legitimate under what conditions?
    a. The conflict is unlikely to be contained within a state, thus posing a threat to international peace and security.
    b. A mass genocide is occurring.
    c. The conflict is likely to be contained within a state, but there is a likelihood that violence in the state will continue perpetually.
    d. A state fails to protect its citizens from mob violence or private militias.

23. International legal restrictions are likely to prevent policymakers from going to war except under what conditions?
    a. When the legal restrictions were enacted prior to 1990
    b. The state perceives going to war as in its vital national interest.
    c. Policymakers have personal vendettas against another state's policymakers.
    d. A state has a large army.

24. According to the principle of state sovereignty, states are normally prohibited from doing what?
    a. Allowing their citizens to vote in another state's elections
    b. Entering into multiple collective security agreements
    c. Intervening in another state's internal affairs
    d. Going to war with another state

25. According to the UN Charter (specifically Article 42), under what conditions may human rights violations be used to justify armed intervention?
    a. When one state does not agree with another state's interpretation of human rights
    b. When such violations threaten international peace and security
    c. When such violations occur in nondemocracies
    d. When one state views intervention as being in its national interests

Asymmetric Conflict

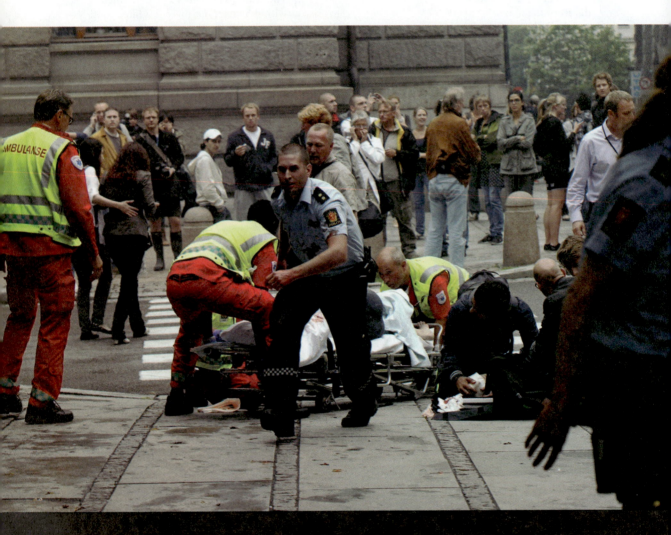

"In the post-9/11 world, threats are defined more by the fault lines within societies than by the territorial boundaries between them. From terrorism to global disease or environmental degradation, the challenges have become transnational rather than international. That is the defining quality of world politics in the twenty-first century." —*9/11 Commission Report*

LEARNING OBJECTIVES

10.1 Compare and contrast asymmetric and symmetric warfare utilizing historical examples.

10.2 Describe the history of international terrorism and key terrorist attacks against the United States over the past sixty years.

10.3 Identify and critique three factors used to explain the causes of terrorism.

10.4 Explain how radicalization, revenge, and networks have increased the threat of terrorism.

10.5 Compare and contrast the strengths and weaknesses of four major policymaking approaches to dealing strategically with the threat of international terrorism.

10.6 Explain how globalization has aided the rise of transnational criminal organizations (TCOs) and their attendant illicit activities.

Read and **Listen** to **Chapter 10** at **mypoliscilab.com**

Study and **Review** the **Pre-Test & Flashcards** at **mypoliscilab.com**

*T*he *Sandbox* (Doonesbury.com) is an online forum for service members in Afghanistan and elsewhere in the "global war on terror," returned veterans, spouses, and caregivers. *The Sandbox's* focus is not on policy and partisanship, but, as stated on the website: "the unclassified details of deployment—the everyday, the extraordinary, the wonderful, the messed-up, the absurd." Entries range from reports on operations to distant Afghani villages that at night are under Taliban control, to the experience of Marines being deployed to protect the U.S. embassy in Cairo during the overthrow of the Mubarak regime in early 2011, to what it is like to arrive at Bagram Airfield for another deployment in Afghanistan, to sobering stories of vets trying to readjust to civilian life after experiencing combat. What is extraordinary is that instantaneous personal communications from war zones even occur. Such a possibility would have been unheard of ten years ago, but are all too common now in an age of globalization.

The conflict these men and women have experienced is not the classic clash of conventional armies on the battlefield. Rather, it involves wars in which there is no frontline or rear area, where it is difficult to distinguish innocent civilians from insurgents, and personal relations with the local population are often more important than the amount of firepower one can bring to bear on a target.

Traditional national security concepts are associated with the exercise of state power and interstate conflict. With the rapid expansion of globalization, however, the role and importance of transnational, nongovernmental actors has been expanded dramatically. Here we will examine one important aspect of the dark side of globalization—the rise of armed groups. Such organizations include terrorist groups, insurgencies, paramilitary organizations, and transnational criminal organizations. Despite their differences, all engage in some form of asymmetric warfare that adversely affects states and societies.

Interstate warfare has historically involved conflicts between states with similar types of capabilities, whether one is speaking of 5th-century B.C.E. Greek city-states, European states since the 17th century, India and Pakistan in the 20th century, or the United States and its coalition allies against Iraq in 1991 and again in 2003. Interstate wars, however, have become relatively rare over the past fifty years, while armed groups have come to pose what some see as the major threat to international security.

ASYMMETRIC CONFLICT

10.1 Compare and contrast asymmetric and symmetric warfare utilizing historical examples.

👁‍🗨 **Watch** the **Video "Peace with Honor in Vietnam"** at **mypoliscilab.com**

symmetric warfare ■ conflict in which two entities have essential equality in terms of amount and types of capabilities and pursue similar strategies

center of gravity ■ metaphor from mechanics that captures the idea that an adversary's military may have a focal point that is critical in holding that structure together

asymmetric warfare ■ involves a lack of congruity in the capabilities and strategies of two foes

Symmetric conflict and symmetric warfare in particular involve a general congruity in the capabilities and strategies of two foes. In the case of 5th-century B.C.E. Athens and Sparta, for example, both sides armed their soldiers with similar long pikes, bows and arrows, and shields. Cavalry was used for scouting missions and harassment of the enemy's lines. Strategy essentially involved one side attempting to crush and rout the enemy on the battlefield and lay siege to and capture cities. Similarly, European armies in the 18th and 19th centuries emulated each other's organization, training, and weapons with the goal of concentrating and using these capabilities on what Clausewitz termed the enemies' center of gravity. (See Chapter 9, "Interstate Conflict.")

Asymmetric warfare involves a lack of congruity in the capabilities and strategies of two foes. More specifically, asymmetric warfare is defined for our purposes as a situation in which the nonstate opponent has developed capabilities and strategies designed to diminish greatly a state's capabilities and strengths or render them irrelevant. An example would be the al-Qaeda attack on September 11, 2001, on the U.S. homeland. Lacking traditional missile capability, the terrorists hijacked American aircraft and essentially turned them into deadly assault missiles. Similarly, inexpensive and simple improvised explosive devices (IEDs) used by insurgents in Iraq and Afghanistan are responsible for the vast majority of U.S. casualties. The insurgents do not have aircraft, helicopters, tanks, or sophisticated technology, so they have devised alternative capabilities and strategies to attack the United States and its allies. The result has been to diminish U.S. military strength, one small attack at a time.

Even within more classic symmetric warfare scenarios, one side can utilize asymmetric tactics on the battlefield. The deployment of small, special operations forces to breach enemy defenses has a long tradition in warfare. The Greeks' use of the Trojan horse to break the siege of Troy is one example. In 1940, the French constructed defensive fortifications in anticipation that the invading Germans would engage in frontal assaults as they had done in World War I. The Germans utilized the tactic of *blitzkrieg* (lightning war), which involved the creative integration of fast-moving tank battalions supported by air power to outflank and paralyze the French army.

Dramatic technological developments historically have allowed one protagonist to break out of an essential symmetry in terms of capabilities and engage in asymmetric warfare at the strategy level. These turning points represent new faces of war and have been termed **revolutions in military affairs**. Examples include the infantry revolution of the 14th century in which English longbowmen and Swiss pikemen gained the upper hand over heavy cavalry; the gunpowder revolution of the 15th century that rendered medieval fortifications virtually irrelevant; the flintlock revolution of the 17th century that allowed armies to amass firepower and contributed to the successful colonization of much of the developing world; the 19th-century Industrial Revolution that led to the development of weapons systems like tanks and combat aircraft; and more recently the atomic revolution and the invention of the A-bomb, and the information revolution marked by the internet and the globalization of telecommunications.

Of course, technology alone was not decisive in and of itself. The state most creative in combining such weapons with new tactics and military organization held the key to success. With each revolution in military affairs, defeated or threatened powers raced to catch up, hoping to turn the strategic asymmetric disadvantage they faced into a more symmetrical conflict or competition.

Armed groups utilizing asymmetric warfare against the ruling states and societies have existed throughout history. A number of examples will be discussed. What they all had in common was that the technology available to them was primitive by today's standards. The specter of mass casualties was limited, and the threats were generally geographically localized in one region or another.

What is historically unprecedented today is how one particular aspect of globalization—the information revolution—has so dramatically changed the strategic landscape in recent decades. Armed groups have been able to acquire weapons on the global arms market of such alarming firepower that security forces are at times outgunned. Witness the situation in northern Mexico involving drug cartels. Insurgents in Somalia, Afghanistan, and Pakistan are similarly awash in weapons, many provided by international arms traders. Terrorist organizations such as al-Qaeda are able to avail themselves of the internet as a way to propagate their message, recruit new followers, solicit funding, and communicate with one another while planning operations.

revolutions in military affairs ■ a major change in the nature of warfare brought about by the innovative application of new technologies which, combined with dramatic changes in military doctrine and operational and organizational concepts, fundamentally alter the character and conduct of military operations

CASE & POINT | The Mumbai Terrorist Attacks

CASE   The terrorist attack on Mumbai, India, in November 2008 by the Pakistani terrorist organization Lashkar-e-Taiba (LT) is a particularly chilling example of technology-enabled terrorism. The operation consisted of ten coordinated shooting and bombing attacks and resulted in the deaths of 175 people with over 300 wounded. While planning the attack the LT downloaded images of Mumbai from Google Earth. A Pakistani-American, David Headley, allegedly went to Mumbai, took photographs of possible targets, and noted GPS coordinates. During the attack the ten terrorists maintained cell phone and VOIP contact with operational planners in Pakistan.

POINT   Technology in an era of globalization can work as much to the benefit of an armed group as it can for the state.

TERRORISM

10.2 Describe the history of international terrorism and key terrorist attacks against the United States over the past sixty years.

👁 **Watch** the **Video** **"Bin Laden Killed in Pakistan"** at **mypoliscilab.com**

terrorism ■

politically motivated violence directed against noncombatants and designed to instill fear in a target audience

Throughout history **terrorism** has been one of the starkest expressions of rejection of authority. Terrorism, as politically motivated violence, aims at achieving a demoralizing effect on publics and governments. The very act of attacking innocents raises the shock value and sends a message that the government is unable to protect its own citizens. The concern is that, over time, terrorism eats away at the social-political fabric of many states, undermines democracy, provides a rationale for a government to delay democratic reforms, and can increase tension among states. The result is often the impression that the world is in a state of chaos, and international order and authority are collapsing. It is understandable why terrorism is considered a major challenge to international security.

Terrorism is usually viewed as a weapon of the weak, so it is associated with such nonstate actors as clandestine terrorist groups and insurgencies. But our definition of terrorism is neutral and can be applied to any number of armed groups, some of whom pose serious threats to ruling authorities. Terrorism continues to be used, for example, by drug traffickers in northern Mexico against government officials, journalists, and photographers like those who worked for *Diario de Juarez*. The insurgent organization al-Shabaab controls large geographic areas of Somalia. Vast areas of Pakistan's Federally Administered Tribal Areas (FATA) are also under insurgent control. Furthermore, terrorism can be and has been a tool of statecraft. Indeed, down through the centuries, states have certainly terrorized many more people than have terrorist groups or insurgencies. The focus in this chapter, however, is on the challenges posed by armed terrorist and criminal groups who use violence to achieve political objectives.

History

Terrorism is certainly not new. In fact, it is deeply embedded in history. The Zealots, for example, were a Jewish sect that appeared in 6 C.E. and assassinated local government officials in an attempt to ignite uprisings and drive the Romans out of Palestine. The Middle East spawned the Assassins (1090–1275), Muslims who killed the political rivals of the potentate for whom they worked. Christian Europe also had its experience with terror during the 15th-century Spanish Inquisition that combined the forces of church and state in trials and the burning of accused witches—a phenomenon that even touched the New World, most notably at Salem, Massachusetts, where witches were hanged in the 1690s. Historically, the vast majority of terrorism in traditional societies has been religiously inspired; indeed, terrorists often claimed they were carrying out the will of God. These historical examples are a good reminder that religiously inspired terrorism—a major contemporary concern—is certainly not new.

It was the French Revolution of 1789, however, that popularized the term *terrorism*. During this period, terrorism was associated with the state, as the guillotine was used to behead publicly those who were declared enemies of the state. In later years, even more highly developed forms of state terrorism were practiced in both the Stalinist Soviet Union and Nazi Germany in the 1930s and 1940s. The "knock at the door" by state authorities, the use of show trials and executions, and purges of large numbers of people were used by these regimes to instill fear in domestic populations, thus assuring greater compliance with the dictates of the state. Such tactics also found their way into Saddam Hussein's Iraq as well as other states and societies whether on the left or right, secular or religious.

The 19th century witnessed the rise of secular or nonreligious terrorism on the part of groups that were opposed to particular governments. During the 1800s, both the creative and destructive effects of the scientific and industrial revolutions became obvious in Europe and North America. Great wealth was created, as was great poverty. The birth of the modern city forever changed the rural ways of life. Humanity grew more confident in its ability to master nature and to design and create the perfect society. Karl Marx (1820–1872) and other communists demonstrated such faith in their vision of a worker's paradise established after the victory of the downtrodden classes over their capitalist oppressors.

Other leftists, however, were impatient with the slow unfolding of history and wished to hasten the revolutionary process. Collectively known as anarchists, they accomplished a number of terrorist spectaculars. In the 1890s alone, anarchist victims included the presidents of France and Italy, the kings of Portugal and Italy, the prime minister of Spain, and the empress of Austria. Anarchists also attempted to assassinate the German *kaiser* (emperor) and chancellor. What distinguished them from modern-day terrorists, however, is that their victims were almost always government officials, not innocent civilians. The Russian anarchist group known as the People's Will, for example, rarely placed bombs in public places and never kidnapped schoolchildren or shot people in the knee to cripple them for life.

anarchists ■
individuals who advocate entirely voluntary human associations or communities, reject authority in general, and may or may not use violence against governments or their officials

With the collapse of the major continental monarchies in Russia, Germany, and the Austro-Hungarian Empire following World War I (1914–1918), factional ethnic violence and terrorism came to the fore. Under the banner of national self-determination, terrorist violence was particularly pronounced in Eastern and Central Europe. A somewhat similar process began to unfold in the so-called "developing world" during and especially after World War II. Having fought Nazi Germany, fascist Italy, and Japan in defense of freedom, Western European leaders found it difficult to answer nationalist leaders in the colonial world who asked why their countries should not also be free from outside control. European reluctance to end colonial rule led nationalist movements, often with a terrorist wing, to fight British, French, Belgian, and Portuguese domination. By the 1960s European colonial rule was effectively ended in most areas of the globe.

The Cold War between the United States and the Soviet Union and their respective allies and supporters, however, lent an ideological cast to much of the terrorism perpetrated from the late 1940s to the late 1980s. Despite the fact that Karl Marx himself believed terrorism to be self-defeating, Marxist-Leninist teachings on revolution helped to inspire and justify revolutionary movements throughout the world and justify, to such participants at least, their use of terrorism. These movements included the Red Army Faction in Germany, Red Brigades in Italy, 17 November in Greece, Revolutionary Armed Forces of Colombia, Shining Path of Peru, Japanese Red Army, and New People's Army of the Philippines.

Particularly in Europe, terrorism became the basic strategy of the organization, meaning it was the defining signature of the group. In the developing world, however, terrorism was generally a tactic on the part of an insurgent organization, meaning it was simply one aspect of a larger revolutionary strategy that included paramilitary attacks on government forces, the liberation of territory, and the extensive use of propaganda.

Throughout the Cold War, insurgent organizations often combined Marxism-Leninism with old-fashioned nationalist appeals. Indeed, all successful revolutions, including Lenin's in Russia and Mao's in China, have relied extensively on such appeals. With the end of the Cold War, however, most Russians acknowledged that their Marxist-Leninist vision for society was bankrupt. Furthermore, despite its socialist pronouncements, China experienced an economic boom as the state encouraged the development of a free market. These policies on the part of the two states most closely associated with Marxist-Leninist ideas on international revolution caused a predictable crisis of confidence for revolutionary movements around the world. Some, like Shining Path, simply condemned Russia and China for backsliding, while others, like the New People's Army, experienced bitter internal divisions that weakened them. Now lacking a transnational ideological justification for their violent campaigns, other groups such as the Kurdistan Workers Party (PKK) shifted their emphasis away from Marxist ideology to more nationalist appeals.

nationalism ■
a mind-set glorifying the national identity, usually to the exclusion of other possible identities, infused with a political content

Nationalism has always provided the dynamism of the various original Palestinian organizations associated with the Palestine Liberation Organization (PLO). Despite couching their agenda in Islamic terms, even organizations such as Hezbollah (Party of God) in Lebanon and Hamas in the Palestinian West Bank of the Jordan River and in the Gaza Strip are also fueled in part by nationalist sentiment. Israel, despite its historical association with the region, is viewed as an outpost of Western interests and values. For some observers in the West, the ideological clash of democracy and communism during the Cold War has been replaced by the clash of Eastern and Western civilizations. If not a clash of civilizations, others see conflicts driven by intercommunal and cultural differences that divide peoples in many parts of the world. Russia, for example, has suffered from a number of deadly suicide bombings related to ongoing ethnic conflicts in the Caucasus region.

Israel was first attacked in the 1960s by terrorist organizations affiliated with the Palestine Liberation Organization (PLO). The PLO terrorist campaign included the murder of Israeli athletes at the 1972 Munich Olympics and massacres of civilians at the Rome and Vienna airports in 1985. Following the Israeli invasion of Lebanon in 1982, which was designed to root out Palestinian terrorists, Islamist groups such as Lebanese Hezbollah, backed by Syria and Iran, began in the early 1980s its ultimately successful campaign to drive Israel out of southern Lebanon. Further trouble for the Israelis began in the 1990s in the wake of the first Palestinian uprising or *intifada* in the Israeli-occupied West Bank and Gaza Strip. Out of this chaos came Hamas and the Palestine Islamic Jihad.

The United States

Aside from actions by Puerto Rican nationalists who desired an independent country and the leftist Weather Underground, which sought to spark a revolution against the government, the United States felt relatively immune from terrorist threats in the 1950s and 1960s. This dramatically changed in the late 1970s.

As one of two superpowers then with a military presence in many countries of the world and economic interests in virtually every country, it is not surprising that the United States has been blamed, rightly or wrongly, for all types of problems and has been viewed as an agent of military, economic, and cultural imperialism.

The United States came face to face with international terrorism in the Middle East. With the overthrow of the U.S.-backed shah of Iran in 1978, a radical Islamic regime came to power not only bent on securing its control over the country, but also desiring to spread its brand of Islamist radicalism to other countries by supporting terrorist organizations. U.S. diplomats were held hostage for over a year in Iran before being released in 1981 with the aid of Canadian officials. In 1983 in Lebanon alone, Lebanese Hezbollah killed 241 U.S. soldiers in a suicide truck bombing of the U.S. Marine barracks; the U.S. embassy was destroyed by another suicide truck bomb, costing seventeen lives; and U.S. citizens were repeatedly taken hostage. In 1985 there were several terrorist spectaculars, including the June hijacking of TWA flight 847 by Islamic extremists, which lasted seventeen days; the takeover of the *Achille Lauro* cruise ship by Palestinians in October, which resulted in the murder of a wheelchair-bound American tourist; and the aforementioned December 27 attacks in the Rome and Vienna airports by the Abu Nidal Organization, which left eighteen dead and 114 wounded.

In December 1988 a bomb placed aboard Pan Am Flight 103 exploded over Lockerbie, Scotland, resulting in the death of 259 passengers and members of the crew. Conducted by Libyan intelligence agents, this act of state-sponsored international terrorism, more than any other single terrorist incident, galvanized cooperation among Western governments. The bombing of the World Trade Center in New York City in February 1993, a nerve gas attack on Tokyo's subway in March 1995, bombings directed against the U.S. embassies in Kenya and Tanzania in August 1998, and the bombing of the USS *Cole* in the port of Aden in October 2000 are all examples of major terrorist incidents predating 9/11. With the exception of the first attack on the World Trade Center in 1993, Americans seemed to be immune from international terrorism on the home front. The fact of the matter is that as long as terrorists focused their efforts on killing Americans overseas, there was no major public or political groundswell of support for anything like the U.S. response following al-Qaeda's attack on September 11, 2001, against New York City and Washington, DC.

CAUSES OF TERRORISM

A great deal has been written on the causes of terrorism. But, as is often the case with human behavior, no single factor can be identified as the root cause. It is possible, however, to break down the major categories as follows.

10.3 Identify and critique three factors used to explain the causes of terrorism.

Psychological/Social-Psychological Factors

Certain analysts—not surprisingly, they tend to be trained psychologists or psychiatrists—view some individuals who engage in terrorism as mentally disturbed or socially maladjusted. Though the mental disorder perspective includes explanations rooted in such physiological factors as chemical imbalances in the brain, the main focus of attention is on the early childhood experiences of terrorists. Analysis of European terrorists points to such factors as abusive or unemotional parents, suggesting that at least some terrorists are rebelling, perhaps, against parental authority figures as personified in their minds by the state.

While undoubtedly some terrorists exhibit pathological behavior, to dismiss all terrorists as mentally ill is simply wrong. In fact, one thing most terrorists have in common is their normality. Consider, for example, the four British suicide bombers who killed 52 and injured over 700 persons on London subways and buses on July 7, 2005. Mohammad Sidique Khan, aged 30, was married and had a young child. Shehzad Tanweer, aged 22, lived with his mother and father and worked in a fish-and-chip shop. Germaine Lindsay, aged 19, lived with his pregnant wife and young son. Hasib Hussain, aged 18, lived with his brother and sister-in-law. Not one of them was a societal outcast.

A young person with few life prospects may choose to join a terrorist organization for the expected thrill of life in the underground, or as a way to enhance his or her self-esteem by becoming a "defender of the community," or even simply as a way to earn money. Such prosaic possibilities have little to do with mental illness, and psychological explanations often have the effect of downplaying terrorism's political component. As one former member of the Provisional Irish Republican Army stated: "The IRA gave these young men a sense of belonging, a status in their community, and a purpose, a cause to believe in and to fight and die for. These were young men without much hope of employment who had seen their communities devastated in sectarian attacks. Now that they were hitting back, their pride and dignity were restored."

To the extent that such group dynamics contribute to the self-worth of individual terrorists, strengthening their commitment to a particular cause, we move beyond the psychological or psychoanalytic understanding into the domain of social psychology—the relationships and interactions among individuals in group settings. Hence, there is the case of men from Arab and Islamic countries who travel to the West for schooling or employment and find themselves alienated from their surroundings. Local mosques become a place of comfort and refuge and also an incubator, in some cases, for radical Islamist views. This was the case for Mohamed Atta, head of the 9/11 hijackers, and several of his colleagues living in Hamburg, Germany. Even more ominous are those cases where young Muslim men who were born and raised in a Western country turn to terrorism. The perpetrators of the July 2005 suicide bombings in London fit this profile.

social psychology ■
the study of the relations between people and groups

Those who risk or sacrifice their lives as perpetrators of terrorism—for example, suicide bombers—set aside what the German sociologist Max Weber (1864–1920) called instrumental rationality (in German, *Zweckrationalität*) one employs in trying to match means to the ends we seek—when considering each alternative, the careful weighing of the costs and benefits in an effort to minimize the former or maximize the latter. They are instead rationally motivated by commitment to cause or duty, perhaps accompanied by notions of honor that comes from sacrifice—what Weber referred to as value rationality (*Wertrationalität*). Ironically, the leaders of movements or groups using terror as a tactic usually do not put their own lives on the line, but know how or learn to use the value-rational, sacrificial efforts of those they employ in an instrumentally rational way.

CASE & POINT | Rational Terrorism

CASE   Leaders like the late Osama bin Laden are indeed highly rational in their instrumental use of terrorism to advance their political-religious agendas. The 9/11 attacks were supposedly designed to get the United States embroiled in wars in South Asia and hopefully the Middle East, eventually sapping American military and economic strength as happened with the Soviet Union's misadventure in Afghanistan from 1979 to 1989. Ironically, it is the instrumentally rational Osama bin Laden as well as other extremist leaders in the Middle East or elsewhere who are able to mobilize the self-sacrificing value rationality of others to commit suicide or take other high-risk actions to advance a cause. The 9/11 hijackers and July 2005 London bombers are examples.

POINT   One way to understand terrorism is to see it as the rational or purposive use of the irrational, that is, the intimidating effects of threats or violence to advance some objective or set of objectives, typically for political ends. Resorting to terrorism is a way relatively weaker parties (those lacking armies, navies, and air forces to do their bidding) can engage in asymmetric warfare to try to level the playing field. Terrorism, then, is a form of what the late-19th, early-20th-century German political sociologist Max Weber, though not writing about terrorism, referred to as instrumental rationality—a means to some desired end. That said, terrorists may be willing to make major sacrifices, even committing suicide, for a cause to which they are deeply committed. This is another kind of rationality—one of complete commitment regardless of costs—that Weber called value rationality.

Ideological Factors

Ideological explanations emphasize the power of ideas. Historically, Marxism-Leninism has proven to be powerfully attractive to individuals who seek a framework that enables them to understand not only why injustices exist in a society but also how to end them. Terrorists, therefore, are true believers, possessed by an idea that a better society can be created if only certain obstacles or threats can be eliminated. For Marxist-Leninists, this threat is the upper classes and bourgeoisie; for fascists, it is often minority groups or foreign immigrants; for nationalists, it is often colonialists; for religious extremists, it is not simply foreigners, but rather the values they represent that threaten the indigenous culture.

> **instrumental rationality** ■ the rational calculation of costs and benefits in pursuit of an end or goal to include available capabilities

> **value rationality** ■ holding and pursuing values such as duty, loyalty, or commitment regardless of costs

Religious motivation, for example, is the recurrent claim made on the part of such organizations as al-Qaeda. Al-Qaeda and affiliated Islamist groups are reacting not only against American and other Western influences and presence in the Middle East, but also against the forces of globalization that are undermining more traditional Islamic societies and their ways of life. They claim their version and interpretation of Islam provides a justification for violent *jihad* as well as a religious-political blueprint for not only Muslims, but also the world as a whole.

Environmental Factors

Environmental explanations that examine where terrorism arises generally fall into one of two related categories: grievances and cultures of violence.

Grievances   Environmental grievances that affect a community can be social, political, or economic in nature. Grievances—real or imagined, just or unjust—are, after all, still grievances that can motivate persons to resort to terrorism against a foreign occupying power or against another community. In this regard, "community" can be broadly defined, referring to either a particular economic class such as exploited peasants or perhaps ethnic or religious groups that have experienced political and economic discrimination over the years.

The Muslims of Lebanon, for example, particularly the *Shia*, see themselves as having historically suffered from discrimination at the hands of the Christian Lebanese. Not only have the *Shia* been at the bottom of the economic ladder, but they have also been politically underrepresented in the government and parliament. Such grievances often fester for a long period of time and then erupt in bloody violence, as they did in Lebanon in 1976. In this particular case the *Shia* were energized by other factors, such as the growing power of the Palestinians, particularly in southern Lebanon. Expelled from Jordan in 1970, many Palestinians fled to Lebanon, where they initially received a warm welcome. But as the Palestinians settled in, many *Shia* grew resentful when they also suffered from Israeli military reprisals directed against the Palestinians who were using southern Lebanon as a base of operations against Israel.

Cultures of Violence   A second environmental source of terrorism can be termed cultures of violence. This does not refer to cultures that are somehow innately violent. Rather, it refers to societies that have experienced high levels of intercommunal violence over a number of years so that violence, not peace, becomes the norm. For young people growing up in Northern Ireland from the 1970s to the early 1990s, intercommunal warfare and the presence of British troops and security forces on the streets were part of their everyday existence. Violence, not peace, was the status quo. Lebanon from the late 1970s through the 1980s represents a similar case. Chechnya in the Russian Federation and Iraq are more recent examples. As intercommunal violence continues, people may forget the original reason for conflict, and instead hatred becomes habitual and violence is a function of revenge.

The key point as we seek to identify what causes terrorism is that the search for a single factor to explain it is self-defeating. As with all human behavior, multiple factors typically come into play. To explain why any single individual turned to terrorism, one would have to consider the relative importance of psychological or social-psychological, ideological, and environmental factors.

For example, an examination of the lives of the 9/11 hijackers certainly shows a high degree of religiously based motivation for persons such as Mohamed Atta, leader of the plot. But it is also interesting to note that the decision to seek support from al-Qaeda was taken after experiencing the alienating environment of living and studying in the West. To assume that all terrorists are ideologically driven zealots is as much an overgeneralization as it is to assume they are all mentally ill. No, rational commitment to cause—whatever its merits in the minds of others—is an extraordinarily strong motivating factor for those who engage in or engage others to carry out terrorist acts.

Finally, as time goes by, the continuation of a terrorist campaign may have perhaps as much to do with maintaining the existence of the organization as it has to do with achieving the originally stated political objective. There is no reason to

cultures of violence
■ when violence becomes commonplace, it may acquire acceptance or even legitimacy in a community

believe that terrorist organizations are any different from any other organization—a primary goal being organizational survival. For some individuals, terrorism undoubtedly becomes a way of life. It is probable that the longer one is with the organization, the more important this factor becomes. Conversely, it is likely that the most altruistic and ideologically driven members of the group are the newest recruits.

THE CHANGING NATURE OF TERRORISM

Today's terrorism is a multifaceted phenomenon consisting of a diverse array of actors, motivations, and tactics that evolves over time. Such a phenomenon requires equal ingenuity and flexibility on the part of those who study it or—as intelligence analysts, operators, and policymakers—deal directly with it. What is occurring today has been an evolution in the who, why, and how of terrorism. Each will be briefly discussed in turn.

10.4 Explain how radicalization, revenge, and networks have increased the threat of terrorism.

Who Are Terrorists?

From the perspective of the West, the single most disturbing development in recent years has been the radicalization of its own residents and citizens who came to support and justify terrorism. This radicalization process can occur whether the individual's belief system is sacred or secular. Certainly, one can hold radical beliefs but not engage in any illegal activity, let alone acts of terrorism. But the number of individuals living in the West who have turned to political violence and professed adherence to the radical *jihadist* worldview offered by the late Osama bin Laden and others has been of particular concern. The case of the London July 7, 2005, bombers was mentioned. The United States has not been immune. Consider the following cases from 2009 and 2010 alone.[1]

radicalization ■ the multifaceted process by which individuals become mobilized to consider or engage in acts of political violence

Abdulhakim Mujahid Muhammad (Carlos Bledsoe). In June 2009 Bledsoe, from Memphis, Tennessee, killed one soldier and wounded another at a U.S. military recruiting station in Little Rock, Arkansas. Muhammad had spent time in Yemen and claimed to be a member of the group al-Qaeda in the Arabian Peninsula (AQAP).

Nidal Malik Hasan. On November 5, 2009, Major Hasan, a military psychologist stationed at Fort Hood, Texas, opened fire on the base with two handguns, killing thirteen and wounding forty-three before security officers shot and disabled him. Hasan was born in Virginia to Palestinian parents. He also had been in touch with AQAP member and American citizen Anwar al-Awlaki.

Michael Finton. A convert to Islam, Finton, of Decatur, Illinois, was arrested in September 2009 after attempting to set off an inert car bomb in front of a federal government building in Springfield, Illinois. Federal agents posing as al-Qaeda members supplied Finton with a fake bomb, and a friend working

[1] Peter Bergen and Bruce Hoffman, *Assessing the Terrorist Threat: A Report of the Bipartisan Policy Center's National Security Preparedness Group*, September 10, 2010. Available at www.bipartisanpolicy.org.

as an FBI informant recorded conversations in which Finton expressed his hatred of the United States and his desire to engage in *jihad*.

Najibullah Zazi. Zazi, an Afghan immigrant and permanent U.S. resident, was arrested in September 2009 while preparing to attack targets including the New York City subway system. Zazi had stockpiled chemicals, including hydrogen peroxide, needed to make an explosive compound known as TATP. He pleaded guilty in February 2010 to conspiring to commit a terrorist act using a weapon of mass destruction. He also admitted to having received training in Pakistan. Zazi had gone originally to fight American forces in Afghanistan, but al-Qaeda leaders convinced him to return to the United States.

David Coleman Headley. A Pakistani-American, Headley was arrested along with Tawahhur Rana in October 2009 on charges that he helped conduct preoperational surveillance of targets for the 2008 Mumbai attacks conducted by the Pakistani militant group Lashkar-e-Taiba. Headley pleaded guilty in March 2010, also admitting to having helped plot an attack that never took place against the Danish newspaper *Jyllands-Posten*, in retaliation for the paper's publication of cartoons depicting the Prophet Mohammed.

The "DC 5." In November 2009 five young Americans of Pakistani, Arab, and African descent were arrested in Pakistan after their families reported them missing and found what appeared to be at least one "martyrdom video." The five reportedly had tried to join multiple Pakistani militant groups, without success, before being picked up by Pakistani police. They were charged in Pakistan and convicted in June 2010 of criminal conspiracy and funding a banned terrorist organization.

Minnesota Somali-Americans. Federal prosecutors in 2009 indicted two groups of men, eight in one indictment, six in another, for recruiting young men in Somali communities in Minnesota and fundraising for the al-Qaeda–linked group al-Shabaab. Seven of those charged as part of the ongoing investigation were indicted in August 2010 on additional charges of providing material support to Shabaab.

North Carolina Cluster. American-born Daniel Boyd, a convert to Islam, was arrested in July 2009 along with six others, including two of his sons, and charged with plotting to wage violent *jihad* abroad. He allegedly performed reconnaissance on the U.S. Marine base at Quantico, Virginia, while planning a possible attack on the base. Members of the "Cluster" allegedly traveled to Gaza, Israel, and Jordan in the hope of fighting Israeli forces.

Faisal Shahzad. A naturalized Pakistani-American, Shahzad pleaded guilty in court to attempting to blow up an SUV in Times Square, New York City, in May 2010. Married, a father of a young child, and a graduate of the University of Bridgeport, he confessed to receiving bomb-making training from the Pakistani Taliban and was inspired in part by Anwar al-Awlaki.

This changing terrorist demographic logically leads one to the question: Why?

Why Terrorism?

As noted, the possible motivations for individuals engaging in terrorism are diverse. They include such possibilities as psychological and social-psychological factors, both sacred and secular ideologies, and political, social, and economic grievances.

To complicate matters, a single campaign may be composed of various groups who turn to terrorism for their own particular reasons. Insurgents in Iraq who targeted the United States, coalition partners, and Iraqi government forces included former members of Saddam's Baath Party and ex-military officers who wished to return to power, religious extremists who desired Islamic rule, foreign fighters who wish to hurt the United States, and criminals motivated by money. As has been the case throughout recorded history, the mix and relative weight will vary depending on the individual and the group.

Having said that, it appears that revenge was a prominent motivating factor beginning in the 1990s. Whether it is a citizen-directed attack against the U.S. government, such as the 1995 bombing of the Alfred P. Murrah Federal Building in Oklahoma City, or carried out by Islamic extremists who resent the pernicious influence of Western values on their societies due to globalization, the potential for high casualties is always there. What is disturbing is that such attacks are not necessarily aimed at achieving a particular political agenda but rather have the generalized goal of inflicting pain and suffering on innocent people.

Religious motivation coupled with a desire for revenge is a particularly explosive combination—it makes it easier to justify in one's mind high numbers of casualties, whether they are military or civilian, government employees or tourists. In other words, no one is an innocent, and no moral, ethical, or religious constraints apply. In fact, religion often acts as a justification as opposed to a constraint on terrorist actions. Consider, for example the martyrdom video recorded by Mohammed Sidique Khan prior to the July 7, 2005, suicide bombings in London:

> I and thousands like me are forsaking everything for what we believe. Our drive and motivation doesn't come from tangible commodities that this world has to offer. Our religion is Islam, obedience to the one true God, and following the footsteps of the final prophet messenger. Your democratically elected governments continuously perpetuate atrocities against my people all over the world. And your support of them makes you directly responsible, just as I am directly responsible for protecting and avenging my Muslim brothers and sisters. Until we feel security you will be our targets and until you stop the bombing, gassing, imprisonment, and torture of my people we will not stop this fight. We are at war and I am a soldier. Now you too will taste the reality of this situation.

Here we find a chilling, yet excellent example of the combination of ideological-religious motivation, grievances, and revenge which, from Khan's perspective, justifies attacks on civilian targets.

Looking back over the past one hundred years, we have come a long way from 19th-century terrorist organizations such as the People's Will that targeted government officials and attempted to avoid killing innocent civilians. For many of today's terrorists, however, the death of innocents not only increases the shock value of the attack—an instrumental goal—but is an end in itself.

How Terrorism Works

Examine any anthology of articles on terrorism and you will find discussions of "the group" as the unit of analysis. The subsequent classification scheme is invariably based on the group's essential goals or ideology—Marxist-Leninist, nationalist-separatist, fascist, religious. Typically, terrorists utilize such nouns as "army," "brigade," or "command" in the name of their organization in order to enhance the legitimacy of their cause by suggesting they view themselves as soldiers. Aside from anarchist organizations whose small numbers preclude a true division of labor, many larger terrorist groups indeed have historically organized themselves along paramilitary lines and hence lend themselves to classic line-and-block organizational diagrams.

What is different about the current *jihadist* terrorist threat is its complexity and diversity. Al-Qaeda still exists despite the death of Osama bin Laden in May 2011—the Egyptian Ayman al-Zawahiri being named his successor. We can still speak of it as an organization with the intent to organize and conduct attacks, despite being forced to maintain a clandestine existence in Pakistan. Operational planners from al-Qaeda, for example, recruited Najibullah Zazi to plan and carry out attacks against the New York City subway in September 2009. Its real, although perhaps waning strength, however, has been its ability to survive and continue to spread the worldwide *jihadist* call to arms. This inspirational role is best reflected in those cases such as the DC Five where individuals not associated with any one particular group have attempted acts of terrorism in the name of al-Qaeda and global *jihad*.

Networks and Netwar   The best expression of al-Qaeda's capability, however, is in its relations with like-minded affiliated armed groups. Al-Qaeda has assiduously worked to create a decentralized transnational network that reflects and encourages the spreading of violent *jihad*. The result has been a particular type of asymmetric warfare termed **netwar**. One element of this network is the Tehrik-e-Taliban Pakistan (TTP) that provided minimal training for Pakistani-American Faisal Shahzad and his May 2010 attempted bombing of Times Square in New York City. An even greater threat comes from al-Qaeda in the Arabian Peninsula (AQAP), which was the group responsible for the attempted midair bombing of Northwest Airlines flight 253 over Detroit on Christmas Day, 2009. Umar Farouq Abdulmutallab, a 23-year-old Nigerian affiliated with AQAP, failed in his attempt to explode a bomb with plastic explosives. As the plane neared Detroit, he tried to initiate the bomb with a chemical injection, setting himself on fire and suffering severe burns. The plot was encouraged by the now deceased Anwar al-Awlaki, a dual U.S.-Yemeni citizen, member of AQAP, and Islamic extremist ideologue with a large following on the internet. He also has been implicated in other plots against the United States through his exchange of e-mails with Major Hasan prior to the latter's attack in Ft. Hood, Texas, and the November 2010 attempt to detonate ink cartridges loaded with explosives on air freight planes. Al-Qaeda also has ties with al-Shabaab of Somalia and al-Qaeda in the Islamic Maghreb (AQIM), which operates out of Algeria.

Al-Qaeda's affiliates' increasing ability to provide training, guidance, and support for attacks against the West, local regimes, and the United States in particular makes it more difficult to anticipate the precise nature of the next attack. Some would argue that by simply managing to persist since 9/11 is a great achievement on the part of al-Qaeda. But a balanced threat assessment that takes into account

netwar ■ conflicts in which a combatant is organized along networked lines or employs networks for operational control and other communications

When it comes to applying theory to armed groups, realists tend to ignore them, and liberals simply list them as another type of transnational actor. Insightful conceptual work on armed groups has come from national security theorists who see warfare in terms of what is called *netwar*.

Netwar refers to "an emerging mode of conflict (and crime) at societal levels, short of traditional military warfare, in which the protagonists use network forms of organization and related doctrines, strategies, and technologies attuned to the information age." The organizational form is not the classic hierarchical structure as reflected in line-and-block organizational charts. Rather, netwar organizational forms may resemble "stars" that have some centralized elements or "chains" that are linear, or most likely all-channel networks in which each principal node communicates and interacts with every other node (see figures below).

ARGUMENT John Arquilla and David Ronfeldt provide examples of armed groups and other organizations that are taking advantage of networked designs: transnational terrorist groups, black-market proliferators of weapons of mass destruction (WMD), drug and other crime syndicates, fundamentalist and ethnonationalist movements, intellectual-property pirates, and immigration and refugee smugglers. Thanks to the worldwide information revolution,

members of networks do not necessarily have to meet face-to-face. From the perspective of terrorists, security is therefore enhanced, and an organization could conceivably have supporters around the world. These actors generally consist of dispersed groups who agree to communicate and act, perhaps without a central leadership or headquarters. It is suggested that hierarchical organizations such as states might be ill-equipped to deal with such organizational innovations.

COUNTERARGUMENT Realists, as noted, believe the focus on armed groups, while useful, overstates their relative importance in international relations and world politics compared to states. Such organizations may indeed pose a threat to national security, but they rarely (in the case of terrorist groups) actually come to power. Earlier transnational armed groups such as pirates were eventually suppressed by the power of states. Similar headway could be made against modern armed groups once they are deemed threats to vital national interests.

APPLICATION The National Counterterrorism Center (nctc.gov) maintains a robust database on terrorist groups and activities. Take some time to navigate around the site. Can you find evidence that terrorist groups actually match the netwar model of armed groups? Based upon the number and types of terrorist incidents, do you agree or disagree with the realist downplaying of the threat from terrorist organizations?

Source: John Arquilla and David Ronfeldt, *Networks and Netwars* (Santa Monica, CA: RAND, 2001). See also David Ronfeldt, John Arquilla, Graham E. Fuller, and Melissa Fuller, *The Zapatista Social Netwar in Mexico* (Santa Monica, CA: RAND, 1998).

Chain
(Smugglers)

Star or Hub
(Drug cartel)

All-Channel
(Peace network)

Basic Types and Levels of Networks

Source: John Arquilla and David Ronfeldt, *The Advent of Netwar*, MR-678-OSD (Santa Monica, CA: RAND, 1996), p. 49.

longer-range, strategic considerations would note the following weaknesses in al-Qaeda. First, al-Qaeda and its affiliates keep killing Muslims civilians. Islamic armed groups account for the greatest number of Muslim casualties around the world. This is not a winning recruitment strategy for an organization that calls for a massive, worldwide Muslim uprising against apostate (nonbelieving) regimes. Second, al-Qaeda has not managed to create a genuine mass political movement. No al-Qaeda political parties exist, and opinion polls have shown a decline in support among Muslims for bin Laden's vision of the world. Third, al-Qaeda's leaders keep expanding the list of their enemies. The organization has publicly stated it opposes all Middle Eastern regimes; Muslims who don't share their views; the *Shia*—the other major branch of Islam; most Western countries; Jews and Christians; the governments of India, Pakistan, Afghanistan, and Russia; the United Nations; and international and nongovernmental organizations. Creating a world of enemies is not a winning strategy. Finally, al-Qaeda has no positive vision of what it hopes to ultimately achieve. Before his death, bin Laden continually stated what he was against, but what was he for? An Islamic caliphate is unrealistic and vague. It would mean the creation of Taliban-style theocracies, which even fewer Muslims would wish to see instituted.[2]

Technology   A great deal has been written in recent years on terrorism and technology. This topic is part of a larger concern over the implications of our increasingly technologically reliant society. The subject can be discussed from the perspective of terrorist use of technology as well as from societies' reliance on it.

Technology certainly increases terrorist options. The media, for example, have always had a symbiotic relationship with terrorists—the latter provide the drama and the former the dissemination of the dramatic story to its readers and viewers. For some critics, the electronic media in particular are to terrorism what oxygen is to a fire, almost deserving to be viewed as unindicted coconspirators. In recent years, technological developments have provided terrorists with another communications option over which they have more control. The internet hosts numerous websites for terrorist groups and their political fronts. Such sites are obviously a source of propaganda and a way to solicit financial contributions. They also serve as a means of recruitment and dissemination of tradecraft such as how to build improvised explosive devices (IEDs).

The internet also reflects the vulnerability of our technologically reliant society. In recent years there has been a steady drumbeat of journalistic and government reports analyzing the vulnerabilities of the air traffic and rail control systems, electrical power grids, government computer networks, and financial exchanges and banking records. Rather than having to be physically present at the chosen target, an adept hacker could be located on the other side of the world, using keystrokes to gain access to computer systems. While the alteration or wiping out of financial records may not have the visual impact or resultant fatalities of a car bomb, such computer hacking, dubbed **cyberterrorism**, could obviously cause economic chaos. Hackers with such goals can use the internet to gain access to military, police, air traffic control, and other networks on which public safety depends.

cyberterrorism ■ computer-based attacks on information systems designed to destroy or manipulate data banks or cause the system to crash with the goal of furthering a political agenda

---

[2] Bergen and Hoffman, p. 23.

To date, such scenarios are mostly the province of novels and Hollywood thrillers. Yet such possibilities are seriously considered by computer security experts and government investigative agencies. The dilemma is that in highlighting technological interdependencies and vulnerabilities, terrorists might be given ideas for new modes of disruption. Ignoring such possibilities, the private sector and government reduce their ability to take preemptive action to neutralize system vulnerabilities.

Weapons of Mass Destruction   One reason terrorism is proclaimed a top international security concern is that in recent years it has been coupled with another international security challenge—the proliferation of nuclear, biological, chemical, and radiological or "dirty bomb" **weapons of mass destruction** (WMD). Newspaper reports have highlighted the dangers posed by "nuclear leakage" from the former Soviet Union, the security of Pakistan's nuclear arsenal, and the erratic nuclear policy of North Korea. Having nuclear material fall into the hands of renegade states is bad enough, but having terrorists get their hands on it is even worse. States have to fear retaliation should they employ such weapons. A small band of terrorists, however, perhaps feels confident that they are difficult to locate, or they simply do not care about retaliation.

> **weapons of mass destruction ■** chemical, biological, radiological, and nuclear weapons as well as large amounts of conventional explosives that cause widespread death and destruction

Raising the specter of terrorist use of nuclear weapons dates from the 1970s. Looking back, such studies are oddly reassuring. Utilizing the rational-actor model associated with realist thinkers, it was assumed by analysts that terrorists recognized that the employment of such weapons was counterproductive in achieving political objectives and gaining public support for one's cause. As noted by Brian Jenkins: "Terrorists want a lot of people watching, not a lot of people dead."[3] Such reasoning can be extended to the use of chemical and biological weapons.

Is this logic still applicable today? Some commentators argue that self-sanctions against the use of weapons of mass destruction may have eroded over the years. It is necessary, however, to distinguish among different types of armed terrorist groups. With some degree of confidence, we can state it is unlikely such weapons will be utilized if we are talking about secular terrorist organizations with a political agenda that requires public support in order to succeed. Note the three critical adjectives— secular, political, and public. Nationalist-separatist movements, for example, often have political as well as clandestine terrorist wings. The terrorist wing may indeed be more likely to consider using WMD for a number of reasons—violence-prone individuals are by definition drawn to operational cells; if cut off from broader society, internal dynamics tend to move a group toward extreme actions.

The political wings of nationalist-separatist movements, however, by definition must take into account numerous factors. First, there is the attitude of the core constituency they claim to represent. As horrible as the effects of bombings may be, crossing the nuclear, chemical, or biological threshold has emotional and psychological effects that go beyond the resultant physical devastation. Death by biological agents is simply viewed differently from death by conventional explosives. Second, political leaders must consider the possibility of retribution against their own community. Third, the employment of weapons of

---

[3] Brian Jenkins, *The Potential for Nuclear Terrorism* (Santa Monica, CA: RAND, 1977), 8.

mass destruction would undoubtedly forsake any international sympathy and support for one's cause.

The limitations in such arguments stem from the fact that the universe of terrorist organizations has been restricted to secular groups with political agendas requiring public support. What about religious groups? Islamic extremist organizations that engage in suicide bombings come to mind. It is often suggested that religious extremists differ from secular organizations in that the audience they are trying to impress is God, as opposed to a segment of the public. Hence, religious convictions supposedly make it easier to engage in actions causing large numbers of deaths when the act is done in the name of God and supposedly with his blessing.

Such logic is not incorrect but simply incomplete. In fact, religious groups have secular as well as sacred motivations. The Lebanese Hezbollah, for example, is best known in the West for its terrorist operations. Yet it also is represented in the Lebanese parliament and wants to be viewed as a legitimate political player. Such ambitions undoubtedly influence the group's approach to terrorism.

Al-Qaeda and affiliated religious extremist groups, however, do not share these secular motivations. Material found in training camps in Afghanistan makes it quite clear that al-Qaeda was actively pursuing the purchase or development of weapons of mass destruction. Furthermore, bin Laden's public statements have explicitly acknowledged this goal. Indeed, bin Laden had called on Islamists to build or procure weapons of mass destruction and claimed it is a duty to use them against the United States and other oppressors of the Muslim peoples. In April 2004, authorities in Jordan disrupted what would have been the largest chemical and terrorist attack ever. The Islamist terrorists had managed to smuggle three cars—packed with explosives, a chemical bomb, and poisonous gas—into the capital city of Amman. It is estimated an incredible eighty thousand people would have been casualties if the bombs had gone off at their intended targets—the Jordanian intelligence headquarters, the U.S. embassy in Amman, and the Jordanian prime minister's office.

The other type of religious organization likely to use weapons of mass destruction can be characterized as cults. In cults, the focus of group loyalty and devotion is not so much to religious precepts as expounded by prophets who have long since departed this Earth, but to a "living god" who issues edicts designed to enforce discipline and complete loyalty among followers. The leader—not the message—is the focus of loyalty. When coupled with physical isolation and a worldview that outside society is corrupt and sinful, a cult can either withdraw into itself and avoid contact with the sinful outside world, or it can work to destroy and transform it. It is when a transformative agenda is coupled with the capability to produce weapons of mass destruction that a threat arises.

Groups that engaged in terrorism from the 1960s through the 1990s had stated political objectives that, however much one might disagree with them, were still fathomable. They developed a particular *modus operandi* and generally stayed with it. State sponsors were consistently the same nefarious lot. Analysts were perhaps no better than today in providing sufficient warning of impending terrorist acts, but at least there was a certain degree of confidence as to the limits to which groups would go to achieve their stated objectives.

Final Observations   We conclude this discussion of the changing nature of international terrorism with two observations. The first is that one of the difficulties in discussing terrorism and international security is that a single event can immediately and dramatically shift perceptions of the relation between the two. Environmental degradation, progress toward global democratization, and even the spread of nuclear weapons allow one to identify and assess trends with some degree of confidence. In the case of terrorism, however, a devastating act by a single individual or small group can make current analyses seemingly irrelevant overnight. Relying on the historical record and simply projecting it into the future is problematic when dealing with terrorism.

Second, terrorist attacks may have an instrumental purpose such as driving the U.S. military out of Afghanistan, derailing the Israeli-Palestinian peace process, or intimidating policymakers into releasing jailed comrades. But such terrorist attacks often derive their real power from their psychological effects on the public. It is highly unlikely that any one individual would fall victim to a terrorist attack, yet events as far away as Mumbai or as near as London or New York City produce a feeling of vulnerability and uneasiness. Similarly, government policies have the instrumental goal to deter, respond, and punish terrorists. We should not, however, underestimate the need for government policies to create a reassuring psychological effect among the public. National security is not simply an empirical fact; it is also a state of mind. It is therefore understandable why in recent years many government policymakers have made what they view as prudent investments in efforts to respond to the evolving phenomenon of terrorism. Possible responses to international terrorism are worthy of further discussion.

POLICYMAKER RESPONSES

Innumerable studies, articles, and reports have been produced over the years on the subject of how best to deal with the specter of terrorism. Both before and after the events of September 11, 2001, terrorism has been on the agenda of international governmental summits and UN resolutions, and it is a favorite topic of congressional hearings and presidential, vice presidential, or other high-level task forces. In the case of the United States, a new cabinet-level department, the Department of Homeland Security, was created to coordinate the multitude of agencies involved in homeland defense. Budgets went up correspondingly. In Washington it was recognized that first responders to a terrorist incident would not be federal or military forces, but rather local fire, police, and emergency medical personnel. Hence, national security planning now involves local and state authorities to a degree never before experienced. U.S. counterterrorism policy, therefore, has had to move beyond deterrence, prevention, and punishment to include what is euphemistically termed "consequence management" or "damage limitation."

Many policymakers are faced with two crucial questions. First, can a counterterrorist strategy be devised that does not compromise civil liberties in the name of fighting terrorism? Second, what might be the unintended effects of pursuing a particular policy and its associated policies? Four of the most prominent suggestions or options for how policymakers should deal strategically with the international

10.5 Compare and contrast the strengths and weaknesses of four major policymaking approaches to dealing strategically with the threat of international terrorism.

Watch the **Video** "Counterinsurgency and Legitimacy in Afghanistan" at mypoliscilab.com

The technological prowess of the United States is evident in the development of unmanned aerial vehicles (UAVs). Whether limited to intelligence collection or actually armed with missiles, UAVs continue to play a key role in the war against terrorist organizations.

Persistent intelligence collection and analysis since 9/11 finally led to the location of Osama bin Laden in a compound in Pakistan. In this famous photograph, President Obama and senior national security advisers receive an update on the military mission via a video teleconference.

Technology, however, is available not only to states but also to nonstate armed groups. In November 2005, militants from the Pakistani group Lashkar-e-Taiba (LT) launched a series of terrorist attacks in Mumbai, India, including the Taj Mahal Hotel. Cellphones allowed the attackers to stay in touch with their LT handlers back in Pakistan. More than 195 persons died.

Mexican drug cartels are another example of armed groups that rely heavily on modern technology and weaponry. Flush with cash, cartels are often better equipped than government forces.

terrorist threat include the following: deal with the underlying causes, use military power, impose the rule of law, and seek international cooperation.

Eliminate the Underlying Causes

This approach assumes that grievances lie at the heart of the problem. In a number of cases, this seems possible. Spain, for example, devolved power to the Basque region, undercutting the appeal of the Basque separatist movement. The peace process in Northern Ireland has been one of fits and starts, progress and reversals. In May 2007, however, two long-time Catholic and Protestant adversaries declared an end to violence and embraced political compromise. In recent years there has also been much discussion in Europe on how better to integrate into society the growing Muslim population. The sheer degree of poverty and social ills found throughout the world, however, always will provide a fertile ground for political discontent, which may be harnessed for terrorist violence. Investment in development is one remedy, particularly when grievances are at the core of the discontent. Progress in accommodating the demands of some groups may reduce the likelihood that they will continue to resort to terrorist actions.

Counterattack

This approach calls for military attacks such as the use of armed Predator drones on terrorist organizations. Such an approach is appealing, as it satisfies demands for punishment and justice and can disrupt terrorist planning. Complications with this approach, however, must be taken into account by policymakers. First of all, excellent intelligence is required to locate members of terrorist groups that by definition are clandestine in nature. This is not easy to do, as witnessed by the almost ten-year hunt for bin Laden. Placing an agent inside a terrorist group is no simple task—terrorists don't openly advertise for new members, and the vetting process is understandably quite rigorous. Satellite or drone imagery might locate possible training sites in the countryside, but it is of limited utility in finding terrorists located in urban environments. Intercepting terrorist communications assumes that one knows where to direct one's electronic gathering capabilities.

Second, even if a government can locate terrorists, a military operation designed to eliminate them faces tactical and political challenges in its actual execution. For example, what if a group of terrorists is training at a site that is also used by the host government's paramilitary forces? Is everyone targeted? If so, what of the political fallout regionally and internationally as photographs of "innocents" are provided to the world media? Would the government that launched the raid be willing to share the intelligence that presumably justifies the action with the public? What if a U.S. military action undermined the political stability of the host government?

There is evident concern over the use of **unmanned aerial vehicles (UAV)** such as the Predator in Pakistan to eliminate al-Qaeda and Taliban operatives. So-called collateral damage in terms of civilians has caused diplomatic problems for the United States and evoked outrage among large segments of the Pakistani populace, even those opposed to militant Islamic armed groups and their agendas.

unmanned aerial vehicles (UAV) ■
pilotless unarmed or armed aircraft such as the Predator

Although UAVs operate with greater accuracy than could have been imagined just a few years ago, this use of force resembles more a blunt instrument than a scalpel used with surgical precision. However unintended, when casualties are sustained by noncombatants—in this case, people not connected to terrorist elements—perpetrators tend to lose the popular support they seek.

Impose the Rule of Law

For many observers, this is the critical pillar of any effective international antiterrorist policy. What is the purpose, they ask, in abandoning democratic principles and legal rights in the name of eliminating terrorism? Is the curbing of civil liberties worth it? History too often shows that in the name of combating terrorism or subversion, temporary states of emergency evolve into dictatorial governments.

Governments can enforce the rule of law in two basic ways: through unilateral domestic efforts and through international cooperative efforts. The United States has used both approaches.

U.S. Domestic Efforts   Legislation designed to undercut terrorism also has implications for the U.S. government, U.S. citizens, corporations, and foreign governments and nationals. The Omnibus Diplomatic Security and Anti-Terrorism Act of 1986, for example, strengthened so-called long-arm statutes that enable the Federal Bureau of Investigation (FBI) to arrest individuals overseas who are charged with committing a terrorist-related criminal act against U.S. citizens. Of particular importance is Section 6(j) of the Export Administration Act, which allows the secretary of state to place a country on what has come to be known as the Terrorism List. If so designated, a whole host of sanctions are employed—no U.S. foreign assistance to the country, no export of weapons, and a negative U.S. vote that amounts to a veto in international economic institutions such as the World Bank or International Monetary Fund should they contemplate assistance to a country on the Terrorism List. The USA Patriot Act passed in the aftermath of the September 11, 2001, terrorist attacks in New York and Washington has substantially expanded law enforcement powers of the federal government, which also extends to cooperative measures among federal, state, and local authorities. Not surprisingly, alarms have been sounded by civil liberties groups that the quest for greater security against terrorist attacks has eroded essential liberties that define civil society.

International Legal Efforts   In terms of international legal efforts, states can pursue bilateral or multilateral approaches. An example of a bilateral agreement—one between two countries—is the U.S.–United Kingdom extradition treaty, which states that, in certain crimes associated with terrorism like skyjackings or the murder of diplomats, the defendant cannot claim to have been engaged in a political act of conscience and hence not be extraditable. Put another way, asylum or protection may be granted to noncitizens with political or religious beliefs that put them in jeopardy in their own or other countries, but when those same individuals commit acts of terror they are not protected.

Examples of multilateral or regional agreements include the Montreal Convention on the Making of Plastic Explosives (1998) and a series of agreements dealing with skyjackings. The problem is that not all states sign such conventions, the most obvious being those that have been accused of supporting or conducting international terrorism, such as Iran and Syria and, in the past, Iraq and Libya. All states, however, can fall back on a particular functional agreement—Article 51 of the UN Charter. This article states that "nothing in the present charter shall impair the inherent right of individual or collective self-defense if an armed attack occurs against a Member of the United Nations." Although this provision was originally intended as a legal basis for defense by sovereign states against aggression by other states, it can broadly be applied to defense against terrorist activity, whether or not it is state sponsored. All sovereign states thus reserve the right to engage in unilateral or, working with other states, collective military action against such threats.

Article 51 ■ UN Charter article stating that if attacked, states have the inherent right of individual or collective self-defense

Encourage International Cooperation

Perhaps even more important than formal legal agreements, however, are various efforts among states to improve international cooperation in the struggle against terrorism. Diplomatic progress, often painstaking and requiring enormous patience and persistence, can reduce resorting to terrorism by some groups. This has occurred, as noted, in the case of Northern Ireland. An unintended, positive consequence of deliberations that resulted in the unification of Germany at the end of the Cold War was the effective denial of sanctuary used by a number of terrorist groups operating from East Germany (the former German Democratic Republic).

Cooperation can take any number of forms—diplomatic support for another state's counterterrorist efforts, combined military operations, intelligence sharing, law enforcement cooperation, or security assistance and training. Such cooperation, however, is not always easily achieved. A concern for international terrorism may be a common concern for most states, but its relative priority among foreign policy issues is not always the same. Prior to 9/11, for example, Europeans often noted that their geographical proximity to the Middle East meant they were more likely than the United States to be the venue for terrorist actions on the part of Islamic extremists. Italy, Germany, France, and the United Kingdom also play host to a large number of foreign nationals from this region. After 9/11, however, there is no doubt that many of the successes against terrorist groups and their plans came about as the result of cooperation among observant law enforcement officials around the world.

A complication arises, however, if democracies have to create even informal alliances with unsavory regimes in the name of fighting terrorism. More often than not, the terrorist problem emanates from areas of the developing world where democratic regimes are more the exception than the rule. By supporting these regimes, Western states can become associated with repressive domestic policies that have more to do with keeping leaders in power than fighting terrorism.

In sum, terrorism is a phenomenon that is here to stay—as history shows, terrorism doesn't end; rather, it evolves. Often the instrument of groups or movements that perceive few, if any, other alternatives to serve their causes, terrorism for them becomes the purposeful or rational use of the irrational—bringing attention to their objectives through the intimidation and fear that terrorism evokes in targeted officials, populations, or institutions. A government simply cannot ignore terrorism even if it might wish to do so. Reporting by mass media, instantaneous communications, and social networking, known as the *CNN effect*, brings terrorist incidents in even remote parts of the globe into our living rooms. Governments must address the clamor of questions raised by a press corps avidly covering all aspects of a newsworthy international terrorist incident.

To believe terrorism's underlying causes can be cured or terroism stamped out purely by military force is naive. If successful, addressing grievances and related causes may reduce the propensity of groups to resort to terrorism; however, defensive measures are still necessary. Combating terrorism requires patience on the part of policymakers and the execution of a strategy that connects a country's capabilities to the antiterrorist goals it seeks to realize. Prevention through good intelligence and effective law enforcement measures is best, but also planning for the worst—mitigating damage and managing consequences by employing well-trained and equipped police, firefighters, medical personnel, and other first responders—is essential. In addition, a successful strategy also requires diplomatic and conflict-resolution approaches that, if successful, reduce substantially the propensity of affected groups to resort to further terrorist activity. In an era of global interdependence, when no state can be sure it will not fall victim to terrorist attacks, international cooperation is particularly important.

TRANSNATIONAL CRIME AND GLOBALIZATION

Scant mainstream international relations literature deals with transnational organized crime. As a result, little theory has actually been applied to the phenomenon. Realists have maintained their focus on states and have not had much to say about transnational criminal organizations in general and criminals groups in particular. As the realist conception of security emphasizes external military threats, when a border is breached the focus is understandably on a military invasion. Liberals are conceptually not much better. Despite an acknowledgment of the importance of transnational actors, they are most concerned with private-sector economic actors, nongovernmental organizations, and international organizations as facilitators of collaboration among states.

While terrorism may currently be the number one transnational threat from the perspective of policymakers, transnational crime is a close second. Although terrorist violence is a type of criminal activity as it violates laws, it is useful to distinguish here between terrorism with a political motivation and forms of organized crime that usually are motivated by economic purposes—making illicit gains. Of course, many terrorist groups also engage in criminal activity to financially support their organizations, just as criminal organizations have used threats and financial enticements to frighten and corrupt politicians to become complicit in their criminal activities. Most organized criminal groups do not seek illicit gains as a means to serve political purposes. Ideally, they work to keep their identities and their activities off the radar of national and international law enforcement agencies. But when threatened, such groups have not hesitated to engage in violent asymmetric warfare against the state.

10.6 Explain how globalization has aided the rise of transnational criminal organizations (TCOs) and their attendant illicit activities.

Watch the **Video** **"Dealing with Piracy in the 21st Century"** at **mypoliscilab.com**

What interests us here is that organized crime, traditionally viewed as a domestic problem for a few states, has become an increasingly global concern. When compared to terrorist acts, it may not make front-page news, but the threat is evident in a number of developments from the 1990s to the present:

- The dramatic increase in violence in Mexico and more recently Central America involving wars among crime organizations as well as attacks against state military and law enforcement officials
- Trafficking in human beings for sexual exploitation and forced labor
- The rise of criminal organizations in Russia and other areas of the former Soviet Union and Eastern Europe
- Extension beyond Japan (*Yakusa*) and China (Triads) of long-established criminal networks
- The dramatic expansion of international money laundering
- Reports of trafficking in nuclear materials
- The sale of pirated and counterfeit products and copyright, trademark, and patent infringement

transnational criminal organizations (TCOs) ■
criminal organizations that operate across borders

Transnational criminal organizations (TCOs), by definition, are groups that operate across state borders. TCOs are not new actors on the world stage, but globalization has impacted the massive scale and geographic spread of their activities. Developments like the continual expansion of international telecommunications allows for the easy electronic transfer of money as well as the removal of political and economic barriers between the East and West after the end of the Cold War that encouraged the expansion of the capitalist economic system.

tariffs ■ taxes placed by governments on imported goods from other countries

To encourage the further liberalization of trade, tariffs on the importation of goods were dropped, and in 1995 the World Trade Organization was created. From 1990 to 2000 world trade increased by over 6 percent per year on average. The establishment of the North American Free Trade Agreement (NAFTA) and similar actions in Latin America and Asia occurred in tandem with the global expansion of trade and transportation. The European Union expanded from fifteen to twenty-five members in 2004, rising to twenty-seven by 2007—further reducing border controls over the same period.

Trade boomed, accompanied by a rise in air cargo and express shipping by companies such as FedEx and DHL, and the ability of states to inspect more than a small percentage of trucks and containers dropped. Express custom clearance schemes were devised as were exports processing zones. As state properties were sold in the former Soviet Union and Eastern Europe, warehouses full of weapons and munitions became available on the open market. Just as legitimate businesses looked for more international opportunities to expand into new markets, so, too, did criminal organizations.[4]

At the same time, technological inventions made sophisticated information encryption techniques available to all. Criminals have taken full advantage of the anonymity of Web-based e-mail accounts and the use of computers in internet cafes and cheap, disposable cell phones. With the reduction in exchange controls, the

exchange controls ■
government restrictions on the amount of domestic currency that can be exchanged for other currencies

---

[4] Examples are drawn from Moises Naim, *Illicit: How Smugglers, Traffickers, and Copycats are Hijacking the Global Economy* (New York: Anchor Books, 2005).

buying and selling of currencies exploded. In 1989, daily transactions in the global currency market totaled $590 million. By 2004 it was up to $1.88 trillion and to-day well over $4 trillion! With the resultant rise of computerized global banking networks, money launderers found it easier to conceal and funnel illicit gains from crime into legitimate businesses and other accounts, becoming ever-more adept at financial smurfing—concealing or avoiding records of financial transactions that can be traced by law-enforcement officials.

Activities of this type are much easier when criminals can take advantage of weak states. In such countries, it is not surprising that criminal organizations with ready cash attempt to influence or capture key institutions such as the courts, customs offices, banks, police, and politicians. Once they gain a foothold, they branch out into legitimate businesses, deeply permeating the political and eco-nomic life of a country. By way of example, the tiny Pacific island nation of Na-uru is a haven for money laundering, particularly from Russia. Suriname, located on South America's northern coast, is a transshipment point for drug traffickers. The experience of Suriname, Mexico, Colombia, Afghanistan, Lebanon, and other countries underscores the increasing importance of TCOs on the supply side of a seemingly insatiable world demand for drugs.

Estimates of the value of all global retail sales of illicit drugs are over $320 bil-lion, making the drug trade one of the largest commercial activities in the world. While Latin American countries such as Colombia and the notorious Medellín and Cali cartels historically have drawn the most attention, Afghanistan is now the world's largest producer of heroin. Other states, while not quite so visible in terms of public awareness, suffer from the plague of criminal activity associated with drug trafficking. Take, for example, South Africa. The government is com-mitted to fighting domestic and international trafficking in illicit narcotic drugs, but reliable evidence suggests that the country continues to be an important transit area for cocaine (from South America) and heroin (from the Far East) primarily destined for Southern African and European markets.

South Africa has for some time been the origin, the transit point, or the termi-nus of many major smuggling routes; this was particularly so during the apartheid period or era of white rule. Trends and practices begun in the sanctions-busting apartheid period continue into the current era; rather than embargoed items, drugs and other illicit items now are smuggled into and out of South Africa. Addition-ally, South Africa has the most developed transportation, communications, and banking infrastructure in sub-Saharan Africa. The country's modern international telecommunications systems, particularly wireless telephones; its direct air links with South America, Asia, and Europe; and its permeable land borders provide opportunities for regional and international trafficking in all forms of contraband, including narcotics.

One of the most appalling developments in recent decades has been the expan-sion in human trafficking. Aided and abetted by a reduction in border controls, victims end up in sweatshops, plantations, and factories. The most infamous exam-ple involves the sex trade. Some countries are notorious destinations for sex-trade tourists—Myanmar, China, Cambodia, Thailand, Colombia, and the Philippines. Former communist countries such as Russia, Ukraine, Moldova, and Romania are well known for the export of sex-slaves. Recruiters promise young women a life in

money laundering ■
financial transactions designed to conceal the identity, source, and/or destination of illegally gained money

smurfing ■
dividing large amounts of currency into smaller transactions that are in amounts below some statutory limit that normally does not require a financial institution to file a report with a government agency

the West in clerical, retail, or modeling work. Many, however, end up working as prostitutes in Western capitals. Japan is often the destination for girls from Brazil, Ecuador, and Colombia. Cambodian teenagers are sent to brothels in Thailand, at times having been sold into servitude by desperately poor families. The United States has not been immune; foreign sex slaves are being brought into the country—imported as if they were commodities bought and sold on the open market.[5]

Blurring the Terrorism-Crime Distinction

As noted, terrorist groups and criminal organizations differ in one basic aspect: Terrorists tend to be more motivated by political objectives than criminals who pursue essentially economic goals. Criminals usually want to be left alone to pursue their criminal activities. Far from wanting to overthrow the capitalist system—the professed goal of many terrorists over the years—criminals embrace the market system and exploit it to their advantage. Instead of attacking governments and law enforcement agencies, they prefer, when possible, to corrupt and intimidate them.

The traditional distinction between terrorists and criminals is eroding. Criminals at times resort to political violence to intimidate government officials, as seen in the assassination campaigns of the Mexican drug organizations. As the drug battlefield has moved south, El Salvador, Guatemala, and Honduras now suffer the world's highest murder rates. Central America forms a bridge between Colombia, the world's biggest cocaine producer, and the United States, the world's biggest market for drugs. It is really not surprising that terrorist organizations operating in such countries as Afghanistan, Colombia, Peru, and Lebanon, which are the source of much of the world's illicit drugs, became involved in the drug trade. On the other hand, as governments gear up to deal with the expanding transnational crime problem, criminals likely will resort more frequently to asymmetric warfare as a means to intimidate officials and coerce policy changes.

If criminals essentially see their operations as businesses, it is not surprising that they at times create strategic alliances that work to their mutual benefit. As with legitimate businesses, the point is to reduce risk and improve profits. One example involves relationships between the Colombian drug cartels and Mexican drug-trafficking families. Mexican criminal organizations have developed over the years an excellent smuggling infrastructure for transporting goods and people across the border into the United States. For the Colombians, employing the Mexican smuggling networks to get their cocaine into the United States lowers the risk of running afoul of U.S. drug interdiction efforts. For the Mexicans involved, the alliance allows them to share some of the profits of the cocaine industry, which has much higher profit margins than marijuana and other smuggled commodities.

A similar alliance has been developed between Mexican smugglers and Chinese criminal organizations that transport illegal immigrants seeking to enter the United States. The Colombians have also worked with Nigerian drug-trafficking organizations, with the latter providing heroin to the Colombians in exchange for cocaine, which the Nigerians sell in Europe. Similarly, the Sicilian Mafia and the

---

[5] Peter Landesman, "The Girls Next Door," *New York Times Magazine*, January 24, 2004.

Colombians worked out an alliance in the late 1980s designed to aid Colombian entry into the European cocaine market. The Sicilians had a well-established distribution system in Europe and knowledge of regional law-enforcement capabilities; they were also making efforts to recapture a portion of the U.S. heroin market they had progressively lost to Asian suppliers.

A comparative study reveals many interesting similarities among several criminal groups such as the Italian Mafia, Japanese *Yakusa*, Russian mafia, and Chinese Triads. Very much a part of their national and local cultures, they were at their origins fraternities also known for good or service-oriented works that built their legitimacy in the communities in which they operated. Indeed, the term *Triad* refers philosophically to an essential three-way linkage among the spiritual (heaven), the material (earth), and human beings. Moreover, the *omerta* or code of silence among members is by no means unique to the Mafia, a commitment to secrecy also being an integral part of Russian mafia, *Yakusa*, Triads, and other criminal groups. Hierarchical structures of social organization based on personal, reciprocal loyalties and protection of other family members are also characteristics in common, albeit with cultural variations. Viewing the criminal organization as a form of extended family with expectations of loyalty is to be found in Mafia and Triad groups; however, reflecting its origins in feudal Japan, the *Yakusa* put greater emphasis on the personal, mutual loyalties between the *oyabun* (senior) and his followers.

TCO Threat Assessment

How big a threat are such TCOs to national and international security? The answer varies depending on the state, TCO, and region of the world. Several generalizations, however, are possible. First, to date it is apparent that such criminal alliances are alliances of convenience, with each organization asking, "What's in it for us?" Such organizations are highly protective of their independence and markets, so there is no movement to create some sort of global criminal organization with central direction and enforcement mechanisms. In fact, just as legitimate international businesses have their disagreements, transnational criminal alliances also have their strains and easily can fall apart. They tend, in other words, to epitomize the netwar type of organization.

Second, large-scale, organized criminal activity, though it is not designed to bring down a state and create a new political order, can have the pernicious and deadly effect of undermining the social fabric of a society and contributing to a host of financial and social ills and political crises of authority. This is particularly the case with narcotics trafficking and the attendant consequences of widespread drug abuse and the financial corruption of governments. Such dangers are particularly pronounced in countries struggling to escape from their authoritarian past but saddled with weak legal, financial, and democratic institutions.

Third, the trend line in terms of narcotics trafficking, human trafficking, and the general spread of illicit activities on the part of TCOs is not encouraging. Law enforcement agencies struggle to keep up. How can governments combat transnational criminal organizations? As with all problems of world politics, there are no easy answers.

One approach is to improve intelligence collection and analytical efforts, aiming at better understanding of TCOs, their networks, and their means of doing business. This "mapping of the terrain" requires the sharing of information and intelligence among interested states. One example is the International Criminal Police Organization (ICPO), more commonly known as INTERPOL, the name adopted in 1956 for a law-enforcement information-exchange network originally established in 1923. From its secretariat in Lyon, France, INTERPOL now connects more than 180 countries that may share information and coordinate law-enforcement efforts against criminal activities of all kinds in an increasingly globalized world. Singled out for particular emphasis these days are terrorism and other forms of violent crime, criminal organizations, narcotics production and trade, human trafficking, financial and high-technology crimes, and alien and fugitive investigation support to national authorities. EUROPOL, a clearinghouse for police information based in Europe, is another example of such an enterprise.

What is required is the development of joint programs and operations among those states that have the interest, will, and capability to make inroads that undermine the power of TCOs. Developing any strategy or policy requires taking into account the possible unexpected consequences of a particular line of attack to minimize the sorts of outcomes evident in counterdrug efforts in some Latin American countries in which indigenous militaries end up violating human rights. One also can be critical of such rhetoric as the "war on drugs" or the "war on crime." Such military phrases imply that such problems can be solved once and for all—a naïve hope—rather than merely reduced—a more reasonable goal. Finally, and perhaps most important, more progress can be made in curbing the demand for illicit drugs—the market that gives incentives to criminal activity in the first place. It is not enough to wage war on the supply side without attending to the difficult social and other factors that lead people to buy and use drugs in the first place—the demand side.

CONCLUSION

As U.S. and Western military involvement winds down in Iraq and Afghanistan, so, too, will the number of dispatches posted on the online forum *The Sandbox*. Yet eventually more postings will occur as efforts are made to suppress if not resolve the myriad of asymmetric conflicts that plague so many parts of the world. While fifty years ago the West could essentially ignore many of these small wars, in an age of globalization, this is harder to do in those cases where local threat groups have an actual or potential global reach.

Terrorism and crime are where realist concern with national security threats to states intersects with the liberal interest in nonstate actors. Terrorism has understandably received more headlines and news coverage than has transnational organized crime. A major terrorist incident, after all, is very dramatic. On the other hand, few of us or anyone we know likely will ever fall victim to a terrorist attack. The impact of global crime, however, is much more pervasive. It is evident in the drug problems in our schools and society in general. Criminal activity has major financial consequences and, like terrorism, can threaten democratic institutions. This is particularly a concern in emerging democratic states.

Terrorism and crime epitomize the dark side of globalization. These asymmetric threat organizations or armed groups both attack or attempt to circumvent existing political authorities. Compared to classic interstate wars, asymmetric conflicts involve not only military force, but the use of the entire range of domestic and international resources available to policymakers—law enforcement, intelligence, support of the general populace, and various types of international cooperation.

✓• Study and Review the **Post-Test & Chapter Exam** at **mypoliscilab.com**

LEARNING OBJECTIVES REVIEW

10.1 Compare and contrast asymmetric and symmetric warfare utilizing historical examples.

Asymmetric warfare involves a lack of congruity in the capabilities and strategies of two foes. In this chapter it specifically refers to a situation in which the nonstate opponent has developed capabilities and strategies designed to diminish the state's capabilities or strengths. Asymmetric warfare in the form of terrorism is not new, as evident by such historical examples as the Zealots and Assassins. After the French Revolution there was a rise in secular-based terrorism on the part of such movements as the anarchists. The 20th century witnessed the rise of ideologically based terrorism that drew strength from Marxism-Leninism and nationalist appeals. Current Islamic terrorism is often traced to 1979—the Soviet invasion of Afghanistan and the fall of the shah of Iran occurred that same year.

KEY TERMS
Symmetric warfare 336
Center of gravity 336
Asymmetric warfare 336
Revolutions in military affairs 337

ADDITIONAL READING
Bruce Hoffman, *Inside Terrorism*, 2nd ed. (New York: Columbia University Press, 2006). The best textbook on terrorism, its evolution, and efforts to combat it.

10.2 Describe the history of international terrorism and key terrorist attacks against the United States over the past sixty years.

Terrorism is as old as recorded history. In the ancient world it tended to have religious aspects (Zealots and Assassins). The French Revolution of 1789 popularized the term *terrorism*, and by the 19th century there were a number of secular (nonreligious) terrorist groups and movements such as the Anarchists. Following World Wars I and II, ethnic and nationalist-based terrorism came to the fore. During the Cold War insurgent organizations in the developing world often used terrorism as part of broader political-military strategies. The United States came face to face with international terrorism in the Middle East in the 1970s, culminating with the 9/11 attacks.

KEY TERMS
Terrorism 338
Anarchists 339
Nationalism 340

ADDITIONAL READINGS
Walter Laqueur, *The Age of Terrorism* (Boston: Little, Brown, 1987). A classic work presenting both a historical and conceptual overview of terrorism.
Lawrence Wright, *The Looming Tower: Al-Qaeda and the Road to 9/11* (New York: Vintage Books, Random House, 2006). Pulitzer Prize–winning book that traces the evolution of al-Qaeda and the attempts of an FBI agent to thwart follow-on attacks after 9/11.

10.3 Identify and critique three factors used to explain the causes of terrorism.

Keeping in mind the complexity of human behavior, there are three basic explanations for terrorist motivation—psychological and social-psychological factors, ideological factors both secular and religious, and environmental factors for grievances and cultures of violence. The search for a single factor to explain terrorism is a dead end. The question is: What is the relative importance of the various factors in any particular individual or group?

KEY TERMS

Social psychology 342
Instrumental rationality 343
Value rationality 343
Cultures of violence 344

ADDITIONAL READING

Walter Reich (ed.), *Origins of Terrorism: Psychologies, Ideologies, Theologies, States of Mind* (Cambridge, England: Cambridge University Press, 1990). A classic, the book covers the ideological, psychological, and social-psychological approaches to explaining terrorism.

10.4 Explain how radicalization, revenge, and networks have increased the threat of terrorism.

Contemporary terrorism consists of a diverse array of actors, motivations, and tactics that evolve over time. Recent trends include the domestic radicalization of individuals living in the West, including the United States; the seeming increase in terrorism motivated by revenge; the rise of transnational network terrorism on the part of Islamic *jihadist* groups; the increasing importance of technology; and the rising threat posed by weapons of mass destruction.

KEY TERMS

Radicalization 345
Netwar 348
Cyberterrorism 350
Weapons of mass destruction 351

ADDITIONAL READING

John Arquilla and David Ronfeldt, (eds.), *Networks and Netwars: The Future of Terror, Crime, and Militancy* (Santa Monica, CA: RAND Corporation, 2001). A classic analysis of a future that has come to pass. Free download from rand.org.

10.5 Compare and contrast the strengths and weaknesses of four major policymaking approaches to dealing strategically with the threat of international terrorism.

Four possible components of a strategy to confront international terrorism include: addressing the underlying causes or grievances; applying military power; imposing the rule of law; and enhancing international cooperation. Eliminating underlying causes is unrealistic. Military attacks against suspected terrorists run into practical problems such as locating them and dealing with the reality of collateral damage when using stand-off weapons such as UAVs. Imposing the rule of law both domestically and internationally is an important element of any counterterrorist strategy, but there is the risk of going so far as to undermine civil liberties.

International cooperation is of paramount importance given the transnational dimension of terrorism.

KEY TERMS

Unmanned aerial vehicles (UAV) 356
Article 51 358

ADDITIONAL READINGS

Christopher C. Harmon, Andrew Pratt, and Sebastian Gorka (eds.), *Toward a Grand Strategy Against Terrorism* (New York: McGraw-Hill, 2011). A comprehensive overview of various policies designed to defeat or at least diminish terrorism. Chapters include legal, military, diplomatic, and international cooperative approaches.

Paul R. Viotti, Michael Opheim, and Nicholas Bowen (eds.), *Terrorism and Homeland Security* (New York: CRC

Press, 2008). The contributors deal strategically with terrorism, laying out both the away and the home games—the domestic and external approaches to dealing with this challenge and thus providing greater homeland security.

10.6 Explain how globalization has aided the rise of transnational criminal organizations (TCOs) and their attendant illicit activities.

Representing the dark side of globalization, transnational criminal organizations have benefited since the 1990s from the lowering of customs and border controls in Europe and elsewhere; the expansion of free trade; technological developments such as the internet, enhanced computing power, and programs that encourage the dramatic increases in trade and financial transactions; and the existence of weak states with officials who are helpless or complicit in the activities of the TCOs. These organizations and their networks have creatively taken what are usually seen as the benefits of globalization and used them for their own nefarious ends.

KEY TERMS

Transnational criminal organizations (TCOs) 360
Tariffs 360
Exchange controls 360
Money launderers 361
Smurfing 361

ADDITIONAL READINGS

Moisés Naím, *Illicit: How Smugglers, Traffickers, and Copycats Are Hijacking the Global Economy* (New York: Anchor Books/Random House, 2005). The title says it all. Disturbing and well-written, this book details the interconnection between TCOs.

David E. Kaplan and Alec Dubro, *Yakuza: Japan's Criminal Underworld* (Berkeley: University of California Press, 2003). A fascinating look at a criminal phenomenon not well understood.

CHAPTER REVIEW

1. Terrorism and transnational crime are examples of
   a. the depraved nature of human beings.
   b. kinds of problems inherent in societies that are not democratic.
   c. worldwide security issues that confront us in an increasingly globalized world.
   d. methods used exclusively by Middle Eastern, European, and Asian religious fanatic fringe groups to advance their agendas.

2. Terrorism is all of the following EXCEPT a
   a. weapon of the weak.
   b. symbol of the rejection of authority.
   c. threat to democratic civil societies.
   d. relatively new phenomenon.

3. The Zealots are (or were)
   a. Peruvian dissidents who resort to terrorist actions.
   b. ancient Jewish dissidents who took terrorist actions.
   c. Indian dissidents who resort to terrorist actions.
   d. Lebanese dissidents who resort to terrorist actions.

4. From the perspective of instrumental rationality, terrorism is
   a. an end to some desired means.
   b. a means to some desired end.
   c. the same as value rationality.
   d. a practice that is morally or legally legitimate, depending on the circumstances that give rise to such actions.

5. Causes of terrorism are least likely to include
   a. profit making through illegal business activity.
   b. psychological factors.
   c. ideological factors.
   d. environmental factors.

6. The thing that most terrorists have in common is that they are
   a. psychopaths.
   b. sociopaths.
   c. never bound by ideology.
   d. apparently normal human beings.

7. Which type of terrorist group is most likely to resort if possible to using weapons of mass destruction?
   a. Religiously based
   b. Politically based
   c. Regionally based
   d. Ethnically based

8. The radicalization process
   a. only involves religious belief systems.
   b. only involves adherence to the Muslim faith.
   c. in recent years has affected a number of Muslims living in the West.
   d. is restricted to ethnic groups.

9. Revenge as a motivation for terrorism has been evident in recent years. It can be particularly dangerous in terms of casualties when combined with
   a. religious justification.
   b. criminal motivation.
   c. secular ideologies such as Marxism-Leninism.
   d. none of the above.

10. Weapons of mass destruction
    a. refers to nuclear weapons.
    b. are just as likely to be used by one terrorist group as another.
    c. are most likely to be used by religious extremists or cults.
    d. would probably not be used by terrorist groups as they would alienate their supporters.

11. Problems associated with a military attack on terrorist organizations and states that support them include all of the following EXCEPT

a. it is financially too expensive.
b. it is hard to locate terrorist organizations.
c. there is a potential for collateral damage and the possible killing of innocents.
d. it may result in retaliation.

12. That a state can defend itself from attacks as an inherent right of sovereignty is underscored in
    a. NATO documents.
    b. Article 51 of the U.N. Charter.
    c. The Hague Conventions.
    d. the Geneva Conventions

13. Examples of known international criminal organizations do NOT include the
    a. Palestine Liberation Organization.
    b. Medellín and Cali cartels.
    c. Sicilian Mafia.
    d. *Yakusa* in Japan and Triads in China.

14. Which of the following does NOT help explain the recent spread of transnational crime?
    a. The end of the Cold War that has facilitated criminal access to worldwide markets
    b. Implementation of NAFTA that has facilitated criminal access to North American markets
    c. Advances in international telecommunications that can be used to facilitate criminal activities around the world
    d. A marked decline in moral or religious education in an increasingly secularized world

15. The single most important difference between terrorist and criminal organizations is that
    a. they have different goals and therefore different means.
    b. criminal organizations usually seek economic gain while terrorist organizations are usually more motivated by political objectives.
    c. terrorist organizations use more violent means, resulting in more deaths than criminal organizations.
    d. criminal organizations typically have a tighter organizational structure than terrorist organizations.

Trade and Money

"*The [IMF's] credibility, and hence effectiveness, rests on its perceived capacity to cope with worst-case scenarios.... We heard loud and clear that the emerging markets in particular were very concerned about the risk of contagion from advanced economies to emerging markets and to low-income countries.... What has been asked of us is instruments that are more flexible, more short term.... With the ability to engage at [a] little under $400 billion, we do have resources available.*"
—Christine Lagarde, Managing Director, International Monetary Fund (IMF)

LEARNING OBJECTIVES

11.1 Explain classical trade theory in relation to comparative advantage, unequal terms of trade, and the adverse implications of competitive devaluations.

11.2 Differentiate between classical and neoclassical economic understandings as they relate to macroeconomic and microeconomic theories applicable to global, regional, national, and local political economies.

11.3 Apply free trade theory to present-day circumstances of uneven development in which some countries have well-capitalized, large-scale producers capable of developing and applying advanced technologies to the products they bring to market, but many other countries do not.

11.4 Illustrate how changes in exchange rates affect prices of both exports and imports.

11.5 Outline how monetary authorities in institutions like the International Monetary Fund (IMF), treasuries and central banks, and the Bank for International Settlements (BIS) relate to each other in global-governance arrangements aimed at maintaining global trade and monetary regimes.

11.6 Evaluate progress made globally and regionally on liberalizing trade and achieving integration goals in Europe, North America, and other parts of the world.

Read and **Listen** to **Chapter 11** at **mypoliscilab.com**

Study and **Review** the **Pre-Test & Flashcards** at **mypoliscilab.com**

The following appeared in the "Weekly Piracy Report" of the ICC Commercial Crime Services (www.icc-ccs.org):

- 318-11 20.08.2011: 2325 UTC: Posn: 05:38N – 002:39E, Off Cotonou, Benin. Twelve pirates armed with guns boarded a chemical tanker involved in STS operations. The pirates took control of the ship and sailed to an unknown location. Owners unable to contact the vessel. Further details awaited.
- 317-11 20.08.2011: 0108 UTC: Posn: 16:54N - 054:03E, Salalah Anchorage, Oman. Armed pirates attacked and boarded a chemical tanker at anchor. They took hostage 21 crewmembers and hijacked the tanker to Somalia.
- 316-11 20.08.2011: 0225 LT: Posn: 03:47.3N - 098:42.1E, Belawan Port, Indonesia. Two robbers boarded a berthed bulk carrier during cargo operations. Four crewmembers on security watch and the 2/O at the gangway

rushed to the poop deck upon hearing a loud knocking sound. The 2/O saw the robbers with a big heavy black bag and he tried to stop them. The robbers pushed the 2/O and threw the bag ashore and escaped with ship's properties.

One of the oldest of crimes on the high seas is still with us. Ever-increasing commerce under globalization provides new opportunities not just for traders, but also for pirates. As with other international challenges, states and nonstate multinational corporations find it to their advantage to work together to meet the threat.

Authorities in governments and international organizations join with the private sector in global-governance arrangements designed not only to curb piracy and other crimes that threaten day-to-day commerce among nations, but also to sustain the trade and finance regimes (the sets of rules and institutions) they have constructed in their enlightened self-interests. Governments can act unilaterally, of course, but imposing one state's will on others invites retaliatory measures by those adversely affected. Working with others either bilaterally or in multilateral, institutional settings usually proves more beneficial for all parties concerned.

In this chapter we examine trade and the exchange of money in the global political economy. Trade and money to finance purchases go hand in hand. When Mexican traders want to purchase goods or services priced in dollars, they need to exchange their pesos for dollars to complete the purchase. Banks and money-exchange firms routinely make these transactions, buying dollars or other international currencies they sell to their customers. Mexico's central bank maintains a supply of international currencies in its reserves, which it can sell to banks using pesos to purchase them.

Maintaining this international liquidity—access to the cash needed to finance trade and other commerce in global markets—is a core task in the politics of global governance. In this regard, we explore the roles institutions play, particularly governments and central banks; the World Trade Organization (WTO) in Geneva, Switzerland; the International Monetary Fund (IMF) in Washington, DC; and central bankers at the Bank for International Settlements (BIS) in Basel, Switzerland.[1]

On global governance arrangements relating to trade and finance, we discuss classical and neoclassical economic thinking—understandings that have influenced profoundly how economists and political leaders craft both domestic and international policy regimes and responses. In Chapter 12, "Development," we revisit trade and finance as they relate to the developing world—also addressing such other concerns as demographics, the environment, and health, which have proven to be further burdens and barriers to economic advancement of the poorest people who comprise the majority of the world.

---

[1]For further details on the structure and workings of trade-related international organizations, see among others the World Trade Organization (wto.org), International Monetary Fund (imf.org), Bank for International Settlements (bis.org), World Bank (worldbank.org), UN Conference on Trade and Development (unctad.org), World Intellectual Property Organization (wipo.int), and the Organization of Petroleum Exporting Countries (opec.org).

TRADE THEORY AND COMPARATIVE ADVANTAGE

11.1 Explain classical trade theory in relation to comparative advantage, unequal terms of trade, and the adverse implications of competitive devaluations.

👁 **Watch** the **Video "U.S.-China Trade Tensions"** at mypoliscilab.com

trade ■ supplying goods or services in exchange for payment from purchasers

exports ■ goods and services sold abroad

imports ■ goods and services purchased abroad

GDP ■ gross domestic product—GNP minus return on foreign investment since the latter is a measure of *foreign*, rather than *domestic* production

global governance ■ set of arrangements and processes by which authorities in governments or international organizations perform certain global tasks like maintaining trade and monetary regimes

The reason we give so much attention in this chapter to understanding the economics of **trade** is that, quite simply, it has a dramatic impact on the economic well-being of countries worldwide. The importance of trade in national economies is apparent in Table 11.1, which depicts **exports** (sales abroad) and **imports** (purchases from abroad) as a percentage of total domestic economic production as measured by **GDP**. As noted earlier, it should not surprise us that anything as important as economics is also highly political. Politics is core to economics as peoples and their governments, and the international and nongovernmental organizations they form inevitably become involved to a greater or lesser degree in the decisions they make about budgets, money, trade, investment, and other commercial matters.

Particularly for states, economic capabilities are one indicator of overall state power and hence of interest to realists and liberals alike. Precisely because of the high stakes involved, anything important, like economics, seems always to become political—authoritative decisions involving choices made by officials in governments or international organizations. We see these choices that relate to economic matters as part of the politics of **global governance**. Directly affected by these authoritative choices and having the financial and other capabilities to represent their interests, firms engaging in trade—both exporters and importers—and other corporations, banks and investment firms, and other nongovernmental organizations not surprisingly seek to influence those making these decisions. As in domestic politics, the interests of workers, consumers, and other individuals in national and global publics depend for the most part upon actions taken in political processes by interest groups, political parties, and other nongovernmental organizations acting on their behalf in efforts to sway officials in governments and international organizations.

Some people think governments have a constructive role to play in managing their economies and working with other governments to manage regional and global commerce. Others prefer a *laissez-faire* approach, minimizing government participation or interference in the marketplace, whether domestically or globally. Having said that, most *laissez-faire* advocates concede that government treasuries and their central banks wind up playing an instrumental role in global commerce by managing the national supply of money and assuming obligations to make payments to other countries that come from international trade, investment, and other commercial or financial transactions. Governments, their courts, and their law-enforcement authorities also play a pivotal role defining, enforcing, and adjudicating disputes concerning property rights. However we look at it, it is difficult to talk about trade and commerce without talking about politics and the roles played by governments and international organizations—once again, the politics of global governance.

Exports and imports are an important part of national economies, although some countries are relatively more dependent on their trade sectors than others. A positive (or favorable) trade balance—when exports are greater than imports—in the dollar difference adds to GNP. Conversely, a negative (unfavorable) trade balance—when imports are greater than exports—in the dollar difference is subtracted from GNP. The following data in Table 11.1 depict the relative importance of trade among different categories of states. As shown, developing countries have increased their reliance on trade as a percentage of GDP in the years since 1990

TABLE 11.1

International Trade and Economic Production

We see in this table the relative size of the trade sector (as % of overall economy measured by GDP) both regionally and in high-income (OECD member countries) and low-income, least-developed countries. Also indicated is the degree to which exports of high-technology products are concentrated in the high-income (OECD) countries located primarily in Europe, North America, and East Asia.

Region	Imports as % of GDP		Exports as % of GDP		High-Tech Exports as % of Manufactured Exports	
	1990	2009	1990	2009	1990	2009
Arab World	38	–	38	–	–	2
East Asia/Pacific	18	23	19	25	20	29
Latin America/ Caribbean	15	21	17	21	7	13
OECD High Income	18	23	17	22	18	19
Least-Developed Countries	21	34	12	23	–	–
Sub-Saharan Africa	25	34	26	30	–	–
Europe/Central Asia	27	34	27	36	14	17
South Asia	12	24	9	19	2	8
Euro Area	28	35	27	36	12	16

while, given their lower level of economic development, lagging far behind the capital-rich, high-income countries in terms of high-technology exports.

Why do countries trade with one another? How does trade translate into a higher standard of living? Why are some countries winners and others losers? Why can't countries do just as well by simply going it alone economically? We examine two approaches to these questions with a long and respected tradition: classical and neoclassical economic theory. Classical trade theory is exemplified in the writings of David Ricardo (1772–1823) and others. For countries or their business firms to engage in international trade requires some reason or rationale for doing so. Classical trade theory predicts that countries (their corporations and their other firms) will tend *ceteris paribus* (other things being "equal" or held constant)[2] to produce and export those products in which they have a comparative advantage. Productive

comparative advantage ■ free-trade principle that countries tend to specialize in producing those goods and services for export in which they are most efficient, leading to a global specialization or division of labor that maximizes aggregate productivity

[2]Economists often use the term "other things being equal," or in Latin, *ceteris paribus*, as a caveat or warning that the model they are describing or the argument they are making contains simplifying assumptions—for example, that factors held as constants in a model or argument are variables in the real world that could otherwise affect the predicted outcome.

capacities and the demand for these products in domestic and external (regional and global) markets will determine the amount produced and the degree of economic return. Thus trade depends upon differences, not sameness in relative efficiency and capacity of production among two or more countries and their businesses in the products they trade regionally or globally. If there were no differences in efficiency of production and domestic production capacity were sufficient to meet demand, in theory there would be no trade at all. States could, indeed, go it alone.

What factors account for comparative advantage? Why don't all countries produce electronics or agricultural products for export? Consistent with Ricardian thinking, the Heckscher–Ohlin theorem developed early in the 20th century makes the obvious point that because different countries have diverse factor endowments— different amounts and quality of land, labor, and capital—they are likely to export those goods or services in which their combination of these production factors gives them a comparative advantage. For example, producers in some countries, having sufficient labor and a favorable climate, might specialize in agricultural production, whereas producers in other countries with larger capital endowments might special- ize in manufactured goods and services such as banking.

This may all sound well and good in theory, but there are at least two major criticisms of classical trade theory that should be mentioned. First, it is one thing to state that countries should produce what is favored by their factor endowments, but that still does not guarantee a significant role or comparative advantage for many developing world countries. You would think, for example, that developed countries should emphasize high-tech production and less-developed countries ag- ricultural exports. We still often think of agriculture—raising animals and growing and harvesting plants for food and other purposes—as a labor-intensive enterprise favoring countries with good soil, favorable growing climate, and abundant popu- lations willing to work the land. Historically, this has been the case. Even today, the composition (proportion of GDP) of many less-developed world economies re- mains 30 percent or more agricultural compared to advanced-industrial or postin- dustrial economies that are perhaps just 1 to 3 percent agricultural.

Capital-rich countries, however, may find that their capital still gives them de- cided advantages over other countries that are rich in natural resources. The United States and other developed, capital-rich economies tend to be relatively more ef- ficient in agricultural production because capital has been effectively substituted for higher-cost labor in these countries. Indeed, the mechanization of agriculture, cou- pled with agricultural research and development of growing-and-producing tech- nologies, requires vast amounts of capital, which the developed countries have in relatively more abundant supply than do less-developed countries. Such technologies include using chemicals as fertilizer and for insect or pest control, developing plant hybrids with greater or more diverse crop yields, and the more controversial area of genetically engineering new plant and animal forms by altering DNA or cell content.

Thus capital-intensive agriculture becomes a comparative cost advantage for many capital-rich countries. Moreover, governments in these countries, enjoying ample access to capital through taxation or borrowing, have also subsidized the politically influential agricultural sectors in their countries. Not surprisingly, in the absence of tariffs, quotas, or other barriers, these capital-rich countries are prone to export agricultural produce to each other and even to less-developed countries.

Classical economist David Ricardo (1772–1823), who, like Adam Smith (1723–1790) before him and Karl Marx (1818–1883) afterward, considered the value of a product (good or service) a function of the labor put into its production, advanced central tenets of trade theory. In an international market free of tariffs or other barriers to trade, a country's firms would tend to produce for export those products in which it enjoyed a comparative advantage, that is, it was more efficient in producing them than foreign competitors.

ARGUMENT   To understand classical trade theory and the concept of comparative advantage, it helps to simplify things a bit. So let's pretend there are only two countries in the world (Insula and Terra), each capable of producing the same two products. Many texts illustrate the concept of comparative advantage as affecting the trade of cloth versus wheat or wine versus textiles, but we will modernize the example by referring to the trade of semiconductors versus lumber.

Insula is an island country with small, well-tended forests and other natural resources. Terra, a continental country, also has natural resources and vast forest lands. Let's assume each country uses the factors of production (land, labor, and capital) it has to produce just two products—semiconductors and lumber. To keep things simple, let's assume that these countries exchange one product for another without using money. We omit in this discussion the effects of such variables as different levels of domestic demand, different size economies and scale of production, changes in exchange rate that affect prices, and government intervention (as in subsidizing production or imposing tariffs or quotas to protect and encourage domestic production of a particular product). Rather, in order to understand classical free-trade theory and its predictions, it is helpful to reduce the trade puzzle to its basic essentials—production trade-offs of just two products produced and traded between just two countries *ceteris paribus* (holding all other factors constant or equal).

Production Possibilities

In addition to land and other natural resources, both semiconductor and lumber production rely heavily on labor (or human resources, especially skilled labor) and capital in the forms of machinery, work space, and finance for these enterprises. Take a look at the graphic presentation of production possibilities for the two countries. The diagonal lines on both graphs represent the maximum possible combinations of semiconductors and lumber that can be produced separately by Insula and Terra.

If Insula produces only semiconductors (putting all of its available land, labor, and capital to that purpose), the most it can produce is 100,000 units, but no lumber at all is produced at that level of semiconductor production. If Insula wants to

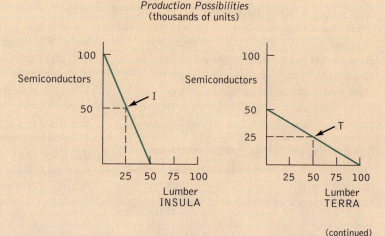

Production Possibilities
(thousands of units)

(continued)

produce at least some lumber, it will have to reduce semiconductor production a bit to free up some land, labor, and capital, reallocating these to lumber production. On the other hand, if Insula forgoes semiconductor production entirely and produces only lumber, the most lumber it can produce is 50,000 units.

As a practical matter, however, firms in Insula actually produce both lumber and semiconductors, as depicted on the graph by point I: 25,000 units of lumber and 50,000 semiconductors. A similar analysis for Terra reveals a maximum production possibility of either 100,000 units of lumber or 50,000 semiconductors with actual production, point T, being a combination of 50,000 units of lumber and 25,000 semiconductors.

The marginal trade-off between producing semiconductors and lumber for Insula is 2:1—for every two units of reduced semiconductor production, Insula can free up enough land, labor, and capital to produce one more unit of lumber instead. The reverse is also true: For every unit of reduced lumber production, Insula can allocate enough land, labor, and capital to produce two more semiconductors instead. (We can also see this by looking at the downward or negative slope of the diagonal line, which is 2.0.)

By contrast, Terra's marginal trade-off between producing semiconductors and lumber is 1:2—for every unit of reduced semiconductor production, Terra can free up enough land, labor, and capital to produce two more units of lumber instead. Alternatively, if Terra forgoes two units of lumber production, it will have enough land, labor, and capital to produce one more semiconductor instead. (Again, we can also see this by looking at the downward or negative slope of the diagonal line, which is 1/2 or 0.5.)

Comparative Advantage and Specialization

These trade-offs show us how Insula, compared to Terra, is relatively more efficient in producing semiconductors than lumber (it can produce two more semiconductors for every unit of lumber production it forgoes), and Terra is relatively more efficient in producing lumber than semiconductors (for every unit of semiconductor production it forgoes, it can produce two more units of lumber). Put another way, efficiency in producing semiconductors allows Insula to produce them less expensively than Terra can. Terra's comparative advantage in lumber allows it to produce lumber less expensively than Insula can.

The idea of trade-offs is captured by the term *opportunity costs*. If a country, or more specifically its corporations or other firms, chooses to invest its capital and allocate labor and other resources to production of some quantity of semiconductors, the same capital and labor will not be available for production of some quantity of lumber. If Insula allocates all of its production to semiconductors, it will not have any labor or capital left to cut trees, process them, and deliver lumber to market. Inability to produce any lumber because production factors have been allocated to producing only semiconductors is referred to as an opportunity cost. As a practical matter, of course, production decisions in the real world are usually not all-or-nothing decisions. Instead, a country may allocate its capital, labor, and natural resources to production of different amounts of semiconductors, lumber, or other products. Still, as the model depicts, Insula's decision this year to produce 50,000 semiconductors and 25,000 units of lumber (point I) also means it is forgoing as opportunity costs the production of up to an additional 50,000 semiconductors.

In any event, if both countries choose not to trade with each other and sustain their current production levels of both products (points I and T respectively), their total production will be 75,000 semiconductors (50,000 for Insula and 25,000 for Terra) and 75,000 units of lumber (25,000 for Insula and 50,000 for Terra). On the other hand, if each specializes according to comparative advantage, total production of semiconductors and lumber can be increased

(continued)

from 75,000 to 100,000 units of each product—the maximum production possibility.

Because of this difference in efficiency in the use of the three factors of production and consequent cost of production, there is an opportunity for trade. If the two countries do specialize in producing those products in which they enjoy a comparative advantage—those in which they are relatively more efficient as producers—aggregate or total production of both products can expand substantially.

COUNTERARGUMENT The theory oversimplifies and thus misses the realities of trade then and now:

1. The labor theory of value accepted by classical economic theorists has long been overtaken by neoclassical understandings in which value indicated by the price at which goods or services sell is a function of supply and demand for them, not the labor put into their production.

2. Ricardian theory omits key variables: different levels of domestic demand, different size economies and scale of production, changes in exchange rate that affect prices, and government intervention (as in subsidizing production or imposing tariffs or quotas to protect and encourage domestic production of a particular product).

3. The theory is often used ideologically to justify unfair terms of trade that work to the disadvantage of less-developed countries. Put another way, it is an ideology masquerading as theory set forth by capital-rich countries for their own benefit, masking the terms of trade that are so unfavorable to less-developed countries, relegating to them the production of commodities in which they allegedly have the comparative advantage. These agricultural products, minerals, and other natural resources typically are purchased at bargain-basement prices by producers in capital-rich, more advanced economies who, by contrast, sell their manufactures and high-technology products at increasing price levels.

APPLICATION Whether applied on a regional or global basis, the claim of classical trade theory is that if we allow free, unencumbered trade, countries will tend to specialize in production of those products (goods and services) in which they have a comparative advantage. A world in which the most efficient producers of particular products tend to specialize in their production results in maximizing or optimizing aggregate, worldwide production, thus enhancing global welfare. As critics are quick to point out, however, enhancing aggregate production through specialization and free trade does not mean an equal or even equitable distribution of these gains. Some countries and their businesses clearly benefit more than others. Can you identify the kinds of countries and businesses that tend to gain from free trade as well as those that do not do so well? ◢

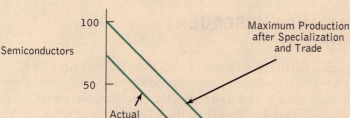

Production Possibilities for Insula and Terra Combined
(thousands of units)

Semiconductors

Maximum Production after Specialization and Trade

Actual Production before Trade

Lumber

Indeed, it was this very point—the demand of a number of developing world leaders that the developed world restrict its agricultural exports to developing countries—that led to the collapse of the World Trade Organization (WTO) talks in Cancun, Mexico, in September 2003. In a capitalist world economy, we should not be surprised that decisive advantages even in agriculture often go to capital-rich countries.

terms of trade ■ ratio of export prices of one country to those of another, which in effect tells us the amount of revenue from a country's export sales to the other that can be used to pay for imports from the other

A second and related objection to classical trade theory is that it ignores unequal terms of trade. Beginning in the 1960s, Latin American and other economists charged that less-developed countries of the South were in a decidedly disadvantageous position compared to more advanced, industrial countries of the North. Economists such as Argentine Raúl Prebisch observed that countries in the South export raw materials and agricultural commodities that tend not to increase (or even tend to decline) in price, whereas countries in the North gain an advantage from production and export of manufactured goods that tend to increase in price.

trade preferences ■ special arrangements allowing easy access on a cost-competitive basis by a foreign producer to a country's domestic market

To address this and other trade problems, less-developed countries have sought trade preferences from rich countries. Trade preferences can take the form of assurances by developed countries that they or their businesses will buy at least a certain minimum quantity of developing world products. Alternatively, they may agree to give trade preferences—not to impose tariffs, quotas, or other barriers against developing world exports even as these countries retain such barriers against imports from the capital-rich, developed world.

European Union (EU) ■ an economic and political partnership between 27 European countries designed to ensure peace, stability, and prosperity by helping to raise living standards and progressively building a single Europe-wide market

For their part, the European Union (EU) countries have developed by political agreement the most extensive set of trade preferences in Africa, the Caribbean, and the Pacific, the so-called "ACP" countries, many of which were former colonies of EU members. In addition to benefits derived by developing world countries from these measures, trade preferences and cooperative monetary measures also tie them economically to the countries granting these favors. Critics thus see extensive trade preferences as actually a means of maintaining neocolonial, political-economic relations that also convey substantial advantages to developed countries. Defenders see little or nothing wrong with trade preferences or arrangements that benefit both sides, however unequally.

NEOCLASSICAL AND SUBSEQUENT ECONOMIC THOUGHT

11.2 Differentiate between classical and neoclassical economic understandings as they relate to macroeconomic and microeconomic theories applicable to global, regional, national, and local political economies.

It is not only critics from the developing world who have taken issue with classical economic theory as advanced by Adam Smith, David Ricardo, and other classical economists. As far back as the late 19th and early 20th centuries, there were developments in economic thought that departed from the labor theory of value. What we now call neoclassical economic theory refers to approaches advanced by English economist Alfred Marshall (1842–1924) and French economist Leon Walras (1834–1910).

Instead of seeing the value of a good or service as determined primarily by the human labor put into its production, neoclassical economists see value in a market context—price as the outcome of demand for and supply of particular products (either goods or services). As such, value is to be found in relative abundance or scarcity and in the utility buyers and sellers place on the goods or services they seek (demand) or provide (supply) to markets. Utility and marginal utility (the value to be found in each additional unit of a good or service) thus became key concepts in market analysis. The equilibrium price is dependent on the intersection of demand and supply curves representing quantities sought or provided at alternative prices in different types of markets (models of "perfect" or "pure" competition among many sellers, oligopoly among a few sellers, and monopoly dominated by one seller).

Bringing the ideas of earlier economists together, Marshall and Walras dealt with different aspects of market equilibrium as a conceptual device for understanding market forces. Although Smith, Ricardo, and other classical writers certainly dealt with individuals and firms as units in the marketplace, they also placed relatively more emphasis in their work on understanding the functioning of the economy as a whole (the subject of **macroeconomics**), whereas neoclassical economists focus relatively more on how purchasers (consumers or buyers) and suppliers (firms or sellers) interact in the marketplace (the subject of **microeconomics**).

Neoclassical economic theorists have developed and explored the applicability of such microeconomic concepts as elasticity of demand and supply—the expected response to changes in price (or income) with respect to quantities of a product buyers want to purchase or suppliers want to sell; externalities—the positive or negative impacts (benefits or costs) of market behaviors on others; efficiency and optimization of utility, production, allocation of resources, and performance of other market activities; and rational expectation, public choice, and collective goods theories that provide a basis for explaining or predicting market behaviors. Other important analytical concepts introduced by neoclassical economists to provide understanding of market processes include marginal cost (the cost of producing and supplying an additional unit), marginal revenue (the amount earned from sale of an additional unit), and diminishing marginal returns, or more simply, diminishing returns (that each additional unit of land, labor, or capital put into production—holding all other factors constant—will produce proportionately somewhat less of a product than the previous unit of land, labor, or capital). In all of this work, most neoclassical theorists have made heavy use of mathematics (stating economic ideas symbolically in algebraic equations), statistics, and **econometrics**—such methods of analysis as correlation, regression, and causal modeling.

At the same time, other economists have also made substantial contributions to macroeconomic theory. Directly influenced by Marshall's earlier work, John Maynard Keynes (1883–1946) and his followers have taken a macroeconomic view, dealing with aggregate demand and supply for an entire economy taken as a whole. They have explored, for example, how demand is stimulated or dampened when government spends and taxes (**fiscal policy**) and influences the money supply and interest rates (**monetary policy**). Keynes also participated in laying political plans in 1944 for global actions through an **International Monetary Fund (IMF)** to assure international monetary flows and facilitate currency exchange so essential to international commerce (discussed more completely later in this chapter). Often at odds with Keynesian economists, the work of Milton Friedman and other monetarists has focused on how the supply and velocity or flow of money in an entire economy affect production and supply as well as demand. For his part, Joseph Schumpeter (1883–1950), a contemporary of Keynes, also took a macroeconomic perspective, particularly in his exploration of how changes in technology,

macroeconomics ■ deals with how an economy as a whole functions, the domain of fiscal and monetary policy, respectively, involving such aggregates as GNP or GDP and money supply

microeconomics ■ deals with how purchasers and suppliers interact in the marketplace, sometimes referred to simply as market or price theory

econometrics ■ economic analyses employing quantitative methods and statistical tools that other social science fields also may use

fiscal policy ■ national budget decisions and actions on taxing and spending

monetary policy ■ national decisions and actions that affect the money supply, interest rates, and exchange rates

International Monetary Fund (IMF) ■ Washington-based international organization that seeks to maintain international liquidity—the availability of foreign currencies used to make international payments for imports of goods and services from abroad

innovation, and other factors influence business cycles. Expressly interested in the linkage between politics and economics, he also investigated how capitalism and socialism relate to democracy and democratic ideas.

These and other economists have made very important contributions to macroeconomic theories and concepts, but they have had an even greater impact on microeconomic theorizing. Originally formulated more with local or domestic markets in mind, microeconomic theories and concepts developed by neoclassical economists have increasing applicability to the global political economy. Markets for many goods and services now have truly worldwide scope. Microeconomic theory offers explanation of the exchange value (or price) of currencies in relation to each other as well as an account of the expected effects of governmental subsidies, regional integration, tariffs, quotas, or other barriers to trade. All of these issues have enormous political importance, given the high economic stakes states, firms, consuming publics, and others have in such matters. In short, neoclassical and other theorists have continued to expand our understanding of the global political economy beyond the foundational insights offered by classical writers.

THE IMPACT OF TECHNOLOGY ON FREE-TRADE THEORY

11.3 Apply free trade theory to present-day circumstances of uneven development in which some countries have well-capitalized, large-scale producers capable of developing and applying advanced technologies to the products they bring to market, but many other countries do not.

👁 ⎯ Watch the **Video** **"Shell Oil in Nigeria"** at **mypoliscilab.com**

economies of scale ▪ efficiencies that come from larger quantities or mass production resulting in lower costs

To summarize the discussion to date: Classical Ricardian free-trade theory focuses primarily on cost differences among producers. If a country is relatively more cost-efficient at producing a particular good or service, it will supposedly tend to specialize in producing and exporting what is not consumed or used domestically. It is the differences among countries that explain trade. In the absence of government intervention to place tariffs, quotas, or any other obstacles in the way of trade, countries will tend to specialize in producing those products in which they enjoy a comparative cost advantage relative to other producers. The result, then, of relegating production to the most efficient producers is, in principle, to maximize total productive capacity or aggregate output of goods and services, enhancing global welfare, however uneven the distribution of these gains from specialization and trade may be. Or so says classical theory.

Not so fast, say some economists. Ricardian theory goes partway but does not really provide a complete answer to why countries trade. Instead of focusing just on differences in production cost efficiencies, we also need to understand how **economies of scale** deriving from technological innovation influence marketing and production for export trade. That the average cost per unit of producing a million semiconductors typically is less than when a production line is set up to produce only a thousand is an example of an economy or unit-cost reduction based on large-scale production. Existing producers, large or small, of particular goods and services thus may look globally to expand their markets and enjoy increasing gains from export trade, dramatically increasing sales by finding many more customers that can be served efficiently by increasing substantially the overall level or scale of domestic production.

In the 1930s and 1940s economist Joseph Schumpeter, a contemporary of John Maynard Keynes, addressed the impact of technological innovation on business cycles. Clusters of new technologies displace older technologies in a process of "creative destruction." Economic growth, particularly in early-21st-century advanced-industrial and postindustrial, information- or knowledge-based economies, is profoundly influenced by such innovations and upward shifts in technology. Investments in technology usually are very costly; however, they are seen as crucial determinants of economic growth and future competitiveness in the global economy. Governments have been active players along with business enterprises in pursuing technological development, particularly "high technologies" with application in such knowledge-intensive industries as electronics, computers, and telecommunications. Know-how in advanced materials, superconductors, semiconductors, computers, and lasers has very real market applicability. Payoffs in these sectors are potentially not only greater but also increasing compared with similar investments in machines for lower-technology manufacturing enterprises. The implication is that countries and firms able to work in this high-technology sector will reap the greater rewards of knowledge-intensive production. Once again, this tends to leave developing world countries in the dust.

Economist Paul Krugman is prominent among those who have raised theoretical challenges to classical Ricardian trade theory. Krugman is careful to note, however, that focusing on increasing gains aided by technological innovation as motivation for export trade is a supplement to (not a replacement for) comparative-cost considerations as to why trade occurs.[3] Engaging in trade for increasing gains is not a new idea but, as Krugman suggests, we may not have given it sufficient consideration.

The increasing-gains argument, however, may actually matter more than merely enjoying a comparative-cost advantage, particularly for high-technology products in some markets in which certain firms have already well established themselves. It is difficult, although not impossible, of course, to start up a new firm and achieve a strong market position when one or a few large firms with ready access to capital already dominate a particular market. It is even harder to compete when new, fast-changing high technologies are difficult to acquire and develop into marketable products that can be produced at sufficient scale to be cost (and price) competitive.

By contrast, because of their ready access to capital, large, established firms in industries with increasing returns to scale are usually quite able not only to beat start-up competition, but also to grow even larger and realize ever-increasing gains from expanding their export-market positions. Aviation is a good example of a market in which only a few firms dominate globally. In fact, mergers and acquisitions of existing firms have continued to reduce the numbers of these large firms to just a few. Capital for production of aircraft and related high-technology products is thus increasingly concentrated in fewer corporations. Thousands of smaller firms offering specialized products are therefore increasingly dependent for contracts on a declining number of major producers. In order to compete on a scale with such U.S. giants as, for example, Lockheed Martin and Boeing, European producers have pooled their efforts in joint development and production agreements for both civil and military aircraft, thus effectively reducing even further the total number of competitors in global markets.

---

[3]For example, see Paul R. Krugman, *Rethinking International Trade* (Cambridge, MA: MIT Press, 1990, 1994).

Although oil as an energy source is well known, coal continues to play an important role, particularly for the poor in the developing world. This photo was taken in Bangladesh.

Large-scale mining and trading of coal are also critical for industrial use in economies such as China's. Even as many Western countries cut back on the use of coal, China imports large quantities from such countries as the United States and Australia to keep its industries going. China burns half of the six billion tons of coal used each year.

Despite environmental concerns, coal also still plays a role in providing energy in Western economies. The Fukushima nuclear reactor meltdown in March 2011 led to a reassessment of plans to decommission power plants in Germany such as this brown coal–fired plant. Because coal provides 42 percent of Germany's power, coal imports will rise through the first half of the decade.

International trade in coal is reflected in activity on the floors of commodity exchanges around the world. Coal is mined commercially in over fifty countries and used in over seventy.

The automobile market is another example. Consider, for example, two sets of transnational mergers in the auto industry that underscore market incentives to remain competitive and realize increasing gains by pooling technologies and other forms of capital. The original mergers were followed during the great recession of 2008 with further "restructuring" by the two American multinationals—offloading their interests to Italian and Chinese firms. Indeed, capital in this increasingly globalized world is truly fluid:

multinational corporation ■
corporate firm based or headquartered in one country, but producing goods or services and conducting other operations in two or more countries

1. The gradual acquisition of Chrysler (a U.S.-based **multinational corporation**) by Fiat, the Italian automaker, beginning in 2009. Previously Chrysler had merged in 1998 with Germany's Daimler-Benz, best known as the manufacturer of Mercedes cars, which in 2007 sold its interest in Chrysler to a private equity firm.
2. The merger in 1999 between Ford (another U.S.-based multinational) and Volvo passenger (the Swedish automaker)—Ford's interest was sold in 2010 to Geely, a Chinese firm.

What about the success of start-up, high-tech companies? Isn't the world market still open to technological innovations advanced by individual entrepreneurs? Indeed, some start-up firms with high-technology applications have been successful challengers to established, large-scale firms. But even these new players have had to secure substantial access to capital to finance and expand their efforts by selling stocks and issuing bonds in financial markets. Furthermore, market forces have ruthlessly eliminated many of these firms.

In sum, existing large-scale producers motivated by the prospects of increasing gains have a decided trade advantage, quite apart from any comparative-cost considerations suggested by classical theory. Following the same logic, of course, even smaller firms marketing specialized products seek to increase both their domestic- and export-market shares to achieve increasing gains. Although not yet fully developed, new thinking on trade and other aspects of the global economy thus challenges old theoretical assumptions and predictions, provides new explanations, and aims to expand our understanding of how international and global trade actually work.

TRADE AND FINANCE

11.4 Illustrate how changes in exchange rates affect prices of both exports and imports.

👁—Watch the Video "The Mexican Peso Crisis" at mypoliscilab.com

Classical free-trade theory also assumes the neutrality of money, which hardly seems to be the case in the real world. By "neutralizing" money, in classical trade theory the exchange of goods and services is influenced only by production costs and related considerations, not fluctuations in the value or exchange rates of currencies. In the earlier example in which the fictional countries Insula and Terra bartered semiconductors and lumber, no consideration was given to the value of currencies.

Again, following classical theory, it is comparative production costs, not changes in the value of money, that are supposed to drive consequent changes in the direction, volume, and types of products traded. These production and delivery-to-market costs are borne by suppliers of the good or service produced. In neoclassical understandings we see prices that are not only a means by which suppliers cover these costs, but also are in relation to demand for these goods or services—what purchasers wanting to buy them are willing to pay. Put another way, prices in these microeconomic, market-oriented understandings are a function of both supply and demand—the most efficient producer, thus the most competitive supplier is able to offer the same good or service at a lower price than competitors seeking the same export sales.

But in the real world, the value of money *does* fluctuate with consequent effects on prices. One country's currency may be worth more in relation to another country's currency today than it was yesterday, but it may be worth less tomorrow. Unfortunately, the prices at which goods and services are traded also change when **exchange rates** between currencies also change.

How Exchange Rates Work

An exchange rate is merely the price at which a currency can be bought (or sold) using another currency. Although exchange-rate arithmetic may seem confusing at first, it's really not so difficult to figure out if we treat a currency just like any product traded in markets, and we take a few moments to sort out how it is priced. Tourists are forced to do this when they travel abroad.

If the British pound (often referred to in currency markets simply as sterling and represented by the symbol £) can be traded for $1.60, we refer to this as the sterling–dollar exchange rate (£1.0 = US$1.60). Put the other way, one U.S. dollar can buy 0.625 of a pound—an exchange rate of US$1.00 = £0.625. This is how to switch from one exchange rate to the reverse:

$$£1.00 = US\$1.60$$

thus, reversing what is on either side of the = sign,

$$US\$1.60 = £1.0$$

and

$$US\$1.00 = £0.625$$

In an example we use in the next section, the dollar–yen exchange rates are US$1.00 = 120 yen (for last week) and US$1.00 = 110 yen (today)—a depreciation in the value of the dollar in that the same dollar buys fewer yen today than it could a week ago. Put the other way, last week's yen–dollar exchange rate can be expressed as 100 yen equaling about $0.83 last week but increasing to about $0.91 today—an appreciation in the value of the yen.

The exchange rate of a currency (its price in relation to other currencies) fluctuates in financial markets in response to shifts in demand for (and supply of) them in much the same way as commodities do. Currencies in demand *ceteris paribus* (all things being equal) tend to rise in price; a drop in demand for a currency means its exchange rate in relation to other currencies falls. When governments or their central banks make the authoritative or political choice to increase or decrease the supply of their currencies by selling or buying them in open-market operations, they also can impact exchange rates for these currencies. These effects are summarized in Figure 11.1. The intersection of the demand and supply curves is the equilibrium exchange rate in a particular financial market. The dashed lines represent

exchange rate ■
price of one currency in terms of another; for example, it may take $1.60 (U.S.) to purchase one British pound, or put another way, one U.S. dollar at this exchange rate will buy 0.625 of a pound

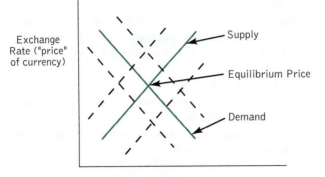

Quantity of Currency

FIGURE 11.1
Effects of Supply and Demand on Currency Exchange Rates

alternative demand and supply curves. Look at what happens to exchange rates when the levels of demand and supply go up (increase) or go down (decrease).

The Impact of Exchange-Rate Fluctuations on Trade

Let's look at an example of how fluctuations in exchange rates affect the prices of imports, exports, and thus the competitive positions of firms in two countries engaged in trade. If one U.S. dollar could purchase 120 Japanese yen last week but today can only purchase 110 yen, we say the dollar has depreciated in relation to the yen. Put another way, the yen has appreciated in relation to the dollar over the same period. A week ago, 120 yen could buy one U.S. dollar, but now the same 120 yen can buy about $1.09.

Let's see how a change in exchange rates affects prices. A Japanese importer wanting to buy a Ford automobile costing $25,000 last week at an exchange rate of 120 yen to the dollar had to come up with 3 million yen. This week the same $25,000 Ford can be bought at 110 yen to the dollar for 2,750,000 yen—a saving to the Japanese importer of 250,000 yen (about $2,272.72 at this week's exchange rate). Savings on the car are to the benefit of the Japanese importer; however, the American exporter is paid the same amount ($25,000) this week as last week. The real gain to the American exporter, of course, is the degree to which Japanese importers are willing to buy more Fords at 2,750,000 yen than they would at 3 million yen. Other things equal, more sales at the same dollar price mean more revenue and profits to Ford and Ford retailers.

Economists describe the impact on markets (and export-import positions) of exchange-rate changes by referring, as in the Ford case discussed earlier, to the **price elasticity of demand** in the Japanese market for Fords. For example, if demand for Fords increases substantially with a small decline in yen price, and as a result many more are purchased, elasticity is said to be high. The American exporter realizes great gains from increased sales to Japanese customers due to a

price elasticity of demand ■ the change in quantity of demand caused by a change in price

reduced price in yen. The American exporter's gain is not caused by increased efficiencies or reduced production costs on the American side. The gain in sales is purely due to a change (a decline) in the dollar–yen exchange rate. This effect is less if Japanese demand for Fords is not very elastic in relation to price or, worse from the American perspective, is perfectly inelastic—demand stays the same (does not change at all in relation to price).

Now let's turn the tables and look at the position of a Japanese exporter (and its U.S. retailer or dealer) of Honda automobiles. At 120 yen to the dollar, a Honda with a 3 million yen retail price that arrived by ship in Los Angeles last week can be sold for $25,000, competing directly with a $25,000 Ford. On the other hand, at an exchange rate of just 110 yen to the dollar, if the export manufacturer of the same type of Honda arriving in Los Angeles today is to receive the same profit margin in yen, it will have to raise the retail price in the U.S. market by more than $2,200. The Honda will be less competitive in this circumstance, not due to any change in quality or cost of production but solely because a change in exchange rate has had an adverse impact on its price. In an elastic market in which U.S. consumers are willing to substitute Fords for Hondas, a price rise can adversely affect Honda's market position, undercutting its sales and revenues.

Given the dollar's decline in value (it now buys only 110 yen compared to 120 yen last week), if the Japanese exporter and its U.S.-based retail dealer judge the American market to be inelastic, the price increase due to the exchange-rate change can be passed directly on to the consumers. On the other hand, if the U.S. market for Hondas is elastic, the exporter and retailer may choose for the time being to hold the American price at $25,000 and absorb more than $2,200 in lost revenue between them on the sale of each vehicle. (Of course, how the loss is distributed is subject to contract or negotiation between the export manufacturer and the importing dealer. Thus, Honda can reduce the price in yen the dealer is charged, or the dealer will have to reduce its dollar profit margin on each Honda it sells.)

To sum up, exchange rates are important to know about precisely because changes in them directly affect prices and thus the revenues earned from international trade. Political decisions or actions taken by governments and their central banks either unilaterally or coordinated multilaterally with their counterparts in other countries thus can affect exchange rates, export-import prices, and the terms of trade:

- If a country's currency depreciates, or falls, in relation to other world currencies, the prices of the products its firms export become cheaper (and thus more competitive) in foreign markets. At the same time, foreign goods its firms and individuals import become more expensive in domestic markets.
- On the other hand, if a country's currency appreciates (or becomes more valuable in relation to other currencies), its firms and people may buy and import more from abroad at lesser prices, but the prices of its exports rise and thus become less competitive in foreign markets.

The Politics of Managing Exchange Rates

Because government and central bank actions can have such effects on the livelihoods or welfare of exporters, importers, and those who produce or own the

CASE & POINT | The Big Mac Index

CASE Did you know that a "Big Mac" that costs you $4.07 in the United States only costs you $2.27 in China? In Europe you'd have to pay slightly more for the same hamburger—$4.93! Although there are some differences in profit margins and cost of production and delivery to the counter of your "Big Mac," these are relatively minor compared to the impact of currency values.

Chinese authorities keep the yuan (or RMB, the *renminbi*—the people's currency, as it is often called) undervalued in relation to both the dollar and the euro. As a result, Chinese goods are priced lower in these foreign currencies than they otherwise would be—a decided trade advantage for China. Put another way, the dollar and the euro are both overvalued in relation to the yuan and thus, as with most Chinese goods and services, can be bought more cheaply from China than if produced domestically. Should we be surprised that the U.S. imports more from China than it exports there? Price matters!

The exodus of U.S. production (and thus jobs) to China and other countries is due not just to less-expensive labor costs abroad, but also because an overvalued dollar goes much further in places like China. Dollar investments buy more plant and production capacity than the same outlays would in the United States. It's much cheaper for large segments of corporate America to produce abroad and import these products for sale in the United States, particularly since the dollar is overvalued. A single dollar buys more in a country like China than if currency values were set in a market free of intervention by government or central banking authorities. Or so theory holds—the market, left to its own devices, would result in an upward revaluation

of the yuan—a devaluation of both the dollar and the euro in relation to the Chinese currency, thus achieving purchasing power parity. A Big Mac would cost the traveler roughly the same whether in Beijing, New York, or Paris!

This "Big Mac" index has an interesting history. In 1983 the *Economist*, a weekly news magazine, well regarded particularly in the professional world, developed the index as a play on one of the McDonald's hamburger offerings—an indicator of what exchange rates should be (and might well become). The index is still calculated and published in the magazine from time to time and is available at the *Economist* website.

Absent substantial differences in production, marketing, or other costs, in principle the price of the Big Mac should be about the same everywhere, but that is usually not the case. In some countries, it is decidedly higher or lower than in others. Critics have advocated that the *Economist* move away from its Big Mac index to a more diverse, market-basket calculation using a number of products. As a practical matter, of course, the magazine never restricted itself to reporting only this one index, but found its iconic Big Mac indicator as telling much the same story as formal indices less familiar to many of its readers outside of the fields of economics and monetary finance.

POINT One can find purchasing power parity and similar statistics compiled in IMF, World Bank, UN Development Programme, and other publications, but they usually do not communicate to noneconomists with the same degree of clarity as the "Big Mac" index. As any consumer knows, purchasing power matters. ▲

goods and services traded, changes in prices or currency values are not just economic, but also highly political decisions.

Indeed, all of this technical discussion—how exchange rates work, how they affect import and export prices, and thus how they can alter competitive positions of traders—becomes very political when governments (or their central banks) choose to intervene in global currency markets to maintain, increase, or decrease a currency's exchange value. For example, in the mid-1980s U.S. monetary authorities (in the U.S. Treasury and Federal Reserve Board, the central banking authority that oversees the U.S. banking system) perceived that, just as in the 1960s and early 1970s, the dollar had become too overvalued in relation to other major currencies. Put simply, an overvalued dollar meant that U.S. firms and individuals could import foreign products too cheaply while U.S. exports were too pricey or expensive to foreigners.

The same decision to allow the dollar to depreciate in value relative to other currencies in global markets occurred more recently in the Great Recession that began in 2008. Market forces—supply and demand for a given currency like the dollar—ultimately drive its price (i.e., its exchange rate *vis-à-vis* other currencies). Any such decision to depreciate and thus reduce the foreign buying power of the dollar, making foreign goods pricier to Americans, also makes U.S. products cheaper to foreigners. This sounds at first like a charitable gesture or good deal to foreigners by U.S. monetary authorities. On closer examination, however, it was a case of "charity begins at home."

Jobs, then and now, are always at stake. So are profits or returns on investment. An overvalued dollar means U.S. consumers tend to pass up buying U.S.-made products in favor of foreign-made goods of comparable quality, but priced at a discount only because of an overvaluation in dollar–foreign currency exchange rates. As a result, when the dollar is overvalued relative to foreign currencies overall, U.S. purchases from other countries tend to be far greater than American sales abroad—a national trade imbalance deeply in red ink. Even more important from a domestic political perspective, however, imports of foreign products stimulate production (and employment) in other countries, but tend to dampen or reduce domestic production with consequent losses of jobs. Labor unions thus argue that overvaluation costs American jobs lost to producers in other countries. Some put it this way: Overvaluation of the dollar tends to shift production to other countries, with job creation abroad to replace jobs cut at home, in effect "exporting" jobs.

U.S. monetary authorities on these occasions might try to depreciate the dollar unilaterally—by themselves—but instead usually work the issue multilaterally, negotiating with their treasury and central bank monetary-authority counterparts in other countries to collaborate in depreciating the dollar. This means refusing to defend the existing exchange rates between the dollar and other currencies, instead letting the dollar slide or helping it down the depreciation road to a new, lower level at which valuation or purchasing power of the dollar and other countries is at least closer or somewhat more comparable.

Treasury officials and central bankers may agree to do this by not buying up surplus dollars in global markets, thus reducing demand for them. Alternatively, when they want to see the dollar appreciate, they may choose to do the opposite—buy dollars and thus increase demand for them. In either case, these officials in conjunction with their counterparts abroad are making essentially political decisions about economic matters—an exercise of global governance, discussed in greater detail in the next section.

The bottom line: Consistent with trade theory, the effort to adjust exchange rates in this way is designed to achieve greater purchasing-power parity between the dollar and other currencies because this shifts competition from artificial, exchange-rate considerations to such factors as efficiency, cost of production, and quality.

Trade theory assumes the neutrality of money, but exchange rates can get out of whack and adversely affect trade that otherwise would be based on comparative advantage with lower-cost, more efficient producers specializing in production of certain products. In the real world, some currencies are overvalued (overpriced in terms of their exchange rates with other currencies), and others are undervalued (underpriced in terms of their exchange rates with other currencies).

To be neutral, money should be in parity or roughly the same in purchasing power to buy goods and services in one country as in another. A practical, but amusing way to measure purchasing-power parity is to compare how much it costs to buy the same hamburger, fries, and cola in one country as in another. If money is really neutral and production and marketing costs are roughly the same, the hamburger, fries, and cola should cost or be priced about the same regardless of which currency one uses. This is what is meant by purchasing-power parity—the equivalent values of all currencies, in principle, should buy about the same number or amount of the same goods or services—assuming, of course, comparable production, marketing, and retail costs for these items.

international monetary regime ■ financial rules, regulations, and institutions agreed on by states to facilitate international trade and other forms of commerce

international liquidity ■ in monetary affairs, the ease with which foreign currencies are available to countries so they can settle their accounts with other countries

GLOBAL GOVERNANCE TASKS: SUSTAINING TRADE AND MONETARY REGIMES

11.5 Outline how monetary authorities in institutions like the International Monetary Fund (IMF), treasuries and central banks, and the Bank for International Settlements (BIS) relate to each other in global-governance arrangements aimed at maintaining global trade and monetary regimes.

In day-to-day international commerce, government agencies, business firms, other groups, and individuals use domestic currency to buy foreign currencies to finance the purchase of goods and services imported from abroad, to loan or invest money in foreign countries, or to have money to spend there. Similarly, foreign government agencies, foreign business firms, other groups, and individuals living abroad use their currencies to buy currencies in other countries needed to conduct the same kinds of transactions. Currencies, usually in the form of deposits in banks and other financial institutions, thus readily move back and forth electronically across national boundaries.

Maintaining International Liquidity

Rules governing the exchange of currencies and conditions for loans have evolved over time, as have the international organizations tasked by member countries with implementing or enforcing them. The sets of rules and institutions associated with them constitute what we can refer to as an international monetary regime, which has as its purpose providing financial arrangements so essential to maintaining and expanding trade and other forms of international commerce. Maintaining international liquidity is the principal global-governance function associated with this international monetary regime.

Liquidity is a financial term referring to having cash available or an ability to raise such funds readily by selling assets. Maintaining international liquidity, the most important IMF task, means providing member countries in need with access to financial assets that can be exchanged for currencies necessary to meet their payments obligations. Financial assets held as reserves by national monetary authorities include gold, special drawing rights (SDRs), and "hard" currencies.

✴ Explore the "International Trade: You Are a Trade Expert" at mypoliscilab.com

Hard currencies are those major currencies (e.g., the U.S. dollar, British sterling or pound, Japanese yen, and the European Union's euro) readily accepted and used by countries for making their payments transactions. What made them "hard" in earlier times was their convertibility to gold (or dollars, which in turn were readily convertible to gold) by national treasuries or at their central banks. By contrast, "soft" currencies lacked this convertibility and thus were less accepted globally.

Nowadays we refer to hard currencies simply as those readily accepted and exchangeable for one another and thus easily used to buy any country's currency whenever needed. In an effort to improve their acceptability, monetary authorities of countries with soft currencies sometimes peg or link these currencies to the dollar or one or another of the hard currencies, allowing their soft currencies to rise and fall in value in the same way as the leading hard currencies do. As a result, their otherwise soft currencies are more readily accepted in commercial transactions.

reserves ■ cash or assets easily converted into cash held out of use by a bank, company, or state to meet expected or unexpected demands

special drawing rights (SDRs) ■ lines of credit that IMF member countries add to their monetary reserves used to settle international payments obligations

Fixed Exchange-Rate Regimes

In earlier centuries, currencies were often defined as being equivalent in value to a fixed weight of some precious metal, such as silver or gold. In the late 19th and early 20th centuries, for example, a U.S. dollar could be exchanged for 1/20th of an ounce of gold. Put another way, it took $20 to buy an ounce of gold from the U.S. Treasury. Stated formally, the dollar's gold parity (a technical term) was $20 an ounce. At the same time the value of the British currency (the pound sterling) was also defined as a fixed weight of gold. Countries willing to exchange their currencies for gold on demand at these fixed rates were said to be on a gold standard.

In fact, relatively little gold was actually exchanged because countries found it more convenient instead to exchange each other's currencies as needed to finance trade and other forms of international commerce. The exchange rate between the U.S. dollar and British pound was easy to calculate because both were defined in terms of specified weights of gold. Thus, at the time, it took about $4.87 (more precisely $4.867) to buy one British pound note. At the core of the international monetary regime at the time was what amounted to a gold-exchange standard.

In the late 1800s and early 1900s the United Kingdom enjoyed financial prominence in Europe and throughout the world. Given its standing and its global access to capital, the Bank of England as a central bank managed not only the British currency—the pound sterling, which was readily convertible into a fixed quantity of gold—but also effectively the worldwide international monetary regime. Other countries often held deposits of the pound sterling as reserves, which could be used to finance their trade and other purchases abroad. Holding sterling deposits as reserves was actually preferable to holding gold because these sterling deposits could even earn interest. Because of its pivotal role in the international monetary regime of the time, sterling came to be regarded in effect as a key currency.

This is how the Bank of England managed the international monetary regime at the time. Because foreigners understood and respected the financial soundness of the Bank of England and the economy it represented, whenever the Bank of England wanted to attract foreign currencies to enhance its own reserves in order to make payments to other countries, it could do so simply by raising its interest rate—referred to technically as its discount rate.

As a central bank, changes in the rate it charged to other British banks would have an impact on their own interest rates as well. By raising its discount rate, the Bank of England in effect encouraged the sale of sterling to holders of foreign currencies seeking greater earnings due to higher interest rates to be found in British financial markets. Put another way, holders of foreign currencies would readily use these holdings to buy sterling for deposit in British banks, thus taking advantage of higher British interest rates. In turn, many of these foreign currencies would wind up in the Bank of England's reserves as British banks exchanged them there for sterling.

During World War I (1914–1918), budgetary requirements to finance the war effort forced Britain (and other countries) to abandon the gold-exchangeability of their currencies. Wartime controls on currency expenditures were eventually removed when the war ended as the United Kingdom tried to reassume its prewar role as manager of a restored international monetary regime. Although the United Kingdom still retained its worldwide empire, Britain's capital base had been significantly eroded by heavy borrowing necessitated by massive wartime expenditures. The United States, although it possessed the capital base to assume the international monetary-management role, was unwilling to do so. Given its financially weakened position, Britain had great difficulty performing the monetary-management role in the 1920s and finally was forced to abandon the effort in 1931 with the onset of a worldwide economic depression.[4]

exchange controls
■ government restrictions on the amount of domestic currency that can be exchanged for other currencies

During the 1930s, countries often resorted to currency exchange controls to limit the amount of money spent abroad, thus avoiding payment obligations. At the same time, imports were restrained by high tariffs, quotas, and other barriers to trade. It was a period described as "beggar thy neighbor" as countries turned inward to protect themselves no matter what the negative externalities—the expense might be to others. Countries also devalued their currencies in an effort to make imports more expensive to firms and individuals at home while, at the same time, promoting their exports by making them cheaper to foreigners.

competitive devaluations ■ since devaluations reduce the export price of goods and services to purchases in foreign currencies, some countries may devalue their currencies merely to gain an unfair competitive advantage, a tactic often matched by devaluations in other countries

The United States did this by raising the price of gold from $20 to $35 an ounce. Raising the official price of gold amounted to a devaluation of the dollar. The process was a bit complicated, but here is how it worked. The exchange value of the dollar depended upon its gold value. Following the increase in gold price, Americans now had to pay $35 for the same amount of foreign goods and services that they previously bought with the dollar equivalent of an ounce of gold when it was priced at $20—in effect, a 75 percent increase in the price of imports. At the same time, foreign purchasers got a good deal designed to promote exports because the foreign currency equivalent to an ounce of gold now bought $35 worth of American goods and services instead of just $20 worth. Of course, more than one country could play this game, and many did. As a result, round after round of competitive devaluations characterized the 1930s, as each country tried to establish a trade advantage over others—maximizing exports and minimizing imports. It was a "zero-sum" political game that countries played, seeking gains at the expense of others.

The net effect of such policies was a drastic reduction in international trade and foreign investment as the worldwide economy continued to stagnate. These economic

---

[4]For an excellent, highly readable discussion of this period, see Charles P. Kindleberger, *The World in Depression, 1929–1939* (Berkeley: University of California Press, 1973).

events were followed in a few years by the onset of another world war in 1939, which many observers at the time and since have understood at least partly as a consequence of the self-serving, nationalistic or neomercantilist political-economic policies pursued throughout the 1930s—trying to maximize positive trade balances—increasing domestic production through export sales while minimizing import purchases, thus dampening production in other countries. It didn't work as other countries retaliated, which set in motion a devastating, downward spiral in the volume of international trade that hurt producers and cost jobs in all countries.

Lessons drawn from this experience led during World War II to political plans for establishing a new international monetary regime that would make possible a reopening of international trade and investment across national borders. Instead of zero-sum thinking, achieving positive gains through expanded trade and commerce took center stage. In game-theoretic terms, there was a visible shift from the zero-sum political game of the Depression years to a positive-sum political game to guide country players in the postwar period. All could gain in principle from international monetary collaboration.

One outcome of this thinking was establishment of the IMF (and also a separate institution to help finance postwar reconstruction and development, the World Bank) by international agreement at a conference held in 1944 at Bretton Woods, New Hampshire. British economist John Maynard Keynes and his American counterpart, Harry Dexter White, were the key proponents of alternative plans. In proposing to allow the new IMF political authority to create reserves (to which Keynes and his followers gave the nickname "bancor"), the Keynes plan was far more liberal than the White plan, which preferred to rely on gold and key currencies for reserves and opposed conferring any such reserve-creation authority on the new IMF. Given the political-economic prominence of the United States in these negotiations, the American view was more influential in determining the final outcome. Nevertheless, a version of Keynesian thinking was evident in the 1960s when member countries authorized the IMF to create SDRs, or special drawing rights that IMF members could count as monetary reserves along with gold, dollars, and other key currencies convertible into gold or dollars.

The task the IMF was given at Bretton Woods, which prevailed during the institution's first quarter-century, was to oversee and manage an international monetary regime of relatively fixed exchange rates. It did this by relying on key currencies like the U.S. dollar, which were readily exchangeable into gold or other currencies. As such, a new gold-exchange standard came into existence with the U.S. dollar at its center—in effect a dollar-gold-exchange standard with the dollar still priced at its 1934 level of $35 an ounce. As in the sterling-gold-exchange standard of the late 19th and early 20th centuries, relatively few actual gold exchanges occurred among national monetary authorities. Most countries held their reserves in the form of U.S. dollar deposits, understood to be at least as good as gold, or even better because these deposits also earned interest.

Floating Exchange Rates

The Bretton Woods fixed-exchange rate regime lasted until 1971 when the United States, confronted by long-standing balance-of-payments deficits and now a substantial deficit in its trade balance as well, decided to go off the gold-exchange standard and made the unilateral political choice to abandon fixed exchange rates. It allowed the value of its currency to float, or be set based on currency market supply and demand. American officials complained that over the years the dollar had become overvalued, which as a practical matter meant that U.S. exports were too expensive to foreigners and imports too cheap to Americans. As a result, the volume of U.S. exports could not keep up with the ever-increasing volume of American imports. By contrast, many other countries were seen as having undervalued currencies, giving them a decisive trade advantage—promoting their exports to (while discouraging imports from) the United States.

With its trade balance slipping into deficit, American officials chose to devalue the dollar by letting its value float, depreciating it in currency markets. Because the exchange values of many other currencies were tied to what had become a floating dollar, their values also fluctuated. A new international monetary regime of flexible exchange rates had come into existence. Fierce debates, however, occurred among monetary authorities as to just how flexible these rates should be.

Fixed exchange rates were credited with having contributed to the enormous growth in international commerce since the end of World War II. On the other hand, they were also blamed for leading to financial crises when currencies were viewed in currency markets as either overvalued or undervalued in relation to other currencies. A compromise position, managed flexibility, allows for some intervention in currency markets by monetary authorities to stabilize or otherwise influence exchange rates.

The new flexible exchange-rate regime established by the mid-1970s remains in effect today. It relies on market forces, but allows treasuries and central banks to intervene in global markets, particularly when they do so multilaterally in coordinated, cooperative actions. The politics of global governance in this regime capture the give-and-take among national and international authorities often disagreeing on what is to be done. When national monetary authorities do coalesce, they may decide to buy or sell each other's currencies to correct under- or overvaluations and maintain international liquidity so important to trade—assuring each country has the cash it needs to cover shortfalls in the balance of trade or overall payment obligations to other countries. In the absence of this liquidity and a political consensus on the need to provide it, countries unable to pay their bills might be forced to reduce or cut imports substantially, perhaps also imposing exchange controls to reduce or keep their country's money from being spent or invested abroad.

Faced with what they understood as destabilizing fluctuations in exchange rates in the 1970s and 1980s, members of what was then called the European Communities (EC)—the European Economic Community, Coal and Steel Community, and Atomic Energy Community—developed a monetary arrangement to stabilize rates among themselves even as their currencies floated collectively in relation to the dollar. As the EC became incorporated in the 1990s in a new European Union (EU), an outgrowth of earlier monetary collaboration was the establishment of an economic and monetary union. This included a common central bank located in Frankfurt managing the new currency, the euro, often viewed as the leading or potential competitor to the dollar as a global key currency. Rather than see this in zero-sum terms, others see the EU and the United States collaborating to make both the euro and the dollar as key currencies used worldwide to pay trade, investment, and other commercial obligations.

The United States and other countries adversely affected by China's persistent trade imbalance—its exports so much greater than imports—continue to pressure China to allow its national currency (the *renminbi* or "RMB" for short) to appreciate somewhat—an "upward revaluation" in relation to the dollar that increases the price of its exports and decreases import prices in China. Doing so makes exports of other countries more competitive. Although China has allowed for some appreciation, it depends on its favorable trade position to sustain domestic production and employment as well as generate capital for investment in its growing economy—a position China's critics call a form of neomercantilism—pursuing national gain without much regard for the costs or negative externalities imposed on other countries.

Financing Trade

The IMF has its headquarters in Washington, DC—separate from, but physically next to the headquarters of the World Bank. Although the World Bank specializes in making loans for investment in economic reconstruction and development, the focus of the IMF is on the finance of trade—assisting member countries to manage their payment obligations to each other. Another institution, the Bank for International Settlements (BIS) in Basel, Switzerland, is a bank for central bankers who engage in buying, selling, lending, and borrowing each other's currencies as needed to sustain international commerce.

Established in 1930, the BIS includes many of the same countries that belong to the IMF. Governments and their treasury officials are typically the principals in the IMF, whereas central bankers are the main players in the BIS. Over the years central bankers participating in the BIS have played an active, often pivotal role in actually making some of the financial arrangements agreed to by treasury and other government officials of IMF member countries.

If there is a shortfall in the supply of foreign currencies available, banks (and governments) can turn to their central banks—national institutions that service the banking needs of both member banks and government treasuries. Countries normally keep reserves of foreign currencies (and gold that can be used to buy these currencies), but sometimes these reserves become depleted, as when charges for imported goods and services and other payments far exceed earnings from exports and other sources. When that happens, member countries can draw on their accounts or borrow from the IMF, which is in a position to keep its members in cash—maintain international liquidity.

The IMF makes advances of hard currencies that can readily be exchanged for whatever currency may be needed to finance transactions. As the IMF itself likes to say, it operates in much the same way as a credit union by offering its member countries a variety of different kinds of loans and other mechanisms to meet their financial needs. If countries did not have such a source of short-term finance for balancing their payments, they probably would be forced to impose exchange controls, severely limiting the amount of domestic currency used to acquire foreign currencies, thus restricting purchases from abroad and disrupting international commerce.

Special Drawing Rights (SDRs)   Policymakers in the 1960s and 1970s addressed the availability of reserves to finance payments in international trade, concluding that reliance on growth in gold, dollars, and other hard currencies was not sufficient. Building on ideas set forth earlier by John Maynard Keynes and other economists, the IMF was authorized in 1969 by its member countries to create special drawing rights (SDRs), dubbed by journalists at the time as "paper gold." In fact, SDR allocations to each IMF member country amounted to a new line of credit that could be drawn on without challenge in a time of need. Because countries having SDRs in their IMF accounts can readily exchange them at any time for hard currencies such as the U.S. dollar, Japanese yen, and other convertible currencies, they are "as good as gold" and thus also can be included as part of a country's official reserves in the same way that gold and hard currencies are counted. So far, the IMF has been authorized to create and allocate SDRs worth a total of about $30 billion.

Advances by the IMF are just that—advances that must be repaid, usually with interest. The IMF has about $300 billion in deposits by its members, which it can use to provide hard currencies to members in need. The amount of each country's required deposit or "quota" is different, depending on the size of its economy and trade requirements. The quota size also determines the voting power a member has on the board of governors that provides policy guidance and direction to the executive board, the IMF managing director, and the IMF staff. In effect, this gives political primacy in the IMF to countries with the largest economies, notably the United States, EU countries (particularly Germany, France, and Britain), and Japan. With 18 percent of the vote, the United States has the largest number of votes. Given the requirement for an 85 percent voting majority on important matters, the European Union members voting as a block and the United States voting alone all enjoy the political advantage of an effective veto on major policy questions and other organizational decisions.

Each member of the IMF meets its contribution quota by putting on deposit 25 percent of the amount in convertible currencies, gold, or SDRs and the remaining 75 percent of the quota by deposit of the country's own currency. When in need, the first 25 percent can be drawn without question (which amounts to a line of credit), but drawings beyond that amount are usually subject to certain conditions.

These conditions are the politically difficult part. In time, these IMF-prescribed remedies are expected to lay a firm basis for producing a viable economy able to sustain growth and finance trade. In the short run, however, these measures often call for substantial government belt tightening—tighter fiscal policies (e.g., cutting expenditures and increasing taxes) and tighter monetary policies (e.g., raising interest rates and constraining growth in the domestic money supply). Unfortunately, such policies, designed to dampen economies, cut inflation, curb imports, and foster greater efficiency in use of factors of production—so-called **structural adjustments** in the fundamental elements of an economy—also impose enormous costs.

structural adjustments ■ when fiscal and monetary policies like cutting spending, increasing taxes, or raising interest rates are used to curb or dampen an economy deemed to be "overheated"

Critics refer to such policies as neoliberal—driven by market-oriented understandings that force national economies to adjust to external or global pressures in the world economy coming from the economically powerful states that use their leverage in the IMF, World Bank, WTO, and other institutions to force compliance with these standards. Businesses, for example, may not readily find capital to finance plans for expansion or may even close, and workers may lose jobs and have difficulty finding new employment. These economically difficult times brought on by such IMF-prescribed neoliberal austerity measures may well have politically explosive consequences for governments complying with IMF loan conditions. The IMF has also been the target of much criticism for insisting on these stringent requirements as conditions for advances to borrowing countries. Critics see these structural adjustment measures as retarding economic growth and development in less-developed countries with unfair, often dire consequences to the peoples affected by these neoliberal policies.

From the IMF perspective, exchange controls come at a great cost. If countries in economic difficulties impose exchange controls (as many did before the IMF became effective as a lending agency), the net effect will be reduction in imports and thus on the global volume of trade, adversely affecting economic growth as well. Moreover, other countries can no longer sell their products freely to countries limiting imports through exchange controls. When export sales go down, profits and jobs are lost. These are real costs borne by other countries, which economists refer to, as noted earlier, as negative externalities.

Resorting to exchange controls thus runs the political and economic risk that countries adversely affected by this policy may choose to retaliate economically by discriminating against the exports of countries adopting such measures. In short, those opposing resort to exchange controls as a way of managing a country's payments not only see such a policy as reducing the volume of trade, but also argue that it is an unfair way of shifting some of the costs of structural adjustments in one's own economy to the shoulders of others. Be that as it may, defenders of managing a country's payments through exchange controls see it as a more desirable, somewhat less intrusive remedy than either bearing the social and political consequences of fiscal and monetary austerity or, worse yet, directly blocking trade by imposing high tariffs or quotas against imports from other countries—an approach sure to invite retaliation in kind.

The Effects of National Macroeconomic Policies *Fiscal policies* deal with government budgetary matters (how much and how to tax and spend), whereas *monetary policies* address government measures that affect size and growth of the money supply and level of interest rates. Together fiscal and monetary policies are sometimes referred to as macroeconomic policies because they affect the national economy taken as a whole.

No matter how necessary imposing fiscal and monetary restraints may seem to finance experts, compliance with loan conditions can be extraordinarily difficult. Certainly this was the case for Indonesia, Thailand, South Korea, and other countries caught in the Asian financial crisis during the late 1990s. For its part, however, Malaysia found its own way out of IMF-imposed austerity by breaking IMF rules and imposing exchange controls—limiting the amount of *ringgit*, the Malaysian currency, that could leave the country. By adopting this monetary policy, Malaysia managed its payment obligations through government actions to limit the amount that could be spent abroad for imports or other purposes. Malaysia is not alone, of course, among countries that over the decades have resisted imposition of stringent IMF requirements seen as too costly.

Imposing exchange controls is a monetary policy for managing a country's payment obligations to other countries. These controls usually take the form of domestic banking regulations in Country X that limit purchase of foreign currencies used to finance imports, other purchases, or investments abroad. People leaving a country also are limited in the amounts of the country's currency they physically can take with them lest these funds be spent abroad. With less money spent abroad, there are fewer payment obligations to meet when the central banks or treasuries of other countries seek hard currencies or other reserves in exchange for amounts of currency from Country X they have acquired.

As discussed earlier, trade of goods and services in trade theory is based on differences in cost of production and market value of products themselves, not on the value of money used to purchase them. Thus it was convenient for classical economic theorists to assume the neutrality of money—that money has no independent impact on the costs of production or market value of goods and services. As established above, however, money is anything but neutral in the real world. Changes in exchange value have a direct influence on the prices of exports and imports and thus on the demand for and supply of them. Accordingly, governments and their national monetary policies do influence both domestic and international trade.

Table 11.2 summarizes domestic and international implications—expected macroeconomic effects—of different monetary policy choices made by government authorities and implemented by treasuries and their central banks. These are economic matters, of course, but they are essentially political decisions made by authorities in a position to make them. All parts of a national economy—owners of capital interests, owners of land and resources, workers and other citizens—typically have high stakes in the implications of these choices for the economy as a whole, as do their counterparts in other countries abroad who either benefit from or suffer losses due respectively to these positive or negative externalities.

TABLE 11.2

Domestic Effects and Externalities of National Monetary Policy

Following is a list of domestic and external effects of political choices to change a country's monetary policy—specified here in terms of both interest rates (the cost of borrowing money) and the money supply (the amount of money in circulation). This table indicates how money, interest rates, and exchange rates are by no means neutral in relation to either their domestic or external effects.

INTEREST RATES UP
(tightening monetary policy; growth in money supply decreased)

Domestic Effects (*ceteris paribus*):

- Dampens domestic economy; slows growth by raising the cost of capital (e.g., borrowing capital for investment in productive enterprises is more expensive at higher interest rates)
- A curb on inflation (slower growth/less demand tends to keep prices stable or at least slow price increases; less money in circulation means there is less to spend)

(continued)

TABLE 11.2 | *Continued*

- Increases fiscal cost of servicing national debt (government pays more interest given higher rates)
- Encourages short-term net capital inflow (as when capital flows in to take advantage of relatively higher interest rates domestically)
- Tends to increase exchange value of domestic currency (increasing capital inflows to take advantage of relatively higher interest rates tends to increase demand for country's currency)
- Stimulates imports; discourages exports (i.e., higher exchange value means imports tend to be cheaper domestically, exports more expensive to foreigners)
- Discourages long-term investment in domestic economy by foreigners (i.e., cost of domestic assets more expensive when purchased with foreign currencies)

External Effects (*ceteris paribus*):

- Stimulates foreign production by promoting imports (see previous examples)
- May export inflation by dampening domestic economy while stimulating foreign production for export
- More difficult for developing world countries and other debtors to pay their obligations

INTEREST RATES DOWN
(loosening monetary policy; growth in money supply increased)

Domestic Effects (*ceteris paribus*):

- Stimulates domestic economy; encourages growth by lowering the cost of capital (e.g., borrowing capital for investment in productive enterprises is cheaper at lower interest rates)
- Could spur inflation (faster growth/greater demand tends to put upward pressure on prices; more money in circulation means there is more to spend)
- Decreases fiscal cost of servicing national debt (government pays less interest given lower rates)
- Encourages short-term net capital outflow (as when capital flows out to take advantage of relatively higher interest rates abroad)
- Tends to decrease exchange value of domestic currency (increasing capital outflows to take advantage of relatively higher interest rates abroad tends to decrease demand for country's currency)
- Stimulates exports; discourages imports (i.e., lower exchange value means exports tend to be cheaper to foreigners, imports more expensive domestically)
- Encourages long-term investment in domestic economy by foreigners (i.e., cost of domestic assets cheaper when purchased with foreign currencies)

External Effects (*ceteris paribus*):

- Dampens foreign production by promoting exports (see previous examples)
- Tends to dampen inflation pressures abroad by stimulating domestic production and curbing imports
- Easier for developing world countries and other debtors to pay their obligations

Political Choices in Global Governance   Before taking up the question of how much capital the IMF or other institutions need to maintain international liquidity, we need to take a closer look at how countries cover their bills—the payments they owe to other countries for trade deficits, investments abroad greater than inflows of capital for these purposes, and other net capital outflows. The balance of payments is composed of four accounts detailed in Table 11.3 and briefly discussed below:

1. The balance of trade or current account (b) refers to exports (X) minus imports (M) of goods (merchandise trade) and services across national borders during a specified period of time (typically a month, quarter [three months], or year). Thus, if Japan has exported more than it has imported in a given year, it is said to have run a surplus or positive balance of trade. By contrast, if the United States imports more than it exports over the same period of time, it is said to have a *deficit* or negative trade balance:

$$\underset{\text{of Trade}}{\text{Balance}} \quad \underset{}{\text{Exports}} \quad \underset{}{\text{Imports}}$$
$$b \quad = \quad X \quad - \quad M$$

TABLE 11.3

Balance of Payments

These four accounts collectively define what we mean by "balance of payments":
(1) **Current Account** (international trade—exports and imports of goods and services);
(2) **Capital Account** (investment and other capital flows in and out of a country);
(3) **Unilateral Transfers** (inflows and outflows of gifts and grants); and (4) **Official Reserves** (inflows and outflows of currencies, gold, and other reserve assets). Transfers into and out of the fourth account bring the total of all four accounts to zero—reserve assets *sent to* other countries to pay for *deficits* in the other three accounts and *received from* other countries to compensate for *surpluses* in these accounts. Some countries like to accrue reserve assets by continually running surpluses—so-called neomercantilist policies, particularly in the trade and capital accounts—chronic surpluses that work to the disadvantage of trade and investment partners. Other (particularly capital-poor) countries have the opposite problem. Chronic deficits run down their reserve assets, sometimes leading to financial crises that require loans from the IMF or other sources of capital needed to "pay the bills."

I. Current Account (Goods and Services)
  A. Examples of Credits/Positive Entries (+):
    1. Merchandise exports (goods)
    2. Transportation abroad provided by domestic carriers (airplanes, ships, and the like) and paid for by foreigners
    3. Expenditures by tourists from foreign countries
    4. Financial services and insurance provided by domestic banks and other firms to (and paid for by) foreigners
    5. Interest, dividends, and other financial payments received by domestic residents from abroad

(continued)

TABLE 11.3 | *Continued*

6. Spending by foreign governments (e.g., the costs of running their embassies and other missions, making official visits, stationing troops [if any], and various other activities)

B. Examples of Debits/Negative Entries (2):
1. Merchandise imports (goods)
2. Transportation abroad provided by foreign carriers and paid for by residents
3. Expenditures by residents as tourists in other countries
4. Financial services and insurance provided by foreign banks and other firms to (and paid for by) domestic residents
5. Interest, dividends, and other financial payments made to foreigners
6. Spending by the government in foreign countries (e.g., the costs of running their embassies and other missions, making official visits, stationing troops [if any], and various other activities)

II. Capital Account
A. Examples of Credits/Positive Entries (+):
1. Increase in foreign-owned deposits or accounts in domestic banks, brokerage firms, or other financial institutions
2. Decrease in domestically owned deposits or accounts in foreign banks, brokerage firms, or other financial institutions
3. Purchase of domestic stocks, bonds, or other securities by foreigners
B. Examples of Debits/Negative Entries (2):
1. Decrease in foreign-owned deposits or accounts in domestic banks, brokerage firms, or other financial institutions
2. Increase in domestically owned deposits or accounts in foreign banks, brokerage firms, or other financial institutions
3. Purchase of foreign stocks, bonds, or other securities by domestic residents

III. Unilateral Transfers (Gifts or Grants)
A. Examples of Credits/Positive Entries (1):
1. Grants, contributions, or pensions received from nongovernmental foreign sources
2. Grants or other payments (including pensions) received from foreign governments
B. Examples of Debits/Negative Entries (2):
1. Grants or contributions made to foreigners or residents in foreign countries (e.g., pensions)
2. Grants or other payments made to foreign governments

IV. Official Reserves (Gold, Foreign Currencies, SDRS)
A. Credits/Positive Entries (+):
1. Export of reserves, thus reducing payment amounts due to foreign countries as a result of net deficits in the other three accounts (current account, capital account, and unilateral transfers)
B. Debits/Negative Entries (−):
1. Import of reserves, thus reducing payment amounts due by foreign countries as a result of net deficits in the other three accounts

Bottom Line: As an accounting tool, the "balance" of payments equals zero when overall surpluses or deficits in the first three accounts are compensated by transfers (gains or losses) of official reserves in the fourth account.

2. The trade balance or current account is only one of several accounts in a country's overall balance of payments. Net investment, the capital account, is another. This is the difference between capital investment by domestic investors in foreign countries and capital investment by foreign investors in the country's domestic economy.

3. Unilateral transfers represent a third account—grants or other transfers received by a country's government (e.g., foreign aid) or residents (e.g., social security or other pensions received) from foreign governments minus grants or other transfers sent by the country's government to other governments or to residents living in other countries.

4. Finally there is the official reserves account (referred to historically as the gold account) composed of assets used to balance payments with other countries; these are generally gold, foreign currencies, and special drawing rights (SDRs) from the International Monetary Fund (IMF) that can be counted as official reserves. If after adding up the balances in the other accounts there is a net deficit, the balance can be made up by sending official reserves to other countries. On the other hand, if the sum of a country's other accounts shows a surplus, other countries may be called upon to transfer a portion of their reserves to add to the official reserves of the surplus country:

$$
\begin{array}{ccccc}
\text{I} & \text{II} & \text{III} & \text{IV} \\
\end{array}
$$

$$
\underset{\text{of Payments}}{\text{Balance}} (B) = \underset{\text{Account}}{\text{Current}} + \underset{\text{Account}}{\text{Capital}} + \underset{\text{Transfers}}{\text{Unilateral}} + \underset{\text{Reserves}}{\text{Official}} = 0
$$

Decisions on how much capital the IMF should have and for what purposes are essentially political choices made by member countries represented in the IMF's board of governors and its executive board. Indeed, as we have discussed, the IMF's central function is to have the necessary funds available to lend to countries in balance-of-payments difficulties, thus precluding their resort either to erecting tariffs, quotas, and other barriers to trade or to imposing exchange controls. The IMF also facilitates dismantling exchange controls already in existence when countries are making the adjustments necessary to open their domestic economies and participate more fully in global trade and other forms of commerce.

To do all this—as a practical matter, to be able to perform its core task of maintaining international liquidity as well as make funds available for other purposes specified by international agreement of its member countries—the IMF requires enormous capital resources. Because 75 percent of the quota contributions made by member countries is in their own currencies, the amount of "hard currency" available for lending is considerably less than half of some $300 billion the IMF has on deposit from quota subscriptions.

IMF lending resources were initially expanded in the 1960s when a new mechanism, the General Arrangements to Borrow (GAB), was constructed to supplement drawings on quotas. Eleven capital-rich countries originally put up GAB funds, which now total about $25 billion, that can be lent to IMF members needing balance-of-payments assistance. Following the same model, twenty-five member

countries decided to contribute hard currencies to another facility, the New Arrangements to Borrow (NAB), which was established in 1997, doubling total resources available under these arrangements to a combined total of some $50 billion.

The IMF also has a gold stock of more than 100 million fine ounces (its
market value fluctuates from day to day, but at, say, $300 an ounce, this is
worth more than $300 billion), which the IMF board of governors can autho-
rize be sold to acquire hard currencies. The political decision to create special
drawing rights or SDRs—so-called "paper gold"—and allocate them to member
countries also expanded capital resources that now amount to close to an additional $30 billion.

As a lending institution, the IMF charges interest on drawings or borrowing
of its funds. Member countries actually earn interest on their quota contributions
when their currencies are borrowed by other countries. The interest rates charged
to borrowing countries, however, are truly concessionary—well below rates countries would be charged if they borrowed in financial markets. Over the years, the
specific purposes for which the IMF may lend funds have expanded substantially,
particularly for low-income, less-developed countries.

For example, since the 1980s some eighty low-income, less-developed countries have been eligible to receive special treatment by borrowing funds for ten-
year terms from what is now known as the Poverty Reduction and Growth Facility
at below-market or concessionary interest rates (just one-half of 1 percent). The
condition for such loans is that borrowing countries use the money for structural
adjustment tasks—implementing a three-year program designed to provide a foundation for sustained economic growth, thus enabling them to meet their payment
obligations. A total of close to $13 billion in loans has been disbursed to more
than fifty needy countries by this facility, with new lending projected at more than
a billion dollars a year. The source of these funds is capital-rich and other more
economically developed countries.

The IMF may extend contingency lines of credit to countries not presently in
balance-of-payments difficulties but that are concerned that the effects of financial
turmoil in other countries might spread to them. The IMF also has special lending
authority for countries recovering from war and other civil conflicts, as well as
emergency assistance or compensatory financing when earthquakes, hurricanes,
floods, droughts, frosts, insect and other pest infestations, or other natural disasters adversely affect exports or disrupt normal trade and payments transactions.
The IMF not only lends money in such circumstances but also renders technical
assistance toward establishing or reestablishing the financial infrastructure that
may have been destroyed or weakened by political or economic turmoil brought
on by natural disasters or armed conflict.

Understanding itself as an agent for global trade and commerce, the IMF sees
this role as encompassing technical tasks as well as fostering market-oriented values in member or would-be member countries willing to avail themselves of such
assistance. Accordingly, the IMF contributes to developing effective central banking and treasury institutions, collecting and refining statistical data on economic
activities, and training officials who can perform technical monetary tasks. Perhaps
even more significant, as an agent of socialization the IMF joins other international organizations and governments in efforts to integrate these officials within

an expanding, worldwide culture of values shared by professionals or technical experts dealing with monetary matters so essential to sustaining and increasing global trade and other forms of commerce. These technical experts can be understood as constituting a transnational professional community conversant with each other across state boundaries, whether in direct meetings or by telecommunications.

GLOBAL TRADE

11.6 Evaluate progress made globally and regionally on liberalizing trade and achieving integration goals in Europe, North America, and other parts of the world.

👁 Watch the **Video "The New European Union"** at **mypoliscilab.com**

Just as an international monetary regime sets forth rules for the exchange of currencies and the finance of international commerce, an international trade regime also has rules relating to how exports and imports are bought and sold, transported, paid for, and delivered. Many of these rules have standing as customary international law and are enforceable in suits brought in national courts.

The topic of rules for international commerce is not a new one. Hugo Grotius (1583–1645) addressed the topic, and both customary international law and the Law of the Sea Treaty identify territorial waters, define rights of passage for commercial vessels, and underscore the primacy of freedom of navigation on the high seas. Similar rules with the force of international law apply to trade across land and by air.

Political opposition, particularly in the United States by those who saw such an institution as potentially threatening to private-sector business interests, blocked efforts after World War II to establish an International Trade Organization (ITO) as a companion institution to the International Monetary Fund and World Bank. Instead, negotiating arrangements known as the General Agreement on Tariffs and Trade (GATT) produced periodic international conferences (or rounds, as they were called) that worked toward reduction of tariffs, quotas, and other barriers to trade, especially those erected in the 1930s when protectionist sentiments had reigned supreme.

Even in the absence of an international organization or specialized agency for trade, participating countries (including the United States) made great progress in liberalizing global trade—opening markets between and across national borders. Most of the existing trade agreements are the result of the 1986–1994 Uruguay Round negotiations, signed at the Marrakesh, Morocco, ministerial meeting in April 1994. There are about sixty agreements and decisions, totaling 550 pages.

The Marrakesh meeting is where the World Trade Organization (WTO) was established as a single institutional framework designed to encompass the GATT, as modified by the Uruguay Round, and all agreements and arrangements concluded under its auspices. The WTO's essential mission is to ensure that trade flows as smoothly, predictably, and freely as possible. In addition to agreements reached on trading rules, WTO global-governance tasks include "administering trade agreements, acting as a forum for trade negotiations, settling trade disputes, reviewing national trade policies, assisting developing countries in trade policy issues through technical assistance and training programs, and cooperating with other international organizations."

The WTO structure is headed by a Ministerial Conference meeting held at least once every two years. A General Council at the WTO's headquarters in Geneva oversees the operation of the agreement and ministerial decisions. Its key function is to act as a Dispute Settlement Body and a Trade Policy Review Mechanism dealing with the full range of trade issues covered by the WTO. Hence, member countries may bring complaints against other members to the WTO's dispute-settlement process. The framework requires a "single undertaking approach" to the results of the Uruguay Round. Therefore, membership in the WTO entails accepting all the results of the Round without exception by some 150 member countries.

Nevertheless, open-trade (if not entirely free-trade) advocates still saw much work to be done. In addition to further reductions in trade barriers, curbing bribery or other illicit practices and assuring global respect for intellectual property rights (patents and copyrights) are issues high on the agenda of both private interests and those wishing to promote growth in international commerce. Moreover, advocates want to head off fears of trade wars or any thought of return to the mutually exclusive, regional trading blocs that had prevailed in the 1930s. Bringing many newly market-oriented countries into the global trading regime was another important motivation in the 1990s for moving beyond GATT to forming a new World Trade Organization (WTO).

Major disputes do surround the WTO, as evidenced by demonstrators at WTO ministerial meetings. WTO opponents are highly critical of trading policies that in their view do not afford sufficient weight to protecting the environment. Labor interests challenge WTO policies that open trade at the expense of workers who lose their jobs in what they argue is unfair global competition brought on by corporate exploitation of foreign workers who are paid very low wages and often suffer poor working conditions in labor-intensive industries abroad. Environmental activists and labor rights advocates thus find common cause in these anti-WTO demonstrations.

These challenges from outside the WTO are matched by conflicts within. Not only are unfair trade practice complaints frequently made by member countries against each other, but members also differ philosophically on practical goals. By no means does global governance suggest unanimity of thought, much less full agreement on what is to be done. Some members, like the United States, argue for open markets as free as possible of government intervention or protectionism. Other members argue not so much for free trade but rather for managed trade that avoids some of the environmental, labor, and other pitfalls encountered in a free-trade environment. From this perspective, the WTO can serve as a forum for discussing and negotiating managed-trade arrangements in which governments intervene in markets to reduce costs to interested parties.

Despite the GATT's and WTO's tremendous success in reducing trade barriers over the years and the resulting increase in overall global prosperity, the collapse of the Cancun, Mexico, conference in September 2003 was a wakeup call highlighting obstacles that lay ahead. The chief goal of the conference was to lower trade barriers in areas where freer trade would help poor countries the most, particularly in agriculture. Suffice it to say there was enough blame to be shared by rich countries, poor countries, and nongovernmental organizations for this serious failure to maintain momentum in the continuing liberalization of international trade.

Regional Economic Integration and Global Commerce

Economic efforts to increase the level of global prosperity have been taken at the regional as well as international level.[5] The post–World War II European experience has been a test-bed for ideas, concepts, and theories as to how to increase regional integration. What has occurred in Europe since the end of World War II in 1945 is one of the more amazing international developments. Here we have a continent twice devastated by world wars, fueled by the nationalist fires and ambitions of century-long rivalries, and divided by the Cold War, but now an economic giant. For realists, the success of the Western European economic enterprise was essentially due to the security protection provided by the United States. There is much truth to that, but liberals are quick to point out that realists expected economic integration and cooperation to slow down or collapse once the unifying threat of the Soviet Union and its allies had passed. Such a crisis of authority for the European Union did not occur until the sovereign debt crisis of 2011. Why not?

The underlying assumption of much of the work on European integration has been quite simple: Enhanced economic ties and exchanges not only will have positive benefits in terms of economic prosperity but will have political benefits as well. A critical objective of regional integration, therefore, is the prospect of enhancing peace among states. In the first decade or so after World War II, Jean Monnet and Robert Schuman from France and German Chancellor Konrad Adenauer were among the important advocates of a new Europe. These elites had made no secret of their objectives and plans for constructing a new Europe. Reacting to the devastation wrought by two world wars, they were trying to put in place an alternative set of positive, constructive relations among former enemies. By fostering economic integration efforts, they were trying at a very practical level to establish new, cooperative links between France and the Federal Republic of Germany, core players in the continental European economy. Theirs was an incremental, step-by-step strategy for attaining economic integration goals over time. A principal motivation was their expectation of a positive impact on political relations among European states to be drawn from progress toward greater economic integration.

Seeking the bases for reconstruction of a world torn apart by World War II, functionalists like David Mitrany noted that international organizations are formed from the recognition that certain tasks need to be performed, such as monetary exchange, trade, multilateral investment, mail service, or parceling out telecommunications frequencies. Writing in the 1950s and 1960s, neofunctionalists like Ernst Haas focused on the political processes orchestrated by politically connected specialists or elites. To the neofunctionalist, integration doesn't just happen, it arises by design. Along the same lines, Andrew Moravcsik claims liberal

---

[5]Regional organizations include the Andean Group (comunida-dandina.org), Asia-Pacific Economic Cooperation (apec.org), Association of Southeast Asian Nations (aseansec.org), Caribbean Community and Common Market (caricom.org), Economic Community of West African States (ecowas.int), European Union (europa.eu.intand, in the United States, eurunion.org), Mercosur [Common Market Southern Cone, South America] (mercosur.org.uy), and the North American Free Trade Association (nafta-sec-alena.org). For UN Regional Economic Commissions, see Africa (Addis Ababa, Ethiopia: uneca.org), Europe (Geneva, Switzerland: unece.org), and Latin America (Santiago, Chile: eclac.org).

intergovernmentalism is the best perspective through which to view the major turning points in European integration. He argues that state preferences are chiefly determined by interdependence, opportunities for international economic exchange, and the dominant interests in a national society, with actual substantive integration outcomes resulting from hard bargaining among state elites.

An internal logic to the economic integration process identified by neofunctionalists is apparent in the European integration experience. For example, free trade and commerce in the 1950s expanded in one economic sector, a **customs union** known as the European Coal and Steel Community, or ECSC. Commercial transactions and ties, however, also spilled over into other economic sectors that in turn were used by commercial and politically connected elites in 1958 to create an enlarged European Economic Community (EEC) as well as a European Atomic Energy Community (EURATOM) to advance peaceful, economic uses of nuclear energy. The ECSC, EEC, and EURATOM—referred to collectively as the European Communities (EC)—carried out their integration tasks for more than thirty years before being incorporated into what is now referred to as the European Union (EU). Another example of spillover occurred when a Common Agricultural Policy (CAP)—painstakingly developed in the late 1960s and early 1970s to set farm prices and price supports within the EEC—came apart. The key precipitating event was when the dollar, to which European currencies were then tied, was allowed to fluctuate in value. To reconstruct a new CAP, integration spilled over into the monetary sector with the creation of a European Monetary System to stabilize currency exchange rates, a necessary step to stabilize prices for agricultural commodities traded within the EEC.

Integration also can occur in response to external challenges. Movement from a Customs Union to a Common Market in 1992 and achievement of a European Economic and Monetary Union were not driven by the internal logic indicated by neofunctionalist theory. These changes were due more to calculations by politically relevant elites that Europe would have to deepen the level of economic integration in order to remain competitive with the United States, Japan, and other countries in 21st-century high-technology and other global markets.

customs union ■ states not only have agreed to eliminate tariffs on imports and other barriers to trade among themselves, but also have established a common external tariff imposed on imports from nonmembers

Trade and Economic Integration

An ongoing, post–Cold War debate within Europe during the 1990s and the first decade of the 21st century involved the issue of whether the widening of the membership of the European Union should be pursued if it came at the expense of deepening the level of integration among member states. In fact, widening membership has exposed substantial macroeconomic differences among EU countries, especially given the deepening of integration that came in 2000 with the euro as common currency for most member countries. To keep members in less capital-rich countries like Greece, Spain, and Ireland tied to the euro, better-off countries like Germany, France, and other northern European countries have resented having to finance those in difficulty, particularly since some have engaged in what they see as profligate spending that helped precipitate these crises. At the same time, however, capital-rich EU countries have been reluctant to abandon their integration goal of greater European unity.

For its part, the United Kingdom chose not to join the euro, preferring to remain with its historic national currency, the pound sterling. Countries tied to the euro like Greece or Spain could withdraw from the euro, returning to its own national currencies—the *drachma* or *peseta* in these cases—but the losses to Greece or Spain of doing so voluntarily have seemed greater than any gains from greater freedom to set their own fiscal and monetary policies independent of preferences advanced by capital-rich fellow EU members in northern, continental Europe. If long-standing members of the EU like Greece, Spain, Ireland, and several others have found it difficult to maintain the fiscal and monetary discipline required to stay in the euro group, EU leaders see newer members in central and eastern Europe facing comparable challenges.

The question of widening at the expense of deepening the level of integration in Europe is by no means new. For example, Britain's first attempt to join the European Communities (EC)—what the present-day EU was then called—was rebuffed in 1967 by France under President Charles de Gaulle's right-of-center leadership (1958–1969). The World War II general saw the United Kingdom as more closely tied to the United States and the British Commonwealth than to continental Europe. After reconsideration of the matter by successor governments in France as well as by the five other EC members, accession to the EC by the United Kingdom, Ireland, and Denmark finally took place in 1973, thus marking the first round of enlargement.

Greece joined in 1981, Portugal and Spain in 1986, and in 1995 came the immediate post–Cold War accessions by Austria, Finland, and Sweden—Norway choosing to maintain a more independent posture and thus remain outside what had now become the European Union (EU). The most extensive enlargement round occurred in 2004 with decisions on widening to include much of Central and Eastern Europe, previously in the Soviet sphere of influence (the Czech Republic, Hungary, Poland, and Slovakia); the Baltic states, previously part of the Soviet Union itself (Estonia, Latvia, and Lithuania); a part of the former Yugoslav Federation (Slovenia); and two Mediterranean states (Cyprus and Malta). Two other central European states (Bulgaria and Romania) joined in 2007, while waiting in line are Macedonia, Montenegro, Albania, Iceland, Serbia, and Turkey, the last of these continuing its long-term, uphill struggle for membership.

For many years, critics of EC or EU enlargement noted that increasing the membership and thus widening its European scope risked undermining efforts to deepen integration—initially moving beyond a customs union to a common market, economic and monetary union, and common social as well as foreign and security policies. Not only was collaboration among larger numbers of states understood to be more difficult than forging agreements among a few had proven to be, but also the asymmetries in levels of economic development and socioeconomic diversities among a larger membership were seen as posing substantial challenges to keeping ever-deeper integration on track.

Although the EC members were often referred to as the "Common Market" countries, a true **common market**—a step deeper on the integration ladder than a customs union that entails free flow within the community of the land (i.e., natural resources), labor, and capital "factors of production"—technically did not come into existence until full implementation in 1992 of the EC's 1987 agreement

common market ■ in addition to the free trade of goods and services, and a common external tariff on imports from nonmember countries, there is also free movement of land, labor, and capital—the three factors of production

TABLE 11.4

A Regional Integration Ladder

There are different degrees or levels of integration. Descent on the ladder denotes movement from relatively shallow to ever-deeper levels of integration. Participants may choose to minimize the degree of integration, staying on upper rungs, or they may decide to deepen the level of integration by moving to lower rungs. Most members of the European Union (EU) are on the fourth rung—some, like the UK, are on the third rung. The North American Free Trade Agreement (NAFTA) countries—the United States, Canada, and Mexico—are on the first rung.

		Characteristics (Characteristics Are Cumulative as Rungs Descend)
First Rung	Free-Trade Area	*Goal:* no tariffs or other trade barriers (e.g., North American and European Free Trade Areas [NAFTA and EFTA]) +
Second Rung	Customs Union	*Goal:* common external tariff against imports (e.g., European Economic Community, EEC, established in 1958) +
Third Rung	Common Market	*Goal:* free movement of factors of production (land, labor, and capital) within integration area (e.g., Europe 1992, Single European Act) +
Fourth Rung	Economic and Monetary Union	*Goal:* common currency and integrated economic policies (e.g., European Union Treaty agreed to at Maastricht in 1991, also calling for common foreign and security policies; implemented by Amsterdam Treaty signed in 1997 and effective in 1999) +
Fifth Rung	Full Political Union	*Goal:* complete economic and political integration (e.g., federations like the United States, a model for some advocates of European integration, but others oppose stepping into this deepest form of integration)

on a set of commercial and related regulations known more formally as the Single European Act (SEA). Work also was under way to create a European Union (EU) with common currency by the end of the 1990s, coordinating social policy and developing a common foreign and security policy (CFSP)—goals set in December 1991 and formally agreed upon in the February 1992 Treaty of Maastricht. The subsequent treaties of Amsterdam (1997) and Nice (2001) addressed organizational matters—an effort to streamline bureaucratic procedures and make other institutional adjustments to the expanded EU role.

To say the least, the EU has made great progress in its quest not only to widen but also to deepen the level of integration. Agricultural policy has always been a problematic issue, particularly given strong political pressures from farmers to continue or expand agricultural protection or subsidies. Admission of new members adds to the challenge in the decades-long effort to develop and implement a Common Agricultural Policy (CAP)—coordinating price structures and taking other cooperative measures to facilitate trade while accommodating farm-sector interests.

On monetary matters, great progress was marked in 2002 with the euro becoming the EU currency managed by a common central bank; however, asymmetries in fiscal and monetary policies and a political preference for retaining a greater degree of independent political control over such matters led the United Kingdom and Denmark to opt out of the monetary union. That said, the euro became the major currency EU leaders sought, designed to facilitate trade, investment, and other forms of commerce across the European continent. The debt crisis that emerged in 2011, however, challenged the solidarity of the 17 "eurozone" countries using the euro as common currency.

Finally, the quest for a common foreign and security policy remains a substantial challenge, as did the effort to establish an agreed EU constitution, which faced a significant setback when rejected by French and Dutch voters in 2005. A substitute for this failed constitutional-ratification process, the Lisbon Treaty, was signed in 2007 and went into force in 2009. Some progress has been made on security since the decision in 1999 to assume the tasks previously performed by the West European Union (WEU), although critics argue that the effort has not received the funding the program needs to establish a viable all-European, independent defense capability.

Of even greater concern to many was the decision in 2003 by the United Kingdom to join the United States in the invasion and subsequent occupation of Iraq (and the decision by France and Germany not to do so), thus effectively splitting the EU, with adverse impact on plans for deepening the level of foreign and security policy integration. Although European members came together with the United States under NATO auspices in Afghanistan, EU members continue to divide on serious foreign and security policy matters to include the 2011 intervention in Libya championed by the French and British with American support, but opposed by the Germans—a venture also joined by the Italians and other NATO members. Bottom line: European collaboration has proven easier to forge under NATO than under EU auspices.

Some realists have noted that perhaps the United States succeeded too well in encouraging European integration—not only does the European Union have the potential to be a formidable economic bloc, but Europeans have developed an ingrained aversion to large military budgets and the use of military force. To put it another way, the Europeans have managed to create for themselves a Kantian peace based upon negotiation and cooperation, and they don't want to jeopardize it. The United States, however, being a superpower, supposedly lives in a Hobbesian world, with conflict being the essential characteristic. Where the two might clash, however, is in the economic realm. The EU now stretches from the Arctic to the Mediterranean and from the Irish Sea to the Black Sea. It comprises 450 million persons and accounts for more than one-fifth of global economic activity. For this reason alone, realists foresee difficult times in U.S.–European relations.

Is Europe Unique?

Our focus above has been on European economic integration because it is the region that has made the most progress toward these goals. Most important, the idea of a war among Western European countries is almost to the point of being far-fetched. The interesting question is, "Why haven't we seen similar progress toward economic and political integration in other areas of the world?" Much more modest efforts include the North American Free Trade Agreement (NAFTA), the Central American Free Trade Agreement (CAFTA), the West African Economic Community (ECOWAS), the Common Market in the Southern Cone of South America (MERCOSUR), the Andean Group, the Central American Common Market (CACM), the Association of Southeast Asian Nations (ASEAN), and other regional integration organizations. Compared to the EU, these associations do not even have as an objective the levels that already have been achieved in Europe, much less those that are anticipated by European integration advocates.

For example, the much-celebrated Canada–Mexico–United States NAFTA accord has only the relatively modest ambition of gradually establishing a regional free-trade area. In this context it also provides for greater mobility of capital and some harmonization of business practices and standards. As yet there has been no serious discussion, however, of moving to a customs union with a common external tariff, much less a common market that would allow for the free flow of labor across borders. This makes the European efforts to establish and sustain an economic and monetary union with a common currency—a much deeper level of integration than ever attempted in other regional integration projects—even more impressive. The current challenge is to maintain the role of the euro and prevent the catastrophic collapse of the European integration project.

free-trade area ■ region where commerce is unobstructed by tariffs, quotas, or other barriers

Perhaps the post–World War II circumstances in Western Europe were unique. As noted, the United States provided a security guarantee against the communist East and encouraged the Europeans to focus on economic recovery. The Marshall Plan certainly helped to jump-start economic recovery. The fact that the states were contiguous geographically was also a factor, a situation quite different from that in Asia. The common aspirations of European elites were also important, and perhaps the common historical European values, despite the fascist experiences in Germany, Italy, and elsewhere, also made a difference. In more recent years, the strong grounding in democratic values and traditions has encouraged the rise of a civil society, with many transnational European organizations encouraging social interactions below the level of the state.

Would the continual integration of Europe encourage the development of regional economic blocs and lead to mercantilist competition? This possibility is constantly raised and debated. Developing and maintaining trade within a region can (but need not) divert trade or displace other commercial relations outside of the regional context. Advances at the regional level should be viewed in the broader context of the continual fast pace of globalization. To the extent that they create trade and promote economic development, regional efforts—however ambitious or however modest—do contribute to the continued functioning of capitalist political economy on a global scale.

CONCLUSION

Economics has been called the dismal science, not just because of an inherent pessimism accompanying many economic theories or theorists but also because of a certain opaqueness of presentation seemingly impervious to penetration by general readers. Yet understanding basic economics is important not only if you wish to enter the business world, but if you are to make sense of what is taking place in an increasingly globalized world. But for the globalization of trade, for example, we probably would not have seen such a resurgence of the types of piracy mentioned at the outset of this chapter. The importance of economics underscores its link to politics—in particular the processes leading to authoritative decisions and implementation of economic policies by governments and international organizations. That is why political economy figures so prominently in this text. It is a term that explicitly recognizes the political dimension of economic matters in domestic as well as international and global contexts.

In this chapter we've addressed a number of important conceptual issues related to trade and finance in an increasingly globalized world. Although subject to challenge by those who see it taking insufficient account of the circumstances in which less-developed countries find themselves, classical trade theory in relation to comparative advantage continues to hold sway among advocates of further trade liberalization. To sustain an open, if not entirely free, trading environment is the goal advanced by authorities in governments and international organizations like the WTO and IMF.

Such global governance requires both bilateral and multilateral cooperation among those committed to these goals, resolving trade disputes, and managing exchange rates that directly affect the terms of trade. Finally, we note movement toward regional integration—an economic and monetary union in Europe, a free trade area in North America, and ongoing efforts particularly in Latin America, Africa, and Southeast Asia. By no means, of course, is continued progress a certainty.

✓—Study and Review the **Post-Test & Chapter Exam** at **mypoliscilab.com**

LEARNING OBJECTIVES REVIEW

11.1 Explain classical trade theory in relation to comparative advantage, unequal terms of trade, and the adverse implications of competitive devaluations.

Classical trade theory holds that under free trade countries will specialize in producing goods and services in which they are more efficient, thus enhancing overall productivity and at lower costs than otherwise would be the case. This perspective, however, does not address either the distribution of gains from trade or that some countries—particularly commodity exporters—may suffer from unequal terms of trade (exports of manufactures tend to rise in price, those of commodities often declining).

KEY TERMS
Trade 372
Exports 372
Imports 372
GDP 372

Global governance 372
Comparative advantage 373
Terms of trade 378
Trade preferences 378
European Union (EU) 378

ADDITIONAL READINGS

Paul R. Krugman, Maurice Obstfeld, and Marc Melitz, *International Economics*, 9th ed. (Upper Saddle River, NJ: Prentice Hall, 2011). A detailed overview of how the global economy works.

Robert O. Keohane, *Power and Governance in a Partially Globalized World* (London: Routledge, 2002). A conceptual discussion of how global governance in various issue areas can be (and has been) achieved.

11.2 **Differentiate between classical and neoclassical economic understandings as they relate to macroeconomic and microeconomic theories applicable to global, regional, national, and local political economies.**

Classical economic theory rested on the labor theory of value, whereas neoclassical (microeconomic) theory shifts the focus to markets and the play of supply and demand as they affect the price of goods and services produced either for domestic consumption or export. Macroeconomic policy—government fiscal (taxing, spending and borrowing) and monetary (money supply, interest rates, exchange rates, etc.) decisions—often affect trade, stimulating either exports or imports.

KEY TERMS

Macroeconomics 379
Microeconomics 379
Econometrics 379
Fiscal policy 379
Monetary policy 379
International Monetary Fund (IMF) 379

ADDITIONAL READINGS

Robert B. Ekelund Jr. and Robert F. Hebert, *A History of Economic Theory and Method*, 4th ed. (New York: Longrove, IL: Waveland Press, 1975, 2004). A highly readable account of the development of both classical and neoclassical thought in economics.

Charles P. Kindleberger, *World Economic Primacy: 1500 to 1990* (Oxford, UK: Oxford University Press, 1995), and *A Financial History of Western Europe* (London: Allen & Unwin, 1984, and Oxford: Oxford University Press, 1993). Now-classic treatments by this prominent economic historian.

11.3 **Apply free trade theory to present-day circumstances of uneven development in which some countries have well-capitalized, large-scale producers capable of developing and applying advanced technologies to the products they bring to market, but many other countries do not.**

Efficiencies occur in large-scale production—the cost of producing each additional unit (referred to as marginal cost) tending to decline. Thus, large economies with large-scale producers tend to have an advantage in lower costs (and thus usually lower prices) for goods or services sold in domestic markets or for export abroad.

KEY TERMS

Economies of scale 380
Multinational corporation 384

ADDITIONAL READING

Robert Gilpin, *The Political Economy of International Relations* (Princeton, NJ: Princeton University Press, 1987) and his two more recent volumes *Global Political Economy: Understanding the International Economic Order* (Princeton, NJ: Princeton University Press, 2001). Cf. Jean M. Gilpin and Robert Gilpin, *The Challenge of Global Capitalism: The World Economy in the 21st Century* (Princeton, NJ: Princeton University Press, 2002). For further background reading on politics and the global economy.

11.4 Illustrate how changes in exchange rates affect prices of both exports and imports.

Money is not neutral (as classical trade theory assumes). When a currency becomes stronger in relation to other currencies (i.e., the exchange rate or price paid for buying foreign currencies declines), the price paid for goods and services imported from abroad also becomes cheaper, thus tending to stimulate demand for imports. By contrast, when a currency becomes weaker in relation to other currencies (i.e., the exchange rate or price paid for buying foreign currencies increases), imports also become more expensive, thus tending to dampen demand for imports. Exports are more attractive to foreigners when the seller's currency weakens (foreign buyers can buy them more cheaply) and less attractive when the seller's currency strengthens (foreign buyers have to pay more for them).

KEY TERMS
Exchange rates 385
Price elasticity of demand 386

ADDITIONAL READINGS
David N. Balaam and Michael Veseth, *Introduction to International Political Economy*, 5th ed. (Upper Saddle River, NJ: Prentice-Hall, 2010). See the chapters on trade and finance.
H. Robert Heller's *International Trade: Theory and Empirical Evidence* (Englewood Cliffs, NJ: Prentice-Hall, 1968, 1973) and Charles P. Kindleberger's *Foreign Trade and the National Economy* (New Haven, CT: Yale University Press, 1962), *Power and Money* (New York: Basic Books, 1970), and *The World in Depression, 1929–1939* (Berkeley: University of California Press, 1973, 1986). Older, easily read volumes—the last three now-classic, nonmathematical presentations on international political economy.

11.5 Outline how monetary authorities in institutions like the International Monetary Fund (IMF), treasuries and central banks, and the Bank for International Settlements (BIS) relate to each other in global-governance arrangements aimed at maintaining global trade and monetary regimes.

International organizations, tasked by their state members with such economic responsibilities as maintaining international liquidity, work closely with national treasuries and central banks to assure traders and investors can buy the foreign currencies they need. Institutions thus play an important role in global governance arrangements essential to sustaining trade relations.

KEY TERMS
International monetary regime 390
International liquidity 390

Reserves 390
Special drawing rights (SDRs) 390
Exchange controls 392
Competitive devaluations 392
Structural adjustments 396

ADDITIONAL READINGS
Robert O. Keohane and Joseph S. Nye, *Power and Interdependence*, 4th ed. (New York: Longman, 1977, 2011). A classic study that combines liberal and realist understandings of world politics and international relations, including case studies on trade and international monetary regime.
Robert O. Keohane, *After Hegemony* (Princeton, NJ: Princeton University Press, 1984, 2005). Focuses on institutions and theories of cooperation in the world political economy.

11.6 Evaluate progress made globally and regionally on liberalizing trade and achieving integration goals in Europe, North America, and other parts of the world.

The European Union has achieved the deepest level of integration. Most members now part of an "economic and monetary union" (EMU) are using the euro as a common currency managed by a European Central Bank; the others (including the U.K.) retain their

national currencies, but are still part of the EU's "common market" (a commitment to allow capital, labor, and natural resources to flow across national borders). Given asymmetries in level of development and substantial differences in fiscal (tax-and-spend) policies, the coordination of monetary policies in the EMU essential to sustaining the euro has proven difficult. By contrast, efforts at regional integration in North America and elsewhere are shallow by comparison; the free-trade areas they have established are much less demanding politically on members than a customs union (common external tariff)—much less a common market or economic and monetary union.

KEY TERMS

Customs union 407

Common market 408

Free-trade area 411

ADDITIONAL READINGS

Margaret Haerens (ed.), *The World Trade Organization: Opposing Viewpoints* (Farmington Hills, MI: Greenhaven Press, 2010). Diverse perspectives on the WTO.

Michael T. Klare, *Resource Wars: The New Landscape of Global Conflict* (New York: Henry Holt & Company/Owl Books, 2001) and Tim Lang and Michael Heasman, *Food Wars: The Global Battle for Mouths, Minds and Markets* (London and Sterling, VA: Earthscam, 2004). Trade is also a domain of conflict.

Neill Nugent, *The Government and Politics of the European Union*, 7th ed. (New York: Palgrave Macmillan, 2010). A well-established text on the EU.

CHAPTER REVIEW

1. Classical trade theory predicts that countries will engage in trade when what condition exists?
   a. calculated advantage
   b. comparative advantage
   c. absolute advantage
   d. equal advantage

2. According to classical trade theory, trade depends on _____ in relative efficiency and capacities of production.
   a. sameness
   b. relative equality
   c. differences
   d. competitive gains

3. Critics of classic trade theory see trade preferences as
   a. a means of productive engagement.
   b. a means of perpetuating inequality.
   c. a means of eliminating colonial relationships.
   d. a means of maintaining neocolonial relationships.

4. The examples of Insula and Terra illustrate
   a. comparative advantage.
   b. labor theory of value.
   c. monetary policy at work.
   d. regional integration.

5. Economists like Raúl Prebisch have observed that _____ often do not increase in price over time and thus cause unequal terms of trade.
   a. capital inputs
   b. land acquisition costs
   c. agricultural commodities
   d. labor inputs

6. Differing from classical economists, neoclassical economists see value in terms of what?
   a. market context
   b. production context
   c. production inputs
   d. market outputs

7. Neoclassical economists have focused on and developed multiple analytical techniques, but they all generally focus on what topic?
   a. how supplies interact with goods in a marketplace
   b. how producers achieve profits in the marketplace
   c. how purchasers and suppliers interact in the marketplace
   d. how purchasers and producers interact in the marketplace

8. John Maynard Keynes and his followers have focused on what two broad concepts in economics?
   a. fiscal and monetary policy
   b. fiscal and countercyclical policy
   c. monetary and quantitative policies
   d. quantitative and fiscal policies

9. Which of the following is not an example of a way microeconomic theory offers an explanation for a global phenomenon?
   a. exchange value of currencies
   b. regional integration
   c. national GDP growth
   d. the effects of tariffs

10. Monetarists have focused on what aspects of economic theory?
    a. how money changes hands through the economy
    b. how the rapidity and liquidity of money changing hands determines production
    c. how the supply and velocity of money affect production, supply, and demand
    d. how the supply and velocity of money affect only the supply of goods

11. What is the main advantage economies of scale possess over others?
    a. They have smaller costs per unit of production.
    b. They produce more goods and services.
    c. They have greater bargaining capacity.
    d. They employ more people.

12. According to Paul Krugman, focusing on increasing gains aided by technological innovation should be seen as _____ comparative cost considerations.
    a. exclusory of
    b. inclusive of
    c. supplemental to
    d. disregarded in

13. The lack of what factor of production makes it difficult for small firms to achieve a strong market position?
    a. land
    b. labor
    c. capital
    d. wages

14. Creative destruction refers to the process of what?
    a. new technologies creatively reworked to match existing systems
    b. large firms creatively buying out smaller firms
    c. small firms finding a niche in the economy and exploiting it
    d. new technologies displacing older technologies in the economy

15. According to the authors, what role have governments played in developing high technologies?
    a. have been active players
    b. have been passive players
    c. have overregulated the business cycle
    d. have unregulated the business cycle

16. Neutralizing money is a scenario in which the exchange of goods and services is influenced only by _____ .
    a. production costs and related considerations
    b. value of currencies and production costs
    c. production costs and intermediary costs
    d. value of currencies and tariff reductions

17. According to the authors, an exchange rate is
    a. the price to exchange one good for another.
    b. the total transaction cost of a currency exchange across borders.
    c. the price of a currency when bought or sold using another currency.
    d. the rate at which money can be exchanged for goods.

18. The concept of price elasticity of demand refers to what?
   a. changes in demand for a product due to changes in price
   b. the impact on markets due solely to currency depreciations
   c. the impact on markets due solely to currency appreciations
   d. the impact on markets of exchange rate uniformity

19. According to the authors, what ultimately drives the price of a currency?
   a. central bank autonomy
   b. market forces
   c. currency elasticity
   d. domestic political decisions

20. Efforts to adjust exchange rates by a central bank are efforts at achieving what?
   a. stronger currencies
   b. weaker currencies
   c. export dominance
   d. purchasing power parity

21. _____ is the principal goal of the international monetary regime.
   a. Decreasing tariff barriers
   b. Encouraging free trade
   c. Maintaining international liquidity
   d. Increasing international currency exchange

22. According to the authors, currency exchange controls are mechanisms designed to do what?
   a. avoid a debt default
   b. avoid artificial currency manipulation
   c. limit the amount of money spent abroad
   d. limit the amount of money spent domestically by foreigners

23. A central bank will most likely engage in a competitive devaluation for what purpose?
   a. to maximize exports and minimize imports
   b. as an attempt to stabilize exchange rates relative to gold
   c. to weaken another country's currency value
   d. to combat inflation

24. Competitive devaluations are akin to what political-economic tradition?
   a. liberalism
   b. neomercantilism
   c. neoliberalism
   d. Marxism

25. Which of the following is *not* one of the goals of structural adjustments directed by the IMF as a condition for a loan of its funds?
   a. cut inflation
   b. curb excessive imports
   c. foster greater efficiency
   d. raise government expenditure

26. _____ was one the first individuals to develop rules for international commerce.
   a. Hedley Bull
   b. Hugo Grotius
   c. Adam Smith
   d. David Ricardo

27. Which of the following is *not* one of the tasks of the WTO?
   a. administering trade agreements
   b. settling trade disputes
   c. reviewing national trade policies
   d. imposing tariffs on the developed nations

28. According to the authors, one critical objective of regional integration is
   a. enhancing peace among states.
   b. diminishing regional wealth.
   c. creating markets for developing countries.
   d. facilitating security cooperatives.

29. The economic integration goal in a common market is to
   a. create a common external tariff.
   b. create a common currency and integrated economic policies.
   c. allow the free movement of the factors of production.
   d. establish no tariffs or other trade barriers.

30. NAFTA can be classified as what type of regional integration scheme?
   a. full political union
   b. customs union
   c. common market
   d. free-trade area

Development

"Globalization, as defined by rich people like us, is a very nice thing.... You are talking about the internet, you are talking about cell phones, you are talking about computers. This doesn't affect two-thirds of the people of the world.... If you're totally illiterate and living on one dollar a day, the benefits of globalization never come to you."—Jimmy Carter, Former President of the United States and Winner of the 2002 Nobel Peace Prize

LEARNING OBJECTIVES

12.1 Illustrate how the differences between capital-rich and capital-poor, less-economically developed countries contribute to the uneven levels of development found around the world.

12.2 Identify the sources of capital sought by developing countries upon which their development depends.

12.3 Explain how population growth, resource depletion and environmental degradation, the absence of effective health care, excessive military spending and war can undermine development efforts.

12.4 Evaluate the various economic-structuralist perspectives on the global capitalist system.

I n his early twenties in the late 1950s, Padre Ricardo Sammon, a socially committed New Yorker, took up residence in Portezuelo, a small rural village reachable only on undeveloped roads west of the Chilean town of Chillon (pron. Shee-yon) south of Santiago. It was his base for reaching out to the indigenous Mapuche (pron. Mah-poo-chay) people, most living off the land in varying degrees of poverty. Over the next half century he traveled regularly throughout the wide area north, south, and west of Portezuelo, coming to know intimately the plight of the Mapuche—family by family, person by person.

Capital formation to fund development was virtually nonexistent in this part of rural Chile. Local contributions were mostly in kind from agricultural produce. He relied instead on funds he received from followers in America and from those Mapuche who had moved away, rising to higher socioeconomic positions in Chilean society. These were the principal sources of capital he needed for such projects as building a free boarding school (primary through 12th grades) and establishing a local-area radio station. Although expanding to television was a possibility, in the years before his death in 2008 he was planning to "leapfrog" telecommunications development by going directly from radio to the internet.

Not surprisingly, politics matter in the conduct of development projects. Although a cleric, he kept his religious duties in second position to development projects, which earned him respect from better-off followers in Chillon. The military regime under Augusto Pinochet, however, distrusted his social-liberal projects and consequent empowerment of the Mapuche in these rural areas. For the same reasons, the Church in Santiago forced him to close his home-grown seminary in Portezuelo lest a socially committed, politicized Mapuche clergy emerge. Nevertheless, his legacy of advancing the level of living of people he cared most about remained in place. It's hardly ever easy—a narrow, twisting path with many setbacks along the way—but socially committed individuals can make a difference.

Read and Listen to **Chapter 12** at **mypoliscilab.com**

Study and Review the **Pre-Test & Flashcards** at **mypoliscilab.com**

In this chapter we review the data and the disturbing facts of poverty in developing countries, noting the enormous obstacles to be overcome to achieve development. We begin with essentially conventional or mainstream accounts of the global political economy but end with emphasizing economic-structuralist perspectives that identify the problem as capital-poor countries in the South subordinated to capital-rich countries in the North or, as Marxists put it, dominant capital-owning classes in the North and South exploiting the laboring classes, particularly peasants and workers in less-developed countries.

UNEVEN DEVELOPMENT AND POVERTY IN DEVELOPING COUNTRIES

12.1 Illustrate how the differences between capital-rich and capital-poor, less-economically developed countries contribute to the uneven levels of development found around the world.

✳ Explore the
"Business: You Are a Foreign Market Analyst" at
mypoliscilab.com

developing world ◼ countries with public and private sectors investing capital (from savings, trade surpluses, grants, loans, corporate or other investments) to increase the country's capacity for domestic production of goods and services

Third World or **South** ◼ capital-poor, low-income, or less-developed countries

In this volume we refer to capital-poor countries generically as the less-developed or, more positively, the developing world. Other writers often use the terms Third World or South, sometimes interchangeably to denote the same capital-poor, low-income, or less-developed countries—those at the lower levels of economic development we've been describing. Although the term "Third World" is still widely in use, many writers now shy away from the term lest it be interpreted negatively—as if using it implies that these countries or their peoples are somehow inferior to those in the "first" or high-income, capital-rich world. As noted in Chapter 5, however, we note the hopeful position in the 1960s of those who originated the term "Third World" as denoting the most populous category of the world's peoples in much the same way as the term "Third Estate" in French revolutionary history referred to the masses of "have-nots" who ultimately triumphed, substantially improving their lot over time.

Why are poor people in these countries the "have-nots," and do they, in fact, have a chance to rise from the depths of poverty? One answer to the first of these questions is provided by postcolonial theorists who see the present state of affairs as the outcome of several centuries of dominance by European powers that inhibited development of the South in the 20th and 21st centuries—First World countries that effectively structured global capitalism to the disadvantage of those on the lower rungs of global and national societies—in Spanish, *los de abajo* (those from below, the bottom of the socioeconomic ladder). Whether one accepts this analysis or not, the remedy lies in generating capital that can be invested to grow the productive capacity of the economies in these countries.

According to some optimists, these are different times. They see harnessing information technology for productive purposes as by no means the exclusive preserve of capital-rich countries. They see possibilities in many less-developed, lower-income economies that acquire the know-how in advanced-production processes that capitalize on information technologies—putting labor and natural resources to work and leapfrogging to ever-higher levels of production and productivity.

They point to the great strides made by the so-called BRIC countries (Brazil, Russia, India, and China). Both China and India during the last quarter century have moved into the upper ranks of countries in terms of aggregate production of goods and services. When we compare the profiles of countries listed in Table 12.1, however, we find substantial diversity among the countries.

ARGUMENT-COUNTERARGUMENT | The Poor Get Poorer

ARGUMENT Technology, in the form of computers and information, drives growth in both advanced industrial and postindustrial service economies in increasingly globalized markets. Although some capital-poor countries have improved their level of development, most have not. Poverty, disease, and malnutrition continue to plague the peoples of sub-Saharan Africa and parts of south and southeast Asia in particular. The economic-development gap between capital-poor and capital-rich countries remains and, in many countries, has grown even larger. Prospects for narrowing, much less closing, this economic divide between haves and have-nots around the world seem dimmer and dimmer: "The rich get richer and the poor stay poor (or worse, get poorer)"—or so says the conventional wisdom. Even in advanced economically developed countries like the United States, the inequality gap among people is growing, not getting smaller. Wealth in the United States has continued to increase substantially during the last four decades, but its distribution has benefited the few at the top far more than the many below them.

COUNTERARGUMENT It may come as a surprise to many people, but between 2000 and 2010, six of the ten fastest growing countries in the world were African. Angola's economy grew faster than that of any other country on the planet. Granted, what these African countries had in common were commodities desired by the rest of the world. A boom in prices spurred investment in mining and drilling as well as bridges, roads, and high-rise office buildings. Unfortunately, with wealth comes corruption and the squandering of income that could be used to benefit the broader population.

APPLICATION Go to Transparency International's website and search for the reports on Africa. Also examine its annual report and its global corruption index.

At the same time, however, most of the income from this productivity is concentrated in the top 20–25 percent of the population; the remaining 75–80 percent still are predominantly a peasant society, engaged as they've always been in labor-intensive agriculture. The same can be said of India. Indeed, both China and India have dual economies—the production and distribution of wealth produced each year concentrated in the upper tiers of their societies, the vast majority of China's 1.3 billion people and India's 1.1 billion decidedly less well off, the bottom 20 percent or more still living in varying degrees of poverty. Although the economies of both countries have grown significantly in recent decades—producing wealthy upper and upper-middle socioeconomic classes—the adverse plight of the less-advantaged masses remains severe with per capital income about $375 in China, just under $120 in India.

Social justice demands better levels of living than most of the world's seven billion people now enjoy. Human rights and socioeconomic well-being require not only sustainable development and growth of economies on a truly global scale, but also a more equitable distribution of wealth—lofty objectives sought by economic development advocates. To the contrary, wishful thinking aside, pessimists see economic development on the scale advocates seek as both consuming resources that cannot be replaced and polluting the environment, making it extraordinarily difficult (if not impossible) to sustain growth, much less extend economic development to all the world's peoples.

sustainable development ■ economic growth that avoids obstacles that would undermine or preclude further growth, particularly depletion of natural resources, pollution, and other environmental damage

TABLE 12.1

Development Indicators for Selected Countries: A Comparative Snapshot

For all the talk of American economic decline, note the striking gap between the size of the U.S. economy and those of the rising BRIC countries. The starkest contrast, however, is between the United States and Chad, an African country. Even given the troubling state of health of many Americans, the U.S. life expectancy is still thirty years more than that of Chad.

Indicator	The "BRIC" Countries				Other Developing Countries		Among the Capital	
	Brazil	Russia	India	China	S. Africa	Indonesia	Poorest: Chad	Richest: USA
Population (Millions)	194	142	1,155	1,331	49	230	10.9	307
Size of Economy (Gross domestic product—GDP in US$ billions)	1,594	1,232	1,377	4,985	285	540	6.8	14,119
GDP per Capita (Gross domestic product divided by population in US$)	8,216	8,676	119	375	582	235	62	45,990
Foreign Debt (External debt as % of GNI—gross national income)	18	32	18	9	15	30	29	—
Life Expectancy (Years at birth)	73	69	64	73	52	71	49	79
Literacy Rate (% of population above 15 years of age who can read)	90	>99	63	94	89	92	34	>99
Size of Business (Private) Sector (Merchandise trade as % of GDP)	18	40	30	44	47	39	70	19
Level of Urban	87	93	54	58	84	67	23	>99
Development (% of urban population with access to improved sanitation facilities)								
Unemployment (% of total labor force)	8	8	4	4	24	8	8	>8

Source: This table constructed by the authors draws from World Bank data, accessed in 2011 from http://data.worldbank.org/indicator. Figures in the table have been rounded.

Beyond assuring some basic, minimum level of living, is the world (or at least large parts of it) to abandon the effort, get off the ever-increasing growth-and-development train, and seek some new way of defining the quality of life? It is an interesting thought, taken more seriously by those who see the exhausting pace prescribed by market capitalism as having eroded core values, the environment (pollution and resource depletion), and the overall quality of life. For understandable reasons, more low-income countries still seem eager to get better seats on—not get off—the growth-and-development train. Progression from local to express and then to bullet-train class seems to be the more common worldwide aspiration. But how realistic is this goal? Most of the developing world or South is, quite frankly, invisible to those in the capital-rich, economically advanced countries that label themselves First World or North. When it make the news, it is invariably bad news—poverty, wars, famines, AIDS. The facts are stark and difficult to comprehend. World Bank statistics tell us that of more than seven billion people on Earth, about 1.4 billion—a fifth of humanity—subsist on less than $1.25 a day. Women and children account for the majority worldwide. Seventy-five percent of global income goes to just 20 percent of the world's population; only 5 percent of global income goes to the bottom 40 percent—the poorest of the poor.[1]

More than a billion people live in the forty-two most indebted, poverty-stricken countries—most of them in sub-Saharan Africa and South Asia.[2] Even though **barter** (exchanges of one agricultural or other good or service for another) is the common way of subsistence as opposed to the use of currency, living standards are appallingly low compared to those of the industrialized North. Malnutrition accounts for the fact that 30 percent or more of children under five years old suffer from severe or moderate stunting and contributes to more than half of the deaths of children under five years old in developing countries. Twenty-one million children do not attend school.[3] Examples of extreme poverty are found throughout the less-developed world, but particularly in more than thirty African countries identified in data collected by the UN Development Programme (UNDP).

The differences between the capital-rich and less-developed capital-poor countries become even more striking when we compare world regions. In Table 12.2, we see the enormous social cost of poverty. The highest mortality rate of 130 per 1,000 for children under age five is found in sub-Saharan Africa where three-quarters of the population lives on less than two dollars per day—fifty-one percent in extreme poverty on less than $1.25 per day. By sharp contrast, in European Union countries only five children die per 1,000 live births in the same age bracket. The absence in less-developed countries of adequate medical or health care malnutrition, disease, and other environmentally related factors are the underlying causes of most premature deaths in the earliest years of life. Also indicative of substantial economic differences are **investments** in, and exports of,

barter ■ trading one good or service for another

investment ■ the input of money or other resources to maintain or expand productive capacity and, in turn, to generate a profit or return on investment for the investor

---

[1] Anup Shah, "Poverty Facts and Stats," *Global Issues* (20 September 2010): http://www.globalissues.org/article/26/poverty-facts-and-stats.

[2] UNDP, *UN Development Report*, 2010. See Table 5.1 in Chapter 5.

[3] See the UNICEF annual *The State of the World's Children*, available at www.unicef.org/sowc.

TABLE 12.2

Uneven Development: The Human Condition in a Globalized World

The best starting point is the European Union. Compare the EU on any number of dimensions with other regions of the world. Military spending and research and development investment are of note.

Asia	Arab World	E. Asia–Pacific	European Union	Latin America & Caribbean	Middle East & N. Africa	Sub-Saharan	South Africa
Urbanization (% living in cities)	56	45	74	79	58	37	30
Urban Development (% of people in cities with access to improved sanitation facilities)	89	64	99	86	92	43	57
Human Cost of Poverty: Mortality Rate (Deaths per 1,000 under age 5)	50	26	5	23	33	130	71
High-Tech Development (High-tech exports as % of total exports of manufactures)	2	32	17	13	2	6	8
Research & Development Investment (% of GDP)	—	1.4	1.8	0.7	—	—	0.8
Military Spending (% of GDP)	6.3	1.9	1.8	1.5	3.5	1.7	2.6
Gender/Social Development (% of seats in legislature held by women)	11	19	24	24	9	20	19
Agriculture (% of land area)	40	48	44	35	23	45	55
Poverty (Percent living on or on less than $2.00 a day)	—	39	—	17	17	73	74
Extreme Poverty (Percent living on or on less than $1.25 a day)	—	17	—	8	4	51	40

Source: This table constructed by the authors draws from World Bank data, accessed in 2011 from http://data.worldbank.org/indicator. Figures in the table have been rounded.

high-technology goods and services—highest in East Asia and the Pacific (particularly China, Japan, and Korea), Europe, and Latin America (notably countries like Brazil, Argentina, and Chile). North America could be added.

POVERTY, CAPITAL FORMATION, AND DEVELOPMENT

Adam Smith (1723–1790) saw the wealth of nations lying not in their stock of gold or other treasure but rather in their productive capacity—effectively combining capital with land (natural resources) and labor (human resources) for production of goods and services. These are referred to as **factors of production**. Figure 12.1 shows the distribution of GNP (gross national product per capita) in the world. All countries have labor, yet in many countries of the developing world it is uneducated and poorly trained. Land may be essentially deserts, mountains, and jungles with scarce natural resources. **Capital formation** on a national basis depends heavily on domestic savings, but millions of people are more worried about their next meal than saving for the future. Thus, many of these countries depend upon capital from abroad:

- Aid provided as grants or subsidized loans at **concessionary rates** (below-market-interest rates)
- Loans (as well as debt forgiveness) by foreign governments, international and private banks, and purchases of government or private-sector bonds
- Direct foreign investment (by multinational corporations and private investors)
- Trade preferences (as when foreign governments agree to quantities or prices of imports from, and favorable to, particular countries)

In the next few pages, we take a more detailed look in turn at each of these four sources of capital.

Aid

Official development assistance (ODA) or aid from governments and international organizations continues to be an important source of investment capital for many developing countries. (See Table 12.3, columns 1 and 2.) Table 12.4 lists providers of foreign aid. Note the low level of official development assistance as percentage of gross national income in terms of the United States—the highest proportionally coming from the small Scandinavian countries in northern Europe.

For years, states and international organizations have provided more than a trillion dollars in aid to developing countries. The logic was straightforward. It was assumed that such aid would boost recipient countries' growth rates and hence help millions escape poverty. Unfortunately, many studies have failed to find a strong link between the amount of aid and faster economic growth. Why? First, a good deal of the aid was not really concerned with stimulating economic growth. During the Cold War the Soviet Union, United States, and their respective allies were primarily concerned with propping up friendly governments. To this day, Israel and Egypt are the two major recipients of U.S. foreign aid. Nor were the economic and financial competencies of governments a primary consideration.

12.2 Identify the sources of capital sought by developing countries upon which their development depends.

👁 **Watch** the **Video "Kenya's Developmental Challenge"** at mypoliscilab.com

factors of production ■ land (including natural resources), labor, and capital as components essential to the production of goods and services

capital formation ■ accruing savings or other sources of finance for new and continuing investment in the means of production of other goods and services

concessionary rates ■ interest rates below market rates, thus allowing reinvestment of a portion of the funds at market rates, the gains compounded and applied toward paying off the loan

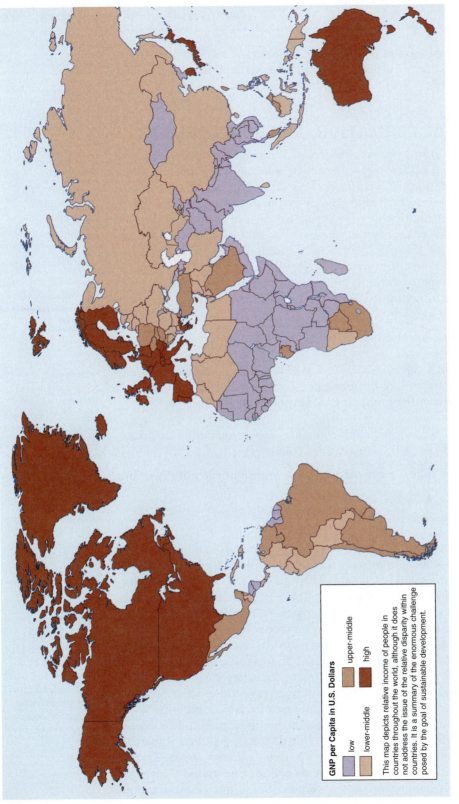

GNP per Capita in U.S. Dollars

- low
- lower-middle
- upper-middle
- high

This map depicts relative income of people in countries throughout the world, although it does not address the issue of the relative disparity within countries. It is a summary of the enormous challenge posed by the goal of sustainable development.

FIGURE 12.1

Gross National Product per Capita

The map shows the very uneven development around the world not only from continent to continent, but also within each of the continents: Europe, Africa, Asia (and the Pacific), and the Americas—North, Central, and South.

TABLE 12.3

North-South Capital Flows: Foreign Aid (Official Direct Assistance) "In" and Debt Payments "Out"

Net official development assistance (ODA) and borrowed funds are important sources of capital for investment, as when a country improves its infrastructure of roads, rail, seaports, airports, power, telecommunications, and other utilities— all of which expand the country's capacity for economic growth. Properly invested, foreign aid and borrowed funds can contribute substantially to economic development; however, whether invested wisely or not, servicing debt (making payments of interest and principal on time) can be a heavy burden, particularly for capital-poor states that find themselves overextended and in need of debt relief.

	Total aid Received (Net ODA in US$ Billions)	Total aid Received (Net ODA as % of GNI)	External Debt (as % of GDP)	Debt Service Ratio (Debt Payments as % of Exports)
Latin America				
Brazil	338	< 0.1	8.9	23.2
Colombia	1.060	0.5	7.9	18.5
Mexico	185	< 0.1	7.6	11.9
Panama	66	0.3	10.2	11.2
Peru	442	0.4	4.0	16.3
Venezuela	67	< 0.1	6.0	10.5
Asia				
Bangladesh	1,227	1.3	1.2	6.9
China	1,132	< 0.1	1.2	1.2
India	2,393	0.2	2.8	19.5
Indonesia	1,049	0.2	7.9	12.7
Pakistan	2,781	1.7	4.5	22.8
Philippines	310	0.2	13.7	16.0
Vietnam	3,744	4.1	1.7	5.9
Africa				
Côte d'Ivoire	2,366	10.6	3.5	4.8
Egypt	925	0.5	2.9	6.8
Nigeria	1,659	1.0	3.3	8.8
South Africa	1,075	0.4	1.8	2.4

Source: http://data.worldbank.org

Second, donors often send inappropriate types of aid. Some, for example, prefer to direct aid to conspicuous prestige projects such as major dams, which may or may not contribute substantially to economic development. Even small donations are regularly ill advised—Somalis have received heartburn pills and Mozambican

TABLE 12.4

Foreign Aid (Official Direct Assistance) to the South from the North

Official development assistance (ODA) from capital-rich countries in the North remains an important source of capital for investment in capital-poor countries in the South and in other countries receiving such aid. In addition to examining the total or aggregate amount of foreign aid disbursed for development purposes, indicators of the degree of commitment by capital-rich countries to development assistance are annual development assistance as a percent of gross national income (GNI) of the donor country (the 0.7 percent international goal met or surpassed only by just a handful of countries) and development assistance on a per capita or per person basis in the donor country (for which no international goal has been set). The data in this table are for high-per-capita-income, capital-rich donor countries with the largest economies—the Group of Seven countries that have the highest GNPs—as well as other relatively high-per-capita-income, capital-rich countries, albeit with economies smaller in aggregate size.

	Total ODA (US$ Millions)	ODA as % of GNI	ODA (US $/Person in Donor Country)
Group of Seven			
United States	19,750	0.17	67
Japan	8,922	0.19	70
Germany	7,534	0.28	91
France	8,473	0.41	137
Italy	2,462	0.15	43
United Kingdom	7,883	0.36	131
Canada	2,599	0.27	81
Other Donor Countries			
Australia	1,460	0.25	73
Belgium	1,463	0.41	141
Denmark	2,037	0.85	377
Luxembourg	236	0.83	524
Netherlands	4,204	0.73	258
Norway	2,199	0.87	477
Spain	2,437	0.24	56
Sweden	2,722	0.78	302
Switzerland	1,545	0.41	210

Source: www.undp.org, UN Development Programme data.

peasants high-heeled shoes. Nomads of northwestern Kenya, long pestered by poorly planned charitable projects, refer to their own government as well as foreign aid workers as *ngimoi* ("the enemy"). Third, wars often destroy the best-laid development plans. Finally, there is no doubt that corruption, incompetence, and poor economic policies have squandered large amounts of donor cash.

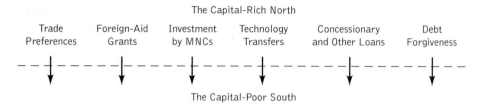

FIGURE 12.2

Foreign Sources of Capital: A New International Economic Order (NIEO)?

The arrows in the figure depict the direction of net capital flows preferred by less-developed countries in the South. Critics note that net capital flows, in fact, often move in the opposite direction when MNCs send their profits or return on investments back to the North, when countries in the South run negative trade balances and must repay their loans (often at market rates) and owners of capital in the South choose to invest in the North, where they expect to realize greater returns.

Yet all is not hopeless. Botswana, for example, gained independence in 1966. At the time, one British official rather undiplomatically termed it "a useless piece of territory." Foreign aid initially kept the new government going. Then diamonds were found in the desert, but the government did not squander its newfound wealth. Profits were plowed into infrastructure, education, and health care. Foreign investment was welcomed, and private business was allowed to flourish. Aid projects proceeded only if it were likely they would provide sustainable development. In succeeding decades, Botswana's economy grew at one of the fastest rates in the world. A key reason was the fact that government ministers were for the most part honest and competent. As the economy slowly diversified, aid donors began to look for other, needier recipients.

Loans

In addition to loans by government, banks, and nongovernmental organizations, a conventional source of capital has been the World Bank. Formally named the International Bank for Reconstruction and Development (IBRD), the institution was established along with the International Monetary Fund (IMF) at an international conference at Bretton Woods, New Hampshire, in 1944. The World Bank's immediate post–World War II goal was economic recovery and reconstruction of major European and Asian economies devastated by the war. Located in Washington, DC, next to the IMF, the World Bank's focus since the 1950s and 1960s has been on loans for economic development to capital-poor countries. The World Bank's capital comes from contributions—a multilateral form of foreign assistance by capital-rich member countries that want to use this institution as a vehicle for lending to less-developed countries. In addition to loans at near-market rates, the World Bank engages in extensive lending at concessionary, below-market-interest rates to capital-poor countries through its affiliate, the International Development Association (IDA). World Bank loans for private-sector projects in developing countries are made through its International Finance Corporation (IFC) affiliate.

To facilitate lending and direct investment to countries where investors fear takeover of their assets by nationalization (expropriation) or face political instability or other political risks, the Multilateral Investment Guarantee Agency (MIGA) is an investment-insurance affiliate that provides political-risk insurance programs. Disputes between governments and private investors can also be submitted for mediation or conciliation to the World Bank's International Center for Settlement of Investment Disputes (ICSID).

Regional lending for development also occurs through such separate international organizations as the Inter-American Development Bank (IADB), Asian Development Bank, African Development Bank, and now the North American Development Bank. Privately held investment banks are also participants, often benefiting from research on investment projects undertaken by multilateral institutions.[4]

Payments of interest and principal on loans to foreign governments or banks can constitute a substantial drain on capital, particularly if developing countries have borrowed too heavily. When global interest rates take a significant turn upward, additional strain is placed on developing countries trying to service (make payments on) existing debt or refinancing and securing new loans. Countries facing financial difficulties, perhaps in danger of being forced to default on their loan payments, often seek debt forgiveness.

Failing that, they ask for cooperation from governments or international or private lending institutions as they try to reschedule or refinance these obligations with new long-term loans at concessionary, below-market interest rates. Such concessionary loans are really a form of grant aid because interest earned from a proportion of the loan invested at higher market rates can actually be used to service the loan. Debtor countries do have some leverage over their lenders, however. Because lenders stand to lose all if borrowers default, the former are usually willing to accommodate reasonable requests from the latter, particularly if these concessions give some assurance that the loan eventually will be repaid.

Direct Foreign Investment

Multinational corporations (MNCs), investment firms, and international banks seeking profits or returns on investment are a third source of capital. In terms of multinational corporations, direct foreign investment may involve building a foreign subsidiary whose assets are controlled by the parent company. Annual revenues of many MNCs are larger than the GDPs of many states.

---

nationalization (expropriation) ■
Governments taking private property for public ownership or use. Under international law such seizures should be nondiscriminatory and accompanied by fair compensation.

---

[4]Inter-American Development Bank (www.IADB.org), Asian Development Bank (www.adb.org), African Development Bank (www.afdb.org), and North American Development Bank (www.nadb.org).

MNCs are also a potential source for the transfer of technologies they use in their production processes if carried out in developing countries. Of course, proprietary interests of the MNCs often lead them to maximize their profits while minimizing technology transfers. Nevertheless, they are an important source of capital as well as training for domestic labor forces.

Continuing and seemingly endless debate goes on between MNC advocates, who see these corporations as well as domestic firms providing jobs and contributing substantially to development, and those who contest this view, seeing MNCs as essentially predatory, engaging in whatever levels of exploitation governments and local elites will tolerate. Critics claim that one reason MNCs organize their operations multinationally is to avoid taxes and circumvent obstacles or barriers imposed by particular states. Nevertheless, private direct investment, portfolio investment (purchase of stock), and bank lending continue to account for substantial sums of capital investment in developing countries.

Trade

Aside from aid, loans, investment, and occasionally debt forgiveness and technology transfers, trade preferences have been a key element of the agenda for a New International Economic Order (NIEO) advanced by developing countries in the South and articulated over several decades in the UN Conferences on Trade and Development (UNCTAD) and in other forums. Efforts that began in the 1960s and 1970s to build an NIEO looked for ways to bridge the great North–South divide. It is not surprising that the General Assembly was at the core of NIEO efforts because less-developed countries have had a controlling majority there after decolonization, and the creation of new states in Africa and Asia in the 1960s tipped the balance of votes in that chamber toward the South.

In a challenge to Ricardian free-trade theory as a basis for policy, discontent in less-developed countries was expressed concerning the uneven or asymmetric distribution of wealth created through free trade—an arrangement that critics claimed clearly favored the North. For one thing, the terms of trade between exporters favor the North's manufactured and higher-technology goods and services over the single-commodity agricultural or mineral exports or relatively low-technology manufactured goods offered by most developing countries. Prices for these exports from less-developed countries barely hold their own or tend to decline over time. By contrast, First World manufactured and higher-technology goods and services tend to hold their own or increase in price over time.

Hence, the South has sought trade preferences from the North as part of the NIEO. The argument is that beginning or infant industries in the South may need the protection of tariffs or other barriers to trade until they have grown sufficiently to be competitive in global markets. At the same time, these countries do not want advanced industrial or postindustrial societies to discriminate against exports from less-developed countries by imposing trade barriers against them. Developing countries, in effect, have argued for unfettered access to First World markets for their exports, without fear of reprisal if in the early stages of industrialization they are allowed to discriminate against First World exports. In point of fact, the value of annual agricultural subsidies in rich nations is substantially

trade preferences ◼ special arrangements allowing easy access on a cost-competitive basis by a foreign producer to a country's domestic market

terms of trade ◼ ratio of export prices of one country to those of another, which in effect tells us the amount of revenue from a country's export sales to the other that can be used to pay for imports from the other

CASE Critics claim that by operating in different countries, multinational corporations (MNCs) avoid paying taxes on their profits or, at least, reduce the amount they have to pay. This case takes up one way they do it—transfer pricing that minimizes MNC tax liability in countries with higher tax rates.

It is fair to say that since the end of World War II, the most controversial aspect of international political economy has been the rise of the multinational corporation. Some see MNCs as eventually superseding the nation-state, muting nationalism by providing economic benefits to all. Others view MNCs as rapacious imperialists, exploiting the weak and poor in their quest for greater profits. The truth is somewhere in between these two views. In direct, open conflict between MNCs and the state, the state will in principle generally prevail, as it always has the option of closing down the corporation's operations. MNCs realize this and prefer to avoid such confrontations. Conflict between states and MNCs, therefore, tends to be more subtle and is usually reported on the business page, not the front page, of daily newspapers.

To illustrate potential conflict between a state and a multinational corporation, consider the following scenario. XYZ Corporation's automobile assembly plant subsidiary in the country of Ruralia needs to import engines, computer parts, and other higher-technology components manufactured in XYZ subsidiaries located in more industrially developed countries.

As it turns out, there is a difference in tax rates on profits in these countries. Because XYZ Corporation is a rational actor that tries to maximize its gains (or minimize its losses), the corporation can be expected to reduce its tax exposure—maximizing legally the amount of profit it makes in countries with lower tax rates. It may choose to do this through transfer pricing—increasing or decreasing the prices its subsidiaries charge each other for components.

Its assembly plant is in low-tax, less-developed Ruralia, a country chosen both because of its relatively low taxes and its abundant supply of relatively unskilled, lower-cost labor. The local government has intentionally set the tax rate low to attract investment by multinational corporations as part of its own economic development plan.

Although the Ruralian government would like XYZ Corporation to put in more than just an assembly plant, it recognizes that at least the assembly plant will employ a substantial number of Ruralians who would not otherwise have these jobs. Opponents who see XYZ and other multinational corporations as exploiting local labor, damaging the environment, or imposing foreign cultural preferences on Ruralians are not as strong politically as local investors and businesses that favor the plant. Some of these interests will participate in the venture directly, whereas others expect to gain indirectly due to the plant's positive contribution to local economic growth. The argument in favor of XYZ is that foreign investment contributes to a rising tide that raises all ships.

Thus, notwithstanding some domestic opposition, XYZ's investment in an assembly plant is compatible with both corporate and state objectives. In short, XYZ Corporation and the Ruralia government are rational (or purposive) actors seeking to make a good business deal. One side may get the better deal, but both see the investment as a potential or expected gain.

Manufacturing computers, carburetors, or other engine components that involve higher technologies, by contrast, requires greater capital investment in machinery, employing relatively fewer but higher-skilled and higher-paid workers than those needed for assembly plants. Countries like Industritania with higher-skilled and higher-paid labor forces are often higher-tax countries as well.

In this circumstance, the corporation's internal sale prices of computers, carburetors, or other engine components needed by the assembly plant subsidiary in Ruralia are set legally at or near cost, thus minimizing profit from producing these components in the high-tax country. Setting lower prices also

(continued)

reduces the tariff or tax that must be paid on the value of components imported by the assembly plant subsidiary in Ruralia, which has relatively high tariffs to protect its new, emergent industries as they compete in global markets.

When the automobiles have been assembled in Ruralia, they are sold or exported at market prices. Because components were imported so cheaply, and labor and other production costs were also held down, profit as the difference between revenue from sales and the overall costs of production is maximized in Ruralia and minimized in Industritania. Because of liberal capital outflow rules, XYZ Corporation spends some of its gain on new investment in Ruralia but moves most of it out of the country, using some to finance investments in other subsidiaries and repatriating (or bringing home) the rest to its corporate headquarters to pay corporate shareholders and other stakeholders.

In this example, Industritania lost tax revenue on profits: Had components manufactured there been exported at market prices well above cost, revenues would have been higher. XYZ Corporation can expect the Industritanian government to object, particularly if XYZ exports components to its Ruralia subsidiary below production cost, thus avoiding payment of any tax at all to Industritania. On the other hand, Ruralia gains by having more profits to tax, even though its tax rate remains low.

POINT When their interests diverge, governments may try through policy, law, and regulation to control multinational corporate operations. The complexity of financial transactions such as transfer pricing among subsidiaries of the same corporation in several countries makes regulation extraordinarily difficult. Moreover, if the corporation finds the local government too hostile, it may choose to close its plants and take operations elsewhere. ◀

greater—as much or more than three times the yearly aid flow to poor countries, which, in effect, allows First World producers to compete unfairly with unsubsidized producers in less-developed countries. Worse yet, the most protected industries in high-income economies tend to include agriculture and textiles, precisely those sectors in which many poor countries are most competitive.

Foreign-exchange earnings that come from exports can be used to purchase capital goods from the advanced industrial and postindustrial economies that produce them. Indeed, trade balances favorable to a less-developed country are an important source of capital that can be invested for economic development purposes. By contrast, when developing countries continue to run negative trade balances, capital that could have been invested in their domestic economies is drained off. That is why favorable terms of trade and trade preferences are so important, particularly to developing countries trying to acquire capital for industrial or other economic development.

Special trade arrangements have in fact been made and preferences granted, most notably under agreements known as the Lomé Conventions (named for negotiations conducted in the African country of Togo) by European Union members with less-developed "ACP" countries in Africa, the Caribbean, and the Pacific, many of which are former colonies of European powers. Critics have been quick to claim that these trade concessions, although of some benefit to the South, also effectively tie these states to the former colonial powers in what amount to neocolonial relations that work to the net advantage of Europe.

transfer pricing ■ accounting mechanism used by multinational corporations to minimize overall tax liability by purposely setting import or export prices of product components (produced in one subsidiary and exported to a subsidiary in another country) to show low or no profit for their subsidiaries operating in higher-tax countries

cartel ■ an association among financial, commodity-producing, or industrial interests, including states, for establishing a national or international market control, setting production levels, and increasing or stabilizing the prices of such diverse products as oil, tin, and coffee

One approach to securing more favorable terms of trade is to form a **cartel** or joint arrangement that allows member states to influence the price of a commodity by regulating its supply to the world market. Efforts to form cartels among coffee producers and tin or other agricultural and mineral exporters have been relatively unsuccessful due to the difficulty of enforcing compliance with cartel production targets and quotas. The ready availability of substitute suppliers outside of cartel arrangements has compounded these difficulties. Moreover, a rising price for one mineral or agricultural product may lead consumers to substitute and import another, less-expensive product. If coffee becomes too high in price, for example, some consumers may switch to tea.

One exception to this generally negative record for cartels, at least for a few years, was the Organization of Petroleum Exporting Countries (OPEC), a cartel that was successful in substantially raising the world price of oil in the 1970s. These oil shocks, as they were called, immediately and dramatically improved the terms of trade of cartel members; however, the industrial world's heavy dependence on imported oil at ever-higher prices significantly raised overall costs of production in oil-buying countries and thus contributed to fueling inflation on a global scale. Efforts were undertaken to find new oil supplies and to develop alternative energy sources. Powerful First World countries also brought great pressures to bear on those OPEC members they could influence.

The dollar price of oil was relatively static in the 1980s and 1990s, actually declining in real terms when we take inflation into account. Until recently, the OPEC cartel thus had not been as successful in keeping prices up as in its early years. Why not? First, rivalry among OPEC members and a desire to produce more oil for export than allowed by cartel agreements kept OPEC production targets higher than they might have been and effectively added enough oil to world supplies to keep prices from rising. Due in part to its security and economic relations with the United States and other Western countries, Saudi Arabia (which has the world's largest oil reserves) has remained committed to maintaining an ample supply to world markets. Second, development of oil fields under the North Sea between Britain and Norway, at Prudhoe Bay in northern Alaska, in the Caribbean, and in the central Asia–Caspian Sea area have added to world oil supplies. Third, although aggregate demand for oil continued to increase over the decades, it was less than what it would have been thanks to some development of alternative energy sources and energy-efficiency measures.

More recently, however, growing demand in fast-growing economies like China and India, coupled with political turmoil and consequent uncertainties in the Middle East from North Africa to the Persian Gulf, have absorbed surplus oil in global markets and put great upward pressure on the market price of oil. The cartel did not increase oil production enough to meet increased demand, and, as a result, OPEC countries gained substantially from the increased price of oil as did the companies producing and marketing it to purchasers around the world.

A great frustration for many in less-developed countries, therefore, is the degree to which they are caught in a seemingly inescapable structure of dependency on capital-rich First World countries. There seems to be no escape. Adverse terms of trade are difficult to reverse, and producing qualitative manufactures that will compete favorably with those produced by firms in technology-endowed and

CASE & POINT | The Internet and the Developing World

CASE An important reflection of globalization is the spread of global communication. The internet epitomizes this global connectivity. But what about the developing world? Developing countries lack easy access to computers, infrastructure to support their use, and skilled users. Does the internet therefore represent yet another technological advancement that leaves the poorest of the world even further behind? As a result of the Rio Conference in 1992, the UN Development Programme (UNDP) launched the Sustainable Development Networking Programme (SDNP) designed to help bridge the information gap between the haves and have-nots. The program was met with much initial skepticism both within and outside the United Nations. How, it was asked, does information technology aid sustainable development? How does one get illiterate farmers from their field to a computer? The answer is, "You don't," but that's hardly the way to look at how and why the internet matters.

The key intermediaries are NGOs that pass on useful information to farmers. In Mexico, for example, the SDNP established an information center for corn producers where farmers learned online what the market price of corn is in the capital. The goal was to help them avoid underselling their crops. Similar information centers were established in Jamaica, Guatemala, Honduras, Costa Rica, and elsewhere.

POINT With the benefit of hindsight, we can now see how farsighted delegates were at the 1992 Rio meeting. Global communications among buyers and sellers, investors and entrepreneurs, lenders and borrowers, producers and consumers all depend on the internet, which now is very much a part of the sustainable-development project worldwide.

capital-rich countries is a formidable task. Some newly industrializing countries (NICs)—for example, South Korea, Taiwan, Singapore, Hong Kong (now part of China), and Brazil—have been able to break into world markets for manufactured goods or such technology-intensive services as banking and insurance by combining substantial domestic capital formation, imported technologies, and access to a lower-wage but skilled and conscientious labor force. As noted above, the BRIC countries (Brazil, Russia, India, and China) have had the greatest impact during the last decade, the economies of South Africa and Indonesia also expanding rapidly.

Most developing countries have not been so successful, as their domestic firms find it difficult to compete in global trading markets or are shut out of rich countries that protect their agricultural and textile industries. Some have formed regional free-trading areas and other arrangements[5] such as the Economic Community of West African States (ECOWAS) among lower-income countries in West Africa, the Southern Cone Common Market (MERCOSUR) in South America, the

---

[5]Regional associations include the Andean Group (www.itcilo.it), Asia-Pacific Economic Cooperation (www.apec.org), Association of Southeast Asian Nations (www.asean.org), Caribbean Community and Common Market (www.caricom.org), Economic Community of West African States (www.cedeao.org), European Union (europa.eu.int; in the United States, www.eurunion.org), Mercosur (Common Market Southern Cone, South America: www.mercosur.com), and the North American Free Trade Association (www.nafta-sec-alena.org). UN-affiliated economic commissions also work to advance trade and other commercial relations—Africa (Addis Ababa: www.un.org/Depts/eca), Asia and the Pacific (Bangkok: www.unescap.org), Europe (Geneva: www.unece.org), and Latin America (Santiago: www.ecla.org)

SLIDESHOW | Land, Labor, Capital

Despite technological developments, labor-intensive agriculture remains critical to food production in developing countries.

Aside from land and labor, the provision of capital is required to facilitate economic development. This photo depicts a trading room at the Dubai International Financial Center in the United Arab Emirates.

Capital and technology come together in the production and international sale of modern harvesters. Such machinery is not always affordable or appropriate in those cases where the result is to displace agricultural workers and disrupt land tenure patterns that provide employment to the poor.

Skilled labor in conjunction with capital is reflected in the establishment of manufacturing subsidiaries of multinational corporations. Thousands of garment workers are employed to work sewing machines in the large-scale Sepal Group factory in Bangladesh to make clothing for the American designer Tommy Hilfiger. Other U.S. companies, such as Wal-Mart, have also outsourced production of clothing to factories in Bangladesh.

Andean Group, the Caribbean Community and Common Market (CARICOM), the Central American Common Market (CACM), and the Association of Southeast Asian Nations (ASEAN). For its part, Mexico has joined the United States and Canada, two First World countries with about ten times its per capita income, in a North American Free Trade Agreement (NAFTA). Given these economic asymmetries in levels of development, Mexico has faced substantial difficulties, as reflected in its having to defend the peso, its currency, with heavy foreign borrowings from time to time. Mexico's hope, of course, is that NAFTA will continue to be a means of access to capital and to the huge, relatively wealthy Canadian and American markets for selling its goods and services now and over the long term.

SUSTAINING DEVELOPMENT

12.3 Explain how population growth, resource depletion and environmental degradation, the absence of effective health care, excessive military spending and war can undermine development efforts.

As we have seen, there are a number of sources for capital available to many developing countries. But if the solution to global poverty and underdevelopment was simply the provision or generation of more capital for investment, the challenge, though daunting, would seem to be achievable. Why, despite all of the aid, loans, foreign investment, and trade preferences, have so many less-developed states still been unable to make much headway against underdevelopment? A number of possible interrelated factors that impinge directly on economic prosperity deal with the domestic and regional issues faced by these states. We will examine the following: population growth, resource depletion and environmental degradation, health care, excessive military spending, and war.

Population Growth

Economies that grow depend on a continuing investment of capital. Populations that grow too fast consume whatever surplus would have been produced for capital investment. Planners who want to lift the capacities of less-developed political economies to provide a better level of living for their peoples seek to reduce birth rates even as improved medical and health conditions also reduce death rates.

Parson Thomas Robert Malthus (1766–1834), a religious man of the cloth, spent much of his professional life studying systematically and writing extensively about human population growth in relation to the societal problem of feeding these geometrically increasing numbers of people. According to Malthus, "Population, when unchecked, increases in a geometrical ratio. Subsistence [i.e., food] increases only in an arithmetical ratio." Put another way, in the absence of measures that might be taken to slow its rate of growth, population tends to outpace the food production necessary to sustain the whole of humanity.

Indeed, his "Essay on the Principle of Population" (1798) and his restatement or "Summary" provided in 1830 foreshadowed present-day efforts to achieve sustainable development. The challenge is to draw from the Earth resources necessary for increasing levels of production and improved human well-being while, at the same time, avoiding resource depletion and environmental degradation that, in turn, will undermine capacity for further production. The application of technology to agriculture, particularly in capital-rich countries, has extended the food-production limits of which Malthus wrote so pessimistically; however, the

---

👁 **Watch** the **Video** **"Go Slows in Lagos"** at **mypoliscilab.com**

resource depletion
■ reduction or exhaustion of nonrenewable resources

environmental degradation
■ pollution or destruction of land, air, and waterways

21st-century world as a whole does still suffer from widespread malnutrition (and even starvation), found today primarily in capital-poor countries.

Since development planners seek to improve the level of living, the quality of life, and longevity, they seek acceptable ways to curb birthrates and thus slow population growth, particularly in less-developed countries where increases in population easily can outstrip the economic growth needed to provide food, shelter, clothing, and other goods and services. Religious and cultural preferences constrain the choices of birth control method both as a matter of individual choice or of national policy.

China's controversial "one child per family" policy—its enforcement now somewhat more relaxed—has reduced birthrates, particularly in urban areas where the Communist Party and government have greater sway. The means used to stay within these limits go beyond contraceptives and medication to include abortion and, in many cases, even resorting to infanticide. The killing of newborns, particularly girls—a clear violation of human rights anywhere—is by no means government policy, but rather is an unintended consequence of limiting the number of live births in a society that has a long-established cultural preference for a family to have at least one boy succeed his father and mother.

Those who by whatever means have complied with the government's one-child policy now have to cope with the absence of centralized social-security systems outside of extended family-support networks to sustain them in old age. Indeed, a principal reason for large and extended families—still more prevalent among the peasantry living in the countryside—is the security one gets from knowing one's children have a family and culturally established obligation to respect and care for their elders. Given the smaller size of Chinese families than historically has been the case, an economically even more developed China will have more resources than before to establish the equivalent of the Medicare, Medicaid, and Social Security pension systems one finds in the United States and other countries that moved in the 20th century away from the nuclear family as the sole means of support for aging parents.

Substantial progress has been made to curb annual growth rates as high as 3 percent or more in the 1960s, now trimmed to less than 2 percent in most countries. Nevertheless, populations have continued to grow at a very rapid rate in many less-developed countries. With a 3 percent growth rate, population doubles in just about a quarter-century, but a 2 percent growth rate slows this doubling time to about three and a half decades. By contrast, population is actually declining in some First World countries. The 0.6 percent average growth rate in the First World taken as a whole means that it will take a much longer time—some 120 years—to double their numbers at this relatively slow rate.

A 1994 UN conference held in Cairo on population issues and economic development was part of an international consensus-building process that included governmental representatives of UN member states, UN and other international organizations' delegates and staff members, and representatives of numerous non-governmental organizations (NGOs). Significant differences of view on what was to be done were readily apparent. The Chinese policy of one child per family discussed above was scrutinized closely by those concerned that enforcement could easily violate human rights, particularly should violators face punitive sanctions or even forced sterilization. Many delegates preferred an approach focusing on empowering women by educating them in the use of contraceptives, medications, and other birth-control devices. Another objective for many was to make birth-control technologies readily available free of charge or at relatively low cost. A separate NGO forum was also attended by almost 4,000 individuals representing 200 nongovernmental organizations.

So what is to be done from a policymaker's perspective? For those who accept family planning as legitimate, are decisions best left to men, women, or both? The obvious answer is both. Vasectomy is a choice many men make, particularly in First World countries, but forced sterilization or government incentives to undergo the procedure for national population-growth policy reasons (as has occurred in India, China, and elsewhere) is offensive to many on moral, human-rights, and legal grounds. Thus, a number of efforts to curb population growth focus primarily on women—educating them on the pros and cons of various options and providing the contraceptives and medications they may need either free or at an affordable cost.

Empowering women has greater likelihood of achieving population-growth goals, but faces enormous obstacles, particularly in many male-dominated, less-developed countries. Since such family-planning support by governments often runs into political opposition, the task often falls to international and nongovernmental organizations not as constrained as governments sometimes are.

Slower-growing (but also better-educated and trained) populations, coupled with substantial capital investment, are key ingredients in the recipe for economic development and continued growth for any economy. Success in curbing population growth removes a significant obstacle or impediment to economic development. As will be discussed below, excessive military spending, engaged in by many less-developed countries, also drains important resources that could be used for more productive economic-development purposes.

Environment

Relatively unconstrained efforts to achieve rapid economic growth can undermine the continued sustainability of economic development. The sheer size of populations in countries now industrializing magnifies the environmental impact of economic development. The adverse environmental impact of industrialization seen in First World societies with populations in the millions when the industrialization process was well under way in the 19th and early 20th centuries can be expected on an even greater scale of damage if China (with more than 1.3 billion people) and India (with some 1.1 billion people) continue to follow the same approach to industrialization in the first decades of the 21st century as they did in the last half of the 20th century.

In addition to bearing the burden of soaring population, agricultural productivity can be destroyed through erosion and misuse of fertilizers, water supplies can be contaminated, and other forms of pollution can wreak havoc on agricultural and other forms of production.

Resource depletion; reduction of wildlife, fishery, and seafood stocks; and other forms of environmental degradation can make continued production unsustainable even at present levels. In northern Africa, desertification continues. Arable land goes out of production as populations increase. These issues were at the core of UN-sponsored meetings in Rio de Janeiro in 1992 and at follow-on meetings attended by representatives of governments and international organizations. About 17,000 individuals, including 2,400 representatives of NGOs, held separate but simultaneous meetings in Rio on these same environmental and sustainable development issues. Subsequent conventions and programs have been instituted under UN auspices. We take up these environmental challenges at greater length in Chapter 14, "The Environment."

Health

It is truly ironic that, as some developing countries worry about the danger of overpopulation to economic viability and quality of life, other countries fear the opposite—a precipitous decline in population due to the alarming increase in infectious diseases, which account for almost half of mortality in developing countries. In some cases the disease is relatively new (AIDS), while in other cases the diseases are reemerging (tuberculosis, malaria and other insect-borne infections). What is frightening to many scientists and doctors is the rapid growth in the number of infectious diseases apparently resistant to antimicrobial drugs. This is not simply a problem for developing countries. Given the speed, ease, and volume of international trade and travel, diseases such as SARS have become a true hallmark of globalization.

The global HIV/AIDS epidemic has killed 25 million people. Though curbed significantly in First World countries by access to drugs, it continues to plague the poorest countries, particularly in sub-Saharan Africa—the region accounting for some three-quarters of the global population living with HIV/AIDS. As adults are struck down and children are orphaned, villages become ghost towns, and economic productivity plummets at the same time overburdened and underfunded clinics and rudimentary health care programs attempt to deal with the disaster. Yet there is some hope. In southern Africa in 2005 the disease killed 2.1 million people. In 2009 the number dropped to 1.8 million. Approximately 5 million lives have been saved by drug treatment.[6]

The death toll caused by malaria in Africa, though significant, is not as high as that caused by AIDS. But, in the memorable words of a Tanzanian researcher, it is equivalent to seven Boeing 747s, filled mostly with children, crashing into Mount Kilimanjaro each day. In the 1950s and 1960s, malarial mosquitoes were in retreat in most of Africa and Asia. It is estimated that hundreds of millions of lives were saved, but the use of the pesticide DDT involved a trade-off, as it also killed millions of birds and animals and poisoned the environment. Malaria seems to be, however, flying underneath the radar in terms of global awareness.

In the case of AIDS, global awareness is high. At a special session of the UN General Assembly in June 2001, members adopted a Declaration of Commitment and time-bound targets to which governments and the United Nations are supposed to be accountable. Approximately two-thirds of the Global Fund to Fight AIDS, Tuberculosis and Malaria goes to fight AIDS. This battle was given a boost when former President George W. Bush, in the 2001 State of the Union speech,

---

[6]"The End of Aids?" *The Economist,* June 4, 2011, p. 11.

pledged $15 billion. NGOs like the Bill and Melinda Gates Foundation have also taken on this challenge. The organization UNAIDS notes that much more money needs to be raised, underscoring the ongoing commitment of resources necessary to meet this challenge. Indeed, so many who could further the development of their countries have been struck down by this plague.

Military Spending and War

Military spending may create employment in the armed forces and the arms industries closely tied to them, but our concern in this chapter is the extent to which it diverts or reallocates resources away from investment for economic development. Technological spinoffs from military spending may benefit the economies of highly developed countries that make these expenditures, but less-developed countries are importers—not producers—of advanced weaponry. Their outlays for arms, in effect, help finance further technological development in First World countries.

Excessive military spending, engaged in by many less-developed countries, thus drains important resources that could be used for more productive economic development purposes. Worse yet, many of the weapons purchased are used in brutal civil wars, military interventions, and conflicts with neighboring states. Most wars now fought are civil wars, and most are in the poorest countries. In almost every case, these wars leave a legacy of persistent poverty and disease in their wake.

Wars also destroy capital, particularly in lands where the combat occurs. Arms sellers may make money from warfare—"merchants of death" to some antiwar critics, part of a military-industrial base essential to national security to others.

TABLE 12.5

Military Expenditure (% of GDP)

It should not be surprising that the Arab world is currently the region with the highest military expenditure as a percent of overall gross domestic product. South Asia includes India and Pakistan, while Europe and Central Asia includes Russia.

Arab world	6.3%
East Asia & Pacific	1.9%
Euro area	1.7%
European Union	1.8%
Europe & Central Asia	3.3%
Latin America & Caribbean	1.5%
Least-developed countries	2.1%
Middle East & North Africa	3.5%
OECD members	2.7%
South Asia	2.6%
Sub-Saharan Africa	1.7%
World	2.6%

Source: data.worldbank.org

The question for us in this chapter, however, is the relation between military spending and development or, more broadly, economic growth. How do you think less-developed countries should try to balance the budgetary demands of defense spending for national security security with the costs of investments necessary for achieving economic development objectives?

Military purchases can be financed when capital is generated domestically (from savings, rather than consuming everything produced) or with revenue from net export earnings (when income received from export sales is greater than what is paid out for imports). If there is insufficient capital available from domestic generation and positive trade balances, capital to finance military purchases has to be borrowed—putting purchasers (typically governments) in the already less-developed countries more deeply into debt, eroding capital, or diverting it from infrastructure and other investment for economic development.

Armaments competition—purchases driven by threats and counterthreats—can draw excessive amounts of national capital and drain precious and often limited monetary reserves in developing countries. Given the high national security stakes at risk should war break out, the arms race continues as each side tries to match or surpass the warmaking capability of the other. When wars finally come to an end, there is new demand for replacement weapons and weapons systems expended during armed conflict.

ECONOMIC-STRUCTURALIST CRITIQUES AND PERSPECTIVES

Liberals and realists of all persuasions may hold differing perspectives as to the utility of aid, loans, investment, trade concessions, technology transfers, and debt forgiveness. But both tend to take for granted the framework within which these economic activities take place—the global capitalist system. There are, however, radical critiques of this system that are theoretically grounded in quite different assumptions and worldviews.

12.4 Evaluate the various economic-structuralist perspectives on the global capitalist system.

👁 Watch the Video "The Bhopal Disaster" at mypoliscilab.com

global capitalist system ■ a focus on class and economic relations and the division of the world into a core, periphery, and semiperiphery

Dependency Theory

Some of the more provocative work in the economic-structuralist tradition was produced by Latin Americans in the 1960s and 1970s. They have come to be referred to collectively as dependency theorists. Several of these writers were associated with the Economic Commission on Latin America (ECLA) and the UN Conference on Trade and Development (UNCTAD). They were concerned with the important problem of explaining why Latin America and other less-developed countries were not developing as had been predicted by mainstream economists. Why wasn't the North American–Western European experience being repeated?

The focus of the ECLA and UNCTAD economists was initially quite narrow. They examined the unequal terms of trade between LDCs that exported raw materials and northern industrialized countries that exported finished manufactured goods. They questioned the supposed benefits of free trade. The ECLA at one point favored the diversification of exports, advising LDCs to produce goods

dependency ■ low-income countries of the South economically subordinated to the advantage of high-income countries of the First World or North; in class-analytical terms, workers and peasants subordinated and exploited by capital-owning classes, the *bourgeoisie*

economic structure ■ class- or other material-based concentration, as in ownership of capital by a *bourgeois* class or its aggregation in capital-rich countries of the North or First World

instead of importing them. This policy did not result in the anticipated amount of success and, in fact, increased the influence of foreign multinational corporations brought in to facilitate domestic production.

Some writers cast their recommendations in terms of nationalism and state-guided capitalism. Others, however, more boldly emphasized political and social factors within the context of a capitalist economic system that binds Latin America to North America. Development, it was argued, is not autonomous. If it occurs at all, it is reflexive—subject to the vagaries and ups and downs of the world's advanced economies. Choices of Latin American countries are restricted or constrained as a result of the dictates of capitalism but also due to supporting political, social, and cultural relations. The result is an economic structure of domination. This multifaceted web of dependency reinforces unequal exchange between the northern and southern parts of the hemisphere. Opportunities for the LDCs are few and far between because LDCs are allocated a subordinate role in world capitalism. Dependency has succinctly been defined as a "situation in which a certain number of countries have their economy conditioned by the development and expansion of another . . . , placing the dependent countries in a backward position exploited by the dominant countries."[7]

Some economic structuralists use Marxist terminology and Leninist insights to explain this situation of dependency. More important than relations between states are transnational class coalitions linking elites in industrially developed countries (the center) with their counterparts in the South (or periphery). This version of class analysis emphasizes how transnational ties within the global bourgeois or capitalist class work to the disadvantage of workers and peasants in the periphery. Multinational corporations and international banks, therefore, are viewed from a much different perspective from that of a realist or liberal. To the liberal, especially "liberal institutionalists," MNCs and international banks appear merely as other, potentially benign, actors. To the realist, they tend to be of secondary importance because of the emphasis on the state-as-actor. To economic structuralists who were part of the dependency perspective, however, they are central players in establishing and maintaining dependency relations.

One doesn't hear as much about dependency theory these days, at least not in the United States. There are a number of reasons. First, empirical studies have shown that terms of trade (the prices of exports relative to those of imports) have not always deteriorated for producers of commodities. Second, critics have raised the question of whether dependency creates social and economic backwardness or whether it is economic and social backwardness that leads to a situation of dependency. In short, there is the issue of causality—whether dependency is the cause of backwardness or whether it is an effect of this condition. Third, some of the protectionist policies engendered by dependency theory were failures, leading to inefficiency and stifled technological progress. Finally, in the 1980s Latin America began a period of trade liberalization policies. Some sectors thrived, others lagged; some countries experienced dramatic growth, others disasters. But under the pressure of

---

[7]Theotonio dos Santos, as cited in J. Samuel Valenzuela and Arturo Valenzuela, "Modernization and Dependency: Alternative Perspectives in the Study of Latin American Underdevelopment," *Comparative Politics* vol. 10, no. 4 (July 1978): 544.

Marxist Perspectives on the Plight of Less-Developed Countries

ARGUMENT-COUNTERARGUMENT |

ARGUMENT   Marxists are not at all surprised by the depressed state of affairs in many less-developed countries. In the Marxist view, the *bourgeoisie* or capitalist class, uses its base in the capital-rich North to reach out to its class allies in the South for new markets in which to sell and new workers and peasants to exploit. In short, the *bourgeoisie* in the North joins with *bourgeois* elements at the top of societies in less-developed countries in exploitative joint ventures. In advanced, global capitalism, older colonial forms of imperialism have been replaced by multinational corporations and banks, the present-day agents of the owners of capital who are able to use neocolonial ties and channels to facilitate their efforts.

Karl Marx (1818–1883), born and reared in Trier in present-day Germany, wrote extensively on political-economic history and the practice of capitalism. Much of his research and writing took place during his stay in London, where he was able to observe firsthand the kind of labor exploitation in early industrial capitalism that also inspired the literary contributions of Charles Dickens. Marx was both a political-economic theorist and a revolutionary who challenged the capitalist or *bourgeois* interests

of his time. Present-day theorists who focus on the South's dependency on the North and the resulting exploitation of peoples in the less-developed countries owe an intellectual debt to Marx, even if they do not share all of Marx's premises.

COUNTERARGUMENT   Marxist analyses oversimplify reality by reducing the complexity of political and economic matters to class and class conflict—artificial constructions that give us a distorted view of how capitalism and capitalist political economy work. Little regard is given to the independent, instrumental roles—collaborative or competitive—played by international and nongovernmental organizations, interest groups, and individuals. Instead, all of these are relegated to being agents of a national or international capital-owning class, the *bourgeoisie*.

APPLICATION   In an era of increasing globalization, what argument can you make that Marxist analysis is becoming increasingly irrelevant as an approach to understanding the world economy? Now make the opposite argument concerning the supposed relevancy of Marxist analysis. ▶

globalization, protectionist policies could not be sustained, and Latin American presidents were active participants in World Trade Organization (WTO) meetings that called for further trade liberalization and the reduction of trade barriers and, more recently, in the new Central American Free Trade Agreement (CAFTA). Nevertheless, critics of these regimes continue to see them as serving U.S. and other First World interests at the expense of less-developed countries. The decline in attention to dependency theory is understandable, they say, since this academic discourse is unpopular in capital-rich countries that object to any critique of neoliberal policies that serve their interests at the expense of capital-poor countries.

bourgeoisie ■
French term used to depict the owners of capital as a class differentiated from other classes—the aristocracy as landowners, workers or peasants defined typically by their labor in factories or on the land, respectively

Capitalist World-System Theory

The dependency theorists pointed the way for scholars who write in what is known as the capitalist world-system perspective. This perspective is another form of economic structuralism that differs from dependency in at least two ways. First, world-system theorists are not only concerned with the lack of development in capital-poor countries, but also wish to understand the economic, political, and social development of regions throughout the entire world. Developed and underdeveloped states, winners and losers, are examined in attempts to explain the global existence of uneven development.

Second, the goal is to understand the fate of various parts of the world at various times in history within the larger context of a developing world political economy. Latin America, for example, is not unique. Its experience is an integral part of the capitalist world-system. The priority is to understand the global system from a historical perspective. Only then can the fates of particular societies or regions of the globe be understood. World-system theorists, therefore, were interested in the nature and effects of globalization long before the end of the Cold War and the subsequent popularization of the term "globalization."

Advocates of this view are not necessarily Marxists, and in fact some adherents differ from classical Marxism in key respects. But world-system theory is essentially grounded in the Marxist conception of social reality because of its emphasis on the primacy of the economic sphere and the role of class struggle. Rather than focusing on domestic class structure, however, the emphasis is on an international hierarchy and the struggle among states and transnational classes.

The writings of Immanuel Wallerstein represent the most ambitious world-system work and have been the catalyst for an extensive amount of subsequent research. In attempting to understand the origins and dynamics of the modern world economy and the existence of worldwide uneven development, he aspires to no less than a historically based theory of global development, which he terms *world-system theory*.[8]

Wallerstein begins by analyzing the emergence of capitalism in Europe, tracing its development into a capitalist world-system that contains a core, a periphery, and a semiperiphery. The core areas historically have engaged in the most advanced economic activities, such as banking, manufacturing, technologically advanced agriculture, and ship building. The periphery has provided raw materials—minerals, timber, and the like—to fuel the core's economic expansion. Unskilled labor is repressed, and the peripheral countries are denied advanced technology in those areas that might make them more competitive with core states. The semiperiphery is involved in a mix of production activities, some associated with core areas and others with peripheral areas. The semiperiphery also serves a number of other functions, such as being an outlet for investment when wages in core economies become too high. Over time, particular countries or regions of the world may gravitate between core, peripheral, and semiperipheral status.

Class structure varies in each zone depending on how the dominant class relates to the world economy. Contrary to the liberal economic notion of specialization based on comparative advantage, this division of labor requires as well as increases inequality between regions. States in the periphery are weak, in that they are unable to control their fates, whereas states in the core are economically,

---

[8]Immanuel Wallerstein, *The Capitalist World-Economy* (Cambridge, Cambridge University Press, 1979).

politically, and militarily dominant. The basic function of the state is to ensure the continuation of the capitalist mode of production.

Given the inexorable nature of capitalism, Wallerstein and his followers were probably less surprised than most theoreticians at the virtual collapse of most of the communist Second World. In a post–Cold War volume, Wallerstein attempts to place the events of 1989–1991 in historical perspective. Liberalism—an ideology he identifies as associated with the capitalist world-system—has served as a "legitimating geoculture." On North–South relations, he depicts the North's wealth as largely "the result of a transfer of surplus value from the South." Vulnerability in a capitalist world economy comes from "a ceaseless accumulation of capital" that approaches its limit "to the point where none of the mechanisms for restoring the normal functioning of the system can work effectively any longer." Grossly unequal distribution of material gains contributes to multiple strains in the world-system and undermines state structures, notably "their ability to maintain order in a world of widespread civil warfare, both global and state level."[9] Hence Wallerstein sees a direct connection between the continual deepening of global capitalism, crises of political authority, and increased conflict.

CONCLUSION

Fostering economic growth and sustaining economic development on a global scale will remain formidable challenges throughout the coming decades. Some have suggested that we must redefine development needs to be more consistent with quality-of-life criteria rather than a seemingly never-ending quest for economic growth. Whether economic well-being, the environment, social justice, human rights, the natural environment, and the overall improvement of the human condition can be served at lower economic growth rates is not altogether clear. It is indeed a tall order. Yet as noted at the outset of this chapter, committed individuals such as Padre Ricardo Sammon can make a difference, even in the face of political obstacles. Individual practitioners of international relations and world politics do not necessarily have to follow the path of Padre Sammon but can make contributions in any number of ways, whether working for a government, international organizations, or nongovernmental organizations including religious institutions and programs.

From the perspective of images of international relations and world politics, realists recognize the reality of poverty in less-developed countries and the developmental gap between North and South. Most doubt, however, that this gap in itself will be a major cause of international conflict, the primary realist concern. It is still national power and the relative power position of states that matters most to realists. Thus, development is important to the extent that it alters the distribution of power—the "pecking order" among states. Furthermore, if developmental problems are to be mitigated, then it will be states that will take the lead and be the final arbiters of whatever global policies are devised. International

---

[9]Immanuel Wallerstein, *After Liberalism* (New York: New Press, 1995).

organizations and nongovernmental organizations can play a role, but only states have the requisite economic clout to improve the situation.

Liberals (including liberal institutionalists), given their pluralist, cosmopolitan view of world politics, usually have a greater interest in international political economy than do most realists, at least in relation to less-developed countries. For them, states tend to think in terms of short- and medium-term objectives lacking a longer time horizon. This is where international organizations such as the United Nations and nongovernmental organizations can play a role by institutionalizing the longer-term interests of states.

✓•—Study and Review the Post-Test & Chapter Exam at mypoliscilab.com

Economic structuralists are most at home with issues of global development—focusing as they do on exploitative relations they observe at play in the postcolonial, capitalist world-system. Their major contribution has been to highlight an alternative to theoretical perspectives offered by realists and liberals on the development of the global political economy. When development is placed in historical context, provocative arguments are put forward that draw our attention to alternative ways of interpreting the poverty of the vast majority of humanity. It is this global poverty, of course, that remains one of the most significant 21st-century challenges as both capital-rich and capital-poor countries proceed down the paths of what they hope will be sustainable development.

LEARNING OBJECTIVES REVIEW

12.1 Illustrate how the differences between capital-rich and capital-poor, less-economically developed countries contribute to the uneven levels of development found around the world.

As capitalism has become ever more global, aggregate production and trade of goods and services have expanded dramatically, but their distribution remains uneven both globally as well as within countries—many are decidedly better off, but many more are still living in varying degrees of poverty.

KEY TERMS

Developing world 420
Third World or South 420
Sustainable development 421
Barter 423
Investments 423

ADDITIONAL READINGS

Reducing Global Poverty (2009), *Global Education* (2010), and *Improving Global Health* (2011). These volumes have been published by Oxford University Press in an ongoing series on *Patterns of Human Progress* edited by Barry Hughes, Dale Rothman, Randall Kuhn, and other colleagues in or in association with the Pardee Center on International Futures at the University of Denver.

UN Development Programme's *Human Development Report* and the World Bank's *World Development Report* provide statistical data. Both are published annually by Oxford University Press and are available on the Web.

Robert J. C. Young, *Postcolonialism: A Very Short Introduction* (Oxford, UK: Oxford University Press, 2003) provides an overview on postcolonial understandings. See also Sankaran Krishna, *Globalization and Postcolonialism: Hegemony and Resistance in the Twenty-first Century* (Lanham, MD: Rowman and Littlefield, 2009).

12.2 Identify the sources of capital sought by developing countries upon which their development depends.

Capital-poor countries look to the capital-rich countries for a better deal—foreign aid grants, loans at concessionary or below-market rates, trade preferences favoring their exports, multinational corporate investment, technology transfers, and debt forgiveness. As a practical matter, efforts by capital-rich countries have been less than many had hoped would be the case.

KEY TERMS

Factors of production 425
Capital formation 425

Concessionary rates 425
Nationalization (expropriation) 430
Trade preferences 431
Terms of trade 431
Transfer pricing 432
Cartel 434

ADDITIONAL READING

Howard Handelman, *Challenge of Third World Development*, 6th ed. (New York: Pearson Longman, 2010). Among other issues, the book explores economic growth and poverty, global warming, ethnic conflict, democratization, and the roles women play in a changing Third-World context.

12.3 Explain how population growth, resource depletion and environmental degradation, the absence of effective health care, excessive military spending, and war can undermine development efforts.

Increasing populations and expanding military establishments both consume more and more of the goods and services produced, thus reducing any surplus that could be invested for development purposes. Rapid industrialization and other development projects not only may deplete scarce resources, but also degrade the environment, undermining further growth. Poor health and nutrition standards render populations less productive economically, particularly since they often lack the education and skills essential to economic development.

KEY TERMS

Resource depletion 438
Environmental degradation 438

ADDITIONAL READINGS

Nancy Birdsall, Allen C. Kelley, and Steven Sinding (eds.), *Population Matters: Demographic Change, Economic Growth, and Poverty in the Developing World* (Oxford, UK: Oxford University Press, 2003). Examines population growth in relation to development.

Chandra Talpade Mohanty, Ann Russo, and Lourdes Torres (eds.), *Third World Women and the Politics of Feminism* (Bloomington, IN: Indiana University Press, 1991) and Ligaya Lindio-McGovern and Isidor Wallimann (eds.), *Globalization and Third World Women: Exploitation, Coping and Resistance* (Farnham, UK: Ashgate, 2009). Women play a decisive role in the economic and social development of capital-poor countries.

Rachel Stohl and Suzette Grillot, *The International Arms Trade* (Cambridge, UK: Polity, 2009). Analyzes the global arms trade in which Third World countries are so much a part.

Michael T. Klare, *Resource Wars: The New Landscape of Global Conflict* (New York: Henry Holt/Owl Books, 2001) and Tim Lang and Michael Heasman, *Food Wars: The Global Battle for Mouths, Minds and Markets* (London and Sterling, VA: Earthscan, 2004). Both examine armed conflicts.

Kelley Lee, *The World Health Organization* (New York: Routledge, 2008). United Nations efforts to manage global health and coping with disease.

Dean T. Jamison et al. (eds.), *Disease and Mortality in Sub-Saharan Africa* (Washington, DC: World Bank Publications, 2006). Commentary on health and infectious diseases in the world's poorest continent.

12.4 Evaluate the various economic-structuralist perspectives on the global capitalist system.

Some say Marxist analyses were dismissed too quickly as communist regimes collapsed at the end of the Cold War. To these scholars and practitioners, the uneven distribution of capital—its increasing concentration in a few hands at the expense of the many—is precisely what economic structuralists have said would happen. Globalization to these critics is no more nor less than the 20th- and 21st-century manifestation of continued exploitation, whether characterized as capital vs. labor or capital-rich countries vs. the capital poor.

KEY TERMS

Global capitalist system 443
Dependency 443

Economic structure 444
Bourgeoisie 445

ADDITIONAL READINGS

Immanuel Wallerstein, *World-Systems Analysis: An Introduction* (Durham, NC: Duke University Press Books, 2004). A good place to start on economic-structuralist understandings of global capitalism in relation to the developing world.

Richard Peet and Elaine Hartwick, *Theories of Development: Contentions, Arguments, Alternatives*, 2nd ed. (New York: Guilford Press, 2009). Overview of diverse understandings of the development challenge.

CHAPTER REVIEW

1. Some experts argue that the current world economy is not negatively structured against less-developed countries because of
   a. the rise of information technologies.
   b. the rise of global shipping.
   c. the rise of transnational centers of production.
   d. the rise of multinational corporations.

2. Social justice would demand not only sustainable development and economies of scale but also
   a. more equitable distribution of wealth.
   b. more equitable concentrations of production.
   c. less equitable distribution of power.
   d. less equitable concentrations of wealth.

3. Capital-rich countries tend to have all of the following characteristics EXCEPT
   a. urbanized.
   b. possess economies of scale.
   c. likely to invest in high-technology sectors.
   d. likely to avoid social welfare programs.

4. According to the authors, _____ is not one of the underlying causes of most premature deaths in less-developed countries.
   a. lack of adequate health care
   b. malnutrition
   c. other environmental factors
   d. civil war

5. According to the authors, _____ and _____ describe a large portion of the labor force in the developing world.
   a. underworked, underpaid
   b. overtrained, underworked
   c. undereducated, poorly trained
   d. undernourished, poorly trained

6. Which of the following investment categories is not considered in the World Bank's annual country assessments on capital formation?
   a. fixed assets
   b. changes in inventory levels
   c. changes in interest rates
   d. net acquisitions of other valuables

7. According to the authors, which of the following is not considered a source of capital?
   a. government spending
   b. foreign direct investment
   c. trade preferences
   d. foreign aid

8. _____ can serve as a drain on capital.
   a. Capital transfers
   b. Currency exchange risk
   c. Debt repayments
   d. Transfer payments

9. _____ and _____ are the most likely benefits of MNC production centers in the less-developed countries.
   a. Capital, training
   b. Capital, technology transfers
   c. Technology transfers, training
   d. Training, domestic consumption

10. OPEC is an example of a(n)
    a. MNC.
    b. preferential trade agreement between the United States and the Arab world.
    c. cartel of oil-producing countries designed to control the price of oil.
    d. affiliate of the World Bank that offers loans at concessionary rates.

11. Growing populations have what effect on surplus capital?
    a. They tend to consume it before it can be invested.
    b. They encourage the production of surplus capital.
    c. They tend to divide the surpluses inequitably, as in Brazil.
    d. They discourage investments due to their high marginal costs.

12. According to the authors, what economic sector can suffer the greatest negative impacts due to environmental degradation?
    a. services
    b. mining
    c. manufacturing
    d. agriculture

13. Diseases can most dramatically affect an economy by
    a. causing the disability or death of workers.
    b. causing the loss of jobs due to disease burdens.
    c. causing productivity gains to be lessened due to decreased education.
    d. causing damage to the environment as disease control mechanisms are implemented.

14. According to the authors, high military spending affects development in what key way?
    a. creates arms dealers
    b. siphons off resources that could be used more productively
    c. destroys international investor confidence
    d. discourages economies of scale in more productive industries

15. Which of the following is one of the ways the authors discuss as a means of population growth control?
    a. slowing economic growth
    b. more equal distribution of wealth
    c. more investment in the health infrastructure
    d. the empowerment of women

16. The structuralist tradition of development developed out of what primary concern?
    a. the structures of capital transfers
    b. why less-developed countries were not experiencing economic development
    c. why less-developed countries experienced high transactions costs
    d. the structures within less-developed countries that hindered economic development

17. The main prescription structuralists advocate is
    a. equitable distribution of production.
    b. decreasing barriers to entry for domestic competitions.
    c. decreasing the economic dependency of less-developed countries.
    d. decreasing the role of Europe in global economic decision making.

18. Capitalist world-systems theorists are primarily interested in the existence of
    a. capitalism throughout the world.
    b. uneven development.
    c. the global existence of ideologically driven development.
    d. further developing a capitalist world-system.

19. The main tensions within the world-systems theory are between what two broadly classified groups?
    a. core and periphery
    b. core and semiperiphery
    c. periphery and semiperiphery
    d. core elite and peripheral elites

20. Wallerstein sees connections among what events in the international system?
    a. conflict, terrorism, and deepening capitalism
    b. transnational crime, political chaos, and deepening capitalism
    c. conflict, political crises, and deepening capitalism
    d. drug trade, human trafficking, and deepening capitalism

Human Rights

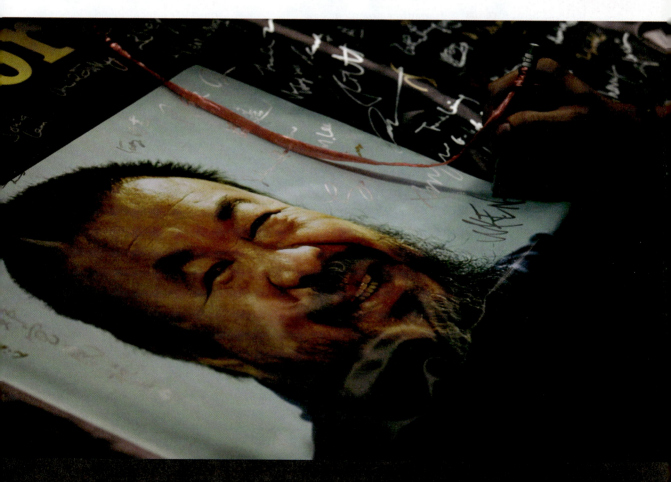

"*All human beings, whatever their cultural or historical background, suffer when they are intimidated, imprisoned or tortured. . . . We must, therefore, insist on a global consensus, not only on the need to respect human rights worldwide, but also on the definition of these rights . . . for it is the inherent nature of all human beings to yearn for freedom, equality and dignity, and they have an equal right to*

LEARNING OBJECTIVES

13.1 Compare and contrast differences in religion and culture to diverse understandings of human rights and the human condition across the globe.

13.2 Differentiate among diverse strains of liberalism, particularly individual and collective variants, that underlie definitions of (and commitments to) human rights in the United States and other countries.

13.3 Evaluate the American perspective on human rights in relation to those of other societies and cultures.

13.4 Identify the universally understood values that transcend diverse cultures and thus provide a common moral or ethical foundation on which human rights rest.

13.5 Describe the plight of refugees produced by wars, natural disasters, and other cataclysmic causes as well as what can be done to serve their best interests.

▶ Read and Listen
to **Chapter 13** at
mypoliscilab.com

✓ Study and Review
the **Pre-Test & Flashcards**
at **mypoliscilab.com**

Indicative of the human rights challenge is the fate of Ai Wei Wei (born 1957), the extraordinarily talented Chinese artist who also provided the "bird's nest" design for the stadium in Beijing used in the 2008 Olympic Games. Notwithstanding this and other artistic accomplishments, his independence of thought, particularly his biting criticism of government officials for their corruption and mismanagement, led to forced shutdown of his widely followed blog, coupled with police assaults against him.

Ai also refused to submit to often arbitrary restrictions on his artistry by the same government and party officials who, among other things, objected to his portrayal in sculpture of the Chinese people as downtrodden, presumably by those in authority. The governmental response was to destroy his new art studio and put him under arrest, the latter on apparently trumped-up allegations of tax evasion.

Cracking down on dissenters—labeled as dissidents—stems from fears among Chinese elites now in power that unless they are curbed, such activists might fuel a movement against governing authorities. Ai Wei Wei is not alone. He and other dissenters enjoy widespread support, particularly among Chinese intellectuals and many young professionals. The regime's reaction to any challenges seems always to crack down from the extreme of turning gunfire on dissidents in the Tiananmen Square massacre in 1989 to detaining or imprisoning them and constraining access to Google and other browsers as well as Facebook, Twitter, and other social networking sites. Informed by societal turbulence in the Middle East and elsewhere, and feeling threatened by the potential for popular movements to challenge the regime's authority, Chinese officials act swiftly and take decisive action when they think conditions warrant.

China's government has long made clear it does not tolerate groups like separatists who want independence (or at least greater autonomy for) Tibet and independent, spiritual movements like *Falun Gong* (founded in 1992) that quickly drew a large following (some 70 million people by some estimates) and launched protests against curbs on its activities imposed by the government in Beijing. The regime finally took action in 1999 to prohibit and disband the group, reportedly subjecting many of its members to human rights abuses. Lest they also become agents of political change, Western churches are prohibited from going outside of the international, "expatriate" community to seek converts or do any other organizational work deemed threatening to the regime.

Given this record, the United States and other governments have used both diplomatic and public channels from time to time to condemn the regime's human rights conduct and to urge the regime to release many of those the government has detained or imprisoned. Much to the dismay of many human rights advocates, economic and commercial interests of China's trade and investment partners have kept these governments from pressing Beijing too strongly on these human rights violations. The pragmatism driven by governmental and commercial interests often trumps human rights advocacy. If politics is the art of the possible, just how far can we push governments in China and other countries to change their conduct? Not surprising is the human rights advocate's response: Much further! What's your answer? Why?

We live in a world of almost seven billion people, a large proportion of whom suffer from political oppression, social discrimination, poverty, starvation or malnutrition, disease, and early death. Freedom from want is an elusive goal in much of the world, where poverty is the norm, life expectancy is much lower than in high-income countries, and infant mortality is still very high. Insecurity reigns supreme, and there is relatively little prospect of eliminating either the fact or fear of political and other abuses. Many human rights advocates lament how President Franklin Roosevelt's "four freedoms" enumerated in his 1941 State of the Union address—freedom of speech and expression, freedom of religion, freedom from want, and freedom from fear—seem so unattainable for most of the world's population.

We approach the subject of human rights in this chapter by examining how rights or values can be considered universal and not just representations of particular cultural or national preferences. In this regard, it is important for Americans (or the nationals of any country, for that matter) to understand the lack of universal agreement on which rights or whose rights ought to be protected. We also examine the problem of refugees not simply in terms of human rights but also as a potentially destabilizing element in international relations and world politics.

13.1 Compare and contrast differences in religion and culture to diverse understandings of human rights and the human condition across the globe.

HUMAN RIGHTS AND THE HUMAN CONDITION

Victimization of other human beings is at the core of human rights concerns high on the global-governance agenda. A belief in certain inalienable human rights is at the core of our understanding of the human condition. Unfortunately, universal

Watch the **Video** "Tiananmen Square" at mypoliscilab.com

human rights ■ persons possess authority within themselves in relation to political, economic, and social choices they make and protections they ought to enjoy from abuse by others

apartheid ■ a state policy of discrimination and strict racial segregation in a society

principles like respecting life, treating others with dignity, and affording others justice or fairness are interpreted across societies through very different cultural lenses. As a result, the human condition is beset by widespread abuses related to intercommunal strife, politically oppressive regimes, and deeply set prejudices within and across different societies and cultures. We focus in this section on some of these circumstances that produce widespread human rights violations.

Racial and ethnic discrimination is a global problem. South African **apartheid** or racial-separation policies were implemented by white-minority governments against the black majority population until the 1990s. Suppression of a majority by a small, powerful minority made the South African case particularly egregious.

Much more common in various countries, however, are racial, national, and ethnic prejudices that result in oppression of minority populations. These are not just developing world issues. Europe, Japan, and North America also offer considerable evidence of discriminatory practices on racial or ethnic lines.

Legalized, racially based slavery in the United States lasted until President Lincoln's Emancipation Proclamation of 1863 and the Thirteenth Amendment to the U.S. Constitution, passed in 1865, prohibited the practice. Outlawing slavery, of course, did not eliminate racial discrimination. Legalized racial segregation continued until Supreme Court rulings beginning in 1954 and passage of the Civil Rights Act of 1965. Notwithstanding considerable progress toward equal rights, there is still substantial evidence of continuing racial discrimination in various forms.

Some societies value free expression and religious choice, but others do not. Brutality directed against other human beings, by no means a new phenomenon, seemed nevertheless to intensify during the 1980s and 1990s, as evidenced by the 1989 massacre of demonstrators at Tiananmen Square in the Chinese capital, Beijing, noted above; the slaying of peasant villagers in the southern Mexican state of Chiapas and in El Salvador, Honduras, Nicaragua, Haiti, and other parts of Central America and the Caribbean; the breakup of Yugoslavia and the intercommunal violence among Croat, Serb, and Muslim populations that followed; and intertribal atrocities committed in Sudan, Ethiopia, Rwanda, and elsewhere in Africa. These incidents gained worldwide attention not just as localized atrocities but also because they are indicative of a pattern of intercommunal violence throughout the world.

refugee(s) ■ A person displaced because of war (usually) or other political or economic causes. Refugees may flee or be forced to leave a country, or they may be internally displaced persons within their own state.

Massive numbers of migrant populations—especially economic **refugees** seeking work and a place to live for themselves and their families—have swelled the ranks of other refugees, most of whom are seeking asylum or protection from various forms of political oppression throughout the world. These growing numbers challenge even those countries historically sympathetic to their plight. Widespread national and ethnic strife in Africa, the Balkans, the Persian (or Arab) Gulf, the Transcaucasus, South and Southeast Asia, and the Caribbean have produced literally millions of displaced persons who have been forced, or who have fled, from their home areas, often across national borders. In sub-Saharan Africa alone, the office of the UN High Commissioner for Refugees (UNHCR) has counted more than six million displaced persons—more than 10 percent of the region's population.[1]

---

[1]For the most recent data on refugees, see the UNHCR website (www.unhcr.org).

Not all countries share a deep commitment to admitting immigrants seeking asylum or refugee status, but even those that do face practical limits to their population-absorption capacities. Large-scale immigration pressures typically are balanced by governments that also are concerned about the impact of immigration on the welfare of their own citizens. The United States certainly has grappled with this issue, given pressures from populations fleeing regimes in Cuba, Haiti, and other locations in Central America and the Caribbean. In addition, there are large numbers of employment-driven migrations from Mexico, many of them illegal.

Widespread gender discrimination also denies equal rights to women. The term gender discrimination hardly captures the nature of existence for the vast majority of women in the developing world, where a combination of culture, laws, and religion not only deprive women of basic human rights but also relegate them in some places to almost subhuman status. In parts of Latin America, Asia, and Africa, women suffer from endless discrimination that begins even before birth with forced abortions of female fetuses in some countries. Infanticide, the practice of killing newborn girls, is a common rural phenomenon in India and China. For cultural as well as economic reasons, boys are preferred. Government policies that limit overall family size have had the unintended consequence of encouraging resort to female abortion and infanticide in these circumstances. They have also led

gender discrimination ■ placing people at a disadvantage on the grounds of their sex or their masculine or feminine identity

CASE & POINT | Women in the Developing World

CASE   As difficult as life may be for the vast majority of humanity, it is even more trying for women and girls.

- An estimated 500,000 women die of pregnancy-related causes each year, more than 90 percent of them in the developing world.
- 100,000 women die each year from unsafe abortions, almost all in the developing world.
- The World Health Organization estimates that seventy million women, most of them Africans, have undergone some form of female circumcision.
- In a typical year bridal dowry disputes led husbands and inlaws to kill more than 5,000 wives in India.
- Approximately 855 million people in the world are illiterate (almost one-sixth of humanity); two-thirds of them are women.
- Of the 1.3 billion persons living in absolute poverty, 70 percent are women.

In South Asia

- One of every eighteen women dies of a pregnancy-related cause.
- More than one of every ten babies dies during delivery.

In Nepal and Bangladesh

- One in every five girls dies before age five.

In India

- Approximately 25 percent of the twelve million girls born each year die by age fifteen.

POINT   Improvement in the lot of women and girls in much of the developing world cannot be simply legislated by United Nations declarations. The obstacles to overcome are political, social, economic, and cultural and must occur in the context of male-dominated societies, which hold traditional views of the role of women. ▲

Source: www.undp.org.

to the development of the notorious "Dying Rooms," which are orphanages filled almost entirely with abandoned female infants and girls.[2]

Even if a baby girl survives her first few years, in some low-income countries life continues to be precarious. As children, girls are fed less than their brothers, often only table scraps. Girls also are provided with less medical care and are much less likely to be taken to a hospital for treatment compared to boys. They are often denied educational opportunities afforded to boys and men, the largest obstacle to advancement of women.

Throughout the developing world, even if girls are allowed to attend school, they are often withdrawn sooner than boys so they can carry water, work in the fields, raise younger siblings, and do other domestic chores. In Pakistan, where schools are segregated by sex, only one-third are for women, and one-third of those have no building. Three out of four women cannot read or write. There has also been a recent rise of Islamic fundamentalism in Pakistan—what some refer to as the "Koran and Kalashnikov" culture—in part due to the spillover effect of the Taliban regime that ruled Afghanistan for so many years. Many mullahs have increased in power and preach against any developments meant to improve the status and condition of females.

Deeply rooted cultural values or prejudices are, of course, not easily changed, even when laws are passed to condemn such practices. In some cases, however, laws have been passed that actively discriminate against women. In some African countries, laws prohibit women from owning houses. In old age, these trials and indignities often become worse. In India, a woman's identity is so intertwined with that of her husband that if she should outlive him, she is often treated as a nonentity. In some parts of the country, women are forced to marry the dead husband's brother so that property stays in the family.

Women also have not achieved equality of opportunity or position in the workplace or in other aspects of social life even in advanced countries. Progress has been made, but only at a relatively slow pace. Women are increasingly rising to higher positions in economic, political and social life, although the numbers reaching the highest positions in industry and government are still relatively small.

One international effort to publicize the problems facing women around the globe has been through UN–sponsored conferences. One held in Beijing, China, in September 1995 aimed to develop a worldwide strategy to advance the situation of women. Parallel to this official conference was a Non-Governmental Organizations Forum on Women that attracted some 35,000 participants, 2,000 organizations, and 4,000 journalists. This gave the forum perhaps even more press coverage than the official conference received.

As diplomats, other government officials, representatives of international and nongovernmental organizations, and private citizens, practitioners have to deal with difficult, controversial issues on human rights agendas. Rather than sidestep them, we present them here in as balanced a way as we can, identifying points of consensus, but also where substantial differences remain within the human rights discourse. Virtually no one challenges genocide or mass murder of a people as a legitimate human rights issue. We underscore, however, that assaults on sexuality

---

[2]See www.gendercide.org.

are another form of violence against other human beings. The violence discussed in the text that follows is a global matter that poses pressing human rights challenges practitioners in international relations and world politics need to understand.

Female genital mutilation (FGM) or cutting (FGC), a severely damaging ritual often referred to euphemistically as "female circumcision," is widely practiced, particularly in parts of Africa. The euphemism is intended by some to make the practice seem less severe than it actually is. The World Health Organization defines this practice as including "all procedures that involve partial or total removal of the external female genitalia, or other injury to the female genital organs for non-medical reasons." Such actions constitute an assault on a woman's sexuality, notwithstanding claims to religious grounds for doing so. Although it is often represented as a measure to protect women from predatory men, most outside observers see the practice, in fact, as part of a larger cultural frame—the subordination of women in certain male-dominant, more traditional societies.

To ensure gender neutrality in this discussion, we also mention practices that affect men or boys. Human rights advocates are divided on the legitimacy of male circumcision (one in three or four males undergo the procedure worldwide), which has much greater acceptance on both religious and cultural grounds and is, in any event, far less severe than female genital mutilation. Apart from the pain it inflicts and other adverse effects, those challenging the practice on human rights grounds, sometimes citing the UN Convention on the Rights of the Child and other human rights treaties, rest their argument primarily on their opposition to any involuntary alteration of a person's natural physiology—man or woman, boy or girl.

FGM is not as commonplace in advanced industrial and postindustrial, high-income societies, although trafficking of girls and women for prostitution or labor-intensive work in slave-like conditions does occur, much as it does in lower-income countries. Trafficking of boys and men also occurs worldwide, but in much smaller numbers.

Other human rights challenges include discrimination or harm done to people for reasons of their sexual orientation or identity. A global trend in recent years, particularly in high-income countries, is the establishment of norms (and passage of laws) mandating acceptance of people regardless of sexual orientation or identity. On the other hand, long-standing prejudices against same-sex relationships in both high- and low-income countries remain in place. Advocacy groups have made some progress on their agendas, as covered by mainstream media. In the United States, for example, some states now allow same-sex marriages, others civil unions. The U.S. military is now integrating openly serving homosexuals and bisexuals, no longer excluding them from military service, which is also commonplace in most European military establishments.

Finally, we mention another human rights controversy between those who claim a woman's right to choose to abort a pregnancy with access to medical care and those who claim the unborn has a right to life regardless of the reasons a woman may offer to terminate her pregnancy. It is an issue discussed extensively in the UN Human Rights Committee and the Committee on the Elimination of Discrimination against Women. American law since a landmark Supreme Court case, *Roe* v. *Wade* (1973), provides a woman a legal right to choose, but this has not ended the controversy. The larger consensus among human rights

female genital mutilation (cutting) FGM (or FGC) ■ The World Health Organization defines female genital mutilation (or cutting) as all procedures that involve partial or total removal of the external female genitalia or other injury to the female genital organs for nonmedical reasons

advocates, particularly in high-income countries, leaves the choice as a private one a woman makes—one in which state authorities (or anyone else) ought not to interfere. Not everyone agrees.

Many emphasize that the decision is an extraordinarily difficult one as the woman facing this choice seeks to balance her rights to life, dignity, and justice or fairness with concerns she may have for the fetus she carries. Some lay out conditions or criteria that ought to be satisfied before making the choice—for example, will carrying the pregnancy to term risk the life or cause harm to the mother? Was the pregnancy due to rape? Even in these circumstance, some very strongly oppose any willful termination of life. We leave this important human rights question for your discussion and debate with others. No one ever said human rights was an easy subject!

THE UNIVERSALITY OF HUMAN RIGHTS VERSUS STATE SOVEREIGNTY

13.2 Differentiate among diverse strains of liberalism, particularly individual and collective variants, that underlie definitions of (and commitments to) human rights in the United States and other countries.

Quite apart from how we may feel about human rights abuses, do we have any obligation to act or any right to do so, particularly if our actions conflict with the prerogatives of sovereign states? Indeed, international or transnational actions in support of human rights often directly challenge or violate state sovereignty. For example, NATO's use of force in 1998 and 1999 against Serbia over Serbian actions in Kosovo seemed to violate state sovereignty because Kosovo was recognized by most states as being a province of Serbia, which still referred to itself as the Yugoslav Republic.

Still, injustices offend the human conscience and cry out for corrective action. If justice is understood universally as fairness, is there agreed or common cause for external action on behalf of human rights? Or does their sovereignty (affirmed by Article 2, Section 7 of the UN Charter) legally preclude intervention in the domestic affairs of states, however just a cause might be? Is a violation of human rights within a country likely to have international consequences, particularly in neighboring countries with tribal or other links to the victims? If so, this may not be just a domestic matter, but rather a danger to international peace and security that allows the UN Security Council to authorize even armed intervention under Article 42 of the Charter as a legal exception to the Article 2, Section 7 provision cited above.

Certainly that was an understanding that led the UN Security Council in 2011 to authorize intervention in Libya—the imposition of a no-fly zone and other actions deemed necessary to protect the civilian population there. Not only were Libyans who opposed the regime facing the prospect of further military attacks by forces under the government's command in Tripoli, but also the possibility that this could spill over borders with Tunisia in the west and Egypt in the east. If this were so, the matter was not just a human rights question, but also one that "endangered international peace and security"—the key phrase the UN Security Council can use to authorize intervention in what otherwise would be a purely domestic matter.

The more this recourse for human rights violations occurs—Darfur in Sudan, the eastern and western border areas of Libya, and other locations—some say there is, as a result, a growing basis in customary international law for armed intervention to stop or prevent human rights abuses even if international peace and security were not endangered. Of course, not everyone agrees with this more liberal position on the use of force under UN auspices, least of all the leaderships of countries subject to unwanted interventions of this kind.

The larger question is to what extent, then, need we be concerned with the welfare of other human beings in different cultural, socioeconomic, and geographic settings? Are there grounds for such concerns that go beyond the bounds of a given state or society? Is it enough to be concerned about justice and human rights within one's own country? Should we seek application of universal norms of justice and human rights? Is the human condition properly a global or supranational concern?

supranational ■ authority beyond or above the level of a state; if one were created, a world government would be a supranational authority, governing the relations among states and other actors in world politics

It is an understatement to say that there is no consensus on the answers to these questions. A traditional response is that sovereign states have an exclusive right to address such questions within their own jurisdictions. As noted above, others argue that universal norms (some of which now are part of international law) apply across national borders. The existence of human rights from this perspective concerns international or global society as a whole, not just an internal matter for particular states to manage or handle.

We may be more likely to address human rights or questions of justice in global terms if we see the world as composed of individuals (or tribes, classes, or other groups of people) rather than of states. By contrast, if we adopt a more abstract, state-centric view, we may see demands for justice and respect for human rights in other countries as unwarranted intrusions into their domestic affairs.

A further significant complication is the absence of agreement on what human rights are (much less on what constitutes justice, either within a particular society or across national boundaries). Efforts have been made to define human rights in formal terms, as in the UN Declaration of Human Rights and in the documents of such regional organizations as the Council of Europe, the Organization for Security and Cooperation in Europe, the European Union, the Organization of American States, and the African Union.

classical liberalism ■ a commitment to individuals as human beings worthy of regard in themselves and not just as part of larger groups or classes

The degree of emphasis on human rights in U.S. foreign policy has varied from one governmental administration to another and even within administrations. Regardless of the degree of emphasis, the U.S. approach has been criticized because of its distinctly American point of view. The American focus on individual rights, a concern deeply embedded in its classical liberal tradition, tends to overlook communitarian, group, or class rights that occupy a more prominent place in other political cultures.

communitarian ■ philosophical position emphasizing collective or group service obligations to one another in society

Americans also tend to place more weight on liberty and its relation to order than on the egalitarian and socioeconomic issues emphasized in other countries. Notwithstanding what may be the best of intentions, American foreign policy pronouncements on human rights that project an individually oriented, libertarian focus are sometimes taken as yet another imposition of American values on others. The severest critics call it quite simply cultural imperialism. As such, U.S. and other national efforts in the human rights field have often been interpreted as intrusions on the sovereign prerogatives of states not sharing the same perspectives on these issues.

libertarian ■ philosophical position emphasizing *individual* rights, often preferring specific limits or restraints on government

The American understanding of human rights stems in large part from the ideas of 17th- and 18th-century Enlightenment thinkers and the American historical experience itself. One of the best summations of this thesis is Louis Hartz's now-classic book, *The Liberal Tradition in America*.[3] Hartz notes that the United States, unlike Europe, lacked any direct experience with feudalism and its hierarchic authority structure. European medieval society was dominated by an aristocracy with antidemocratic values. By contrast, the new American political culture had embedded within it what Hartz calls "the liberal idea."[4] What, then, is the nature of "liberal society" from the American point of view?

The term *liberal* as used by Hartz in its classic meaning should not be confused with contemporary American political usage that places liberals and conservatives into opposing categories. Although modern-day American social liberals and conservatives differ on many political issues, they are all liberals in the classical meaning of the term used by Hartz; that is, they share a belief in individualism, a commitment to individuals as human beings worthy of regard in themselves and not just as part of larger groups or classes.

Individualism built further on notions of equality among individuals; however, this egalitarianism would not readily support a redistribution of property or other socialist design. Alexis de Tocqueville, an early-19th-century French observer of the American scene, commented how the egalitarian spirit in the United States existed among individuals who were part of a very individualistic society.

Because the United States had not experienced feudalism in its national history, the country lacked even the vestiges of aristocratic titles and deference to authorities that, by contrast, were integral parts of European societies. Feudalism, of course, had long since given way to preindustrial market capitalism in Europe, but many of the class inequalities of feudalism had survived into the modern era.[5] Notwithstanding actual differences among individuals in wealth and opportunity in the United States, its society and culture exhibited a stronger spirit of equality than in most early-19th-century European societies.

To many Americans of Tocqueville's time, government was a necessary evil at best. As he noted: "Whenever the political laws of the United States are to be discussed, it is with the doctrine of sovereignty of the people that we must begin."[6] The best way for people as equal individuals to remain sovereign was to constrain the authority and power of government. In the America that Tocqueville observed, it was the "people"—understood not in some abstract way as society as a whole but rather as individual "citizens" (or groups of them)—who were "the real directing power."[7]

---

[3]See Louis Hartz, *The Liberal Tradition in America: An Interpretation of American Political Thought since the Revolution* (New York: Harcourt, Brace & World, 1955).

[4]That "the absence of feudalism and the presence of the liberal idea" are key factors in "an analysis of American history and politics" is a core thesis in the entire book, first discussed by Hartz on pp. 20–23.

[5]See Alexis de Tocqueville, *Democracy in America,* Henry Reeve, trans. (New York: Schocken Books, 1961). The first English translations were published in 1835 and 1840, accompanied by introductions written by the English liberal and political philosopher John Stuart Mill. In developing his thesis, Louis Hartz draws directly from Tocqueville's observations of early American society.

[6]Ibid., 48.

[7]Ibid., 193–194.

The framers of the U.S. Constitution, educated in the Greek and Roman classics, also drew heavily from the writings of such Enlightenment thinkers as Locke (1632–1704) and Montesquieu (1689–1755). Following the late Greek historian Polybius (ca. 203–120 B.C.), Montesquieu developed the idea of separation of powers in his *Spirit of the Laws*. This idea was adopted in the U.S. Constitution as a means of keeping the central government from growing too strong at the expense of the governed. Human rights were to be conserved by restricting government's size and involvement in the private affairs of individual citizens.

Locke advocated an important but relatively minimal role for government at the service of individuals, primarily the protection of their lives, liberties, and property. Consistent with Locke, the U.S. Constitution explicitly prohibits government infringing on individual rights; citizens grant their consent to be governed and do not delegate all their rights to government. Isaiah Berlin and other political writers have called this a "negative" construction of libertarian rights. Liberties are negatively maintained by constraining government rather than by empowering it in some positive way to serve individual rights. The government role was thus to be as small as possible. The framers of the U.S. Constitution understood that this liberal philosophy of governmental *laissez-faire* offered the most consistent and effective means of protecting individual liberty.

In the course of its history, American government in practice would depart from this strict *laissez-faire* philosophy, particularly in the twentieth century. Even the meaning of the term liberal in its American context took on a more positive orientation toward governmental action for social and economic purposes. By contrast, American conservatives have articulated greater skepticism toward governmental activism, preferring to underscore their preference for governmental *laissez-faire*.

The key point is that what survived alongside new and expanded governmental attention to social and economic issues was a tendency for Americans to see and deal with human rights in individualist terms. American social liberals and social conservatives have differed on the means by which individuals are to be served and the role government is to play in this regard, but both groups have retained their classical liberal focus on individuals. Thus, laws passed since the 1930s have the government do such things for individuals as guarantee a minimum wage, provide for a safer workplace, give unemployment and disability compensation, establish retirement pensions, offer job training, make higher-education loans and grants, and provide medical care.

Keeping the state at bay, opposing tax increases needed to fund programs—"starving the beast [i.e., the state]"—is a present-day echo of this 18th- and 19th-century preference for a minimal state. Reforms—an expansion of the welfare state that date in the United States from the Roosevelt New Deal era in the 1930s—have long been challenged by social conservatives. Social security—pensions and unemployment insurance, medical care, organized labor's right to collective bargaining, government assistance to diverse groups such as farmers, students, families, and others—are part of the expanded state social conservatives want to reduce, if not dismantle. Their preference is for government to focus primarily on maintaining law and order at home and security from threats coming from abroad, leaving welfare to individuals themselves or to private charities.

social liberals ■ political perspective that, while sharing the commitment to individualism, puts emphasis on government programs or other social actions as means to improve the position or conditions of individuals

social conservatives ■ doubt the efficacy of social engineering or other governmental programs that would effect substantial changes in the status quo, preferring instead to rely more on private, nongovernmental efforts—any changes implemented incrementally, slowly, and carefully

As social constructivists observe, ideas like human rights evolve over long periods of time. Advocates of one position or another do not always realize that the threads they are making on their spinning wheels will, in time, become part of a larger cloth. We examine in this discussion two strands of liberal thought. The Anglo-American tradition historically placed more emphasis on individual rights and liberties—a more libertarian position. Following the French Revolution, the continental tradition has also included more in the way of socioeconomic rights, not just for individuals, but also for groups or classes of people—a more egalitarian and communitarian stance. Modern-day understandings of human rights are built upon these two traditions in liberal thought, although the emphasis each receives varies substantially among human rights advocates.

ARGUMENT   Human rights advocacy should focus on individual rights and liberties. This more libertarian view holds that rights apply to individuals as free agents. Groups are merely a band of individuals who find value in joining with others, but all are still individuals. The English tradition on civil rights and liberties begins with *Magna Carta* (1215) when the king, faced by a rebellion, finally granted his barons and clergymen as individuals a free church, rights to trial, *habeas corpus* (a right to be released from unlawful arrest; that a person ought not to be imprisoned without legal grounds, that is, sufficient evidence to legitimate detention as a criminal suspect), due process of law, and equitable punishment for offenses, rights later extended throughout the kingdom. These individual rights form the bedrock of Anglo-American law to the present day.

COUNTERARGUMENT   Human rights include, but go well beyond, individual rights and liberties to include concerns with equality not just on an individual, but also on a collective basis. This is a more communitarian and egalitarian French revolutionary (and, later, continental European)

tradition on human rights. Much inspiration is drawn from the writings of Jean Jacques Rousseau (1712–1778). Rousseau not only bound *equality* to *liberty*, but in his *Social Contract* underscored that human beings enjoy rights in society subject to the general will—the interest they hold in common. The French revolutionary slogan "*liberté, égalité, fraternité* [or community]" captures eloquently the idea that individual rights are integral to—part of—the community or society in which individuals reside.

APPLICATION   Philosophical underpinnings matter. Human rights are, after all, social constructions—a synthesis of sometimes competing strands that, over time, blend into a larger fabric. Both the individual or libertarian and the communitarian, more egalitarian understandings of rights were at play in framing the Universal Declaration of Human Rights (1948), an effort led by UN Ambassador Eleanor Roosevelt. Given the position of the United States at the time, the principal advocate of this declaration, its wording puts greater emphasis on individual rights. To a decidedly lesser extent, it does include concerns with inequality framed in more communitarian language, thus also reflecting the continental tradition—not just civil liberties and rights as in the Anglo-American tradition. The declaration is also foundational to subsequent human rights conventions (see Table 13.1 on page 475), which also address these communitarian concerns and economic, social and cultural rights.

Do an internet search on the Universal Declaration of Human Rights and note the emphasis on individual rights. But also examine more communitarian understandings in Articles 16, 21, 22, and 26–29 as well as the explicit acknowledgment in Article 22 of economic, social, and cultural rights in the continental tradition. Do you agree that, taken as a whole, this document reflects a balance more on the individual-libertarian than on the communitarian-egalitarian side? ▸

Even advocacy of civil rights in the United States has been based primarily on the constitutional view that individuals as citizens are entitled to equal protection under the law. With few exceptions (e.g., group rights for Native Americans or the right of organized labor to bargain collectively), Americans have been much less comfortable with recognizing rights on a group or class basis. Even collective bargaining by labor unions was understood as a tactical means for representing individual worker interests; groups of individuals were understood in this context as being more effective than individuals standing alone in disputes with managers or owners of firms.

Arguments in favor of socioeconomic rights for large groups, classes, or society as a whole have enjoyed far less support in American thinking and practice than claims in favor of individual political rights and liberties. Even though the doctrine of eminent domain allows public need to supersede individual property rights (e.g., when government takes private property in order to build a highway or school), the law upholds individual rights at the same time with specific provisions to assure just compensation. Such property is also to be taken in a nondiscriminatory way; no individuals are supposed to receive either more favorable or unfair treatment compared to anyone else.

HUMAN RIGHTS ACROSS CULTURES

It should not be surprising, therefore, that Americans (whether social liberals or conservatives) tend to view human rights through these same individualist and classical liberal lenses, focusing more on individual rather than collective rights and liberties. Not everyone agrees with this decidedly American perspective. In fact, when we examine the issue as it is addressed in different cultures, we find a lack of consensus on whose rights and what rights are bases for legitimate claims.[8]

Some cultures perceive rights less in relation to individuals than to tribes, classes, or other groups. The state and society as a whole also may claim to have rights. States thus claim to be sovereign with rights to exercise complete jurisdiction over their domestic affairs and to be independent or autonomous in the conduct of their foreign affairs. The existence of rights belonging to the world's population taken as a whole—human civilization or humankind (to include generations not yet born)—is a claim quite different from the liberal idea that rights are primarily an individual matter.

Does a tribe, for example, have rights as a tribe that supersede rights claimed by individuals, whether or not they are members of the tribe? Can the same be said of society as a whole in relation to the individuals, tribes, classes, or other groups of which it is composed? For human civilization as a whole? Unfortunately there is no consensus across societies and cultures on this question of whose rights are to take priority when they conflict.

Cross-cultural disagreement also exists even on what rights are to be considered human rights. Consistent with their focus on individual, civil or political, and legal rights, Americans often fault foreign governments for failure to provide equal

> **13.3** Evaluate the American perspective on human rights in relation to those of other societies and cultures.

---

[8]See Ernst B. Haas, *Global Evangelism Rides Again: How to Protect Human Rights without Really Trying* (Berkeley: University of California Institute of International Studies, 1978).

protection of the laws and adequate due process (afforded the legal process in civil and criminal matters to which they are entitled). This is particularly troublesome for Americans who are arrested while traveling abroad who may not have the same rights to a fair and speedy trial as at home and may suffer mistreatment or what they consider to be cruel and unusual punishments.

A celebrated case in which Singapore administered severe corporal punishment by caning an American youth who was found guilty of vandalism is by no means unique. In any given year, more than 2,500 Americans are incarcerated abroad for crimes or alleged crimes, often involving drug use or trade. Complaints concerning abuses of rights claimed by these American citizens in custody abroad are commonplace. The U.S. State Department's Bureau of Consular Affairs monitors the issue, but U.S. consular officials stationed abroad must rely for the most part on persuasion to extricate Americans unjustly implicated or mistreated. The host government and local authorities claim complete jurisdiction or sovereign authority over the acts of individuals committed on their own territory, regardless of the citizenship of these alleged offenders or convicted felons.

This American focus on **legal and political rights** (especially relating to life, liberty, and property), which puts much less emphasis on claims to social, cultural, and economic rights, is by no means universally shared. For citizens merely to be equal before the law is considered in many other cultures to be too narrow and a rather abstract construction of human rights. If they have human rights sensitivity at all, human welfare or social security in its fullest sense may be more highly valued.

Do people have sufficient food, clothing, shelter, medical care, and other necessities? Do they have **socioeconomic rights**? From this perspective, ignoring or doing little about conditions that promote disease, hunger, and high mortality rates are understood as human rights violations of greater consequence than the more abstract legal and political rights concerning liberty or property. This priority stands quite apart from whether rights are understood in individual terms or as applying to tribes, classes, or other groups in a given society.

It is sometimes tempting to adopt a moral or **cultural relativism** and assert that rights or any other values can be understood only within their separate cultural contexts. Cultural relativists reject claims to human rights as universal, arguing that such universal claims are artificial constructions. To a relativist, values cannot be separated from the cultural context. Who is to say which culture's values should supersede another's?

It is not hard to show that different cultures (and subcultures within a given society) have different ways of thinking about and doing things. For example, the time of day and the size and content of different meals considered appropriate varies across cultures and subcultures. How one eats—with one's hands, with chopsticks, or with fork, knife, and spoon—is also quite variable. We refer to such practices as customs or manners. Even though there may be a correct way to act in a particular cultural context, we usually do not understand the values associated with manners or customs as having moral content.

Other values in a particular cultural context may be part of its moral code. Thus respecting the elderly as a group or as individuals may be seen as a moral obligation in some cultures but not in others, at least not to the same degree. The

legal and political rights ■ a narrow construction of rights—for example, free speech, rights to assemble and to vote, due process of law

socioeconomic rights ■ a more expansive view—that human beings have rights to such essentials as food, clothing, shelter, health care, and education

cultural relativism ■ belief that moral or ethical principles are not universal, but rather are tied to particular situational or cultural contexts

same is true for children. Providing for some minimum level of living may be understood in moral terms as social responsibility in some cultures, whereas others prefer to hold individuals primarily responsible to provide for themselves. Children are usually the least able to fend for themselves, of course. Exploitation of child labor is widespread, particularly in low-income countries. The International Labor Organization estimates there are some 215 million child laborers forced to work long hours in difficult conditions.

Thus many societies hold governments, whether democratic or authoritarian in character, responsible for assuring at least a basic level of living and welfare for their people, but this is not a universally held view. In American society, for example, there may be a higher value placed on equality of opportunity rather than on fairness of socioeconomic outcomes. Although Americans disagree among themselves on such matters, many who are well off may not feel there is any individual or societal obligation to assist those who are not. This perspective views charity as properly a voluntary effort undertaken primarily by individuals, not by governments. Value is often placed on the marketplace as the best mechanism for allocating goods and services, a view challenged, of course, by Americans with greater social-liberal (or social-democratic) commitments.

The American approach to such matters not only differs from that of most other advanced industrial countries, which expect a larger government role in assuring a greater degree of socioeconomic welfare, but also from that of many less-developed countries, which have social security systems based on tribal or clan loyalties. The more *laissez-faire* perspective still prevalent in the United States is not in any way typical of the rest of the world.

VALUES THAT TRANSCEND DIVERSE CULTURES

Although some values do vary across cultures from one society to another, does this mean that all values are dependent on certain societal or cultural contexts? Do any values apply to human beings or humanity as a whole independent of cultural context?

Students of philosophy observe that if we really believe in a strict cultural relativism—that values and rights are only to be defined by separate cultures and can have no independent standing of their own—then we are saying, in effect, that there is no such thing as morality or ethics. Can morality, ethical principles, and human rights really be said to exist if they can be changed so readily within and across cultures and subcultures? Is there no basis independent of a given society or culture for moral or ethical standards of behavior?

One significant problem with moral or cultural relativism is that it gives us no universal basis for condemning atrocities and such human tragedies as the Holocaust. Just because eliminating the Jews as a people may have been considered legitimate within a Nazi political subculture, this belief did not make it right. Even if we have difficulty agreeing on many other values, genocide is so offensive to the human spirit that it is condemned as mass murder on universal, not just on cultural, grounds. Any rational human being, regardless of cultural origin, would understand the immorality of such atrocities.

13.4 Identify the universally understood values that transcend diverse cultures and thus provide a common moral or ethical foundation on which human rights rest.

Explore the "Human Rights: You Are a Refugee" at mypoliscilab.com

genocide ■ mass murder of a people typically because of their racial, ethnic, religious, or other particular identity

deontology ■ human understandings we have within us of universal moral principles that transcend time and space

categorical imperative ■ Ethicist Immanuel Kant identified two: (1) one ought to act "according to the maxim that you can at the same time will [such conduct] to be a universal law," and (2) one should treat others "as an end [worthy in themselves] as well as a means, [but] never merely as a means."

utilitarian ■ philosophical school associated with Jeremy Bentham and John Stuart Mill based on the principle that right conduct is that which brings the greatest good or happiness for the greatest number

social contract ■ idea that human beings, acting in their own enlightened self-interest, would agree to bind themselves to one political or governing arrangement or another to include rules for the society they construct

What about a religious basis for universal human rights? Islam, Christianity, Judaism, Hinduism, Buddhism, and other religions do not just limit themselves to their followers but frequently also make universally applicable moral claims. As a practical matter, rejection of religion by some and the absence of theological consensus even among the followers of various religious groups prevent us from using particular religions as the solitary bases for common, worldwide acceptance of human rights and other moral claims.

Instead, many writers have tried to identify secular or nonreligious bases for their universalist positions. Aristotle identified certain virtues exhibited by virtuous persons we might emulate. Also attributed to Aristotle is the ethical maxim "do no harm." For his part, the 18th-century German philosopher Immanuel Kant identified what he called categorical imperatives, or absolute obligations—a duty-oriented ethics, which he argued had applicability to all reasoning human beings, regardless of religious or other cultural differences. Because these understandings of ethical universals come from within ourselves as human beings—knowable through the human reason with which we are endowed—Kantian ethics are said to be deontological, meaning reflective of the human understandings we have of the world around us. Capturing the essence of this Kantian meaning—transcendence across time and space of universal moral principles—is the phrase "the starry sky above me, the moral law within me."

Thus, according to Kant, we should follow only those maxims that we would be willing to make into universal laws. This categorical imperative binds all human beings. Regardless of cultural or religious identity, rational human beings would not want to legitimize murder, lying, stealing, or other forms of dishonesty by making them into universal "laws" or maxims to guide human conduct. Even though human beings engage in such activities, they cannot be considered right by rational human beings in any cultural context.

In short, a difference is recognized between how human beings should act and how they do act. Kant also understood as universal the obligation to treat human beings as ends worthy in themselves, not just as means to other ends. From the Kantian perspective, this categorical imperative is also universally binding as a moral or ethical guide to behavior, even though it too is often violated. Again, even though the actual conduct of human beings deviates from these norms or maxims, they are not any less morally binding. According to Kant, human beings have a duty to follow those ethical principles that are discoverable through their rational faculties.

Kant was not the only writer to provide a secular basis for universal norms of right conduct. The 19th-century English utilitarians Jeremy Bentham and John Stuart Mill argued that we should act in accordance with the maxim of assuring the greatest good (or greatest happiness) for the greatest number. Utilitarians take this abstract principle and apply it to a wide range of human circumstances, including a defense of liberty and other human rights as representing the greatest good for the greatest number.

The 17th-century English writer John Locke reasoned that human beings have certain natural rights to life, liberty, and property, which they surrender only as part of a social contract. The notion among social-contract theorists that, quite apart from cultural context, human beings have rights as part of their nature obviously provides another secular ground for making universalist moral claims. To Locke (and to Thomas Jefferson, who followed Locke's lead), human rights are thus part of human nature. The citizenry or people who empower governments in the first place must therefore strictly limit the authority of governments to abridge them. In fact, governments are created in part to guarantee certain civil rights, which are those entitlements that individuals have as members of the particular societies to which they belong.

Locke and Jefferson clearly put particular emphasis on individual liberties, although another social-contract theorist, the 18th-century French-Swiss writer Jean-Jacques Rousseau (1712–1778), placed relatively greater emphasis on equality and on the obligations to one's community. In his "Discourse on the Origin of Inequality," Rousseau found fault with the division of property among individuals, believing it to be the source of much that is wrong in society. That "the fruits of the earth belong to all and the earth to no one" is at once egalitarian and communitarian, a universalist moral.

At the same time, in his *Social Contract* Rousseau argued in favor of liberty, lamenting that "man is born free" but that "everywhere he is in chains." Rousseau's thoughts on such matters are more complex, of course, than merely providing an endorsement of liberty and equality. He saw human beings as part of a larger community or society in which decisions are to serve the general will or interest of society as a whole, rather than the particular wills or interests of certain individuals.

The important point for this discussion, however, is that some human rights advocates in Europe and elsewhere have been influenced by this mode of thought. They have tended to offer a vision of a just world society based more on egalitarian and communitarian values than is present in the more individualist, Lockean mode of thought. John Rawls (1921–2002), a late-20th-century theorist in the social-contract tradition, comes closer to Rousseau in his focus on the equity or fairness we would expect in a just society. If human beings did not know in advance how they would fare (behind what Rawls referred to as a "veil of ignorance" as to what their personal circumstances might be), what rules would they establish to assure fair or just outcomes?[9]

The lack of intellectual agreement among social-contract theorists, utilitarians, Kantians, and others who think about values in universal terms is part of the global confusion on such matters. This lack of consensus on human rights—how we are to understand rights and values and what we are to do about them—underlies the global debate on what commitments and obligations we have to fellow human beings throughout the world. Disagreement on what and whose human rights ought to be recognized hinders the construction of a just world society.

civil rights ■ rights established by generally accepted rules or law in society—claims typically made by or on behalf of individuals concerning their equal status and role as citizens

general will ■ Individual rights are integral to or part of the community or society in which individuals reside

From Theory to Fact

English, French, and American theories of rights, developed in the 17th and 18th centuries as part of liberal revolutions then underway in these societies,

---

[9]See Rawls, *A Theory of Justice* (Cambridge, MA: Harvard University Press, 1971).

SLIDESHOW | Human Rights Abuses

The trials of accused Nazi war criminals in Nuremberg, Germany (1945–1946), are the best known and most significant early international efforts to deal with crimes against humanity.

Aung San Suu Kyi is an internationally known human rights activist, Nobel Peace Prize winner, and leader of the democratic movement in Myanmar (Burma). She has spent many years under house arrest. During a thaw in relations with the outside world, Suu Kyi met with U.S. secretary of state Hillary Clinton in November 2011.

An innovative approach to dealing with extensive human rights abuses and their emotional and political legacy was the Truth and Reconciliation Commission established in South Africa after the end of apartheid. Here Archbishop Desmond Tutu greets former South Africa president Nelson Mandela.

The extensive recruitment of children and teenagers in Third World conflicts is a troubling and unfortunately established trend. Often war refugees, runaways, and orphans, these young males not only commit human rights abuses, but are victims themselves. These teenagers are members of an Eritrean separatist group in the Horn of Africa.

positivism ■
concept that law is
what lawmakers,
following
constitutional
procedures, define
it to be

remain important as philosophical underpinnings of present-day, global concerns about justice and human rights. The idea of agreeing on principles of human rights and then declaring them as binding obligations is also consistent with a positivist view. From this perspective, whether or not rights exist as part of human nature, their existence as civil rights can be declared as a positive act. Indeed, when states ratify treaties to this effect, human rights become binding as part of international law.

The idea of constraining government authority by the positive assertion of rights is contained in the English *Magna Carta* (1215), by which the English nobility set limits on their own monarch. The English civil war of the 1640s was followed by a period of turmoil that finally resulted in Parliament's restoration of a constitutional (or limited) monarchy in 1688, proclaiming an English Bill of Rights in 1689. The American understanding of rights was profoundly influenced by the British experience in general and English and Scottish writers in particular. The Declaration of Independence (1776) and the addition of a Bill of Rights to those rights specified in the original draft of the U.S. Constitution underscored an American commitment to the civil rights and liberties of individuals.

Following in this liberal tradition, a Universal Declaration of the Rights of Man was proclaimed in 1789 by the French revolutionary National Assembly. The 18th-century English writer Thomas Paine (1737–1809), who was widely read by Americans at the time, provided an eloquent defense of the French position on human rights.[10] In doing so, he directly contradicted the conservative Edmund Burke (1729–1797), then a member of Parliament, who saw the French Revolution as dangerous in the extreme. Paine justified French claims by expounding a theory of natural human rights. Going beyond individual rights and liberties, Paine also provided justification for egalitarian and communitarian claims.

The Universal Declaration of Human Rights (1948) and subsequent efforts to codify human rights as treaty obligations owe much to a historical legacy of constitutional liberalism in which governments were constrained and citizen rights were declared. On this and the following pages a few of these are presented. Because of their global influence in the 19th and 20th centuries, this bedrock of predominantly Anglo-American and French ideas has provided the foundation for the universal declaration and international conventions on human rights promulgated since 1945.

Whether or not we are satisfied with one or another of the intellectual justifications that have been offered for the universality of human rights in Kantian, natural, utilitarian, religious, or other terms, we should take note of several positivist constructions since the end of World War II. These are part of a growing body of human rights principles, some of which have the binding character of international law. Consistent with its preamble, Articles 1 and 55 of the UN Charter (1945) established the principle of "universal respect for, and observance of human rights and fundamental freedoms for all without distinction as to race, sex, language, or religion." Many of these rights were also specified in the Universal Declaration on Human Rights, passed by the UN General Assembly in 1948.

---

[10]Thomas Paine published *Rights of Man* in two parts in 1791 and 1792.

The U.S. ambassador to the UN, Eleanor Roosevelt (1884–1962)—President Franklin Roosevelt's widow—chaired the UN committee that drafted the declaration and was its principal advocate.

The declaration did not establish these specified rights in international law with the binding force of a treaty. Some have argued, however, that the declaration did give formal recognition to rights as they have come to be accepted in practice and thus have become in effect part of customary international law. Whatever the outcome of this argument among international lawyers, what is most important for our purposes in this chapter is that by vote of the United Nations General Assembly, sovereign states formally acknowledged the legitimacy of human rights as universal rights.

Ambassador Roosevelt joined with others seeking to legitimize the idea that rights exist independently of particular sovereign states and their respective societies. Not surprisingly, given the dominant position of the United States in world politics at the time, the declaration conformed more to American and other Western preferences for individual, political rights in the liberal tradition and gave relatively less emphasis to communitarian and socioeconomic interpretations of human rights.

Nevertheless, six of the thirty articles in the universal declaration did address such socioeconomic and cultural rights, but even these were cast largely in

---

CASE & POINT | Children and Human Rights

CASE The worldwide population of children under the age of fourteen who work full-time is estimated to exceed 200 million. Pakistan illustrates the gap between a government's declared commitment to protecting the welfare of its children and its actual policies. According to the Human Rights Commission of Pakistan, some eleven to twelve million children work full-time, about half under the age of ten. They are found in virtually every factory, workshop, and field in situations best characterized as indentured servitude. The carpet-making industry is a good example. According to UNICEF, between 500,000 and one million Pakistani children between the ages of four and fourteen work long hours as full-time carpet weavers, accounting for up to 90 percent of the workforce.

A carpet master in the Punjab village of Wasan Pura states that he aggressively pursues boys from poverty-stricken families who are between the ages of seven and ten: "They make ideal employees. Boys at this stage of development are at the peak of their dexterity and endurance, and they're wonderfully obedient—they'd work around the clock if I asked them. I hire them first and foremost because they're economical. For what I'd pay one second-class adult weaver I can get three boys, sometimes four, who can produce first-class rugs in no time." The low cost of child labor allows Pakistan to undersell its foreign competitors that prohibit child labor.

A Pakistani human rights nongovernmental organization known as the Bonded Labor Liberation Front (BLLF) has worked hard since its founding in 1988 against bonded and child labor, liberating some 30,000 adults and children from brick kilns, carpet factories, and farms. It has won some 25,000 court cases against unscrupulous employers.

POINT The plight of children in the developing world at times fails to receive the amount of publicity that other human rights cases receive. ◣

individual rather than collective terms.[11] Further specification of these rights was contained in two 1966 covenants that entered into force in 1976—one for civil and political rights and the other for economic, social, and cultural rights. Reference in these later documents to "peoples" indicated some acceptance that rights could be understood in terms of collectivities, not just individuals.

In any event, these two covenants, built as they are on the foundation of the UN Charter and the Universal Declaration of Human Rights, are the main pillars of the United Nations' human rights "structure." Other documents include the International Convention on the Elimination of All Forms of Racial Discrimination (1966), the Convention on the Elimination of All Forms of Discrimination against Women (1979), Convention against Torture and Other Cruel, Inhuman or Degrading Treatment or Punishment (1984), and a Convention on the Rights of a Child (1989). Documents produced by the UN Educational, Scientific, and Cultural Organization (UNESCO), the International Labor Organization (ILO), the World Health Organization (WHO), and other specialized agencies have contributed directly and indirectly to the corpus of this emergent UN human rights regime. See Table 13.1 for a list of documentary sources that specify human rights.

Machinery for Human Rights Issues and Cases

Sovereign states have jealously guarded their legal jurisdiction and have been very reluctant to surrender such authority to international institutions on all types of cases, including human rights. A Permanent Court of International Justice (PCIJ) was established under the League of Nations in 1922 at The Hague in the Netherlands. Its jurisdiction was limited to cases involving states. Legal accountability of individuals was left to the courts of individual states. Germany's invasion of Poland in 1939 marked the de facto end of the PCIJ, which was officially disbanded in 1946.

Following World War II, a new International Court of Justice (ICJ) or World Court was established at The Hague in the Netherlands as a principal organ of the UN organization and successor to the earlier PCIJ. The ICJ also meets to hear only those cases brought voluntarily by states agreeing to submit to its jurisdiction. Moreover, the ICJ does not have jurisdiction in cases involving individuals; the ICJ's jurisdiction thus fully respects the sovereignty of states.

Even the Universal Declaration of Human Rights has been viewed with a certain degree of skepticism. It was easy to agree on high principles when the matter of enforcement was left unresolved. Nowhere in the Declaration was it mandated that a member state had the right to intervene in another country's affairs to stop human rights abuses; state sovereignty still ruled.

Individual accountability for such crimes against the law of nations such as piracy on the high seas was established in international legal practice centuries ago. It was left, however, to the domestic courts of states to try pirates and other alleged offenders of the law of nations. War crimes trials of individuals following World War II under the International Military Tribunal at Nuremberg, Germany, set an enormously important precedent for the assertion of international jurisdiction

---

[11]Articles 22–27 specifically address social security, rights to work and leisure, adequate standard of living, education, and participation in cultural life.

TABLE 13.1

Selected Documents Defining a Global Human Rights Regime

To find the legal bases of human rights claims, we consult the treaties or conventions that address these matters. We also may consider customary practice, writings of jurists, and general principles established in international law as additional sources.

1948	Universal Declaration of Human Rights
1948	Convention on the Prevention and Punishment of the Crime of Genocide
1949	Geneva Conventions for Amelioration of the Condition of the Wounded and Sick Members of Armed Forces in the Field
	Amelioration of the Condition of Wounded, Sick, and Shipwrecked Members of Armed Forces at Sea
	Treatment of Prisoners of War
	Protection of Civilian Persons in Time of War
1951	Convention Relating to the Status of Refugees
1966	International Covenant of Civil and Political Rights
1966	International Covenant on Social and Cultural Rights
1966	International Convention on the Elimination of All Forms of Racial Discrimination
1977	Protocols to the Geneva Conventions (see 1949 above)
	Protection of Victims of International Armed Conflicts and Non-International Armed Conflicts
1979	Convention on the Elimination of All Forms of Discrimination against Women
1984	Convention against Torture and Other Cruel, Inhuman, or Degrading Treatment or Punishment
1989	Convention on the Rights of the Child
1989	Second Optional Protocol to the International Covenant on Civil and Political Rights (aiming at abolition of the death penalty)
1999	Optional Protocol to the Convention on the Elimination of Discrimination against Women
2000	Optional Protocols to the Convention on the Rights of Children (children in armed conflict, the sale of children, child prostitution, and pornography)
2002	Optional Protocol to the Convention against Torture and Other Cruel, Inhuman, or Degrading Treatment or Punishment

over such cases. The Nürnberg (in English, Nuremberg) Tribunal was given its authority in 1945 by the victorious "Big Four" allied powers or "united nations" of World War II—the United States, the Soviet Union, the United Kingdom, and France—which had just defeated the German Reich and its allies. War crimes trials were also conducted in Tokyo under U.S. occupation authority over Japan.

The Nuremberg Tribunal dealt not only with war crimes ("violations of the laws or customs of war") but also with two new crimes under international law—crimes against peace ("planning, preparation, initiation or waging of a war of aggression") and crimes against humanity ("murder, extermination, enslavement, deportation, and other inhumane acts committed against any civilian population"). The concept of crimes against humanity was affirmed further when the General Assembly adopted the Convention on the Prevention and Punishment of the Crime of Genocide in December 1948. The convention declared genocide to be a crime under international law and stated that persons charged with genocide shall be tried "by a competent tribunal." After adjournment of the Nuremberg Tribunal, states reassumed first jurisdiction in such matters, but a precedent for international hearing of criminal cases involving individuals had been set.

Calls for new international war crimes trials have occurred from time to time. Global horror over atrocities in Bosnia and elsewhere in the former Yugoslavia finally produced enough pressure for war crimes trials to be organized, the first since Nuremberg after World War II. The statute establishing the International Criminal Tribunal for the Former Yugoslavia (ICTY) was adopted by the UN Security Council in May 1993. The tribunal was mandated to prosecute persons responsible for serious violations of basic international humanitarian laws (war crimes, crimes against humanity, and genocide). The tribunal is an independent body consisting of sixteen judges, an Office of the Prosecutor, and staff of more than 1,300 persons from eighty-three countries.

A UN investigative commission reported to the Security Council in 1994 its findings of "crimes against humanity" that "constitute genocide" in Bosnia. Human rights violations were committed by all sides, but the principal victims were Bosnian Muslims. The report indicated that among the tactics used was rape of women "for the purpose of terrorizing and humiliating them often as part of the policy of 'ethnic cleansing.'" Beyond regrouping and forcing movements of peoples based on their ethnic identities, humiliation of women apparently was part of "a systematic rape" campaign designed to break up Muslim families and communities because of the shame rape victims would carry, particularly in these more traditional Muslim communal settings. Further victimization of innocent rape victims by shunning, ostracizing, or holding them somehow responsible or guilty is common enough in many societies. To use this vulnerability as a calculated tactic in the destruction of a people, however, is what makes mass rape part of an overall program of genocide. In March 1998, the tribunal's Office of the Prosecutor announced the extension of its jurisdiction over events also occurring during the armed conflict in Kosovo. Trials began two years later.

A major weakness of the tribunal was the fact that it had no constabulary to enforce its indictments. It had to rely on the voluntary cooperation of states, including the very governments whose officials it sought to prosecute. In effect, the tribunal had to rely on NATO forces to enforce its rulings. In the case of Bosnia, NATO forces were given the authorization, but not the responsibility, for apprehending indicted war criminals. Significantly, the June 1999 peace plan to end the war in Kosovo did not give NATO forces a mandate to arrest Slobodan Milošević, the president of Serbia and an indicted war criminal. Milošević was eventually arrested, and his long, drawn-out trial began in February 2002. Nevertheless, the tribunal gained the grudging respect even of its critics. Milošević died of a heart attack in 2006 before a verdict was delivered, much less sentencing. Those found guilty of crimes against humanity received sentences ranging between five and forty years of imprisonment, depending upon the gravity of their offenses.

Similarly, an International Criminal Tribunal for Rwanda (ICTR) was established in Tanzania to prosecute those suspected of committing genocide and other serious human rights violations during Hutu-Tutsi tribal warfare in 1994. Specifically listed offenses included widespread murder of civilians, torture, and mass rape. The first-ever sentencing for the crime of genocide by an international court occurred in 1998. Two individuals, including the former prime minister of Rwanda, were given life sentences. So-called "hybrid courts" composed of local and international judges applied a mix of local and international law to cases in Kosovo, East Timor, and Sierra Leone.

An international conference in Rome did take a major step forward in 1998 when it formulated as a treaty for signature and ratification a new statute for an International Criminal Court (ICC) with global jurisdiction, complementary to national courts, for genocide, war crimes, and crimes against humanity. Unlike previous war crimes courts with jurisdiction limited to specific conflicts, the ICC is a permanent institution. Unlike the International Court of Justice (ICJ), it is not an organ of the United Nations.

The Clinton administration supported creation of the ICC, but this position was reversed by the Bush administration (2001–2009). Fearing that American soldiers and peacekeepers abroad (not to mention U.S. political and military leaders) could be brought before the court on politically motivated charges, the United States joined Israel and China in rejecting the new tribunal. The "war on terror" following the September 11, 2001, al-Qaeda attacks in New York and Washington only exacerbated these concerns.

In May 2002, a month after the ICC formally came into existence, President George W. Bush informed the United Nations that the United States would not ratify the Treaty of Rome, raising questions about the court's legitimacy. Gains in criminal accountability before international courts have not been matched, however, by expansion of international jurisdiction for civil cases (as when individuals or corporations sue each other for violations of contracts, torts, and other offenses, or when allowed by domestic law, try to sue or petition governments for redress of grievances). For the most part, civil law remains the domain of states exercising jurisdiction within their territorial boundaries.

Even though the United States was not a participant in the ICC in its first decade of work, U.S. policymakers in the Obama administration have supported use of the ICC, particularly for those committing war crimes, genocide, and other crimes against humanity. Since its founding, the court has actively pursued cases in the Central African Republic, Democratic Republic of the Congo, Sudan (Darfur), Kenya, Libya, and Uganda. Although support for ratification of the Rome Treaty falls short of the required two-thirds of the U.S. Senate, continued endorsement by the Obama administration of the court as the proper venue for such trials adds legitimacy to the ICC.

Regional Human Rights Efforts in Europe

Efforts to build upon the base established by the Universal Declaration have continued within the United Nations, expanding the scope of rights to include social, economic, and cultural concerns that retain—but go well beyond—the liberal, individual commitments embodied in the original declaration. Further specification of rights by treaty (and thus with a firmer basis in international law) has been achieved by states participating on regional bases in the Council of Europe, the Organization for Security and Cooperation in Europe (OSCE), the European Union, and the Organization of American States.

Some of these regional efforts have made substantial progress in the human rights field. Members of the Council of Europe (an international organization formed in 1949 and located in Strasbourg, France) are democratically oriented European states seeking to expand civil society and the rule of law. In 1950, the council adopted the European Convention for the Protection of Human Rights and Fundamental Freedoms. As an international organization composed of European democracies, the council oversees the work of an executive agency (the European Commission on Human Rights) and a judicial arm (the European Court of Human Rights), both of which are located in Strasbourg. Only member states or the commission may actually bring cases before this court. Europeans as individuals, however, may petition the European Commission on Human Rights after exhausting domestic legal remedies. In turn, the commission (or states) may refer such matters to the European Court of Human Rights. Although individuals thus do not have direct access to this court, individual cases deemed worthy by the commission or states belonging to the Council of Europe may be heard. Moreover, the European Court of Human Rights not only may award compensation to individuals for damages but also may exercise limited judicial review by requiring states to change domestic laws found in violation of the convention.

Not to be confused with the Council of Europe and its European Court of Human Rights is the European Union's European Court of Justice (ECJ), located in Luxembourg. In the European Union's legal system, ECJ rulings supersede domestic laws of EU members when these laws are in conflict with EU law. Significantly, the ECJ hears not only cases brought by states and EU institutions but also cases brought by or against individuals or corporations (so-called natural or legal persons, respectively). Thus, in addition to states and EU institutions, individuals and corporations may take cases directly to the European Court of Justice without having secured the consent of their national authorities. Indeed, its caseload has grown substantially in recent years, and it has ruled on thousands of cases involving contract and other economic issues, some of which have had human rights aspects. International courts in Europe have thus acquired some jurisdiction for certain civil and criminal cases involving persons. It should also be noted that the European Union has a Charter of Fundamental Rights, and acceptance of these rights is a precondition for countries who seek to join the EU.

Relying on regional courts and asserting legal arguments and decisions that overrule national courts is mainly a European development. In addition to the Council of Europe and the European Union, the human rights obligations assumed by OSCE member states have been invoked many times since the Act of Helsinki (1975) that specified these rights in the first Conference on Security and Cooperation in Europe (CSCE). With more than fifty members, the OSCE also includes the United States and Canada and almost all countries in Europe from the Atlantic to the Urals. Review conferences allow an opportunity for the airing of human rights violations and the application of public and private pressures for their correction.

During the 1980s, for example, the United States and other Western states used various CSCE review conferences to criticize the USSR and other Eastern European states for human rights violations.

More recently, however, human rights questions have been dealt with as part of the OSCE's commitment to the "human dimension." This refers to commitments made by OSCE participating states to ensure full respect for human rights and fundamental freedoms. Since 1990, the OSCE has developed institutions and mechanisms to promote respect for these commitments, such as the Office for Democratic Institutions and Human Rights. The current approach of the OSCE is to assist states in living up to their obligations rather than isolating them.

Whether within the OSCE, other international organizational settings, or in bilateral diplomacy, public airing of human rights violations usually contributes very little to correcting these violations. In fact, such publicity often contributes to a hardening of the offending state's position lest it lose face in submitting to such public rebuke. China, for example, has been reluctant to change its policies despite foreign criticism. It is true that accusing states may use human rights to score propaganda points against alleged offenders, but this is use of the human rights issue for other purposes.

States and governments genuinely committed to rectifying perceived human rights abuses usually find confidential, behind-the-scenes diplomacy—however forceful—more effective in achieving these ends. Positive incentives for compliance may be offered in these quiet, diplomatic efforts on behalf of human rights. Of course, accusing states may also choose to use the threat of public exposure as a negative tactic. It may become necessary to act on the threat, however, when quiet efforts have failed.

In the final analysis, the OSCE and its human rights charter can claim at least some degree of credit for changes since the fall of the Berlin Wall in 1989 and the subsequent demise of the Soviet bloc and the Soviet Union itself. Indeed, democratic reforms and human rights assurances offered by the new governments in many of these countries have enabled them to join the Council of Europe with its more developed legal structure for human rights cases. These are modest but still very positive developments that seemed unthinkable just a few years earlier.

Other Regional Human Rights Efforts

Efforts in Latin America and Africa, in contrast to Europe, have been far more modest. Human rights obligations were specified in 1948 as part of inter-American law in the OAS Charter and the American Declaration of the Rights and Duties of Man. The Inter-American Commission on Human Rights was created in 1960, and in 1969 the American Convention on Human Rights established an Inter-American Court of Human Rights.

The OAS Charter revision in 1970 gave the Inter-American Commission a greater role in human rights matters, which was underscored by OAS approval in 1979 of a revised statute for the commission. The commission engages in human rights education and awareness efforts and receives petitions and complaints, even from private persons. It may publicize human rights violations, but it has no real enforcement authority. For its part, the Inter-American Court of Human Rights, located in Costa Rica, has heard a small number of cases but has not played the decisive role of its European counterparts in carving out authority over member states on human rights matters. Its opinions have tended to be advisory in nature.

The human rights structure of the African Union is even less developed on a continent plagued by violence and atrocities committed within and among states. Nevertheless, the 1981 African Charter on Human and People's Rights (the "Banjul Declaration") did enter into force in 1986. In addition to individual and collective rights, a list of duties to humanity and to state and society also was prescribed. The mandate to the African Commission on Human and People's Rights was explicitly limited to interpretation, promotion, and protection of human rights. No judicial arrangements or enforcement authorities were provided. Nevertheless, it has played a role in publicizing human rights violations, such as sending a fact-finding mission to the Darfur region of Sudan in 2004 and establishing a venue for peace talks.

NGOs and Human Rights

Particularly in the post–World War II era, states, international organizations, and nongovernmental organizations have all contributed to raising the international profile of human rights. For some states, pointing out human rights violations in another state may be a matter of principle, or it may simply be a way to embarrass a government. At times, a state may issue a condemnatory statement due to the efforts of NGOs such as Amnesty International, which relies heavily on global letter-writing campaigns, press releases, and publications to shame governments into releasing political prisoners or shame other states into making good their publicly stated support for human rights.

The origins of Amnesty International date to 1961 when a London lawyer, Peter Benenson, read about a group of students in Portugal who had been arrested for toasting freedom in a restaurant. This event prompted him to launch an "Appeal for Amnesty," calling for the release of all people imprisoned because of their peaceful expression of beliefs, politics, race, religion, or national origin. The campaign caught on and spread to other countries. By the end of 1961 Amnesty International had been formed. Amnesty's initial activities involved letter-writing campaigns on behalf of prisoners of conscience. Groups of volunteers were assigned to a particular prisoner whose fate was closely monitored. Unfortunately, few of these letters were ever answered, so in the late 1960s adoption groups were formed at the local level. These groups adopted a particular prisoner, country, or issue and helped with publicity, education, and fund-raising at the grassroots level. Outreach activity included churches, schools, businesses, professional organizations, and labor unions. New members and more financial contributions aided Amnesty's growth. In the early 1980s, the number of college campus groups expanded. Today Amnesty International has more than one million members, subscribers, and regular donors in more than 160 countries and territories.

The largest human rights organization in the United States is Human Rights Watch. The organization was founded in 1978 as Helsinki Watch. Local human rights groups in Moscow, Warsaw, and Prague had been established in the mid-1970s to monitor their governments' compliance with the Helsinki accords. Not

Nonviolent resistance is a tactic pioneered by Mahatma Gandhi against British imperialism in India, which has been emulated by others opposed to repression. The central question is how effective nonviolent resistance can be against regimes that rely on the coercive power of the state to maintain the status quo.

ARGUMENT   Nonviolence works to effect change when there is a popular support base against the coercive power of state authorities. Aung San Suu Kyi is one of the most famous political activists in the world today. Due to her defense of human rights and nonviolent opposition to the military regime in Myanmar (formerly known as Burma), she was awarded the Nobel Peace Prize in 1991. Viewed as a threat to state security, she was held under house arrest from July 1989 to July 1995. The daughter of the revered father of Burmese independence, Suu Kyi returned to Burma in 1988 to take care of her dying mother. She became actively involved in the democracy movement, helping to form the National League for Democracy (NLD). The NLD is the largest legally recognized political party. The military, however, which came to power in a bloody military coup in September 1988, reigned supreme.

Nonviolent resistance to martial law led to a series of arrests in 1989. In July of that year Suu Kyi and her colleagues had planned a Martyrs' Day March but called it off when extensive military preparations were evident. Returning home, she found eleven truckloads of troops waiting for her. During most of her six years of house arrest, she was denied access to the outside world. In April 1995 she was finally allowed two visits from her husband and sons, the first in over two years.

Her husband, terminally ill with cancer and living in London, applied for a visa in 1999 to pay a farewell visit to his wife in Myanmar, his first in three years. The junta refused, hoping Suu Kyi would go to Britain instead. Suu Kyi's husband died in March 1999, but she has continued to work for democracy and human rights in Myanmar. This activism led to a 19-month house arrest between 2000 and 2002 and a three-month imprisonment in 2003 followed by house arrest. Yielding to both international and domestic pressures, the regime finally released her in November 2010. Although detaining her and putting her under house arrest were intended to curb such activities, these actions actually strengthened her base of strong supporters at home and abroad. Indeed, even under house arrest she continued to work from behind the scenes, helping inspire, for example, monk-led protests in September 2007 that led to a major roundup of pro-democracy activists.

COUNTERARGUMENT   Even when there is a popular support base, the coercive military and police power of the state usually is enough to thwart the efforts of nonviolent, popularly supported movements. Actions like those taken by Aung San Suu Kyi, though well-intentioned, accomplish very little in the interest of human rights and only exacerbate conditions in conflict-prone settings. It would have been better for the safety of her supporters if she had acted quietly from behind the scenes to advance her cause.

APPLICATION   Unless leaders rise up peacefully to challenge their oppressors, there can be little hope of change. Regimes that control the military and police forces can continue to repress human rights unless both domestic and international pressures are brought on them by movements led by people like Aung San Suu Kyi. She conducts herself in the same nonviolent fashion as Nelson Mandela did against the racist regime in South Africa, Martin Luther King against similar segregation by race in the United States, and Mahatma Gandhi in India against British colonialism. How do you weigh in on this controversy on the efficacy of nonviolent means to effect political or social change? Alternatively, does repression of people warrant a violent response directed against the authorities perpetrating such abuses? Or does violence merely beget more violence—needless bloodshed without anything positive accomplished? Do you agree with the nonviolent path taken by Gandhi, King, Mandela, and now Aung San Suu Kyi? Why do you take the position you do? ▲

surprisingly, they came under pressure from the communist governments, and Helsinki Watch was created to provide support for these embattled groups. A few years later, Americas Watch was created to monitor human rights abuses in North and South America. The strategy of Human Rights Watch is straightforward— painstaking documentation of abuses and vigorous advocacy in the media and halls of governments and international organizations. As the organization notes: "We challenge governments and those who hold power to end abusive practices and respect international human rights law."

Amnesty International is only the best-known NGO working for human rights. Indeed, recent years have seen a veritable explosion in the number of such organizations. Not only is the number of groups significant, but also the fact that these NGOs form coalitions and communication networks to link them together, continuing from the 20th into the 21st century. The growth of the Internet has certainly facilitated this networking by providing data and information on websites. Now anyone can easily gain access to information about the latest advocacy campaigns or learn how to become directly involved in supporting human rights around the globe. These human rights organizations are in turn linked to domestic movements and organizations in countries suffering from human rights abuses.

REFUGEES

13.5 Describe the plight of refugees produced by wars, natural disasters, and other cataclysmic causes as well as what can be done to serve their best interests.

⊙—Watch the **Video** "Carteret's Climate Refugees" at **mypoliscilab.com**

migration ■ the movement of peoples from one country or area to others; immigration involves arrivals, emigration departures

Migration and refugee issues are no longer the sole concern of midlevel bureaucrats and advocates of human rights; they have become a topic of conversation and negotiation among heads of state. This is because these issues have generated conflict both within and between states, no matter what the underlying cause for an outflow of migrants might happen to be. International migration has implications for sovereignty, stability, and security for a growing number of states. In fact, the issue promises to become even more salient due to three political, economic, and environmental trends that cause international migration.

First, with the end of the Cold War, barriers to movement were lifted for many people living in former communist states. As the Soviet empire collapsed and independent states came into existence in January 1992, new minorities were created within these borders who now felt less secure. One option was for minorities to create secessionist movements and demand their own states; another option was to migrate. This scenario is all too familiar to many people living in Africa and South Asia, areas that have been plagued by civil wars.

Second, the huge gap in income and employment opportunities among countries motivated thousands of persons to become economic migrants. Western European countries have remained very concerned over the immigration issue. In the 1970s and early 1980s, about 100,000 people left the Warsaw Pact countries for the West for essentially political reasons, and they were welcomed there. But, as communism began to collapse, the number of migrants rose dramatically as their motivation became economic as well as political.

In 1989 alone, 1.2 million people left the former Warsaw Pact states. The economic restructuring and privatization process in the former Soviet Union and Eastern Europe also increased the number of those who wanted to migrate. The mass migration of people westward—many of them among the most skilled or talented—hampered post–Cold War economic development efforts in eastern countries. Emigration to newly industrializing countries (NICs) in Asia and oil-producing countries of the Middle East also drained important population segments in many less-developed countries.

Finally, drought, floods, and famines may also stimulate migration. According to one estimate, three million Africans were displaced at the end of 2005. This does not even take into account refugees created by conflict in such places as Somalia, Congo, Darfur, Rwanda, and Burundi. One can begin to sense the magnitude of this ongoing problem.[12]

In this section we focus on refugees, who can be viewed as one type of immigrant. A true "immigrant" certainly is influenced by both push (adverse conditions at home) and pull factors (such as better options in another country). By contrast to immigrants who have some degree of choice on where they will reside, refugees are unwillingly forced from their homes. The most generally accepted definition of a refugee comes from the United Nations: A refugee is a person who "owing to a well-founded fear of being persecuted for reasons of race, religion, nationality, membership of a particular social group or political opinion, is outside the country of his nationality and is unable, or unwilling to avail himself of the protection of that country."[13]

Thanks to the wonders of modern global communications, refugees trek across our television screens on a regular basis. The report may come from Africa, Asia, Latin America, or Europe, but the image is always the same—men, women, and children trudging down dusty roads, their few possessions on their backs or in horse-drawn carts or dilapidated automobiles and trucks. No matter who the unfortunate inhabitants may be, refugee camps share similar characteristics—smoky cooking fires, endless rows of tents, skinny children with saucer-sized eyes, and long lines of the ill and infirm waiting patiently to see a specialist from organizations such as Doctors Without Borders. Most media reports include the obligatory thirty-second interview with the representative from the UN High Commissioner for Refugees (UNHCR), who once again emphasizes the need for a sustained global response to the latest humanitarian crisis. Other refugees are not so lucky. Some refugees are separated from their families and subjected to armed attacks and exploitation.

The humanitarian response to refugee crises is in part a moral argument. How can the comparatively wealthy of the world sit idly by and watch fellow human beings exist in unspeakable conditions and subject to extreme deprivations? But watching the endless replay of refugee crises and scenes of famine sometimes induces what has been referred to as "compassion fatigue"—a numbing of our sensitivities when we become overwhelmed by the dire plight of so many fellow human beings. Eventually, television viewers and those linked to these adverse circumstances from internet connections may feel that investing emotion and money in what seems to be an inalterable fact of life on this planet is pointless.

---

[12]For current data on migrations in Africa, see http://unstats.un.org/unsd/demographic/sconcerns/migration/.

[13]The definition comes from the 1951 UN Convention Relating to the Status of Refugees.

As noted, some people may be victimized by such natural disasters as drought, floods, or typhoons. Most refugee crises, however, are not a function of "acts of God" or weather, but rather of politics. Political turmoil is most often at the root cause of the crisis, dictating the type and level of international response. The plight of Palestinians displaced in 1948 upon creation of the new state of Israel has yet to be resolved.

In 1971, ten million East Pakistani refugees fled to India, most not returning until the creation of an independent Bangladesh. The disintegration of the former Yugoslavia in the 1990s displaced some four million people within the former communist state and scattered another half million across Europe. Throughout many other areas of the world, men, women, and children flee their homelands because of armed conflict, intimidation, and repression.

Particularly when the political conflict has racial, religious, and ethnic overtones, those who have been expelled from their homeland will find it increasingly difficult to integrate into neighboring host nations or be resettled in distant countries. But thanks to modern means of travel, those refugees with the financial wherewithal have the ability to travel by sea or air to more distant lands. Those who manage to reach their destination are often viewed with fear and resentment. Others are kept in a legal limbo.

The exodus of refugees is as old as repression. It was not until 1951, however, that the Office of the UN High Commissioner for Refugees was established, principally in response to the large number of refugees fleeing the oppression of Eastern European communist regimes. These refugees were resettled and generally integrated into Western states, aided by sympathy for their plight as well as cultural and ethnic affinities. As a result of this experience, international standards concerning the treatment of refugees were adopted and are reflected in the 1951 UN Convention Relating to the Status of Refugees.

This convention states that the international community will treat refugees as a distinct category of human rights victims who should be accorded special protection. As noted above, refugees are defined as people who have been forced for political, racial, or ideological reasons to flee their home countries. According to the convention, the host nation should not compel refugees to return to their homes if doing so would place them in danger of persecution. Furthermore, refugees have the right to apply for asylum and be given a chance to plead the political nature of their plight. While their appeal is in process, refugees are to be granted adequate assistance. The convention was essentially written with the European case in mind, but since the United Nations was involved, nods were made toward universalizing these norms.

In the 1960s, however, the focus of international efforts began to shift to less-developed countries, which had been undergoing the pains of decolonization and wars of national liberation. Compared to later years, the early reaction of African states and the international community to the displacement of hundreds of thousands of people went relatively smoothly, in part because many African states shared a common colonial experience. Regional norms for the treatment of refugees were embodied in a 1969 Organization of African Unity agreement, and the 1951 convention added a protocol in 1967.

In the 1970s, however, the size and complexity of the problem dramatically increased in a manner the signatories of the 1951 convention could not have foreseen. In terms of sheer numbers, little can match the ten million refugees from East Pakistan in 1971. But with the era of decolonization almost over, political conflicts now involved independent developing states. Developed countries increasingly looked askance at asylum seekers from countries that had achieved independence years before as well as from countries with no historical ties to a European state. What did the developed world owe to these people? Were these refugees really seeking **political asylum**, or were they actually economic refugees or, less charitably as some suggested, fortune seekers? Could they contribute economically, socially, and culturally to the host nation, or would they simply be a drain on resources?

Such questions and attitudes are found in Europe, which has had to absorb the brunt of refugees resulting from the end-of-the-Cold-War fall of communism, but they also resonate in immigration debates in the United States and Canada. Downturns in the business cycle marked by sluggish economic growth rates particularly tend to heighten public awareness of the numbers of refugees and legal or illegal immigrants competing with citizens for employment and other opportunities.

As noted, the 1951 convention was the first international and transnational response to the refugee problem. Since that time, basic norms concerning the treatment of refugees have been institutionalized in refugee-receiving nations and also in the complex structure of international and private transnational organizations that attempt to deal with the problem. In other words, we can speak of an international regime, or agreed set of rules, for dealing with refugees. As with all such regimes, it requires the support of the major powers that dominate world politics. As such, the norms and programs of the regime effectively cannot run counter to the interests of these key states. The United States, for example, was initially quite suspicious of yielding authority to the UNHCR. Over time, however, it has become apparent to most states that the network of international agencies and voluntary organizations is critical if the refugee problem is not going to spin out of control. Unilateral ad hoc responses to crisis conditions are deemed unsatisfactory.

Nevertheless, the treatment of refugee groups under this international regime varies widely. A number of factors come into play, all of them involving politics:

- Domestic support for certain refugees in the receiving country
- The publicity the refugees receive
- The financial cost incurred by accepting them
- Foreign policy concerns of the receiving country in terms of the country of origin or other interested countries

During the Cold War, for example, local conflicts drew in outside powers. These conflicts generated large numbers of refugees in the Horn of Africa, southern Africa, and Central America. The United States and other donor countries responded out of humanitarian concern but also for reasons of national interest and broader foreign policy objectives. As the former U.S. Coordinator for Refugee Affairs stated in 1982, refugee policy helped to counter Soviet expansionism because it could be used to "wean away client states from Soviet domination."

political asylum ■
protection granted to individuals who face persecution, violation of human rights, or other denial of civil rights and liberties in their home and other countries

Similarly, Western Europe welcomed refugees from the Eastern bloc who, by voting with their feet, symbolically demonstrated the bankruptcy of communist regimes in the East. In some cases, such as in Central America, support for refugees went beyond humanitarian assistance and a desire to score propaganda points; refugees were armed and sent back to fight their oppressors. In general, therefore, states will be more positively disposed toward involvement in refugee crises if they believe their interests and foreign policy objectives are at stake—no surprise to a realist.

The interests of the major donors to UN programs—the United States, Western Europe, Japan, Australia, and Canada—in particular ultimately decide the nature and extent of the international refugee regime. The UNHCR and voluntary transnational organizations, given limited resources, are constrained in what they can do. Voluntary organizations in an age of instantaneous global communication, however, can help sway domestic public opinion.

This was evident in the case of the conflict and resultant creation in 1995 of refugee camps in Rwanda, Africa. Based upon a cold, hard calculation of U.S. national security interests, there was little reason to expect U.S. relief and logistical support to such a country. The American public and leadership, however, were willing to help, in part due to humanitarian concerns and worldwide appeals on the part of international and transnational refugee-relief organizations. By this time, however, 800,000 Rwandans had been murdered.

It is not only foreign policy considerations that influence the attitude of potential host and donor countries. Refugees can also be created by regimes that want to rid themselves of political dissidents or other undesirables. This was the case in Vietnam's expulsion of hundreds of thousands of Vietnamese of Chinese origin in the early 1980s as well as Fidel Castro's expulsion of criminals and mentally ill people in 1980 during the Mariel boatlift. Once such an action occurs, states may attempt to score political points, such as anticommunist states did by accepting the Vietnamese boat people in the 1980s.

The international refugee regime essentially deals with the appropriate responses expected of states, IOs, and NGOs *after* a crisis has occurred. Indeed, the UNHCR's mandate prohibits it from protesting against the *cause* of refugee outflows, allowing it to respond once refugee flight has happened. Little headway has been made in dealing with the roots of refugee crises, although doing so might help the international community extricate itself from a reactive mode. The problem is evident: To prevent refugee crises may require outside powers to intervene before people flee or are expelled from their country even though any such interference violates the sovereignty of such states.

Quite apart from legal considerations, in the post–Cold War era the advanced industrial states have relatively little appetite for intervention. This is the case in particular with the less-developed countries, where the West sees few if any vital interests. Yet it is in the less-developed countries that refugee crises will most likely continue to occur. Not just plagued with drought and famine, the developing world is the primary setting for armed conflict. From 1945 to 1990, for example, there were over one hundred internal and interstate wars in the developing world. Since 1945, nearly twenty million people have died in wars or as a result of civil strife and the use of force. Out of this total, some 200,000 or about 10 percent occurred in Europe in conflicts such as the Greek civil war in the late 1940s and Soviet military intervention in Hungary in 1956. The rest died from wars in the less-developed countries. Even taking into account the deaths caused by conflicts in the former Yugoslavia and Chechnya in the Russian Federation, interstate wars are primarily a developing world phenomenon, and this is where refugee crises will most likely continue to occur.

It has also been in the less-developed countries where outside interventions have challenged the concept of sovereignty held by political leaders and many analysts of the international state system. In 1991, the UN Security Council passed Resolution 688, demanding that the government of Iraq "allow immediate access by international humanitarian organizations to all those in need of assistance." Subsequent UN resolutions and state actions regarding Haiti, Rwanda, and Somalia overrode the principle of noninterference in the domestic affairs of states on the legal ground that these conflicts also endangered international peace and security, a condition allowing UN–authorized actions consistent with Article 42 of the UN Charter.

Compared to the Cold War and given their humanitarian concerns, the major powers are now much more willing to acknowledge that events that take place within a country can constitute a threat to regional and international peace and security, although it may be difficult to identify a threat to a particular state's "national security." Notwithstanding difficulties encountered during the UN peacekeeping effort in Somalia and the international consensus that the UN peacekeeping effort failed to halt the war in the former Yugoslavia, the West still was willing to introduce NATO troops into Bosnia in December 1995 and go to war with Serbia over Kosovo in 1999.

Twenty-first-century wars in Iraq and Afghanistan as well as interventions in the Middle East and Africa have all disrupted the lives of domestic populations and produced refugees from these conflicts. Put another way, refugee crises have continued to increase in number and severity, leading to the understandable perception that the situation is out of control.

Traditional solutions and procedures appear to be inadequate in the current environment. For example, voluntary repatriation of refugees to their homes is virtually impossible when the country is plagued by continual war and economic devastation. At the same time, few host countries are willing to allow refugees to take up permanent residence in their countries. In fact, even UN officials recognize that the very success of resettling Vietnamese boat people in the 1980s as well as the expensive long-term assistance programs for refugees in Africa have actually made the global situation worse, as states that create refugees believe they have no responsibility for finding viable solutions. Or consider the case of Iraq where, for example, thousands of Sunnis fled neighborhoods in Baghdad now occupied by Shias. Can dislocated persons really expect to return easily to their previous homes in such ethnically divided societies?

Donor states also grumble over the increasing costs of these humanitarian missions. In one year, for example, UNHCR received $1.3 billion in contributions, and this did not include the large sums of money provided to other international organizations such as the World Food Programme and the International

Committee of the Red Cross, nor the money spent by nongovernmental organizations and bilateral state programs.

Finally, the conventional categories used since the early 1950s have proved inadequate to deal with the refugee crises of the current era. Traditionally, humanitarian organizations made fairly rigid distinctions among refugees, returnees, internally displaced persons, and the resident population. But in the border areas of a number of African countries such as Congo, Ethiopia, and Somalia, people from all four categories live side by side in similarly appalling circumstances. The same situation has existed in parts of the former Yugoslavia and persists in many Middle East and African countries. In this case the UNHCR, which has always seen itself as an organization concerned with refugees, has provided food and shelter to persons besieged in their own communities. Little has been done to resolve the legal status of displaced persons, some of whom may be able to return to their homes, but thousands of others cannot or will not return.

CONCLUSION

It seems that one continually hears of human rights abuses and refugees crises. It is understandable that what could be termed "compassion fatigue" may set in. That is why it is important to keep in mind the fate of real individuals such Ai Wei Wei who was mentioned at the outset of this chapter. As noted, his independence of thought poses challenges to the Chinese government and party officials. There are, of course, thousands of others who live in oppressive conditions, yet are not often well known outside human rights circles and do not have even minimal protection provided by international publicity and support.

Perhaps international human rights efforts and attempts to deal with refugee crises in recent years need to be assessed not just solely for what they have accomplished in concrete terms but rather in terms of the contribution to developing a universal consensus on human rights and proper responses in what is still an anarchic world society. The UN-sponsored World Conference on Human Rights held in Vienna in 1993 illustrated the different interpretations of human rights concepts. In particular, there was an obvious gap between Western norms and those of many developing countries. These differences remain unresolved some twenty years later.

The difficulty in pursuing international human rights is particularly evident when it is discussed in the context of some of the other themes addressed in this book. By definition, a concern for human rights raises the basic issue of what the term *sovereignty* means today. If, as we have noted, the internal aspect of sovereignty traditionally has meant that how a state treats its own citizens is a matter of domestic jurisdiction, then criticizing a state on the grounds of human rights violations undermines the concept of sovereignty. Although some states such as China or Myanmar may continue to claim that no state, international organization, or transnational organization has the right to criticize how it treats its dissidents, the reality of the world today is that they do, whether they have a "right" to do so or not.

The violation of a person's rights due to his or her political beliefs and activities is relatively easy to condemn. In other cases it is not quite as easy. Consider, for example, how the AIDS epidemic in Africa changed the international debate about human rights of these victims. AIDS can not only devastate a country's workforce and worsen its economic prospects, but also weaken its military forces. How far should a state go to prevent the spread of AIDS?

In the case of Cuba, for example, mandatory testing, immigration controls, and quarantine were implemented, testing Western human rights precepts about an individual's dignity and privacy. How should a state balance the rights of AIDS or other victims with its concurrent responsibilities for economic and national security? Do foreigners have the right to criticize a state's decision, demand an end to discriminatory policies, and proclaim that access to health care and treatment should be a basic human right?

Reconciling diverse interpretations of human rights is not an easy task. Nevertheless, we can expect to see continuing efforts to cast human rights and human rights enforcement in global terms. This quest is pursued not just by diplomats, but also by such NGOs as Asia Watch, Americas Watch, Human Rights Watch, Amnesty International, and other similarly motivated transnational and domestic interest groups. Even if states are reluctant to act, such NGOs and movements continue to give human rights issues a high profile, contributing in their own way to the development of human rights norms in an emerging global civil society. Assuming such trends continue, the idea that basic human rights of individuals are not the exclusive domain of a state but also are a legitimate concern of the larger international community will continue to be strengthened.

✓ **Study** and **Review** the **Post-Test & Chapter Exam** at **mypoliscilab.com**

LEARNING OBJECTIVES REVIEW

13.1 Compare and contrast differences in religion and culture to diverse understandings of human rights and the human condition across the globe.

Those concerned with advancing human rights globally find substantial differences across cultures on the way women and men, girls and boys are treated. At the core of human rights concerns are violence and other forms of victimization of fellow human beings that are high on the global-governance agenda. Human rights advocates seek a global civil society that in its laws and norms respects life, treats fellow human beings with dignity, and affords others justice or fairness.

KEY TERMS
Human rights 455
Apartheid 456
Refugee(s) 456
Gender discrimination 457
Female genital mutilation (cutting) FGM (or FGC) 459

ADDITIONAL READING
Micheline R. Ishay (ed.), *The Human Rights Reader*, 2nd ed. (London and New York: Routledge, 1997, 2007) and her *History of Human Rights: From Ancient Times to the Globalization Era*, 2nd ed. (Berkeley: University of California Press, 2005, 2008). A general overview of the human rights field.

13.2 Differentiate among diverse strains of liberalism, particularly individual and collective variants, that underlie definitions of (and commitments to) human rights in the United States and other countries.

Both social liberals and social conservatives are liberals in the classic meaning of the term—both groups emphasize the importance of individuals and what they do. They differ ideologically on the role of government—social liberals tending to see it as a helping hand, conservatives tending to reduce the role of government, seeing individuals as helping themselves. What they have in common in the United States, however, is a commitment to individual rights and liberties. Many other countries tend to be more communitarian, prone as well to favor socioeconomic rights.

KEY TERMS
Supranational 461
Classical liberalism 461
Communitarian 461
Libertarian 461
Social liberals 463
Social conservatives 463

ADDITIONAL READING
Jack Donnelly, *Universal Human Rights in Theory and Practice,* 2nd ed. (Ithaca, NY: Cornell University Press, 1989, 2003) as well as his *International Human Rights,* 3rd ed. (Boulder, CO: Westview Press, 1993, 2006). Discusses the evolution of human rights regimes and human rights as a field of study.

13.3 Evaluate the American perspective on human rights in relation to those of other societies and cultures.

Although moral absolutes are always subject to cultural interpretation (for example, exactly how the manners or customs by which we afford dignity to others may vary across cultures and change over time), what remains unchanged is a moral or ethical obligation to treat others with the dignity due fellow human beings. Cultures can be wrong. No matter how some cultures rationalize practices like FGM, for example, the procedure violates life, undermines a woman's dignity, and is inherently unfair—unjust to the victim.

KEY TERMS
Legal and political rights 466
Socioeconomic rights 466
Cultural relativism 466

ADDITIONAL READING
Andrew Clapham, *Human Rights: A Very Short Introduction* (Oxford, UK: Oxford University Press, 2007). On defining and balancing rights as well as an overview of different kinds of human rights violations.

13.4 Identify the universally understood values that transcend diverse cultures and thus provide a common moral or ethical foundation on which human rights rest.

Respect for life, human dignity, and justice as fairness are foundational values underlying human rights. We reaffirm their compelling quality every time we learn of yet another human rights violation whether genocide, a war crime, or something less extreme. When rights or obligations conflict, we try as best we can to find a just or fair balance among these competing imperatives.

KEY TERMS
Genocide 467
Deontology 468
Categorical imperative 468
Utilitarian 468
Social contract 468
Civil rights 469
General will 469
Positivist 472

ADDITIONAL READING
Gordon Lauren, *The Evolution of International Human Rights,* 2nd ed. (Philadelphia, PA: University of Pennsylvania Press, 2003). The origins and 19th- and 20th-century progress on human rights.

13.5 Describe the plight of refugees produced by wars, natural disasters, and other cataclysmic causes as well as what can be done to serve their best interests.

Quite apart from what nature may do to the human condition, war and intercommunal strife tear the fabric of human societies, dislocating noncombatants from their dwellings, cities, towns, and other settlements. These are the very real and enduring costs of armed conflict—an ongoing, global-governance challenge on human rights agendas.

KEY TERMS

Migration 482

Political asylum 485

ADDITIONAL READING

Alexander Betts and Gil Loescher (eds.), *Refugees in International Relations* (Oxford, UK: Oxford University Press, 2010). The challenges facing refugees and the countries seeking to accommodate their needs.

CHAPTER REVIEW

1. _____ is/are the largest obstacle to the advancement of women.
   a. Lack of educational opportunities
   b. Female circumcision
   c. Patriarchal societies
   d. Infanticide

2. Which of the following is the main way in which the international community has attempted to focus attention on human rights issues?
   a. direct mailings
   b. UN conferences
   c. articles in scholarly publications
   d. economic sanctions

3. Human rights opponents of infant circumcision espouse which of the following arguments?
   a. Since infants do not remember the pain they experience, it is acceptable after all.
   b. Parents should receive consent from the infant prior to circumcision.
   c. Parents should not alter the physiology of a child—leaving such decisions to him or her upon reaching adulthood.
   d. Society must accept circumcision as a practice in order for it to be legitimate.

4. The authors suggest which of the following concerning the interaction between cultural values/prejudices and legislative law?
   a. Cultural values/prejudices are often superseded by legislative law in most regions.
   b. There is no interaction between cultural values/prejudices and legislative law.
   c. Cultural values/prejudices often supersede legislative law in the many regions.
   d. Cultural values/prejudices always complement legislative law.

5. Countries accepting immigrants try to balance _____ with the human rights values they espouse.
   a. the ability to defend immigrants
   b. the ability to provide adequate services for immigrants and native citizens
   c. the ability to raise revenues
   d. the ability to transport immigrants to inaccessible areas

6. _____ was/were a driving cause to impose a no-fly zone in Libya in 2011.
   a. Possible spillover of corruption into world oil markets
   b. Possible spillovers of democratic movements from neighboring countries, thus endangering international peace and security
   c. Possible spillovers of terrorism from Libya into France and Italy
   d. Possible spillovers of violence into neighboring countries, thus endangering international peace and security,

7. Those who view the world as composed of individuals are more likely to view human rights and justice questions on a _____ scale.
   a. global
   b. local
   c. regional
   d. national

8. Those who have a state-centric view of the world are more likely to view human rights and justice questions as the purview of _____ actors.
   a. national
   b. supranational
   c. global
   d. grassroots

9. A communitarian view of human rights takes into account _____ or _____ rights that an individualistic view overlooks.
   a. natural, systematic
   b. inalienable, universal
   c. global, international
   d. group, class

10. According to Louis Hartz, the United States adopted its individualistic view of human rights due to a lack of experience with which governing system?
    a. dictatorship
    b. participatory democracy
    c. feudalism
    d. egalitarian socialism

11. Cultural relativists would agree with which of the following statements?
    a. Universal rights supersede cultural norms.
    b. Human rights are inextricably linked to cultural values/norms.
    c. Universal rights are separate and distinct from cultural rights.
    d. Human rights are independent of cultural values/norms.

12. According to the authors, which cultural value is *not* normally associated with having moral content?
    a. manners and customs
    b. the treatment of the elderly
    c. the treatment of children
    d. providing for a minimum level of living

13. _____ rights and _____ rights are the basis of dispute when it comes to determining the definition of human rights.
    a. Whose, what
    b. National, global
    c. Cultural, universal
    d. Community, individual

14. Americans tend to focus on _____ and _____ rights over social, cultural, or economic rights.
    a. property, speech
    b. legal, political
    c. extrajudicial, extralegal
    d. individual, communitarian

15. Defining human rights depends in large part on determining the _____ of analysis.
    a. complexity
    b. nature
    c. unit
    d. contribution

16. Kant argued that we should only follow principles that we would be willing to
    a. proselytize to others.
    b. adhere to under all conditions.
    c. set aside in the face of new evidence.
    d. make into universal maxims.

17. According to the authors, utilitarians, such as John Stuart Mill and Jeremy Bentham, argue what?
    a. Individuals should follow principles that realize the greatest good for the greatest number of people.
    b. The greater or greatest good is the best option only if it does not interfere with personal preference.
    c. Individuals should apply cultural norms to determine the greater or greatest good.
    d. The greater or greatest good should be overlooked in favor of personal accountability.

18. Many social contract theorists believe
    a. human beings are subject to government authority.
    b. human beings have rights as part of their very nature.
    c. governments should shape the debate on human rights.
    d. social contracts should protect governments from incursions on their rights.

19. An individual espousing a positivist viewpoint of human rights would most closely associate with which of the following statements?
    a. Human rights can be declared by a positive act such as in a treaty or convention.
    b. Human rights cannot be created but are rather inherent in all people.
    c. Only universal human rights should be accepted.
    d. All human beings are born with a blank slate and can adopt whatever rights they believe in.

20. Which of the following is one of the first attempts to use positive acts to determine rights?
    a. the United States Bill of Rights
    b. the Declaration of Independence
    c. the *Magna Carta*
    d. The Universal Declaration on the Rights of Man

21. Refugees represent a special category of migrants due to what unique factor?
    a. They are poor.
    b. They have little prospect of finding a job.
    c. They were forced by circumstance to leave their countries.
    d. They are connected by family ties.

22. What is most often the root cause of refugee crises?
    a. political turmoil
    b. acts of God
    c. famine
    d. ethnic migrations

23. The 1951 UN Convention Relating to the Status of Refugees states that the international community will
    a. mitigate the flow of refugees.
    b. issue ID cards to all refugees and treat them fairly.
    c. give political asylum to all refugees as well as employment.
    d. treat refugees as a distinct category of human rights victims.

24. Which of the following is one of the factors that contributes to the treatment of refugee groups?
    a. the publicity refugees receive
    b. the financial cost incurred by accepting them
    c. foreign policy concerns of a receiving country
    d. all of the above

25. The principle of _____ has contributed to the inability of the international community to prevent refugee crises, but the strength of this principle seems to be weakening of late.
    a. noninterference in domestic affairs
    b. the balance of power
    c. equality of states in the international system
    d. the responsibility to protect

The Environment

"In China's thousands of years of civilization, the conflict between humankind and nature has never been as serious as it is today. The depletion, deterioration and exhaustion of resources and the worsening ecological environment have become bottlenecks and grave impediments to the nation's economic and social

LEARNING OBJECTIVES

14.1 Explain the environmental challenges the world faces in terms of the atmosphere, land, biodiversity, freshwater, coastal and marine areas, and fisheries and associated economic considerations.

14.2 Describe and evaluate the argument that environmental issues undermine international

security by impacting resources and precipitating group-identity conflicts.

14.3 Describe the limitations of UN-sponsored environmental conferences and the roles played by nongovernmental organizations in attempts to establish international norms and environmental regimes.

aniel Pauly is a French-born marine biologist, well known as a professor and the leader of the Sea Around Us Project at the Fisheries Centre at the University of British Columbia. His career has been devoted to studying, documenting, and promoting policies to mitigate the impact of fisheries on the world's marine ecosystems, and his research and Ecopath modeling approach and software (www.ecopath.org) have been adopted by other research institutes and NGOs.

Even up until the 1990s, the one word often used to describe the sea as a source of food was "inexhaustible." As Dr. Pauly and various IOs and NGOs have documented, this is clearly not the case. Atlantic bluefin tuna have been fished virtually into extinction. Cod, once so plentiful off the coast of Newfoundland, Canada, are now scarce, as is the case with halibut, haddock, swordfish, marlin, and skate. While sharks kill five to eight humans worldwide each year, we kill approximately 100 million sharks.

One reason for this state of affairs is the global spread of technology. Purse seines, introduced in the 1930s, are giant nets that surround entire schools of fish and which are then gathered up with drawstrings, like huge laundry bags. Factory freezer trawlers are now so large and efficient they have become virtually seafaring towns. Fishing fleets utilize echo-sounding sonar, which can detect fish schools long before they surface. Buoys known as "fish aggregating devices," or FADs, attract species like yellowfin tuna and blue marlin.

In the late 1980s, the total world catch topped out at around eighty-five million tons. Over the past twenty years, the global catch has been steadily declining. Meanwhile, as the size of the catch has fallen, so, too, has the size of the creatures being caught. This phenomenon, which has become known as "fishing down the food web," was first identified by Pauly in his book, *Five Easy Pieces: How Fishing Impacts Marine Ecosystems* (Island Press, 2010). Pauly follows this trend to its logical conclusion—all that will be left in the oceans are organisms that people won't, or can't, consume, like sea slugs and toxic algae. Humans have become such a dominant force on the planet that we've ushered in a new geological epoch,

Read and Listen to **Chapter 14** at **mypoliscilab.com**

Study and **Review** the **Pre-Test & Flashcards** at **mypoliscilab.com**

which Pauly proposes should be called the Myxocene. The term comes from the Greek *muxa*, meaning "slime."[1]

Imagine a village in England. On the edge of the village is a pasture or commons owned by the local herdsmen. It is a peaceful scene, as cows contentedly munch the grass and produce milk and calves. Gradually the size of the herd expands. As long as there is enough grass for the number of grazing cows, the carrying capacity of the commons is fine. But what happens as the grass becomes depleted and the herd continues to grow in number? Everyone sees that, at the current rate, the entire commons will be destroyed, and all will suffer. What to do? Focus on selfish short-term benefits? If everyone does that, the commons will rapidly disappear. Reduce the size of one's herd so the commons can replenish itself? That's all very fine, assuming everyone does the same. But can one trust others to do the same? Immediate self-interest may clash with the long-term common interest.

collective or public goods ■ the allocation of, and payment for, goods that, once provided, cannot easily be denied to others

The commons represents a collective or public good, meaning one that cannot be withheld from any member of the group. The tragedy of the commons is that the situation encourages short-term consumption of a good, even though it will undermine the value of the good in the long term. This analogy is often applied to the issue of the global environment. Assuming the environmental problems can be identified, what can be done for the collective good of the world's population?

In this chapter we will first provide a brief overview of key global environmental challenges and how the impact of economic considerations must be weighed by policymakers. We then turn to the contentious matter of the relation between environmental issues and political-military conflict, and end with an assessment of how practitioners in IOs and NGOs have contributed to the policy debate on the global environment.

A GLOBAL PERSPECTIVE

14.1 Explain the environmental challenges the world faces in terms of the atmosphere, land, biodiversity, freshwater, coastal and marine areas, and fisheries and associated economic considerations.

Everyone agrees that the environment should be protected, and it is recognized that this is a collective action problem. Some see the environment as an international security problem, while others take a more expansive view and see it as a human security issue. Research has done a good job of identifying the myriad of environmental problems, but the key question is: What should be done? A particular challenge is the trade-off between concern for the environment and concern for the economic well-being of persons, particularly in the developing world. It is all very well to worry about the spreading of deserts in Africa, but do we tell the local herdsmen and farmers not to cut down scrub brush for cooking fires and not to expand the size of their herds as precious grassland is trampled and destroyed?

In this chapter we provide brief overviews of the major global environmental concerns as enumerated by the UN Environment Programme (UNEP).[2] We

[1]Elizabeth Kolbert, "The Scales Fall: Is There Any Hope for Our Overfished Oceans?" *The New Yorker*, August 2, 2010, available at www.newyorker.com/
[2]UNEP, *Year Book 2011: Emerging Issues in Our Global Environment*, available at www.unep.org.

will highlight some of the challenges faced by practitioners in achieving collection action in each area.

Atmosphere

The discovery of the ozone "hole" in the atmosphere in 1985 led to many years of debate over its importance and what to do about it. The ozone layer absorbs most of the harmful ultraviolet-B radiation from the sun. Depletion of the ozone layer allows more harmful rays to reach Earth, resulting in more skin cancer, eye cataracts, weakened immune systems, reduced plant yields, and damage to ocean ecosystems. In the early 1970s, researchers suggested that nitrogen oxides from fertilizers, supersonic aircraft, and chlorofluorocarbons (CFCs) break apart in the atmosphere and release chlorine atoms that cause ozone depletion. International agreements aim to reduce and eventually eliminate CFC production. Even so, CFCs already produced (e.g., freon in old air conditioners, refrigerators, and spray cans—many of which are rusting in garbage dumps) will continue to pollute the upper atmosphere. Measurements taken of the ozone layer over the Antarctic show a weakening of the ozone layer. No hole has appeared elsewhere. The first general ozone agreement, the Vienna Convention for the Protection of the Ozone Layer, was simply a pledge to protect the ozone layer. Specific commitments are listed in the 1987 Montreal Protocol. Even with full compliance of the Montreal Protocol, scientists believe the ozone will remain particularly vulnerable for at least the next decade.

Industrial societies consume enormous quantities of oil, gas, coal, or wood (so-called fossil fuels) in factories, households, and transportation vehicles of all kinds. Burning these hydrocarbon fuels contributes to acid rain—production of carbonic, hydrochloric, and sulfuric acids that fall to Earth mixed with rainwater, thus increasing the acidity of soils, lakes, and streams and killing fish, trees, and other forest plant life. States have taken some steps to reduce the atmospheric pollution that contributes to acid rain (as in reducing sulfur content in industrial smokestack emissions or curbing auto emissions) and have tried to deacidify affected areas by adding calcium carbonate or other bases to lakes and streams. The problem, however, remains an enormous one as scientists try to identify more precisely the causes of undesired effects and suggest possible remedies or approaches to policymakers.

Even more devastating in terms of climatic consequences is the degree to which burning hydrocarbon fuels contributes to **global warming**. If atmospheric scientists are correct (and there are only a few who still disagree), burning such fuels over many decades increases the overall volume of carbon dioxide in the atmosphere, creating a greenhouse effect or thermal blanket that keeps more heat from escaping into space. Clearing rain forests and other forested areas exacerbates the problems by removing an important natural recycling mechanism—trees and other plant life take carbon dioxide in and release oxygen as part of the photosynthesis process. Even a degree or two in overall global temperature increase can produce seasonal variation, rainfall, and other effects that can reduce or even eliminate agricultural production in some regions, flood some landscapes, create deserts in other areas, and increase sea levels (due to melting polar ice caps) with consequent

✴ Explore the "North-South Gap: You Are a Coffee Farmer" at mypoliscilab.com

human security ■ emphasis on security of all human beings, not the more common and limited focus on national or state security

global warming ■ an increase in the volume of carbon dioxide in the atmosphere contributing to a greenhouse effect that traps heat from the sun's rays and raises the average temperature around the world

flooding of coastal and other low-lying areas. The prospect of runaway climate change also increases dramatically if global temperature rises more than 2°C, according to the International Climate Change Taskforce (2005). Such catastrophic climate change would cause rising sea levels, large declines in food production, water shortages, irreversible damage to ecosystems including the Amazon rain forest, and shutdown of the Gulf Stream that gives Europe its temperate climate. Aside from the current and future cataloguing of climate change, the ongoing Intergovernmental Panel on Climate Change (IPCC) issued a report in 2007 on the opportunities to mitigate the complex global warming problem (www.ipcc.ch).

In the face of such evidence, why isn't more done to mitigate these threats? Part of the problem is that from a policymaker's perspective, "going green" by severely restricting the sources of pollution can come at the expense of current jobs in so-called smokestack industries. This domestic consideration is compounded by the fact that countries such as China and India understandably resent being told by Western countries that they should curtail their dramatic economic rise when those same Western states rose to economic prominence with scant concern for the environmental impact.

Land

The main driving force leading to pressure on land resources has been increasing food production. Today food is needed for two billion more people than lived on the Earth three decades ago. Inefficient irrigation schemes can cause salinization and alkalization of soil, resulting in an estimated ten million hectares (38,610 square miles) of irrigated land abandoned annually. Humans also contribute to land degradation through poor soil management practices, deforestation, removal of natural vegetation, use of heavy machinery, overgrazing of livestock, and improper crop rotation.

Deforestation is caused by the expansion of agricultural land; overharvesting of industrial wood, fuel wood, and other forest products; and overgrazing. Underlying these practices are such factors as poverty, population growth, markets, and trade in forest products. Forests also can suffer from natural factors such as insect pests, diseases, and fire. The net loss of the global forest area (deforestation plus reforestation) in the last decade of the 20th century was about 94 million hectares (363,000 square miles), the equivalent of 2.4 percent of total world forests. Deforestation of tropical forests is almost 1 percent annually.

The 1972 UN-sponsored conference in Stockholm, Sweden, recognized forests as the largest and most complex and self-perpetuating of all ecosystems. The need for sound land- and forest-use policies was emphasized as well as the introduction of forest management planning. Most of these recommendations remain unfulfilled, particularly due to the competing demands for environmental conservation and economic development and subsistence. Some 75 million people live in the three largest tropical wilderness areas: the Upper Amazon, the Congo River Basin, and the New Guinea–Melanesia complex of islands. Population in these areas is growing at 3.1 percent per year, more than double the world average.

More encouraging is the fact that the rate of deforestation in Brazil's Amazon has dropped. In 2004, 10,700 square miles were razed, but in 2009 the number

ARGUMENT In his study of organizations, J. D. Thompson noted how uncertainties can make decision making difficult for practitioners. If we apply his insights to environmental problems like global warming, we find uncertainty among atmospheric scientists about possible outcomes as well as the relative importance of different causes for global climate change. Given this uncertainty, it is extraordinarily difficult to form a global political consensus on what is to be done, particularly because proposed remedies are usually very costly.

By contrast, the scientific understanding of ozone-layer depletion caused by chlorofluorocarbon (CFC) emissions has been far clearer, making a political consensus on remedies to be implemented much easier to achieve in what became the Montreal Protocol and later the Vienna Convention, which aim to eliminate or reduce CFC emissions. Somewhere in between global warming and ozone-layer depletion in terms of degree of uncertainty is the case of increased acidification of precipitation—acid rain.

COUNTERARGUMENT The primary problem in dealing with many global environmental challenges is not so much the issue of a need for scientific consensus to achieve a plan of action. The problem is that some states have understandably made economic development the primary goal. In countries with a large youth population with few prospects, creating jobs is the concern. Indeed, dismal life prospects even for educated young people was one reason for the protests in Tunisia and Egypt that brought down the regimes. While the long-term effects of global environmental degradation may be recognized, it is the challenges of the here and now that are of immediate concern to policymakers.

APPLICATION Putting aside the political trade-offs for policymakers between concern for the environment and economic development, Thompson's matrix below may help us understand environmental problems analytically as we explore building political consensus nationally and globally on appropriate remedies. In which of the four cells would you place global warming, ozone-layer depletion, and acid rain? Or are you even uncertain about how to categorize them? ◤

Preferences regarding Possible Outcomes

	Certainty	Uncertainty
Certainty	A	B
Uncertainty	C	D

Beliefs about Cause-Effect Relations

Decision-Making Matrix

Source: J. D. Thompson, *Organizations in Action* (New York: McGraw-Hill, 1967), 134–135.

had dropped to 2,900 square miles. The only notable success of the Copenhagen climate-change conference (2009) was a commitment to pay people in developing countries to leave trees standing. Four and a half billion dollars was promised by a half dozen rich countries including Norway, the United States, and the United Kingdom.[3] This initiative is known as REDD (Reducing Emissions from Deforestations and Forest Degradation).

Biodiversity

The extent of the loss of biodiversity is calculated against what is termed the natural rate of extinction. Unfortunately, the loss of biodiversity is many times higher due to land conversion, climate change, pollution, and the harvesting of natural resources. Land conversion is most intensive in tropical forests, but other contributing factors to the loss of biodiversity include waste and pollution, urban development, and wars. Yet as much as 40 percent of our modern pharmaceutical medicines are derived from plants or animals. The rosy periwinkle from Madagascar, for example, produces substances effective in fighting two types of cancers—Hodgkin's disease and leukemia. But it is rapidly disappearing as its environment is being destroyed to supply firewood and farmland to impoverished people. How can policymakers be expected to tell the poor that they shouldn't scavenge for firewood to cook meals for their families?

Scientists have noted an apparent increase in the decline and extinction of species over the past thirty years. Lack of data does not allow for a precise determination of how many species have become extinct in the past several decades, but it is estimated that 24 percent of mammals and 12 percent of bird species are currently globally threatened. With continued global warming that upsets ecosystems throughout the world, some estimate the extinction of as many as half of the Earth's species of plants and animals in a matter of decades.

Freshwater

Approximately one-third of the world's population lives in countries that suffer from what scientists term moderate-to-high water stress. This is defined as a situation where water consumption is more than 10 percent of renewable freshwater resources. By the mid-1990s, eighty countries, constituting 40 percent of the world's population, suffered from serious water shortages. With population growth comes industrial development and the expansion of irrigated agriculture, resulting in increased water demands. The flip side of the coin is untreated water. About 1.1 billion persons lack access to safe water, and 2.4 billion lack access to adequate sanitation. The result is hundreds of millions of cases each year of water-related diseases and more than 5 million deaths. Water management programs vary from place to place, and there has been a move in some countries to emphasize demand as opposed to supply management by introducing pricing policies.

---

[3]"The World's Lungs," *The Economist*, September 25, 2010, p. 15.

Coastal and Marine Areas

Marine and coastal degradation is the result of increasing pressure on both land and marine natural resources as well as the use of the oceans to deposit wastes. The root causes are increased population growth, urbanization, industrialization, and tourism in coastal areas. It is estimated that some 37 percent of the world's population lives within 60 kilometers of the coast. This is more than the entire world population in 1950. Sewage remains the largest source of global ocean contamination, and coastal sewage discharges have increased dramatically in the past three decades. Blooms of toxic phytoplankton are increasing in frequency, intensity, and geographic location. In several enclosed or semienclosed seas, including the Black Sea, plant and animal life is dying. Finally, there is particular concern about the possible effects of global warming on coral reefs. During the intense weather of *El Niño* in 1997–1998, extensive coral bleaching occurred worldwide. Some reefs recovered quickly, but others in the Indian Ocean, Southeast Asia, the far western Pacific, and the Caribbean suffered high mortality rates, in some cases more than 90 percent.

Global demand for seafood and other fish-related products has put great pressure on fish stocks, endangering some species—for example, tuna, sea turtles, and sharks—and causing other forms of environmental damage. Some environmental advocates would halt many, if not all, forms of deep-sea fishing to allow the natural populations the time they need to recover from overfishing. Another approach favored by others is managing both the intensity and modalities of fishing. Of course, prohibiting or putting restrictions on fishing tuna or hunting whales requires policymakers to reach international agreement and agree to adequate enforcement measures to assure compliance.

Partial remedies include reducing the number and size of fishing boats, installing "trap doors" that help sea turtles or other species escape from shrimp-fishing nets, pulling up fishing nets regularly to release turtles or other species inadvertently trapped, and using harpoons or fishing poles for tuna and swordfish instead of long lines that unnecessarily take other, unwanted species of sea life. Even fish farms at sea and their freshwater counterparts on land pose additional environmental challenges. Raising fish in sea pens often requires extensive fishing to feed them; genetically altered fish that escape their breeding areas at sea threaten natural populations. Sanitary conditions in these pens may also be problematic, not to mention feed residues and antibiotic effects on fish populations. On the demand side, environmental advocates urge people to avoid consumption of endangered fish species and publish updated lists on such websites as montereybayaquarium.org. Yet to further restrict fishing comes at the expense of even further reduction in employment in the fishing industry.

Global Population

Although we have noted that a number of factors place stress on the global environment, the key underlying factor is the growing world population. Some demographers project that within three decades or so world population will have passed nine billion persons. The concern, however, over the carrying capacity of the Earth is certainly not new. Thomas Malthus (1766–1834), a minister and social analyst, published "An Essay on the Principle of Population" on the eve of the 19th century in 1798. He published a shorter summary in 1830 for "those

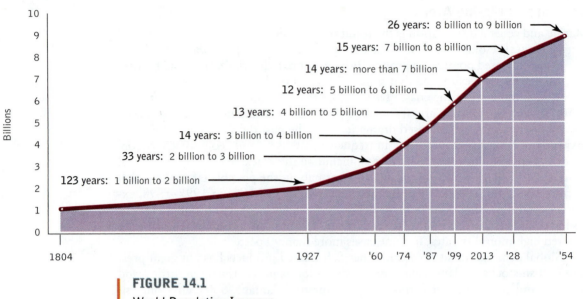

Billions

10	
9	26 years: 8 billion to 9 billion
8	15 years: 7 billion to 8 billion
7	14 years: more than 7 billion
6	12 years: 5 billion to 6 billion
5	13 years: 4 billion to 5 billion
4	14 years: 3 billion to 4 billion
3	33 years: 2 billion to 3 billion
2	123 years: 1 billion to 2 billion
1	
0	

1804   1927   '60 '74 '87 '99 2013 '28   '54

FIGURE 14.1

World Population Increase

Source: UN Population Division.

who have not had the leisure to read the whole work."[4] Noting the "prodigious power of increase in plants and animals," Malthus observed that human "population, when unchecked, increases in a geometrical progression of such a nature as to double itself every twenty-five years."

He worried that food supplies would not keep pace with population growth. How would humanity cope with its tendency "to increase, if unchecked, beyond the possibility of an adequate supply of food?" He foresaw "diseases and epidemics, wars, infanticide, plague, and famine." Malthus acknowledged that technology would contribute to increased food production. At some point, however, he believed that human ingenuity would run up against the Earth's limits to produce, resulting in awful consequences for the human condition.

In the almost two centuries since Malthus made these predictions, global population has grown dramatically from the hundreds of millions of his time to more than six billion people today. Through industrialization and modern medicine, population has continued to grow even more significantly. From the 1820s to the 1920s the global population doubled and reached two billion. From 1925 to 1976 it doubled again to four billion. By 1990 the figure was 5.3 billion, increasing by more than 700 million people in the last decade of the 20th century. Doubling populations when numbers are in the millions is challenging enough; doubling when the base is in billions is potentially catastrophic. Indeed, current estimates for the end of the 21st century put the numbers in a wide range from about 11 billion to more than 15 billion people. Can Earth sustain so many? Are there limits to growth? Figure 14.1 graphically presents data on world population growth.

---

[4]See Thomas Malthus, *An Essay on the Principle of Population* and *A Summary View of the Principle of Population* (London: Penguin Books, 1982, 1985), 221.

CASE & POINT | Estimating Population Growth

CASE   Annual population growth rate (usually expressed as a proportion or percentage) for a given population is calculated by subtracting the number of deaths from the number of births at the end of a given year and dividing that figure by the total population at the beginning of that year.

A convenient way to estimate the impact of population growth rate on total population over time is the "Rule of 72," which is also used by financial analysts as a quick rule of thumb in estimating the effect of compound interest rates on the growth of principal over time. The length of time in years that a population can be expected to double is 72 divided by the growth rate. Thus a 2 percent growth rate means that population can be expected to double in 36 years (72 divided by 2), assuming, of course, that the 2 percent rate remains constant over the period.

POINT   It is easy to overestimate future population size by projecting present growth rates. Reduction in population growth rates will slow the doubling time. Because population growth rates tend to decline as societies industrialize, there is a danger in projecting present population growth rates for developing countries too far into the future. Unexpected catastrophes due to natural disasters, widespread famine, disease, or warfare will also have a negative impact on population growth rates. On the other hand, if assumptions on reduced population growth rates are too optimistic, future population size can just as easily be underestimated. ▶

In the early 1970s, a nongovernmental organization known as the Club of Rome sponsored studies and conferences on limits to growth. The push for industrial development that got underway in Europe and North America in the 19th-century world of Thomas Malthus had enormous impact on the environment as forests were cleared, resources mined, and factories put into operation. Consumption of nonrenewable energy resources and other minerals increased dramatically, reducing stocks and adding to ground, sea, and air pollution levels.

Production of goods and services for increasing numbers of peoples has had adverse environmental impact, but continued development thus far has still been sustainable. The negative environmental impact of the Industrial Revolution, however, was less than it would have been had population levels been as high as they are today. If the more than 1.3 billion people currently in China and some 900 million now in India (not to mention projected increases in these numbers and additional billions in other less-developed countries) continue to industrialize following the European, American, or Japanese models, the result could be truly devastating, not only for these countries but also for the world as a whole. Resource depletion and environmental degradation on a global scale could undermine any capacity to continue producing at ever-increasing levels. Renewable resources would also suffer from growing scarcity as demand dramatically increases, with obvious implications in terms of arable land, fisheries, and the degradation of aquifers, rivers, and lakes. Development in these circumstances would not be sustainable. The limits predicted by Malthus might finally be reached.

Desertification is directly tied to human activity. It is unreasonable, however, to expect the poor of the developing world to refrain from exploiting their immediate natural environment.

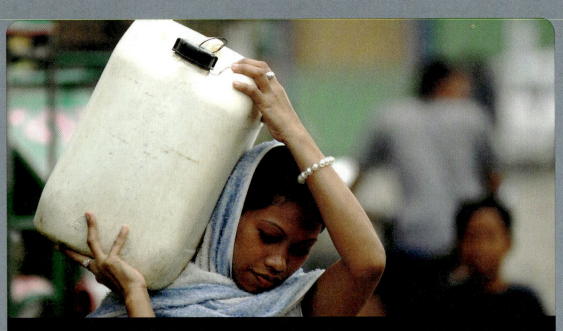

As a result of desertification, the poor often have to travel great distances to secure potable water. Some observers of international relations and world politics are concerned resource wars might become more likely in the near future.

Major cities in the developing world are ringed with slums as a result of migration from the countryside. As population growth outpaces available public services, the quality of life including the physical environment inevitably suffers.

Whatever the causes of the incremental rise in global temperature, the impact is evident around the globe. In this photo a slab of ice falls from a glacier in Disko Bay, Greenland.

THE ENVIRONMENT AND SECURITY

14.2 Describe and evaluate the argument that environmental issues undermine international security by impacting resources and precipitating group-identity conflicts.

A key question is whether environmental issues undermine international security. This requires us to bring politics back into the discussion. The Project on Environmental Change and Acute Conflict, which involved the efforts of thirty researchers from ten countries, asked three specific questions: (1) Do decreasing supplies of resources such as clean water and arable land provoke interstate **resource wars**? (2) Does large-scale migration caused by environmental stress lead to **group-identity conflicts**, particularly ethnic clashes? (3) Does severe environmental scarcity increase economic deprivation, disrupt key institutions, and hence contribute directly to civil strife?[5]

👁 **Watch** the **Video** "Brazil's Biofuel Boom" at **mypoliscilab.com**

resource wars ■ the hypothesis that state and group rivalry, especially over nonrenewable resources such as oil and minerals, contributes to conflict

group-identity conflicts ■ the hypothesis that environmental stress exacerbates conflict among ethnic groups

Resource Wars

Conventional wisdom suggests that resource wars are rather prevalent. But scarcity of renewable resources such as forests and cropland rarely cause resource wars between states. It is rather conflict over nonrenewable resources that occurs. Examples include Japan's attempts to secure oil, minerals, and other resources in China and Southeast Asia during World War II and, in part, Iraq's invasion of Kuwait in 1990 to secure disputed oil fields. Oil and minerals are understandably of greater concern to states, as they can more easily be converted into state power than can land, fish, and forests.

The most likely renewable resource to generate conflict among states is freshwater in lakes, rivers, and aquifers shared by two or more states. No society can survive without adequate water supplies. In the Middle East and Southwest Asia, the Jordan, Tigris-Euphrates, and Indus rivers provide the only significant sources of water to the approximately 500 million persons who live in the area, and the number is expected to double by 2050. Shared water resources that have caused disputes include the Nile, Jordan, and Euphrates rivers in the Middle East; the Indus, Ganges, and Brahmaputra rivers in south Asia; and the Rio Grande, Colorado, and Parana rivers in the Americas.[6] Because rivers often pass through more than one state, they are a constant source of potential tension. States upstream may not only pollute the water; as a means of coercive diplomacy, they may also threaten to dam the river, thus reducing downstream flow. Particularly in those cases in which the state downstream believes it has the military capabilities to rectify the situation, the chances for conflict increase.

In 1986, for example, North Korea announced it would build a hydroelectric dam on a tributary of the Han River, which flows down to South Korea's capital of Seoul. South Korea feared the dam could be used to limit its water supplies

---

[5]The framework, evidence, and conclusions of this impressive effort are presented in Thomas F. Homer-Dixon, "Environmental Scarcity and Violent Conflict: Evidence from Cases," *International Security*, vol. 19, no. 1 (Summer 1994): 5–40.

[6]Michael T. Klare, *Resource Wars: The New Landscape of Global Conflict* (New York: Holt and Company, 2001), 161; Peter H. Gleick, "Water and Conflict: Fresh Water Resources and International Security," *International Security*, vol. 18, no. 1 (Summer 1993): 80. See also Michael Specter, "The Last Drop: Confronting the Possibility of a Global Catastrophe," *The New Yorker*, October 23, 2006, pp. 60–71.

or perhaps as a military weapon if the dam were destroyed and most of Seoul flooded. In the Middle East, the Euphrates flows from Turkey through Syria and Iraq and into the Persian Gulf. Syria and Iraq both rely on the Euphrates for drinking water, irrigation, industrial use, and hydroelectric power. In 1974, Iraq threatened to bomb the al-Thawra Dam in Syria, claiming the dam had reduced Iraq's share of the water. Then, in 1990, Turkey completed the Ataturk Dam, the largest of twenty-one proposed dams in a major water supply plan to improve hydroelectric power and irrigation. Both Syria and Iraq protested, viewing the project as a potential source of Turkish coercive diplomacy. The fears were perhaps not unwarranted—in mid-1990 the president of Turkey threatened to restrict water flow to Syria in the hope of forcing Syria to end support for Kurdish rebels operating in southern Turkey. While Turkey later disavowed the threat, the fact remains that completion of the Turkish projects reduces water to Syria by up to 40 percent and to Iraq by up to 80 percent. Numerous other states also depend on surface water from outside their borders.

More recently, Egypt and Ethiopia have been quarreling over Nile River water. The world's longest river, the Blue Nile tributary, begins in the Ethiopian highlands. Egypt is the largest consumer of the water, but now Ethiopia and also the upstream countries of the White Nile—Burundi, Congo, Kenya, Rwanda, Tanzania, and Uganda—have banded together to rewrite the 1959 water treaty that favors Egypt. This is understandable from the perspective of Ethiopia, which has overtaken Egypt as Africa's second-most populous state and needs not just water but also hydroelectric power. Chinese banks are underwriting part of the cost of the turbines and electrical equipment.

Group-Identity Conflicts

The second question—whether there is a link between group-identity conflicts and large-scale migration caused by environmental stress—is supported by substantial empirical evidence. The link in any particular case has to be carefully traced, as the environmental factors that may lead people to migrate occur slowly over time, just as the social and political problems that arise in a host country also may take time to develop; there is no sudden explosion of ethnic conflict. In fact, ethnic conflict may not even occur, as in many cases immigrants simply suffer quietly in isolated misery.

But the situation is quite different in such cases as Bangladesh and northeast India. Over the years, large numbers of Bangladeshi have moved to India, causing group-identity conflicts. Degradation of the soil is less problematic than the increasing size of the Bangladeshi population. The United Nations estimates that Bangladesh's current population of more than 120 million will nearly double to some 235 million by the year 2025. Almost all of the arable land is already under cultivation, and land scarcity and poverty are exacerbated by flooding. It is estimated that migrants from Bangladesh have increased the population of neighboring regions of India by 12 to 17 million, with at most 2 million accounted for by migration resulting from the 1971 war between India and Pakistan that created Bangladesh.

This massive influx of peoples has affected land distribution patterns, economic relations, and the balance of political power among ethnic and religious groups. The result has been intergroup conflict and violence. In the state of Assam, for example, members of the Lalung tribe have accused Bengali immigrants of taking the best farmland. In 1983, during an election campaign, nearly 1,700 Bengali were massacred in the village of Nellie. Similar tensions exist in Tripura, where the Bengali influx has reduced the original Buddhist and Christian inhabitants to less than 30 percent of the population. This change in the local balance of power led to an insurgency between 1980 and 1988 that ended only after the central government agreed both to return land to the native Tripuris and work to stop the influx of Bangladeshi.

Civil Strife

The third question—whether severe environmental scarcity increases economic deprivation, disrupts key institutions, and hence contributes directly to civil strife—is partially supported by empirical evidence. The first part of the equation—environmental scarcity leading to economic deprivation—is well established. Soil erosion in upland Indonesia costs the agricultural economy about half a billion dollars in loss of income per year. The destruction of the dry land in Burkina Faso in Africa reduces the country's gross domestic product by an estimated 9 percent a year due to fuel-wood loss, lower yields of crops, and reduction in numbers of livestock.

China provides an interesting example as it is best known for its booming economy—at least in the coastal regions—over the past thirty years. It is estimated that the combined costs of environmental degradation are about 15 percent of China's gross national product. The cost derives from such factors as lower crop yields because of water, soil, and air pollution; higher death rates from air pollution; lost farmland caused by soil erosion and construction; flooding and loss of soil nutrients from erosion and deforestation; and loss of timber because of poor harvesting practices.

The last part of the equation concerning the political effects of environmental scarcity and economic deprivation applies to the state. Particularly in the Third World, the effect has been to undermine the legitimacy and hence the authority of certain states. Given the precarious finances of many governments, the loss of water, soil, and forests results in demands for new dams, irrigation systems, and reforestation programs. If those living in the countryside do not receive adequate government support, rural poverty increases. This may lead to an exodus to the city in the often vain hope of finding a better livelihood. The demands then take the form of calls for housing, transportation, food, and employment. With the increase in urban population come subsidies that strain financial coffers and misallocate capital. Such state intervention often breeds corruption and tends to concentrate financial and political power in the hands of a small elite.

When the elites are drawn from one ethnic group, urban unrest is possible, if not likely. This is not to suggest that conflict in the Third World is simply a function of environmental scarcity and economic deprivation. The idea that poverty in and of itself leads to political violence has proven simply to be untrue. Other factors, such as conceptions of what is economically just, perceptions of economic and political opportunities, the coercive power of the state, and the ability of political elites to exploit and politicize the poverty issue, all play a role. But such scarcity certainly exacerbates the myriad of problems faced by people of the Third World and works to undermine the legitimacy of many developing states.

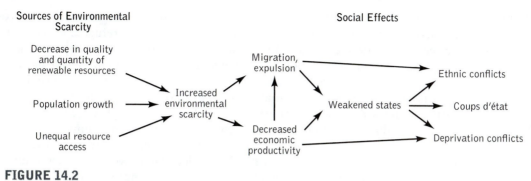

FIGURE 14.2

Some Sources and Consequences of Environmental Scarcity

Source: Thomas F. Homer-Dixon, "Environmental Scarcities and Violent Conflict: Evidence from Cases," *International Security,* vol. 19, no. 1 (Summer 1994): 5–40. © 1994 by the President and Fellows of Harvard College and the Massachusetts Institute of Technology.

We would also note the link between resources and civil wars. In such domestic power struggles, financing is obviously a key factor. In 2000, a UN report was issued on illicit "blood diamond" trafficking and arms procurement by the UNITA rebel group in Angola. The report noted, "Diamond revenues constitute the essential component of UNITA's ability to wage war." That same year, a World Bank study was issued on the relation between "natural resource predation" and the incidence of civil war. Based on a statistical analysis of all major internal conflicts between 1960 and 1995, the greatest risk factor for civil war was not ethnic antagonism, but the availability of easily procured "lootable" resources.[7]

In sum, environmental scarcity will only worsen over the next few decades as population growth leads to a decrease in the quantity and quality of renewable resources, with some groups enjoying disproportionate access to them. The population explosion will occur in the developing regions of the world, those least able to deal with such a development. The political and social effects are outlined in Figure 14.2. Finally, nonrenewable resources such as precious minerals will continue to be fought over to finance wars and civil wars.

14.3 Describe the limitations of UN-sponsored environmental conferences and the roles played by nongovernmental organizations in attempts to establish international norms and environmental regimes.

IOs AND NGOs

In our discussion of states and national security, we noted that realists claim the anarchic structure of the international system makes it difficult for states to work together. National interests and anarchy emphasize what divides states and people from one another. In the case of the physical environment, however, it is apparent to even the most obtuse leader that environmental concerns transcend state

[7]UN Security Council, *Report of the Panel of Experts on Violations of Security Council Sanctions against UNITA,* UN doc. S/200/203, March 10, 2000; Paul Collier, "Economic Causes of Civil Conflict and Their Implications for Policy," unpublished paper, World Bank, Washington, DC, June 15, 2000. Both cited in Klare, *Resource Wars,* 210–211.

Watch the Video
"Establishing Carbon
Markets" at
mypoliscilab.com

environmental regimes ■ sets of rules and associated institutions that have been constructed by states to coordinate, manage, or regulate their relations in a particular environmental issue area

borders. Industrial pollution in one country can drift downstream or blow across borders; environmental degradation can lead to economic refugees looking for a better life; the implications of global warming and ozone-layer depletion affect people around the world. Not surprisingly, liberal institutionalists have been particularly interested in tracking the drafting and implementation of environmental international agreements and analyzing the evolution of international norms and their role in the construction of environmental regimes. (See Table 14.1.)

As noted at the outset of this chapter, even when the environmental implications of industrial and economic practices are accepted, agreement on what needs to be done can be difficult to achieve. Many developing world countries, for example, suffer from massive unemployment and underemployment and resent being told by developed countries that industrialization is bad for the environment, particularly when during their own early phases of industrialization these latter countries paid little or no heed to the impact of their activities on the environment.

International Organizations

sustainable development ■ economic growth that avoids obstacles that would undermine or preclude further growth, particularly depletion of natural resources, pollution, and other environmental damage

The concept of sustainable development has gained increasing acceptance, particularly given both developing world emphasis on economic development and worldwide concerns for the global environment. A term popular with the United Nations and its various affiliate organizations, sustainable development is based on the premise that there needs to be a balance between consumption and population size within overall limits imposed by nature. Environmental degradation can also impede production of food and other goods and services needed to sustain increasing populations. Without an improvement in resource and environmental stewardship, development ultimately will be undermined, as eventually there will be little or nothing left of nature to be exploited. But without accelerated economic growth in the poorest countries in the near term, environmental policies will fail, as poor peasants are likely to exploit the land to the maximum merely in order to survive.

The United Nations recognizes that trying to implement such a balancing act is not a function of the "ignorant" poor failing to understand the implications of their actions; for example, ranchers and farmers in developed countries often also focus on the near term, tending to discount considerations that lie in the future. Indeed, given the massive scale of their agricultural and industrial production and extraordinarily high consumption patterns, it is the advanced economies in wealthier countries that have the greatest adverse impact, resulting in resource depletion, pollution, and other forms of environmental degradation. In any event, to avoid turning the concept of sustainable development into a buzzword or slogan lacking any meaningful content, hard thinking has to take place on the trade-offs between protecting the environment and economic development. Such a dialogue is not simply a matter of scientific evidence, but political debate as well, because it is through politics that policies will be decided.

As noted previously, UN-sponsored conferences have addressed many of these issues. The UN Conference on Environment and Development held in Rio de Janeiro, Brazil, in 1992 is a good example of a forum that brought diverse governmental and nongovernmental actors together. As the formal UN members, states controlled most

Selected International Environmental Regime Agreements

The key to successful environmental agreements is not policymakers signing the protocols, but creating enforcement and monitoring mechanisms that encourage or shame states to keep their written commitments. Do an internet search on three of these agreements and try to determine what has actually been done to solve the problems that are supposedly being addressed by the international community.

Environmental Agreements Relating to Atmospheric Regimes

Air Pollution	Convention on Long-Range Transboundary Air Pollution (1979)
Air Pollution: Nitrogen Oxides	Protocol to the 1979 Convention on Long-Range Transboundary Air Pollution Concerning the Control of Emissions of Nitogen Oxides or Their Transboundary Fluxes
Air Pollution: Sulphur	Protocols to the 1979 Convention on Long-Range Transboundary Air Pollution on the Reduction of Sulphur Emissions or Their Transboundary Fluxes by at Least 30 Percent (1985); further reductions (1994)
Air Pollution: Volatile Organic Compounds	Protocol to the 1979 Convention on Long-Range Transboundary Air Pollution Concerning the Control of Emissions of Volatile Organic Compounds or Their Transboundary Fluxes
Ozone Layer	Montreal Protocol on Substances That Deplete the Ozone Layer and Vienna Convention for the Protection of the Ozone Layer
Climate Change	UN Framework Convention on Climate Change
Environmental Modification	Convention on the Prohibition of Military or Any Other Hostile Use of Environmental Modification Techniques

Environmental Agreements Relating to Regimes for the High Seas

Law of the Sea	UN Convention on the Law of the Sea (LOS)
Marine Dumping (London Convention)	Convention on the Prevention of Marine Pollution by Dumping Wastes and Other Matter
Marine Life Conservation	Convention on Fishing and Conservation of Living Resources of the High Seas
Ship Pollution	Protocol of 1978 Relating to the International Convention for the Prevention of Pollution from Ships (MARPOL) (1973)
Whaling	International Convention for the Regulation of Whaling

Environmental Agreements Relating to Regimes for Land Areas

Antarctic: Environmental Protocol	Protocol on Environmental Protection to the Antarctic Treaty
Desertification	UN Convention to Combat Desertification in Those Countries Experiencing Serious Drought or Desertification, particularly in Africa
Hazardous Wastes	Basel Convention on the Control of Transboundary Movements of Hazardous Wastes and Their Disposal

(continued)

▶ **TABLE 14.1**	*Continued*	
Tropical Timber	International Tropical Timber Agreements (1983 and 1994)
Wetlands	Convention on Wetlands of International Importance, Especially as Waterfowl Habitat (also known as Ramsar)
Organic Pollutants	Stockholm Treaty on Persistent Organic Pollutants (2000)
Agreements for Other Environmental Regimes	
Biodiversity	Convention on Biological Diversity
Endangered Species	Convention on the International Trade in Endangered Species of Wild Flora and Fauna (CITES)
Comprehensive Nuclear Test Ban	Bans all nuclear tests in the atmosphere, underground or under water, or in outer space

Source: UN Environment Programme and *The World Fact Book* (Washington, DC).

of the action, but parallel meetings by nongovernmental actors also contributed substantially to the professed consensus reached on a sustainable development approach, assuring a sensitivity to the environmental impacts of economic activities and demographics. The distillation of this consensus was the Rio Declaration later endorsed by the UN General Assembly and the creation of the Commission on Sustainable Development, an intergovernmental body of some fifty-two members that serves as a focal point within the UN system for coordination of various UN programs.

From the perspective of some environmental activists, however, much of the Rio Conference consisted of world leaders posturing and mouthing platitudes about their concern for the environment. Hundreds of pages of proposals for international and national action were produced, but not much has happened. For the poorest countries, the problem is not simply lack of will but lack of resources to implement a program of sustainable development that balances economic and environmental needs at a time when population continues to grow. Environmental activists note, however, that the sustainable development concept also places developed countries on the hook. These countries, after all, far and away consume more both per capita and in the aggregate than do those in the developing world. Indeed, it is not always certain whether developing world population growth rates or the expanding appetites for the consumption of raw materials on the part of the industrial nations is the greater danger.

A related international effort was undertaken in 1994 at a meeting under UN auspices in Cairo, Egypt, to address global population growth in relation to economic development, the environment, and social concerns. Although a Cairo declaration addressing measures to slow population growth rates eventually passed, conflicting views were not easily reconciled—some Islamic countries even refused to send representatives to the conference. As such, some international conferences may well reflect the absence of consensus among the parties. Table 14.2 lists examples of UN conferences that have examined global political economy and society.

TABLE 14.2

UN Conference Diplomacy on Global Political Economy and Society

Conference diplomacy under UN auspices has brought states, nongovernmental organizations (NGOs), and individuals together to address issues of common concern in the global economy and society. In a number of cases the recurrent problem has been lack of follow-through to verbal commitments or fundamental clashes over divergent interests, as was the case in the 2009 Copenhagen conference on the environment.

Major Conferences

World Summit for Children, New York, 1990

Survival, protection, and development of children, setting goals for children's health, nutrition, education, and access to safe water and sanitation

UN Conference on Environment and Development, Rio De Janeiro, 1992

Continuing work that began in 1972 at the UN Conference on the Human Environment in Stockholm, this Earth Summit developed Agenda 21—a global blueprint for sustainable development (dealing with poverty, excess consumption, toxic and other hazardous wastes from production processes, alternative energy sources, greater reliance on public transportation systems, environmental impact of national economic decisions, etc.); drafted a Declaration on Environment and Development; prepared a Statement of Forest Principles; and took up both the UN Framework Convention on Climate Change and the Convention on Biological Diversity

World Conference on Human Rights, Vienna, 1993

Reaffirmed international commitment to human rights, strengthening mechanisms for monitoring and promoting human rights globally; led to the appointment of the first UN High Commissioner for Human Rights; made human rights integral to UN peacekeeping missions; linked democracy, development, and human rights

International Conference on Population and Development, Cairo, 1994

Worked toward consensus on family planning as part of development programs, seeking education and empowerment of women as the most effective way to reduce population growth rates and promote sustainable development, reaffirming that voluntary family planning decisions are a basic human right, and encouraging donor countries to increase funding for population-related activities; follow-up special session of the UN General Assembly held in June 1999

World Summit for Social Development, Copenhagen, 1995

Committed governments to eradicating poverty "as an ethical, social, political and economic imperative"; raised the negative side of economic globalization—growing gaps between rich and poor, shrinking social safety nets, and increasing insecurity about jobs and social services in both developed and developing countries; formulated a plan for meeting basic human needs, reducing economic and social inequalities, and providing sustainable livelihoods

Fourth World Conference on Women, Beijing, 1995

Addressed advancement and empowerment of women in relation to women's human rights, women and poverty, women and decision making, violence against women, and other areas of concern; supported efforts to fight violence against women and afford them greater legal protection; follow-up special session of the UN General Assembly in June 2000

(continued)

▶ **TABLE 14.2** | *Continued*

Second UN Conference on Human Settlements (Habitat II), Istanbul, 1996

Adopted a global plan and policy guidelines to improve living conditions in urban and rural settlements and to implement the "full and progressive realization of the right to adequate housing," identifying mayors and other local officials as key players in implementation of the Habitat action plan

The Millennium Assembly of the United Nations, New York, 2000

Set forth "animating" vision "to strengthen the role of the United Nations in meeting the challenges of the twenty-first century" for the United Nations in the new era of "global society"—underscoring the relation between development on the one hand and peace and security on the other, promoting peace and sustainable development; agenda included disarmament and other aspects of peace and security, development and poverty eradication, human rights; separate "Millennium Forum" for NGOs and other individuals

Copenhagen, 2009

Viewed across the board as a failure as it only resulted in a nonbinding accord to limit temperature rises but included no emissions targets. A global fund was pledged to help poor countries adapt to climate change.

Even when an international consensus is worked out, such as in the Law of the Sea negotiations in the late 1970s, which dealt with navigation rights and economic uses of offshore waters and the seabed, domestic political processes may preclude ratification of treaties and other agreements reached. Treaties may go for decades without ratification when effective domestic opposition is in place. Reservations or interpretations appended to international agreements can even alter concessions made by negotiators or change substantial portions of agreements made in the give-and-take of international negotiations. Of course, other parties may not accept such changes made unilaterally by individual countries.

Transnational Nongovernmental Organizations

The impact of transnational nongovernmental organizations (NGOs) on environmental issues is perhaps more evident than in any other area of global politics. At the international conferences in Rio and Cairo, private transnational organizations influenced the agenda, actively participated, and pressured states to hold these conferences in the first place. They have also played an important watchdog role in a wide variety of functional areas, ranging from environmental protection of the oceans and forests, Antarctica, and the ozone layer, always reminding political leaders of their public commitments. Such environmental organizations as the World Wildlife Fund, Greenpeace, Conservation International, Friends of the Earth, World Business Council for Sustainable Development, Earth Council, and the International Council for Local Environment Initiatives exemplify the diversity of actors that compose global civil society.

Transnational organizations demonstrate that instruments of power are not solely available to the state. One instrument has been modern communications.

global civil society ◼ the gradual worldwide emergence of the rule of law and networks or relationships among people in a world composed of both state and nonstate actors

Greenpeace, for example, has created wonderful photo opportunities for journalists by climbing aboard whaling ships, parachuting from smokestacks, and floating hot air balloons into nuclear test sites. Greenpeace has its own media facilities, allowing it to produce video spots and photographs for news organizations. Through dramatic actions and publications, Greenpeace and other environmental organizations can change public perceptions of the activities of states as well as nonstate actors. A good example involves Greenpeace's antiwhaling efforts. They have changed whaling's original image of man versus vicious, Moby Dick–like monsters of the deep, substituting the image of rapacious hunters slaughtering peaceful, nurturing mammals.

Using the power of modern communications to alter how people view topics of potential international concern requires money, an obvious source of power in the world. Since the 1970s the budgets of the largest transnational environmental groups have been greater than the amount spent by most states on environmental issues. Some of these organizations have budgets that are quite impressive even compared to the UN Environment Programme. For example, Greenpeace International took in $290 million in 2010 and the World Wildlife Fund $224 million, while UNEP's 2010–11 budget was $446 million.

Finally, initial successes of such organizations are often followed by further successes. Greenpeace and the World Wildlife Fund have enrolled over seven million members around the globe, supported by a well-developed staff and cadre of scientific experts able to contest the arguments and evidence put forward by state bureaucracies and corporations. These experts often provide input into the development of programs such as the Global Environment Outlook, sponsored by the UN Environment Programme. Such NGOs illustrate that the state is not the only focus for collective efforts to affect world politics.

Governance therefore is not necessarily synonymous with government. Transnational environmental organizations as practitioners contribute to global governance through their influence on how publics, states, and corporations perceive international issues. Such organizations rely not on force but rather on persuasion to help change and define the boundaries and conceptions of what are considered "good" ecological policies. In other words, they work to restructure the "environment" within which environmental policies are framed by politicizing such actions as whaling or pollution, issues that historically have been viewed as simply economic in nature. Most important, transnational environmental organizations have used this noncoercive power in efforts designed to change the behavior of states and corporations

governance ■ the political interaction of transnational actors aimed at solving global problems that affect more than one state or region when there is no power of enforcing compliance, as would be the case within a state

CONCLUSION

Despite the disturbing and dramatic research conclusions of scientists such as Daniel Pauly, interest in the global environment as a topic in international relations and world politics is relatively new. Access to natural resources has always been of concern to realists analyzing competition among states, but such topics as fish and ozone depletion, biodiversity, and water pollution seem to many realists to border on the trendy or faddish. This is quite different from the perspective of many liberals, who see the environment as another important chessboard of international

✓—[Study and **Review**
the **Post-Test & Chapter
Exam** at mypoliscilab.com

politics. Not only are environmental issues directly tied to economic and development concerns, but they may also stimulate conflict among states and groups.

The environment is also a topic that raises the issue of "What is meant by security?" To pursue a policy based on a narrow definition of "national security" may be counterproductive if the issue at hand transcends borders and requires international cooperation. Avoiding the tragedy of the commons is in everyone's interest. If so, "international security" or "human security" may therefore be the most appropriate concept when discussing the global environment.

LEARNING OBJECTIVES REVIEW

14.1 Explain the environmental challenges the world faces in terms of the atmosphere, land, biodiversity, freshwater, coastal and marine areas, and fisheries and associated economic considerations.

Garrett Hardin's famous "Tragedy of the Commons" makes an important point about the difficulty of achieving collective action. The commons—the environment—can be understood as a collective or public good. Some see the environment as an international security problem, while others take a more expansive view and see it as a human security issue. Brief overviews are provided of the major global environmental concerns as enumerated by the United Nations Environmental Program (UNEP): atmosphere, land, forests, biodiversity, freshwater, coastal and marine areas, fishing. In each case practitioners and policymakers often have to weigh a concern for the environment with economic considerations such as jobs.

KEY TERMS
Collective or public goods 496
Human security 496
Global warming 497

ADDITIONAL READINGS
Al Gore, *An Inconvenient Truth: The Planetary Emergency of Global Warming and What We Can Do About It* (Emmaus, PA: Rodale Books, 2006). The former U.S. vice president and senator focuses global attention on climate change.

Mark London and Brian Kelly, *The Lost Forest: The Amazon in the Age of Globalization* (New York: Random House, 2007); Stephen Sloan, *Ocean Bankruptcy: World Fisheries on the Brink of Disaster* (Guilford, CT: The Lyons Press, 2003). Both volumes take up other aspects of environmental crisis predictions on the global agenda.

14.2 Describe and evaluate the argument that environmental issues undermine international security by impacting resources and precipitating group-identity conflicts.

Researchers have posed the following questions on the relation between the environment and international security: (1) Do decreasing supplies of resources such as clean water and arable land provoke interstate "resource wars"? (2) Does large-scale migration caused by environmental stress lead to group-identity conflicts, particularly ethnic clashes? (3) Does severe environmental scarcity increase economic deprivation, disrupt

key institutions, and hence contribute directly to civil strife and crises of authority? In each case the answer quite often is "it depends." Conflict is most likely over nonrenewable resources such as oil and minerals, while the most likely source of conflict over a renewable asset is freshwater. Ethnic conflict may occur due to environmental stress, while empirical evidence partially supports the hypothesis that economic deprivation contributes to civil strife.

KEY TERMS
Resource wars 506
Group-identity conflicts 506

ADDITIONAL READINGS
Michael T. Klare, *Rising Powers, Shrinking Planet: The New Geopolitics of Energy* (New York: Holt, 2009) and his earlier *Resource Wars: The New Landscape of Global Conflict* (New York: Holt and Company, 2001). Both volumes underscore the national security implications of competition for scarce resources.

14.3 Describe the limitations of UN-sponsored environmental conferences and the roles played by nongovernmental organizations in attempts to establish international norms and environmental regimes.

International conferences sponsored by international organizations draw attention to global environmental problems. But they are often long on rhetoric and planning documents, but fail due to conflicting state interests and lack of follow-through. Transgovernmental organizations play an important role in publicizing environmental issues and have managed to secure enough financial contributions to hire their own scientists and experts and act as watchdogs on the behavior of states and international organizations on environmental issues.

KEY TERMS
Environmental regimes 510
Sustainable development 510
Global civil society 514
Governance 515

ADDITIONAL READINGS
Publications of the United Nations organization, the World Bank, the UN Development Programme, the UN Environment Programme, and other international organizations are rich sources of information available on their websites. The same is true for transnational organizations such as Greenpeace and World Wildlife Fund.

CHAPTER REVIEW

1. The tragedy of the commons illustrates
   a. the danger of mad cow disease.
   b. the dangers of collaboration.
   c. the challenge of collective action.
   d. the impact of high population growth rates in the Third World.

2. A major issue concerning the atmosphere involves
   a. pollution caused by high-altitude jets.
   b. high-energy radon emissions.
   c. nuclear leakage from satellites.
   d. a hole in the ozone layer.

3. Burning fossil fuels over many decades increases the overall volume of
   a. carbon dioxide in the atmosphere.
   b. lead in the atmosphere and oceans.
   c. CFCs in the oceans.
   d. water in the ocean.

4. Which of the following is the least likely to be a major cause of deforestation?
   a. expansion of agricultural land
   b. overharvesting of industrial and fuel wood
   c. overgrazing
   d. infestation of birds

5. The extent of the loss of biodiversity is calculated against what is termed
   a. the tragedy of the commons.
   b. the stag hunt outcome.
   c. the CFC index.
   d. the natural rate of extinction.

6. Approximately one-third of the world's population lives in countries that suffer from what scientists term
   a. little or low water stress.
   b. moderate water stress.
   c. moderate-to-high water stress.
   d. no water stress.

7. Which of the following is the largest source of oceanic pollution?
   a. dead fish and fowl
   b. sewage
   c. seaweed spores
   d. leakage from nuclear reactors on submarines

8. Thomas Malthus wrote about
   a. population growth.
   b. environmental degradation.
   c. the causes of war.
   d. pollution in the British Isles.

9. Countries involved in disputes over water include all of the following EXCEPT
   a. Syria.
   b. North Korea.
   c. Iraq.
   d. Brazil.

10. Which of the following—in and of itself—is LEAST likely to cause political violence directly?
    a. the coercive power of the state
    b. perceptions of injustice or inequity
    c. the condition of poverty
    d. perceptions of economic and political opportunity

11. The premise that there needs to be a balance between consumption and population size within the overall limits imposed by the environment is referred to as
    a. ecological awareness.
    b. sustainable development.
    c. environmental protocol.
    d. environmental awareness.

12. International environmental agreements have addressed all of the following EXCEPT
    a. whaling.
    b. tropical timber.
    c. environmental modification and biodiversity.
    d. water levels in underground aquifers.

13. The conference in Cairo, Egypt, that addressed population issues achieved
    a. a consensus on the nature of the problem.
    b. a consensus on the goals to be reached.
    c. a consensus on the methods of population control.
    d. little if any consensus then or subsequently.

14. Transnational organizations (NGOs) concerned with environmental issues include all of the following EXCEPT
    a. World Wildlife Fund.
    b. Amnesty International.
    c. Greenpeace.
    d. Friends of the Earth.

15. One of Greenpeace's most famous campaigns involved
    a. whaling.
    b. coral reefs.
    c. the launching of satellites into space.
    d. nuclear testing on Pacific atolls in the 1950s.

GLOSSARY

Actor A participant or player such as a state, international organization (IO), multinational corporation (MNC) or bank, and other nongovernmental organization (NGO)

Alliance A formal agreement between two (bilateral) or more (multilateral) states to cooperate in security matters—a formal security coalition of states with specified commitments

Ambassador A state's highest-ranking representative assigned to an embassy in a foreign country

Anarchists Individuals who advocate entirely voluntary human associations or communities, reject authority in general, and may or may not use violence against governments or their officials

Anarchy The absence of political authority. International politics or the international system is said to be *anarchic* as there is no world government—no central or superordinate authority over states, which retain their sovereign rights.

Apartheid A state policy of discrimination and strict racial segregation in a society

Armed intervention Use of force by a state in another country

Arms control A negotiation process aimed at producing agreements on weapons and their use—quantitative and qualitative limits on armaments, regional or other spatial restrictions, and functional measures related to telecommunications ("hot" lines between adversaries) and other confidence- and security-building measures (CSBMs)

Article 51 UN Charter article stating that if attacked, states have the inherent right of individual or collective self-defense

Assimilation A strategy, often oppressive, to create a common identity among diverse peoples

Asymmetric warfare Involves a lack of congruity in the capabilities and strategies of two foes

Autarky An independent posture of self-sufficiency as when a state as a matter of policy attempts to exist in economic isolation from other states

Balance of payments Accounting concept by which a state's international economic transactions (inflows and outflows) are tracked to include exports and imports (balance of trade), capital investment and other "invisible" or financial flows, and official reserve transactions (gold, certain national currencies acceptable as reserves, and SDRs—special drawing rights in the International Monetary Fund [IMF]). "Balance" is achieved when reserves flow in or out to cover differences in other accounts.

Balance of power A key concept among realists that is often defined as a condition of equilibrium among states either constructed by them or an outcome that emerges from the interactions of states over time

Balance of trade One account in the balance of payments—the difference in value between the goods and services a country *exports* and what it *imports*. A negative value (or deficit) is the amount by which imports exceed exports, a positive value (or surplus) the amount by which exports exceed imports.

Ballistic missiles Missiles that when launched follow a trajectory to the ground subject to gravitational forces; as their range and warhead explosives increase, so does the perceived threat to other countries

Barter Trading one good or service for another

Bellicism Idea that war and war preparations have positive value to state and society

Bilateral diplomacy Negotiations involving two states

Bourgeoisie French term used to depict the owners of capital as a class differentiated from other classes—the aristocracy as landowners, workers, or peasants defined typically by their labor in factories or on the land, respectively

BRIC Refers to Brazil, Russia, India, and China as rising economic political powers

Capabilities Material and nonmaterial resources that can serve as the basis for power

Capital Savings that can be used for investment in the means for producing goods and services

Capital controls Restrictions placed by a state on the export of money or wealth

Capital formation Accruing savings for new and continuing investment in capital goods for production and consumption

Capital goods Refers to goods used in the production of other goods or services, e.g., the machinery and tools in a factory

Capitalism An economic system, form of political economy, or mode of production that emphasizes money, market-oriented trade, capital investment for further production, and a set of values or culture legitimating investment and market-oriented behaviors

Capitalist world-system A focus on class and economic relations and the division of the world into a capital-rich *core*, a capital-poor *periphery*, and a *semi-periphery* of states between the first two categories

Cartel An association among financial, commodity-producing, or industrial interests, including states, for establishing a national or international market control, setting production levels, and increasing or stabilizing the prices of such diverse products as oil, tin, and coffee

Cartography The drawing of maps

Categorical imperative Ethicist Immanuel Kant identified two: (1) one ought to act "according to the maxim that you can at the same time will [such conduct] to be a universal law," and (2) one should treat others "as an end [worthy in themselves] as well as a means, [but] never merely as a means."

Causes, causality, causal Factors that occur prior to and appear to produce certain outcomes or effects. Some causes may be *necessary*, but not *sufficient* to produce a given effect; some are *efficient*—the proximate, immediate, or direct cause(s), while others are *permissive* underlying cause(s) that allow or pose no effective obstacle to certain outcomes or effects to occur as, for example, when international anarchy—the absence of central authority over states—is said to pose no obstacle to the onset of war between or among them. What is to be explained causally (for example, war) is the *dependent variable*, the factors explaining it referred to as *independent* variables. Factors that may facilitate, constrain, or block the effect of an independent variable are referred to as *intervening variables*.

Center of gravity Metaphor from mechanics that captures the idea that an adversary's military may have a focal point that is critical in holding that structure together

Civil liberties Freedoms from governmental interference in matters of speech, press, religious choice, movement, assembly, and the like guaranteed to citizens typically by the constitution and laws of a particular state and society

Civil rights Rights established by generally accepted rules or law in society—claims typically made by or on behalf of individuals concerning their equal status and role as citizens (essential ingredients in the functioning of democracies)

Civil war War within a state and society as two or more factions compete for governmental power and authority

Class A unit in society with identifiable interests or characteristics that differentiate it from other such units

Classical economics 18th- and 19th-century view shared by Adam Smith, David Ricardo, Karl Marx, and others that the value of a product was the direct result of labor put into the production of the particular good or service brought to market for sale. Later, *neoclassical* economists would see value (or price) as a function of supply and demand.

Classical liberalism A commitment to individuals as human beings worthy of regard in themselves and not just as part of larger groups or classes

Collateral damage Death and destruction to human beings and property coincident to (or following) the intentional destruction of military targets; the damage is not confined to the intended targets, but spills over to harm other victims and property

Collective defense A strategy relied upon by states that pool capabilities to balance the power of rivals or enemies

Collective good Goods (or services) to which others (including other states) cannot be excluded even though they have not contributed to paying for them, for example, the security produced by an alliance

Collective or public goods The allocation of, and payment for, goods that, once provided, cannot easily be denied to others

Collective security The idea that if one state behaved aggressively, other states have a legal right to enforce international law by taking collective action

Commodity Broadly, any article bought or sold; agricultural products, metals, and other minerals including fossil fuels are often referred to as commodities

Common market In addition to the free trade of goods and services, and a common external tariff on imports from nonmember countries, there is also free movement of land, labor, and capital—the three factors of production.

Communitarian   Philosophical position emphasizing collective or group service obligations to one another in society

Comparative advantage   Free-trade principle that countries tend to specialize in producing those goods and services for export in which they are most efficient, leading to a global specialization or division of labor that maximizes aggregate productivity

Competitive devaluations   Since devaluations reduce the export price of goods and services to purchases in foreign currencies, some countries may devalue their currencies merely to gain an unfair competitive advantage, a tactic often matched by devaluations in other countries

Concert of Europe   Early 19th-century effort by policymakers in Great Britain, Austria, Russia, Prussia, and France to create a society of states to maintain the balance of power and thus sustain the peace

Concessionary rates   Interest rates below market rates, thus allowing reinvestment of a portion of the funds at market rates, the gains compounded and applied toward paying off the loan

Confederalism   Weak central governments and strong political authority at state and local levels

Consociational model   Formal division of power among different national or ethnic groups—for example, as in Lebanon the president routinely may be from one ethnic group, the prime minister and other cabinet posts distributed across the other ethnic groups; government institutions, as in Belgium, may be duplicated with separate ministries accommodating the different parts of the country where the different national or ethnic groups reside

Constructivism   Ideas and concepts about international relations are not essential attributes but are rather of human origin and humanly constructed. The world is the image that states and others choose to make it.

Containment   The grand strategy of the United States to deal with the Soviet Union during the Cold War. Containing enemies or would-be adversaries through diplomatic means backed up by the threat of force remains an alternative short of actually having to use force in armed interventions.

Crisis   A situation characterized by surprise, high threat to a state's values or interest, and short decision time

Critical theory   Argues that theory must be connected to practice. This also entails a critique of positivist–empiricist approaches to knowledge, with critical theorists claiming all knowledge is historical and political in nature.

Cultural relativism   Belief that moral or ethical principles are not universal, but rather are tied to particular situational or cultural contexts

Cultures of violence   When violence becomes commonplace, it may acquire acceptance or even legitimacy in a community.

Customary international law   Law found in the common practice of states established over time

Customs union   States not only have agreed to eliminate tariffs on imports and other barriers to trade among themselves, but also have established a common external tariff imposed on imports from nonmembers.

Cyberterrorism   Computer-based attacks on information systems designed to destroy or manipulate data banks or cause the system to crash with the goal of furthering a political agenda

Cyber-war   Politically motivated computer network hacking designed to conduct sabotage and espionage

Defense   Programs and capabilities designed to repel or deter an enemy attack

Delian League   Alliance of city-states headed by Athens

Démarche   A diplomatic representation, request, or protest from one government to another

Demography   Collection and study of data on populations

Deontology   Human understandings we have within us of universal moral principles that transcend time and space

Dependency   Low-income countries of the South economically subordinated to the advantage of high-income countries of the First World or North; in class-analytical terms, workers and peasants subordinated and exploited by capital-owning classes, the *bourgeoisie*

Dependent variable   The thing that is to be explained or accounted for

Détente   An easing of tensions among states as in the late 1960s and 1970s between the United States and the Soviet Union and their respective allies

Deterrence   Keeping an opponent from doing something by threat of punishment or by possessing capabilities the adversary knows will block or deny any such attempt

Developing world   Countries with public and private sectors investing capital (from savings, trade surpluses, grants, loans, corporate or other investments) to increase the country's capacity for domestic production of goods and services

Diplomacy   The management of international relations by communications, including negotiations at times leading to a bargain or agreement

Diplomatic immunity   A reciprocal privilege among states by which diplomats are not subject to arrest, prosecution, or penalty in the foreign state to which they are assigned

Disarmament   Reducing to zero either all weapons in national arsenals (as in general or complete disarmament) or all weapons of a particular type (as in biological weapons)

Division of labor   In international trade, the specialization in production of goods and services—countries tending to produce those things in which they are relatively more efficient—a *comparative advantage* they have for producing these goods and services compared to other products more efficiently produced in other countries

Division of powers   Power is distributed among a central and constituent state or provincial governments as in a federal republic

Dual or double effect principle   A single act that may have more than one effect, perhaps some good and others not

Econometrics   Economic analyses employing quantitative methods and statistical tools that other social science fields also may use

Economic leverage   The ability to use economic power to extract political concessions

Economic sanctions   Coercive means to influence a state's behavior such as by a boycott, embargo, freezing bank assets, or blockade

Economic structuralism   An image of world politics that argues one must comprehend the global context within which states and other entities interact—a context defined by class or other materially defined structures and exploitative relations

Economic structure   Class- or other material-based concentration, as in ownership of capital by a *bourgeois* class or its aggregation in capital-rich countries of the North or First World

Economies of scale   Efficiencies that come from larger quantities or mass production resulting in lower costs

Economy   The production, distribution, and consumption of goods and services. While conventionally focusing on the state, it can also be applied to the economic well-being of individuals.

English School   An image that combines aspects of realism and liberalism in the context of international society as well as finding a middle path that takes both realism and idealism into account

Environmental degradation   Pollution or destruction of land, air, and waterways

Environmental regimes   Sets of rules and associated institutions that have been constructed by states to coordinate, manage, or regulate their relations in a particular environmental issue area

Epistemology   A theory of knowledge about how we come to know what we think we know about the world and what we observe in it; a pursuit that leads us to adopt various methods and methodologies for testing and expanding our knowledge

European Union (EU)   An economic and political partnership among 27 European countries designed to ensure peace, stability, and prosperity by helping to raise living standards and progressively building a single Europe-wide market

Exchange controls   Government restrictions on the amount of domestic currency that can be exchanged for other currencies

Exchange rate   Price of one currency in terms of another; for example, it may take $1.60 (U.S.) to purchase one British pound, or put another way, one U.S. dollar at this exchange rate will buy 0.625 of a pound

Executive agreement   Agreement made between leaders of two or more states that does not have the more formal characteristics of treaties

Exports   Goods and services sold abroad

Extended deterrence   Threats designed to deter and protect other countries from an attack by a common enemy

Externality   When a state or other actor takes an action that has a positive or negative impact on other states, whether intended or not

Extraterritoriality   The legal fiction that an embassy or consulate and the ground it stands on are part of the sovereign territory of the foreign country

Factors of production   Land (including natural resources), labor, and capital as components essential to the production of goods and services

Federal state   A system of government in which power is apportioned between a national-level government and states or regions

Federalism   Division of powers between states or provinces and the central government

Female genital mutilation (FGM) or cutting (FGC)   The World Health Organization defines female genital mutilation (or cutting) as all procedures that involve partial or total removal of the external female genitalia or other injury to the female genital organs for nonmedical reasons.

Feminism   Provides an alternative lens—gender—through which to view world politics and offers insights on the often-overlooked political, social, and economic roles that women play in IR

Feudal system   Power is claimed by a diverse group of governmental units including kings, barons, trading houses, and popes in a very decentralized system

First-strike capability   The ability to launch an attack against an enemy so that its ability to retaliate is severely degraded

First-Third Worlds   *First World*: capital-rich countries of the North; *Third World*: capital-poor countries of the South

Fiscal policy   National budget decisions and actions on taxing and spending (and borrowing—government or "sovereign" debt)

Fixed exchange rates   A system in which the value of a country's currency, in relation to the value of other currencies, is maintained at a fixed conversion rate through government intervention or the actions of monetary authorities

Fog of war   Metaphor that captures the uncertainties in warfare—factors not considered or, quite simply, that bad luck may have adverse effects

Force posture   Numbers, types, locations, and other qualitative factors concerning a state's military forces

Foreign direct investment   Money invested in countries aside from one's own

Free rider   Actor not making payments for (or other contributions to) establishing or maintaining the collective good, as when nonalliance states also benefit from the security provided and paid for by alliance members

Free trade   Commerce unobstructed by tariffs, quotas, or other barriers to trade

Free-trade area   Region where commerce is unobstructed by tariffs, quotas, or other barriers

Friction   Metaphor from mechanics that captures the idea that implementation of a plan likely will face impediments or obstacles

Game theory   Decision-making approach based on the assumption of actor rationality in a competitive situation in which each party tries to maximize gains or minimize losses

GATT   General Agreement on Trade and Tariffs, signed in 1947 and lasted until 1993 when it was replaced by the WTO, which incorporated GATT into its organizational framework

GDP   Gross domestic product—GNP minus return on foreign investment since the latter is a measure of *foreign*, rather than *domestic* production

Gender discrimination   Placing people at a disadvantage on the grounds of their sex or their masculine or feminine identity

General will   Individual rights are integral to or part of the community or society in which individuals reside

Geneva Conventions   Prescribing right conduct toward both combatants and noncombatants in warfare and defining war crimes, crimes against the peace, and related offenses

Genocide   Mass murder of a people typically because of their racial, ethnic, religious, or other particular identity

Geopolitics   An attempt to understand the issue of national power almost exclusively in terms of physical geography

Global capitalist system   A focus on class and economic relations and the division of the world into a core, periphery, and semiperiphery—"capitalist world system," another term that captures this meaning

Global civil society   The gradual worldwide emergence of the rule of law and networks or relationships among people in a world composed of both states and nonstate actors

Global governance   Set of arrangements and processes by which authorities in governments or international organizations perform certain global tasks like maintaining trade and monetary regimes

Global system   Encompasses the entire globe and is characterized by economic and technological interdependence and diverse actors

Global warming   An increase in the volume of carbon dioxide in the atmosphere contributing to a greenhouse effect that traps heat from the sun's rays and raises the average temperature around the world

Globalization   The continual increase in transnational and worldwide economic, social, and cultural interactions that transcend the boundaries of states and the resultant political implications. These interactions are aided by advances in technology.

Governance   The political interaction of transnational actors aimed at solving global problems that affect more than one state or region when there is no power of enforcing compliance, as would be the case within a state

Gross national income (GNI)   GNP minus indirect (like sales and excise) business taxes and gross imports of goods and services

Gross national product (GNP)   A country's annual output of goods and services, calculated as the sum of consumption, investment, government spending, and exports minus imports

Group-identity conflicts   The hypothesis that environmental stress exacerbates conflict among ethnic groups

Groupthink   Tendency over time for members of a group to think alike; screening out ideas or perspectives that contradict what has become their commonly accepted wisdom

Hegemonic state system   One or more states dominate the system. Variants include unipolar, bipolar or dual hegemony, and multipolar or collective hegemony.

Human geography   The visual depiction of human activities overlaid on physical terrain maps, which includes cultural, religious, and other factors related to the world's peoples

Human rights   Persons possess authority within themselves in relation to political, economic, and social choices they make and protections they ought to enjoy from abuse by others

Human security   Emphasis on security of all human beings, not the more common and limited focus on national or state security

Humanitarian intervention   Application of force within another country in order to stop the fighting among competing groups, provide the necessary security to feed starving people, or halt ethnic cleansing

Hypothesis   An explanatory proposition subject to empirical test for its veracity

Idealism   Tradition of political thought that advances universal, uniting concepts found in moral and legal principles

Identity   Consists of the answer to the question "Who am I?" It may be associated with a state, religion, or ethnicity, and have political implications.

Identity politics   The political implications of individuals identifying with religious, national, ethnic, tribal, or clan values

Image   A general perspective of international relations and world politics

Imperial system   Consists of separate societal units associated by regular interaction, but one among them asserts political supremacy and tends to manage the affairs of a subject state or colony

Imperialism   A position or policy of preeminence or dominance vis-à-vis foreign elements as in the establishment of colonies or by virtue of the capabilities a great power has over less powerful states, perhaps in the form of economic, social, or cultural imperialism

Imports   Goods and services purchased abroad

Independent state system   Political entities that each claim to be sovereign with the right to make both foreign policy and domestic decisions

Independent variable   A factor used to explain some outcome or effect

Instrumental rationality   The rational calculation of costs and benefits in pursuit of an end or goal to include available capabilities

Integration   Process by which such political units as states come together in varying degrees of unity, often to serve specific functions or purposes

Interdependence   A situation in which actions and events in one state affect people in other states and assumes some degree of reciprocal effect

International Court of Justice (ICJ)   A United Nations judicial body

International Criminal Court (ICC)   Tribunal located in The Hague, Netherlands, for prosecution of war crimes, genocide, and other crimes against humanity

International law   Binding rules or law that transcend borders and apply to states as well as to individuals (natural persons) and organizations or corporations (legal persons)

International liquidity   In monetary affairs, the ease with which foreign currencies are available to countries so they can settle their accounts with other countries

International Monetary Fund (IMF)   Washington-based international organization that seeks to maintain international liquidity—the availability of foreign currencies used to make international payments for imports of goods and services from abroad

International monetary regime   Financial rules, regulations, and institutions agreed on by states to facilitate international trade and other forms of commerce

International organization (IO)   An institution composed of states as members (for example, the

United Nations [UN], European Union [EU], and the North Atlantic Treaty Organization [NATO]).

International regime   Voluntarily agreed-upon sets of principles, norms, rules, and procedures constructed by states to coordinate, manage, or regulate their relations in a particular issue area

International relations   Conventionally refers to relations among states

International security   Defense matters among states or, more broadly, issues that affect the welfare of human beings—not just defense, but also economics, health, environment, human rights, and other social questions

International system   An aggregation of similar or diverse entities linked by regular interaction that sets them apart from other systems, for example, the interstate or international system of states, or world politics understood as a system composed of both state and nonstate actors

Internationalization   Increasing interactions between or among states; by contrast, the term *globalization* refers to global transaction that transcend state boundaries

Interstate conflict   Use of armed force in conflict between two or more states

Intervening variable   A factor that comes between the cause (independent variable) and the outcome or effect (dependent variable), either facilitating, opposing, or even blocking the effect

Investment   The input of money or other resources to maintain or expand productive capacity and, in turn, to generate a profit or return on investment for the investor

Issue area   Military, economic, and political issues in which different types of power are most relevant

Jus ad bellum   Latin term for moral criteria establishing the right to go to war

Jus gentium   Laws applicable to all humanity, states, and individuals

Jus in bello   Latin term for moral criteria establishing right conduct in war

Jus naturale   Natural law or the laws of nature that some writers see as superseding man-made law

Just war   Specific conditions must be met both to establish the right to use force (*jus ad bellum*) and to assure right conduct while engaged in warfare (*jus in bello*).

Just-war theory   Arguments as to the accepted circumstances in which states can go to war and conduct warfare

LDC   Less-developed country, a euphemism for an economically poor country

League of Nations   International organization established after World War I—forerunner to the UN

Legal and political rights   A narrow construction of rights—for example, free speech, rights to assemble and to vote, due process of law

Legitimacy   A right to govern and exercise power based on popular acceptance

Levels of analysis framework   A way to organize thinking about world politics and generate hypotheses. Individuals, groups, states and their societies, or the overall international system are points of focus.

Liberalism   An image of world politics that emphasizes the multiplicity of international actors—states, international organizations, and transnational organizations—and the conditions under which international cooperation can be achieved

Libertarian   Philosophical position emphasizing *individual* rights, often preferring specific limits or restraints on government

Liquidity   Availability of cash—in international monetary affairs, the ease with which foreign currencies are available to countries so they can settle their accounts with other countries

Macroeconomics   Deals with how an economy as a whole functions, the domain of fiscal and monetary policy, respectively, involving such aggregates as GNP or GDP and money supply

Markets   Refers to the exchange of goods and services, money, and other financial instruments between buyers and sellers

Means of production   The combination of land, labor, and capital used to produce goods and services

Mercantilism   The concept that national wealth is a function of the amount of gold and other accumulated treasure—present-day neomercantilist policies pursued by some states trying to maximize trade surpluses, accumulating large monetary-reserve balances

Microeconomics   Deals with how purchasers and suppliers interact in the marketplace, sometimes referred to simply as market or price theory

Migration   The movement of peoples from one country or area to others; immigration involves arrivals, emigration departures

Minimum or finite deterrence   A doctrine in which a state maintains a relatively small number of nuclear or other weapons of mass destruction for use in making deterrence threats

Mode of production   The form of political economy associated with the production of goods and services at different historical periods—a term used in Marxist understanding of ancient slavery, feudalism, and capitalism as different modes of production

Monetary policy   National decisions and actions that affect the money supply, interest rates, and exchange rates

Money   An instrument that provides a store of value, a unit of account, and a medium of exchange

Money laundering   Financial transactions designed to conceal the identity, source, and/or destination of illegally gained money

Monotheism   Belief that there is only one god

Most-favored-nation (MFN)   Status given by one state to another state as in setting tariffs at the lowest level charged on imports from any other country

Multilateral diplomacy   Negotiations involving three or more states.

Multilateralism   Working on international issues jointly rather than unilaterally by a single state—often a means to achieve mutual gains

Multinational corporation (MNC)   Corporate firm based or headquartered in one country, but producing goods or services and conducting other operations in two or more countries

Mutual assured destruction (MAD)   A nuclear deterrence doctrine that aims to avoid war by reciprocal threat of punishment through an unacceptable level of destruction

Nation   People with a common identity based on certain characteristics that distinguish them from other social groups

National interest   A state's core security interests and values

National self-determination   The assertion that nations have the right to choose their political status, which in practice often means the creation of a new state

Nationalism   A mind-set glorifying the national identity, usually to the exclusion of other possible identities, infused with a political content

Nationalization (expropriation)   Governments taking private property for public ownership or use. Under international law such seizures should be nondiscriminatory and accompanied by fair compensation.

Nation-state   People with a common identity who live within a given state

Natural law   Obligations and rights that exist in nature, discoverable through reason

Neoclassical economics   Late-19th- and early-20th-century developments in economic thought that departed from the labor theory of value held by such classical economists as Adam Smith, David Ricardo, and Karl Marx by focusing on price as a function of supply and demand as well as introducing such market-related concepts as utility, marginal utility, marginal revenue, and marginal cost. Prominent neoclassical economists included Alfred Marshall (English) and Leon Walras (French).

Neocolonialism   Relations of economic, social, cultural, and even political dominance by a former colonial ruler of a now independent state

Netwar   Conflicts in which a combatant is organized along networked lines or employs networks for operational control and other communications

Nongovernmental organizations (NGOs)   Transnational organizations that have a standing independent of governments, often with a diverse membership that works to fulfill specific political, social, or economic objectives

Normative theory   Value-oriented or philosophical theory that focuses on what *ought to be* as opposed to *what is*. As such, it is usually different from empirical theories, which try to explain the way things *are* or predict what they will be.

Norms   Values that states or people take seriously and that influence behavior, such as concern for human rights

North-South   *North*: advanced-industrial or postindustrial, high-income countries and societies generally in the northern hemisphere; *South*: less industrially developed, lower-income countries and societies generally in the southern hemisphere

Objectives   Specific goals of a state, international organization, or transnational organization

Opportunity cost   When a decision is made to do one thing, it precludes doing something else

Pacifism   Commitment to peaceful, nonviolent approaches to conflict

Pacta sunt servanda   Latin term for treaties or conventions that are binding on states party to these agreements

Papacy   The office held by the pope as head of the Catholic Church

Parliamentary government A form of government in which the executive (the prime minister and cabinet) is part of the legislative branch

Patterns of life Repeated human behavior and tendencies

Peacekeeping Task performed by UN or other multilateral forces in an effort to keep conflicting parties from resorting (or returning) to armed hostilities

Physical geography Material manifestations of terrain such as continents, mountains, rivers, lakes, and oceans

Political asylum Protection granted to individuals who face persecution, violation of human rights, or other denial of civil rights and liberties in their home and other countries

Political culture Those norms, values, and orientations of a society's culture that are politically relevant

Political economy The intersection of politics (or authoritative choice), particularly in relation to trade, money, finance, and investment—the flows of capital across national boundaries

Polytheism Belief in more than one god

Positivism Concept that law is what lawmakers, following constitutional procedures, define it to be; also refers to application of scientific method not just to the *natural*, but also the *social* sciences

Postmodernism What we see and how we analyze international phenomena rely on our perception, which is particularly influenced by prior understandings and meanings. Even the language we use reflects values.

Power Means by which a state or other actor wields or can assert actual or potential influence or coercion relative to other states and nonstate actors because of the political, geographic, economic and financial, technological, military, social, cultural, or other capabilities it possesses

Presidential government A form of government in which the executive branch is separate from the legislature

Preventive diplomacy Efforts taken to address international problems with constructive approaches, avoiding if possible the deterioration of relations that could lead to armed conflict

Price elasticity of demand The change in quantity of demand caused by a change in price

Protectionism Policies favoring a country's industries, agriculture, or other producers by imposing tariffs or quotas on imports, subsidizing production, and erecting other barriers to free trade

Qualitative methods Comparative case studies, historical methods, and reasoned arguments to develop explanations of outcomes

Quantitative methods The use of statistical data and related measures to develop explanations of outcomes

Race Identifiable physical characteristics used to categorize people

Radicalization The multifaceted process by which individuals become mobilized to consider or engage in acts of political violence

Raison d'état Literally "reason of state," which is seen as the realist rationale for foreign and national security policies pursued by state authorities

Rational choice Decisions based on maximizing benefits or minimizing costs of alternative courses of action directed toward attaining one or more objectives

Realism An image of international relations or world politics that can be traced back more than two thousand years. Realists tend to hold a rather pessimistic view, emphasizing the struggle for power and influence among political units acting in a rational, unitary manner in pursuit of objectives grounded in their separate, often divergent interests.

Realpolitik German term for *power politics*

Refugee(s) A person displaced because of war (usually) or other political or economic causes. Refugees may flee or be forced to leave a country, or they may be internally displaced persons within their own state.

Regimes Sets of rules and associated international organizations that have been constructed by states to coordinate, manage, or regulate relations in a particular issue area

Religion A system of belief in a divine or superhuman powers(s) with accompanying practices and values

Reserves Cash or assets easily converted into cash held out of use by a bank, company, or state to meet expected or unexpected demands

Resource depletion Reduction or exhaustion of nonrenewable resources

Resource wars The hypothesis that state and group rivalry, especially over nonrenewable resources such as oil and minerals, contributes to conflict

Revolutions in military affairs A major change in the nature of warfare brought about by the innovative application of new technologies which, combined with dramatic changes in military doctrine and operational and organizational concepts, fundamentally alter the character and conduct of military operations

Satraps   Local Persian governors

Second-strike capability   The ability to absorb a nuclear first strike with sufficient retaliatory forces surviving to launch a counterattack

Security   The basic survival and protection of a state, but can also refer to individuals

Separation of powers   A political system in which power is distributed between two or more branches of government—sometimes referred to as *presidential government*

Shariah   Islamic law

Shiah   Second largest of the two great divisions of Islam

Smurfing   Dividing large amounts of currency into smaller transactions that are in amounts below some statutory limit that normally does not require a financial institution to file a report with a government agency

Social conservatives   Doubt the efficacy of social engineering or other governmental programs that would effect substantial changes in the status quo, preferring instead to rely more on private, nongovernmental efforts—any changes implemented incrementally, slowly, and carefully

Social constructivism   Identities are not essential or given attributes but rather are constructed by individuals and groups

Social contract   Idea that human beings, acting in their own enlightened self-interest, would agree to bind themselves to one political or governing arrangement or another to include rules for the society they construct

Social liberals   Political perspective that, while sharing the commitment to individualism, puts emphasis on government programs or other social actions as means to improve the position or conditions of individuals

Social network analysis   Software designed to place individuals in the context of their social network and hence discern personal ties and relationships

Social psychology   The study of the relations between people and groups

Socioeconomic rights   A belief that human beings have rights to such essentials as food, clothing, shelter, health care, and education

Soft power   Nonmaterial capabilities such as reputation, culture, and value appeal that can aid the attainment of a state's objectives

Sovereignty   A claim to political authority to make policy or take actions domestically or abroad; based on territory and autonomy, historically associated with the modern state

Special drawing rights (SDRs)   Lines of credit that IMF member countries add to their monetary reserves used to settle international payments obligations

Strategy   Plan that connects capabilities (or means) to ends or objectives sought

Structural adjustments   When fiscal and monetary policies like cutting spending, increasing taxes, or raising interest rates are used to curb or dampen an economy deemed to be "overheated"

Structure (systemic)   In realist usage, structure usually refers to the distribution of power among states. Thus, a world subject to the influence of one great power is unipolar, to two principal powers is bipolar, and to three or more is multipolar.

Sunni   Largest of the two great divisions of Islam, the other being Shiah

Supranational   Authority beyond or above the level of a state; if one were created, a world government would be a supranational authority, governing the relations among states and other actors in world politics

Sustainable development   Economic growth that avoids obstacles that would undermine or preclude further growth, particularly depletion of natural resources, pollution, and other environmental damage

Symmetric warfare   Conflict in which two entities have essential equality in terms of amount and types of capabilities and pursue similar strategies

Tactics   The methods or way in which one takes actions or conducts operations

Tariffs   Taxes placed by governments on imported goods from other countries

Terms of trade   Ratio of export prices of one country to those of another, which in effect tells us the amount of revenue from a country's export sales to the other that can be used to pay for imports from the other

Territoriality   Geographic area under the administrative control of an overriding authority

Terrorism   Politically motivated violence directed against noncombatants and designed to instill fear in a target audience

Theory An intellectual construct that helps us explain or predict what we observe—interpreting facts and identifying regularities and recurrences or repetitions of observed phenomena

Third World or **South** Capital-poor, low-income, or less-developed countries

Trade Supplying goods or services in exchange for payment from purchasers

Trade integration The level of a country's participation in world markets through trade

Trade preferences Special arrangements allowing easy access on a cost-competitive basis by a foreign producer to a country's domestic market

Transfer pricing Accounting mechanism used by multinational corporations to minimize overall tax liability by purposely setting import or export prices of product components (produced in one subsidiary and exported to a subsidiary in another country) to show low or no profit for their subsidiaries operating in higher-tax countries

Transnational criminal organizations (TCOs) Criminal organizations that operate across borders

Treaty A written agreement or contract between two or more states pledging adherence to any number of commitments

Tribalism People with a common identity but often reserved for Africans

Unitary state A system of government in which most powers are reserved for the national-level government

United Nations An international organization created in 1945 with universal membership, dominated by the major powers in the Security Council

Unmanned aerial vehicles (UAV) Pilotless unarmed or armed aircraft such as the Predator

Utilitarian Philosophical school associated with Jeremy Bentham and John Stuart Mill based on the principle that right conduct is that which brings the greatest good or happiness for the greatest number

Value rationality Holding and pursuing values such as duty, loyalty, or commitment regardless of costs

Verification Finding out whether another party to a treaty or other agreement is living up to its obligations

Voluntarism The philosophical position that humans can influence, if not control, outcomes such as in international relations

Wahhabi Conservative Muslim group found mostly in Saudi Arabia

Warfighting The application of violence to achieve one's political and military objectives

Weapons of mass destruction Chemical, biological, radiological, and nuclear weapons as well as large amounts of conventional explosives that cause widespread death and destruction

Weapons proliferation The spread of weapons and weapon systems to countries not previously possessing them (horizontal proliferation) or the stockpiling of weapons or weapons systems by particular countries (vertical proliferation)

World Bank An IO created in 1944, currently designed to be a source of financial and technical assistance to developing countries around the world

World federalists Those seeking international order or peace through the rule of law as in constructing federations or confederations of states

World politics Refers to relations among states but also international organizations and nongovernmental organizations

World Trade Organization (WTO) Geneva-based international organization created in 1995 that seeks to lower, if not eliminate, tariffs and other barriers to international trade

Zero-sum Concept in game theory that one side's gain amounts to the other side's loss

CREDITS

INDEX

Note: *Italicized* page numbers indicate illustrations; page numbers followed by *b* indicate boxed text

ANSWER KEY

CHAPTER 1

1. a	6. c
2. d	7. c
3. d	8. c
4. a	9. b
5. d	10. a

CHAPTER 2

1. d	11. a
2. e	12. d
3. c	13. c
4. a	14. a
5. c	15. b
6. a	16. c
7. c	17. d
8. c	18. a
9. a	19. a
10. d	20. d

CHAPTER 3

1. c	11. b
2. d	12. c
3. d	13. d
4. d	14. b
5. b	15. d
6. a	16. d
7. d	17. a
8. a	18. b
9. a	19. a
10. b	20. d

CHAPTER 4

1. d	11. a
2. d	12. d
3. b	13. d
4. c	14. c
5. d	15. b
6. c	16. a
7. b	17. b
8. d	18. d
9. c	19. b
10. a	20. c

CHAPTER 5

1. a	11. a
2. c	12. b
3. d	13. c
4. c	14. b
5. d	15. e
6. a	16. a
7. c	17. d
8. a	18. a
9. a	19. c
10. c	20. b

CHAPTER 6

1. a	9. d
2. b	10. c
3. d	11. c
4. b	12. c
5. d	13. d
6. d	14. d
7. b	15. d
8. c	

CHAPTER 7

1. c	11. c
2. b	12. b
3. d	13. d
4. c	14. a
5. d	15. a
6. c	16. b
7. b	17. c
8. a	18. d
9. b	19. b
10. a	20. b

CHAPTER 8

1. a	7. a
2. d	8. b
3. c	9. c
4. a	10. c
5. b	11. a
6. a	12. b

13. d	17. a
14. b	18. d
15. a	19. c
16. b	20. a

CHAPTER 9

1. a	14. b
2. c	15. d
3. b	16. d
4. d	17. b
5. a	18. a
6. b	19. d
7. a	20. b
8. b	21. a
9. c	22. a
10. a	23. b
11. b	24. c
12. a	25. b
13. c	

CHAPTER 10

1. c	9. a
2. d	10. c
3. b	11. a
4. b	12. b
5. a	13. a
6. d	14. d
7. a	15. b
8. c	

CHAPTER 11

1. b	12. c
2. c	13. c
3. d	14. d
4. a	15. a
5. c	16. a
6. a	17. c
7. c	18. a
8. a	19. b
9. c	20. d
10. c	21. c
11. a	22. c

24. b
25. d
26. b

27. d
28. a
29. c
30. d

CHAPTER 12

1. a
2. a
3. d
4. d
5. c
6. c
7. a
8. c
9. a
10. c

11. a
12. d
13. a
14. b
15. d
16. b
17. c
18. b
19. a
20. c

CHAPTER 13

1. a
2. b
3. c
4. c
5. b
6. d
7. a
8. a
9. d
10. c
11. b
12. a
13. a

14. b
15. c
16. d
17. a
18. b
19. a
20. c
21. c
22. a
23. d
24. d
25. a

CHAPTER 14

1. c
2. d
3. a
4. d
5. d
6. c
7. b
8. a

9. d
10. c
11. b
12. d
13. d
14. b
15. a